The Ne

Histori

Genealogical Register

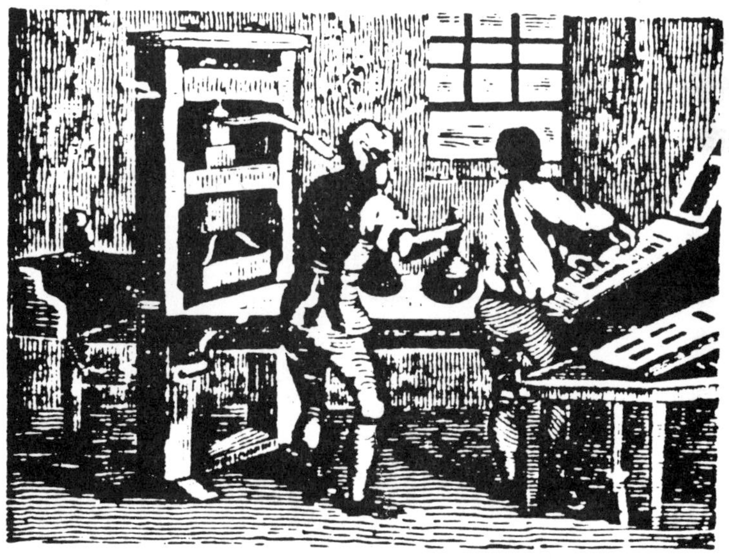

Volume III

1849

A HERITAGE CLASSIC

Facsimile Reprint

Published 1992 By
Heritage Books, Inc.
1540-E Pointer Ridge Place
Bowie, Maryland 20716
(301) 390-7709

ISBN 1-55613-641-2

- Notice -

The foxing, or discoloration with age, characteristic of old books, sometimes shows through to some extent in reprints such as this, especially when the foxing is very severe in the original book. We feel that the contents of this book warrant its reissue despite these blemishes, and hope you will agree and read it with pleasure.

martin frobisher

THE

NEW ENGLAND

Historical & Genealogical Register,

PUBLISHED QUARTERLY UNDER THE PATRONAGE OF THE

New England Historic, Genealogical Society.

FOR THE YEAR 1849.

VOLUME III.

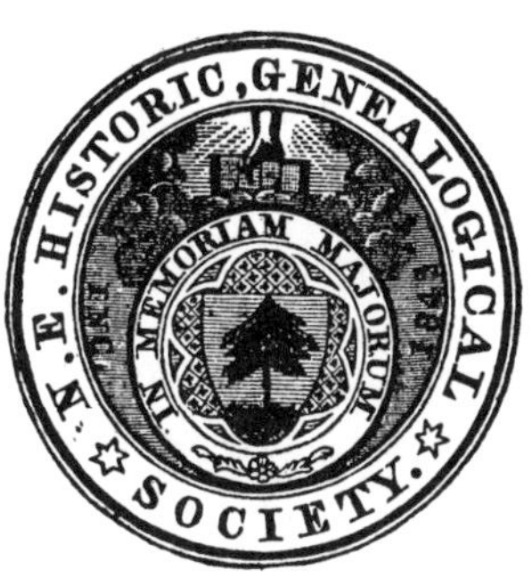

A HERITAGE CLASSIC

1849.

ADDITIONS AND CORRECTIONS.

IN VOL. I. — Page 120, line 14, for *Rev. John Brazier, D. D.*, read *Rev. John Brazer, D. D.* — Page 256, line 48, for (21—3) read (321—3). — Page 340, line 44, for *Rev. B. B. Drane, D. D.*, read *Rev. R. B. Drane, D. D.* — Page 342, line 12, after *Rebecca Hovey*, insert, *m. James B. Curwen, Feb.* 3, 1848. — Page 396, column 2, line 75, read *Richardson, Lydia*, 9, 29, 30. — Same page, column 2, after line 75, insert *Richardson, Mary*, 26, 27.

IN VOL. II. — Page V, line 20, for 398, read 395. — Page 64, column 3, line 21, for *Roger Goddspeed*, read *Roger Goodspeed.* — Page 157, line 10, Mr. Endicott writes: "Owing to different records conflicting with each other, some doubt is expressed in Vol. 2, p. 157, as to who was the wife of Ensign David Peabody, (7) 111. Since the publication of that account, I have received through the politeness of a gentleman at Fairhaven, positive proof that the wife who survived him, (for perhaps he may have married twice,) was Sarah Pope, of Dartmouth, Mass., as stated in the Boxford Records. She was the daughter of Seth Pope, a man of much consequence in his day, who left her at his decease, in 1727, £469 — which legacy was settled by his Executor, Lemuel Pope, with her oldest son, Thomas Peabody, (53.—1) 22 Dec. 1735." — Same page, line 40, for *Louisa*, read *Lucy.* — Page 196, line 6, for *John Manton*, read *John Martin.* — Same page, line 21, John Otis. *See Vol.* III. *p.* 274. — Page 229, column 1, line 20, for 1848, read 1847. — Same page, column 1, line 50, for 1848, read 1847. — Page 308, line 7, for 1780, read 1700 — Page 368, line 46, for *Keith*, read *Kiff.* — Page 372, line 5, for *Eben Perkins*, read *Ezra Perkins.* — Same page, line 12. Error. *See Vol* III *p.* 359. — Page 376, column 3, line 29, insert "*lived on Boston Neck, R. I.*" — Page 378, line 30, for *dau.*, read *wife.* — Page 379, line 13, for *John Parker*, read *John Barker*; line 34, after *Andrew Allen, Jr.*, insert *of Small Pox*; line 35, after *John Allen*, insert *of Small Pox* — Page 395, line 30, for *Hon. James Fitch*, read *Rev. James Fitch*; line 33, for *Barshuah*, read *Bathsheba*; line 37, for *Mr. Benjamin Church*, read *Rev. Benjamin Cotton*; line 40, after 1699, insert *m. Rev. William Gager*; line 49, after 1736, insert *m. an Ashley.* — Page 396, line 1, for *Sarah*, read *Tirzah*; line 38, the children of Rev. John Taylor were, Elizabeth; Jabez Terry; John; Harriet, m. Roderick Terry, Esq., of Hartford; Henry Wyllys; Mary, m. Josiah Wright; Nathaniel Terry.

IN VOL. III. — Page 58, line 43, for *Copps*, read *Copp's.* — Page 65, line 16, Mr. Boltwood writes, "I am *sure* that this woman's name is not Pope. The first letter is *R*, the second *o*, and the third *c*. Respecting the third letter I am somewhat in the dark. I think, however, it is either *s* or *c*, making the reading *Rose* or *Rofe.* (perhaps for *Rolfe.*)" — Same page, line 17, for *Unity Smylolary*, read *Eunice Singletary*; line 19, for *Richard Margun*, read *Richard Margin.* — Page 66, line 15, for *Elizabeth Ping*, read *Elizabeth Ring*; line 22, for *Peturne Johnson*, read *Returne Johnson*; line 33, for 9*ber* 21 1677, read 9*ber* 22 1677. — Page 67, line 15, for *Daniel Ennes*, read *Daniel Eimes*; line 25, for *Andrew Peters and Elizabeth*, read *Andrew Peters and Elizabeth Farnum.* — Page 68, line 11, for *Elizabeth Merritt*, read *Elizabeth Merrill?*; line 19, for *Martha Farnum*, read *Tabitha Farnum* — Page 84, line 16, for *Lezaia*, read *Lydia*; line 39, for *Lezaia*, read *Lydia.* — Page 88 last line, for *Jan.* 1, 1810, read *Jan.* 1, 1801. — Page 100, line 50, column 1, for 9 *Oct.*, read 12 *Oct.*; line 51, column 1, for *Segar*, read *Seger.* — Page 108, line 7, for *shot*, read *short.* — Page 123, line 43, the reference to the note is misplaced. It should have been inserted after *Lord*, line 46. — Page 134, Note. A slight mistake. Lewis was grandfather of Capt. Nathaniel Hamblen, but *not* of Hon. Frederick Hamblen, whose paternal ancestor was *Thomas* Mr. Hamblen writes, with reference to his valuable articles on the "First Settlers of Barnstable," as follows: "I have published all the Births, Marriages, and Deaths, contained in the first book of Records of Barnstable, and may, at some future day, give something more" — Page 156, line 9, for *Riard Haffeeld*, read *Richard Haffeeld.* — Page 158, line 37, for *Mr. Robert Say*, read *Mr. Robert Lay.* — Page 159, line 3, for *Mr. Robert Say*, read *Mr Robert Lay.* — Page 182, at the end of note §, read *ED.* — Page 183, line 19, for *Pease*, read *Peage.* — Page 188, line 44, column 1, for 7 *Oct.* 1650, read 7 *Oct.* 1640 — Page 197, line 54, column 1, for *Josiah*, read *Isaiah.* — Page 202, line 28, for *Cochituate*, read *Chechichowick.* — Page 212, line 31, for 1848, read 1849. — Page 233, last line, the autograph of Nathaniel Pease, accidentally omitted in this its appropriate place, will be found on page 390. — Page 245, line 37, column 3, for *Zache Marsh*, read *Zacke Marsh*; line 48, column 3, for *David Ashley*, read *David Ashly.* — Page 246, line 5, column 1, for *Ralph King*, read *Ralp King*: line 37, column 1, for *Enos Kinsly*, read *Enos Kinsly*; line 28, column 2, for *Nicholas Whilmarsh*, read *Nicholas Whitmarsh*; line 34, column 2, for *Nathan Smith*, read *Nathani Smith*; line 42, column 2, for *Abijah Whitman*, read *Abjah Whitman.* — Page 254, line 45, for *Knowles*, read *Rolls*; line 47, for *Knowles*, read *Rolls.* — Page 257, line 27, for *Maltahouse*, read *Mattahanada* — Page 279, line 19, for *Mr. Thomas Watirman*, read *Mr. Thomas Waterman.* — Page 282, line 42, after *execution*, insert a comma — Page 283, line 31, for *any*, read *an.* — Page 286, line 64, column 1, for *Vinton, Mr. C. M.*, read *Vinson, Mr. C. M.*, (*Harv. Coll.* 1839) — Page 287, line 32, column 2. We are informed, upon perfectly reliable authority, that in the obituary notice of Rev. Sylvester Dana, as compiled from the work therein indicated, there are several inaccuracies. Our limited space not allowing us to make the necessary corrections at this time, we are obliged to defer the matter until the next Number — Page 294 line 37, column 1, for 69, read 60; line 41, for *April* 1780, read *April*, 1789. — Page 336, note †, for 1727, read 1827. — Page 337, line 10, for *no 9 on list*, read [*no 9 on list.*]; line 43, for *Superscribed*, read [*Superscribed*] — Page 352, line 49, for *line* 36, read *line* 37; line 50, for *line* 47, read *line* 48. — Page 392, line 1, for *Mr. Pease*, read *Judge Pease.*

PREFACE.

Another year is drawing to a close, and time, in its onward course, has brought us to the point whence it has been customary for the editor of the Genealogical Register to look back upon the field of his labors, to make his obeisance to the Public, return thanks for the indulgence which has kept even pace with his steps, and to crave the continuance of that indulgence for the ensuing year.

But to the present Editor — an untried traveller upon the course of popular favor — the return of this season of retrospection brings a novel task. He finds himself obliged, for the first time, to appear before the patrons of the Register, to most of whom he is a stranger, and to explain his connection with a work, which has generally been considered the foster-child of one far more worthy of the Editorial chair.

In the month of January last the subscriber was appointed "Chairman of the Publishing Committee of the N. E. Historic-Genealogical Society, and *ex-officio* Editor of the Genealogical Register." Since that appointment he has devoted a considerable portion of his time, and such talents as he possessed, to the discharge of the duties of his responsible office, cheered by the hope that his efforts might not be entirely unsuccessful, and that his labors might not be wholly unacceptable to an enlightened community. Fortunate, indeed, must he consider himself, in having had the benefit of the counsel and aid of one, whose long experience eminently qualified him for an adviser; one who, as Publisher of the Register, still continued to watch with anxious solicitude over the interests of this favorite object of his care.

The first (January) number of this year, was issued under the auspices of Mr. Drake. For the remaining three numbers — April, July, and October — the subscriber is alone responsible. Sufficient reason for the particularity of this statement will be found in the fact, that *the Publisher* has been called to account for articles which he had never seen until they were in print, and been favored with comments, which, if made at all, should have been addressed to *the Editor*.

And now, inasmuch as his good friend the Publisher reminds him that *he* should like to say a few words to his patrons, the Editor hastens, in conclusion, to return his grateful acknowledgments to all who have in any way lent him assistance; and to assure them that their kindness and attention will ever be remembered by their obedient servant,

William Thaddeus Harris.

Cambridge, Mass.,
Oct. 1, 1849.

OUR WORK.

Having brought a third volume of the NEW ENGLAND HISTORICAL, GENEALOGICAL, AND ANTIQUARIAN REGISTER to a close, a word or two may be expected from its Publisher to those patrons who have continued to sustain him thus far; and so long as he has the privilege of saying what he pleases, it is his own fault whether he says nothing, or whether he speaks acceptably on the occasion.

That we have not exactly satisfied ourself, we are free to confess. Owing to circumstances which have occurred since we wrote our last preface, (to the second volume,) we have, in some measure, been compelled to depart from the fundamental principles therein laid down; and furthermore, circumstances are still such, that it is judged best not to make any new promises, that we may be sure not to break any:—but to say to our patrons, one and all, that so long as we continue our labors in this way, we shall do all in our power to make the work what it should be; namely, a TREASURY OF MATERIALS; to which all the sons of NEW ENGLAND may, with the utmost confidence, appeal, for the HISTORY AND ANTIQUITIES of their ANCESTORS.

Whatever (if any thing) may be contained in the present volume not generally desirable, it is the humble opinion of the Publisher, that, as a whole, it will be one of the most permanent value. The complete list of FREEMEN from the records of the General Court of Massachusetts is nowhere else to be found in print; and we are persuaded that this feature of the volume alone will give it a value above the cost of the whole subscription of all the volumes thus far; especially, as the accuracy of the list cannot be questioned, nay, will not be, guaranteed, as it is, by the name that accompanies it.

It is not proposed to point out faults in what we have done, for we doubt not too many will readily present themselves to such as seek for them. We only desire to remind *such co-workers*, that while errors, mistakes, and omissions are easily detected, and easier denounced, it would become them quite as much, were they to give due credit for the *many that have been avoided.*

Should any be disposed to complain that we have printed some genealogies in a more extended form than it will be expedient hereafter to do, we must in the present case reply, that it is *not done* at the expense of our subscribers, inasmuch as we have extended our number of pages to comprehend them.

THE PUBLISHER.

Boston, 56 Cornhill,
1 October, 1849.

GENERAL INDEX.

NEW ENGLAND

HISTORICAL AND GENEALOGICAL REGISTER.

VOL. III. JANUARY, 1849. NO. I.

MEMOIRS OF SIR MARTIN FROBISHER, KNIGHT.

1536 to 1594.

One of the most determined, resolute, and practical men of the time of QUEEN ELIZABETH was MARTIN, afterwards SIR MARTIN FROBISHER.* But we scarcely know which we should most admire, the man who, through a period of *fifteen years*, struggled with adversity and all kinds of disappointments before he could find himself able to undertake a voyage of discovery, or the man who travelled *two hundred miles*† (in those days) to learn the truth of such discoveries, that he might be enabled to transmit an account of them to posterity.

It is often the case that great men who have been benefactors of mankind, have gone off the stage without leaving behind them any key to their parentage or ancestry. Many took no pains to transmit any account of themselves, while many others may have left accounts, but which, owing to some one of numerous accidents, have been lost or destroyed. And thus MARTIN FROBISHER comes to us late in life, as is judged, without telling us whence he came; and when he leaves us, his death is merely mentioned by the chroniclers, because they could not well avoid it.

It is pretty certain that Frobisher was born in or near Doncaster‡ in

* Like almost every other name which would admit of permutations, that of *Frobisher* was in early times written with great variation; but there is probably little doubt, if any, that the name was originally derived from the occupation of a *polisher of arms*. It was most probably imported from France. A *sword-cutler* is called in that country a *fourbisseur*. Hence the name was of old often written *Furbisher*, which was more correct than that which obtained.

† Hakluyt's *Voyages*, iii. 169–70. HAKLUYT himself tells us that he made such a journey to learn an account of the voyage of "The Trinitie and Minion" in 1536, "set forth by Master Hore of London," upon discoveries in the North. HAKLUYT made his journey of two hundred miles to see the only survivor of the voyage, of the termination of which he thus speaks: "They arrived at S. Ives in Cornwall about the ende of October, from thence they departed unto a certain castle belonging to Sir John Luttrell, where M[aster] Thomas Buts, and M. Rastall, and other gentlemen of the voyage, were very friendly entertained; after that they came to the Earl of Bathe at Bathe, and thence to Bristol, so to London. M. Buts was so changed in the voyage with hunger and miserie, that Sir William his father, and my Lady his mother, knew him not to be their sonne, until they found a secret mark, which was a wart upon one of his knees, as he told me, Richard Hakluyt of Oxford, himself; to whom I rode 200 miles to learn the whole trueth of this voyage from his own mouth, as being the onely man now [about 1589] alive that was in this discoverie." The voyage spoken of was to Newfoundland. *We use the edition of Hakluyt in 5 vols., 4to, 1809–12.*

‡ So named from its situation upon the *Don* or *Dun*; hence *Don Castle* was originally understood, that is, the *castle* upon the *Don*. The castle has long been in ruins. The

Yorkshire, and there seems to be a pretty strong probability that he was a son of *Francis Frobisher*, who, as early as 1535, was mayor of that place.

MARTIN FROBISHER belongs to American biography and history as much as he does to those of England. By his firmness, perseverance, and enterprise, the discovery and settlement of North America were vastly promoted. And notwithstanding his great services, we may look in vain for anything like a tolerable biography of him, although his name is found in the ordinary and common dictionaries of biography and naval memoirs.

We have nothing that enables us to state with any degree of certainty the time of his birth; but from some circumstances it is thought to have been about the year 1536. If that date be *about* right, then Frobisher was *about* forty years of age in 1576, the year he undertook his discoveries into the American seas. He must have been full forty at this time, or he must have been very young when he conceived of the undertaking; for we are assured by Hakluyt, his cotemporary, that he had been upon the enterprise fifteen years before he was able to set out in it.

That Frobisher belonged to a family of respectability there is no doubt. In one of the earliest mentions we find made of him, he is styled "gentleman," which never was bestowed on ordinary persons in his time. Between 1560 and 1570 he was appointed a commissioner of the coal trade. Such abuses were practised at that time in the sale of coal, that a petition to the queen, setting forth the "greate deceit that is used aboute the measuring of sea coales in New Castell and elsewhere throughout Yorkshire, by the bellmen and others, to the greate damage of manie," desiring her "to graunte letters patents to Martyn Furbusher, gentleman, and Richarde Morley of London, gentleman," was set on foot.*

We hear nothing further of him till 1572, at which time he was residing at Lambeth. While there overtures seem to have been made to him to aid in the liberation of the Earl of Desmond, then a prisoner in England, but no steps appear to have been taken by him to further the design, and it was suspended.

The next year, 1573, there was a rumor, probably without any real foundation, that "Furbisher was allured by certaine decayed men" into a conspiracy they had formed of joining one Thomas Stukely in Spain, where they were to collect followers and invade the English in Ireland. Although the plot was partially carried out, we hear nothing further implicating Frobisher.

What has been said of men by cotemporaries is generally interesting, though often to be taken with much allowance. We shall therefore give what several of Frobisher's cotemporaries have said about him, and as Camden is more full than any of them within our knowledge, his account shall be given first, and in his own words. As for Stow and Speed, they are very brief, especially the latter; and the former appears to have hurried over his notice; and as though aware he was doing so, he makes

church of Doncaster is famous for a monument with what our author calls an uncouth inscription, to the memory of *Robert Byrks*, a benefactor to the town. It is in these words:

How, how, who is heare?
I Robin of Doncastre
And Margaret *my Feare.*

That I spent, that I had,
That I gaue, that I haue
That I left that I lost
A. D. 1597.

Quoth Robertus Byrks, *who in this World did reign*
Three score years & seven, & yet liued not one.

Magna Britannia, vi. 429.

* Wright's "*Queen Elizabeth and her Times*, i. 222

amends for it by referring his reader to Hakluyt, in this passage: "**Concerning the rest of the English Nauigators and voyages, I will referre you vnto the Reuerend Father, Master** Richard Hackluit, **Batechelor of Diuinitie, in his Booke*** **of English voyages.**" We now proceed with Camden.

"At this time [1576] some studious Heads, moved with a commendable Desire to discover the more remote Regions of the world and the Secrets of the Ocean, put forward some well monied men, no less desirous to reap Profit by it, to discover whether there were any Streight in the North part of *America* through which men might sail to the rich Country of *Cathay*, and so the Wealth of the East and West might be conjoyned by a mutuall Commerce. These learned men argued that probably there was some Streight opened a way in that part; taking it for granted that the nearer the Shoar a man cometh, the shallower the Waters are. But they who sail from the Western Coast of *Iseland* find by experience the Sea to be deeper: so as it may probably seem to joyn with that Sea which the Mariners call *Mare del Sur*, on the other side of *America*. Then they argued, That whereas the Ocean is carried with the daily Motion of the *Primum Mobile*, or the uppermost Heaven, being beaten back by the Opposition of *America*, it runneth Northward to *Cabo Fredo*, that is, the Cold Cape or Promontory, about which place it should be emptied through some Streight into the Sea *del Sur*; otherwise it would be beaten back with the like violence upon Lapland and *Finmarck*, as it is in the South part of the world beaten back from the Streight of *Magellan* (a Streight full of Isles, and, by reason of the Narrowness of the Streight, being so full of Isles, uncapable of so great a quantity of Waters,) along the Eastern Coast of *America* to *Cabo Fredo*." "Herewith these monied men being perswaded, they sent *Martin Frobisher* with three Pinnaces to discover this Streight, who, setting out from *Harwich* the 18. of *June*, entred on the ninth of *August* into a Bay or Streight under the Latitude of 63 Degrees, where he found men with black Hair, broad Faces, flat Noses, swarthy-coloured, apparelled in Sea-calves Skins; the Women painted about the Eyes and Balls of the Cheek with a blew Colour, like the ancient Britans. But all being so frozen up with Ice in the moneth of *August* that he could not hold on his Voiage, he returned, and arrived in *England* the 24. of *September*, having lost five Sea-men, whom the Barbarians had intercepted. Nevertheless the two years next following he sailed to the same Coasts, to perfect his Enterprise: but being incountred every-where with Heaps of Ice like Mountaines, he was kept from entring any farther into the Bay. Being therefore tossed up and down with fowl weather, Snows, and unconstant winds, he gathered a great quantity of Stones, which he thought to be Minerals, and so returned homewards: which Stones, when neither Gold nor Silver nor any other Metall could be extracted from them, we have seen cast forth to mend

* When Stow wrote, Hakluyt had published but one volume of his voyages, namely, that of 1589.

We know not that the name of Frobisher even exists in America, unless it be in those of Furbush, Furber, &c., which may have had the same origin; and so far as we know it is rare in England. So late as 1807, not one of the name was to be found in London, that immense cauldron of almost every name under the sun; at least none is to be found in its *great directory* for that year. The only time we recollect to have met with it, is in an account of a shocking calamity at Exeter in the county of Devon, where, in 1800, Mrs. *Rachel Charlotte*, daughter of *Joseph Frobisher*, Esq., was burnt to death in endeavouring to rescue her child from the flames. She was the wife of Capt. E. J. O'Brien. See Lyson's *Hist. of Dev.*, ii. 208.

the High-ways. But these matters are published at large and every where to be sold."*

As has been remarked, the account of Frobisher by Stow is very brief, but brief as it is, it seems to have been about all that is known of him, aside from the narrations of his maritime expeditions. It is in this:

"Martin Frobusher, borne neere Doncaster, in Yorkeshire, in his youth gaue himselfe to Nauigation, he was the first Englishman that discouered the North way to China, and Cathay, and at his first discourie of the way to Cathay at which time for tryall of what he could find there, brought thence a black soft stone like sea coale, supposed to be gold, or siluer Oare, & in that perswasion made two seuerall voyages againe to Cathaye, bringing with them great quantitie of the sayd supposed Oare, the which after due tryall & much expence prooued not worth anything, neither fit for any vse, a great quantity of which stuffe was layed in the nursery at Darford, no man regarding it, he was vice-admirall to Sir Francis Drake, at the winning of Saint Domingo, Saint Iago, Carthagena, and Saint Augustino.

Hee did great seruice in the yeere one thousand fiue hundred eightie and eight, vpon the inuincible Spanish Armado, for which he was Knighted, after that hee was General of tenne ships, to keepe Brest-hauen in Britaine, where the Spaniardes neere thereunto had strongly fortified themselues, in whose extirpation he did speciall seruice by Sea and Land, and was there shotte into the side with a Musket, the wounde not mortall, he liued vntill hee came to Plimmouth, through the negligence of his surgeon that onely tooke out the Bullet, not sufficiently searched the Wound, to take out the Bombaste strucke in with the shotte the sore festered, whereof he dyed,† & was buried in Plimmouth, he was very valiant, yet harsh & violent."‡ To these facts thus briefly stated we shall have occasion again to refer. The account of SPEED, being short, it follows entire:

"For the searching and vnsatisfied spirits of the *English*, to the great glory of our Nation, could not be contained within the bankes of the *Mediterranean or Leuant Seas*, but that they passed farre, towards both the *Articke* and *Antarticke* Poles, inlarging their trades into the *West* and *East Indies*: to the search of whose passage, that worthy Sea-Captaine Sir

* CAMDEN, *Annals of Elizabeth*, 215–16. In another account it is said that in his first voyage, "one of his Company bringing back with him a large Piece of the said black Stone, much like Sea-coal, carried it to the refiners of Gold, who extracted from it so great a quantity of Gold, that they gave it the name of Gold Ore; which encouraged him to load his Ships with it, though it proved to no Purpose." — *Mag. Brit.*, vi. 430. It seems likely that the alchemists deceived Frobisher and his friends, or he would not have brought a second quantity of the same kind of stone. It is difficult too to see what object they could have had in view. "Yet (says Fuller) will no wise man laugh at his mistake, because in such experiments they shall never hit the mark who are not content to miss it." Perhaps adventurers were slow for such an undertaking, and the gold story may have been contrived to quicken them.

† FULLER, in his *Worthies of England*, had evidently nothing but this account of STOW from which to make one for his work, but he seldom fails to add something to every thing he takes up, which increases its interest. "Swords and guns (he says) have not made more mortal wounds than probes in the hands of careless and skill-less chirurgeons, as here it came to pass."

‡ "*Annales, or A Generall Chronicle of England.* Begun by IOHN STOW. Continued and Augmented with matters Forraigne and Domestique, Ancient and Moderne, vnto the end of this present yeere, 1631." p. 809. We give the entire title-page of STOW, except the "horid pictures," which seem to have frightened it into an exceeding small space upon the verge of the lower margin, as though it would gladly escape such company. Yet to us the whole title-leaf of the venerable old volume is most gratifying; and how Dibdin could say "it was enough to give a man the cholic to behold it," is beyond OUR comprehension. However, even antiquaries must be allowed *sometimes* to indulge in a conceit where the *real* truth cannot be mistaken. The imprint of Stow is LONDINI, Impensis RICHARDI MEIGHEN, 1631. Folio, 1087 pages, and an index of about 100 pages.

Martin Furbusher,* made Saile into the *North-East-Seas*, farre further then any man before him had euer done, giuing to these parts the name of *Queene Elizabeths Foreland.*

"The next yeere hee attempted thirty leagues further, when finding *Gold Ore* (as was thought) and taking a man, woman, and child, of the *Sauage Catayes*, he returned into *England;* but as his gold prooued drosse, so these liued not long, neither turned that discouery to any great profit, though it was againe the third time assaied by himself, and since by other most *famous Nauigators*, the *Northwest* by Englishmen being lately descried, to bee Seas more safe, and the passage of farre better hope."† We shall now proceed to narrate in as intelligible a manner as we can the voyages and expeditions of Frobisher.

When an individual undertakes any great or extraordinary enterprise, the reasons or motives which led him to it are sought for by every one, and not without good reason. For there is a vast difference whether a man ventures his life and fortune merely for the accumulation of wealth, or whether it is for the enlargement of the bounds of human knowledge, and the consequent promotion of happiness to the human race. That Frobisher had other views than merely the acquirement of gold will not be questioned, when the circumstances upon which he undertook his first voyage of discovery are considered.

But the first inquiry which will naturally take possession of the mind of the reader of the memoirs of Sir Martin Frobisher will be, What grounds had he to think he might find a passage into the South Seas to the north of America? What intimations had he that even such a thing were at all practicable? Had there not been northern voyages in many years before, nearly all of which had terminated in losses and distress?

It appears pretty clear from the various treatises contained in Hakluyt's collection, that the subject of a north west passage had been long in agitation, and reports had been circulated that even a passage had been made around the extreme north of the American continent many years before Frobisher set out upon his voyage. This latter fact, or statement as such, was no doubt known to him as well as to the rest of the enterprising men of his time, which, although probably false, had the effect to spur on the spirit of adventure in England, and resulted in the undertaking in question.

To set this matter in its proper light, the following passage from Sir Humphrey Gilbert's able treatise‡ is extracted:

"There was one Saluaterra, a Gentleman of Victoria in Spain, that came by chance out of the West Indias into Ireland, [where Sir Humphrey was at that time serving] Anno 1568. who affirmed the Northwest passage from vs to Cataia, constantly to be beleeued in America navigable. And further said in the presence of Sir Henry Sidney (then lord Deputie of Ireland) in my hearing, that a Frier of Mexico, called Andrew Vardeneta, more than

* In his index SPEED has "*Frobisher or Furbisher.*"

† "*The Historie of Great Britaine vnder the conquests of the Romans, Saxons, Danes and Normans.* Their Originals, Manners, Habits, Warres, Coines, and Seales: with the Successions, Liues, Acts, and Issues of the ENGLISH MONARCHS from IVLIVS CÆSAR, vnto the Raigne of King IAMES of famous MEMORIE. *The Third Edition.* Reuised, enlarged, and newly corrected, with sundry descents of the Saxons Kings, Their Marriages and Armes. By IOHN SPEED." p. 1167–8. The imprint is "AT LONDON, Printed by IOHN DAVVSON, for GEORGE HVMBLE, and are to be sold in Popes-head Pallace, at the signe of the White Horse. *Cum Priuilegio.* Anno 1632." Folio, 1243 pages besides the Index, of about 200 more.

‡ "*A Discourse* written by Sir Humphrey Gilbert Knight, to proue a passage by the Northwest to Cathaia, and the East Indies," in *Hakluyt*, iii. 41–2.

eight yeeres before his then comming into Ireland, told him there, that he came from Mar del Sur into Germany through this Northwest passage, and shewed Saluaterra (at that time being then with him in Mexico) a Sea Card* made by his owne experience and trauell in that voyage, wherein was plainly set down and described this Northwest passage, agreeing in all points with Ortelius mappe."

To give the greater credibility to his statement, Vrdaneta† [Urdeneta] stated that he had communicated an account of the discovery to the king of Portugal, and that the king charged him not to make it known to any nation. Because if the English knew it, "it would greatly hinder bothe the King of Spaine and me."

Another account‡ of a similar kind was afterwards promulgated, which produced the same encouraging effect. It states that one *Thomas Cowles*, an English seaman of Badminster in Somersetshire, made oath, that being some six years before (1573) in Lisbon he heard one *Martin Chacque*, a Portuguese mariner, read out of a book which he had published six yeares before that, that twelve years before, (1556) he, Chacque, the author of it, had set out of India for Portugal, in a small vessel of the burthen of about eighty tons, accompanied by four large ships, from which he was separated by a westerly gale; that having sailed among a number of islands he entered a gulf, which conducted him into the Atlantic, in the 59th deg. of latitude, near Newfoundland, from whence he proceeded without seeing any more land till he fell in with the northwest part of Ireland, and from thence to Lisbon, where he arrived more than a month before the other four ships with which he set out.§

We leave the reader now to form his own opinion of the influences which may have acted upon the mind of Frobisher, which caused him to undertake "the only thing of the world that was left yet vndone,"‖ and proceed to give a summary of his voyages.

Full journals of all Frobisher's three voyages are contained in Hakluyt; the first of which, "written by Christopher Hall, Master in the Gabriel," thus commences:

"The 7. of Iune [1576] being Thursday, the two Barks, viz. the Gabriel, and the Michael, of which M.[aster] Matthew Kinderslye was Captaine, and our Pinnesse set saile at Ratcliffe, and bare down to Detford, [Deptford] and there we ancred: the cause was, that our Pinnesse burst her boultsprit, and foremast aboard of a ship that rode at Detford, else wee meant to have past that day by the Court then at Grenewich.

"The 8. day being Friday, about 12 of the clocke we wayed at Detford, and set saile all three of vs, and bare downe by the Court, where whe shotte off our ordinance and made the best show we could; Her Maiestie Beholding the same, commended it, and bade vs farewell, with shaking her hand at vs out of the window. Afterward shee sent a gentleman aboard of vs, who declared that her Maiestie had good liking of our doings, and thanked vs for it, and also willed our Captaine to come the next day to the Court to take his leaue of her."

* Charts went by this name at that time.

† The same, we are told by John Barrow, F. R. S., (afterwards Sir John Barrow, Knight, not the present Sir John Barrow of the Admiralty office, but his father,) who accompanied Magelhanes in his voyage.

‡ Barrow, *ut supra*, pronounces it "utterly false."

§ *A Chronological Hist. of Voyages into the Arctic Regions, &c.* By John Barrow, F. R. S., (before cited) pp. 80, 81.

‖ Hakluyt, iii. 86.

No particular* entry appears in the journal of the precise time the little fleet weighed at Gravesend, but it was probably on the following Monday, as on Tuesday it is recorded, "being ouer against Grauesend, we observed the latitude, which was 51. degrees 33. min. and the variation of the Compasse 11. degrees and a halfe." For the twelve following days nothing is noted. On the 11th of July, "at a Southeast sunne we had sight of the land of Friesland bearing from vs West northwest 16. leagues, and rising like pinacles of steeples, and all couered with snowe." Here the latitude was 61 deg. "We sailed to the shoare and could find no ground at 150 fathoms, we hoised out our boate, and the Captaine with 4. men rowed to the shoare to get on land, but the land lying full of yce, they could not get on land, and so they came aboord again."†

Frobisher was now in great danger from ice, but he continued to press onward in his discovery, and on the 11th of August, in latitude 63 deg. 8 min., he discovered and entered the straights which ever since have borne his name. On the 14th of the same month he "ranne into another sownde, where we ankered in 8. fathome water, and there calked our ship, being weake from the wales vpward, and took in fresh water."

Before discovering the straits which bear his name, Frobisher met with several trying discouragements, such as men only like him could meet and overcome, without changing their purpose. When he was near the coast of Friesland "he lost company of his small pinnesse, which by means of the great storme he supposed to be swallowed vp of the sea, wherein he lost onely four men. Also the other barke named the Michael mistrusting the matter conueyed themselues priuily away from him, and returned home, with great report that he was cast away.

"The worthy captaine notwithstanding these discomforts, although his mast was sprung, and his toppe mast blowen ouerboord, with extreame foule weather, continued his course towards the northwest, knowing that the sea at length must needs have an ending, and that some land should haue a beginning that way."

But we have seen his entry into the straits. "After he had passed 60 leagues into the same, he went on shore and found signs where fire had been made. He saw mighty deere that seemed to be mankinde, which ranne at him, and hardly he escaped with his life in a narrow way, where he was faine to vse defence and policy to saue his life."

The details and particulars of this first voyage being few, we have comprehended them almost entirely, thus far. The remaining part consists of an account of the Indians, and what occurred between them and the English, and is of an exceedingly interesting character; it is therefore judged best to comprehend that also.

"In this place [where Frobisher so narrowly escaped from the deer] he saw and perceiued svndry tokens of the peoples resorting thither. And being ashore vpon the top of a hill, he perceiued a number of small things fleeting in the sea afarre off, which he supposed to be porposes or seales, or some kinde of strange fish; but coming neerer, he discouered them to be

* But in "Master George Best's" account of Frobisher's voyages (in Hakluyt) he says, "He (Frobisher) departed vpon the sayd voyage from Blacke-wall the 15 of Iune anno Domini 1576." There can be no doubt the old journal is right, and that though "Master George Best, a Gentleman employed in the same voyages," did "penn" a more full account, it is not a more correct one.

† Which was also accompanied with an extreame Fogge, as double gard to that Iland (vncertaine weather [whether] to fortifie it, or to imprison them.) — *Purchas's His Pilgrimage*, 739.

men in small boats made of leather. And before he could descend downe frō the hill, certaine of those people had almost cut off his boat from him, hauing stolen secretly behinde the rocks for that purpose, where he speedily hasted to his boat, and bent himselfe to his halberd, and narrowly escaped the danger and saued his boat. Afterwards he had sundry conferences with them, and they came aboord his ship, and brought him salmon and raw flesh and fish, and greedily deuoured the same before our mens faces. And to shew their agility, they tried many masteries vpon the ropes of the ship after our mariners fashion, and appeared to be very strong of their armes and nimble of their bodies." "After great curtesie, and many meetings, our mariners, contrary to their captaines direction, began more easily to trust them; and fiue of our men going ashore were by them intercepted with their boat, and were neuer since heard of to this day againe: so that the captaine being destitute of boat, barke, and all company, had scarcely sufficient number to conduct backe his barke againe. He could now neither conuey himselfe ashore to rescue his men (if he had been able) for want of a boat; and againe the subtile traitours were so wary, as they would after that neuer come within our mens danger. The captaine notwithstanding desirous to bring some token from them of his being there, was greatly discontented that he had not before apprehended some of them; and therefore to deceiue the deceiuers he wrought a prety policy; for knowing wel how they greatly delighted in our toys, and specially in belles, he rang a pretty cowbell, making signes that he would giue him the same that would come and fetch it. And because they would not come within his danger for feare, he flung one bell vnto them, which of purpose he threw short, that it might fall into the sea and be lost. And to make them more greedy of the matter he rang a louder bell, so that in the end one of them came nere the ship side to receiue the bel; which when he thought to take at the captaines hand, he was thereby taken himself: for the captaine being readily prouided let the bell fall, and caught the man fast, and plucked him with maine force boat and all into his barke out of the sea. Whereupon when he found himselfe in captivity, for very choler and disdaine he bit his tongue in twaine within his mouth: notwithstanding he died not thereof, but liued vntil he came in England, and then he died of cold which he had taken at sea.

"Now with this new pray (which was a sufficient witnesse of the captaines farre and tedious trauell towards the vnknowen parts of the world, as did well appeare by this strange infidell, whose like was neuer seene, read, nor heard of before, and whose language was neither knowen nor vnderstood of any) the sayd captaine Frobisher returned homeward, and arriued in England in Harwich the 2 of October following, and thence came to London 1576, where he was highly commended of all men for his great and noble attempt, but specially famous for the great hope he brought of the passage to Cataya."*

The notion that gold ore had been discovered in this voyage has been adverted to. A seaman by the name of Hall brought home a stone, which from its singular dark color had attracted his attention. This stone accidentally fell into the hands of some sailor's wife, who threw it into the fire. After it was heated she poured vinegar on it, and "it glistened with a bright marqueset of gold." Thence it went into the hands of an assayer of metals, and the result we have before stated.

* "He had taken possession of the Countrey in right of the Queene, and commanded his company to bring euery one somewhat, in witnesse of the same. One brought a peece of blacke Stone, like a Sea-coale, which was found to hold Gold in good quantity."—*Purchas*, 739.

The northwest passage soon grew to be a mighty matter, and preparations for a second voyage were carried on with such gold-stimulating alacrity that all could by no means be accommodated who desired to share in it. The government now took the lead. Early in March, 1577, a council was convened at Westminster, in which appeared the Lord Treasurer Burleigh, the Lord Chamberlaine, the Earl of Leicester, the Comptroller, (Sir James Crofts*) and Secretary Walsingham. At this council the voyage of "Master Furbussher" was the topic of admiration, and another was energetically recommended, because "there is great likelihood that the continuance thereof will be beneficial to the whole realme."

With such spirit was preparation carried on, that by the 26th of the following May, Frobisher was again ready for sea, "furnished with one tall ship of her Maiesties, named the Ayde of 200 tunne," and two small barks, the Gabriel, and Michael, of about thirty tons each. The Ayde was admiral, and her complement of men was one hundred, "of all sorts, whereof 30 or moer were Gentlemen and Souldiers, the rest sufficient and tall sailers."

Several persons who accompanied Frobisher in this voyage were afterwards noted captains; especially Gilbert Yorke, captain of the Michael, and Edward Fenton, captain of the Gabriel.

Upon his departure for his second voyage, Frobisher was honored with the privilege of kissing the hand of the Queen. Our limits not allowing us to go further into details concerning it, we shall, after a few brief notes, pass to his third voyage.

In this voyage Capt. Frobisher took along with him certain persons denominated gold-finders. The place where the stone was found in the last voyage appears to have been named *Hall's* Island, which was within Frobisher's Straits. On arriving here they landed, but could not find "a piece as bigge as a walnut."† They provoked the natives and were attacked by them. *Frobisher* was himself wounded as he narrowly escaped on board his boat. In York Sound they had a skirmish with a party of Indians, and unfortunately killed five or six of them. Two women they took captive, "whereof the one being old and ugly, our men thought she had been a devil or some witch, and therefore let her goe." The other was a young woman with a child on her back; being mistaken for a man she was fired upon by one of Frobisher's party, and the child was wounded in the arm. The wound was dressed by the English, but the mother, not knowing what such treatment meant, tore off the bandages and salves, "and with her own tongue, not much unlike our dogs, healed up" the wound.

Frobisher had now two captives; a man taken a little before the women just mentioned, and the young woman with the wounded child. By means of these he obtained an intercourse once more with the natives, and learned from them that the five men lost in the former voyage were yet living. They agreed to carry a letter to them and to bring back an answer; nothing, however, was ever heard of the five men, and it is more than probable

* Sir Simonds D'Ewes *Parliaments of Elizabeth.*

† "They found a great dead Fish, round like a Porcpis, twelve foote long, hauing a Horne of two yardes, lacking two ynches, growing out of the Snout, wreathed and straight, like a Wax Taper, and might be thought to be a Sea Unicorne. It was broken in the top, wherein some of the Saylers said they put Spiders, which presently died. It was reserued as a Iewell by the Queenes commandment, in her Wardrobe of Robes. Such a horne was brought home two yeeres since, [1611] found on shore in *Greeneland* by the Carpenter of *Ionas Pooles* ship, 7. foot and a half long, and sold since at Constantinople, proued good against poisons: and such a one was taken vp *A.* 1588 in the coast of Norfolke, and sould by an ignorant woman for 18. pence, which proued effectuall against poisons as I was told by Mr. *Rob. Salmon* of Leegh, who had a peece of it."— *Purchas, id.*

that it was all a sham on the part of the Indians, by which they hoped to gain some advantage over their bold and troublesome enemy.

Upon this affair with the Indians PURCHAS has this passage: "The English had some encounter with the inhabitants, which were of so fierce and terrible resolution, that finding themselves wounded, they leapt off the Rockes into the Sea, rather than they would fall into the hands of the English. The rest fled. One woman, with her child, they tooke and brought away. They had taken another of the Sauages before. This Sauage had before, in the Ship seene the Picture of his Countryman, taken the yeere before, thought him to be aliue, and began to be offinded that he would not answer him; with wonder thinking, that our men could make men liue and die at their pleasure. But strange were the gestures and behauiour of this man and the woman, when they were brought together; which were put into the same cabin, and yet gaue such apparent signes of shamefastnesse and chastity, as might be a shame to Christians to come so far short of them."

The letter intended for the *five men* was dated on "Tuesday morning the 7th of August, 1577." Having dispatched this Frobisher waited thereabouts for a return of his messengers till the 22d. None came, and as the season was getting late, and as his commission was for procuring gold ore rather than the further discovery of a passage to the Pacific Ocean, he set about loading the ships with such dirt and stones as could be found, (calling it ore,) then making bonfires on a high mount in an island where they now were, he fired a volley for a farewell, in honor of the Lady Anne, Countess of Warwick, (for whom he named the island,) and then set sail for England.

Thus ended Frobisher's second voyage, unprofitable in every point of view; dishonorable, even, in some points, and disgraceful in others. The vessels were separated on their return voyage by a storm, but they all arrived at different ports in Great Britain, with the loss of but one man by sickness, and one was washed overboard. The name of the latter was *William Smith*, "a young man, a very sufficient mariner," who was master of the Gabriel. The Indian captives are presumed to have been set at liberty in their own country.

FROBISHER'S THIRD VOYAGE.

Notwithstanding the result of the second voyage of Frobisher, the Court seem to have been highly delighted with the report brought by those concerned in it, and (no doubt before trial was made of *the ore*) immediately determined that the voyage should be succeeded by another with all dispatch. The Queen gave the name *Meta Incognita* to the country visited, and it was resolved that a colony should be sent out to inhabit there. No one of course thought of any man but Frobisher to conduct the colony to its destined country.

Accordingly *fifteen* ships were got ready, and *one hundred* persons were selected as settlers. They were to remain a year, and to retain for their use three of the ships. The rest of the fleet were to return *with cargoes of gold ore.* Frobisher was now constituted General and Admiral, and received from the queen a gold chain, and his captains were allowed to kiss her Majesty's hand.

Frobisher sailed on his third voyage from Harwich, May 30th, 1578. In this voyage many of his old companions were found by his side. Capt. Fenton was his Lieut. General; York, Best, Carew, Filpot, and many others, old captains in the former voyages were also there. They had a most perilous voyage, the ships were scattered, and one, which had on board the chief part of the frame of a house, and provisions for the settlers, was crushed by mountains of ice and sunk immediately, but the people were saved.

When the ships were at length assembled, their commanders were so bewildered by fogs, mist and snow, that they were in extreme doubt where they were. But nothing could discourage Frobisher, and "he perswaded the Fleete alwayes that they were in their right course, and knowen straights."* And however he was thought to dissemble, he soon conducted them to the Countess of Warwick's Sound in the Strait.

It was intended to settle the colony on the Countess of Warwick's Island, but taking a survey of the effects for its support and sustenance, it was found that so much had been lost that it was judged by the Admiral inexpedient to make the attempt. Nothing therefore could further be done but to freight the ships with ore and then make the best way they could back to England. They had a stormy passage homeward, but the chief of them arrived in various ports in England about the beginning of October, 1578. About forty persons had died during the expedition, which was a large proportion of the original number, which consisted of one hundred and forty-three.

It was pretended that gold was found among the rubbish brought home, and the ore (as it was called) was put in safe keeping in the queen's storehouse on Tower Hill. Extensive works were erected for assaying and refining, and the most able assayers were employed in them. For some time very extravagant reports were abroad concerning the richness of the ore, and the great per cent. it yielded. The truth appears to be, that those concerned, on finding themselves in possession of a great quantity† of dirt and stones of no value whatever, to avoid immediate and popular obloquy, kept up the idea for a time that the rubbish was actually producing gold. Such confidence had obtained abroad, that even the old chronicler of the time, Holinshed, put it down as his belief that Solomon must have got his gold from the same place whence Frobisher brought this rich ore!

How Frobisher employed his time for the next seven years nothing remains of which we are at all aware, that can inform us. We have, therefore, to pass over the intermediate years, from 1578 to 1585, which brings us to the stupendous enterprise against the dominions of PHILIP II., in the West Indies, in which he was engaged. Meantime a great excitement was kept up by one signal event after another, which pervaded the whole realm, among all ranks and conditions of men. Elizabeth had dared to aid the Netherlands in its resistance to the cruel oppressions of the Spaniards in that quarter, and an Englishman had sailed quite round the world, to the admiration of all mankind, and the astonishment of believers in its practicability themselves. And, from the known character of Frobisher, we doubt not of his active participation whenever his counsel or sword was required.

In 1585, Philip II. had virtually declared war against England by an embargo on all the vessels, men, and merchandise of that country in his ports. Whereupon one of the most powerful fleets that had ever sailed out of England was prepared to reduce the Spaniards in South America and the West Indies. It consisted of twenty-five ships and two thousand three hundred seamen and soldiers. Of this fleet SIR FRANCIS DRAKE was

* Hakluyt, iii. 112.

† About *thirteen hundred* tons was the produce of the third voyage.—*Barrow, the younger.*

appointed General and Admiral, CAPT. MARTIN FROBISHER Vice Admiral, FRANCIS KNOLLES Rear Admiral, and CHRISTOPHER CARLEILL was Lieutenant General of the land forces.

The accounts of this expedition, while they give our Admiral due credit in general terms, give us no particulars or incidents with which to elucidate his biography. The particular history of the enterprise belongs to the life of Drake. Suffice it to say, it was completely successful. St. Jago, Carthagena, St. Domingo, and St. Augustine were reduced, a spoil of £60,000 in money was taken, two hundred brass and forty iron cannon were brought to England.

The time employed in this expedition was about ten months. The fleet sailed on the 14th of September, 1585, and returned to England the 28th of July, 1586. After Drake and Frobisher had taken St. Augustine in Florida, they sailed to Virginia, where, finding the colony in distress, they took the people into their ships, at their request, and carried them to England. In the voyage with Drake, Frobisher commanded a ship called the *Primrose.*

We next meet with Capt. Frobisher early in 1588. The war with Spain was approaching a crisis. The great struggle was between papist and protestant. Complete annihilation of the heretics of England was confidently anticipated by all papal Europe. Frobisher was one among the foremost who stood up to breast the threatened storm. Philip had prepared an immense navy with which to attack England. To this he gave the name of the *Invincible Armada.* Lord Howard was the nominal commander of the English fleet, and in writing to the queen he mentions Frobisher and others as "men whom the world doth judge of the greatest experience that this realme hath."

When the Spanish fleet arrived on the English coast, it was drawn up in order of battle. Frobisher was one of the three commanders who in the most undaunted manner began the attack upon it. His separate achievements are but indifferently recorded, but in his first onset a sensible impression was made on the Spanish galeons; some being crippled and others dispersed. Soon after, the English fleet was divided into squadrons, the command of one of which was given to Frobisher. Such were his immediate services, that the Lord High Admiral knighted him on board of his own ship, as he did also Capt. John Hawkins at the same time. He was one of the very few knights created during this memorable invasion by the Spaniards, if indeed there were any others made during the expedition, saving himself and his valiant companion in arms just mentioned.

The naval operations of the English against the *Armada* commenced in May and ended in August. The discomfiture of the Spaniards was most complete. Out of *one hundred and thirty-four sail* (ninety-one of which were immense ships, then called "galleons") only *thirty-three* ever returned to Spain. In men their loss was more deplorable; upwards of *thirteen thousand five hundred* either fell in battle, perished by famine, or were swallowed up by shipwreck!

The rejoicing in all parts of England at this signal deliverance was unbounded; shows, bonfires, and processions lasted many days. The streets of London were decorated in the most superb manner that could be devised to honor the heroes who walked in proud procession along them. Frobisher was conspicuous there — it was the proud day of his life.*

* Those who would have a correct idea of those doings and days would do well to read STRYPE's account of them in his *Annals.*

The next year we find Sir Martin cruising upon the coast of the Netherlands, apparently to watch the actions of the Spaniards, and to give intelligence should there be any appearance of another *Armada*, which some anticipated. Several of the letters which he wrote while on this service are extant, but their orthography is stranger than any thing we have ever met with, even of that age, and their substance, so far as can be guessed out, of no very great importance.

In 1590 he sailed to the coast of Spain with a fleet of five ships, commissioned by the queen as Admiral. The chief object of the expedition was to intercept the Spanish treasure ships, but none could be discovered. King Philip was aware of the intentions of Frobisher, and he ordered twenty ships to be got ready to proceed in quest of him. His fleet actually put to sea, but learning that five other English ships, under Sir John Hawkins, were also cruising in aid of Frobisher, Philip sent after and recalled his fleet, being "better advised (says Monson*) than to adventure twenty of his ships to ten of ours."

Before returning to England Frobisher stood over to the Azores. Here he sent a trumpet to the governor of Fayal "in a friendly manner" upon some pecuniary business, but the messenger was fired upon, and probably killed, as Frobisher sent the governor word that the city should suffer severely for the barbarous conduct he had received. He then departed for England.

In 1592 Sir Martin Frobisher was sent to recall Sir Walter Raleigh from an expedition he had undertaken against South America, and to take command of Sir Walter's fleet himself; which consisted of fifteen ships. During this enterprise one immensely rich carrack was taken "with a prodigious slaughter" of its men. It was called the *Madre de Dios*, (Mother of God) and was one hundred and sixty feet in length, of one thousand six hundred tons burthen, with a crew of six hundred men. In her was found treasure to the value of £150,000 sterling, besides what was plundered by the English sailors.

Spain had formed a league with France, and Philip had sent three thousand men for the protection of Brest. The faction in France in league with Spain consisted of the Catholic French, who had revolted from their king. To aid Henry against these revolters and their abettors, Elizabeth sent Sir John Norris at the head of three thousand men to besiege Brest, and Sir Martin Frobisher with a fleet consisting of four of her own ships and several others, to support Norris. This was the last expedition in which Frobisher was engaged. In a joint attack made by the forces under him and those under Norris upon Fort Crozon, Sir Martin received a wound in his side, from the effects of which he died, as before related.

The English took the fort, but with a wretched sacrifice of life, at which Elizabeth was much grieved. She wrote to Norris complaining of his rashness, "but (says Camden) this Letter came too late."† In storming this place the barbarity of the English was equal to the prodigality of their own lives. "During the heat of this Siege (says our author) *D'Aumont* and *Norris* thought good to undermine the Eastern Bulwark on that Side where the French were posted, and to blow it up: which took effect, and opened a great Breach. Now they fall upon the Fort on all sides. *Latham*, *Smith* and others, with the English, stormed the Western Bulwark, whilst the French set upon the Eastern, and the rest the Wall betwixt both

* *Naval Tracts.*

† Verum hæ literæ serius allatæ — *Annales rerum Anglicarum*, etc., 668.

on the South; and this lasted from Noon till four of the clock. At length the English made themselves Masters of the Western Work, and *Thomas de Parades*, the commander of the Spaniards, being slain, entered the Fort, plucked down the Spanish Flags, and opened an entrance for the rest, who put the Garrison Souldiers, in number about 400, to the Sword, and laid the Fort level with the Ground." "Neither was this Victory gotten by the English without Bloud; many valiant Souldiers being slain, and Sir *Martin Forbisher* wounded with a small shot in the hip, who brought back the Fleet to Plymouth, and there died. A valourous and stout man he was, and to be reckoned among the famousest men of our age for Counsell and Conduct, and Glory gotten by Navall Exploits, as what I haue before spoken of him plainly appeareth."

There is an entry in the register at Plymouth of his death, but no monument any where to his memory. His body, after being embowelled, (a custom of those days) was sent to London for interment. A portrait of him is said to be in the picture gallery of Oxford. There was an engraved portrait of him published a few years after his death, and is contained in the Heroology. It is from this we have caused our copy to be taken. We have no doubt of its faithfulness, and it fully justifies the character given of him by the early writers.

Although the name of Frobisher is not less poetical than many others often met with in poetry, yet we scarcely remember to have met with his above two or three times in our limited reading of that class of authors. Among the commendatory effusions poured out upon CAPTAIN JOHN SMITH, and published in his curious book of "Trve Travels, Adventvres," &c., our discoverer comes in for a share, in the following lines:

From far fetcht *Indies*, and Virginia's soyle,
Here *Smith* is come to shew his Art and skill.
He was the *Smith* that hammered famins foyle,
And on *Powhatan's* Emperour had his will.
Though first *Columbus*, *Indies* true *Christofer;*
Cabots braue *Florida*, much admirer;
Meta Incognita, rare *Martin Frobisher;*
Gilberts braue *Humphrey*, Neptunes deuourer;
Captaine *Amadis*, *Raleighs* discourer;
Sir *Richard Grenvill*, *Zelands* braue coaster:
Drake, doomes, drowne, death, *Spaines* scorner;
Gosnolds Relates, *Pring* prime observer.
Though these be gone, and left behinde a name,
Yet *Smith* is here to Anvile out a peece
To after Ages, and eternall Fame,
That we may haue the golden *Iasons* fleece.
He *Vulcan* like did forge a true Plantation,
And chain'd their Kings to his immortall glory;
Restoring peace and plentie to the Nation,
Regaining honor to this worthy Story.

A WORD TO MODERNIZERS.

The old style of composition, without the old mode of orthography to convey its meaning, is a falsification of the times of the original. To alter an original to suit modern orthography is to bastardize a performance; such is neither the original author's production, nor can the modernizer with decency claim it. It always reminds us of that couplet of Pope, beginning "As heavy mules are neither horse nor ——"

INDIAN WAR PAPERS.

[Communicated for the Antiquarian Journal by CHARLES W. PARSONS, M. D., of Providence, R. I., member of the N. E. H. Gen. Society.]

I.

Capt. Frost and sergnt neall

Gentelmen I thought to have mett with you here at maior Sheply's [Shaplegh] but understandng the guns were herd about Stargeon Creeck it is well you tooke your march as you did — my dasier and order is that you garrison you owne house with 10 men and doe your beste now the snow is vpon the grond which will be Aduantadge upon ther tracks. Your letter I reseued about garrisoning your house. We have a party of men upon your side comanded by goodman banmore (?) and John wingut [Wingate?] and Joseph Fild are going out this night: and in Case you want men goe to the garrisons aboue and especially Samon faull and take men for any expedition: and all the Comanders of the garrisons are hereby requierd to Atand your order herin and this shall be your surficant warrant.

dated this 8 nomber 1675 about 3 oclock.

Your servent Richard Waldern
Sergent Maior

I intend god willing to be at
nachwanack to morrow morning
therfor would dasier to her from you
R: W.

II.

Instructions for Capt. Charles Frost

You must take notice that the party of souldiers now sent you are designed cheifely for the defense of Yorkeshire & the dwellinges on the upper parts of Pascatay. You are therfore principally so to improve them, by your constant marches about the borders of Wells, Yorke, Nochiwannick Cochecho Exeter Haueril &c. as you shal have intelligence of the enemies' motion, whom you are upon every opportunity without delay to persue & endeavor to take Capteve, kill & destroy

Having notice of any partie of the enemy at any fishing place or other rendevous you shall lay hold on such opportunity to assault the enemy.

If you shall understand the enemy to be too numerous for your smal partie you shall advise wth Major Walderne and desire his Assistance to furnish you wth a greater force for a present service, but if you judg the opportunity or advantage may be lost by such a delay you shall for a present service require the inhabitants or garrison souldiers of the place where you are or so many as may be necessary for you & safe for the place im̄ediately to attend you upon such present service for destroying the enemy.

In all your motions & marches, silence & speed will be your advantage & security.

You must supply your present wants of victuals & amunition for your souldiers out of the townes & places where you come, especially from Portsmouth to whom I have writt for that end, & if a larger supply be wanting you shal give notice thereof to my selfe or the Govern^r^ & Counsel

The necessity & distress of those parts & confidence of your Courage & industry doe require your utmost activity in the management of this business w^thout^ spending needeless expensive delayes up and be doing & the Lord prosper your endeavors

You shall from time to time give intelligence of all occurrences of moment to Major Walderne, & my selfe, & as much as may be w[thout] prejudice of the service advise wth Major Walderne & the Gentelmen of Portsmouth upon whom you must principally depend for your present supplyes

[Then follows in another hand:]

for Charles Frost

These ar the Instructions Received from y[e] Maj[r] Generall at the same time as his Comiss of Aprill 1677 & delivered to him the 13th according to order

Yours Rob[t] Pike
Serg[t]

III.

To Capt Charles Frost

You are hereby Required in his Maj[ties] name to Impresse six able Souldiers either of yo[r] Own town or others compleatly ffitted wth Armes & Amunition to Attend y[e] Service of y[e] Country in yo[r] Garrison or otherwise as you shall see meet, & this shall be yo[r] sufficient War[tt] from

Richard Waldern Serget maior

2: May 1677

IV.

Province
of Mayne.

To Major Charles Ffrost
Instructions as followeth.

Pursuant to the Comission signed, & bearing same date with these p[r]sents

You are with all care & speed to hasten gathering of your Soldjers together, and in case Cap[t]. Simon Willard be in any wise disinabled that he can[t] attend y[t] service you are to comissionate such other meet person as you shall Judge meet. & appoynt all other officers as you shall have occasion.

You shall in all places & by all wayes & meanes to your power take, kill, & destroy y[e] enemy without limitation of place or time as you shall have opportunity. & you ar also inpowred to comissionate any other person or persons to do the like.

You shall carefully inspect all the Garisons in y[r] Province, & reduce them to such a number, & appoynt such places as shall in yo[r] wisdome most conduce to the preservation of the people, & y[t] y[e] great charge now expended for y[e] same may be abated.

Comitting you to y[e] Co & pe
of God almighty upon whom you
have all yo[r] dependance

I subscribe

Ffeb. 17. 1689. Yo[r] Loveing friend

Tho: Danforth. Presid[t].

[Along the margin is written]

I have prevailed with L[t]. Andrews to come back esteemeing him a fitt man for your L[t]. and I would y[t] you accordingly enterteyn him.

[Superscription.]

To Maio[r] Charles
Ffrost in
P. L[t]. Andros Q. D. C. Kittery

V.

Province of
Maine Scarborough the 11th Nour 1689.

Att a Councill of warr held at the point Garrison Present Majr Benjemen Church, Capt Sylvanus Dauis, Capt. Wlm. Bassitt, Capt Simon Willard, wth the Rest of ye Comission Offecers of Saco, Ffelmouth & Scarborough

Itt is Ordered that one hundred theire Majesties Horses now in this present Exspedition against the Coman Enimie, be detatched out of the seuerall Companyes, wch sd numbr for ye security of ye Garrisons there Resident, & in Case any of ye Enemie be discovered or Any tracks of them be made in this winter Season, untill further force be sent that may Advance to theire head Quarters.

Souldiers Quartered in ye towne Ship of Saco twenty men; in theire two Garrisons. In ye township of Scarborough twenty men in theire Garrisons viz: three Sperwink Included.

Ffelmouth the 13 Nour: Att a Councill of Warr held in persuance of wt is above written, by Majr. Benjamen Church & the officers abovesd. Added Capt Nathl Hall, Leiut Thaddeus Clark, Leiut Elisha Andrews, Mr Elisha Gallison, Leiut George Ingersoll, Leiut Ambrous Davis, Mr. Robt. Lawrance, Mr. Jno Palmer & othrs &c.

Itt is ordered that sixty souldjers be Quartered in Felmouth, besides the Inhabitents, and, the Souldjers that shall Belonge to the ffoart, wch shall be ffifteen Souldjers besides the Comander & Guner, & ye Remayner to be sent to Boston, to be Ready to Returne Accordinge to Order.

Itt is Ordered that there be A Sufficiant Garrison Erectd about Mr Gallisons house for a mayne Court of Guard, Together wth Mr Robt Lawrance. his Garrison, wch two Garrisons are to be supplyed with ye Sixty Souldjers left for to guard the sd towne.

Itt is Ordered that Capt Nathll Hall is to take Charge as Comandr in Cheife of those fforces that are lefft for the defence of the Above sd three Townes, Those Souldjers that belong to ffoart Loyall only to be undr the Comandr of said ffoart.

Ordered that Leiut Richd Huniwell, is to Take the Charge & Conduct of the twenty Souldjers quartered at Blew-point Black point & Spurwinck Garrisons, as he the sd Leiut. Huniwell, shall Recaive orders from time to time from ye sd Comandr in Cheife.

Itt is Ordered that Ensigne John Hill is to take the Care and Conduct of those twenty Souldjers Quartered at Saco Garrison as the sd Ensigne Hill shall Recaive orders from time to time, from his sd Comandr in Cheife.

Itt is Ordered that ye fforty Souldjers posted att Saco, Scarborough & Spurwinke are to be obedient unto ye Comanders of ye severall Garrisons where they shall be posted whilst in Garrison, but to Atend the Comands of Leiut Huniwell & Ensigne John Hill respectively as they are Concerned upon theire scoutinge or marchinge out:

Given undr my hand this
14th of Nouembr: 1689: By Concent of sd: Councill
p mee
Benjamin Church
Comandr in Cheife.

[To be continued.]

INDIAN SUMMER.

As connected with the history of the Indian Wars of the western country, it may not be amiss to give an explanation of the term "Indian Summer."

The reader must here be reminded, that during the long continued Indian Wars, sustained by the first settlers of the western country, they enjoyed no peace excepting in the winter season, when, owing to the severity of the weather, the Indians were unable to make their excursions into the settlements. The onset of winter was therefore hailed as a jubilee by the early inhabitants of the country, who throughout the spring and the early part of the fall, had been cooped up in their little uncomfortable forts, and subject to all the distresses of the Indian War.

At the approach of winter, therefore, all the farmers excepting the owner of the fort, removed to their cabins on their farms, with the joyful feelings of a tenant of a prison on recovering his release from confinement. All was bustle and hilarity in preparing for winter, by gathering in the corn, digging potatoes, fattening hogs, and repairing the cabins. To our forefathers the gloomy months of winter were more pleasant than the zephyrs of spring and the flowers of May.

It however sometimes happened, that after the apparent onset of winter, the weather became warm, the smoky time commenced, and lasted for a considerable number of days. This was the INDIAN SUMMER; because it afforded the Indians an opportunity of visiting the settlements with their destructive warfare. The melting of the snow saddened every countenance, and the general warmth of the sun chilled every heart with horror. The apprehension of another visit from the Indians, and of being driven back to the detested fort, was painful in the highest degree, and the distressing apprehension was frequently realized.

A man of the name of John Carpenter was taken early in the month of March, in the neighbourhood of this place [Wellsburgh, Va.] There had been several warm days, but the night preceding his capture there was a heavy fall of snow. His two horses which they took with him, nearly perished in swimming the Ohio. The Indians as well as himself suffered severely with the cold before they reached the Moravian towns on the Muskingum. In the morning after the first day's journey beyond the Moravian towns, the Indians sent out Carpenter to bring in the horses which had been turned out in the evening, after being hobbled. The horses had made a circuit, and had fallen into the trail by which they came the preceding day, and were making their way homewards.

When he overtook the horses and had taken off their fetters, as he said, he had to make a most awful decision. He had a chance, and hardly a chance, to make his escape, with a certainty of death should he attempt it without success. On the other hand, the horrible prospect of being tortured to death by fire presented itself; as he was the first prisoner taken that spring, of course the general custom of the Indians of burning the first prisoner every spring, doomed him to the flames.

After spending a few minutes in making his decision, he resolved on attempting an escape, and effected it by way of forts Laurens, M'Intosh, and Pittsburgh. If I recollect rightly, he brought both his horses home with him. This happened in the year 1782.—*Doddridge's Notes on the Settlement and Indian Wars of the Western Parts of Virginia and Pennsylvania*, p. 265–8.

THE PEASE FAMILY.

[By FREDERICK S. PEASE of Albany, N. Y., member of the N. E. Hist. Geneal. Soc.]

The ancient arms of Pease are here represented, having been preserved in the branch of which Joseph Robinson Pease is a member, and used as a family seal for one hundred and fifty years, viz:

Per fesse Argent and Gules, an Eagle displayed counterchanged.

Crest — An Eagle's head erased, the beak holding a stalk of Pea-haulm, all proper. Said to signify that the person to whom it was granted had been a commander, but not in chief.*

ORIGIN OF THE NAME.†

So subtle are the clues which guide us in tracing out the origin of family names that in many cases it seems impossible to arrive at any positive conclusion. But in the present case it seems highly probable, that while the name was variously rendered into English, in some instances it retained its Celtic appellation; and the transformation of PEA into Peas, as the name was often found in early records, and Pease being so very easy and natural, that for the want of a better derivation, we ought not to hesitate to adopt this as the most probable one.‡

The name has always been common in England; but as there were no

* Arms often give a very certain clue to the origin of the name of the bearer, especially if they be ancient. May not the name of this family be derived from the plant so conspicuous in its most ancient arms? If the individual who introduced that valuable esculent into England, or from being the first to cultivate it successfully, took its name, he is more to be honored than a thousand Napoleons. — ED.

† The author having the same account from the COLLEGE OF ARMS upon the origin of the name PEASE as that we have printed for PEABODY, (in our last volume, p. 153, &c.,) it becomes necessary only to refer to that curious paper. — ED.

‡ That is, the one derived from the paper referred to in the last note. — ED.

parish registers kept prior to 1570, no particulars can be learned previous to that date. The earliest record that can be found is, that John Pease married Margaret Wilson, at the Holy Trinity Church, Hull, June 9th, 1583.

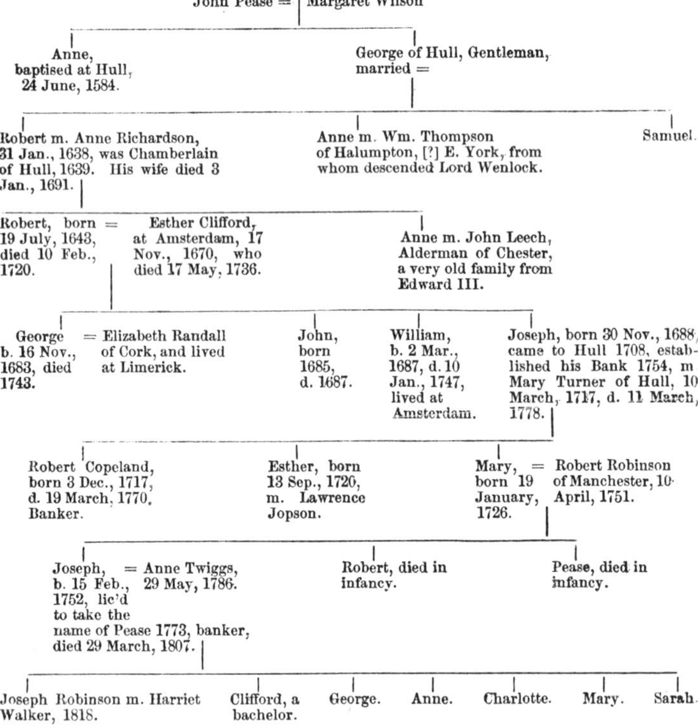

It appears that about 1660, Mr. Robert Pease emigrated to Amsterdam, and died there. His son William lived with him and died without issue. George Pease settled at Limerick, married and died without issue. Joseph, the youngest son, came to Hull, (where the family had resided for some generations,) in 1708. His descendants, Joseph Robinson Pease and family, still reside in that neighbourhood.

Joseph Robinson Pease is successor in the bank that was established in Hull by Joseph Pease, his great-grandfather, in 1754. His residence is Hesslewood, near Hull. His late father's connections are among the large landed proprietors in Staffordshire, and his mother's among those in Derbyshire. His own are amongst some of the most highly respected landed proprietors in East Yorkshire. His youngest brother, a clergyman, and two of Sir Robert Peel's brothers, married sisters.

There are several families, respectable yeomanry, in the neighbourhood of Doncaster and Pontefract.* There is another highly respectable branch residing in the county of Durham.

John Pease of Darlington, who is a preacher of the society of Friends, states that the branch of which he is a member has been located in Darlington for five generations, and the first of the name who settled there came

* Usually pronounced *Pomfret*, in England. — Ed.

ADDENDA ET CORRIGENDA.

Page 27. For "and used as a family seal for one hundred and fifty years," read "who has letters one hundred and fifty years old, which bear the impress of this seal."

Page 27 – 28. For "no parish registers," read "no *regular* parish registers."

Page 28. For "Anne m. Wm. Thompson of H*alu*mpton," read "Hulmpton."

" For "Robert *Copeland*, born 3 Dec. 1717," read "Robert."

" For "Joseph = Anne Twigg*s*," read "Joseph Robinson = Anne Twigge."

" For "Clifford, *a bachelor*," read " = Sarah Cookson."

" Read "George M. A. (in holy orders) = Jane Swinfen of Swinfen."

" Read "Anne = Col. Maister, East York militia."

" Read "Charlotte = Capt. Mason, R. N.

Page 29, third line. For "Joseph," read "Joseph, Jun."

The sign manual of ROBERT PEASE, dated 1711, in his 69th year.

The sign manual of JOSEPH PEASE, dated 1738, in his 51st year.

The sign manual of EDWARD PEASE of Darlington, at about the age of 70, whose mind first practically grasped the question of improved communication by means of a public railway; and by whose influence and means it was carried into successful operation—he having been chairman of the Board of Directors. The Stockton and Darlington Railway was opened in 1825 (See Vol. II, page 313). From it rose George Stephenson, the first English railway engineer, who was selected by Mr. Pease, when an obscure engine-wright at Killingworth Colliery; to which, and his own native genius, he owed his subsequent celebrity. Mr. P. is now in his 83d year, and unusually vigorous; devoting his time to philanthropic objects, and the service of the Society of Friends.

The sign manual of JOSEPH PEASE junior, son of Edward Pease of Darlington. (He had an uncle Joseph.) He was chosen the representative of the south division of the county of Durham, about the close of the year 1832. The Reform bill had just passed, and the electors were determined to select a man in place of the sons of the nobility, for their future representative, and succeeded beyond all expectation; the votes standing for Pease 2273, the next highest 2218, and the lowest 1841. This was considered a great triumph by the liberal party; for the other two not only professed in some degree the same political sentiments, but were of the aristocracy, and supported by that class.

The election of a "Friend," or, as he was sometimes called, "the Quaker member," was quite an event; and some urged that the simple declaration or affirmation would not be accepted, and that he could not take his seat. He was, however, admitted into the house *without the formality of an oath* (which he had declared he would not take) by acclamation. At that time, also, being previous to the penny postage, every member could receive a certain number of letters, and forward a certain number free of postage; but to prevent fraud, they were required to write the date and direction in full, in their own hand. Here another objection arose: some declaring that the Friends' plain way of superscribing would not frank a letter. Here again the liberal spirit of the day triumphed, and a Friend as member, and a Friend's frank, ceased to be a curiosity. He continued to be returned for each successive parliament after this, being a very good and industrious member, until he declined on account of the pressure of duties at home.

[To face page 28, vol. iii.]

from the West Riding of the county of York. A village between the towns of Pontefract and Barnsly, named Scarcroft, was once pointed out to him as the abode of his ancestors. His brother Joseph, also a member of that society, has been several times returned to Parliament for the southern division of the county of Durham. Also, Edward Pease of Darlington, a member of the society of Friends, who has the credit of designing and establishing the Stockton and Darlington Railway, the first one in England.*

No connection as yet can be established between the ancestors of the family in this country and the name in England, although there is no doubt of the fact of such connection.

The following arms have been borne by different branches of the family:

PEASE (Hull, county of York.) Vert. a Chevron between three Bucks trippant Or, in the middle Chief point a Bezant on a Chief per fesse Gu. and Ar. an Eagle displayed counter changed.

Crest, an Eagle's head erased, holding in the beak a slip of Pea-haulm ppr.

PEASE (as borne by Robert Copeland Pease, Esqr., of Ottery St Mary, county of Devon,) son of Joseph Pease and Mary Turner, born 3 Dec., 1717, died 19 March, 1770. Gu. a Saltire Ar. between four Plates, each charged with a Leopard's face ppr.

Crest, a Leopard's head guardant couped at the neck holding in the mouth a sword barways ppr. collared Az.

PEASE (London, granted to Robert Pease, Gent., 1763.) Per pale Gu. and Vert. a Fesse indented, Erminois between three Lambs pass. Ar.

Crest, on a Mount Vert. a Dove rising, Ar. holding in the beak Gu. a Pea-stalk, the blossoms and pods ppr., legs as the beak. — *Burke's Ency. of Heraldry.*

PEASE (Sr George Pease, 1642.) Az. a Chevron between three Lozenges Or.

Crest, a Leopard's head erased ppr. languid Gu.

Those of the name who came first to this country were John and Robert Pease; and their arrival has been variously accounted for by history and tradition as follows, viz:

One traditionary account is, that in the fall of 1632, or a year or two later, a vessel bound from England to South Virginia, fell in with the south shoal of Nantucket, came up through the Vineyard sound and anchored off Cape Poge, on account of a distemper which, like a plague, raged among the passengers and crew, twenty-five of whom died. Or, according to another account, scarcity of provisions was the occasion. Four men with their families, requested to be put on shore, preferring rather to take their chance with the natives, than to pursue the voyage under such distressing circumstances. They landed at the spot since called (Pease's Point,) Edgartown. Their names were John Pease, Thomas Vincent, —— Trapp, and —— Browning or Norton. A red coat, presented on landing, by Pease to the Chief or Sachem, secured at once the good offices of the tribe; and they were treated with hospitality.

In order to shelter themselves from the approaching winter, Pease and his company made excavations in the side of a hill near the water, whence they could command a full view of the harbor and adjacent bay. Some vestiges of these caves still remain. They remained here through the cold season, and were joined by others at different times until, in 1642, the whole number of families amounted to twenty-four.

* Vol. II. page 313.

Another tradition that has obtained credit, and justly, because history has at length come to its support, is, that two brothers came over and landed at Boston.

John Pease aged 27, and Robert Pease aged 27, are proved by the custom-house books to have embarked in the Francis, John Cutting master, in the end of April, 1634, from Ipswich. This ship arrived at Boston without the loss of a single passenger.

Neither of them appear to have had wives with them, but John had with him Robert, aged three years, and a Miss Clark, aged 15, daughter of a fellow passenger, and a Miss Greene, aged 15, perhaps a servant.

The names of John and Robert Pease are found next among the inhabitants of Salem, in 1637. The following is according to the records of the first church of that town:

Widow Pease joined the church 1639, Robert Pease joined it 1643. Both dead in 1660. (Robert died in 1644.) Nathaniel, Sarah, and Mary, children of Robert Pease, baptized 15th day of 8th month, 1643. John, Robert, Mary, and Abraham, children of John Pease, baptized 3d day of 5th month, 1667. John Pease, admitted to the church, 4th day of 5th month, 1667. James, son of John Pease, baptized November, 1670. Isaac, son of John Pease, baptized September, 1672. On sacrament day John Pease and his wife had a letter of recommendation granted to the church at Springfield, (now Enfield, Ct.,) Oct. 6, 1681. Ann Pease was admitted to the church from Ipswich in 1672.

Who widow Pease was there is no present means of ascertaining certainly; but there can hardly be a doubt that John Pease, whose children were baptized at different times from 1667 to 1672, who joined the church in 1667, and who, with his wife, was dismissed and recommended to the church at Springfield, (Enfield) was the son of widow Pease.

It seems most natural to suppose that John and Robert Pease, whose names are found at Salem in 1637, were the same who came over in the *Francis*. But there is a tradition relative to the subject, which may pass for what it is worth: Capt. Valentine Pease of Edgartown, who is upwards of 80 years of age, has heard his father and grandfather say that the two eldest sons of John Pease, who, according to tradition, landed at Martha's Vineyard, removed from there to Salem, and that their names were James and John.

Among a large number of persons of Salem, owning estates there "before 1661," are the names of Nathaniel and Isaac Pease.

Miss Caulkins, in her *History of Norwich, Ct.*, states, that a person named John Pease was there among the first settlers in 1660. This may admit of a rational doubt; for in Vol. I. p. 315 of the *New England Hist. and Geneal. Register*, there is a list of the first settlers of Norwich, which has no John Pease, but John *Pearce*, and agreeing with the authoress above cited in all the other names. It is hardly credible that there should have been three men named John Pease in the colonies of about the same age, at that early period; but admitting it to have been so, the one in Norwich in 1660, could hardly have been the same person who was in Salem, and was enrolled a member of the artillery company in 1661; for it is most probable that he was a resident of Salem from his first arrival there until his removal to Enfield, Ct.

The following notices are to be found in the Annals of Salem:

1643. Lucy Peas of Salem is arraigned before the Genl. Court chard. with having embraced the opinions of Samuel Gorton.—On renouncing them she is dismissed.

1682. Capt. John Peas, Sen. æ. 52, had moved lately from Salem to Enfield. He had been a deputy to the general court.
1689. Capt. Samuel Peas is sent after Pirates in the Sloop Mary of Boston. He came up with & fought one in "Martin Vineyard Sound." Capt. Pease is killed, but the pirate is taken by his crew.*
1692. Sarah Pease is prosecuted for witchcraft at Salem, & imprisoned.

FIRST GENERATION.

(1) I. JOHN, who came in the *Francis* from Ipswich in 1634, aged 27, and whose name appears among the inhabitants of Salem in 1637.

SECOND GENERATION.

(2) II. JOHN, who removed to Enfield, Ct., in 1681. He was twice married. His first wife was Mary ——, who died January 5, 1668; the name of the second was Ann Cummings, to whom he was married Oct. 8, 1669. He died at Enfield 1689, aged 60. His children by his first wife were,

1—1.—John, b. March 30, 1654. (3)
2—2.—Robert, b. March 14, 1656. (4)
3—3.—Mary, b. Oct 8, 1658.
4—4.—Abraham, b. April 5, 1662, m. Jane Mentor, d. 1735, without issue.
5—5.—Jonathan, b. Jan. 2, 1668. (5)

By his second wife he had

6—6.—James, b. Oct. 23, 1670. (6)
7—7.—Isaac, b. July 15, 1672. (7)
8—8.—Abigail, b. Oct. 15, 1675.

[To be continued.]

DEATHS IN WRENTHAM.

1673 to 1704.

[Copied from the Records by MR. G. W. MESSINGER of Boston, member of the N. Eng. Hist. Geneal. Soc.]

The first person buried in the Burying-Place in this town was an infant

son of John and Mary Ware who	died	Feb 10 1673
Mary Littlefield wife of John	"	Jan 13 1674
Jonathan son of Cornelius & Sary ffisher	"	Nov 9 1675
Eliazur son of John & Mary Ware	"	Sept 1675
Sarah wife of Corn[s]. Fisher	"	Feb 28 1675
Elizabeth dau of James & Anna Mostman	"	Mar 6 1675–76
Nath[l]. Crosman son of Rob. & Sarah killed by the Indians	"	Mar 8 1675–76

March y[e] last the Inhabitants were drawn off by reason of the war.

* In Vol. II. page 393, is given from the original depositions of Capt. Pease's crew a circumstantial account of the action in which the captain lost his life. As a further elucidation of this affair, we add from Mr. FELT's *Annals of Salem*, as follows:

"The Council having been informed, that Thomas Hawkins and others were acting as pirates order the sloop Restitution with 40 men, *Joseph Thaxter* master to go after them. These pirates took the Ketch Mary. Capt. *Hellen Chard*, of Salem the 9th [August, 1689,] 3 leagues from Half Way Rock. They captured the brig Merrimack of Newburyport, Capt. *John Kent*, on the 22d, in 'Martin Vineyard Sound.' [Then as above in the text.] They killed him, and wounded some of his crew; but were taken by his Lieut. *Benjamin Gallop*, and in October brought to Boston, where four of them belonged. They were condemned to die, but reprieved."

Mary wife of Joseph Kingsbury	died	July 31 1680
William son of W^{m} & Ruth Maccane Killed by his own Gun accidentally	“	July 6 168–
Sarah dau of John & Sarah Guild	“	Dec 7 1682
Silence Wilson in the 10th year	“	Feb 24 1683
Sarah Lawrence	“	Mar 25 1684
Mehitable wife Thom^{s} Thurston	“	Aug 11 1692
Ichabod son “ “	“	Aug 29 “
Mary dau “ “	“	Mar 30 1688
Joseph Kingsbury died in an awful and dreadful way		Dec 16 1688
Isaac Blake	“	March 8 1689
Hezakiah son of Benj & Judith Rocket	“	1689
Solomon Shears	“	May 6 “
Sarah Lawrance wife of John	“	Aug 30 1690
Sarah dau of John & Sarah Fairbanks	“	Sep 19 1690
Hannah dau of Saml. & Hannah	“	Oct 26 1689
Hannah wife of John Pond	“	Jan 2 1691
Abigail dau of John & Abg^{l} Day	“	1692
Elizabeth dau of John & Melitiah Fisher	“	1693
Ruth Fisher	“	July 28 “
Judith wife of James Meads	“	Oct 9 1694
Priscilla dau of Benj & Priscilla Grant	“	July 14 1694
Mary dau of John & Sarah Laurance	“	Dec 8 “
Mary “ “ Edwd. & Robt. Gay in her 7th year	“	Oct 7 1695
Robert son of Robt. & Joanna Pond	“	May 28 1694
—None Puffer son of Rich^{d}. & Ruth	“	Jan 16 1697–8
Cornelius Fisher died being the first head of a family who died in the town in a natural way for 30 years		Jan 2 1699
John Blake	“	May 25 1700
Sarah dau of Benj & Sarah Hall	“	May 6 1697
Sarah Hancock	“	Nov 17 1700
Thomas Thurston	“	Dec 15 1704
Ephraim Pond	“	Dec 22 “
Mary Gay in her fifth year	“	May 30 1705
Thomas son of Thomas & Hannah George	“	Sep 17 1704
Hannah daughter “ “	“	Sep 17 “
Thos George — the father	“	Oct 31 “
John George	“	Sep 21 “
John Maccane son of John & Eliz^{h}	“	Jan 9 1701
Hannah wife of Cornelius Fisher	“	March 6 “
Ebenezer Guild son of John & Sarah	“	Sept 13 “
Thos Puffer of Providence	“	July 11 1702
Dea Samuel Fisher	“	Jan 5 1703
Mehitable daughter of Jona Wight	“	Sept 3 1704
Samuel Whiting	“	April 2 “
Anna Blake daughter of John & Joanna	“	April 8 “
Mary Shears wife of Samuel	“	April 26 “
Theodoras Man daughter of Theodore	“	Sep 1 1703
Eleazer Metcalf	“	May 14 1704

THE WYMAN FAMILY.

[Collected by T. B. WYMAN, JR., of Charlestown, Mass.]

The name of WYMAN is of German derivation, and was originally spelled WEYMANN. The two individuals first named in the following genealogy are the progenitors of the largest portion of the Wyman family in this country. The first mention made of them is in Charlestown, Dec. 18, 1640, (see *Frothingham*, p. 106) as signers of the "town orders" coeval with the settlement of WOBURN. Their descendants have been numerous and chiefly among the "sturdy yeomanry," possessing substance and a fair estimation in the ordinary ranks of life. At the present time the family is chiefly comprised in that class so ably apostrophized by the poet in the thrilling lines —

> "Heart of the people — WORKING MEN!
> Marrow and nerve of human powers;
> Who on your sturdy backs sustain,
> Through streaming time, this World of Ours."

FIRST GENERATION.

(1) I. JOHN, Lieut., a tanner, m. Nov. 5, 1644, d. May 9, 1684. Wife Sarah, dau. of Miles Nutt of Woburn, who, after his death, m. Thomas Fuller of Woburn, Aug. 25, 1684.

(2) II. FRANCIS, a tanner, m. (see wives) d. Nov. 28 or 30, 1699, aged 82. He married 1, Judith Peirce of Woburn, Jan. 30, 1645; m. 2, Abigail, dau. of William Read of Woburn, Oct. 2, 1650.

(3) III. Name unknown. See issue No. 27.

(4) IV. Name unknown. See issue No. 28.

SECOND GENERATION.

Issue of John, No. 1.

(5) I. SAMUEL, b Sept. 20, 1646, d. Sept. 27, 1646.

(6) II. JOHN, b. March 28, 1648, m. ——— ———, d. at Narraganset, Dec. 19, 1675. He married Mary, dau. of Rev. Thomas Carter of Woburn, who after his death, m. Nathaniel Bachelder of Hampton, Oct. 31, 1676, and d. in 1688.

(7) III. SARAH, b. April 15, 1650, m. Joseph Walker, Dec. 15, 1669, d. Jan. 26, 1729.

(8) IV. SOLOMON, b. Feb. 26, 1652.

(9) V. DAVID, a tanner of Woburn, b. April 7, 1654, m. April 27, 1675, d. of small pox, 1678. Wife Isabel, dau. of John Farmer of Concord, Mass., who afterwards m. James Blood of Concord, Nov. 19, 1679.

(10) VI. ELIZABETH, b. Jan. 18, 1656, d. Nov. 21, 1658.

(11) VII. BATHSHEBA, b. Oct. 6, 1658, m. Nathaniel Tay, May 30, 1677, d. July 9, 1730.

(12) VIII. JONATHAN, Cornet, of Woburn, farmer, b. July 13, 1661, m. (see wives) d. Dec. 15, 1736. He m. 1, Abigail, dau. of James Fowle of Woburn, July 29, 1689, who d. Jan. 3, 1690; m. 2, Hannah, dau. of Peter Fowle of Woburn, July 31, 1690.

(13) IX. SETH, Lieut., of Woburn, farmer, b. Aug. 3, 1663, m. Dec. 17, 1685, d. Oct 26, 1715. He m. Hester, dau. of Wm. Johnson of Woburn, Dec. 17, 1685, who d March 31, 1742.

(14) X. JACOB, of Woburn, tanner, b.   m. (see wives) d. March 31, 1742. He m. 1, Elizabeth, dau. of Samuel Richardson of Woburn,

Nov. 23, 1687, who d. Nov. 21, 1739. He m. 2, Elizabeth Coggin of Woburn, Feb. 4, 1740.

Issue of Francis, No. 2.

(15) I. JUDITH, b. Sept. 29, 1652, d. Dec. 22, 1652.

(16) II. FRANCIS, b. about 1654, d. unm. April 26, 1676.

(17) III. WILLIAM, of Woburn, farmer, b. about 1656, d. 1705. He m. Prudence, dau. of Thomas Putnam. (?)

(18) IV. ABIGAIL, b. about 1660, m. Stephen Richardson, Jan. 2, 1675, d. Sept. 17, 1720.

(19) V. TIMOTHY, of Woburn, farmer, b. Sept. 15, 1661, d. 1709. His wife's name was Hannah.

(20) VI. JOSEPH, of Woburn, tailor, b. Nov. 9, 1663, d. unm. July 24, 1714.

(21) VII. NATHANIEL, of Woburn, farmer, b. Nov. 25, 1665, m. June 28, 1691 or 1692, d. Dec. 8, 1717. His wife was Mary Winn of Woburn, who afterwards m. John Locke of Woburn, Nov. 30, 1720.

(22) VIII. SAMUEL, of Woburn, farmer, b. Nov. 29, 1667, m. in 1692, d. May 17, 1725. His wife was Rebecca, dau. of Matthew Johnson of Woburn.

(23) IX. THOMAS, of Woburn, farmer, b. April 1, 1671, m. May 5, 1696, d. Sept. 4, 1731. His wife was Mary, dau. of Nathaniel Richardson of Woburn, who, after his death, married Josiah Winn of Woburn, Aug. 17, 1733, and d. June 7, 1743.

(24) X. BENJAMIN, of Woburn, farmer, b. Aug. 25, 1674, m. Jan. 20, 1702, d. Dec. 19, 1735. He married Elizabeth, dau. of Nathaniel Hancock of Cambridge, who afterwards married Jonathan Bacon of Bedford, Aug. 22, 1739, and d. at Medford, Mar. 2 or 3, 1749.

(25) XI. STEPHEN, b. June 2, 1676, d. Aug. 19, 1676.

(26) XII. JUDITH, 2d. b. Jan. 15, 1679, m. Nathaniel Bacon, and was living in 1715.

Issue of ———, *No.* 3.

(27) I. JOHN, of Woburn, wheelwright, m. Dec. 14, 1685, d. Apr. 19, 1728. His wife's name was Hannah Farrar, of Woburn.

Issue of ———, *No.* 4.

(28) I. THOMAS, of Boston, tailor. He d. before 1735, and was a soldier in the Narraganset war. Wife's name unknown. See deed, Middlesex Records, 1739.

The name in this branch was sometimes spelled Wayman.

THIRD GENERATION.

Issue of John, No. 6.

(29) I. JOHN, of Woburn, b. Apr. 23, 1672. Descendants in Lunenburg and Cambridge.

(30) II. MARY, b. June 25, 1674, m. Thomas Peirce Jr., Feb. 27, 1693.

Issue of David, No. 9.

(31) I. DAVID, b. May 29, 1676, d. June 15, 1676.

(32) II. ISABEL, b. July 5, 1677, m. John Green, of Malden, in 1700, d. Aug. 9, 1765.

Issue of Jonathan, No. 12.

(33) I. ABIGAIL, b. June 1, 1691, m. Samuel Buck, d. Dec. 2, 1720.

(34) II. Hannah, b. Nov. 1694, m. Israel Reed, June 1, 1717, living in 1753.

(35) III. Mary, b. Jan. 26, 1696, m. Jeremiah Center, before 1718.

(36) IV. Elizabeth, b. Feb. 15, 1700, m. Zerubbabel Snow, Aug. 11, 1721. She was living in 1755.

(37) V. Jonathan, of Woburn, b. Sept. 13, 1704. Descendants in Burlington, Mass., and Dummerston, Vt.

(38) VI. Sarah, b. Aug. 18, 1706, m. Nathan Brooks, d. Feb. 21, 1747.

(39) VII. Zachariah, b. July 19, 1709, a soldier, 1740–8.

Issue of Seth, No. 13.

(40) I. Seth, of Woburn, b. Sept. 13, 1686. Descendants in Haverhill and Shrewsbury.

(41) II. Hester, b. Oct. 25, 1688.

(42) III. Sarah, b. Jan. 17, 1690, m. Caleb Blodgett.

(43) IV. Jonathan, b. Nov. 5 or 19, 1693, d. Jan. 19, 1694.

(44) V. Susanna, b. June 30, 1695.

(45) VI. Abigail, b. Feb. 6, 1698, m. Timothy Brooks, Jan. 19, 1725, d. March 16, 1780.

(46) VII. Love, b. Feb. 14, 1701.

Issue of Jacob, No. 14.

(47) I. Jacob, of Woburn, b. Sept. 11, 1688. Descendants in Bradford and Haverhill.

(48) II. Samuel, of Woburn, b. Feb. 7, 1690.

(49) III. Elizabeth, b. Jan. 5 or 7, 1691, m. Josiah Waters, d. before 1742.

(50) IV. David, of Woburn, b. Apr. 14, 1693. Descendants in Boston and Danvers.

(51) V. Martha, b. Oct. 13, 1695, m. Joseph Richardson.

(52) VI. Mary, b. July 8, 1698, d. before 1742.

(53) VII. John, b. Dec. 11, 1700, graduated at H. C., 1721, d. July 9, 1721.

(54) VIII. Solomon, b. Apr. 24, 1703, d. Sept. 22, 1725.

(55) IX. Patience, b. Apr. 13, 1705, m. John Coggin of Sudbury, 1734–7.

(56) X. Ebenezer, of Connecticut, b. May 5, 1707, graduated at H. C., 1731, m. Mary Wright, May 22, 1739, d. April 29, 1746.

(57) XI. Isaiah, b. Feb. 28, 1709, d. Feb. 9, 1746.

(58) XII. Peter, of Woburn, b. Sept. 27, 1711.

(59) XIII. Daniel, of Sudbury, b. May 27, 1715. Descendants in Philadelphia.

Issue of William, No. 17.

(60) I. William, b. Jan. 18, 1683, d. Jan. 20, 1683.

(61) II. Prudence, b. Dec. 26, 1683, m. Jacob Winn, Jr., June 28, 1704.

(62) III. William 2d, of Woburn, b. Jan. 15, 1685. Posterity in Charlestown.

(63) IV. Thomas, of Pelham, N. H., b. Aug. 23, 1687.

(64) V. Elizabeth, b. July 5, 1689, d. June 25, 1690.

(65) VI. Francis, of Maine, b. July 10, 1691.

(66) VII. Joshua, of Woburn, b. Jan. 3, 1693. Posterity in Roxbury and Keene, N. H.

(67) VIII. A daughter. Name unknown, d. 1694.

(68) IX. EDWARD, of Pelham, N. H., b. Jan. 10, 1696. Posterity in Cambridge, Mass., and Cornish, N. H.

(69) X. ELIZABETH 2d, b. Feb. 16, 1697.

(70) XI. DELIVERANCE, b. Feb. 28, 1700, m. Esekiel Gowin Jr., of Lynn, Jan. 1, 1732.

(71) XII. JAMES, of Maine, b. March 16, 1702.

Issue of Timothy, No. 19.

(72) I. HANNAH, b. July, 7, 1688.

(73) II. TIMOTHY, of Woburn, b. Apr. 5, 1691, m. Hannah Wyman. (88) Descendants in Vermont and New Hampshire.

(74) III. SOLOMON, of Woburn, b. Oct. 24, 1693. Descendants in Templeton and Chesterfield, N. H.

(75) IV. JOSEPH, of Pelham, N. H., b. Nov. 1, 1695. Descendants, in Westminster and Jaffrey, N. H.

(76) V. EUNICE, b. Feb. 24, 1697, m. Henry Tottingham, Sept. 7, 1721, d. before 1748.

(77) VI. ANN, b. Mar. 26, 1700, d. unm. at Andover, Mar. 25, 1774.

(78) VII. JUDITH, b. June 16, 1702, m. John Wright of Ashford, Conn., Mar. 23, 1725, living 1748.

(79) VIII. ELI, b. Mar. 11, 1704, d. unm. Aug. 22, 1728.

(80) IX. EBENEZER, of Townsend, b. Mar. 21, 1706. Descendants in Maine.

(81) X. HESTER.

(82) XI. ELIZABETH.

(83) XII. PRUDENCE, b. Mar. 8, 1709, m. Thomas Phelps. She was living in 1772.

Issue of Nathaniel, No. 21.

(84) I. NATHANIEL, b. May 23, 1693, d. unm. Dec. 13, 1715.

(85) II. MARY, b. May 28, 1694, d. about May 23, 1763, insane.

(86) III. ABIGAIL, b. Oct. 5, 1695, m. Benjamin Gowin.

(87) IV. RUTH, b. Apr. 17, 1697, m. Thomas Gould of Charlestown, Aug. 1, 1721.

(88) V. HANNAH, b. Apr. 23, 1699, m. Timothy Wyman (73.)

(89) VI. ELIZA, b. Nov. 11, 1700, m. John Geary of Charlestown, Mar. 12, 1723.

(90) VII. PHEBE, b. June 11, 1702, m. Thomas Geary of Stoneham, before 1729.

(91) VIII. REBECCA, b. Apr. 14, 1704, m. Thomas Holden, Mar. 7, 1723.

(92) IX. JOANNA, b. July 25, 1705, m. Jonathan Holden, Dec. 30, 1731, d. Nov. 11, 1786.

(93) X. INCREASE, of Woburn, b. Mar. 1, 1707.

(94) XI. SARAH, b. Aug. 21, 1710, m. Ezekiel Walker, July 6, 1732, d. before 1756.

(95) XII. KEZIA, b. Apr. 5, 1713, m. John Reed, Dec. 9, 1735, d. Jan. 14, 1756.

Issue of Samuel, No. 22.

(96) I. REBECCA, b. Nov. 11, 1693, m. Thomas Richardson of Woburn, Sept. 29, 1713, d. before April 11, 1771.

(97) II. ABIGAIL, b. Feb. 5, 1695, m. Jonathan Richardson before 1726.

(98) III. HANNAH, b. Dec. 10, 1696, m. Samuel Parker, May 10, 1725.

(99) IV. Sarah, b. Feb. 2, 1698, m. John Cogin, Aug. 31, 1726, d. May 22, 1732.

(100) V. Samuel, of Woburn, b. Mar. 18, 1700. Posterity in Boston.

(101) VI. Oliver, of Leominster, b. Sept. 5, 1701.

(102) VII. Lydia, b. Jan 1, 1703, m. Oliver Richardson of Woburn, July 24, 1729, d. Oct. 26, 1754.

(103) VIII. Patience, b. Jan. 11, 1705, m. Edward Dean, May 1, 1740, d. June 15, 1741.

(104) IX. Matthew, of Lancaster, b. Aug. 3, 1707.

(105) X. Esther, b. Feb. 25, 1709.

Issue of Thomas, No. 23.

(106) I. Thomas, of Woburn, b. May 12, 1697. Descendants in Pelham, N. H.

(107) II. Josiah, b. March 18, 1700.

(108) III. Phineas, b. 1701. Insane, 1747.

(109) IV. Timothy, b. March 1, 1702.

(110) V. Benjamin, of Woburn, b. June 12, 1704. Descendants in Maine.

(111) VI. John, b. July 6, 1706, d. unm. March 26, 1739.

(112) VII. Mary, b. March 10, 1708, m. Nathaniel Clark of Watertown, June 13, 1726.

(113) VIII. Aaron, of Woburn, b. Dec. 6, 1709.

(114) IX. Eleazer, of Woburn, b. April 13, 1712. Descendants in Winchendon.

(115) X. Nathaniel, of Hopkinton, b. May 18, 1716. Descendants in New York.

(116) XI. Elizabeth, b. Dec. 19, 1718, m. ——— Blodgett.

Issue of Benjamin, No. 24.

(117) I. Elizabeth, b. May 1, 1705, m. Jacob Richardson, June 11, 1724, d. Oct. 20, 1749.

(118) II. Benjamin, of Woburn, b. Nov. 13, or Dec. 17, 1706. Posterity in Lexington, Cambridge, and New York.

(119) III. Lucy, b. April 17, 1708, m. Nathaniel Davenport of Shrewsbury, 1729, d. Oct 25, 1730.

(120) IV. Zebadiah, of Woburn, b. June 21, or 26, 1709. Descendants in Cambridge.

(121) V. Eunice, b. Nov. 16, 1710, m. Robert Peirce, Oct. 28, 1736, d. May 5, 1774.

(122) VI. Jerusha, b. July 23, 1712, m. Edward Richardson, Feb. 24, or April 14, 1730, d. April 10, 1784.

(123) VII. Tabitha, b. April 7, 1714, m. Josiah Kendall, March 17, 1736, d. April 24, 1800.

(124) VIII. Abijah, of Lancaster, b. Sept. 20, 1715.

(125) IX. Catherine, b. May 6, 1717, m. William Tufts of Medford. Feb. 28, 1732, d. Feb. 20, 1749.

(126) X. Nathaniel, of Lancaster, b. Jan. 26, 1719.

(127) XI. Abigail, b. Aug. 26, 1720, m. Jacob Snow, April 8, 1740, d. Oct. 31, 1771.

(128) XII. Martha, b. May 7, 1722, m. Samuel Dean, Sept. 6, 1739.

(129) XIII. Noah, b. July 30, 1724, d. Dec. 10, 1726.

(130) XIV. Jonas, b. July 26, 1725, d. unm. Jan. 20, 1746. He was a soldier at Louisburg.

(131) XV. REUBEN, of Wilmington, b. Nov. 9, 1726. Descendants in Concord, N. H.

Issue of John, No. 27.

(132) I. JOHN, of Wilmington, b. Nov. 16, 1686, d. before Jan. 6, 1748.
(133) II. THOMAS, b. March 25, 1689, d. before 1749, insane.
(134) III. JASHER, of Townsend, b. Jan. 6, 1691. Descendants in Hollis, N. H.
(135) IV. NATHAN, of Woburn, b. Jan. 8, 1695.
(136) V. HANNAH, b. Aug. 8, or 28, 1703, living unm. 1748.
(137) VI. ANN, b. April 10, 1705, m. Samuel Bathrick of Portsmouth, N. H., published May 5, 1739.
(138) VII. RACHEL, b. Oct. 24, 1707.

Issue of Thomas, No. 28.

(139) I. THOMAS, of Boston. Descendants in Concord.
(140) II. DANIEL, of Boston. Descendants in Concord.
(141) III. MARY, m. Joseph Turner, July 11, 1706.
(142) IV. SARAH, m. Robert Karheet, mariner.
(143) V. ABIGAIL, m. John Durham, Dec. 9, 1717.

MISCELLANEOUS.

STEPHEN WAYMAN is mentioned in the "Mass. Colony Book," in the Narraganset expedition, Feb. 29, 1675–6. Also, a STEPHEN WAIMAN (perhaps the same) died intestate. Administration granted to George and Rebecca Bonfeld. See Ipswich Court Record, 21, 10, 1675.

ELINER WAYMAN and George James of Salem, Great Britain, were m. in Boston, Feb. 6, 1711.

SARAH WAYMAN and Edward Jones of Great Britain were published in Boston, June 19, 1714.

SARAH WEYMAN and Samuel Marshall were m. in Boston, Dec. 26, 1717.

JOHN WEEMAN came from Germany, and settled in Maine.

RECORDS OF BOSTON.

[Copied for the Antiquarian Journal by MR. DAVID PULSIFER, member of the N. E. H. Geneal. Society.]

[Continued from Vol. II., page 402.]

Jane the daught^r of Evan Thomas & Jane his wife was borne the 16° (3°) 1641. *Thomas.*

Dorcas the daughter of Evan Thomas & Jane his wife was borne 5° (12°) 1642 & dyed the 28° (12°) 1642.

Deborah the daught^r of Benjamin Thwing & Deborah his wife was borne 17° (3°) 1642. & dyed (6°) 1642. *Thwing.*

Elisabeth the daught^r of William Ting & Elisabeth his wife was borne 6° (12°) 1637. *Ting.*

Annah the daughter of William Ting & Elisabeth his wife was borne 6° (11°) 1639.

Bethiah the daught^r of William Ting & Elisabeth his wife was borne 17° (3°) 1641.

Mercie the daughter of William Ting & Elisabeth his wife was borne 13° (11°) 1642.

Hannah the daught^{r} of Edward Ting & Mary his wife was borne 7° (1°) $\frac{1639}{1640}$. *Ting.*

Mary the daught^{r} of Edward Ting & Mary his wife was borne 17° (2°). 1641.

Jonathan the sonne of Edward Ting & Mary his wife was borne 15° (10°) 1642.

Hannah the daught^{r} of William Townsend & Hannah his wife was borne 4° (2°) 1641. *Townsend.*

Peter the sonne of William Townsend & Hannah his wife was borne the 26° (8°) 1642.

Ephraim Turner the sonne of Robt Turner & Penelope his wife was borne 13° (10°) 1639. *Turner.*

Sarah the daught^{r} of Robt Turner & Penelope his wife was borne 11° (1°) 1640.

John the sonne of Robt Turner & Penelope his wife was borne the 1° (10°) 1642.

Richard Tuttle Dyed 8° (3°) 1640. *Tuttle.*

Tapping see afterward. *Tapping.*

Hopestill the daughter of John Vyall & Mary his wife was borne 14° (6°) 1639. *Vyall.*

Mary the daughter of John Vyall & Mary his wife was borne 30° (9°) 1641.

Isaac the sonne of Richard Waite & Elisabeth his wife was borne 9° (6°) 1638 & dyed the 21° (6°) 1638. *Waite.*

Returne the sonne of Richard Waite & Elisabeth his wife was borne 8° (5°) 1639.

Hannah the daught^{r} of Richard Waite & Elisabeth his wife was borne the 14° (7°) 1641.

Moses the sonne of Gamaliel Waite & Grace his wife was borne (4°) 1637, & dyed (1°) $\frac{1637}{1638}$. *Waite.*

Grace the daughter of Gamaliel Waite & Grace his wife was borne 10° (11°) 1638.

Moses the sonne of Gamaliel Waite & Grace his wife was borne (7°) 1640, & Dyed (7°) 1641.

Samuel the sonne of Gamaliel Waite & Grace his wife was borne ——, 1641.

Elishua the sonne of Robt Walker & ——, his wife was borne the 14° (12°) 1635. *Walker.*

Zachary the sonne of Robt Walker & ——, his wife was borne the 15° (7°) 1637.

John the sonne of Robt Walker & ——, his wife was borne the 22° (7°) 1639.

Sarah the daught^{r} of Robt Walker & ——, his wife was borne the 15° (9°) 1641, & buried 19° (10°) 1643.

Meribah the daught^{r} of William Werdall & Alice his wife was borne 14° (3°) 1637. *Werdall.*

Vsal the sonne of William Werdall & Alice his wife was borne 7° (2°) 1639.

Elihu the sonne of William Werdall & Alice his wife was borne the (9°) 1642.

Jonathan the sonne of Thomas Wheeler & Rebecca his wife was borne 20° (8°) 1637. *Wheeler.*

Joseph the sonne of Thomas Wheeler & Rebecca his wife was borne 15° (3°) 1640.

Rebecca the daughter of Thomas Wheeler & Rebecca his wife was borne 17° (4°) 1643.

Ruth the daughter of Nathaniel Williams, & Mary his wife was borne 1638. *Williams.*

Elisabeth the daughter of Nathaniel Williams & Mary his wife was borne 21° (8°) 1640.

Nathaniell the sonne of Nathaniel Williams & Mary his wife was borne 16° (7°) 1642.

Joseph the sonne of Robert Williams & —— his wife was borne (5°) 1641. *Williams.*

Mary the daught^r^ of m^r^ John Wilson & Elisabeth his wife was borne 12° (7°) 1633. *Wilson.*

Shoreborne the sonne of William Wilson & Patience his wife was borne 6° (6°) 1635. *Wilson.*

Mary the daught^r^ of William Wilson & Patience his wife was borne 11° (11°) 1637.

John the sonne of William Wilson & Patience his wife was borne (11°) 1639.

Joseph the sonne of Wm Wilson & Patience his wife was borne 10° (9°) 1643.

John the sonne of Robert Wing & Joan his wife was borne the 22° (5°) 1637. *Wing.*

Hannah the daughter of Robert Wing & Joan his wife was borne 14° (12°) 1639.

Jacob the sonne of Robert Wing & Joan his wife was borne 31° (5°) 1642.

Elisabeth the daught^r^ of m^r^ John Winthrope the yonger & Elisabeth his wife was borne 24° (5°) 1636. *Winthrop.*

ffitz–John sonne of Mr John Winthrop Esq; the yonger & Elizabeth his wife 14° (1°) 1638.

Luce the daught^r^ of John Winthrop Junio^r^ Esq; & Elisabeth his wife borne 28° (11°) 1639.

Waite–still the sonne of John Winthrop Junio^r^ Esq; & Elisabeth his wife borne 27° (12°) 1641.

Mary the daught^r^ of Richard Woodhouse & Mary his wife was borne & buried (11°) 1637. *Woodhouse.*

Mary the daughter of Richard Woodhouse & Mary his wife was borne 14° (11°) 1638.

John the sonne of Richard Woodhouse & Mary his wife was borne 9° (2°) 1641.

Hannah the daught^r^ of Richard & Mary Woodhouse borne 15, (1) 1643.

Joseph the sonne of Robt Woodward & Rachell his wife was borne 24° (8°) 1641. *Woodward.*

Nathaniel the sonne of Robt Woodward & Rachell his wife was borne 38° (8°) 1642.

EPITAPH ON HUDDLESTONE.

Here lies Thomas Huddlestone, reader don't smile,
But reflect as this tombstone you view,
That death who has killed, in a very short while
May HUDDLE A STONE upon you.

NOTICES CONCERNING THE EARLY "FREEMEN" IN NEW ENGLAND.

Before a member of society could exercise the right of suffrage, or hold any public office, he must be made a *freeman* by the general or quarterly court. To become such he was required to produce evidence that he was a respectable member of some Congregational church. "This regulation was so far modified by Royal order in 1664, as to allow individuals to be made Freemen, who could obtain certificates of their being correct in doctrine and conduct, from clergymen acquainted with them."*

"In 1631, a test was invented which required all freemen to be church-members. This was upon the first appearance of a dissent in regard to religious opinions. But even this test, in the public opinion, required great caution, as in 1632 it was agreed that a civil magistrate should not be an elder in the church."†

The "FREEMAN'S OATH" was the first paper printed in New England. It was printed at Cambridge, by STEPHEN DAYE, in 1639,‡ upon a single sheet, in the manner of a handbill, and without date. It was in these words, as established in 1634:—

I (*A. B.*) being by Gods providence, an Inhabitant, and Freeman, within the Jurisdiction of this Commonwealth; do freely acknowledge my self to be subject to the Government thereof: And therefore do here swear by the great and dreadful Name of the Ever-living God, that *I* will be true and faithfull to the same, and will accordingly yield assistance & support thereunto, with my person and estate, as in equity *I* am bound; and will also truly endeavor to maintain and preserve all the liberties and priviledges thereof, submitting my self to the wholesome Lawes & Orders made and established by the same. And further, that *I* will not plot or practice any evill against it, or consent to any that shall so do; but will timely discover and reveal the same to lawfull Authority now here established, for the speedy preventing thereof.

Moreover, *I* doe solemnly bind my self in the sight of God, that when I shal be called to give my voyce touching any such matter of this State, in which Freemen are to deal, *I* will give my vote and suffrage as I shall judge in mine own conscience may best conduce and tend to the publike weal of the body, So help me God in the Lord Jesus Christ.§

The first General Court in Massachusetts was held on the 19th of October, 1630, not by representatives, but by every one that was free, of the corporation, in person. None had been admitted *freemen* since they left England. It was ordered, that for the future the *free-*

* Felt, *Hist. of Ipswich*, 18.

† Bentley, *Description of Salem*, 1 *Colls. Mass. Hist. Soc.*, vi. 236.

‡ Thomas, *Hist. Printing*, i. 231.

§ Copied from "New England's JONAS *cast up at* London," "by Major *John Childe*," 1647. [In the body of the tract the name of *Childe* is spelt without the *e*.] Mr. Felt has also printed the oath in his *Ipswich*, from the records, and it is likewise to be found in the "*Charters and Laws of Massachusetts Bay.*" We have copied from MAJOR CHILDE to preserve the old orthography.

men should choose the assistants, and the assistants from among themselves choose the governor and deputy governor. The court of assistants were to have the power of making laws and appointing officers. This was a departure from their charter. *One hundred and nine* freemen were admitted at this court. MAVERICK, BLACKSTONE, and many more who were not of any of the churches, were of this number. The next General Court was the court of election for 1631. The scale was now turned, and the *freemen* resolved to choose both governor, deputy, and assistants, notwithstanding the former vote, and made an order, that, for the time to come, none should be admitted to the freedom of the body politic but such as were church members.* "None have voice in elections of Governor, Deputy and Assistants, none are to be Magistrates, Officers or Jurymen, grand or petit, but *Freemen.* The Ministers give their votes in all elections of Magistrates. Now the most of the persons at *New England* are not admitted of their Church, and therefore are not *Freemen;* and when they come to be tried there, be it for life or limb, name or estate, or whatsoever, they must be tried and judged too by those of the Church who are, in a sort, their adversaries; How equal that hath been or may be, some by experience doe know, others may judge."†

"This," remarks Hutchinson, "was a most extraordinary order of law, and yet it continued in force until the dissolution of the government, it being repealed, in appearance only, after the restoration of King Charles the Second. Had they been deprived of their civil privileges in England by an act of parliament, unless they would join in communion with the churches there, it might very well have been the first in the roll of grievances. But such were the requisites to qualify for church membership here, that the grievance was abundantly greater."

It is supposed by Mr. Savage,‡ that "near three fourths of the present [1826] inhabitants of the six New England states," are descended from such as were made freemen before the death of Governor Winthrop. This conjecture would seem plausible enough were we to end our inquiries here; but if we extend them to the revolution of 1688, the time when the practice of making freemen ceased, by a similar course of reasoning we should not *now* find inhabitants enough in New England for our purpose. However, our opinion is, that from the "OLD FREEMEN" before the Revolution, *above seven eighths* of all the present inhabitants of New England, and no inconsiderable portion of those of New York, New Jersey, Pennsylvania, and Ohio are descended.

In 1663, "the practice of freemen's meeting in Boston to elect magistrates was repealed. This repeal, however, was so unpopular, that the same practice was renewed the next year; but it seems to have gone down soon after. At first, danger from Indians was pleaded, why

* Hutchinson's *Hist. Mass.*, i. 25, 26.

† Lechford, *Plain Dealing*, 23, 24.

‡ Winthrop, *Jour.*, ii. 74. In his edition of this invaluable work, Mr. S. has printed lists of the FREEMEN to the time of his author's death.

border and distant towns should retain part of their freemen from General Election. At last, the greatness of the number, when assembled from the whole colony to choose the magistrates, and the concurrent inconveniencies of this custom, appear to have been the cause of producing an alteration, which substantially accords with present usage."*

At as early a day as practicable, it is intended that the most perfect list of FREEMEN possible to be obtained shall occupy a prominent space in our pages. At present we can give only a few items, enough, however, for our students to form some opinion of what the undertaking will be to do the OLD FREEMEN justice. It is proposed here to notice only such as offered themselves for freemen, or such of them as have come to our knowledge in a single year, viz:—

1677.

The: 22: 3: 77. These may Certifye the much honred Generall Court sitting at Boston the: 23. of the: 3. 77: that the psons Whose names ar vnder wretten being in full communion with the Church of christ in Medffeild and otherwise quallified according to Law Desire that they may be admited to the ffredom of this Comon Welth.

Obediah Morse
Jonathn Morse
Joseph Bullin
Edward Adams
Eliezur Adams

p George Barbur.

May 23 1677. This may signify to whom it may Concern y^t
Mr. Richard Dumer &
Mr. Henry Shorte
are members in full Comunion wth ye Church of Newbury as affirms
Jno Richardson *Minister.*

---

1. 4: 77.
ffranses ffletcher
Timothy Wheeler
John Meriam
Samuel Jones
are in full communion with the Churche at Concord as attests
John fflint.

June 9th 1677.+† Mr. John Holyoke of Springfeild a member of ye church there in full comunion: a householder & above 24. yeare of age desires to be admitted to ye freedome of this Collony attested
John Pynchon.

---

‡ These psons are in full Comunion with the Church of Christ in Wooburn desiring their freedome

John Walker
John Carter
John Berbeane

[On the same paper.] James Blake in full Comunion with ye church in Dorchester & 24 years of age. [No signature.

* Felt, *Ipswich*, 18, 19. See, also, *Annals of Salem*, 219, 220.
† This mark is on the original paper, but why is not fully apparent.
‡ The following entries are without date, but are believed to be all of 1677.

Steuen Greenlef Junir
Jacob tapin
Retcherd bartlet Junir

these are Members of the Churtch of Nubery in full Comunion.

[No signature.]

John Eaton
Samuel Lamson
Henery Merow
Sebred Tailor

These are members in full Comunion in yᵉ Church of Redding.

[No signature.]

The names of such as Are in full Communion with the Church of Christ in Charlstowne: for freedom

Mr. Samuell Nowell
Mr. John Phillips
Christofer Goodin
James Millar
Mr. John Blaney. [No signature.]

Samuell Stodder
Andrew lane
John tucker

Are members of the Church of Hingham in full Co̅munion desire to be freemen. [No signature.]

Joseph Parmeter

a householder & member of the Church of Brantry in full Co̅munion Desires to be a freeman of this Co̅monwealth.

[In another hand.] Samuel Wintworth

a householder & in full comunion with yᵉ Church of Douer desires the ffreedom of this co̅mon wealth. [No signature.]

John Wales Senior

A member of the Church of Christ in Dorchester desires his freedome.*

[In another hand.] John White senʳ

of Muddy Riuer [now Brookline] being in full Comunion with the Church of Roxbury desiereth his Freedom. [No signature.]

Salem

Mr. Jnᵒ Hathorne
Manasser Marsten
Henry Skery Jun

all in full Co̅munion. [No signature.]

* A cross stands in the margin against both these entries. They signified, probably, that the matter of each had been disposed of or acted upon.

The names of those men which desiar to tak ther freedum

Nathaniell Gay*	William Auery
Thomas Aldridge	Jonathan Auery
Nathaniell Kingsbery	John Weare

these ar all members in full Cōmunion in Dedham Church as attest
Daniell ffisher

John Rogers
John Baylie
are householders & members of the Church of Waymouth in full Communion desire the freedome of this Cōmon wealth.
p[r]sented by the Deputy of y[t] Towne

Members of the of y[e] first Church [Boston] To be made ffree
William Gibson
Nathaniell Barnes
Edward Ashley
of y[e] North Church
Theophilus Thornton
John Jonse [Jones.]

In the above collection of applicants for *freedom* it is not certain that we have all or any considerable part of those who did apply. Such are given as happened to be within our reach. They may, however, be all that applied in the year 1677 at the General Court. The number applying at the Quarterly County Courts may have been much greater. From hence some notion may be gathered of what the number of freemen may have amounted to in the course of *fifty-seven years.* From 1630 to 1648, there are recorded† *one thousand eight hundred and nine.* This number arose through a course of *eighteen years.*

At some future time, as already hinted, we intend to give as full a list of the early FREEMEN of New England as we can procure. Meantime our correspondents are requested to consider this a direct call upon them to help us in this CORNER STONE of our New England history.

AN OLD PRINTING PRESS.

The following appears to have been cut from the St. Mary's (Md.) Gazette, and inserted in the Boston Transcript of 30 October, 1848. It comes fully within the range of our work, and we therefore give it a place:—

"But few of our readers are aware, we expect, that the press upon which our little sheet is printed, is the oldest now in use in the United States and probably in the world. Yet such is the fact. The press now used by us has been in almost constant service for more than a *hundred years.* Upon it was printed The Maryland Gazette, the earliest paper published in the province of Maryland, and one among the very first in America. Upon it, also, was printed the first volume of the laws of Maryland that ever appeared. It is constructed somewhat on the Ramage principle, and requires three pulls, though two were originally sufficient to produce a good impression. It is truly a venerable object.

* A large cross follows these three names.
† As printed by Mr. Savage in his edition of *Winthrop's Journal.*

WOBURN BURYING-GROUND.

[Communicated by Mr. N. Wyman, Jr.—Continued from p. 387, of Vol. II.]

Richardson	Mathew s of Thomas & Rebeckah	Feb 11 1723	1-10-8
Buck	James s of Samuel & Abigail	Dec 3 1723	9y
Tyng	Johnathan Esq[r]	Jan 19 1723–4	81
Stone	Abigail w of Dea Samuel	May 11 1718	71
Wyman	Samuel	May 17 1725	about 58
Coggen	Capt John	Feb 17 1725	50
Winn	Elisalett w of Timothy	May 14 1714	about 34
Walker	Judeth w of Dea Samuel	Nov 14 1724	57
Hartwell	Precilla d of Joseph & Ruhamah	Aug 28 1725	15y 3-8
Wright	Phebe d of Josiah & Ruth	Dec 7 1724	3y
Carter	Ruth w of Lieut John	Jan 10 1724	55
Hill	Doct Isaac	Jan 9 1723	29
Richardson	Susanna w of Samuel	Aug 6 1726	42
Flegg [Flagg]	Col Eleazer Esq	July 12 1726	56

A faithful Christian, and a pious liver
to any in distress, a cheerful giver.
The widovs solace in a doubtful case,
Yea and a father to the fatherless.
A Tender husband, and a parent kind,
a Faithful friend, which who, O who can find.
All this was he and more, but now at rest,
the memory of the righteous man is blest.

Richardson	Susanna w to Josiah	Mar 6 1726	about 29
Wright	Abigail w of John	Apr 6 1726	84
Carter	Lieut John	Apr 8 1727	75
Richardson	Esther wid to Nathan	Nov 10 1727	27y
Blanchard	Jonathan s of Jacob & Abigail	Sept 14 1727	7y
Carter	William s of Samuel & Margery	Oct 6 1728	1-11-11
"	Margery	Sept 23 1728	3-8-6
Convers	Benjamin s of Cap[t] Robert & Mary	Aug 17 1729	11[th]y
Belknap	Ruth d of Samuel & Lydia	June 27 1734	2-7-16
Hartwell	John s of Joseph & Ruhamah	May 1 1734	9y 6m
Alexander	Philip s of Philip Jr & Sarah	May 13 1734	18y
Wright	James	Jan 6 1734–5	59
Reed	Abigail d of Lieut Thomas & Sarah	Dec 7 1736	15-6-14
"	Lieut Thomas	Aug 18 1736	54-1-23
Pool	Jonathan s of Jonathan Esq & Esther	July 23 1736	7-11-16
Wood	Ruth d of Josiah & Abigail	Aug 2 1736	37y
Richardson	Bridget d of Capt Stephen & Bridget	Sept 27 1736	14y
Snow	Esther w of Isaac	Mar 30 1737	33
Reed	Sarah wid of Lieut Thomas	June 21 1737	49-1-17
Richardson	Tabitha w of Nathan	Nov 25 1739	33y
Sawyer	Joshua	Mar 1 1737–8	54
Snow	Esther d of Isaac & Esther	Apr 12 1739	5y
Richardson	Mary w of Thomas d to John & Joanna Russell	Jan 11 1741–2	29-3-7
Brooks	Hannah w John	Apr 14 1742	26
Richardson	Lucy d Joshua & Eunice	Dec 2 1741	1y
Kendall	Elisabeth w Lieu[t] Samuel	Jan 10 1741–2	54y

[To be continued.]

BIOGRAPHICAL SKETCHES OF THE EARLY PHYSICIANS OF MARIETTA, OHIO.

[By S. P. Hildreth, M. D., of Marietta.*]

The colony founded by the New Englanders on the banks of the Ohio in 1788, marks an interesting era in the history of our country. From that feeble beginning in the wilderness, surrounded by savage and hostile tribes, has proceeded the gigantic state of Ohio, with all its magnificent improvements and numerous population.

Steamboats crowd the tributaries as well as the mighty waters of the Mississippi, the father of rivers, while canals and railroads intersect the country, uniting the distant portions with each other. The sons of the puritans were the projectors of these improvements, as well on the vast fresh water seas of the West, as on the shores of the Ohio. It is a tribute justly due to the memory of the men who witnessed these events, and whose lives and characters have been creditable to the land of their birth, that their names should be preserved. As a class, no order of men has done more to promote the good of mankind and develop the resources and natural history of our country, than physicians; and wherever the well educated in that profession are found they are uniformly seen on the side of order, morality, science, and religion. Of the nine individuals noticed in the following sketches, seven were born in New England.

DOCTOR JABEZ TRUE

was born in Hampstead, N. H., in the year 1760. His father, the Rev. Henry True, was born in Salisbury, Mass., in 1725, prepared for college at Dummer's Academy, and graduated at Cambridge in 1750. The Rev. Mr. Bernard of Haverhill, was his instructor in the study of Divinity, and in 1752 he was settled in the ministry at Hampstead. His wife was a Miss Ayers of Haverhill. He was the father of ten children, nine of whom lived to adult age. In the "Old French War" he served as chaplain to one of the colonial regiments at Ticonderoga and Fort Edward. It was the practice of that day with the New England clergymen, when academies and high schools were rare establishments, to prepare young men for college. Mr. True had a class of this kind, amongst whom was his son Jabez, where he obtained a knowledge of the learned languages and English grammar sufficient to read medicine to advantage. Having selected this branch for a profession, he studied the healing art under Dr. Flagg of Hampstead, a popular but very eccentric man, highly eminent as a physician and much esteemed by his friends. Dr. True having finished his studies near the close of the Revolutionary War, volunteered his services in the defence of the country by entering as the surgeon of a privateer, fitting out for a cruise at the town of Newburyport, distant fifteen miles from his home, and sailed for Europe. Soon after reaching their cruising ground and before many prizes were taken, the vessel was wrecked on the coast of Holland, thus closing abruptly his prospect of wealth. The shipwrecked mariners were received kindly by the Hollanders, amongst whom the doctor remained until the cessation of hostilities, when he returned to America. In a few months

* We beg pardon of the author for inserting his name without his special liberty; but he has done too much for the literature and history of the West not to be credited appropriately in our work. It is unnecessary to specify the works of Dr. Hildreth at this time, as they must be known to most of our readers as well as to us.

after this he entered on the practice of medicine in Gilmanton, N. H., where he remained three or four years. The Ohio company was organized in 1787, and feeling a strong desire to visit the enchanting regions in the valley of the Ohio so admirably described by the writers and travellers of that day, he became an associate, and bidding adieu to the land of his birth, came out in company with a family from Newburyport, reaching the mouth of the Muskingum early in the summer of 1788. The settlement at Marietta had then but few persons in it. The country was covered with a dense forest, and there was more employment for able bodied men in clearing lands and building log cabins than for physicians. Nevertheless he was not disheartened, but erected a small log office for his books and medicine, a short distance from the bank of the Muskingum, on what is now called Muskingum street, near the dwelling of Mr. William Moulton, a goldsmith, from Newburyport, in whose family he boarded for several years. At the breaking out of the Indian war in January, 1791, he received the appointment of surgeon's mate to the infantry and rangers, employed by the Ohio company's directors at Marietta, with a salary of twenty-two dollars a month, which was a welcome and timely aid during the years of privation which attended the war, and sorely tried the resources of the most able among the inhabitants. This appointment was held until near the close of the war. During the most gloomy and disheartening periods, schools were kept up by the inhabitants, as they all had to go into garrisons; the New Englanders deeming the instruction of their children one of their most important duties. Dr. True taught a school a part of the time in a large lower room of one of the block-houses in the garrison at "the point." While they were in their military defences the small pox and scarlet fever, in addition to other diseases of the climate, broke out amongst the inhabitants, and the doctor had to visit several of the stations to attend on the sick. At that period there were neither roads nor bridges, and the intercourse between the posts was carried on by water in canoes, no one travelling the forests but the rangers and hunters. It was several years after the peace of 1795 before roads were opened, and the visits of the physician, as well as the intercourse of the settlers, were still kept up on the water. In descending the Ohio, by keeping in the middle of the stream, little danger was apprehended; but in returning up stream, the canoe was necessarily near the shore, and the traveller in constant danger from the rifle of the savage. During many hazardous trips on visits of mercy to the sick and wounded, he was providentially preserved from harm. In after life he was celebrated for his sympathy with the afflicted, having himself suffered much from disease. So tender was he to the prejudices of his patients, that he seldom prescribed without first consulting their opinion as to the medicine to be taken; and if they had any particular objection to the article, it was changed to suit their taste, unless it was *really* necessary in treating the disease that the objectionable medicine *should* be taken. The result of his calm, deliberate judgment was generally correct, and his treatment of diseases remarkably successful, which was doubtless in part owing to its simplicity; for it is a lamentable fact that many die from too many and improper remedies, as well as from the disease itself. After the close of the war he built a small frame dwelling house and office, turning his attention to the clearing and cultivating a little farm about a mile above the town, on the bank of the Ohio. He still remained a bachelor, until the year 1806, when he married Mrs. Mills, the relict of Capt. Charles Mills, a very amiable and excellent woman. Her maiden name was Sarah Boardman, a native of the town of Wrentham, Mass. In the year 1798, he became united to the Congregational church in Marietta, under the pastoral care of the Rev. Daniel Story, an uncle of the late Judge Story of Cambridge; this was the earliest religious society in Ohio. In this church he was for many years a deacon, fulfilling the duties of that sacred office with great fidelity. His charity for the poor, and especially the sick poor, was unbounded, and only limited by his scanty means; often bestowing on them a large portion of the avails of his attendance on richer patients. It was many years after the settlement of the Ohio company before bridges were built. During this time he was the principal physician for Marietta and the adjacent country; extending his rides to twenty and thirty miles, swimming his horse across the streams, with no road but foot paths and the old Indian trails marked out by blazes on the trees. The people were generally poor and had but little to spare for the services of the doctor. With him, however, it made but little difference whether the patient was poor or rich; he was always ready, when his health permitted, to attend on their calls and to divide his last dollar with those who needed. A practical proof of his equanimity of temper, generosity, and forgiving disposition, even to those who had done him an injury, was related to the writer by the transgressor himself. The doctor was an ardent admirer of fine fruit, and had cultivated with much care some of the choicest varieties of apples and pears in a small garden near his house. Amongst them was a tree of the richest kind of summer sweeting apple, to which the neighbouring boys paid daily visits whenever the doctor was out of the way. James Glover, a partially blind, near sighted man, well known to the inhabitants of Marietta many years since for his natural, ready, and keen wit, but then a stout boy, fourteen or fifteen years of age, hearing the other lads speak of the fine apples in the doctor's garden, concluded he would also try them; so one night a little after bed time he mounted the tree and began filling his bosom and pockets with fruit. Making a rustling among the branches the doctor happened to hear him, and coming out into the garden, looking up into the tree he espied James and hailed him. James was obliged to answer and give his name. "Oh, James, is that you? Why James you are on the wrong tree; *that* is the summer sweeting. Come down, come down my lad, and I will help you to get some." This was indeed the fact, but in his hurry he had not yet made the discovery of his mistake. James came down very slowly, expecting rough treatment, and the kind language of the doctor only a "*ruse*" to get him within his reach. But he was pleasantly disappointed. The doctor, instead of using harsh words or beating the aggressor, as most men would have done, took a pole and knocked off as many apples as he could carry, and dismissed him with the request that when he wanted any more to call on him and he would assist him in getting them. James, however, never visited the tree again, and did all in his power to prevent the other boys from doing so.

For several of the last years of his life, he held the office of county treasurer, which afforded him a moderate salary without much toil, and enabled him to extend his charities to the new societies for the propagation of the gospel, and other benevolent purposes, which came into notice about thirty years ago, and of which he was a zealous promoter. His house was the home of all itinerating preachers of the Congregational and Presbyterian sects who visited the town and were engaged in the cause of religion. Samuel J. Mills, the projector of foreign missions, spent two weeks with him in 1812, when was formed the "Washington County Bible Society," which is still in full operation, and was the first in the valley of the Ohio. He was the "Gaius" of Marietta, although for its population it abounded in men zealous and liberal in promoting all good works. In his domestic relations the doctor was very happy. His wife was a cheerful, humble and sincere Christian, with a lively, benevolent temperament, ever ready to aid in all his works of charity. By this union he had no issue, but the children of his wife were treated with all the love and tenderness he could have bestowed on his own. In person Dr. True was tall and spare, with simple but not ungraceful manners. His eyes grey and small, one being destroyed by a disease of the optic nerve; with full, projecting brows; nose large and aquiline; forehead rather low, but face mild and expressive of benevolence. He was a man of whom no enemy could say hard things, and whom every one loved and respected. He died in 1823, aged 63 years, of the prevailing epidemic fever. His memory is still cherished by the descendants of the early pioneers, for his universal charity, simplicity of manners, and sincere piety.

DOCTOR THOMAS FARLEY

Was the son of General Farley of old Ipswich, Mass. The year of his birth is unknown, but probably was about the year 1761; as by an old manuscript recipe book now in the possession of the writer, it is ascertained that he studied medicine in 1782, at Salem, with Dr. Holyoke. He came to Marietta in the spring or summer of 1788, the same year with Dr. True. He was the attending physician of General Varnum, one of the judges of the North West Territory, who died at Marietta of consumption, in January, 1789, as appears from his bill of attendance found among the papers of the administrator. Col. Joseph Barker, one of the early settlers, says of him, "He was a modest, amiable young man, always ready to obey the calls of humanity, and had the good will and confidence of all who knew him." The country being new, and but few people in the settlements, he became discouraged and returned to his former home in the autumn of 1790, and did not return again to the territory. His subsequent life and place of residence are unknown.

DOCTOR SOLOMON DROWN

Was a native of Rhode Island, and came out to Marietta as one of the proprietors and agents of the Ohio Land company, in the summer of 1788. It does not appear that he intended to settle in the country as a physician, although he attended on General Varnum as consulting physician in the sickness of which he died, in January, 1789. He was educated at Brown University, R. I., and was a man of literature and classical elegance as a writer. The directors of the Ohio company selected him to pronounce the eulogy at the funeral of General Varnum, which was published at Newport, R. I., the same year. He also delivered the first address on the seventh of April, 1789, the anniversary of the landing of the settlers at Marietta, which day was strictly observed for many years as a public festival, and is yet commemorated by "picnic" parties. This was also published but is now rare. At the breaking out of the war with the western tribes, he returned to Rhode Island and was appinted Professor of Botany and Natural History in Brown University, which post he filled for many years. The time of his death is unknown.

DOCTOR WILLIAM PITT PUTNAM

Was the fourth son of Col. Israel Putnam of Brooklyne, Connecticut, and the grandson of General Israel Putnam. He was born the 11th of December, 1770. His boyhood was spent on a farm in the country, on which he worked in the summer, and attended the public schools of the town in the winter. At the age of fourteen years he, with his brother Daniel, about two years older, was placed under the tuition of the Rev. Josiah Whitney, D. D., the minister of Brooklyne, who remained for sixty years the pastor of a Congregational church in that town, and died at the age of ninety. With him they boarded through the week, going home on Saturdays. Under his care he studied English Grammar and Latin for two years. At the age of eighteen he began to read medicine under the instruction of Dr. Albigense Waldo of Pomfret, Connecticut, who was distinguished as a surgeon in the army during the war of the Revolution, and now practised in that branch only. With him he remained two years. In 1791, he attended a course of medical lectures at Cambridge University, delivered by Drs. Warren and Waterhouse, both celebrated as professional men and teachers of that day. In May, 1792, he left his home for Marietta in the N. W. Territory, as appears from a letter from his father to Griffin Green, Esq., recommending him to his favor and patronage. Col. Putnam was a proprietor in the Ohio company, and had visited Marietta in 1788, returning just before the breaking out of the war in 1790 for his family, but thought it imprudent to bring them on until peace was restored, which took place five years after. On his arrival, which was in the midst of the war, he commenced the practice of medicine, spending a portion of the time at Belpre, where his brother, A. W. Putnam, had resided since the departure of his father. The encouragement was little or none; inhabitants few in number, while the savages constantly watched the settlements, and every one's life was in danger who ventured out many rods from the garrison. Under these circumstances he remained at Marietta until the year 1794, when he returned to Connecticut, and married Miss Bethia Glyssan, the daughter of Dr. Glyssan of Woodstock in that state. In 1795, in company with his father and family, he returned with his wife and resumed the practice. In 1797 he purchased the city square on which Col. Mills now resides, containing six acres, and erected a small frame house on the spot where the mansion now stands, in which his brother David and family lived on their removal to Marietta the following year. Finally, in 1799, finding many difficulties in the practice of medicine in a new country, and the people generally poor, although he had a full share of their patronage and confidence, he purchased a tract of two hundred acres on the Ohio river, eight miles above Marietta, and commenced clearing a farm. The fatigues and exposures of this new occupation in the heat of summer brought on an attack of bilious fever, of which he died the 8th of October, 1800, leaving no issue to bear onward his name. His widow subsequently married General Edward Tupper, and is yet living in Gallipolis. In person Dr. Putnam was tall and commanding, with a cheerful, lively countenance and genteel address. He was a successful practitioner, and his early death was a serious loss to the country.

DOCTOR NATHAN M^c^INTOSH

Was the son of Col. William McIntosh of Needham, Massachusetts, and born in the year 1762. His father was a man of considerable note, commanding a company of infantry in the continental army, and subsequently a colonel in the militia. He was one of the delegates in the convention at

Boston, in January, 1788, on the adoption of the Constitution of the United States. After receiving a suitable education, his son Nathan studied medicine in Boston, about the year 1786. Soon after the formation of the Ohio company, he decided on seeking his fortune in the West, and left his father's house in 1788, travelling on horseback as far as Harrisburg, Pa, where he was attacked with the small pox, suffering severely with that loathsome disease. After his recovery, in 1789, he proceeded into the vicinity of Hagerstown, Md., and commenced the practice of medicine. It is unknown how successful he was, but in 1791, after remaining a while in Clarksburg, Va., he moved to Marietta, soon after the breaking out of the Indian war, nothing daunted by the hazard of such a step. Soon after his arrival, in the spring of that year, he was appointed surgeon's mate to the garrison at Waterford, twenty miles above the mouth of the Muskingum, with rations and pay of twenty-two dollars a month. This amount, though small, was at a time when there was little opportunity for private practice, and was an acceptable service. In this post he remained about two years, and becoming acquainted with Miss Rhoda Shepherd, the daughter of Col. Enoch Shepherd and the niece of General Shepherd of Massachusetts, he married her in 1792. In the spring of the next year he received an invitation from the inhabitants of Clarksburg, Va., to come and practise medicine in that place, which he accepted. In July following he returned for his wife and child, a distance of eighty miles, with an escort of eighteen men to conduct her through the wilderness to Harrison county. The journey was performed on horseback, at the imminent hazard of life from the Indians, who constantly waylaid the paths on the routes between the settlements. His professional business was very successful and quite profitable, as it was a settlement many years older than that at Marietta. Being full of adventure and the New England spirit of improvement, he contracted to build a bridge across the west branch of the Monongahela river at Clarksburg, and warranted it to stand for a certain period of time. It is a large stream, and subject to sudden floods, from its vicinity to the mountains. Soon after its completion a great freshet swept it away, to the great damage of the doctor. In 1795, he returned with his family to Marietta and again resumed the practice of medicine. He was now quite a successful operator in surgery, and some difficult cases treated skilfully increased his reputation with the public, so that he had at command a large share of business. His fine personal appearance, aided by a rich fashionable dress and gentlemanly manners, greatly promoted his favor with the community. He was naturally possessed of a kind, conciliating disposition, ready to attend to the calls of the distressed, or oblige his neighbours by any act of courtesy within his power. In proof of his charity and good feeling for the unfortunate, his treatment of the present Elder Jacob Young, a noted Methodist preacher, may be favorably cited. Mr. Young was one of the earliest ministers of that sect in the North West Territory. In 1805, during one of his itinerant rambles through the forests of the West, he was attacked with a fever, and lying at a house about a mile distant from the doctor's, sent for him to visit him. Perceiving his unpleasant predicament amongst strangers, he offered to take him to his own home, where he could both nurse him and administer medical aid to better advantage. The offer was accepted; and after a long and tedious illness he was restored to health. For ten days and nights of the most dangerous period of his disease, he remained constantly by the bed side of his patient. Like the good Samaritan of old, all this was done without the hope of fee or reward, save the pleasure of doing a good act. In the summer of 1847, forty-two years after this event, the venerable elder, now near 80 years old, when at Marietta, visited the house, that he might once more look at the room in which he so long lay under the care of the benevolent doctor. About this time a new era commenced in his affairs, which changed all his future views of life. In the year 1801, Abel M. Sargent, who had been a Baptist preacher in New Jersey and latterly at Clarksburg, Va., moved to Belpre, twelve miles below Marietta, where he preached for the Congregational society one season. Soon after this he originated a new religious sect, the followers of which were called "Halcyons." In one of his publications, which were numerous, he styles himself the "Halcyon, Itinerary, and true Millennium Messenger," saying "that the millennium has commenced its first openings, and that Christ's second coming is now at hand." "I have received my authority to make this report from the Lord. I have received it by divine revelation, and have received my commandment of God to bear this Testimony, and to deliver this message publicly, *first* to the visible church, *then* to the world at large." Filled with the importance of his message, which he appeared fully to believe, he travelled from place to place along the Ohio river, from Louisville to Morgantown on the Monongahela, preaching the new doctrine and spreading his faith by numerous printed tracts. In this wild region, where preachers of any kind were scarce, the novel doctrine caught the attention of the borderers, and many followers soon joined his standard. The Halcyon tenets seem to have embraced many of the views of the modern Millerites, combined with a portion of the Mormon faith. He pretended to hold intercourse with angels, heal the sick, and procure immediate answers from heaven to his prayers. He was a man of considerable learning, profound in the knowledge of the Scriptures, as well as a ready, fluent speaker. Purity of heart and life was inculcated on all his followers, and the indulgence of the animal passions forbidden. Among the stricter members vegetable food and milk formed their diet. By living in a pure and temperate manner it was taught that man might prolong his days, without sickness, to the age of the patriarchs. Immortality and happiness was the reward of those who anxiously strove for and desired it with all the heart; while the wicked and the careless were annihilated at death, or literally burnt up. Members were admitted to the church on a confession of their faith in the Halcyon doctrine, and their initiation manifested by the rite of baptism, which was done by wading into the river and pouring water over the head from a silver cup, which Sargent kept for this use. A continual warfare was waged with all other sects, as this was the only true one. A number of preachers sprung up under his instructión, amongst whom were several females. They had frequent prayer meetings, and assembled often for exhortation and singing from the Halcyon hymn book, exhibiting much love and hospitality in their intercourse with each other. Many of Sargent's tenets harmonized with the feelings and views of Dr. McIntosh, and he became a sincere and devoted believer of his doctrines. From the extravagances of some of the leaders, professing to work miracles and raise the dead, the sect, in the course of six or eight years, greatly declined and finally became extinct, the members generally becoming Universalists. Dr. McIntosh, however, continued to write and to lecture on that and other kindred subjects, especially on the mystery of the Urim and Thummim and against all *secret* societies; to which and to slavery he was violently opposed. The favorite spot for his public discourses was the market house, where he often harangued the assembled citizens with great earnestness and considerable eloquence, having a ready flow of language and agreeable address. Soon after the period of his adopting the new doctrine, he in a great measure declined the practice of medicine, and turned his attention to the manufacture of bricks, erecting many buildings on contract, working diligently in the brickyard as well as with the trowel. He was a man of great industry, temperate in all his habits and of the strictest honesty; possessing the good will and confidence of the community. He published a volume on the science of "Scripture Correspondencies," which is now rare. He died of the epidemic fever in September, 1823, aged 61 years, leaving a family of four sons and a daughter. His two remaining sons rank among the most enterprising men for wealth and activity in business.

DOCTOR JOSIAH HART

Was born in Berlin, Connecticut, about the year 1738. Of his early life little is known to the writer. He was prepared for college by the Rev. Dr. Norris, and graduated at Yale, in 1762. At this time he had expected to study divinity, but for some cause he changed his views and read medicine under Dr. Potter of Wallingford, Ct., a celebrated physician and preceptor of that day. In 1765, he married Miss Abigail Sluman of Stonington, and commenced the practice of medicine in Wethersfield. At the breaking out of the War of Independence he was found on the side of his oppressed country, and turned out in defence of her rights by serving as a surgeon of a regiment in the United States Army for several years, and used, in after life, to describe with great minuteness some of the capital operations under his care. In June, 1777, during the most exciting period of the war, when Burgoyne threatened to overrun the country by dividing the New England states from the Middle ones, he lost his wife, then the mother of seven children, four sons and three daughters. The latter are yet living at very advanced ages in New England. Two of the sons settled in Ohio. In 1778, he married Mrs. Abigail Harris. She was a descendant of John Robbins, one of the first settlers of Wethersfield, and a blood relation on the mother's side to the celebrated Miles Standish. By the second marriage he had three daughters. They accompanied him to Marietta, Ohio, where he removed after the death of his second wife, in 1796. One of them is yet living near that place, as well as several of his grandchildren. Of his standing and character as a man and physician while living in Wethersfield, Mr. Hezekiah Belden, the town clerk, thus writes: "He was highly esteemed in this town as a physician. His naturally kind feelings and his religious views made him at once the attentive physician, tender nurse, and the persuasive teacher of righteousness. As a member of society he was respected, beloved, and trusted; discharging the duties of the trusts conferred upon him not only with fidelity, but with ability. He more than once was a representative of the town in the General Assembly of the state, and often filled the more important town offices, as well as that of deacon in the church. I knew him well and loved him much; for from my earliest recollection until he removed to the West, he was the family physician and intimate friend of my father." The writer of this sketch first knew him in 1806, at which time he was practising his calling in Marietta, but had become infirm and feeble from age. He had been married for several years to his third wife, Miss Anna Moulton, a maiden lady from Newburyport, Mass. At the formation of the Congregational church in Marietta, in 1797, he was elected one of the deacons, which station he filled for several years. As a proof of the love of science which he still retained in old age, it may be stated that he became a member of a chemical society, composed of a few young men and some of the physicians of Marietta, for their mutual improvement. Meetings were held two or three evenings in a week, for about four months. A decent chemical apparatus was procured, and most of the experiments exhibited in college lectures were performed, under the direction of D. C. Wallace, a very intelligent druggist The transactions of each evening were recorded in a journal, and the theory of each experiment fully explained.

Dr. Hart took a deep interest in the subject and was a regular attendant. In 1811, having become too aged for practice, he moved on to a farm ten miles from Marietta. He died in August, 1812, of the spotted fever, aged 74 years. His wife died a few hours after, and they were both buried the same day. In person Dr. Hart was below the medium size, but well formed; countenance mild, pleasing, and intelligent. In manners very gentlemanly and kind, exhibiting a true Christian spirit in his intercourse with his fellow men. Col. Jonathan Hart was his brother, a captain in Harmar's regiment, a fine officer and engineer, killed in St. Clair's defeat by the Indians, in November, 1791.

[To be continued.]

ORIGINAL SETTLERS OF SALISBURY, MASSACHUSETTS.

[Communicated by MR. THORNTON.]

The first or Original list of ye townsmen of Salisbury in ye booke of Records.

1 Mr Sam: Dudley
2 Mr Wm Worcester
3 Mr. ffrances Doue
4 Mr. Henry Byly
6 Edward ffrench
7 Rich: Wells
8 Jno Rolfe
9 Jno: Sanders
10 Isaac Buswell
11 John Severans
12 Mr Tho: Bradbury
13 Jno Hodges
14 Josiah Cobham
15 Jarett Haddon
16 Jno Bayly Senr
17 Henry Brown
18 Ant: Sadler
19 Rodg: Eastman
20 John Steuens
21 Rob: ffitts
22 Mr Sam: Hall
23 John Hoyt
24 Wm Holdred
26 Th^{o} Barnett
27 John Ilsley
28 Wm Allin
29 Wm Barnes
30 Rich: North
31 Abraham Morrill
32 Wm Osgood
33 Mr Wm Hook
34 Mr John Hall
*36 Mr Christo: Batt
37 Robert Pike
38 Wm Partridg
39 Mr Tho: Dum̄er
40 Mr. Henry Mondey
41 Georg Carr
42 Sam: ffelloes
43 Wm Sargent
44 Jno Harison
45 Phil: Challis
46 Luke Heard
47 Ant: Colby
48 Jno Bayly jun^{r}
49 Christian Brown
50 Rich: Singletary
51 Tho: Hauxworth
52 Jno Eyer Sen:
53 Tho: Rowell
54 Jno Dickson
55 Danieli lad
56 Jno ffullar
57 Tho: Carter
58 Enock Greeleaf
59 Rich: Goodale
60 Rich Currier
61 Joseph Moys
62 Andrew Greely
63 Ralf Blasdall
64 Robert Codnam
65 John Wheelar
66 Tho: Macy
67 Joseph Parker
68 John Coles

* No. 35 in the original, or that from which I copy.—ED.

This is a true Copie as they were first listed in ye book of Records: as attests
Tho: Bradbury rec^{r}.

At a gen^{ll} meeting of ye towne of Salisbury 3^{d}: 12th m^{o} 1650
Also it was ordered att ye same meeting that all whose names are herevn-

der written shall be accompted townsmen and com̄oners and none but ȳ to this psent, y^{t} is to say

Mr. Wm Worcester
Robt. Pike
Wm Partridg
Rich: Wells
Mr. Christo: Ball
Wm Buswell
Jno Gill
Rich: Singletary
Jno Stevens
Jno Dickison
Tho: Carter
Rich: Goodale
Rich: North
Wm Huntington
Tho: Rowell
Tho: Macy
Phil: Challis
Josiah Cobham
Mr. ffrancis Doue
Joseph Moys
+Rich: Coy
Georg Golduyer
Jno: Coles
Jno: Rolf
Jno Ilsley
Mr. Sam: Winsley
Mr. Tho: Bradbury
Sam: Getchell
Steven fflanders
Robert Fitts
Wm Brown
Roger Eastman
Mr. Sam: Hall
Abrahā Morrill
Mr. Georg Carr
Jaret Hadon
Jno: Weed
Anthony Colby
Tho: Barnett
Georg Martyn
+Jno Sanders
Rich: Ball
Rich: Goodale jun^{r}
Mr. Sam. Groom
Jno Eaton
Edward ffrench
Mr. Henry Monday
Andrew Greely
Isaac Buswell
Jno Severance
Sam: ffelloes
Mary Hauxworth
Jno Clough
Hen: Brown
Wm Allin
Wm Barns
Mr Wm Hooke
Jno: Bayly Sen:
Nat: Rowell
Rich Currier
Wm Sargent
Jno: Hoyt
Wm Osgood
+Hen. Ambros
Anthony Newland
Widow Blasdall

This is a true Copie taken out of ye town Records for Salisbury
As attests Tho: Bradbury.

All y^{t} ye crosses ar against w^{r} disallowed for being townsmen and Com̄oners Tho: Bradbury rec^{r}.

This is a true copie of ye originall on file
as attests Tho: Bradbury rec^{r}.

Mr Wosters rate for 30^{ls}: the 25: of December 1650.

	s	d			s	d
John Bayly	12	6	Willi: Allin		11	6
Willi: Huntington	3	5	Georg Carr		16	6
Jarret Haddon	6	10	Tho: Carter		8	6
Tho: Rowell	6	8	Sam: Hall		17	2
Josiah Cobham	8	5	Robt. Ring		1	11
Willi: Sargent	7	4	Robt. Pike		10	8
Phillip Challis	7	6	Jno: Cole		8	6
Jno: Weed	4	6	Willi: Partridg		10	0
Vallentine Rowell	4	6	Willi: Barnes		12	6
Tho: Barnett	5	10	Georg Golduyer		18	3
Tho: Macy	15	8	Jno. Eaton		7	8
Rich: Currier	4	6	Jno: Rolf	£1	00	5
Georg Martyn	3	6	Mr. Moodey	1	9	4
Jno: Hoyt	6	6	Abrahā Morrill	0	19	2
Antony Colby	13	2	Rich: North	0	10	4
Willi: Osgood	14	8	Rich: Goodale	0	14	0
Jno: Clough	9	5	Edward ffrench	1	2	0
Rodg: Eastman	8	3	Joseph Moys	00	4	0
Jno. Dickison	8	4	Mr. Hooke	0	10	1
Henry Brown	7	4	Jno: Illsley	0	11	10

	£	s	d
Andrew Greely	0	6	0
Mr. Sam: Winsley	0	11	0
Rich: Wells	0	10	0
Nathll: Winsley	0	4	11
Sam: Winsley	0	4	9
Mr. Tho: Bradbury	0	13	4
Isaac Buswell	0	10	6
Wm. Buswell	0	7	0
Sam: Buswell	0	6	0
Jno: Severans	0	8	2
Jno: Gill	0	06	5
Sam: Getchell		4	6
Sam: ffelloes		9	0
Rich Singletary		7	6
Steven fflanders		3	9
Bell Willix		4	7
Jno: Stevens		11	5
Rob: ffitts		11	3
Widdow Sadler		2	8
Mr. Batt	1	03	0
He Blasdall		6	10

Samuel Hall
The J mark of Isaac Buswell
Edward ffrench
Rich: Wells

This is a true copie of ye originall on file as attests Tho: Bradbury
Recorder.

A rate made 18th 5th mo. 52 for his halfe year due 24: 4: mo

	£	s	d
Edward ffrench	1	00	04
Leift: Pike	1	10	00
Georg Goldnger	0	15	03
Jno: Eaton	0	4	7
Wm: Partridg	0	19	8
Jno: Rolfe	0	17	3
Mr. Monday	1	03	08
Jno: Ilsly	0	08	05
Andrew Greely	0	07	03
Josiah Cobham	0	12	00
Sam: Winsly Senr	0	09	00
Isaac Buswell	0	11	00
Willi: Buswell	0	7	08
Mr. Bradbury	0	17	06
Jno: Severans	0	12	11
Jno: Gill	0	06	06
Sam: ffelloes	0	07	07
Sam: Buswell	0	06	06
Rich: Wells	0	07	08
Rodg: Eastman	0	06	10
Jno: Stevens	0	06	09
Robt. Fitts	0	09	07
Jno: Clough	0	12	02
Jno: Dickson	0	08	07
Sam: Getchell	0	03	05
Steven fflanders	0	02	11
Willi: Brown	0	05	00
Willi: Osgood	0	17	04
Willi: Allin	0	12	03
Henry Brown	0	6	09
Thomas Carter	0	05	10
Mr. Hall	1	02	02
Mr. Hooke	0	03	04
Rich: Goodale Senr	0	10	02
Rich: Goodale Jr.	0	03	07
Rich: North	0	07	11
Rich: Ormsby	0	12	06
Mr. Carr	0	15	07
Mr. Coffyn	0	12	01
Jno: Coles	0	04	10
Mr. Rusels	0	01	06
Sam: Winsly Senr	0	05	04
Nathll Winsley	0	03	08
Barnabas Lams[on?]	0	02	06
Joseph ffrench	0	04	04
Robert Ring	0	04	09
Tho: Robenson	0	02	10
Widow Hawxworth	0	04	06
Jo: Moys	0	04	06
Edmond Elliot	0	02	06
Jno: Wheler	0	01	06
Jno: Bayly	0	01	06
Jno: Maxfeild	0	02	06
Sum	23	01	10

Sam: Hall
Richard Wells
Sam: Winsley
Jno: Stevens

This is a true copie of ye originall Rate on file as attests
Tho Bradbury Recr.

EPITAPHS.

The following inscription is taken from a copy in the autograph of the REV. SAMUEL SEWALL of Burlington, Ms.:

"Inscription in Concord Burying-Ground Nov. 22. 1811."

GOD
Wills us free;
MAN
Wills us slaves;
I will, as God wills;
God's will be done.
Here lies the body of JOHN JACK, a
Native of Africa, who died March 1773,
Aged about sixty years.
Tho born in a land of Slaves,
He was born free;
Tho' he lived in a land of liberty,
He lived a Slave,
Till by his honest, tho' stolen labors
He acquired the source of slavery,
Which gave him his freedom;
Tho' not long before
Death the grand tirant
Gave him his final emancipation,
And set him on a footing with kings.
Tho' a slave to vice
He practiced those virtues,
Without which kings are but Slaves.

Buckland Clark
aged 3 years &
4 months died Nov^{r}
6th 1748.
Also Elizabeth Clark
aged 1 year & 2 months died
Oct. 20. 1751. The children
of Mr. James & Mrs. Ruth Clarke.

Here lyes ye body of Mrs. Elizabethy
Honewell, who died October ye 23. 1731.
in ye 46th year of her age.

Here lies the body of
Mrs. Elizabeth Belcher —
Widow to Mr. Joseph
Belcher who departed this life
Aug. 23. 1762. aged 61 years. b. 1701.

Copied from Copps Hill Burying-Ground, April 9, 1848. J. W. T

PRINCIPAL EVENTS IN THE LIFE OF THE INDIAN CHIEF BRANT.

[Continued from p. 348, Vol. II.]

Since the publication of our article in the Journal, designated above, several important facts have been discovered by us, serving to settle some circumstances in the life of the chief which before were quite uncertain; as, for instance, it was merely a conjecture resting, for aught we could discover, upon that almost certainly fallible source — tradition, that one of the five chiefs who visited the court of Queen Anne in 1710, was the grandfather of Brant; but it is not remembered that there was a pretension that the grandfather's name was the same as that of our chief, namely, Brant. Now we are able to set at rest a part, at least, of this unsettled question. There has come into our hands an engraving of one of the five chiefs, on a quarto sheet, executed during his stay in England, with this inscription: —

Sa Ga Yean Qua Rash Tow.
King of ye Maquas. alias King Brant.

Done from ye Life by I: Faber.
Sold by I: Faber near ye Savoy. & J: King in ye Poultry Lond^n^: 1710.

It is proved by this that, first, one of the chiefs' name was Brant; second, that our chief thus derived his name, and not from a white man, as was before concluded. And notwithstanding the costume and style of the picture are different from the first described in our former article, yet that they were done from the same painting (or "ye life," as above expressed,) there is no doubt. The little variation in the spelling of the name weighs nothing against this conclusion.

It was contrary to the custom of the Indians for children to be named after their father, yet *Brant* bore that of his *grand*father. This circumstance is most likely to be accounted for in this way. His grandfather was a chief of distinction, but there is nothing to show that his father was of any special consideration, further than from the mere fact of his being a son of a distinguished chief. Young Brant seems early to have been destined for distinction, and there is no doubt, or at least it is extremely probable, that Sir William Johnson was the cause of his being named for his grandfather.

There was printed in London in 1767, a pamphlet of this title: "A BRIEF NARRATIVE of the INDIAN Charity-School in Lebanon in Connecticut, New England: Founded and carried on by That Faithful Servant of GOD The Rev. Mr. *Eleazar Wheelock*. The SECOND EDITION with an APPENDIX."

In this work is contained the following memoir of Brant: —

"*Joseph Brant*, a *Mohawk Indian*, and of a Family of Distinction in that Nation, was educated by Mr. *Wheelock*, and was so well accomplished, that the Rev. *Charles Jeffry Smith* (a young gentleman, who, out of Love to CHRIST and the Souls of Men, devotes his Life, and Such a fortune as is sufficient to support himself and an Interpreter, wholly to this glorious Service;) took him for his Interpreter, when he went on his Mission to the *Mohawks*, near Three Years ago. But the War* breaking out at that Time between the back *Indians* and the *English*, Mr. *Smith* was obliged to return; but *Joseph* tarried, and went out with a Company against the *Indians*, and was useful in the War; in which he behaved so much like the Christian and the Soldier, that he gained great Esteem. He now lives in a decent manner, and endeavors to teach his poor Brethren the Things of GOD, in which his own Heart seems much engaged. His House is an Asylum for Missionaries in that Wilderness."

When we had proceeded thus far in our account we received other important matter from the REV. WILLIAM ALLEN, D. D.,† which is as follows: —

Extract of a letter from Dr. E. Wheelock to the marquis of Lothian, dated

"Lebanon, 7 July, 1763.

"Mr. Charles Jeffrey Smith, a well accomplished young gentleman, was ordained here last week with a view to a mission among remote tribes of Indians, and he is this week set out on his long journey into the Indian country, with a promising young *Mohawk* from this school as his Interpreter."

That this young Mohawk was *Joseph Brant* is made evident by a letter of Dr. Wheelock to Sir Wm. Johnson, dated "Hartford, May 16, 1763," in which he says, "I received last evening a paper with your seal, inclosing a letter to *Joseph* from his sister, wrote, I suppose, in the Mohawk language." "In my last I informed you of the truly noble and charitable design of Mr. C. J. Smith, who has been Joseph's tutor last winter; his purpose to come with Joseph to you as soon as he could get ready for the business of his proposed mission; and that I designed to take Joseph with me to Boston and Portsmouth, &c, &c." In the same letter he says, that Mr. Smith depended on Joseph "for a pilot and companion."

Since writing the above another letter has been found, which furnishes other evidence and most conclusive, dated "Hartford, 5 July, 1763," to Sir W. J. "I hope you will please to receive as sufficient excuse for Joseph's staying so long beyond the time, which I set in my last to you, that the Rev. Mr. Smith was not prepared for the business of his mission sooner. I hope you will find he has made such proficiency in the knowledge of things useful, as you will esteem sufficient proof of his past diligence in improving his time and advantages. I can't but hope he may be much perfected in the English tongue by associating with Mr. Smith and serving as his *Interpreter*. He has much endeared himself to me, and I think to every body else, by his good behavior, and I should be very sorry, if any thing should prevent his pursuing his studies. I hope he will return to the school in the fall of the year and continue through the winter," &c.

The following is an extract of another letter, to Dr. Gifford, dated "Lebanon, Feb. 24, 1763:"

* The war of 1763 is evidently meant. It is often called *Pontiac's War*. After the fall of the French power in Canada, in 1760, the Indians remained tolerably quiet for a time; but affairs under the rule of the English differed so widely from those under the French, that their uneasiness broke out into open and fierce hostility, in 1763.

† Now of Northampton, formerly president of Bowdoin College; than whom few if any are better acquainted with the whole range of our history. To speak of American Biography is to speak of him.

"A young Mohawk of a family of Distinction in that nation, (his English name is Joseph), of a sprightly genius, a manly and genteel deportment, and of a modest, courteous, and benevolent temper, I have reason to think began truly to love our Lord Jesus Christ several months ago; and his religious affections seem still agreeably increasing."

It thus appears that Joseph and Mr. Smith left Lebanon or Hartford to proceed to the Indian country, July 5 or 6, 1763; and he remained in the school till this time, and not merely till May 27, 1762, as stated in the Register, p. 347. On the same page this journey of Mr. Smith is said to be in 1762; the mistake may be taken from Col. Stone's book. Being in the school from Aug. 1, 1761, to July 5, 1763,* the advantages of it were enjoyed by a young man of good talents and character for nearly two years.

The interest which Sir Wm. Johnson took in Joseph is explained by the circumstance that after the death of his lady he had taken Joseph's sister *Molly*, either by marriage or without, for his wife; and he lived with her till his death.

You say, p. 346, that the scholar Joseph was "beyond question THAYENDANECA." If there was any doubt, it is removed by a list of his scholars in the writing of Dr. W., as follows:—

"1761. Aug. 1. Joseph Brant }
do. Negyes } Mohawks."
do. Center, dead }

In one of his letters Dr. W. writes the name of Joseph—*Thayendenagen*, a little different from the three forms in which you give it; and in his letter dated March 14, 1764, he speaks of a report, which he did not credit, that Joseph 'is gone over to the enemy.'"

We now resume our chronological form of events in the life of the chief.

1779, July 22. A party of sixty Indians and twenty-seven white men led by Brant, attack the Minisink† settlement, in Orange county, N. Y., burn ten houses, twelve barns, a fort, and two mills, carry off considerable booty and several prisoners.‡

In 1822,§ the citizens of Orange county collected the bones of the gallant band who were cut off by the Indians at Minisink, and which had been exposed to the suns and snows of 43 years. The remains of forty-four persons were found and publicly interred. The line of procession was led by the Cadets from West Point, and extended about a mile. Major Poppino, who bore a distinguished part in the battle, though at this celebration 96 years old, walked in the procession, and was one of the pall bearers.||

In the burying-ground adjacent to the Presbyterian church in Goshen is a monument with this inscription:"¶

* Excepting the time he was absent with Kirtland, and on a visit to his friends, as before stated.—ED.

† Signifying, according to the author of the history of Schoharie, *The water is gone.*

‡ In Stone's *Life of Brant*, the incidents of this affair occupy several pages.

§ The preparatory meeting was held in December, the preceding year, when a committee was chosen to collect the bones and make the arrangements for the celebration.—*Spofford's Gazetteer*, Art. MINISINK.

|| *New York Spectator*, 2 Aug., 1822, in *Holmes's Annals*, ii. 302.

¶ Barber & Howe, *Hist. Colls. of New York*, 418.

"Erected by the inhabitants of Orange county, 22 July, 1822. Sacred to the memory of 44 of their fellow citizens, who fell at the battle of Minisink, 22 July, 1779.

Benj. Tusten, Col.	Roger Townsend	John Carpenter
Bezaleel Tyler, Capt.	Saml. Knapp	David Barney
Samuel Jones "	James Knapp	Jonathan Haskell
John Little "	Benjamin Bennet	Abm. Williams
John Duncan "	William Barker	James Mosher
Benj. Vail "	Jonathan Pierce	Isaac Ward
John Wood, Lieut.	James Little	Baltus Nierpos
Nathaniel Finch, Adj.	Joseph Norris	Galmatiel Bailey
Ephm. Mastin, Ens.	Gilbert Vail	Moses Thomas
Ephm. Middaugh, "	Abm. Shepherd	Eleazer Owens
Gabriel Wisner, Esq.	Joel Decker	Adam Emleler
Stephen Mead	Nathan Wade	Samuel Little
Maths. Terwilliger	Simon Wait	Benjamin Dunning
Joshua Lockwood,	—— Talmadge	Daniel Reed."
Ephraim Forgerson	Jacob Dunning	

We have copied the names contained on the monument, for the double reason that the names themselves are a monument to Brant as well as to those who ended their days then and there, and to show that nearly the whole list are our New England family names.*

Aug. 29. Battle of Chemung, called by the whites Newtown, but now Elmira. Two grand expeditions seem to have been nearly simultaneously undertaken; one by the refugees and Indians upon the borders of Canada, and the other by General Washington, to break up the power of the tories and Indians in the direction of Canada. The battle of Chemung was the result of these expeditions, and the overthrow of the power of the disaffected part of the Five Nations, of whom Brant was.

Of the precise number opposed to the Continentals there is no data to be depended upon; but from the ground occupied by them, the resistance they made, and other signs known to warriors, their number, it was judged, could not have been less than about *one thousand*; while the Continentals, under Sullivan and Poor, amounted to about *fifteen hundred.* The Indians and tories, though they had the disadvantage in numbers, had the advantage of position, which was well chosen, and time to fortify it, which they appear to have improved to good advantage. But against this the Americans were provided with artillery.

Notwithstanding the terror which cannon always excite among Indians, they at this time stood their ground manfully, and "Brant seemed everywhere present" to keep their spirits up. "The battle was long," but was at length decided by the brigade under Gen. Poor. This division of the army performed nearly all the fighting, its advance being disputed by Brant in person, until at length he saw he was in

* Nearly every surname may be found in the publications of Judge Hinman. And although we have not seen it expressly stated, there may be no doubt that the Minisink country was chiefly settled from Connecticut. That Goshen and its vicinity furnished many settlers in that region is more than probable; as a part of the ancient Minisink was named *Goshen.*

danger of his retreat being cut off. He then sounded the retreat halloo. In a moment their strongholds were abandoned; tories and Indians, officers and soldiers, fled with all precipitation, and they made no formidable resistance to the invading army afterwards.

It was a matter of much surprise to Sullivan* and his men that their loss was no more than some "five or six" in killed, considering "the duration" of the battle. "It was small, almost to a miracle." But the wounded was out of all proportion to the killed, amounting to near fifty. Among the latter were Major Titcomb of the artillery, Capt. Clayes, and Lieut. Collis; the last named mortally.

No correct estimate could be formed of the loss of the Indians, but it was thought to have been severe. Though in all possible cases they carry off their dead, yet at this time *eleven* were left on the field of battle, and *fourteen* more found partially buried.

Elated by this signal victory the Continentals pressed forward, and laid waste nearly the whole Indian country.

1780. The first notice we find of Brant after his defeat by Sullivan, is his marriage to a third wife at Fort Niagara, "under circumstances somewhat peculiar. Among the prisoners taken to that post from Cherry Valley, was a Miss Moore, who, being detained in captivity with Mrs. Campbell and others, was courted and married by an officer of the garrison. Brant was present at the wedding, and although he had for some time previous been living with his wife, bound only by the ties of an Indian marriage, he nevertheless embraced the opportunity of having the English marriage ceremony performed, which was accordingly done by Col. Butler, acting as one of the king's commissioners of the peace for Tryon county."†

April 7. Brant surprises a number of men making sugar near Harpersfield, (eleven in number,) and carries them to Canada. At the head of the captured party was Lieut. Alexander Harper. He and his party were sent out from the Schoharie forts by Col. Vrooman, for the double object of discovery and sugar making.‡

August. The Indians under Brant commit extensive depredations at Canajoharie and its vicinity.

Oct. 17. About eight hundred Indians and all sorts of whites appear at Schoharie. The Indians under Brant and the whites under Sir John Johnson. They commit very extensive ravages; eighty thousand bushels of grain are supposed to have been destroyed. The whole valley of the Schoharie-kill is laid in ruins. Above one hundred people, chiefly the inhabitants, lost their lives.

Having saved the life of a child taken at Schoharie, Brant sends it to its mother with this note, addressed "To the commanding officer of the rebel army:—

* General John Sullivan was a son of John Sullivan of Berwick, Me., whose epitaph is copied in our first volume, p. 376. The father was a man of education and distinction, a native of Ireland, who emigrated to New England about 1723. Governor James Sullivan, author of the *Hist. of Maine* and several other works, was his brother. The subject of this note died at his seat in Durham, 23 Jan., 1795, æ 54. He left the army immediately after the Indian campaign, and resigned his commission.

† Stone, ii. 55.

‡ Simms's *Schoharie*, 325.

"Sir: I send you by one of my runners, the child which he will deliver, that you may know that whatever others may do, *I* do not make war upon women and children. I am sorry to say that I have those engaged with me in the service, who are more savage than the savages themselves."

We find nothing further worthy of notice during the war.

1784. A grant of land is conferred on Brant and his followers by the authorities of Canada. It was located on the Ouise, or Grand river, and extended from its entrance into Lake Erie to the head of said river, and "in that proportion of six miles breadth from each side of the river." On this tract of land Brant made his home the remainder of his days.

Oct. Brant attends the famous treaty of Fort Stanwix, where Oliver Wolcott, Richard Butler, and Arthur Lee appeared on the part of the Americans. Lafayette was also there. There was never, perhaps, a greater display of Indian eloquence. Here Cornplanter and Red Jacket took opposite sides. Brant was now an advocate for peace.

1785. He visits England and is received with great attention. The object of his visit seems to have been claims for services and losses of his Indians in the war, and perhaps countenance from the government in his endeavors to unite the Indians generally against the United States.

1786. He returns from England, but at what time in the year is not ascertained.

Dec. A great Indian Council is held at the Huron village, near the mouth of the Detroit river. Here Brant exerts his influence to form a confederacy.

1791, Nov. 4. Gen. St. Clair's army is defeated with great loss by the Indians. A biographer* of Brant thinks he was "the master spirit of the Indians" in that bloody affair, but we can come to no such conclusion.

1792. Brant visits Philadelphia, by invitation from the United States government.

1793. The Indians of the country of the lakes hold a council at the Miami rapids, where Brant meets them.

July. Brant meets Col. Timothy Pickering, Gen. Benjamin Lincoln, Mr. Beverly Randolph, and Gen. Chapin, at Gov. Simcoe's at Fort Erie.

1794. Brant erects a Council House for his nation at Grand River. Prepares for a war with the United States.

The news of the terrible defeat of the Indians by Gen. Wayne is received by Brant with despondency. He is said to have been detained from sharing in the disaster by sickness.

This year closed Brant's open hostilities to the United States.

1795. The civilization of the Indians occupies much of the remaining period of the life of Brant.

He is perplexed about the title to his lands by the Canadian government and land jobbers, which continues nearly to the close of his life.

The time of his death has been given.

* Col. Stone, *Life of Brant*, ii. 313.

MARRIAGES IN THE TOWN OF ANDOVER, MS.

FROM 1647 to 1700.

[Copied for the N. E. Hist. Geneal. Register by LUCIUS MANLIUS BOLTWOOD, member of the N. E. H. G. Soc.]

Edmund Fawkner & Dorathy Robinson were married at Salem by Mr John Winthropp 4 Feb. 1647.

Henry Engolls & Mary Osgood were married at Andover the 6. July 1653 by Mr Simon Bradstreet.

John Osgood & Mary Clemance were married at Haverhill the 15 Nov 1653 by Mr Robert Clemance.

John Lovejoy & Mary Osgood were married at Ipswich 1 June 1651. by Mr Simons.

Thomas Johnson & Mary Holt were married at Andover 5 of July 1657. by Mr Simon Bradstreet.

Daniel Pore & Mary Farnum were married at Boston Oct 20. 1650.

George Abbot & Sarah Farnum were married at Andover Apr 26. 1658. by Mr. Bradstreet.

Ralph Farnum & Elizabeth Holt were married Oct 26. 1658. by Mr. Bradstreet.

Nicholas Holt & Hannah Pope (widdow) were married June 12. 1658.

Thomas Eaton, & Unity Smylolary both of Haverhill were married at Andover Jan 6. 1658. by Mr Bradstreet.

Richard Margun of Dover & Rebecca Houldride of Haverhill were married May 21. 1660 at Andover by Mr Simon Bradstreet.

Mr Seaborn Cotton & Mrs Dorothy Bradstreet were married June 14. 1654. by Mr Bradstreet.

Mr Andrew Wiggin & Mrs Hanna Bradstreet were married June 3. 1659.

Ephraim Davis of Haverhill & Mary Johnson of Andover were married Dec 29. 1660.

William Chandler & Mary Dane of Ipswich were married Aug 24. 1658 by Mr Simons.

Robert Russell & Mary Marshall were married July 6. 1659 by Mr Bradstreet.

John Browne & Elizabeth Osgood were married Oct 12. 1659.

Samuel Archer & Hanna Osgood were married May 21. 1660.

Thomas Farnum & Elizabeth Sibborns were married July 8. 1660.

John Fry & Eunice Potter were married Oct 4. 1660. by Mr. Bradstreet.

Robert Stileman & Elizabeth Fry were married Oct 4. 1660 by Mr Bradstreet.

John Stevens & Hanna Barnard	married	June 13 1662
Andrew Foster & Mary Ruse	"	June 7 1662
Samuel Hutchins & Hanna Johnson	"	June 24 1662
Stephen Johnson & Elizabeth Dane	"	Nov 5 1661
Benjamin Cadye & Mary Peyes[?]	"	Feb 16 1663
John Ruse & Deborah Osgood	"	Aug 28 1663
Stephen Osgood & Mary Hooker	"	Oct 24 1663
Thomas Abbot & Sarah Steward	"	Dec 15 1664
Joshua Woodman & Elizabeth Stevens	"	Jan 22 1665
Joseph Ballerd & Elizabeth Philps	"	Feb 28 1665
Nicholas Holt & Widow Prestone	"	May 21 1666

Moses Tyler & Prudence Blake	married	July 6 1666
Mark Graves & Elizabeth Farrington	"	Nov 14 1667
Jonathan Cady of Rowly & Hester Chandler	"	Nov 12 1667
John Farnum & Rebecca Kent	"	Nov 12 1667
Walter Wright & Susanna Johnson	"	Feb 26 1667
Hew Stone & Hanna Foster	"	Oct 15 1667
Henry Holt & Sarah Ballerd	"	Feb 24 1669
John Barker & Mary Stevens	"	July 6 1670
Joseph Wilson & Mary Louejoy	"	July 4 1670
Stephen Barnard & Rebecca How	"	May 1 1671
Joseph Marble & Mary Fawkner	"	May 30 1671
Joseph Robinson & Phebe Dane	"	May 30 1671
Moses Haggett & Joanna Johnson	"	Oct 23 1671
Samuel Fry & Mary Aslett	"	Nov 20 1671
Nathaniel Griffin & Elizabeth Ping	"	Aug 26 1671
Samuel Preston & Susannah Gutterson	"	May 27 1672
Alexander Sessions & Elizabeth Spaford	"	Apr 24 1672
Nathaniel Deane & Deliverance Heazletine	"	Dec 12 1672
Mr Nathaniel Wade & Mrs Merry Bradstreet	"	Oct 31 1672
Samuel Wardle & Sarah Hawkes	"	Jan 9 1672
John Abbot & Sarah Barker	"	Nov 17 1773
Mr Peturne(?) Johnson & Mary Johnson	"	Sep 7 1673
Mr Dudley Bradstreet & Mrs Ann Price	"	Nov 12 1673
Timothy Johnson & Rebecca Aslett	"	Dec 15 1674
Daniel Bigsbie & Hannah Chandler by Wm French	"	Dec 2 1674
Francis Fawkner & Abigail Dane	"	Oct 12 1675
James Holt & Hannah Allen	"	Oct 12 1675
John Stevens & Esther Barker	"	Aug 10 1676
John Chandler & Hannah Abbot	"	Dec 20 1676
William Barker & Mary *D*ix (or *M*ix)	"	Feb 20 1676
John Lovejoy & Hannah Prichard	"	$11^{\text{th}}_{\text{mo.}}$ 12 1676
Samuel Martin & Abigail Norton	"	Mch 30 1676
Mr Francis Deane & Mrs Mary Thomas by Mr Danforth	"	9ber 21 1677
Samuel Marble & Rebecca Andrew	"	Nov 26 1675
Lawrence Lay & Mary Foster	"	Aug 5 1673
George Abbot & Dorcas Graves	"	Apr 17 1678
William Johnson & Sarah Lovejoy	"	May 23 1678
Benjamin Fry & Mary Parker	"	May 23 1678
Joseph Wilson & Sarah Lord	"	Apr 24 1678
Zachariah Eires & Elizabeth Chase	"	June 27 1678
John Bridges & Mary Post (widdow)	"	Mch 1 1677–8
John Lovejoy & Naomi Hoit	"	Mch 23 1677–8
William Chandler & Bridgett Richardson	"	Oct 8 1679
Joseph Stevens & Mary Ingalls	"	May 28 1679
Nicholas Holt & Mary Russell by Jonathan Danforth	"	Jan 8 1679
James Fry & Lydia Osgood	"	Jan 20 1679
John Granger & Martha Poor by Capt Adams of Chelmsford	"	Feb 9 1679
John Aslett & Mary Osgood by Capt Saltonstall	"	July 8 1680
Joseph Parker & Elizabeth Bridges	"	Oct 7 1680
Eph. Stevens & Sarah Abbott	"	Oct 11 1680
William Lovejoy & Mary Farnum	"	Nov 29 1680
Stephen Parker & Mary Marstone	"	Dec 1 1680

Christopher Osgood & Hannah Barker	married	May 27 1680
Abraham Foster & Esther Foster	"	July 13 1681
John Osgood & Hannah Eires	"	Oct 17 1681
Francis Deane & Hannah Poor	"	Nov 16 1681
John Ballard & Rebecca Hooper	"	Nov 16 1681
Andrew Allen & Elizabeth Richardson	"	Jan 1 1681
Richard Barker & Hannah Kimball	"	Apr 21 1682
William Ballard & Hannah Hooper	"	Apr 20 1682
William Abbott & Elizabeth Geery	"	June 19 1682
Samuel Phelps & Sarah Chandler	"	May 29 1682
Samuel Ingalls & Sarah Hendrick	"	June 4 1682
John Faulkner & Sarah Abbott	"	Oct 19 1682
John Tyler & Hannah Parker	"	Sept 14 1682
Edward Phelps & Ruth Andrews	"	Mch 9 1682
Daniel Ennes & Lydia Wheeler by Mr Woodman	"	Apr 25 1683
William Chandler & Sarah Buckmaster	"	Dec 28 1682
John Farnum & Elizabeth Parker by Mr Saltonstall	"	Apr 10 1684
Walter Wright & Elizabeth Sadir	"	Sep 9 1684
Benjamin Abbot & Sarah Farnum	"	Apr 22 1685
Jonathan Blanchett (Blanchard?) & Anna Lovejoy	"	May 26 1685
Christopher Lovejoy & Sarah Russ	"	May 26 1685
Joseph Lovejoy & Sarah Prichard	"	May 26 1685
John Holt & Sarah Geery	"	July 3 1685
Ralph Farnum & Sarah Sterling	"	Oct 9 1685
Andrew Peters & Elizabeth	"	Feb 8 1685
Jacob Marstone & Elizabeth Poor	"	Apr 7 1686
John Allen & Marcy Peters	"	May 22 1686
Thomas Chandler & Mary Peters	"	May 22 1686
Ebenezer Barker & Abigall Wheeler	"	May 25 1686
Mr Thomas Barnard & Mrs Elizabeth Price	"	Dec 14 1686
William Chandler & Eleanor Phelps	"	Apr 21 1687
John Parker & Hannah Browne by Capt Browne of Redding	"	May 24 1687
Stephen Barker & Mary Abbott	"	May 13 1687
Samuel Hutchinson & Elizabeth Parker	"	Apr 26 1686
Abraham Moore & Priscilla Poor	"	Dec 14 1687
Eph. Davis & Mary Eires	"	Mch 19 1687–8
John Carleton & Hannah Osgood	"	Aug 27 1688
Benjamin Barker & Hannah Marstone	"	Jan 2 1688
John Gutterson & Abigail Buckmaster	"	Jan 14 1688
Timothy Osgood & Deborah Poor	"	May 29 1689
Pascoe Chubb & Hannah Faulkner	"	May 29 1689
John Marstone & Mary Osgood	"	May 28 1689
Henry Ingalls Sen[r] & Sarah Abbott	"	Aug 1 1689
George Abbott & Elizabeth Ballard	"	Sept 13 1689
John Johnson & Elenor Ballard	"	Sept 13 1689
Timothy Abbott & Hannah Graves	"	Dec 27 1689
John Stevens & Ruth Poor	"	Dec 20 1689
Edward Farington & Martha Browne	"	Apr 9 1690
Thomas Astin & Hannah Foster	"	Sept 15 1690
John Stone & Mary Russ	"	Nov 14 1690
Nehemiah Abbott & Abigail Lovejoy	"	Apr 9 1691
Joseph Chandler & Sarah Abbott	"	Nov 26 1691

Samuel Astin & Lucy Poor	married	Oct 11 1691
James Johnson & Elizabeth Peters	"	Apr 26 1692
Hooker Osgood & Dorothy Wood	"	Apr 13 1692
James Bridges & Sarah Marstone	"	May 24 1692
Joseph Ballard Sen & Rebeccah Horn (widdow)	"	Nov 15 1692
Nathan Stevens & Elizabeth Abbott	"	Oct 24 1692
Thomas Farnum & Hannah Hutchinson	"	May 14 1693
Francis Johnson & Sarah Hawkes	"	Feb 1 1693
Ebenezer Lovejoy & Mary Foster	"	July 11 1693
John Farnum & Mary Tyler	"	June 30 1693
Joseph Emerie & Elizabeth Merritt	"	Oct 2 1693
Peter Johnson & Mehitabell Farnum	"	Nov 29 1693
Samuel Holt & Hannah Farnum	"	Mch 28 1693
Nathaniel Lovejoy & Dorothy Hoyt	"	Mch 21 1693–4
Samuel Preston & Sarah Bridges	"	Apr 2 1694
Dane Robinson & Mary Chadwick	"	Jan 18 1693–4
Richard Carrier & Elizabeth Sessions	"	July 18 1694
Joseph Carleton & Abigail Osgood	"	Aug 2 1694
John Fry & Martha Farnum	"	Nov 1 1694
Stephen Parker & Susannah Devereux	"	Jan 10 1694–5
James Ingalls & Hannah Abbott	"	Apr 16 1695
Joseph Marble & Hannah Barnard	"	Apr 23 1695
John Russ & Hannah Ross	"	May 6 1695
Nathaniel Abbot & Dorcas Hibbert	"	Oct 22 1695
Henry Chandler & Lydia Abbott	"	Nov 28 1695
Mr Thomas Barnard & Mrs Abigail Bull	"	Apr 28 1696
John Ingalls & Sarah Russell	"	June 10 1696
Joseph Stevens & Mary Fry	"	Dec 22 1696
John Wright & Mercie Wardwell	"	Aug 31 1697
Robert Busswell & Hannah Tyler	"	Dec 9 1697
Thomas Abbott & Hannah Grey	"	Dec 7 1697
Samuel Farnum & Hannah Holt	"	Jan 4 1697–8
Samuel Peters & Phoebe Fry	"	Dec 15 1696
Oliver Holt & Hannah Russell	"	Mch 9 1697–8
Joseph Ballard & Rebecca Johnson	"	Aug 17 1698
Thomas Blanchard & Rose Holmes of Marshfield	"	Mch 22 1698–9
George Holt & Elizabeth Farnum	"	May 10 1698
Henry Gray & Mary Blunt	"	May 3 1699
Stephen Osgood & Hannah Blanchard	"	May 24 1699
Joseph Wilson & Mary Richardson		Jan 25 1699–70 [1700]
Ephraim Farnum & Priscilla Holt		Mch 20 1699–70 [1700]
Joseph Osgood & Mary Marble		May 8 1700
Moses Haggett & Martha Granger		Feb 21 1699–70 [1700]

When we say that Otis, Adams, Mayhew, Henry, Lee, Jefferson, &c., were authors of independence, we ought to say they were only awakeners and revivers of the original fundamental principle of colonization.

John Adams.

ANCIENT DEEDS IN WOODBURY, CONN.

COPIED FROM THE TOWN RECORDS, BOOK I.

BY WILLIAM COTHREN.*

Whereas I, John Davis am proposed to go in ye service for ye Country against ye Common enemy, I do in short and in great brevity, and earnestly make over and confirm all my interest in my whole accommodations in Woodbury to my two sons, John and Samuel, equally to be divided between them, when they attain their respective ages, with this only proviso, that they do each of them pay to their sister, my daughter Mary Davis ye third part of their then valued accommodations, which shall be valued at ye time aforesaid; and that this my Act and deed is to stand of full force and validity as any will or testament whatsoever at my decease is confirmed and signified by my subscribing hereto ye 29 of April 1690.

Witnessed by us
John Minor
Joseph Minor

JOHN DAVIS.

Woodbury T. R., Book I., page 48.

INDIAN DEED.

A Record of a parcell of Land to Lewis Wheeler by Tautannimo a Sachem at Pagasett is as followeth.

This present writing witnesseth that I Tautannimo a Sachem at Pagasett, Considerations moveing me thereunto, do fully and freely make over, alienate and give from myself and heirs, and all other Indians and their heirs, a parcell of Land bounded as followeth: Potateuk River Southwest, Naugatunck River Northeast, and bounded on ye Northwest with trees marked by me and other Indians, ye said Land I do with ye consent of all Pagasett Indians, freely give it to Leu. Thos. Wheeler and his heirs forever. And I do fully give s^d^ Leu. Thomas Wheeler full power to have it recorded to him and his heirs according to ye Laws and Customs of ye English, in witness hereunto I interchangeably set to my hand this 20 of April 1659 ye names of ye Indians that subscribed.

Subscribed in presence of
John Wells
Richard Harvey
Thomas Uffoot
John Curtiss
John Minor

Tautannimo
Paquaha
Pagasett James
Monsuck
Sasaazo

This is a true copy of ye deed
by me Joseph Hawley.
Woodbury T. R., B. I., p. 67.

INDIAN DEED.

Know all men by these presents that I, Ockenonge, ye only Sachem of Pagasett, do freely give and bequeath unto my loveing friends, Ensign Joseph Judson, Mr. Joseph Hawley and John Minor of Stratford in ye Colony of Connecticut, a parcell of Land, be it more or less, lying on ye West side

* Mr. COTHREN informs us that he is preparing for publication a history of Woodbury. He has furnished us with a list of marriages and deaths in that town, which we shall lay before our readers at some future time.

of ye Land, which ye aforesaid Town of Stratford hath purchased of me, and it being all that lyeth on ye West of what is already purchased, that belongs to me and Pagasett Indians, that I give ye above said tract of land to ye aforenamed, to have and to hold without molestation or trouble by any Indian or Indians whatsoever, I say to them and their heirs forever, as witness my hand this 22nd of April 1665.

Witnessed by us
Henry Tomlynson
Jabez Hardger — Witnessed by us

Ockenonge Ξ his mark
Nansantaways T mark
Chipps C his mark
Pr John Minor, Recorder.

Woodbury T. R., B. I., p. 81.

Indian Deed.

Be it known unto all men by this present, that we, Wompeag and Sequackana and Sewatams do sell to Moses Wheeler, Ferryman, a parcell of ground lying alongst Potateuk River, ye East end being on a small brook, which they say is Nagumpe, ye West end bounding to a great Rock, which reaches ye full length of all that plain piece of ground, and also to have two Mile and a half of ground on ye upland, and all ye meadow within ye bounds, we whose names are above written do sell to ye said Moses, and do bind ourselves, that he shall peaceably enjoy it, he or his assigns, in witness whereof we set to our hand and seal.

Sealed and delivered
in presence of
Wombe ϒ Witness
Samuel Wheeler
Moses Johnson

Wompeag Ω mark
Sequackana Σ mark
Sewatams χ mark
Apl 12th 1659.

In consideration of this we are to have five Pounds and one Girdle of which we have received three Pounds sixteen shillings, Received by me with ye Consent of ye others this full sum of Five Pounds and one Girdle in full satisfaction for this Land.

W Wompeag, mark

This is a true Copy this 24 January 1666.
Woodbury T. R., B. I., p. 82–3.

THE VICAR OF BRAY.

The origin of the proverb "*The Vicar of Bray will be Vicar of Bray still,*" is found thus expounded in Fuller's Worthies of England:

"Bray is a village well known in Barkshire; the vivacious Vicar whereof, living under King Henry the Eigth, King Edward the Sixth, Queen Mary and Queen Elizabeth, was first a papist, then a protestant; then a papist, then a protestant again. This Vicar being taxed by one for being a turn-coat, Not so, (said he,) for I always kept my principle; which is this, to live and die Vicar of Bray. To this Fuller adds, 'such are men now-a-days, who, though they cannot turn the wind, they turn their mills, and set them so, that wheresoever it bloweth, their grist should certainly be ground.'"

Ray.

EARLY RECORDS OF WEYMOUTH.

[Copied by Mr. Cyrus Orcutt, for the N. E. Genealogical and Antiquarian Register.]

These records are said to have been copied from an old quarto book which is now lost.

Edward son of John & Susan Bate	born	Dec 10 1655
Phebe daughter of John and Jane Lovell	"	Feb 19 1655
Jonas son of Jonas & Martha Humphry	"	Feb 24 1655
Elizabeth Daughter of John & Alice Shaw	"	Feb 26 1655
James & Alice Luddens child	"	Jan 12 1656
Ebenezer son of	"	May 30 1656
Ephraim son of John & Mary Osborn	"	Aug 11 1657
Samuel son of Samuel & Mary Pittee	"	Aug 12 1657
Thomas of William & Elizabeth Chard	"	Sept 27 1657
Naomi Bicknell	"	June 21 1657
Abraham son of John & Alice Shaw	"	Oct 10 1657
& Mary Phillips	"	Dec 6 1657
Lidda of James & Elizabeth Preist	"	Feb 12 1657
William son of William & Elizabeth Holbrook	"	Jan 20 1657
Enoch son of Ephraim & Ebbot Hunt	"	Mar 29 1658
Nathaniel son of Andrew & Eleanor Ford	"	Mar 31 1658
Joseph son of Joseph & Elizabeth Green	"	April 2 1658
John son of John & Jane Lovell	"	May 8 1658
Lois & Eunice Daughters of John Holbrook	"	May 12 1658
Ebenezer son of John & Sarah Whitmarsh	"	May 14 1658
John son of Jonas and Martha Humphrey	"	Aug 31 1658
John son of Thomas & Abigail Whitman	"	Sept 5 1658
Samuel son of Samuel & Mary Bagley	"	Sept 7 1658
Thomas son of John & Rebecca Burrell	"	Feb 2 1659
William son of Thomas Pratt	"	March 6 1659
John son of Thomas & Jane Drake	"	March 12 1659
John son of John & Esther King	"	April 12 1659
Susanna of Samuel & Experience King	"	May 6 1659
John son of William & Mary Pittey Drowned		May 28 1659
Samuel son of Josiah & Mary Chapin	"	Nov 11 1659
Nicholas son of Walter Cook	"	Feb 9 1659
Mary daughter of John & Ann Reynolds	"	Mar 15 1660
Mary Daughter of John & Alice Shaw	"	March 24 1660
John son of Nathaniel & Susan Blancher	"	Mar 27 1660
Ebenezer son of Andrew & Eleanor Ford	"	Mar 18 1660
Mary Daughter of John & Phebe Taylor	"	May 18 1660
Benjamin son of William & Grace Richards	"	May 19 1660
Mary of Richard & Mary Phillips	"	May 21 1660
Benjamin son of Richard Newbury	"	May 22 1660
Caleb son of William Chard	"	Oct 19 1660
Ruth Daughter of John & Mary Bicknell	"	Oct 26 1660
Elizabeth of John & Jane Lovell	"	Oct 28 1660
Simon son of John & Sarah Whitmarsh	"	Mar 11 1661
Hannah of Nicholas & Hannah Whitmarsh	"	Mar 25 1661
Mary of Samuel & Mary Bayley	"	April 30 1661
William son of William & Mary Pittey	"	May 12 1661
Sarah of Jonas & Martha Humphrey	"	May 16 1661

Experience of John & Elizabeth Holbrook	born	May 23 1661
Mary of Richard & Mary Phillips	"	May 24 1661
William son of Thomas & Jane Drake	"	May 30 1661
Judah son of Samuel & Hannah Pratt	"	June 25 1661
John son of Joseph & Elizabeth Green	"	July 16 1661
Silence of Andrew Ford	"	Nov 13 1661
John son of John & Esther King	"	Dec 25 1661
Christian of Thomas & Ruth Bayley	"	Feb 26 1661
Joshua son of Richard & Mary Phillips	"	May 10 1662
Lidda Daughter of James Preist	"	Mar 16 1662
Mary of James & Mary Smith	"	Mar 22 1662
John son of John & Mary Vining	"	April 15 1662
Mary of Stephen & Hannah French	"	May 11 1662
Ichabod son of John & Elizabeth Holbrook	"	May 30 1662
Nicholas son of John & Alice Shaw	"	May 23 1662
Sarah of John & Sarah Comar	"	July 10 1662
Elizabeth of Samuel & Experience King	"	Sept 23 1662
James son of John & Jane Lovell	"	Oct 23 1662
Corneilus son of William Holbrook	"	Nov 19 1662
Hannah of Thomas & Experience Bolter	"	Nov 30 1662
Mary of Nathaniel & Susanna Blancher	"	Dec 1 1662
Joseph son of Joseph & Lidda White	"	Dec 16 1662
Joanna Bicknell	"	March 2 1663
Mary Daughter of William & Elizabeth Chard	"	April 8 1663
of John & Sarah Whitmarsh	"	Aug 14 1663
of Samuel & Hannah Pratt	"	Aug 17 1663
Mary of John & Deliverance Porter	"	Oct 12 1663
Joseph son of Thomas & Jane Drake	"	Octo 28 1663
Prudence of Andrew & Ellen Ford	"	Dec 22 1663
Ruth of John & Abigail Whitman	"	Feb 1 1663
James son of Samuel & Mary Bayley	"	Feb 21 1663
John of John & Elizabeth Holice	"	Mar 28 1664
Nicholas son of Richard & Mary Phillips	"	Mar 30 1664
Mary of John & Mary Rodgers	"	April 3 1664
Joanna of James & Mary Smith	"	April 4 1664
Elizabeth of Joseph & Elizabeth Green	"	April 5 1664
Jane of Nicholas & Hannah Whitmarsh	"	April 8 1664
Joseph son of John & Alice Shaw	"	April 15 1664
John son of John & Elizabeth Kingman	"	April 30 1664
Sarah of Joseph & Sarah Pratt	"	May 31 1664
Stephen son of Stephen & Hannah French	"	June 11 1664
Mary of John & Mary Vining	"	June 18 1664
Rebecka of Thomas Kingman	"	July 2 1664
Ephraim son of John & Rebecca Burrell	"	July 19 1664
Esther of John & Esther King	"	Sept 28 1664
Experience of Samuel & Experience King	"	Oct 6 1664
Deborah of James & Jane Lovell	"	Jan 8 1664
Joseph son of Richard & Rebecca Gurney	"	Feb 23 1664
William son of John & Jane Lovell	"	Feb 24 1664
Susanna of John & Deliverance Porter	"	June 2 1665
James son of Jonas & Martha Humphrey	"	Sept 16 1665
Matthew son of Matthew Pratt	"	Sept 18 1665
Nathaniel son of Nath & Susanna Blancher	"	Sept 25 1665

[To be continued.]

SOME ACCOUNT OF DEACON JOHN BUTLER OF PELHAM, N. H., AND OF HIS DESCENDANTS.

BY CALEB BUTLER OF GROTON.

[Continued from p. 36, Vol. II.]

(I. 3. II. 3.)

III. CALEB BUTLER m. REBEKAH FROST.

1 *Benjamin, b. Oct. 5, 1767, m. Lydia Page.
2 *Miriam, b. Feb. 27, 1769, m. John Cutter.
3 *Samuel, b. Aug. 28, 1770, m. { Clarissa Buck, Hannah Lund.
4 *Deborah, b. Aug. 10, 1774, d. unm.
5 Caleb, b. Sept. 13, 1776, m. Clarissa Varnum.
6 *Rebekah, b. Mar. 28, 1780, d. young.
7 *Theodore, b. Dec. 6, 1781, d. unm.
8 *Rebekah, b. July 12, 1784, d. unm.
9 Joanna, b. Feb. 5, 1787.
10 *Solomon, b. Jan. 4, 1789, d. unm.
11 Phinehas, b. Mar. 29, 1791, m. { Sarah Barker, Betsey Wyman.

(I. 3. II. 6.)

III. BULAH BUTLER m. DR. JOHN MUZZEY. { Pelham, N. H. Amherst, " Peterboro', "

1 *Jonathan, b. May 23, 1771, d. young.
2 Sally, b. June 18, 1773, m. Nathan Fisher of Francistown, N. H.
3 *Polly, b. Dec. 4, 1775, m. Solomon Prince of Amherst, N. H.
4 *John, b. March 12, 1778, m. Sally Robb.
5 Reuben Dimond, b. June 23, 1780, m. { Mary Sewall, Mehitabel Osgood.
6 Lydia, b. Aug. 9, 1782, m. John Felton of Amherst, N. H.
7 *Jonathan, b. June 4, 1785, d. young.
8 Bulah, b. Dec. 26, 1789, m. —— Warren.

(I. 5. II. 1.)

III. ABIGAIL BUTLER m. JOSEPH WILSON of Dracut.

1 Joseph, b. April 19, 1762, m. Phebe Wyman.
2 *Benjamin, b. Oct. 30, 1763, d. young.
3 Thaddeus, b. Feb. 18, 1765, m. { Dolly Flint, —— Shattuck, wid.
4 Nabby, b. Dec. 19, 1766, m. James Butterfield.
5 Lydia, b. May 2, 1768, m. William Webster.
6 Life, b. July 20, 1769, m. Sally Jameson, wid.
7 David, b. March 30, 1771, m. Sibyl Abbott.
8 Polly, b. March 7, 1773, m. Benjamin Hamblet.
9 Hulda, b. Oct. 3, 1775, m. Josiah Coburn.
10 Benjamin, b. May 30, 1780, m. —— Alds.
11 Cyrus, b. March 3, 1784, m. —— Bowers.

(I. 5. II. 2.)

III. NEHEMIAH BUTLER m. LYDIA WOOD.

1 *Joseph, b. Aug. 20, 1774, d. young.
2 Lydia, b. Aug. 31, 1775, m. Elijah Trull of Billerica and Townsend.
3 Nehemiah, b. Nov. 25, 1776, m. Olive Davis.
4 Phebe, b. Aug. 23, 1778, m. Eliphalet Parker of Bucksport, Me.
5 Josiah, b. Dec. 4, 1779, m. Hannah Jenness.
6 Delilah, b. April 28, 1781, m. Dole Butler.

(I. 5. II. 3.)

III. GIDEON BUTLER m. MARY ROGERS. Lived in Nottingham West.

1 *Lois, b. June 17, 1776, d. young.
2 Joseph, b. Jan. 18, 1779, m. Hannah Butler.
3 Catharine, b. April 15, 1781, m. Reuben Coburn.
4 Lois, b. Feb. 4, 1784, m. Hugh Smith.

(I. 5. II. 4.)

III. MOLLY BUTLER m. TIMOTHY LADD of Dunbarton.

1 Polly, b. m. —— Jones.
2 Heman, b. m. —— Messer.
3 Hannah, b. m. —— Colby.

(I. 5. II. 5.)

III. JESSE BUTLER m. { MOLLY GREELY, MEHITABEL DUTY.

1 Polly, } by Molly. { m. Jacob Stiles.
2 Abihail, }
3 Moody, m. { Sally Dustin, Lydia Burtt.
4 Mehitabel.
5 Hannah, m. Joseph Butler.
6 Richard.
7 Jesse.
8 James.
9 Betsey, m. Marstin.
10 Roxa, m. Orra May.
11 William.

(I. 5. II. 9.)

III. ELIJAH BUTLER m. —— FIFIELD. Lived at Weare, N. H. Had six or seven sons.

(I. 8. II. 1.)

III. JACOB BUTLER m. SALLY MORGAN.

1 Sarah, b. Oct. 23, 1774, m. { Nathaniel Gage, Asa Careton.
2 Polly, b. May 22, 1776, m. Theodore Wyman.
3 Betsey, b. March 21, 1778, m. Solomon Barker.
4 Hannah, b. March 19, 1781, m. Caleb Johnson.
5 Jacob, b. Sept. 30, 1782, m. Nabby Butler.
6 *Joseph, b. April 29, 1784, d. unm.
7 *Samuel, b. June 14, 1785, d. unm.
8 *Isaac, b. Oct. 5, 1789, d. unm.
9 William, } b. May 4, 1792, { m. Sarah Grosvenor.
10 Clarissa, } { d. unm.

(I. 8. II. 2.)

III. DANIEL BUTLER m. MOLLY TENNEY.

1 Dole, b. Oct. 23, 1777, m. Delilah Butler.
2 Polly, b. May 2, 1779, m. Daniel Varnum.
3 *Phebe, b. March 31, 1780, d. young.
4 Nabby, b. March 20, 1782, m. Jacob Butler.
5 Daniel, b. Oct. 18, 1784.
6 Phebe, b. Jan. 22, 1786, m. Amos Hazleton.
7 Manly, b. July 21, 1788, m. Sarah Hamblet.
8 *Betty, b. Oct. 11, 1790, d. young.
9 *Betty, b. May 21, 1793, d. young.
10 Olivia, b. Jan. 4, 1796, m. Noyes Tenney.
11 Belinda, b. March 17, 1798, m. Samuel P. Hadley.
12 *Thomas J., } b. July 15, 1802, d. young.
13 *Joseph B. V., }

(I. 8. II. 3.)

III. MARY BUTLER m. HON. JOSEPH B. VARNUM of Dracut.

1 Mehitabel, b. Nov. 2, 1773, m. Daniel Swett of Haverhill.
2 Polly, b. Feb. 24, 1775, m. Gen. Simon Coburn of Dracut.
3 *George W., b. Feb. 21, 1779, d. unm.
4 *Nabby, b. Jan. 7, 1781, m. *Josiah Brown, Esq., of Tewksbury.
5 *Hannah, b. Feb. 18, 1783, m. Major Ephraim Coburn of Dracut.
6 Joseph B., b. Jan. 3, 1785, m. Loiza Graham of New York.
7 *James M., b. Aug. 2, 1786, m. Mary Pease of Washington, D. C.

8 Jacob B., b. June 13, 1788.
9 Phebe, b. July 14, 1790, m. *Josiah Brown, Esq., of Tewksbury.
10 *John H., b. June 21, 1792, d. young.
11 *Benjamin F., b. April 11, 1795, m. Caroline Bradley of Dracut.

(I. 8. II. 5, and I. 2. II. 1. III. 1.)

III. PHEBE BUTLER m. BENJAMIN BARKER.

1 *Mary, b. Oct. 28, 1780, d. young.
2 *Phebe, b. May 18, 1784, m. Daniel Ordway.
3 *Benjamin, b. April 13, 1786, d. unm.
4 *Theodore, b. Sept. 14, 1787, d. unm.
5 *Polly, b. May 15, 1789, m. Daniel Ames.
6 *Sarah, b. April 1, 1791, m. Phinehas Butler.
7 *Betsey, b. March 3, 1794, d. unm.
8 *Abigail, b. Jan. 15, 1797, d. unm.
9 *Mehitabel, b. June 22, 1799, d. unm.
10 *Ascenath, b. Feb. 10, 1802, d. unm.

(I. 8. II. 6.)

III. JONATHAN BUTLER m. REBEKAH HARDY.

1 Mehitabel, b. Jan. 20, 1786, m. *David Gage.
2 *Eliphalet, b. April 10, 1788, d. unm.
3 *James, b. July 19, 1790, d. young.

Three of the above named descents of the fourth degree received a collegiate education, viz:—

CALEB, son of Caleb, received his first degree at Dartmouth College, 1800, was preceptor of Moore's Charity School, appurtenant to the college, one year, and twelve years principal of Groton Academy. He afterwards read law and practised as attorney and counsellor a few years, and was chairman of the commissioners of highways, and of the county commissioners for the county of Middlesex, fifteen years in succession.

REUBEN D. MUZZEY, son of Bulah and John Muzzey, received his first degree at Dartmouth College, 1803, studied physic and surgery, and became eminent in the practice of his profession. He sustained a professorship in various branches of the medical science, for many years, in the college of which he was an alumnus, and since in a literary institution in Ohio.

JOSIAH, son of Nehemiah, was graduated at Harvard University, 1803, read law, practised in the courts, and was afterwards sheriff of the county of Rockingham, N. H., a judge of the Court of Common Pleas, and a representative in Congress from 1817 to 1823.

ISAAC, son of Jacob, entered Dartmouth College, but died before the expiration of the regular term of study.

The descendants of the fifth and sixth generations have become so numerous and so widely dispersed, that the following registers will be much less complete than the foregoing.

(I. 2. II. 2. III. 1.)

IV. ASA BUTLER m. REBECCA GOULD.

1 Asa, b. Dec. 9, 1810, m. Phebe Roby.
2 Rebecca, b. May 9, 1812, m. Roswell Hobbs.
3 John, b. March 20, 1814.
4 Lavina, b. July 12, 1816, m. David Roby.
5 *Mary Ann, b. Sept. 2, 1821, d. unm.
6 *Eliphalet, b. Oct. 26, 1824, d. unm.
7 *Albert, b. Nov. 12, 1826, d. unm.

(I. 2. II. 2. III. 6.)

IV. JOEL BUTLER m. DEBORAH GAGE.

1 James M., b. Feb. 5, 1824.
2 Henry, b. Oct. 10, 1826, m. —— Temple.

(I. 2. II. 2. III. 7.)

IV. *RICHARD BUTLER m. SARAH J. JONES.

1 *Mary E., b. Sept. 11, 1820, d. unm.
2 Charles, b. June 30, 1822.
3 Sarah J., b. Mar. 7, 1825.
4 Mary G., b. June 17, 1827.
5 Joel, b. May 27, 1829.
6 Silvester, b. Oct. 29, 1831.
7 Eliphalet, b. June 21, 1834.
8 *Abigail, b. May 11, 1837, d. y.
9 *Pamelia, b. Nov. 6, 1839, d. y.
10 Amanda, b. Feb. 20, 1842.

(I. 2. II. 2. III. 8.)

IV. JOSHUA BUTLER m. PERSIS GAGE.

1 Jane H., b. April 17, 1826.
2 Ann G., b. Mar. 19, 1829.
3 Mary, b. Dec. 31, 1830.
4 Davis, b. Oct. 9, 1832.

(I. 2. II. 2. III. 9.

IV. JAMES BUTLER m. MARY E——.

1 James H., b. May 18, 1820.

(I. 2. II. 4. III. 2.)

IV. DAVID BUTLER m. POLLY CHICKERING.

1 Oliver Deane, b. July 14, 1800.
2 *Maria, b. Nov. 13, 1802, d. y.
Abigail
Mary or Sarah.
Rebecca.
Fanny.
David.

The above family reside in the state of Maine.

(I. 2. II. 4. III. 3.)

IV. *ISAAC BUTLER m. NANCY CHAPLIN.

1 Nancy, b. May 20, 1805, m. Jonathan Gould.
2 Diana L., b. Aug. 11, 1806, m. Joseph Gould.
3 David, b. Dec. 16, 1809, m. Mary Ann Russell.
4 *George P., b. July 4, 1821, d. young.

(I. 2. II. 4. III. 5)

IV. ENOCH BUTLER m. SUSANNA MARSH.

1 Warren A., b. m. Eliza.
2 *Susan, b. d. young.
3 Rebecca, b. m. Eli Hamblet.
4 Diana G., b. Oct. 16, 1836.

(I. 2. II. 4. III. 6.)

IV. NATHAN BUTLER m. SALLY ROBY. Reside at Bedford, N. H.

1 Eliza C., b. April 1, 1811.
2 Hannah, b. Nov. 17, 1812, m. William Cady.
3 Sarah J., b. March 18, 1816, m. Truman Parker.
4 Maria, b. June 27, 1818.
5 Emeline, b. Sept. 23, 1820.
6 Rebecca A., b. Oct.
7 Nathan, b. Jan. 1, 1827.
8 Cordelia, b. July 25, 1833.

(I. 2. II. 7. III. 8.)

IV. DARIUS BUTLER m. LAURA S. WHITTIER.

1 Sarah E., b. June 7, 1838.
2 Juliette, b. June 20, 1840.
3 Roxana, b. Mar. 28, 1842.
4 Ellen J., b. Oct. 31, 1844.

(I. 3. II. 3. III. 1.)

IV. *BENJAMIN BUTLER m. *LYDIA PAGE of Weare, N. H.

1 *Polly, b. June 5, 1795, d. unm. } at Weare.
2 *Rebekah, b. April 5, 1797, d. unm. } at Weare.
3 Benjamin P., b. March 4, 1800, m. Cyrene Brett. } At Minot, Me.
4 Betsey P., b. Aug. 29, 1802, m. Nathaniel True. } At Minot, Me.
5 Caleb P., b. May 23, 1805, m. Sarah Lord. } At Minot, Me.
6 *Lucretia, b. Jan. 30, 1808, d. unm. } At Minot, Me.
7 *Sarah O., b. Dec. 17, 1810, d. unm. } At Minot, Me.

[To be continued.]

ABSTRACTS OF THE EARLIEST WILLS UPON RECORD IN THE COUNTY OF SUFFOLK, MS.

[Continued from p. 386, of Vol. II.]

[Continued from p. 386, of Vol. II.]

EDWARD HOW.

*1644, June 3. I doe make this my last will I do thus dispose of my estate. First I giue to *Nathaniell Treadaway*† about three acres of Upland lying behinde his dwelling howse & one acre vnbroken before ye said howse with nine acres purchased lately of *John Vahan* further I giue to my wife, *Nathaniel Treadaway*, & *Anne Stonne* ye wife of *John Stonne* of Sudbury ye wares wth all y^r previldges therto belonginge & all y^t is due to me from *Mr. Thom: Mayhew*: to either of them one third part. I give to *Mary Knowlse* & *Elisabeth Knowlse* each of them one sheep: And all ye rest of my estate, howsinge Lands Chattles & Moveable goods & Debts I give to my wife. If she shall not make vse of or dispose of my estate during her life what she Leave *Anne Stonne* shall haue one third part of all ye Cattle: & all ye rest of ye Cattle howsinge Lands Debts & movables I giue to *Nathaniell Treadaway*: my wife *Nathaniell Treadaway* & *John Stonne* Excecutors of this my last will: & I doe Appoint *John Sherman* Suprovisour of this my last will. & I giue vnto him fiftye shillings to be paid by my wife in half a year after my Decease.

By me EDWARD HOW.

witnes *John Sherman* who was sworne y^e: 25 of ye 5th 44 in Court

Steph. Winthrop Recor^r.

ELISABETH HOBERT.‡

Boston in New England the 29° of the 10th month 1643. [In margin] 4°. (7°)1644. [Date of proof.]

The said *Elisabeth Hobert* being not well & yet being in perfect sence & vnderstanding do make this as my last will & testament, that my daughter *Hannah Hobert* & my sonne *Benjamin Hobert*, I do make them my whole executors joyntly together of all those goods wch are mine, with this provisor, my executors to pay three score & ten pounds & ten shillings to *Hannah Carrington* as soone as the goods can be sould. Also to pay to the said *Stoctdell Carrington* foure pounds & some odde money: also to my sonne *Richard Hobert* twelve pence. Also to dau. *Hanner Hobert* & to sonne *Benjamin Hobert*, & to dau. *Sarah Hobert*, & to dau. *Rachhell Hobert* equall portions of what is left when all cost & chardges is paid. Youngest dau. *Rachell* to haue three pounds more than the rest of my three children, that is to say Hannah, & Benjamin & Sarah. The executors to haue a tender care of their youngest sister *Rachel.*

* This as well as the following wills in this article is slightly abridged; but the phraseology is always preserved.

† Spelt *Treadway* in FARMER. In the REV. MR. BARRY'S *Hist. of Framingham*, are many facts concerning descendants of the name.

‡ She died 6 Jan., 1643–4, at Boston.—*Shurtleff.*

Robert Hull & *Thomas Clarke* desired to be overseers of will, to see it fulfilled as neere as they can. ELISABETH HOBBERT.

Witnes Robert Hull
Thomas Clarke.

proved 4°. 7°. m°. 1644.
before me Samuell
Symonds & me
Increase Nowell.

GEORG PHILLIPPS.

D. I. (M. 5)* 1644.

Wee do hereby testify this to be the last will of *Georg Phillipps* Pastor of Watertowne. [Date of proof pr. margin] 6° (7°) 1644.

1. I giue to my wife the Thirds of all mine estate.
2. The remainder to be divided amongst my Children. *Samuel* the Eldest to haue a double portion, & the rest to haue equally alike.

Witnes *Symon Eire*
Apphia ffreeman
The mark of *Elisabeth Child*

Presently after his wife putting him in mind of the bond in *Elder Howes* hand, he called *Samuel* to him and tould him he had given him a double portion, and bade him let the bond alone & give it in to yor mother when yow come to age, but if yow take that yow shall haue no more.

Witness *Symon Eyre*
Apphia ffreeman..

This was taken vppon the oathe of the said *Symon Eyre* & *Apphya ffreeman* before m^r. *John Winthrop* D Govr. & Mr. *William Hibbins*.

THOMAS PIG.

14° (7°) 1644 [in margin.]

Be it knowne to all men that this is the will of *Thomas Pig*,† that he doth give to his sonne *Thomas* the house wth the home lott, 2 acres of fresh marsh, also my lott by the dead swamp, & all the land in the neck both upland & Marsh, & the 5 acres at the great lots end. He to pay his brother *John* ten pounds, 5 at 21 years of age, & and the other 5 a year after. To sonne *Thomas Pig* also the land in the Calues Pasture, paying his sister *Hany*‡ *Pigg* 5 pounds, 3 pounds a yeare after his mothers death and the other three pound the year after that, and for defect not paying this sixe pounds at these tymes appointed, the land to returne to her. To dau. *Saray*, dau. *Mathew* my Eight Acre Lott lyeing vppon *Pigs hill*, & I give To them also my last Division of ground. To dau.

* 1° of the 5th month (i. e. 5 July, 1644.) is probably the date intended.

† The name of *Thomas Pigge* is found in our list of Roxbury people printed in Vol. II. p. 53. It undoubtedly represents the same person. Pigs hill, mentioned in this will, we are told is still known by that name; but that no person of the name of *Pigge* has resided there for a long time.

‡ Mr. Ellis, in his *Hist. of Roxbury*, enumerates a *Henry* among the children of Thomas Pigge, but *this* name we are inclined to think stands for *Hannah;* yet when we come to a "daughter Mathew," we confess we are somewhat puzzled. The reader may be sure, *we have not mistaken the manuscript.*

Mary my allotment in the thousand Acres lyeing at Dedham. Wife to haue all I haue so long as she liues to bring vp my children. After her death my children to have their portions as aforesaid.

Giles Payson *Robert Williams*

Testifyed before mr *Winthrop* Dep: Gov: & *Mr. Nowell* the (7°) 12–1644.

John Lovran.

A true Copie of the testimony of *Elisabeth Child*, *Elisabeth Pierce* & *Margaret Howe* examined vppon oath before vs, *Richard Browne* & *Wm. Jennings* appointed 9° (9°)

Elizabeth Child being wth *John Lovran** of watertowne some three dayes before he dyed, did move him to make his will, to wh he answered, That he had but little, & that his wife was sickley, & so he would leave that he had to her.

Elisabeth Pierce at the same tyme being present, heard him speake to this purpose, Alas, that I have is but little, & that he had a sickly wife, & what he had was little inough for her.

Margaret How in the presence of her Husband *Mr. How* & of the wife of *John Lovran* deceased, not long before the death of the said *John*.

Only a trifle or twoe; He would give his brother that had children one hundred pounds, & twenty pounds vnto the Church after her life.

Richard Browne
William Jennison.†

Thomas Finson.

23. (2) 1645.

Whereas *Thomas ffinson* mariner late of Dartmouth Dyed abord the Shipp Gilbert in September last, *Oades*‡ *Bayle* being present, the said *Thomas ffinson* by word of mouth declared this to be his last will & testament. To son *Samuel* fyve pounds of English money; to his child that his wife went withall fifty shillings; to wife one Hogshead of Tobacco; to his father in lawe *Andrew Harwood* all his wages. The fifty shillings for the Child & the Tobacco to be delivered to *Andrew Harwood* for the vse aforesaid.

Deposed the
first of the (9°) month
1644 by *Oads Bayle*
before the Court.

Gabriell Wheatley.

27 (8) 1645.

Thomas Rogers of Watertowne sworne before *John Winthrop* Governor 13 (5) 1637, saith that *Gabriell Wheatley* being of pfect vnderstanding

* Probably since *Lovering*. On this name Farmer has but a line and one third in his *Register*, which is this: "John, freeman 1636, might be the same who lived at Dover in 1665."

The "freeman" of 1636 of Farmer was probably our *John Lovran*; but that he was the same at Dover in 1665, is improbable. There are many of the name in New Hampshire at this day, and elsewhere in New England.

† Seems at first to have been written *Jennings*, like that at the commencement of the document, but subsequently altered to *Jennison*.

‡ Possibly *Oates* is meant, and perhaps *Otis Bayley*.

even to the time of his death, said in the presence of *Bryan Pendleton* and this deponent that he would haue the said *Bryan* to take charge of his estate & out of it to pay himselfe what was due to him; the rest to go to his daughter — to be gathered vp & reserued by the said *Bryan*. Vppon this the said *Bryan* was granted to administer, & to be accountable when required. The summe that was due to her amounted to £16 16s.

Witnes { *Richard Browne*
{ *Edward Howe.*

THOMAS KNOCKER.*

An Inventory of the Goods of *Tho: Knocker* prised of *Will Stitson Will Brackenburye Augustion Walker* & *Jo: Allen* ye 19 Nov. 1641.

[His whole effects amounted to some £30. The following names we find among the list of his debtors & creditors:]

Persons owing: *Rich^d. Graues* of Salem, 6s. *John Penticost*, 6^d. *Tho: Poyston*† of Watertown, 12s. *Nic Jewett*, 12^s. Mr. *Robert Woarye*, 4s. 6^d. *Jo Burridge*, £1. 3s. *Gd* [goodman] *Paddock*, 3 pecks of Corne. *Edward Fuller*, 4s. 6^d.

Thomas Knocker was debtor to *James Browne*, £1. 9s. *Austin Walker*, 5s. *Abram Palmer*, 4s. His bro: *Geog Knocker*, 4s. *Wid^o Wilkinson*, *Jo Lawrence*, £3. 2s. *Ryse Cole*, 9^d. *Robt. Heath*, 1 bu. Corne. *Tho Moulton*, 14s. *Edwd. Convers*, 6s. *Jer Swayne*, 2s. *Gd Hawkins*, £8. 12s. 6^d. *Good Brackenburye*,‡ *Gon Drinker*, 3s. 1d. *Will Smith*, 6^d.

ABIGAIL SUMER.§

31 (8) 1643.

The goods of Abigail the late wife of Tho: Sum̄er deceased praised by the psons subscribed.

Amount £7. 9s. 8^d.
Oweth 1. 18. 0.

witnes
Joseph Jewet
William Boynton.

* The will of this individual does not appear to have been recorded. The abstract of the inventory which we here give is taken from the 2d volume of our Registry, entitled "Inventories," and is called No. 2 FARMER seems not to have met with the name of *Knocker*, at least not in this form. It is possible that it may have been curtailed into that of *Nock*.

† I can make nothing else of this name, and it is a perfect stranger in my catalogue of New England names. Probably *Boylston*.

‡ The family of *Brackenbury* was anciently of much note in England. As late as the 32d of ELIZABETH, "*Richard Brakinbury* was an old courtier." In 1575, in a visitation, he is mentioned as Gentleman Usher to Queen Elizabeth. and was the fifth son of *Anthony Brakenbury* of Denton, by Agnes, dau. of Ralph Wycliffe of Wycliffe in Yorkshire.—*Lodge's Illustrations*, ii. 421. *Dale's Hist. Harwich*, 177.

§ Perhaps *Sumner*. We do not find either *Summer* or *Sumner* at Watertown in 1636, though we infer that this person died resident there. There is no will on record. FARMER found a *Thomas Sumner* at Rowley, 1643. In the index of our volume of Inventories (a modern work,) we find "Abigail Sumner," which is probably right.

Edward Wood.

Inventory of goods and money belonging to Edward Wood of Charlestown, deceased being valued by Robert Long, William Brackenbury and Richard Russell the 4th day of the 18 Month 1642, in New England.

Edward Skinner.*

13 (   ) 1643.

The Inventory of *Edward Skinners* of late prised by *Gregory Stone* & *Gilbert Crackborne* November, 1639.

	£ s. d.
Paid out of this estate to *Wm.* *Merchant* for debt	6 – 0 – 0
To *Thomas Warrish* [Warwick?]	4 – 19 – 6
To *Goodman Rise*	4 – 0 – 0
To *Goodwife Merchant* of his gift	4 – 4 – 0
To *Mary Slanney*	2 – 7 – 0
lost in the sale of the goods & debts	0 – 6 – 0
	£21 – 16 – 6

Deposed the 8 of ye first month 1642
by *Gregory Stone* & *Gilbert Crackborne*
before the Court *Increase Nowell* Secr.

Athagered Knight.

An Inventory of *Athagcred Knights* goods departed & prysed by Lieftenant *Mason* & Goodman *Cooledge*.

[Amount of effects,] £7. 14s. 8d.

Hugh Mason
John Coolidge.

Thomas Axtell.

6 (3) 1646.

The Inventory of the goods of *Thomas Axtell* of Sudbury late deceased. Imprimus his land & house £8. 10. Cattle £8. 10. Wearing apparell & bedding wth his Armes £10. for Brasse & pewter £5. prised by *Edmund Rise*, *Philemon Whale*, *Edward Rice*. He expressed that *Mary* his wife should haue all his estate for to bring vp his children. Testifyed by Edmund Rice vppon oath the 6 (3) 1646 before the Governor, Dep. Govr. & *Increase Nowell* Secr.

Alexander Bradford.

12. (4) 1646.

The last will of *Alexander Bradford* being made this xviith day of the vi month 1644 witnesseth. I the said *Alexander Bradford* of Dorchester

* In extracting the will of *Edward Skinner* (Vol. II. p. 103) the inventory of his estate was inadvertently omitted. The following is all Mr. Farmer has in his *Genealogical Register* upon this name:

"Skinner, Thomas, Malden, 1653—a name common in New England, and which has furnished 14 graduates at the different colleges."

apprehending myself much weakned & naturall life impayred through Sickness & dissease. vnto *Sarah* my now wife all my Masion house & other buildings with the houshold stuffe as it now stands in Dorchester Wife sole executrix. I intreate my brother *Walter Merry* of Boston to be my Supvisor to help my wife in managing her affaires, & for three pounds wth my brother *John Bradford* did owe mee I release him of that, it to be equally divided among his children.

ALEXANDER BRADFORD.

Signed in ye presence of
*Philemon Pormort**
Walter Merry.

Testifyed vppon oath *Walter Merry* 2 (8) 1645 before *John Winthrop* Dep. Gov & *Herbert Pelham.*

Moreover After the death of my wife I giue unto the children of my brother *John* all my housen & lands, the said *Alexander Bradford* haue giuen to *Robert Stowton* his Moose Suite & a musket & Sworde & bandilieres & vest. *Alexander Bradford.*

William Ireland also
testified this addition to be
made by the said Alexander
Bradford being of disposing memory.
Sworne before *John Winthrop* Dep. Gov. &
Herbert Pelham.

REFUGEES IN LONDON.

1775.

The following curious document has been handed us by J. WINGATE THORNTON, ESQ., for publication. Such documents of the Revolutionary era are not only curious but of intrinsic value on historical accounts. It is hoped that whoever may be in possession of such, they will not keep them *so safely* as to defeat their own purposes ; fires, floods, and vermin are daily devouring these *safely kept* materials of history. When they are once put into our pages there are no fears to be entertained for their safety. "Old papers are good for nothing," is a common saying, even among those who, were they to allow themselves a moment's reflection, would censure the remark in every body else.

We whose names are undersigned do mutually agree to meet and dine together at the Adelphi Tavern, on every Thursday, weekly under the following regulations.

1st That the expence of the dinner, exclusive of liquor and waiters, shall be two shillings and sixpence for each person present, and no more.

2dly That a dinner every Thursday, shall be accordingly ordered for twelve persons at least.

3dly That one of the members present shall officiate as steward each day, who alone shall order the liquors, collect and pay the Bill, and manage the general concerns of the Company.

* Perhaps afterwards written *Pimer*. There was a *Matthew Pimer* at Dorchester, who died before 1639. See *Blake's Annals*, 53.

4thly That, when less than twelve members shall attend, those present shall not be liable for more than their own dinners together with the liquor order'd and the waiters; the residue of the bill to be paid by the Steward or his substitute, and repaid him by the absentees in equal proportions.

5thly That any Gentleman, belonging to the four N. England Governments, may be admitted a member provided he is first proposed to the Club at any meeting, and there be not two dissenting votes.

6thly That each person subscribing or agreeing to these Rules, is to be considered as a member, untill he shall give notice to the Steward, of his desire to withdraw himself, and to have his name erased from the list of members.

7thly That any member may invite his friend, giving notice to the Steward of his intention and paying his bill.

Daniel Silsby	Saml. Porter	J. S. Copley
Joseph Taylor	Wm. Cabot	Geo Brinley
Isaac Smith Jr.	Thos. Flucker	David Greene
Harrison Gray Jr.	R: Clarke	Edward Oxnard
Samuel Quincy	S. Curwen	S S Blowers
I. W. Clarke	Joñ Sewall	Fras. Waldo
Jona Bliss	Samuel Sewall	

Whether the above paper were drawn up by one of the signers, it is difficult to determine. The hand writing, however, might be attributed, judging from the signatures, to either Taylor, Smith, or Copley. There is no date upon it, but on a paper accompanying it is this memorandum:

THE COMPANY'S EXPENCE.

1775 Augt.	31	pauls head tavern Bill for		1 — 0 — 3
Sept	7	Queens Arms " " "		2 — 4 — 4
	14	" " do	do	1 — 6 —
	21	" " "		17 — 9
	26	" " "		1 — 2 —
Oct.	5	" " "	"	19 — 6
	12	"	"	1 — 19
	19			17 — 6
	26			17
Nov.	2			16 — 6
	9			" — "

Some account of nearly every individual in the above list may be found in Mr. Sabine's "BIOGRAPHICAL SKETCHES OF AMERICAN LOYALISTS." He finds but few of them in London so early as 1775, or that they had left New England at that date. In his account of Blowers he does not seem to be aware that he was the author of a history of Boston; but such is believed to be the fact, although we do not remember ever to have seen it. How much of a history it was we are therefore unable to state.

Upon one side of the paper containing the signatures is an indorsement in these words: (evidently unfinished.)

Stewards at ye Crown and Anchor.
Mr. Quincy
Pickman
Mr. 7. Porter.

FIRST SETTLERS OF BARNSTABLE.

[Communicated by MR. DAVID HAMBLEN.—Continued from page 390, Vol. II.]

ELEAZER CROCKER m. Reuth Chipman, 7 April, 1682; children, Benoni, b. 13 May, 1682, d. 3 Feb., 1701; Bethiah, 23 Sept., 1683; Nathan, 27 April, 1685; Daniel, 23 March, 1686–7; Sarah, 23 March, 1689; Theophelus, 11 March, 1691; Eleazer, 3 Aug., 1693; Ruth, 3 Aug., 1693; Abel, 15 June, 1695; Rebekah, 10 Dec., 1697. Mrs. Ruth Crocker d. 8 April, 1698.

NATHAN CROCKER m. Joanna Bursley, 10 March, 1708–9; children, Jabez, b. 10 June, 1709; Benoni, 24 Feb., 1711–12.

ROBERT CLAGHORN m. Bethiah Lathrop, 6 Nov., 1701; children, Abia, b. 13 Aug., 1702; Joseph, 25 Aug., 1704; Nathaniel, 10 Nov., 1707; Samuel, 23 June, 1711.

SHOBAL CLAGHORN m. —— ——; children, James, b. Aug., 1689; Thankful, 30 Jan., 1690, d. Jan., 1696; Thomas, 20 March, 1692–3; Shobal, 20 Sept., 1696; Robert, 18 July, 1699; Benjamin, 14 June, 1701; Mary, 1707; Jane, 1709; Ebenezer, 30 July, 1712.

ISAAC CHAPMAN m. Rebecca Leonard, 2 Sept., 1678; children, Lezaia, b. 15 Dec., 1679; John, 12 May, 1681; Hannah, 26 Dec., 1682, d. 6 July, 1689; James, 5 Aug., 1685; Abigail, 11 July, 1687; Hannah, 10 April, 1690; Isaac, 29 Dec., 1692; Ralph, 19 Jan., 1695; Rebecca, 10 June, 1697.

DEACON SAMUEL CHIPMAN m. Sarah Cob, 27 Dec., 1686, d. 1723: she died 8 Jan., 1742. Children, Thomas, b. 17 Nov., 1687; Samuel, 6 Aug., 1689; John,* 16 Feb., 1691; Abigail, 15 Sept., 1692; Joseph, 10 Jan., 1694; Jacob, 30 Aug., 1695; Seth, 24 Feb., 1697; Hannah, 24 Sept., 1699; Sarah, 1 Nov., 1701; Barnabas, 24 March, 1702.

JOHN CHIPMAN m. Hope Howland, dau. of John Howland, which came over in the Mayflower.

JAMES COHOON, (son of widow Mary Davis,) b. 25 Oct., 1696.

STEPHEN CLAP m. Temperance Gorham, 24 Dec., 1696.

NATHAN DAVIS m. Elizabeth Phinney, 25 Nov., 1714; children, Jabez, b. 7 Oct., 1715; Sarah, 12 Aug., 1717, d. 23 Aug., 1717; Elizabeth, 15 Sept., 1718; Isaac, 9 Jan., 1720.

JOSIAH DAVIS m. Ann Tayler, 25 June, 1679; children, John, b. 2 Sept., 1681; Hannah, April, 1683; Josiah, Aug., 1687; Seth, Oct., 1692; Ruth, Feb., 1694; Sarah, Feb., 1696; Jonathan, about 1698; Stephen, 12 Dec., 1700; Anna, 5 April, 1702.

JOSEPH DAVIS m. Hannah Cob, March, 1695; children, Robert, b. 7 March, 1696–7; Joseph, 23 March, 1698–9; James, 30 July, 1700; Gershom, 5 Sept., 1702; Hannah, 5 March, 1705; Mary, 4 June, 1707; Lezaia, 12 Feb., 1709; Daniel, 28 Sept., 1713.

JOSEPH DAVIS m. Mary Claghorn, 28 March, 1682; children, Simeon, b. 19 Jan., 1683; Mary, June, 1685; Joseph, April, 1687; Robert, 13 June, 1689.

†DOLLAR DAVIS m. Hannah Linnil, 3 Aug., 1681; children, Shobal, b. 23 April, 1685; Thomas, Aug., 1687; Hannah, Dec., 1689; Stephen, Sept., 1690; Thankful, March, 1696; Daniel, July, 1698; Job, July, 1700; Noah, Sept., 1702; Remember Mercy, 15 Oct., 1704.

* Rev. John Chipman graduated at Harvard University, 1711, d. 23 March, 1775.
† This name is spelt Dolor, Dollar, Dollor, and Doller.

JABEZ DAVIS m. Experience Linnel, 20 Aug., 1689; children, Nathan, b. 2 March, 1690; Samuel, 25 Sept., 1692; Bethsheba, 16 Jan., 1694; Isaac, 23 April, 1696; Abigail, 26 April, 1698; Jacob, Oct., 1699; Mercy, 16 Feb., 1701.

JOHN DAVIS, JR., m. Ruth Goodspeed, 2 Feb., 1674; children, John, b. Nov., 1675, d. Aug., 1681; Benjamin, 8 Sept., 1679; John, 17 March, 1684; Nathaniel, 17 July, 1686. Married 2d, Mary Hamblen, 22 Feb., 1692. She d. Nov., 1698; Shobal, 10 July, 1694; James, 24 March, 1696; Ebenezer, 13 May, 1697. Married 3d, widow Hannah Bacon, 8 May, 1699; Nicholas, 12 March, 1699–1700.

JOSIAH DAVIS m. Mehitable Tayler, 10 July, 1712; children, Edward, b. 19 June, 1713; Mary, 8 Aug., 1714; Josiah, 2 Aug., 1718.

CAPT. THOMAS DIMOCK* m. ——— ———; children, Mehitable, b. Oct., 1686; Temperance, June, 1689; Edward, 5 July, 1692; Thomas, 25 Dec., 1694; Desire, Feb., 1696.

JOHN DEMOCK m. Elizabeth Lumber, Nov., 1689; children, Sarah, b. Dec., 1690; Anna, July, 1693; Mary, June, 1695; Theophilus, Sept., 1696; Timothy, July, 1698; Ebenezer, Feb., 1700; Thankful, 5 April, 1702; Elizabeth, 20 April, 1704.

SHOBAL DIMOCK m. Tabitha Lothrop, 4 May, 1699; children, Samuel, b. 7 May, 1702; Joanna, 24 Dec., 1708, d. about 3 weeks after; Mehitable, 20 June, 1711.

JOSEPH DIMOCK m. Lydia Fuller, 12 May, 1699; children, Thomas, b. 26 Jan., 1699–1700; Bethiah, 3 Feb., 1702; Mehitable, 22 March, 1707; Ensign, 8 March, 1709; Ichabod, 8 March, 1711; Abigail, 31 [30?] June, 1714; Pharoh, 2 Sept., 1717; David, 22 Dec., 1721.

STEPHEN DEXTER m. Anna Sanders, 27 April, 1696; children, Mary, b. 24 Aug., 1696; a son, 22 Dec., 1698, d. Jan., 1698–9; Abigail, 13 May, 1699; Content, 5 Feb., 1701; Anna, 9 March, 1702–3; Sarah, 1 June, 1705; Stephen, 26 July, 1707; Mercy, 5 July, 1709; Marion, 8 March, 1712; Cornelius, 21 March, 1713–14

SAMUEL DOANE of Eastham, m. Martha Hamblen, 30 Dec., 1696.

JOHN EWER m. Elizabeth Lumbard, 5 July, 1716; children, Shobal, b. ———; Joseph; Benjamin, 5 Sept., 1721.

SHOBAL EWER m. ——— ———; children, Rebakah, b. 27 April, 1715. Mr. Shobal Ewer d. 6 Aug., 1715.

THOMAS EWER m. widow Sarah Warren, 18 Sept., 1712, and died June, 1722.

NATHANIEL FITTSRANDLE† m. Mary Holley, Nov., 1662; children, John, b. 1 Feb., 1662; Isaac, 7 Dec., 1664.

DR. JOHN FULLER m. ——— ———; children, Bethiah, b. Dec., 1687; John, Oct., 1689; Reliance, 8 Sept., 1691.

JOHN FULLER m. Thankful Gorham, 16 June, 1710; children, Hannah, b. 1 April, 1711; John, 3 Aug., 1712; Mary, 1 Sept., 1715; Bethiah, 1 Sept., 1715; Nathaniel, 10 Dec., 1716; Thankful, 19 Sept., 1718.

JOSEPH FULLER, JR., m. Joanna Crocker, 9 Feb., 1708–9; children, Rebekah, b. 29 Dec., 1709; Bethiah, 2 March, 1712.

THOMAS FULLER m. Elisabeth Lathrop, 29 Dec., 1680; children, Hannah, b. 17 Nov., 1681; Joseph, 12 July, 1683; Mary, 6 Aug., 1685: Benjamin, 6 Aug., 1690; Elisabeth, 3 Sept., 1692; Samuel, 12 April, 1694; Abigail, 9 Jan., 1695–6.

* This name is spelt Dimock, Dimmock, and Dimick.
† This name is spelt Fitzrandle and Fittsrandle.

Jabez Fuller m. ——— ———; children, Samuel, b. 23 Feb., 1687; Jonathan, 10 March, 1692; Mercy, 1 April, 1696; Lois, 23 Sept., 1704; Ebenezer, 20 Feb., 1708–9; Mary, no date.

Matthew Fuller m. Patience Young, 25 Feb., 1692; children, Anna, b. Nov., 1693; Jonathan, Oct., 1696; Content, 19 Feb., 1698–9; Jean, 1704, d. 1708; David, Feb., 1706–7; Young, 1708; Cornelius, 1710.

Barnabas Fuller m. Elizabeth Young, 25 Feb., 1680; children, Samuel, b. Nov., 1681; Isaac, Aug., 1684; Hannah, Sept., 1688; Ebenezer, April, 1699; Josiah, Feb., 1709.

Samuel Fuller m. ——— ———; child, Sarah, b. 16 April, 1719.

Joseph Fuller m. ——— ———; children, Remember, b. 26 May, 1701; Seth, 1 Sept., 1705; Thankful, 4 Aug., 1708.

Benjamin Fuller m. ——— ———; children, Temperance, b. 7 March, 1702; Hannah, 20 May, 1704; John, 25 Dec., 1706; James, 1 May, 1711.

Nathaniel Goodspeed* m. Elizabeth Bursley, Nov., 1666; child, Mary, b. 18 Feb., 1667.

Benjamin Goodspeed m. Mary Davis; child, Mary, b. 10 Jan., 1677.

John Goodspeed m. Experience Holley, 9 Jan., 1668; children, Mercy, b. 18 Feb., 1669; Samuel, 23 June, 1670; John, 1 June, 1673; Experience, 14 Sept., 1676; Benjamin, 31 March, 1679; Rose, 20 Feb., 1680; Bathshua, 17 Feb., 1683.

John, son of John Goodspeed, m. Remembrance Buck, 16 Feb., 1697; children, Elizabeth, b. 10 Dec., 1698; Temperance, 17 Feb., 1699; Samuel, 17 March, 1701; Cornelius, 2 Feb., 1703; John, 16 Nov., 1708; Experience, 24 June, 1710; a daughter, 24 April, 1712.

Benjamin Goodspeed, Jr., m. Susannah Allen, March, 1710; children, Joseph, b. 1 Jan., 1711; Mary, 12 Oct., 1713; Mercy, 26 Sept., 1725.

Benjamin Goodspeed m. Hope Lumbart, 1707; children, Jabez, b. 26 Jan., 1707–8; Jane, 7 Sept., 1709; James, 31 [30?] June, 1711; David, 13 Nov., 1713; Nathan, 7 Oct., 1715, d. 29 April, 1731; Patience, 25 March, 1718; Jonathan, 23 April, 1720.

Ebenezer Goodspeed m. Lydia Crowel, Feb., 1677; children, Benjamin, b. 31 Oct., 1678; a son, 21 Jan., 1679, d. 20 Dec., 1680; Mehitable, 4 Sept., 1681; Alice, 30 June, 1683; Ebenezer, 10 Sept., 1685; Mary, 2 Aug., 1687; Susannah, 7 Nov., 1689; Patience, 1 June, 1692; Ruth, 12 July, 1694; Lydia, 14 Oct., 1696; Roger, 14 Oct., 1698; Reliance, 18 Sept., 1701; Moses, 24 Nov., 1704.

James Gorham† m. Hannah Huckins, 24 Feb., 1673; children, Desire, b. 9 Feb., 1674; James, 6 March, 1676–7; Experience, 28 July, 1678; John, 2 Aug., 1680; Mehitable, 20 April, 1683; Thomas, 16 Dec., 1684; Mercy, 22 Nov., 1686, d. 12 June, 1689; Joseph, 25 March, 1689; Jabez, 6 March, 1690–1; Sylvanus, 13 Oct., 1693; Ebenezer, 14 Feb., 1695–6.

James Gorham and Mary Joyce m. 29 Sept., 1709; child, Thankful, b. 25 May, 1711.

Capt. John Gorham m. Desire Howland, 1643, daughter of Mr. John Howland, the one that came over in the Mayflower, who died in Plymouth, 23 Feb., 1672, æ. 80 years.

Col. John Gorham m. Mary Otis, 24 Feb., 1674; children, John, b. 18 Jan., 1675, d. 1 April, 1679; Temperance, 2 Aug., 1678; Mary, 18 April, 1680; Stephen, 23 June, 1683; Shobal, 2 Sept., 1686; John, 28

* This name is spelt Godspeed and Goodspeed.

† This name is spelt Gorum and Gorham.

Sept., 1688; Thankful, 15 Feb., 1690; Job, 30 Aug., 1692; Mercy, Dec., 1695. Col. Gorham d. 11 Nov., 1716.

SHOBAL GORHAM m. Puelia Hussey, May, 1695; children, George, b. 29 Jan., 1696–7; Abigail, last of March, 1699; Lydia, 14 May, 1701; Hannah, 28 July, 1703; Theodate, 18 July, 1705; Daniel, 24 Sept., 1708; Desire, 26 Sept., 1710; Ruth, 7 May, 1713.

THOMAS, (son of James,) Gorham m. —— ——; children, Benjamin, b. 8 Sept., 1708; Reuben, 10 Dec., 1709; Priscilla, 18 Dec., 1711; Samuel, 18 Dec., 1713; Peter, 19 Dec., 1715; Paul, 6 Jan., 1717–18; Abraham, 10 July, 1720; Gershom, 22 June, 1725; Abigail, 13 May, 1729; James, 23 June, 1723.

[To be continued.]

DESCRIPTION OF JAMES THE FIRST.

The following quaint and graphic description of James the First, king of England, whose name will ever be associated with the history of our puritan ancestors, towards whom he ever exhibited the most bitter and persecuting spirit, is by a cotemporary, Anthony Weldon. This writer also gives portraits of other distinguished men of his time. His picture of James, however, is the most complete, and is said to give a very perfect idea of his personal appearance and peculiar habits.*

"He was of a middle stature, more corpulent through his clothes than in his body, yet fat enough, his clothes ever being made large and easy; the doublets quilted for stiletto proof; his breeches in great plaits and full stuffed; he was naturally of a timorous disposition, which was the reason of his quilted doublets; his eye large, ever rolling after any stranger that came in his presence, insomuch that many for shame have left the room, as being out of countenance; his beard was very thin; his tongue too large for his mouth, which made him drink very uncomely, as if eating his drink, which came out into the cup of each side of his mouth; his skin was as soft as taffety sarsnet, which felt so because he never washed his hands, only rubbed his fingers' ends slightly with the wet end of a napkin: his legs were very weak, having had (as some thought) some foul play in his youth, or rather before he was born, that he was not able to stand at seven years of age; that weakness made him for ever leaning on other men's shoulders; his walk was ever circular."†

AN OLD PROVERB.

Never trust much to a new friend or an old enemy.

Remember man and keep in mind
A faithful friend is hard to find.
Suddaine friendship, sure repentance.
If you trust before you try
You may repent before you dy.—BAILEY.

* *Retrospective Review*, Vol. VII., p. 45.

† *The Court and Character of King James*, whereunto is added the court of King Charles, continued unto the beginning of these unhappy times, with some observations upon him instead of a character. Collected and perfected by Sir A. W. (Anthony Weldon.) Qui nescit dissimulare, nescit regnare. Published by authority. Printed at London, by R. J., and are to be sold by J. Collins in Little Brittaine, 1651.

Table of Kings and Queens since the Conquest.

Names.	*When began to Reign.*	*Reigned.* Y. M. D.	*Cause or Manner of Death.*	*Age.*
William I.	1066 Oct 14	20 8 15	Rupture.	60
William II.	1087 Sept. 9	12 10 7	Shot by an arrow.	43
Henry I.	1100 Aug. 1	35 3 27	A surfeit of lampreys. .	67
Stephen.	1135 Dec. 2	18 10 0	The piles.	49
THE SAXON LINE RESTORED.				
Henry II.	1154 Oct. 25	34 6 18	Grief.	55
Richard I.	1189 Aug. 13	9 7 3	Wound of an arrow. . .	43
John	1199 Apr. 6	17 4 23	Course of nature.	49
Henry III	1216 Oct. 17	56 0 19	Age.	63
Edward I.	1272 Nov. 16	37 7 17	Diarrhœa. . . , ...	65
Edward II.	1307 July 8	19 6 12	Was murdered.	47
Edward III.	1327 Jan. 25	50 4 27	Course of nature.	63
Richard II.	1377 June 22	22 3 7	Consumption.	35
THE LINE OF LANCASTER.				
Henry IV.	1399 Sept. 30	13 5 20	Apoplexy.	46
Henry V.	1413 Mar. 21	9 5 10	Pleurisy.	33
Henry VI.	1422 Sept. 1	38 6 3	Murdered.	49
THE LINE OF YORK.				
Edward IV.	1461 Mar. 4	22 1 5	Ague.	41
Edward V.	1483 Apr. 9	0 2 16	Was smothered.	12
Richard III.	1483 June 22	2 1 26	Killed in battle.	42
The two families of YORK *and* LANCASTER *united.*				
Henry VII.	1485 Aug. 22	23 7 30	Consumption.	52
Henry VIII.	1509 Apr. 22	37 9 6	Ulcerated leg and Fever.	55
Edward VI.	1547 Jan. 28	6 5 9	Consumption.	15
Q. Mary	1553 July 6	5 4 11	Dropsy.	42
Q. Elisabeth	1558 Nov. 17	44 4 7	Course of Nature.	69
The union of the two Crowns of ENGLAND *and* SCOTLAND				
James I.	1603 Mar. 24	22 0 3	Ague.	58
Charles I.	1625 Mar. 27	23 10 3	Was beheaded.	48
Cromwell				
Charles II.	1649 Jan. 30	36 0 7	Apoplexy.	54
James II.	1685 Feb. 6	3 10 5	Course of nature.	67
Mary II.	1689 Feb. 13	5 10 15	Small-pox.	32
William III.	1689 Feb. 13	13 0 20	A fall from his horse. . .	52
The union of the Parliaments of ENGLAND *and* SCOTLAND.				
Q. Anne	1702 Mar. 8	12 4 24	Apoplexy.	49
George I.	1714 Aug. 1	12 10 10	Paralytic attack.	67
George II.	1727 June 11	33 4 14	Died suddenly.	77
George III.*	1760 Oct. 25	59 3 4	Course of nature.	82
George IV.	1820 Jan. 29	10 4 28	Bursting of a blood vessel	68
William IV.	1830 June 26	6 11 25	Course of nature.	72
Q. VICTORIA	1837 June 20		Whom GOD preserve. .	

* The Parliaments of Great Britain and Ireland were united Jan. 1, 1810.

LIST OF FREEMEN.

[Communicated by REV LUCIUS R. PAIGE of Cambridge, member of the N. E. Hist. Geneal. Society.]

Under the first charter of the Massachusetts colony, none were regarded as freemen, or members of the body politic, except such as were admitted by the General Court and took the oath of allegiance to the government here established. This custom continued in existence until, by the second charter, the colony was transformed into a province. Mr. Savage, in his edition of Winthrop's Journal, published a list of persons admitted freemen, up to May 10, 1648; and he justly remarked, that "these are probably ancestors of near three fourths of the present inhabitants of the six New England states, with almost half of New York and Ohio." Having occasion to use a more full list of freemen, I transcribed, nearly eight years ago, the names of all the persons admitted freemen, up to the time when the practice was discontinued, as recorded in the office of the Secretary of State. Agreeably to the request of the editor of the Register, this list is now furnished for publication. The names stand in the same order as in the original, and the orthography is carefully preserved. To guard more effectually against mistakes, I have recently, after so long an interval, compared my copy with the original, and I believe it to be correct, so far as the original remains legible. It is not surprising that many of the names are incorrectly spelled. They are not autographs; but they were written by the Secretary, according to the sound, as the names were pronounced to him. Moreover, it sometimes occurred, doubtless, that he did not catch the sound accurately, and therefore mistook the true name. I have endeavoured to exhibit an exact transcript; so that all readers may have the same opportunity to make proper corrections, which a perusal of the original would afford.

The oath administered to freemen is a document not without interest, and is here inserted, both in its original and its revised form, the orthography only being changed.

" *The oath of a Freeman, or of a man to be made Free.*

"I, A. B. &c. being by the Almighty's most wise disposition become a member of this body, consisting of the Governor, Deputy Governor, Assistants and Commonalty of the Massachusetts in New England, do freely and sincerely acknowledge that I am justly and lawfully subject to the Government of the same, and do accordingly submit my person and estate to be protected, ordered and governed by the laws and constitutions thereof, and do faithfully promise to be from time to time obedient and conformable thereunto, and to the authority of the said Governor and Assistants, and their successors, and to all such laws, orders, sentences and decrees as shall be lawfully made and published by them or their successors. And I will always endeavor (as in duty I am bound) to advance the peace and welfare of this body or commonwealth, to my utmost skill and ability. And I will, to my best power and means, seek to divert and prevent whatsoever may tend to the ruin or damage thereof, or of any the said Governor, Deputy Governor, or Assistants, or any of them, or their successors, and will give speedy notice to them, or some of them, of any sedition, violence, treachery, or other hurt or evil, which I shall know, hear, or vehemently suspect, to be plotted or intended against the said commonwealth, or the said Government established. And I will not, at any time, suffer or give consent to any counsel or attempt, that shall be offered, given, or attempted, for the impeachment of the said Government, or making any change or alteration of the same, contrary to the laws and ordinances thereof; but shall do my utmost endeavor to discover, oppose and hinder all and every such counsel and attempt. So help me God." — *Col. Rec. Vol. I. page* 1.

"At a General Court holden at Boston, May 14, 1634.

"It was agreed and ordered, that the former oath of freemen shall be revoked, so far as it is dissonant from the oath of freemen hereunder written; and that those that received the former oath shall stand bound no further thereby, to any intent or purpose, than this new oath ties those that now take the same." *

19 Oct. 1630. The names of such as desire to be made ffreemen.

Mr. Sam^{ll} Mav^{r}acke
Mr. Edw. Johnson
Mr. Edw. Gibbins
Mr. Will. Jeffries
Mr. John Burslin
Mr. Sam^{ll} Sharpe
Mr. Tho. Graves
Mr. Roger Conant
John Woodbury
Peter Palfry
Mr. Nath. Turner
Mr. Sam^{ll} ffreeman
Eprahim Childe
Mr. Willm Clerke
Mr. Abraham Palmer
John Page
Mr. Robte ffeake
Mr. Willm Pelham
Mr. Ben. Brand
Mr. Will: Blackstone
Mr. Edmond Lockwood
Mr. Rich. Browne
John Stickland
Ralfe Sprage
Mr. George Ludlowe
James Peñ (62)
Henry Woolcott
Thomas Stoughton
Willm Phelpes
George Dyar
John Hoskins
Thomas fford
Nich. Upsall
Stephen Terree
Henry Smyth
Roger Willms
John Woolridge
Tho. Lumberd
Bigatt Egglestone
John Grinoway
Christopher Gibson
John Benham
Thomas Willms als. Harris
Rich. Garrett
John Howman
John Crabb
Capt. Walt^{r} Norton
Mr. Alex. Wignall
Mr. Willm Jennison
Mr. Thomas Southcoate
Mr. Rich. Southcoate
James Pemb^{r}ton
Mr. John Dillingham
John Johnson
George Alcocke
Mr. Robte Coles
John Burr
Thomas Rawlins
Rich. Bugby
Rich. Hutchins
Ralfe Mushell
Thomas Lambe
Will: Throdingham
Willm Chase
ffoxewell
Mr. Charles Gott
Henry Harwood
Mr. George Phillips
Mr. John Wilson
Mr. John Mav^{r}acke
Mr. John Warham
Mr. Sam^{ll} Skelton
Mr. Will. Colbron
Mr. Will. Aspinwall
Edw. Converse
Mr. Rich. Palgrave
John Taylour
Rich. Church
Rich. Silvester
Will. Balstone
Robte Abell
Mr. Giles Sexton
Robte Seely
John Mills
John Cranwell
Mr. Ralfe Glover
Willm Hulberd
Edmond James
John Pillips
Nath. Bowman
John Doggett
Laurence Leach
Daniel Abbott
Charles Chadwicke
Will. Drakenbury
John Drake
John Balshe
Mr. Sam^{ll} Coole
Mr. Will. Traske
Will. Gallard
Will. Rockewell
Henry Herricke
Sam^{ll} Hosier
Rich. Myllett
Mr. Abraham Pratt
Willm James
Willm Allen
Sam^{ll} Archer (63)
Col. Rec., Vol. I. pp. 62, 63.

18 May 1631.

The names of such as took the oath of ffreemen.

Mr. John Mav^{r}acke
Mr. Jo: Warham
Mr. Willm Blackestone
Mr. George Phillips
Mr. Rich. Browne
Capt. Dan^{ll} Pattricke
Capt. Jo: Und^{r}hill
Capt. Southcoate
Mr. Tho. Graves
Capt. Walt^{r} Norton
Mr. George Throckm^{r}ton
Mr. Wm. Colbran
S^{r}ieant Morris
S^{r}ieant Stickland
Mr. Roger Conant
Mr. Charles Gott
Ralfe Sprage
Laurence Leach
John Horne

* Having printed the oath here referred to, (see p. 41 of this number of Journal,) it is here omitted. It is in the *Col. Recs*, Vol. I. p. 114.

Mr. Sam^ll^ Coole
John Woodbury
Mr. John Oldeham
Edmond Lockewood
John Page
Mr. Rich. Palgrave
John Doggett
Rich. Sprage
ffraunes Johnson
Tho. Stoughton
Abraham Palmer
John Johnson
Robte Coles, — erased in the record.
Eprahim Childe
Bray Rossiter
Robte Seely
Biggott Egglestone
Mr. Will. Clearke
Willm Noddle
Mr. Robte ffeakes
Willm. Agar
Nich Stower
John Benham
Willm Balstone
Stephen Terre
Sam^ll^ Hosier
Robte Hardinge
Willm Woods
Mr. George Alcocke
Robte Moulton
Pet^r^ Palfry
Mr. Edw. Belchar
John Edmonds
George Phillips
Roger Willms
John Balche
John Moore
Henry Herricke
John Hoskins
Math. Grant
John Burr
Simon Hoytt
Charles Chadwicke
Willm Parks
Ralfe Mushell
Willm Hudson
Walt^r^ Palmer
Henry Smyth
Tho. fford
Jonas Weede
Mr. Edw. Tomlyns
Mr. Rich. Saltonstall
Edw. Gibbons
Mr. Alex. Wignall
Mr. Willm Gennison
Dan^ll^ Abbott
Tho. Rawlins
Rich. Bugby
John Warren
Mr. Willm Jeffry
Davy Johnson
Nich. Upsall
Willm Bateman
Dan^ll^ ffinch
Mr. Jo. Burslyn (73)
Mr. John Maisters
John Peirce
Griffin Crofte
George Dyar
Willm Rockewell
Tho. Moore
John Taylour
Ezekiell Richardson
Edw. Converse
Robte Abell
Mr. John Dillingham
Isaacke Sterne
Roger Mawry
Tho. Dexter, — erased in the record.
Tho. Lambe
Tho. Willms
John fferman
John Gosse
John Grinnoway
Gyles Sexton
Tho. Lumberd
Mr. Edw. Jones
Willm Gallerd
Willm Allen
Rich. Bulgar
Rich. ffoxewell
Willm. ffelpes
John Perkins
Mr. Sam^ll^ Skelton
Mr. Edw. Johnson
Wm. Cheesebrough
Anthony Dixe
ffraunes Smyth
ffrauncis Aleworth (74)

C. R., Vol. I. pp. 73, 74.

March 6, 1631-2.

Mr. John Ellyott
Jacob Ellyott
Abraham Browne
James Pennyman
Isaack Perry
Gregory Baxter
Willm ffrothingham
Sam^ll^ Moore
John Blacke
John Mylls

C. R., Vol. I. p. 74.

April 3, 1632.

Mr. John Winthrop jun^r^
Mr. Willm Aspinwall
John Sampeford
Willm Hulbert

C. R., Vol. I. p. 74.

July 3, 1632.

Mr. Nath. Turner
John Ruggles
Elias Stileman
Mr. Willm Dennison
Mr. Sam^ll^ Sharpe
Mr. John Wilson
John Moore

C. R., Vol. I. p. 74.

August 7, 1632.

John Phillips
Valentine Prentice
John Hull
Sam^ll^ Wakeman

C. R., Vol. I. p. 74.

Oct. 2, 1632.

Mr. Sam^ll^ Mav^r^icke

C. R., Vol. I. p. 74.

Nov. 6, 1632.

Mr. Tho. Weld
Mr. Tho. James
Mr. Jo. Willust
Mr. Jo. Coggeshall
Mr. Rich. Dumer
Mr. Tho. Ollyver
Mr. John Branker
Mr. Tho. Beecher
Tho. ffrench
Willm Goodwin
John Beniamin
John Talcott
James Olmstead
John Clerke
Willm Leawis
Nath. Richards
Willm Wadsworth
Rich. Webb

C. R., Vol. I. p. 74.

March 4, 1632-3.

Willm Curtis
Thomas Uffott
John Perry
Isaack Morrall
Willm Heath
George Hull
Eltweed Pummery
Nich. Denselow
Gyles Gibbs
John Neweton
John White
Willm Spencer
John Kirman
Tymothy Tomlyns (74)

Henry Harwood
Richard Collocott
Willm Brakenbury
John Smyth (79)
C. R., Vol. I. pp. 74, 79.

April 1, 1633.

S'ieant Greene
Rise Coles
Willm Dady
C. R., Vol. I. p. 79.

June 11, 1633.

Willm Stilson
Rich. Millett
Rich. Lyman
Jes^pr Rawling
Tho. Smyth
David Wilton
John Witchfield
Elias Mav'acke
C. R., Vol. I. p. 79.

Nov. 5, 1633.

Mr. Israell Stoughton
Mr. John Coggin
Mr. Willm Hill
Mr. John Moody
John Porter
ffrauncis Weston
John Watson
John Holgrave
C. R., Vol. I. p. 79.

March 4, 1633–4.

Thomas Grubb
Edmond Hubbert
Edw. Hutchingson
Mr. Tho. Leveritt
Mr. Gyles fferman
Edmond Quinsey
Willm Collishawe
Thomas Minor
Tho. Howlett
John Gage
Sam^ll Wilboare
John Levens
John Cranwell
Edw. Mellowes
James Browne
Mr. John Woolridge
Josuah Hewes
Robte Turner
John Biggs
Tho. Matson
Walter Merry
Rich. Tappin
Mr. Atterton Hough
Willm Andrewes
Rich. Walker
George Ruggles
Mr. Nich. Parker.
C. R., Vol. I. p. 79.

April 1, 1634.

Mr. Dan^ll Dennison
George Minott
Rich. Gridley
Thomas Reade
George Hutchingson
Robte Roise
John Pemerton
Bernard Lumbert
Henry Wulcott
Rich. Hull
John Gallop
Richard Silvester
Willm Horseford
C. R., Vol. I. p. 79.

May 14, 1634.

John Haynes Esq.
Phillip Sherman
Daniell Brewer
Tho. Gaildthait
Robte Gamlyn Senr
Thomas Hale
Edward Riggs
John Walker
Thomas Wilson
Sam^ll Basse
Tho. Pigg
Willm Hill
Sam^ll ffinch
George Williams
Edw. Gyles
Willm Dixy
George Norton
Thomas Eborne
Dan^ll Wray
Abraham Mellowes
John Ollyver
Robte Hale
Tho. Cakebread (79)
Tho. Squire
Robte Houlton
John Odlyn
Roger Clapp
Josuah Carter
Thomas Talmage
Richard ffairebancks
Phillip Tabor
Gregory Taylour
John Chapman
Willm Learned
Mr. Tho. Hooker
Mr. Sam^ll Stone
Edw. Howe
Bartholmewe Greene
Rich. Wright
John Steele
Edm. Stebbins
Andrewe Warner
George Steele
Rich. Butlar
Thomas Spencer
Edw. Muste
Rich. Goodman
John Pratt
John Haward
Andrewe Ward
Joseph Twitchwell
Tho. Hatch
George Whitehand
Jerad Hadden
Joseph Reddings
Anthony Colby
John Bosworth
ffrauncis Plumer
Humfry Pynny
Bray Wilkins
James Rawlyns
Jacob Barny
Tho. Lowthrop
Steven Hart
Jeffery Massy
Rich. Brakenbury
Tho. ffaireweath^r
Willm Hedges
John Hoskins
Peter Woolfe
Willm Chase
Willm Talmidge
Mr. John Cotton
Nath. Gillett
Dan^ll Howe
Myles Reddin
John Eales
Mr. Willm Peirce
Mr. Tho. Mahewe
Robte Walker
Phillipp Randill
Tho. Holcombe
Tho. Dewey
Tho. Jeffry
James Parker
Walter ffiler
John Haydon
Edmond Harte
Willm Hathorne
Steven ffrench
Christopher Hussey
Edw. Bendall
John Button
Rich. Raymond
Jonathan Wade
Tho. Coldham
James Tompson
Tho. Hubbard
John Hall
John Baker
Mr. Willm Brenton
John Capen

ffrauncis Dent
Henry ffeakes (112)
C. R., Vol. I. pp. 79, 112.

Sep. 3, 1634.

Beniamin Hubbard
Edmond Hubbard
John Mousell
Willm Baker
Willm Nashe
Thomas Goble
Ollyver Mellowes
Robte Gamlyne
Ralfe Hiningway
Jes^pr^ Rawlyns
John Stowe
John Cumpton
Willm ffreeborne
Willm Perkins
James Everill
Jonathan Negos
Nicholas Willust
Alex. Becke
Henry Pease
Sam^ll^ Crumwell
Joseph Rednape
Edw. Hutchingson
John Sibley
Hugh Hillyard
Moses Mav^r^acke
Mr. John Spencer
Robte Mussey
Henry Shorte
Phillip ffowler
Bryan Pendleton
Abraham ffinch
Anthony Peirce
John Bernard
Martyn Und^r^wood
Sam^ll^ Smyth
John Browne
John Edy
Robte Abbitt
Robte Coe
Nathanell ffoote
Rich. Davenport
Mr. Tho. Newbery
John Pope
John Hawkes
Ralfe ffogg
Robert Reynolls
Robte Potter
John Hardy
Thomas Thorneton
Matthias Sension
Mr. Tho. Parker
Mr. Nicholas Easton
Mr. James Noise
Josuah Hubbard
C. R., Vol. I. p. 113.

March 4, 1634–5.

Capt. John Mason
Hugh Mason
George Munings
John Brandishe
Sam^ll^ Hubbert
Edward Dixe
Thomas Bartlett
George Buncar
Robte Blott
Rich. Kettle
Willm Johnson
Thomas Lynd
Mr. Willm Andrewes
Willm Westwood
Mathewe Allen
Guy Bambridge
Willm Pantry
Tho. ffisher
John Hopkins
John Bridge
Willm Kelsey
John Bernard
James Ensigne
Sam^ll^ Greenehill
Tymothy Stanley
Rich. Lord
John Prince
Edw. Winshipp
Sam^ll^ Greene
Joseph Clerke
John Wulcott
Abraham Newell
Rich. Pepper
Isaac Johnson
Christopher Peake
Thomas Woodford
Thomas Scott
Tho. Boreman
Roger Lanckton
John Webster
Hugh Sheratt
Joseph Metcalfe
Will. Bartholmewe
Tho. Dorman
Rich. Kent
James Davis
John Newegate
Mr. Will. Hutchingson
Tho. Marshall
Rich. Cooke
Willm Neth^r^land
Tho. Wardall
Rich. Hutchingson
ffr. Hutchingson
Gamaliell Wate
Rich. Trusedale
Edw. Hitchin
Robte Parker
Joseph Easton
John Tylley
Tho. Stanley
C. R., Vol. I p. 113.

May 6, 1635.

Philemon Portmorte
Henry Elkines
Christ. Martial
Edmond Bulckley
Eward Browne
Jarrett Bourne
Willm Pell
Beniamyn Gillom
Tho. Alcocke
Edmonde Jacklinge
John Sebley
Tho. Peirce
Mr. Sachariah Syms
Barnaby Wynes
Jeffery fferris
John Reynolls
Henry Bright
Tho. Hastings
John Lethermore
John Batchel^r^
John Tompson
John Clerke
Tho. Swifte
Robte Wincall
Tho. Hosmer
Willm Butlar
John Arnoll
George Stockin
Nathanaell Ely
Robte Day
Jerymy Adams
Joseph Maggott
John Hall
Sam^ll^ Allen
Humfry Bradstreete
Thomas Pyne
John Gay
George Strange
Nathanaell Duncan
Thomas Marshall
Thomas Hoskins
Richard Kemball
Robte Andrewes
Henry Wright
Jonathan Jellett
Tho. Gun
Robte Dibell
Henry ffowkes
Elias Parkeman
John Blackeleach
Dan^ll^ Morse
Joseph Morse
Edward Garfield
Rich. Browne
Willm Moody

Christ. Osgood
Tho. Buckland
Richard Jacob
Aron Cooke
George Phelpes
Boniface Burton
Robte Bootefishe
Robte Dryver
Willm Edmonds
John Ravensdale
John Legg
George ffarr
Robte Cotty
Mr. Steven Batchel^r^
C. R., Vol. I. p. 153.

Sep. 2, 1635.

Willm Blumfeild
Joseph Hull
Willm Reade
Richard Adams
John Upham
Robte Lovell
Willm Smyth
Richard Woodward
Peter Hubbert
Mr. George Byrditt
Mr. Townsend Bishopp
Phillip Vereing
Mr. John ffawne
Thomas Scraggs
C. R., Vol. I. p. 153.

March 3, 1635–6.

Mr. Clem^t^. Chaplaine
Willm Mosse
Willm Dyar
Joseph Wells
John Cogeswell
Richard Tuttle
Robte Lord
Willm Walton
Tho. Loreing
Clem^t^ Bates
John Astwood
Tho. Wakely
Willm Norton
George Ludkin
George Marshe
John Ottis
Nicholas Baker
Nicholas Jacob
David Phippin
Edmond Batter
Philemon Dolton
John Whitney
Willm Swayne
Henry Kingman
Thomas White
Angell Hollard
John Kingsbury
John Levett
Tho. Rawlyns
Roger Harlakendine Esq.
Mr. Joseph Cooke
Mr. George Cooke
Mr. Nich. Danforth
Tho. Marryott
Mr. Sam^ll^ Shepheard
Willm ffrench
Simon Crosby
Tho. Cheeseholme
John Russell
Passevell Greene
Mr. Hugh Peters
Thomas Bloyett
Edmond ffrost
Mr. Tho. Shepheard
Henry Vane Esq.
Tho. Ewer
Tho. Brigden
Michaell Bastowe
Joseph Andrewes
C. R., Vol. I. p. 153.

May 25, 1636.

Jasper Gun
Thom: Bell
Mr. Samuell Apleton
Isaack Heathe
Philip Elliot
Adam Mott
William Webbe
Edward Woodman
Thomas Judd
John Knight
Rich^rd^ Knight
Anthony Mosse
Rob^rt^ Longe
Rob^rt^ Hawkins
Edward Carington
Bernard Capen
Will. Hamond
John Saunders
Robert Kaine
Daniel Maude
Ralph Hudson
Thomas Hassord
James Johnson
John Davy
George Bate
Nathaniell Heaton
Will. Benseley
Will. Townsend
Rich^rd^ Bracket
Thom. Savage
Mr. Henry ffiinte
Will. Courser
James Browne
Zacheus Bosworth
Mathias Ives
Will. Wilson
Will. Salter
Anthony Harker
Edward Goffe
Rich^rd^ Champnyes
Edmond Lewis
John Stowers
John Smythe
John Eaton
Edmond Sherman
John Coolidge
Gregory Stone
Symon Stone
George Hepburne
Will. Kinge
Augustine Clement
Rich^rd^ Karder
John Higgenson
John Mylam
Thom. Dimocke
John Loverin
Willi. Wilcocks
Edward Bennet
Thom. Mekyn junior
Hugh Gunnison
Edmond Jackson
Bernaby Doryfall
Mr. Rich^rd^ Bellingham
Mr. John Winthrope sen.
Mr. John Humfrey
Mr. Thom. Dudley
Mr. Will. Coddington
Increase Nowell
Symon Bradstreete
C. R., Vol. I. p. 194.

Dec. 7, 1636.

James Bate
Edward Clapp
John Smythe
Edward White
David Price
George Aldridge
Oliver Purchase
John Webbe
Alexand^r^ Winchester
Robert Scotte
Steven Winthrope
Will. Goodhewe
Gilbert Crackborne
Samuell Whiteing
Thomas Brooke
Willi. Wilcockson
Will. Beadseley
Alexand^r^ Knolls
Thom. Atkinson
John Holland
Walter Nicoles
C. R., Vol. I. p. 194.

Dec. 8, 1636.

Mr. Thom. Jenner

ffrancis Lightfoote
Edward Howe
John Cooper
John More
Thom. Beale
C. R., Vol. I. p. 154.

March 9, 1636–7.

Edward Ketcham
Rich'd Roots
Joseph Isaack
John Hassell
Rich'd Betsham
Anthony Eames
Samuell Warde
Thomas Hamond
Thomas Underwood
Nicolas Hudson
John Winchester
Abraham Shawe
Rob't Lockwood
Will. Barsham
Rich'd Beares
Edward Bates
Jenkin Davies
Mathewe West
Gerret Spencer
Thomas Tylestone
Henry Collins
Robert Sedgwick
James Heyden
Thomas Samford
John Stronge
Thomas Carter
Joseph Armitage
Rich'd Wayte
Robert Hull
Rich. Wayde
Will. Dinny
Thomas Meakins
C. R., Vol. I. p. 194.

April 18, 1637.

Thomas Parish
Thomas Briggam
William Cutter
Willi. Towne
John Gore
Robert Sever
John Ruggles
Laurence Whitamore
John Graves
Gyles Pason
George Kinge
C. R., Vol. I. p. 195.

April 17, 1637.

Christopher ffoster
Thom. Browninge
Symon Eyre
William Dodge
ffrancis Smythe
Nathani. Porter
Edward Dinny
Willi. Dineley
ffranc^s East
Nathani. Woodward
John Smythe
Edward Rainsfoard
Thomas Wheeler
John Laurence
C. R., Vol. I. p. 195.

May 17, 1637.

Thom. Olney
Thom. Gardner
Joseph Pope
Willi. Bounde
Henry Bartholomewe
Joseph Grafton
ffrancis Skerry
Edmond Marshall
Henry Seawall junior
Henry Bull
Thomas Smythe
Nicolas Holt
Nicolas Noise
Archelaus Woodman
James Browne
John Bartlet
Robert Pike
Thomas Coleman
Mathewe Chafe
George Burden
George Hunn
Willi. Sumner
George Proctor
Thomas Millet
Thomas Dible
Philip Drinker
John Cheney
John Norton
John Syverens
Thom. Wells
John Perkins
Willi. Lampson
Thom. Bircher
Edward Porter
James Howe
Thom. Rogers
John Sharman
John Rogers
Myles Nutte
James Osmer
Rich'd Johnson
Thomas Parker
John Hanchet
John Gibson
C. R., Vol. I. p. 195.

Sep. 7, 1637.

Mr. George Moxam
Mr. Tymo. Dalton
C. R., Vol. I. p. 195.

Nov. 2, 1637.

Nathaniell Wales
Edw^n Sale
Will. Casely
Mr. John ffiske
Mr. John Harvard
C. R., Vol. I. p. 195.

March — 1637–8.

Thom. Spooner
Thomas Venner
James Moulton
James Haynes
Henry Skerry
Joseph Bachiler
John Symonds
John Gedney
Micha: Spencer
John Pearce
Nico. Busbey
Ralph Woodward
Samu. Symonds
Mr. Thom. fflint
Rich'd Griffinn
John Evert
George Haywood
Thom. ffoxe
George Hochens
Edward Rawson
Henry Rust
David ffiske
Willi. Harsye
Willi. Ludkin
Thom. Linkorne
Henry Tuttle
C. R., Vol. I. p. 195.

May 2, 1638.

Samuell Rich'dson
Rob't Cutler
Thomas Rich'dson
Edward Johnson
John Brinsmeade
Isaack Mixer
Henry Kemball
Willi. Nickerson
Henry Dow
Nicho. Byram
Samu. Hackburne
Abraham Howe
John Tatman
Rob't Williams
Humfrey Atherton
Gabriell Meade
Ralph Tomkins
Rich'd Hawes
Alexander Miller
Joseph Wilson

Michaell Willes
John Sill
George Willis
Thomas Swetman
Edward Hall
Mr. William Hubberd
Rich'd Lumkin
Willi. Warrener
Marke Symonds
Thomas Rawlinson
Thomas Carter
Willi. Knight
George Taylor
John Gould
Thomas Cobbet
Daniell Peirce
William Ballard
Willi. Thorne
Abraham Tappin
Henry Lunt
John Browne
Henry Burdsall
C. R., Vol. I. p. 196.

June 9, 1638.

Mr. Natha. Eaton
C. R., Vol. I. p. 196.

Sep. 6, 1638.

The magistrates of Ipswich had order to give Mr. Natha. Rogers the oath of Freedom.
C. R., Vol. I. p. 196.

Sep. 7, 1638.

Thomas Hale
Rich'd Singletery
Steven ffosditch
Nicholas Browne
Zachary ffitche
Thomas Tredwell
Geo. Giddings
C. R., Vol. I. p. 196.

March 13, 1638-9.

Mr. John Allen
Mr. Edward Alleyne
Mr. Ralph Wheelocke
Mr. Willm Tynge
John Leuson
John Frayrye
Eleazer Lussher
John Hunting
Rob't Hinsdall
Edward Kempe
John Dwite
Henry Phillips
Mr. Joseph Peck
Henry Smythe
Edward Gilman
Thomas Cooper
John Beale
Henry Chamberlin
Thomas Clapp
John Palmer
John Tower
Henry Webbe
James Mattucke
John Tuttle
Theophi. Wilson
Jeremy Belcher
Willi. Cockeram
Edward Bates
John Rogers
Christopher Batte
Samuel Neweman
Mr. Robert Peck
Edmond Greenliffe
Thomas Bulkeley
Luke Potter
Ephraim Wheeler
Robert Merriam
James Bennet
John Whiteman
William Palmer
William Eastowe
Thom. Moulton
Rich'd Swayne
Willi. Wakefeild
Thom. Joanes
C. R., Vol. I. p. 196.

March 14, 1638-9.

Nicho. Butler
Mr. Thom. Wills
Mr. Edward Holliock
Mr. Rich'd Sadler
Mr. Edward Howell
Thomas Townesend
Edward Baker
Henry Gaynes
Nicholas Batter
James Boutwell
Rich'd Wells
Willi. Langley
Robert Parsons
Godfrey Armitage
Arthur Geeree
Joseph Pell
Thomas Layton
Willi. Partridge
Roger Shawe
Robert Dannell
Hezechi. Upher
Christopher Cayne
Rob't Steedman
George Keezar
Edward Burcham
Joseph Merriam
Thomas Browne
George ffoule
Willi. Busse
Henry Brooke
Henry ffarewell
Roger Draper
John Miles
Sethe Switzer
Isaack Cole
John Wisewall
John Maudsley
Joseph ffarnworth
William Reed
William Blake
Thomas Dickerman
Thomas Clarke
"Mr. Endicot and Mr. John Winthrope jun. had order to give Mr. Emanuel Downeing the oath of ffreedome."
C. R., Vol. I. p. 196.

22 May, 1639.

Mr. Willi. Sergent
Mr. Thom. Hawkins
Mr. Sam. ffreeman
Thomas Marten
Nichol. Guye
Mr. Samu. Winsley
Steven Dumer
John Osgood
John Gooffe
John Mussellwhit
Steven Kent
John Rimington
Thomas Browne
John Moulton
Hulling
Rich'r Waters
Thomas Ruggles
Joseph Shawe
ffrancis More
Walter Edmonds
Willi. Bowstreete
Hopestill ffostere
Thomas Scotto
Willi. Adams
Thomas Says
John Alderman
Griffin Bowen
John Spooer
Rich'd Hollidge
John Clarke
Giles ffirman
Josua Tedd
Beniamin ffelton

[To be continued.]

ADDITIONAL NOTE ON THE JOSSELYN FAMILY.

An error or misprint, on the 308th page of the Register for July, 1848, requires correction. As it now stands, it makes Rebecca, the daughter of Abraham and Beatrice Josselyn, to have married her third husband in 1780, the date being one hundred and eleven years after her second marriage. The records inform us that Edward Stevens and Rebecca Harris, both of Boston, were married by the Rev. Samuel Willard, on the 8th of October, 1700; and this is doubtless the correct date.

In the article to which this correction pertains, it was proved that Henry Josselyn of Scituate, was the brother of Abraham Josselyn, Jr., and that the latter was the son of Abraham Josselyn, Sen., who was the son of Thomas and Rebecca Josselyn of Hingham and Lancaster. Although no record of the birth of Henry Josselyn had been discovered, it seemed justifiable to conclude that said Henry was the son of Abraham, Sen., and the grandson of Thomas. Since the publication of the article, there has been found on record a deed which fully confirms the foregoing inference. By this deed it appears that on the 19th of Nov., 1695, "Henry Josselin, of Scituate, blacksmith, and wife Abigail, sold to John Langley, of Hingham, innholder, for £5. 10. a lot of fresh meadow, being the 41st lot, 3d division of Conahasset meadow, as it was granted by the inhabitants of Hingham to *Thomas Josselyn his grandfather.*" — *Suffolk Deeds, XVII,* 253. It is believed that sufficient evidence has now been produced to show conclusively that Henry Josselyn of Scituate, was not the son of Henry Josselyn, Esq., of Scarborough.

JOSEPH JOSSELYN of Abington, son of Abraham and Beatrice, settled first at Hingham, where he was married, March 17, 1687, to Hannah, dau. of John Farrow. Their daughter *Mary* was born at Hingham, May 24, 1695.

T. W. H.

NOTICES OF NEW PUBLICATIONS.

Poems. By JOHN G. WHITTIER. Illustrated by H. Billings.

> —— "WAS IT RIGHT,
> While my unnumbered brethren toiled and bled,
> That I should dream away th' entrusted hours
> On rose leaf beds, pampering the coward heart
> With feelings all too delicate for use?" — S. T. COLERIDGE.

Boston: Benjamin B. Mussey & Co. 1849. 8vo. pp. 384.

Such is the title-page of a magnificent volume from the enterprising house of Messrs. MUSSEY & Co. If the author lacked any thing, which is by no means the case, to attract readers of poetry, the defect would be fully supplied by the style in which the publishers have executed their part of the work.

Poets are not very apt to be antiquaries, but we discover in the poems of Mr. Whittier a genuine taste for things time-honored, and we regret that space in our pages does not admit us to sustain our judgment by such extracts as we could wish to make, and such as we may make at some future time.

Who has not read "MOGG MEGONE"? If any can answer "No," we say to such, Go now, Negative, and read it. Should the eye light on the exquisite illustration facing these lines,

"Two forms are now in that chapel dim,
The Jesuit silent and sad and pale,
Anxiously heeding some fearful tale
Which a stranger is telling him"—

resistance would be vanquished; the idle beholder would be compelled to read with interest that beautifully composed tale of the latter days of the Red Men.

The Dudley Genealogies and Family Records. [With a cut of the] Arms of Hon. Thomas Dudley, first Deputy Governor and second Governor of Massachusetts Bay. By DEAN DUDLEY.

"Children's children are the *crown* of old men;
And the glory of children are their fathers."

Boston: Published by the Author. 1848. 8vo. pp. 144.

Besides the genealogy of the Dudley family contained in this volume, there is a large amount concerning numerous other families, among which are those of *Avery, Bailey, Bartlett, Bixby, Bean, Bennoch, Blaisdell, Blanchard, Bradstreet, Buck, Child, Coit, Cotton, Cressy, Dennison, Dodge, Emerson, Emery, Fellows, Folsom, Gilbert, Gould, Greely, Hardie, Harthorn, Hill, Hall, Hilton, Hubbard, Kinsley, Kimball, Ladd, Langdon, Lovell, Lovering, Manwaring, Munford, Miller, Moody, Morrill, Orcutt, Page, Parker, Peabody, Philbrick, Perkins, Perryman, Pilsbury, Richards, Rogers, Rumrill, Saltonstall, Seaver, Sewall, Sidney, Thing, Thurston, Tucker, Treat, Tuffts, Wanton, Webster, Weston, Washburn, Whiting, Williams, Winthrop, Woodbridge, Woodward, Young.*

The work of MR. DUDLEY, though one of great labor and must have cost him much money as well as time, he tells us in his preface, is only an "introduction" to what he intends to do for his name and family. We heartily commend his zeal, and we hope in the end he will find himself amply remunerated for the sacrifices it must cost him. Should he go unrewarded, those he has strived so hard to benefit deserve to go *unremembered.*

A Brief General History of the Welles, or Wells, Family. By ALBERT WELLS. New York. 1848. 8vo. pp. 25.

The "Prefatory Remarks" in MR. WELLS's work being brief, we extract it entire.

"This publication is intended as an introduction to a large work, now and for nearly nine years in progress of compilation—embracing a Genealogical History of about ten thousand of the lineal descendants of THOMAS WELLES, the original emigrant and founder of the family in this country. Those who are connected, are respectfully solicited to communicate whatever information they may possess, including family registers of births, marriages and deaths, to the author, post paid, as it is very desirable to make the collection as complete as possible before publication. A lithographic genealogical tree will accompany the large work, including all the descendants ascertained."

This "introduction" to a history of the WELLS family is good evidence of what the author is able and competent to do, and we hope nothing will prevent his bringing his materials into form in a short time, that those now far advanced in years may have the pleasure of knowing the work has been done before closing their pilgrimage here.

An Address, delivered at the opening of the New Town Hall, Ware, Mass., March 31, 1847. Containing sketches of the early history of that town, and its first settlers. By WILLIAM HYDE. Published at the request of the Town. Brookfield, Ms. Merriam & Cooke, Printers. 1847. 8vo. pp. 56.

The work before us is quite a formidable pamphlet, and to make even a slight synopsis of its contents would exceed our limits. From the cursory glance which we have been able to give to its pages, we are of opinion that it comprehends an excellent history of the town of Ware. Although this town is comparatively of recent date, yet we are told that, as early as 1686, December the 27th, its eastern part was included in a purchase made of the Indian proprietors, "*John Magus*, Lawrence *Nassowanno*, attorneys to *Anogomok*, sachem of the tract of land called Wombemesiscook, *James* and *Simon*, sons and heirs of *Black James*, sachem of the Nipmug [usually *Nipmuck*] country." The price paid was "£20. current money of N. England," and "divers good causes and considerations." The value of what was understood by the latter clause not being very apparent.

For other particulars we must refer the reader to the work itself, *if he can find it.* The author has kindly sent one copy to the Genealogical Society. To that we are indebted for our knowledge of its existence. We ordered some copies from the printers, but it being published by the town, we presume it is not for sale.

Honorable Old Age. A Discourse occasioned by the Centennial Anniversary of Hon. TIMOTHY FARRAR, LL. D. Delivered at Hollis, N. H., July 11th, 1847. By TIMOTHY FARRAR CLARY. Printed by request. Andover: Printed by William H. Wardwell. 1847. 8vo. pp. 28.

The occasion which gave rise to this discourse is, from the nature of it, one which can but rarely occur, and when such an occasion does occur, it is highly gratifying to see it embraced in a manner worthy of it.

To this truly philosophical as well as eloquent discourse, there is appended a notice of JUDGE FARRAR. It would be appropriate for our pages, but as it has appeared elsewhere in print of late, it might be thought superfluous at this time. Therefore we will close our brief notice of the work by a single paragraph from the body of it.

"Look upon the two extremes of such an age, and mark the space between them. What mighty changes has earth undergone! Nations have sprung into being; thrones have crumbled into dust, and the requiem of empires has been sung. Revolution upon Revolution has rolled its mighty billows over the face of the earth. Kingdoms have become desolate, and the wilderness populous with far-spreading tribes of men. What marshalling of forces; what marches and countermarches; what perpetual antagonism; what running to and fro among the busy inhabitants of the earth! In the moral world what changes has so long a period wrought! New institutions have supplanted old. Society has been cast and re-cast, in new and still newer forms. Strong minds and stout hearts have rushed into the field of conflict, where truth was the prize of victory. Error, assuming new and still newer forms, retreating and still retreating, has been driven from successive hiding places, and progress, in every department of life, has marked the lapse of an hundred years."

A History of the County of Westchester, from its first Settlement to the present time. By ROBERT BOLTON, JR., author of the "Guide to New Rochelle," and a member of the N. Y. Historical Society.

"It is the privilege of History to impart the experience of age, without its infirmities; to bring back things long obscured by time, or sinking into oblivion; and enable us to form some reasonable conjectures of what may happen to posterity." — *Poulson's Hist. of Holderness.*

2 Vols. 8vo. New York: Printed by Alexander S. Gould, 144 Nassau st. 1848. pp. 1141.

This work, we are free to confess, has somewhat astonished us. It has, indeed, been long known to us that Mr. Bolton was engaged on such a work, or on a history of that county, but that he was going to eclipse all the works of his (American) predecessors in this department in respect to magnitude, was what we were not prepared to witness.

From some acquaintance with Mr. Bolton, we felt satisfied that if energy and perseverance would accomplish an undertaking, his would not be left undone; and we have now before us two stout thick octavo volumes, profusely set off with numerous appropriate engravings of family arms, views of residences, churches, noted places and maps. But that which will attract the attention of many of our readers in a particular manner is the family pedigrees. In this department of his work the author has taken great pains. He has made long and expensive journeys to examine family papers, converse with old people, and so on. To be brief, Mr. Bolton seems to have followed the English manner of drawing up his work, that is, the manner adopted by the county historians of that country, much further than any of our local historians have hitherto done. His genealogies are chiefly displayed in the legal tabular form, and are folded into his work like maps. Some of the pedigrees thus displayed are of the families of *Cortlandt, Lawrence, Pinckney, Ward, Thomas, De Lancey, Disbrow, Philipse, Quinby, Allaire, Sands, Pell, Jay, Heathcote, Tomkyns, Bartow, Underhill, Leggett, Morris,* and *Strangs.*

It is but very recently that we have had an opportunity to catch even a glance of Mr. Bolton's work, no one having (as yet) served us with a copy, but we have no doubt we shall be favored with one before long, — nor do we know of its being for sale among us.

In index to the work under notice would vastly enhance its value.

The American Almanac and Repository of Useful Knowledge, for the year 1849. Boston: CHARLES C. LITTLE and JAMES BROWN. 1848. 12mo. pp. 370.

Although this most important of American annuals has changed hands (publishers) since its last appearance, it has certainly not lost any thing in value. It is in fact the greatest embodiment of every day matters and things that can well be conceived of. After carefully looking through its index, every one must be surprised at the vast range it comprehends — Fleets, Armies, States, Kingdoms, Cities, Mississippis, Ohios, Ontarios and Eries, all pass in review before us, giving the most satisfactory accounts of themselves.

We wish the publishers could afford to give us a *lee-tle* better paper.

The New Hampshire Annual Register, and United States Calendar, for the year 1849. By G. PARKER LYON. No. XXVIII. Concord: Published by G. P. Lyon. 18mo. pp. 168.

The following important little memorandum Mr. Lyon has included in brackets on his title-page: " The numbering of the Register commenced with 1822, by Dr. John Farmer, who was then engaged as compiler. The first Register published for New Hampshire, was in 1772." There is no other prefatory matter accompanying the work. We are particularly pleased with the appearance of this number, because it is in keeping with its predecessors, especially those on which the name of FARMER appears. It is in every respect a most valuable little manual for not only the inhabitants of the *Granite State*, but for those who have gone from it.

The Massachusetts Quarterly Review. No. V. December, 1848. Boston: Published by Coolidge & Wiley. 8vo. pp. 136.

When this work was announced for publication, very considerable interest was manifested by the reading community. The occasion of the interest thus excited was at the same time fully explained, as it was understood that the REV. THEODORE PARKER was to be a principal contributor to its pages; and with the name of Mr. Parker were given several others, any one of whom alone was a sufficient guarantee that the work would not be wanting in interest. It has now reached the first number of a second volume. The matters discoursed upon in the present number are, I. The Political Destination of America. II. Legality of American Slavery. III. The Law of Evidence. IV. The Works of W. S. Landor. V. A New Theory of the Effects of the Tides. VI. Postal Reform. VII. The Free Soil Movement.

MARRIAGES AND DEATHS.

MARRIAGES.

AMES, MR. FRANKLIN K., of Mansfield, 30 Nov., at S. Scituate, to MISS ABBY A. OTIS of Scituate.

ANDREWS, MR. HENRY G., of Boston, 19 September, at Plymouth, to ELIZABETH BLISS, dau. of the late Hon. Nathaniel M. Davis.

ATHERTON, MR. OTIS, of Newton Lower Falls, 26 Oct., to MISS JANE R. RICE of the same place.

CLAPP, MR. OTIS W., in New York, 20 Nov., to MISS MARION L., only dau. of Hon. George Briggs of New York.

CUTLER, MR. JOHN L., of Farmington, Me., at Augusta, 18 Oct., to MISS ZYLPHIA, dau. of Hon. Ruel Williams.

DRAKE, AMOS G., of Boston, to MISS MARIA S. POTTER of Charlestown, 9 Nov.

FRENCH, HON. BENJAMIN VINTON, of Braintree, 9 Oct., to MISS HARRIET A. SEGAR of Brooklyn, N. Y.. at St. Paul's Church, N. Y.

HINCKLEY, E. R., ESQ., Boston, to MISS FANNIE E. HILL, 9 Nov.

JEWETT, DANIEL T., ESQ., of Bangor, Me., at Roxbury, 1 Dec., to MISS SARAH J., dau. of the late Hon. John Wilson of Belfast, Me.

KELLOGG, ELLIOT G., ESQ., of Burlington, Vt., 7 Nov., to HANNAH B. FOSTER of Roxbury.

KING, REV. THOMAS STARR, pastor of Hollis St. Church, Boston, 17 Dec., to MISS JULIA MARIA, dau. of Noah Wiggin, Esq.

LAWRENCE, T. BIGELOW, of Boston, 5 Dec., to SALLIE, dau. of Robert J. Ward, Esq., of Louisville, Ky., at L.

LEWIS, MR. JOSEPH W., of Philadelphia, to MISS ANNE H. KIDDER of Boston, 9 Nov.

LOMBARD, MR. ISRAEL, JR., of Boston, to MISS SUSAN, dau of Francis Kidder, Esq., of Bristol.

LORING, MR. GEORGE, of Concord, 22 Nov., to MISS ANN D., dau. of the late Rev. Samuel Ripley.

MELCHER, MR. JAMES F., of Exeter, N. H., 31 Aug., to MISS SUSAN L., dau. of the late Samuel Dearborn of North Hampton, N. H.

OTIS, BENJ. F., in St. Louis, 21 Aug., to MISS SARAH K. SWAN of Worcester.

PAIGE, MR. WEST, of Hardwick, 13 Dec.,

to Miss Caroline M. Warner, also of H.

Pike, Wm. F., of Saco, Me., (master of ship Adeline) 19 Oct., at Liverpool, Eng., to Miss Emma Elizabeth Gorsuch of L.

Rice, Mr. Jas. W., of Waltham, at Nashville, N. H., to Miss Maria Farwell, also of Waltham, 26 Oct.

Richardson, Mr. J. Coolidge, of Woburn, 5 Dec., to Miss Mary Myrick of Duxbury, at D.

Robinson, Mr. T. L., of Roxbury, 15 Nov., to Miss H. V. Durfee, dau. of Mr. C. Durfee of Fall River.

Robinson, Mr. Wm. S., editor of the Boston Republican, Salem, 30 Nov., to Miss Harriet J. Hanson of Lowell.

Sawyer, Hon. Thomas E., Dover, N. H., 12 Oct., to Miss Elizabeth Moody.

Sprague, Mr. S. E., of Boston, to Harriet Bordman, dau. of William Lawrence, Esq., 11 Sept.

Stebbins, Mr. Alfred, principal of the High School, Northampton, 27 Nov., to Miss Emily, eldest dau. of Mr. Charles Wheelock, formerly of New York, at Rosedale, N. Y.

Stone, John O., M. D., of New York, 2 Dec., to Miss Catharine, dau. of the late P. T. Jackson, Esq., of Boston.

Turner, Mr. F. A., Boston, 26 Oct., to Miss Ellen H. Frothingham.

Upham, Dr. Jabez B., Boston, 31 Oct., to Miss Catharine Choate, dau. Hon. Joseph Bell.

Wentworth, Mr. Stephen, Milton, 19 Nov., to Miss Susanna Adams.

Winthrop, Wm., Esq., U. S. Consul in Malta, 7 Sept., to Emma, dau. of the late Sir William Curtis, Bart.

Young, Mr. Calvin S., of West Scituate, Oct., to Miss Morgiana A., dau. of Mr. Thomas Bancroft of Boston.

DEATHS

Adams, Mrs. Martha, Boston, 23 Dec. wife of Rev. Nehemiah Adams, D. D.

Albee, Mr. Simeon, Milford, 8 Oct., æ. 88. He was a drummer in the Revolutionary Army.

Barrett, Mrs. Esther, Brookline, N. H., 15 Sept., in her 100th year.

Bartlett, Dr. Ezra, Haverhill, N. H., 6 Dec., æ. 78, the last surviving child of Hon. Josiah Bartlett, one of the signers of the Declaration of Independence.

Bartlett, Mr. Moses, Northampton, 26 Nov. æ. 87.

Bartlett, Mr. George, Roxbury, 25 Dec., æ. 82.

Bigelow, Abijah, Esq., Michigan City, Ind., 28 Oct., æ. 92, a soldier of the Revolution, a native of Waltham.

Bliss, Mrs. Sarah, widow, Springfield, 21 Oct., æ. 89.

Breck, Edward, Esq., China, Me., (formerly of Medfield) 23 Sept., æ. 58.

Bridge, Mr. Samuel, of Dorchester, at Newport, R. I., 8 Oct., æ. 68.

Buel, Mrs. Nancy, widow, Schaghticook, N. Y., formerly of Medford, æ. 74.

Burbeck, General Henry, New London, 2 October, æ. 94. He was born in Boston, June 8th, 1754. Much of the early part of his life was spent in Castle William, now Fort Independence, in Boston harbor, his father being an officer of the ordnance department in the service of Great Britain. He had just attained his majority when the war of Independence broke out. His father promptly took part with the popular cause and entered into the service of the country. He also joined the American army; and his first commission, as a lieutenant in a company of which his father had command, is dated at Cambridge, 19th of May, 1775, and signed by Gen. Joseph Warren. This commission ranks among the earliest in the American service. He received the commission of a captain in a regiment of artillery of the Massachusetts line, 12th September, 1777, and continued in that regiment and line till the close of the war.

In the toils and sufferings of the Revolution General Burbeck bore a full share. In 1775 he was with the army at Cambridge, Mass.; in 1776 he was employed in the vicinity of New York, till the evacuation of the city in September, and in 1777 he joined the army in Pennsylvania under General Washington, and participated in the bloody conflicts of Brandywine and Germantown, and in the terrible deprivations and sufferings of the winter at Valley Forge. The following year he shared the perils of the memorable retreat through New Jersey, and was present at the battle of Monmouth. He continued in active service until the close of the war in 1783, and when the army was disbanded, he returned to private life with the brevet rank of major.

Three years subsequently he again entered the service of his country, with the rank of captain, and was for several years actively engaged in the Indian wars along the Western frontier, under General Anthony Wayne. His death has left Gen. Solomon Van Rensselaer the only surviving officer of Wayne's army. Four years he held the command of Fort Mackinaw, then a solitary post almost entirely cut off from communication with the civilized world. In the war with Great Britain, which commenced in 1812, he commanded at New

York, Newport, New London and Greenbush, with the rank of brigadier general; and on the declaration of peace in 1815, retired from public service to spend the evening of his days in the tranquillity of domestic life; having spent 38 years almost incessantly in active military service. It was at that time that he fixed his abode in this city, of which he continued a resident till his death.

Gen. Burbeck was one of the original members of the society of Cincinnati, and was the last survivor of those whose names were first subscribed to the articles of association. At the time of his decease he was president of the Cincinnati of Massachusetts.— *New London Chronicle.*

He retained his faculties in a wonderful degree. In an interview with him a few months before his death, we found him reading a newspaper with apparent ease. His recollections of Boston before the Revolution, as then related, were exceedingly interesting. He located with seeming accuracy the houses all along what is now Tremont street, gave the names of their occupants, &c.

Carpenter, Mr. Jona. N., at Montpelier, Vt., 19 Oct.

Champion, Mr. Reuben, Lyme, Ct., 10 Dec., æ. 92, a soldier of the Revolution.

Clagett, Miss Emma, at Roxbury, 20 Oct., dau. of the late Hon. Clifton Clagett of Amherst, N. H.

Cleveland, G. W., Esq., of Salem, at Pontotoe, Miss., 20 Sept., of congestion of brain. H. C. 1832.

Clark, Mrs. Betsy, Plymouth, 22 Sept., æ. 92.

Clarke, Mrs. Esther, Salem, 25 Sept., æ. 90, widow of the late Rev. John Clarke, D. D., of Boston.

Coffin, C. Parker, Boston, 25 Oct., æ. 15 mos., son of N. W. Coffin, Esq., of B.

Collins, Mr. Joseph, Gardiner, Me., 6 Dec., æ. 89, a soldier of the Revolution.

Cook, Mr. Sylvanus, Windham, Me., 22 Nov., æ. 74, formerly of Kingston, Ms.

Dean, Mrs. Abigail, Woburn, 13 Sept., æ. 67.

Dearborn, Mrs. Mary, North Hampton, N. H., 7 Nov., æ. 68, wife of Mr. Simeon Dearborn.

Dickinson, Mr. Samuel N., at his residence in Roxbury, 16 Dec., of consumption. Mr. Dickinson is probably known as widely as the typographic art in this country. He was a man of remarkable order, fine taste, great energy, and under his hands arose one of the best arranged job and book printing establishments in the land. At a recent period he added to his business of printing that of type founding and stereotyping. It was his untiring application to business that planted the disease of which he died. He gave himself no respite, not from a passion for amassing, but from a natural impulse to do every thing well. He made himself useful, enjoyed the high satisfaction of honoring a noble art, and will long be remembered. His Almanac, the favorite year-book of Boston, was edited to the last by himself. He indeed took special pains with the last number, and had just finished it, with all his accustomed accuracy, when he died. His age was 47 years.— *Chronotype.*

Dodge, Mr. Abraham, Newburyport, 12 Oct., æ. 85, a Revolutionary pensioner.

Durgin, Lieut. John, Sanbornton, N. H., 21 Oct., æ. 92, a Revolutionary pensioner.

Eddy, Mrs. Abby A., E. Middleboro', 28 Oct., æ. 55, wife of Nathaniel Eddy, Esq.

Felt, Capt. John, New Orleans, 8 Sept., æ. 34, a native of Boston.

Foster, John, Esq., S. Scituate, 16 Sept., æ. 80.

Fuller, Mary Ann, Boston, 17 Nov., æ. 40, dau. of the late Seth Fuller.

Gay, Rev. Samuel, Hubbardston, 16 Oct., suddenly, æ. 63. H. C. class of 1805.

Hale, Hon. William, Dover, N. H., 9 Nov., æ. 84, formerly M. C.

Hancock, Allen, Esq., Dudley, 11 Oct., æ. 94.

Hartwell, Mr. George H., of Cincinnati, O., at Albany, N. Y., suddenly, 9 Sept., æ. 39, a native of New England.

Herrick, Mr. John, Brighton, 21 Oct., æ. 39, son of the late John H.

Hewitt, Mr. Thomas, Taunton, 25 Oct., æ. 92, a soldier of the Revolution.

Hollis, Mrs. Pamela, in Charlestown, 20 Oct., æ. 76.

Hollister, Mr. Joseph, Salisbury, Ct., 30 Sept., æ. 96, a soldier of the Revolution.

Hooper, Mrs. Ellen, wife of Dr. R. W. Hooper of Boston, and dau. of Wm. Sturgis, 3 Nov.

Ingraham, Joseph, Esq., East Thomaston, Me., 23 Oct., æ. 90.

Jordan, Mrs. Hannah, widow, Monroe, Me., 27 Sept., æ. 90.

Lawrence, William, Esq., Boston, 15 Oct., æ. 65, brother of Hon. Abbot Lawrence.

Le Mercier, Mrs. Mary Sigourney, Boston, 5 Dec., æ. 90, widow of the late Pierre Le M. of St. Malo, France.

Lunt, Mrs. Emily Ashton, at the residence of Mr. J. L. Tucker of W. Cambridge, 19 Nov., æ. 23, wife of Hon. Geo. Lunt of Boston.

Lyman, Deacon Solomon, Easthampton, 15 Oct., æ. 85.

Mack, Mrs. Harriet E., Salem, wife of Elisha M., Esq., 21 Nov., æ. 56, last surviving child of the late Rev. John Clarke, D. D., of the first church in Boston.

Mallard, Mr. Thomas, Warwick, 30 Sept., æ. 88, a soldier of the Revolution.

MASON, HON. JEREMIAH, Boston, 14 Oct., æ. 80, formerly of Portsmouth, N. H.

MAYHEW, MRS. ROAMA, at Edgarton, 15 Nov., æ. 53.

MAYHEW, MRS. MARY MAGDALEN, Edgarton, 22 Sept., æ. 79, widow of Mr. Matthew Mayhew.

MAYHEW, MRS. PARNELL, Edgarton, 26 Oct., æ. 23, widow of the late Deacon Wm. M.

MEANS, CAPT. THOMAS, Etna, Me., 9 Oct., æ. 94 yrs. 3 mos., a soldier of the Revolution, and also of the last war with Great Britain.

MONROE, MRS. RUTH L., Charlestown, 21 Dec., æ. 35, wife of Mr. George M., dau. of Mr. Bickford Pulsifer of Ipswich, and sister of Mr. David Pulsifer of Boston.

OTIS, HON. HARRISON GRAY, Boston, 28 Oct., æ. 84. He was son of Samuel Allyne Otis of Barnstable, by Elizabeth, dau. of Hon. Harrison Gray, and the 6th in descent from the first American progenitor. See *Genealogical Register*, Vol. II. p. 292, &c. Mr. Otis was an early member of the N. E. Hist. Gen. Soc., and one of its considerable benefactors.

PARKER, MRS. EDITH, Jaffrey, N. H., 26 Oct. æ. 96 yrs. 9 mos., widow of the late Hon. Abel Parker.

PATCH, CAPT. JOSEPH, Hamilton, 17 Oct., æ. 86, a soldier of the Revolution.

PAYSON, MRS. ANN LOUISA, Williamston, 17 Nov., æ. 64, widow of the late Edward Payson, D. D. of Portland, at the residence of her son-in-law, Prof. Hopkins.

PERKINS, MRS. LUCY, Kennebunkport, 23 Sept., æ. 89 yrs. 9 mos.

PHELPS, ABEL, Esq., Watertown, 27 Sept., æ. 47.

PHILBRICK, MRS. RUTH, widow, Epsom, N. H., 22 Oct., æ. 92.

PIERCE, JOSHUA V., Boston, 10 Dec., æ. 39, consumption.

PLAISTED, MR. ROGER, Buxton, Me., 9 Oct., æ. 94, a Revolutionary pensioner.

POOR, DR. SYLVANUS, Andover, Me., 1 Nov., æ. 80.

PRINCE, JOHN, Esq., Salem, 22 Sept., æ. 66, eldest son of the late Dr. Prince, and a grad. H. C. 1800.

PUTNAM, REV. ISRAEL A., N. Danvers, 31 Oct., æ. 27, son of Hon. Elias Putnam.

ROGERS, MR. W. E. P., Haverhill, 16 Nov., formerly editor of the Gazette of that town.

SILSBEE, FRANCIS H., Esq., Salem, æ. 37, a graduate of H. C. in the class of 1831.

SIMONDS, MRS. MARY B., Boston, wife of Artemas S., Esq., æ. 54.

SMITH, MRS. LUCY, Ipswich, 6 Oct., æ. 94, relict of the late Aaron Smith.

SMITH, MR. NATHAN, Waltham, 8 Oct., æ. 91, the oldest male inhabitant of that town.

SNELLING, MR. WM. J., late editor of the Boston Herald, suddenly, at his residence in Chelsea, 24 Dec., æ. 44. He was son of the late Col. S., a distinguished officer in the last war with England. The deceased was author of several works, poetry as well as prose. His "Truth" will live as long as the "Dunciad," compared to which the latter is a tame performance. Thus much must be said of it, but of the *truth* of "Truth" we have nothing at this time to say. His "Tales of the North West" contain the best descriptions of Indian life any where to be found. Mr. S. commenced writing in 1828, and from that time his pen has been constantly employed, chiefly for the newspapers.

Within four hours after the death of Mr. Snelling, his father-in-law, Mr. Simon Jordan, (with whom Mr. S. lived,) fell from his chair and suddenly expired also.

STEARNS, MRS. ABIGAIL, North Andover, 16 Sept., æ. 85.

STONE, MR. CHARLES, Cincinnati, 31 Oct., æ. 92, a native of Stockbridge.

STRONG, H. WRIGHT, Esq., Troy, N. Y., 7 Oct., æ. 80, formerly of Amherst.

TABER, MRS. MARTHA, Newport, R. I., 17 Sept., in her 105th year.

TE-HO-RA-GWA-NE-GEN, a distinguished Indian chief, (usually called *Thomas Williams*,) 16 Sept., in his 90th year. The Montreal papers contain the following obituary, near which place (Cah-no-wa-ga, C. E.) he resided:

"He was a distinguished chief of the Iroquois nation, and descended from the Rev. John Williams of Deerfield, Mass., who, with his family and parishioners, were taken captives at the sacking of his native town, by the French and Indians, in the year 1704. The deceased was an active participant in the scenes of the Revolution, espousing the cause of the British at Bennington and Saratoga. During the war of 1812, by special invitation of the United States government, he placed himself under the protection of its flag, and was present at the battle of Plattsburgh. He had for many years maintained the tenets of the Christian faith, and died as he had lived, respected and beloved by his people, and in the full hope of a blissful immortality." —*Boston Daily Journal, of* 17 *Oct.*, 1848.

TYLER, REV. EDWARD R., New Haven, 28 Sept., æ. 46. Mr. Tyler was the able conductor of the New Englander.

WHITING, MR. OLIVER J., New Orleans, 12 Nov., æ. 31, formerly of Charlestown.

WILLARD, SAMUEL SHEAFE, Cambridge, 18 Oct., æ. 67, son of the late President Willard.

WILSON, MRS. MARY S., Keene, N. H., 5 Oct., æ. 50, wife of Hon. James Wilson.

YOUNG, MR. JAMES, Fayette, Me., 27 Sept., æ. 89, a Revolutionary pensioner.

OFFICERS OF THE SOCIETY FOR THE YEAR 1849.

Charles Ewer, Esq., *President.*
Lemuel Shattuck, Esq., *Vice President.*
Samuel G. Drake, A. M., *Corresponding Secretary.*
Rev. Samuel H. Reddel, *Recording Secretary.*
William H. Montague, *Treasurer.*

DONATIONS TO THE SOCIETY.

Since the issue of our last number of the Register, (in October last,) many valuable manuscript communications have been received, all, or nearly all, suitable for the pages of the work; which when used, will be accompanied by the names of the contributors. The names of those who have contributed printed works, &c., for the Library of the Society, are as follows:

Frederick S. Pease, Esq., Albany, N. Y.,
Rev. William Hyde, Brookfield,
Prof. Edward North, Clinton, N. Y.,
Hon. Edward Everett, Cambridge,
J. Wingate Thornton, Esq., Roxbury and Boston,
Caleb Bates, Esq., Hingham,
William H. Montague, Esq., Boston,
E. G. Ware, "
Horatio Hammond, "
William Allyne, "
Col. Samuel Andrews, "
William F. Stone, Esq., E. Cambridge,
James Odiorne, Esq., Boston,
James B. Thornton, Esq., Saco, Me.,
John Marsh, Esq., Quincy.

Regular meetings of the Society, the first Wednesday in every month, during the winter at 7 in the evening; during the summer, 3½ P. M. Rooms of the Society No. 8 Massachusetts Block, Court Square.

☞ Valuable additional information has been received for the Breck genealogy, but it will for the present be deferred in the hope of receiving other facts in the early generations of it.

☞ The present number has been delayed a few days in consequence of not receiving the portrait which accompanies it; more time having been required to do it justice than the engraver at first anticipated. This our subscribers will cheerfully bear with, we doubt not, being assured that the artist has given a better finish to his work than he was under obligation to do.

☞ Mr. Ward desires it to be understood that he has discontinued his list of Hingham Settlers, in consequence of information that a new edition of the history of that town is in preparation, and will embrace his design.

Benjamin Colman

NEW ENGLAND

HISTORICAL AND GENEALOGICAL REGISTER.

VOL. III. APRIL, 1849. NO. II.

MEMOIR OF REV. BENJAMIN COLMAN, D. D.

BENJAMIN COLMAN, the second son of William and Elizabeth Colman, was born in Boston, Oct. 19, 1673. His father, "who came from London not long before,"* was the son of Matthew and Grace Colman, of Satterly, near Beccles, in the County of Suffolk, and was baptized there Aug. 31, 1643.

The subject of this notice is said to have been "of a tender constitution from his birth, and very backward in his speech and reading 'till he arrived to the age of five years, when at once he grew forward in both, and entred young and small into the Grammar School under the tuition of the venerable and learned Mr. Ezekiel Cheever."† Although but seven years of age when he became

* Perhaps he and his wife, Elizabeth, may be the persons whose names are given as "—— Cooleman" and "Eliza Coleman," in "A List of the Names of the Passengers on board the Ship Arabella, Richard Sprague Master, for New England, May y[e] 27th, 1671," which is printed in the New England Historical and Genealogical Register, II. 407. The first notice, with which we have as yet met, of William and Elizabeth Colman, in Boston, is the record of the birth of their daughter Mary, Dec. 3, 1671.

† It is not our intention, even had we the ability, to give, at this time, a biographical sketch of the renowned "Corderius Americanus," whose praises have come down to our day. "He was born," says Cotton Mather, "in London, many years before the birth of New England. It was Jan. 25, 1614 [i. e. 1614–15.] He arrived into this country in June, 1637, with the rest of those good men, who sought a peaceable secession in an American wilderness, for the pure, evangelical, and instituted worship of our great Redeemer, to which he kept a strict adherence all his days. He then sojourned first, a little while, part of a year, at Boston; so that at Boston he both commenced and concluded his American race." He accompanied Eaton to New Haven, and his name stands prominent among the one hundred and eleven who subscribed the "Plantation Covenant," June 4, 1639. Here "he began the laborious work of a School-master," occasionally, too, officiating as a Preacher, and devoting some portion of his time to the public service. And here "he continued for twelve years," and then removed to Ipswich, Mass., where he taught the "Grammar School" from Dec. 30, 1650, to November, 1660, and then removed to Charlestown, "where he labored nine years. From Charlestown he came over to Boston, Jan. 6, 1670, [i. e. 1670–1] where his labors continued for eight and thirty years," as Master of the Public Grammar School. He died on Saturday morning, Aug. 21, (Dorchester Church Records say Aug. 23,) 1708, "after he had been a skilful, painful, faithful School-master for seventy years; and had the singular favor of Heaven, that, though he had usefully

connected with "the Grammar School," "his sprightly genius and advances in learning were soon with pleasure observed by his Preceptor," and "fired with a laudable ambition of excelling at his book, and a fear of being out-done, he always, by his industry at home, kept foremost, or equal to the best of the Form at school."

Although he met with a severe loss in the death of his intimate companion and only rival, Prout, inasmuch as he was thereby left "without a spur to daily care and labor," yet still young Colman made such progress in his studies that he was qualified for admission to Harvard College in the year 1688. Remarkable for his serious deportment, even in childhood, "after his admission into College," says his biographer, "he grew in piety and learning, and in favor with God and man." He became a member of the Second Church in Boston, at that time under the pastoral care of Increase and Cotton Mather. As a student he disgraced not his former master, in whose praise it has been said, "it was noted, that when scholars came to be admitted into the College, they who came from the *Cheeverian education* were generally the most unexceptionable." Performing "all his exercises to good acceptance, many of them had the applauses of his learned Tutor, Mr. John Leverett.* He was much animated to the study of the liberal sciences, and to make the utmost improvement in them, from the shining example

spent his life among children, yet he was not become twice a child, but held his abilities, with his usefulness, in an unusual degree, to the very last.

His work he lov'd: O had we done the same!
Our play-days still to him ungrateful came.
And yet, so well our work adjusted lay,
We came to work as if we came to play.
Our lads had been, but for his wond'rous cares,
Boys of my Lady *More's* unquiet pray'rs.
Sure, were it not for such informing schools,
Our Lat'ran too would soon be fill'd with owls.
'Tis *Corlet's* pains, and *Cheever's*, we must own,
That thou, New-England, art not Scythia grown.
The Isles of Silly had o'er run this day
The Continent of our America."

* Afterwards, for sixteen years, President of the Institution at which he was now performing the duties of a Tutor. He was the son of Hudson Leverett, grandson of Governor John Leverett, and great-grandson of Elder Thomas Leverett, and was born in Boston, Aug. 25, 1662. Having received his early education at the Public Grammar School, mostly under the instruction of Ezekiel Cheever, he proceeded Bachelor of Arts at Harvard College in 1680, and Master in due course, received the Degree of Bachelor of Theology in 1692, and was a Tutor and Fellow of the Institution. He was chosen a member of the House of Representatives, and then Speaker of that body. He was a member of his Majesty's Council for the Province, and sustained the offices of a Justice of the Superior Court, and Judge of Probate. Having been chosen to succeed Vice-President Willard as the head of the "School of the Prophets," he was inducted into office, Jan. 14, 1707–8, in which station he continued, "a pillar both of the Church and State, an honor and ornament to society, and the glory of New England," until his sudden death, May 3, 1724. He was one of the very few on this side of the Atlantic who have become Fellows of the Royal Society of England.

of the excellent Pemberton,* who was a year before him in standing."

Receiving the Degree of Bachelor of Arts in 1692, Colman, "being devoted to the work of the evangelical ministry by his Parents, and inclining to it from his childhood," immediately entered upon the study of Divinity, and began to preach, "first privately and then publicly," the next year. For several months he was engaged in preaching at Medford, where there was no settled Minister, and the inhabitants of the Town seem to have been very desirous to have retained him as their Pastor. But, for some reason or other, Colman did not see fit to accept their invitations to a settlement, and returned to Cambridge, where he remained, pursuing his studies, until he received his Second Degree, that of Master of Arts, in 1695;† on which occasion he pronounced the usual Oration, "when," says his biographer, "his thin and slender appearance, his soft and delicate voice, and the red spots in his cheeks, caused the audience in general to conclude him bordering on a Consumption, and to be designed but for a few weeks of life."

About this time young Colman was sent, at the expense of the Second Church in Boston, to Newport, R. I., to preach one Sabbath. He succeeded in accomplishing the object of his mission, notwithstanding the manœuvres of some of the inhabitants, and was much praised, on his return to Boston, for the prudence which he had displayed on this occasion.

* Ebenezer Pemberton, the son of James Pemberton, one of the founders of the Old South Church, was baptized Feb. 11, 1671; graduated at Harvard College in 1691, where he was afterwards a Tutor; was ordained colleague with Rev. Samuel Willard, Pastor of the Old South, Aug. 28, 1700; preached his last sermon, Jan. 20, 1716–17; died Feb. 13, 1716–17, and was buried, on the 18th of the same month, "between 4 and 5, in Mr. Willard's tomb." "He was," says a cotemporary, "of a strong genius, extensive learning, a preacher of raised thoughts, and a masculine style, of flaming zeal in the cause of God and religion, violent in his passions, and as soft as you would wish for out of them, a good Christian, and a faithful pastor." Colman, in one and the same discourse, paid a deserved tribute to the memory of his old friend, as well as to that of Rev. William Brattle, of Cambridge, who died two days after Pemberton, Feb. 15, 1716–17, aged 55 years, "respected as a man, a scholar, and a Divine."

† We have been unable to find the "Order of Performances" for this Commencement, but here give a copy of the

"QUÆSTIONES *Quas pro modulo* DISCUTIENDAS Sub Clarissimo VIRO, D. CRESCENTIO MATHERO, Academiæ HARVARDINÆ, quæ est CANTABRIGIÆ Nov-Anglorum, PRAESIDE Literatissimo; Die Comitiorum Proponunt Inceptores in ARTIBUS. *Die Tertio Quintilis* [i. e. July 3,] MDCXCV.

An Detur in non-Renatis Liberum Arbitrium ad bonum Spirituale?
Negat Respondens BENJAMIN COLMAN.

An Sola Fides, quatenus apprehendit Christi Merita. et Illis innititur, Justificet?
Affirmat Respondens EBENEZER WHITE.

An Gentes ex Naturæ Lumine Salutem possint Consequi?
Negat Respondens JOHANNES MORS.

An Pontifex Romanus sit Ille Antichristus, Quem futurum Scriptura prædixit?
Affirmat Respondens CALEB CUSHING."

"Having a strong desire to see England, and make improvement by what he could see and learn there," Colman, in less than three weeks after he had proceeded Master of Arts, embarked for London, in the Ship Swan, Captain Thomas Gilbert, Master. A war at this time raged between England and France; and before they had been two months at sea, the Swan was chased by a French Privateer, of superior force, and after a shot conflict, during which she was reduced to a wreck, was obliged to surrender. When the boats of the enemy approached the captured vessel, Colman had in his hands a piece of gold, of the value of nineteen pounds. This was seen by "an ingenious French Gentlewoman," named Madam Allaire, who, with her four children, to whom Colman had endeared himself during the voyage, was on her way to join her husband at London. She requested him "to let her save it for him," to which he consented. The prisoners being transferred to the deck of the Privateer, were there stripped of everything, even to their last garment, and were then covered with a few rags, and thrust into the hold. Arrived at Nantz, they were there committed to prison. Here Madam Allaire* sent to Colman his gold, and his first care, upon the receipt thereof, was to clothe himself "from head to foot," at an expense of about three pounds and ten shillings. After various adventures Colman was at length set at liberty, and succeeded in reaching Portsmouth, with but a few shillings in his pocket, of which he was soon relieved by "a young spark from New York," whom he imprudently assisted with money, on a promise of being repaid by "a rich uncle he had, half way to London." But upon arriving at the house of this "rich uncle," "no credit would he give to this his nephew; he knew him too well, he said;" and notwithstanding Colman's representations that he had "saved him from the expences of Portsmouth," he was obliged to remain satisfied with a night's lodging, a loan of twenty shillings, and a horse and guide to London the next morning.

Arrived in London without money, without friends, and having lost all his letters of introduction, his first night in the vast metrop-

* "May 12, 1734, this Gentlewoman paid a visit to Boston, from St. Christopher's, and was received by Mr. Colman with a surprising joy, after so melancholy a parting thirty-eight years before; and after mutual expressions of the most sincere joy, she gave him a large and particular account of her sufferings in France, and deliverance from them, after a wonderful trial of constancy and experience of Divine support and assistance in times of need, till she arrived safely in Holland, which Mr. Colman penned down, and left among his papers; — a most entertaining history." Colman continued to correspond with his former benefactress until his death; after which there was found in his Study a letter from her, dated at London, May, 1747, "wrote with her own hand, in the French tongue," although she was then upwards of eighty years of age.

olis could not have been otherwise than, as his biographer tells us, "melancholy." "With difficulty he found out the house of a reverend Minister, but he could not be seen; it grew dark, and he prayed Madam to direct him to some sober house where he might lodge that night." The next morning he succeeded in finding Mr. Ives, upon whom his brother, John Colman,* "a young man and beginning the world," had given him a bill of exchange for thirty pounds Sterling; and by him was kindly received. Mrs. Ives found him good lodgings, and also a nurse to attend him during a dangerous fever, with which he was soon visited. "Dr. Moreton visited him, and God healed him," writes his biographer. The Rev. Mr. Quick, of London, "a very affectionate gentleman," with whom he had become acquainted, visited him frequently during his illness. "Before he got abroad he was surprised with an invitation from Mr. and Madam Parkhurst, in Cheapside, to accept of half a year's board at their house. This happy lodging at one of the most known and frequented booksellers among the Dissenters, brought him soon into an acquaintance with the City Ministers, which was a singular advantage and pleasure."

"The family attended the ministry of the reverend and learned Mr. How,† and Mr. Colman with them." This circumstance introduced Colman to Mr. How's pulpit; where his performance was so satisfactory, that Mr. How proposed to him to go over to Rotterdam, in Holland, at the expense of his Church, to preach as candidate for the situation of colleague with "the reverend, aged, and learned Mr. Joseph Hill,"‡ whose kinsman and former assistant in the ministry, the Rev. Mr. Spademan, had recently received and accepted an invitation from Mr. How's Church to be his assistant and successor in the pastoral office. Colman expressed his satisfaction with the offer, and accepted Mr. How's invitation; but Mr. Hill himself calling upon him not long after, and expressing his great unwillingness to part with Mr. Spademan, and his sense of injury at Mr. How's proceedings, Colman promised not to go to Rotterdam without his consent. This delicate consideration for Mr. Hill's feelings, although it gave offence to Mr. How, and caused

* Colman's elder brother, born, doubtless, in England, as we find no record of his birth in Boston.

† Probably Rev. John Howe, a Nonconformist Divine, born at Loughborough, in the County of Leicester, in 1630. He was ejected from his ministry at Torrington, Devonshire, in 1662. He subsequently settled in London, where he died in 1705.

‡ Also one of the "Ejected Ministers." He was born at Leeds, in 1624, and educated at St. John's College, Cambridge, and Magdalen, of which he became a fellow. Going over to Holland at the Restoration, he was, in 1667, Pastor of the English Church at Middleburg, and at last settled at Rotterdam, where he died in 1707.

a temporary coolness on his part towards the young Bostonian, established Colman's reputation for integrity and high moral principle.

Scenes of new and varied interest were now continually opening to Colman. He heard Dr. Bates* make one of his finest speeches to King William, at Kensington, upon the discovery of the Assassination Plot. Being invited to preach for Rev. Daniel Williams,† who had gone to Bath, "for the benefit of the waters," he thereby became acquainted with his colleague, Dr. Calamy,‡ who expressed his wish that they might "spend their lives in one Church." At Whitehall he conversed with Dr. Bray.§ He enjoyed the privilege of listening to the conference between How, Bates, Williams, Mather,|| and others, for the reconciliation of the Congregationalists and Presbyterians, and after the meeting had the pleasure of dining with these gentlemen. He saw Dr. Annesley,¶ now drawing toward the end of his mortal pilgrimage; and also Mr. Beverly, "a good man," who "had, in print, fixed on the year 1697 for the accomplishment of all the great *Expectanda*, the fall of Antichrist, &c.," and who, "when his year came, and produced nothing extraordinary, did, in the most humble and public manner, confess his error and presumption, asking pardon of God and his people." Sir Henry Ashurst, at this time Agent for the New England Colonies, took him to his country-seat, near Oxford. Here he became acquainted with Dr. Hall, Bishop of Bristol, "a venerable, humble, grave, Divine"; Dr. Hough,** Bishop of Oxford, and Master of

* Rev. William Bates, D. D., another Ejected Minister, was educated at Emanuel and King's Colleges, Cambridge. He died at Hackney, Middlesex County, where he had spent the last years of his life, in the year 1699, aged 73.

† Afterwards Dr. Williams; a native of Wrexham, in Denbighshire. He was created D. D., by the Universities of Glasgow and Edinburgh, in 1709, and died Jan. 26, 1716, aged 72.

‡ Edmund Calamy, the distinguished author of the History of the Ejected Ministers. He was born April 5, 1671, and, after a life of honorable usefulness, died June 3, 1732.

§ Rev. Thomas Bray, D. D., the best part of whose life was spent as a Commissary for settling the affairs of the Church in the American Colonies; in several parts of which he established Libraries for the information and improvement of the missionaries employed in preaching the Gospel. In this work he sacrificed his whole fortune; and it is to his exertions that many of the Societies established in London for the propagation of the Gospel, and the advancement of religious culture, owe their existence. He died Feb. 15, 1730, aged 73.

|| Rev. Nathaniel Mather, the son of our Richard Mather, (born March 20, 1630.) was at this time Pastor of a Congregational Church in London, where he died July 26, 1697, aged 67. A Latin inscription upon his tombstone, in the burying-ground near Bunhill Fields, from the pen of Dr. Watts, commemorates his genius, learning, piety, and ministerial fidelity.

¶ Rev. Samuel Annesley, LL. D., an Ejected Minister. He died Dec. 31, 1696, aged 77.

** John Hough, celebrated for his opposition, when President of Magdalen College, Oxford, to the arbitrary proceedings of James II. He was born in 1650; and having held, successively, the Sees of Oxford, Lichfield, and Worcester, and having once declined, through modesty, the Primacy, which was offered to him at the death of Tenison, he died March 8, 1743, in his 93d year.

Magdalen College, "a bright and lofty gentleman, polite in dress and behavior"; and Dr. Gastrell,* afterwards Bishop of Chester, who "did him the honor to shew him the several Colleges, and what was rare and curious in them."

Colman was called from Oxfordshire by an invitation from the Presbyterian Board at London, to take charge of a small congregation at Cambridge. Accepting the invitation, he found his hearers few in number, and "sadly tinged with Antinomian principles, and his texts were too legal for them." "They liked illiterate preachers," and whenever an opportunity occurred, would leave him to hear some noisy declaimer. "So he was ashamed of his post, and wrote earnestly to London to be released from it," and left at the end of twelve weeks.

He soon received an invitation to "the great Town of Ipswich, in Suffolk," where he spent eleven weeks. Here he became acquainted with "the venerable" Mr. Burkit,† of Dedham, where Colman preached "every other Lord's Day almost, and the people spake of calling him to be their Minister; but there happened at this time to pass by an itinerant, powerful, illiterate preacher, who had been a taylor, and he 'cut Mr. Colman out of the whole cloth,' and left him but three votes."

Soon after his return to London, the Presbyterian Board appointed him to succeed the Rev. Christopher Taylor, at Bath. This was regarded as a very advantageous and important situation, on account of the annual resort of the gentry thither, to enjoy the benefit of the mineral waters. He was assured that "it was the best stirrup in England, whereby to mount the best pulpits that might be vacant," and was promised that, "if he would serve the Dissenting interest there a few years, they would get him settled at London." To Bath, then, he went, and there spent two years, "and found good acceptance with the people and with the strangers there. Before he had lived among them two months he became acquainted with more families of fashion in London than he had done by living there two years."

It was at this time that he became acquainted with Miss Eliza-

* Francis Gastrell, born at Slapton, Northamptonshire, about 1662, and educated at Christ-Church, Oxford, as distinguished for his eloquence, as for his writings in defence of the Christian religion. In 1711 he was Chaplain to Queen Anne, and in 1714 was raised to the See of Chester. He died Nov. 24, 1725, and was buried in Oxford Cathedral.

† Rev. William Burkitt, probably, who was born July 25, 1650, and educated at Cambridge; and, first as Curate of Milden, in Suffolk, and afterwards as Vicar of Dedham, in Essex, is said to have "adorned his office by a pious and practical elocution, and by a friendly and charitable demeanor."

beth Singer, the daughter of Mr. Walter Singer, of Agford, near Frome, then celebrated under the name of "Philomela," and afterwards as Mrs. Rowe;* and the acquaintance soon ripened into the closest intimacy. Indeed, Mr. Singer seems to have wished and expected a still nearer relation than that of elevated friendship and esteem, between his daughter and the young Dissenter.†

But Colman's visit in England was now drawing to a close. The comparative liberality and moderation in religious views which had succeeded the accession of William and Mary to the throne of England, when Nonconformity was partially rescued from the opprobrium which had so long attached to it, had extended itself to New England, to Massachusetts, the head-quarters of Puritanism, the strong-hold of "the good old Scriptural ways." A few enlightened men in Boston and its vicinity, men distinguished alike for learning and piety, determined to establish a Church, constituted on principles deviating from those set forth in the "Platform of Church Discipline," and more in accordance with their own enlarged and catholic views. By a deed dated Jan. 10, 1698, "in consideration of the sum of two hundred and fifty pounds," and "for other good causes and considerations thereunto moving" him, THOMAS BRATTLE‡ con-

* This Lady was born at Ilchester, Sept. 11, 1674, and early in life displayed a poetical genius. Universally respected and esteemed for her talents and virtues, she had many suitors, among them the poet Prior. In 1710 she gave her hand to Mr. Thomas Rowe, a gentleman of literary attainments, with whom she lived happily until his death, which occurred, after a lingering illness, in May, 1715. After the death of her husband Mrs. Rowe lived in retirement, at Frome, devoting herself to literary pursuits. She ever carried on a correspondence with Mr. Colman. Her death took place on the 20th of February, 1736–7. Colman thus records her character. "She was an Heavenly maid, of sublime devotion and piety, as well as ingenuity and wit; her wisdom and discretion outshone her knowledge. She was a poet, a philosopher, and a Divine; and, above all, a most devout worshipper of God, in secret and in public. Music, poetry, and painting were her three beauties and delights. She used her pencil almost as well as her pen. She never was idle, but either her needle or her pencil was going in all conversations; and what she drew she gave to the company."

† Upon his first visit to Mr. Singer, in company with Rev. Timothy Rogers, after the beauties of the surrounding grounds and the favorite bower and walks of his daughter had been pointed out by the fond and doting father, Colman was requested by Mr. Rogers "to make a compliment on the place"; and Mr. Singer joining in the request, he penned the following lines.

"So Paradise was bright'ned, so 'twas blest,
When Innocence and Beauty it possest.
Such was it's more retired path and seat,
For Eve and musing Angels a retreat.
Such Eden's streams, and banks, and tow'ring groves;
Such Eve herself, and such her muse and loves.
Only there wants an Adam on the green,
Or else all Paradise might here be seen."

‡ An opulent merchant, brother to Rev. William Brattle, of Cambridge. He was born Sept. 5, 1657, graduated, with *two others*, at Harvard College in 1676, and was Treasurer of that Institution from 1688 till his death, May 18, 1713. He was distinguished among his cotemporaries for his intellectual powers and scientific attainments; "a great ornament," writes Judge Sewall, "to our College, on account of his eminent learning, especially in the mathematics."

veyed to twenty persons,* associated with himself, a piece of land, in Boston, called BRATTLE'S CLOSE; and upon this land did they lay the foundations of a house for Public Worship — completed in the autumn of the following year — now known as "THE CHURCH IN BRATTLE SQUARE."

The first care of the associates was to obtain a Pastor, and their eyes were at once turned to BENJAMIN COLMAN, their fellow townsman, a graduate at the neighboring College, the chosen friend of Leverett, of Brattle, and of Pemberton, one whom many of them knew personally, and all by reputation. To him, then, did they send letters,† in the Summer of 1699, informing him "that they had chosen him to be their Minister, and urging him to make what haste he could to them." This invitation was "very acceptable and pleasing" to Colman, "for his heart was always very much in his native country"; and he himself says of it, in his Church Records, "the more acceptable it was by reason of the kind and encouraging letters, which accompanied it, from my excellent friends, the Hon. Mr. John Leverett, the Rev. William Brattle, Ebenezer Pemberton, Simon Bradstreet,‡ and others." "I believe, Sir," writes Leverett, "you have as advantageous a prospect as any our country can offer. The Gentlemen engaged in that affair are able, vigorous, and sincere; they are men of honor, and can't, in an ordinary way, fail a reasonable expectation. The work they have begun had its rise from a zeal that is not common, and the progress of it is orderly and steady. I am heartily pleased," he adds, "with the motion they have made towards yourself, because I shall exceedingly rejoice at your return into your country. We want persons of your character. You will, I doubt not, let the name of your country have a weight in the balance of your consideration. The affair

* Thomas Clark, John Mico, Thomas Bannister, Thomas Cooper, Benjamin Walker, Benjamin Davis, Timothy Clark, Stephen Minot, William Keen, Richard Draper, William Harris, Abraham Blush, Zechariah Tuthill, Thomas Palmer, John Colman, James Meers, Joseph Allen, Elkanah Pembroke, John Kilby, and Addington Davenport.

† Subscribed by Thomas Brattle, Benjamin Davis, John Mico, Thomas Cooper, and John Colman, "in the name of the rest."

‡ A son of the Rev. Simon Bradstreet, of New London, Conn., and grandson of Simon Bradstreet, Governor of Massachusetts. He graduated at Harvard College in 1693, and succeeded Colman at Medford, where, however, he did not remain long, but removed to Charlestown, where he was ordained, as successor to Rev. Charles Morton, Oct. 26, 1698. After a ministry of more than forty years, he died Dec. 31, 1741. He is represented as having been "a most learned man," and so accomplished a Greek scholar, that he was introduced by Lieutenant-Governor Tailer to Governor Burnet with the words, "Here is a man who can *whistle* Greek." He was possessed of "strong mind, tenacious memory, lively imagination, but subject to hypochondriac complaints, which made him afraid to preach in the pulpit some years before he died. Governor Burnet spoke of him as one of the first literary characters and best preachers he had met with in these American regions."

offered to you is great, and of great moment; I pray Almighty God to be your director in it."

"This waits on you with my desires and hopes," writes Brattle,* "that your circumstances will allow you to entertain and accept the invitation. The good respect the Boston Ministers have for you (as well as others) should, methinks, encourage your embracing the motion now made to you. As for my own part, I shall account it a smile from Heaven upon the good design of these Gentlemen, if you can send them an answer of peace, and would hope that your so doing will result to your mutual rejoicing. May God direct you in the matter!"

"With this you will receive a kind invitation," thus writes the ardent Pemberton, "to return to your own country, which you cannot but have a great tenderness for, and your affection will, I trust, constrain you to comply, and hope it will not be to your disadvantage. The Gentlemen who solicit your return are mostly known to you, men of repute and figure, from whom you may expect generous treatment; and among them I doubt not but you may be peculiarly serviceable to the Lord Jesus Christ, which is the highest of your ambition. I believe your return will be pleasing to all that know you; I am sure it will be inexpressibly so to your unfeigned friend and servant."

His friends, apprehending difficulty in obtaining ordination for him at home, in consequence of the prevailing prejudices against the new Church among the Clergy, had advised Colman to "ask ordination at London." Accordingly, having taken leave of his people at Bath, by heading a subscription "to pay a debt of fifty pounds, which they yet owed for their Meeting-house," he repaired to London, where, "being arrived," to use his own language, "August 1, 1699, I asked ordination of the Presbytery there, and on the 4th day of said month the solemnity was attended, after a Public Lecture, at the Meeting-house of the Rev. Mr. Christopher Taylor, to whom I succeeded at Bath. I was ordained by prayer, with the imposition of the hands of the Rev. Richard Stratton,† John Spade-

* William Brattle, the son of Thomas Brattle, was born in Boston, in 1662, and graduated at Harvard College in 1680, was a Tutor and Fellow of that Institution, and its Treasurer from 1713 to 1715. He and his classmate Leverett were honored with the Degrees of Bachelor in Theology at the Commencement in 1692, at which time Increase Mather, also, received the Degree of Doctor in Divinity, this being the first instance of either Degree being conferred by the Corporation of Harvard College. Brattle was ordained pastor of the Church at Cambridge, as successor to Rev. Nathaniel Gookin, Nov. 25, 1696, and died, after a ministry of twenty years, Feb. 15, 1717.

† "An aged and eminent Pastor in the City, much reverenced and honored for his learning, gravity, piety, and wisdom."

man,* Robert Fleming,† and Christopher Taylor. Mr. Stratton prayed, Mr. Spademan made the exhortation." "The Rev. and aged Mr. John Quick," the same of whom mention has been already made, and who subsequently writes to Colman, "no one in England loves you more, or wishes you better," happened to be out of Town at this time, and was "highly displeased that he was not sent for out of the country, *that he might have done him some more public honors at the ordination.*"

In London Colman again found a hospitable welcome at the house of Mr. Parkhurst. His brother John, who, as we have already seen, was one of the committee of the proprietors of the Church which invited his return to New England, having transmitted to him an unlimited order upon Sir James Eaton for such moneys as he should require, he drew twenty pounds, which he expended in the purchase of books. Having received "ample testimonials of his good conversation while in England,"‡ he embarked at Gravesend, about the 20th of August, 1699, and after a fortnight's delay in the Downs, and an eight weeks' voyage, arrived at Boston on the 1st of November, "where he was received by his relations, acquaintance, and the brethren who sent for him, with a great deal of love and joy unfeigned, after an absence of four years and three months." The next day the "Undertakers," as they style themselves, of the new Church presented him with fifty pounds, and soon after they kept a day of Thanksgiving, in private, for his safe arrival, Colman preaching on the occasion from 1 Chron. xxix. 13, 14.

Notwithstanding the general character and station in society of the "Undertakers" of the new Church, some of them, indeed, being men in public office, their innovations upon the old established forms of Church Government and Public Worship exposed them to much jealousy and opposition on the part of the neighboring Churches, which still adhered to the "Platform"; and they found it necessary, "for preventing all misapprehensions and jealousies,"

* The same whose successor Colman was invited to become at Rotterdam. He had come over to England, and was now settled in London. He was "a very judicious and learned man, and so was Mr. Taylor," mentioned below, Colman's predecessor at Bath.

† Son of Rev. Robert Fleming, an Ejected Minister, who was, for some years before his death, Minister of the Scots' Congregation at Rotterdam. This his son was educated at Leyden and Utrecht, and having been settled in the Ministry, successively, at Leyden and Amsterdam, removed, finally, to London, where he was at this time Pastor of a Scotch Church, and was, subsequently, it is believed, "Principal of one of the Colleges in Scotland."

‡ From "Rev. Dr. Daniel Williams, John Quick, Matthew Sylvester, John Shower, Timothy Rogers, Edmund Calamy, Thomas Cotton, Isaac Mauditt, &c. &c."

to make a formal exposition of their views "to all the world," in a paper entitled "A Manifesto or Declaration, set forth by the Undertakers of the New Church now erected in Boston in New England, Nov. 17th, 1699." In this instrument, while they declare that they "approve and subscribe the Confession of Faith put forth by the Assembly of Divines at Westminster"; that they "design only the true and pure worship of God, according to the rules appearing plainly in his word"; they say that they "judge it, therefore, most suitable and convenient that, in Public Worship, some part of the Holy Scripture be read by the Minister, at his discretion." They declare, moreover, that it is their "sincere desire and intention to hold communion with the Churches here, as true Churches, and openly protest against all suspicion and jealousy to the contrary, as most injurious to" them; "and although," say they, "in some circumstances we may vary from many of them, yet we jointly profess to maintain such order and rules of discipline as may preserve, as far as in us lies, evangelical purity and holiness in our communion. In pursuance whereof we further declare, that we allow of baptism to those only who profess their faith in Christ and obedience to him, and to the children of such; yet we dare not refuse it to any child offered to us by any professed Christian, upon his engagement to see it educated, if God give life and ability, in the Christian religion. But this being a ministerial act, we think it the Pastor's province to receive such professions and engagements. We judge it, therefore, fitting and expedient, that whoever would be admitted to partake with us in the Holy Sacrament be accountable to the Pastor, to whom it belongs to inquire into their knowledge and spiritual state, and to require the renewal of their baptismal covenant. But we assume not to ourselves," they continue, "to impose upon any a public relation of their experiences; however, if any one think himself bound in conscience to make such a relation, let him do it. For we conceive it sufficient if the Pastor publicly declare himself satisfied in the person offered to our communion, and seasonably propound him. Finally, we cannot confine the right of choosing a Minister to the communicants alone; but we think that every baptized adult person, who contributes to the maintenance, should have a vote in electing." In conclusion, "these are the principles we profess, and the rules we purpose, through the grace of God, to govern ourselves by; and in some of these particulars, only, and in no other, do we see cause to depart from what is ordinarily professed and practiced by the Churches of Christ here in New England."

Notwithstanding the peaceful spirit which pervades this "Declaration," and the noble sentiments of Christian charity and toleration of which it is an avowal, its effect upon the public mind was, by no means, adequate to its merits; it did not remove the prejudices of those who were fain to imagine that the whole scheme savored strongly of Presbyterianism, nor of those who, on the other hand, apprehended it to be little better than Episcopacy; the Church was, in contempt, called "*the Manifesto Church*"; and its leaders were stigmatized by the Mathers and their adherents as "innovators," "a company of headstrong men, full of malignity to the holy ways of the Churches," "ignorant, arrogant, obstinate, and full of malice and slander," who had published, "under the title of a *Manifesto*, certain articles that utterly subvert the Churches," filling "the land with lies," and inviting "an ill party, through all the country, to throw all into confusion on the first opportunities."

Regardless, alike, of the frowns of their opponents, and the doubts of the wavering, the associates pursued their course, conscious of the purity of their intentions, and certain of the "gracious smiles of Divine Providence on this their undertaking"; and on Tuesday, the 12th of December, at a private meeting, fourteen brethren,* "after solemn calling upon God, declared their consent and agreement to walk together in all the ordinances of our Lord Jesus Christ." On the 20th of the same month the Proprietors voted "that the Psalms in our Public Worship be sung *without reading line by line.*"

On the 24th of December was opened for Public Worship, for the first time, their "pleasant new-built house," when Mr. Colman preached from 2 Chron. vi. 18. *But will God in very deed dwell with men on the earth? Behold, Heaven and the Heaven of Heavens cannot contain thee; how much less this house which I have built!* "I omit on purpose," he writes, under this date, "the differences and troubles we had with any neighbors about our proceedings; only am obliged to leave this acknowledgment of our great obligation to the Hon. William Stoughton, Esq.,† Lieutenant-Governor

* Thomas Brattle, Thomas Clark, Thomas Cooper, Benjamin Walker, Benjamin Davis, William Keen, Richard Draper, William Harris, Zechariah Tuthill, John Colman, Joseph Allen, John Kilby, of the "Undertakers," with John Noyes and Oliver Noyes.

† This eminent man was the son of Col. Israel Stoughton, whose name is familiar to many, as the Commander-in-chief of the Colonial forces in the Pequot War, and afterwards a Lieutenant-Colonel in the Parliamentary Army, in England. He was born in Dorchester in 1631; graduated at Harvard College in 1650; and after pursuing his Theo-

of the Province, the Rev. Mr. William Brattle, of Cambridge, the Rev. Mr. Clark,* of Chelmsford, and Mr. Danforth,† of Dorchester, for their good and kind endeavors for our peaceable settlement."

Meanwhile, although firmly resolved to adhere to the principles and rules laid down in their "Manifesto," the Pastor and brethren

logical studies in this country, went to England, and enjoyed a Fellowship at New College, Oxford, where he also received the Degree of Master of Arts. During his stay in England, he preached with great acceptance in the County of Sussex; but being among those who were ejected from their livings after the Restoration, he returned to New England, and here acquired a high reputation as a preacher; and his Sermon at the Annual Election, April 29, 1668, was pronounced by a cotemporary to be "among the very best delivered on that occasion." Declining all invitations to a settlement as Pastor of any Church, he turned his attention to public affairs, and was, in 1671, chosen an Assistant, which office he held, by annual reëlection, until the dissolution of the government in 1686. On the 30th of October, 1676, he, with Peter Bulkley, sailed for England, in obedience to the requisitions of King Charles, to answer the numerous complaints against the Colony. The agents, after a tedious attendance in England, arrived at Boston again, Dec. 23, 1679. Next followed, in 1685, the revocation of the Charter. On the 12th of May, 1686, Stoughton was elected Governor, but, inasmuch as Dudley was "left out, from complaisance to him, refused to serve." Three days after arrived a Commission from King James, appointing Dudley President, and Stoughton Deputy-President, of the Colony. On the 26th of July, Stoughton was placed at the head of the Courts in the Colony, an office which he held until the arrival of Andros, Dec. 20, 1686, when he became a member of Sir Edmund's Council, and one of the Justices of the Superior Court, Dudley being Chief-Justice. His name stands at the head of those who, on the 18th of April, 1689, requested Andros to "forthwith deliver up the government and fortifications," in order to prevent the effusion of blood; and he was one of the self-constituted "Council of Safety," which assumed the government until the people should have an opportunity of acting on the subject. But he was admitted to no participation in the subsequent administration, until the arrival of the Charter of William and Mary, in May, 1692, under which he was appointed Lieutenant-Governor, an office which he sustained until his death. He was appointed by the Council, Dec. 22, 1692, Chief-Justice of the Superior Court, and this office, also, was held by him until just before his death, which occurred on the 7th of July, 1701, at Dorchester, where he was buried on the 15th of the month, "with great honor and solemnity, and with him much of New England's glory"; and where a monumental inscription perpetuates the remembrance of his public services and his private virtues. He was "a person of eminent qualifications, honorable extract, liberal education, and singular piety"; but his fair fame is obscured by his criminal participation in the melancholy witchcraft delusion, he being the Chief-Justice of the special tribunal constituted for the trial of the unhappy victims of popular infatuation. His name, however, will long be held in affectionate remembrance as a generous and liberal benefactor of Harvard College.

* Rev. Thomas Clarke, son of Elder Jonas Clarke, of Cambridge, by his second wife, Elizabeth, whom he married July 30, 1650, was born March 2, 1653, graduated at Harvard College in 1670, was ordained Minister of the First Church in Chelmsford, as successor to Rev. John Fiske, in 1678, and died Dec. 7, 1704. His death is thus noticed by Chief-Justice Sewall. "1704. Dec. 7th. Mr. Clark of Chelmsford dies of a Fever; was taken very suddenly the Friday before, after he had been at a Funeral: buried the 11th." The Dorchester Church Records contain the following, under date of Dec. 10, 1704:—"Rev. Mr. Thomas Clarke's death, of Chelmsford, lamented in a Sermon on Acts xx. 25, &c."; and a cotemporary writes of him that he was "a great loss to all our towns, and especially to our frontiers on that side of the country, who are greatly weakened with the loss of such a worthy man."

† Rev. John Danforth, son of Rev. Samuel Danforth, of Roxbury, was born Nov. 8, (or 5,) 1660, graduated at Harvard College in 1677, and was afterwards a Fellow of that Institution, was ordained Pastor of the First Church in Dorchester, as successor to Rev. Josiah Flint, June 28, 1682, and continued in the ministry till his death, May 26, 1730. In Blake's Annals is the following notice of him. "He was said to be a man of great learning; he understood the Mathematics beyond most men of his function. He was exceeding charitable, and of a very peaceful temper. He took much pains to eternize the names of many of the good Christians of his own flock; and yet the world is so ungrateful that he has not a line written to preserve his memory, no, not so much as upon his tomb, he being buried in Lt. Govr. Stoughton's tomb, that was covered with writing before; and there, also, lyeth his Consort, Mrs. Elizabeth Danforth."

of the "New Church" were, nevertheless, disposed to do all in their power to conciliate the "neighbor Churches"; and they accordingly sent letters to them, desiring their aid and countenance on the 31st of the next month, when they had determined to keep a day of fasting and prayer "for public imploring the presence of God, his pardon and blessing." To this request Rev. James Allen* and the Mathers† returned answer, that they could not take part in the exercises on that occasion, "lest," say they, "our joining with you in such an action be interpreted as an approbation of the miscarriages, which, both before and since the publication of the *Manifesto*, it seems to us that you are fallen into."

But it soon became apparent that the violent party, at the head of which stood the Mathers, would not be sustained in their crusade against the "innovators," as they were pleased to style the adherents of the "Manifesto Church." It was seen that, as might have been expected, persecution was followed by its usual result, the increased strength and zeal of the persecuted; and an anxiety was soon manifested that the storm of theological controversy might be hushed. At this juncture Lieutenant-Governor Stoughton and Chief-Justice Sewall‡ united with the Rev. Messrs. Willard,§ Clark,

* Rev. James Allen, an Ejected Minister and Fellow of New College, Oxford, came to New England in 1662 or 3, and was installed Teacher of the First Church in Boston, Dec. 9, 1668, Rev. John Davenport being at the same time installed Pastor. After a ministry of forty-two years, he died Sept. 22, 1710, aged 78. John Dunton, in his Life and Errors, says:—"I went to visit the Reverend Mr. Allen. He is very humble and very rich, and can be generous enough, when the humor is upon him. His son was an eminent minister here in England, and deceased at Northampton." The historian of the First Church thus writes concerning him. "He was equally moderate and lenient in his concessions to others, on the score of individual freedom, as he was strenuous for the enjoyment of his own rights. He was willing to render to Cæsar all proper tribute; but he was unwilling that Cæsar, in the capacity of civil magistrate, should interfere in holy things. He was equally desirous of shielding the Church against the power of the Clergy, as against that of the civil ruler." He "enjoyed a long, virtuous, and happy life of seventy-eight years, forty-six of which he had been a member, and forty-two a vigilant ruler and instructer, of the Church. His wealth gave him the power, which he used, as a good Bishop, to be hospitable."

† Of the Mathers, father and son, nothing need be said. Their names, their lives, their works, whether good or evil, are familiar to every one. There always have been, probably there ever will be, as many different estimates of their characters and motives, as there are different phases of the human mind.

‡ For an account of this eminent man, and of his family, the reader is referred to the First Volume of the Register, pp. 105—13.

§ Rev. Samuel Willard, son of Major Simon Willard, a gentleman highly distinguished both in military and civil life, and one of the principal settlers of Concord, was born at Concord, Jan. 31, 1640, graduated at Harvard College in 1659, and was subsequently a Fellow of the Institution. He was ordained the First Minister at Groton, July 13, 1664, where he continued until the breaking up of the Town and the dispersion of his flock by the Indians, in March, 1676, when he removed to Boston, and, on the 10th of April, 1678, (N. S.) was settled as colleague with Rev. Thomas Thatcher, the first Pastor of the Old South Church. In 1700 Rev. Ebenezer Pemberton was ordained his colleague. On the 6th of September, 1701, Mr. Willard took upon himself the superintendence of Harvard College, as successor to Rev. Increase Mather, with the title of Vice-President, still retaining his connection with his Church in Boston. He continued to sustain this two-fold relation, with popularity and success, until Aug. 14, 1707, when he resigned his office as

and Danforth, to pour oil upon the troubled waters, to effect a reconciliation which they all so much desired. Chief-Justice Sewall has left us a record of the steps which were taken to accomplish the desired object.

head of the College, as appears from the following entry in the Diary of Chief-Justice Sewall. "Monday, Aug. 11, 1707. Mr. Willard goes to Cambridge to expound, but finds few scholars come together, and, moreover, was himself taken ill there, which obliged him to come from thence before Prayer-time. Tuesday, August 12, between 6 and 7, I visited Mr. Willard, to see how his journey and labor at the College had agreed with him, and he surprised me with the above account; told me of a great pain in his head and sickness at his stomach, and that he believed he was near his end. I mentioned the business of the College. He desired me to do his message by word of mouth, which I did Thursday following, to the Governor and Council. Quickly after I left Mr. Willard, he fell very sick, and had three sore convulsion fits, to our great sorrow and amazement. Thursday, Aug. 14. When the Governor enquired after Mr. Willard, I acquainted the Governor and Council that Mr. Willard was not capable of doing the College work another year; he thanked them for their acceptance of his service, and reward. Governor and Council ordered Mr. Winthrop and Brown to visit the Revd. Mr. Willard, and thank him for his good service the six years past. Sent down for concurrence, and Deputies to name persons to join in their thanks and condolence. Deputies concur, and nominate the Revd. Mr. Nehemiah Hobart to officiate in the mean time, till October next. This the Governor and Council did not accept, and so nothing was done."

"Sept. 12. Mehetabel Thurston tells me Mr. Willard was taken very sick. I hoped it might go off, and went to dinner. When I came there Mr. Pemberton was at prayer, near concluding. A pretty many in the chamber. After prayer many went out. I staid and sat down; and, in a few minutes, saw *my dear Pastor* expire. It was a little after 2, just about two hours from his being taken. There was a doleful cry in the house." Rev. Dr. Joseph Sewall's Diary furnishes the following additional particulars. "1707, Sept. 12. The Rev. Mr. Willard, after he had cut his finger, while eating oysters, went up to his study, called his wife, thanked her for her kindness, prayed God to bless them all; then fell into a convulsion, about noon, which, in two hours time (plus minus) despatched him, to the great grief and sorrow of all good men." — "Sept. 15. Mr. Willard is buried. The members of the College, the Corporation, &c., go before the corpse. We all have gloves. A vast body of spectators. He is laid in our tomb." Mr. Willard was, in disposition, quiet, unpretending, and retiring. "He is well furnished with learning," says Dunton, in his account of his visit to Boston, "has a natural fluency of speech, and can say what he pleases." Says Dr. Barnard, in his "Sketch of Eminent Ministers in New England, "he was an hard student, of great learning for that day, of a clear head, solid judgment, excellent both in preaching and in prayer, an exemplary Christian, pleasant in conversation, whose works praise him." In the words of the historian of the Old South Church, "his powers of mind were of a superior order. He had a copious fancy, and a quick and accurate perception; and in argument was profound and clear. His piety was consistent, devoted, self-denying, and confiding. His learning was extensive and solid, especially in Theology, which was his favorite study, and for his proficiency in which he was greatly celebrated. 'His style was masculine, not perplexed, but easy as well as strong.' His delivery was characterised by 'gravity, courage, zeal, and prudence; and, when the matter required it, no man could speak with greater pathos and pungency. He knew how to be a son of thunder to the secure and hardened, and a son of consolation to the contrite and broken in spirit.' As a Pastor he was distinguished for 'prudence, faithfulness, and impartiality. All his talents and acquisitions were consecrated' to the service of Christ, and over the whole, it is said, was shed the lustre of a 'remarkable and unaffected modesty,' and a 'spirit truly pacific.'" The position which Willard maintained throughout the witchcraft delusion is, in the highest degree, honorable to his heart and mind; and Thomas Brattle, the uncompromising denouncer of the prominent men and measures of the time, bears ample testimony to his prudence, firmness, and courage; "whose good affection to his country, in general," says he, in his "Full and Candid Account of the Delusion called Witchcraft," printed in Mass. Hist. Coll. V., "and spiritual relation to three of the Judges, [Stoughton, the Chief-Justice, and Samuel Sewall and Wait Still Winthrop, two of the Associate Justices, of the special tribunal, were members of Willard's church] in particular, has made him very solicitous and industrious in this matter; and I am fully persuaded that, had his notions and proposals been hearkened to and followed, when these troubles were in their birth, in an ordinary way, they would never have grown unto that height which now they have. He has, as yet, met with little but unkindness, abuse, and reproach from many men; [according to Robert Calef, on a certain occasion "one of the accusers cried out publicly of Mr. Willard, as afflicting of her"!]

"1699–1700. Jan. 24. The Lieutenant-Governor calls me," thus he writes, "with him, to Mr. Willard's, where, out of two papers, Mr. William Brattle drew up a third, for an accommodation, to bring on an agreement between the New Church and our Ministers. *Mr. Colman got his brethren to subscribe it.*"

"Jan. 25. Mr. I. Mather, Mr. C. Mather, Mr. Willard, Mr. Wadsworth,* and S. S. wait on the Lieutenant-Governor, at Mr. Cooper's, to confer about the writing drawn up the Evening before. *Was some heat*, but grew calmer, and, after Lecture, *agreed to be present at the Fast, which is to be observed Jan. 31st.*"

On Wednesday, then, the 31st of January, was kept the appointed day of fasting and prayer; and Allen and the Mathers were compelled so far to smother their resentments, as to take part in the exercises on the occasion, although they had expressly refused so to do, when invited, a month previous. Says Chief-Justice Sewall, to whom we are again indebted for a record of the proceedings: —

"1700. Jan. 31. Fast at the New Church.

A. M. Mr. Colman reads the writing agreed on. Mr. Allen prays. Mr. Colman preaches, prays, [and] blesses.

P. M. Mr. Willard prays. Mr. I. Mather preaches. Mr. Cotton Mather prays. Sing the 67 Psalm *without reading*. Mr. Brattle sets Oxford Tune. Mr. Mather gives the blessing.

His text was, 'Follow peace with all men, and holiness;' doctrine, — must follow peace *so far as it consists with holiness.* Heb. XII. 14. Mr. Colman's text was, Rom. XV. 29, 'And I am sure

but I trust," he adds, "that, in after times, his wisdom and service will find a more universal acknowledgment; and if not, his reward is with the Lord." Mr. Willard's published works were very numerous. The largest of them, the first folio volume of Divinity printed in this country, was published in 1726, under the title of "A Complete Body of Divinity."

* Rev. Benjamin Wadsworth was born at Milton, in 1669, being the son of Capt. Samuel Wadsworth, who was slain by the Indians, Sept. 18, 1676. In 1690 he graduated at Harvard College, of which he was subsequently a Fellow. On the 8th of September, 1696, he was ordained colleague to Rev. James Allen, of the First Church in Boston; where he continued until his election as the successor of President Leverett, in June, 1725. His inauguration took place on Commencement Day, July 7, 1725. His death, which occurred on the 16th of March, 1737, "was lamented with more than ordinary demonstrations of sorrow." "Of good learning, most pious, humble, and prudent, an excellent, plain, pathetical preacher," his powers of mind "were rather strong than brilliant, and his manners rather grave than animated. His memory was uncommonly retentive; though he wrote his sermons with care, he always delivered them *memoriter*. As a preacher he was perspicuous and solemn; as a Pastor, watchful and exemplary; and as a Christian, so liberal and exact in his charities, as to give to the poor a tenth part of his income." Inferior to his predecessor, Leverett, as well in dignity of deportment, as in versatility and brilliancy of talent, he was, nevertheless, respected and beloved as the head of the College. Fifty-six years of age when he accepted, with the greatest reluctance, the Presidency, "his health began to fail soon after he entered upon its duties, which were performed to general acceptance, under all the disadvantages of bodily infirmity. His conduct in their discharge was marked by firmness, prudence, and judgment. Faithful to every trust, kind to all, calm, cautious, moderate, self-possessed, and affectionate, he left a name precious to his own, and appreciated highly by after, times."

that, when I come unto you, I shall come in the fulness of the blessing of the Gospel of Christ.'

[Principal Ministers, "many Scholars," the Lieutenant-Governor, and Council, present.]

Mr. Willard prayed God to pardon all the frailties and follies of Ministers and people; *and that they might give that respect to the other Churches due to them, though not just of their constitution.*

Mr. Mather in his Sermon, and Mr. Cotton in his prayer, to the same purpose. Mr. Willard and C. Mather prayed excellently and pathetically *for Mr. Colman and his flock.* 'Twas a close, dark day."

[To be continued.]

WILL OF BRIAN PENDLETON.

[For the copy of this most interesting document we are indebted to LIEUT. A. W. WHIPPLE, of Washington, D. C.]

Portsm°. 9th August 1677. I Brian Pendleton sometime of Saco in ye County of York, now resident in Portsm°. on Pascataq. River in N. E. doe make & ordain this to be my last Will & Testament hereby revokeing all former wills by mee made.

1°. I give to my beloved wife Eleanor Pendleton (besides wt. I have reserved for her in a deed of Gift to my Gran-child Pendleton Fletcher) all my Household Goods together with all that piece of land belonging to mee lying between my son James's & Mr Deerings upon the Great Island wh. I have excepted & reserved out of my Deed of Gift of all

2°. to my son James. Furthermore I give to my wife all my huseing & Land at Cape-Porpus wh. Richd Palmer's wife hath the [defaced] dureing her Life, together with my Sixe Hundred & forty Acres of Land more or lesse lying on ye East side of Westbrook near Saco Ffalls wch I bought of Jno West & Majr Wm Philips as ye Deeds will appear, as also Timber Island at ye Little River, All wh. I give to my wife absolutely to bee at her disposeall.

2.°—Unto my Gran-child James Pendleton Junr. I give my Hundred Acres of Upland & ten Acres of meadow wch I bought of Jno. Bush & lies within ye Township of Cape-Porpus, adjoining to Prince's Rock.

3°.—All my Houseing & Land at Wells, wth all ye Priveledges & Appurtenances I give unto my two Grand-children Mary & Hannah Pendleton wch my son had by his fformr wife, to bee equally divided between ym.

4°.—I give to my wife all my wearing Clothes to be diposed of as shee shall see meet, desiring her to [remembr some poor.*]

5°.—Finally I make my wife my Executrixe & joyn my beloved son James Pendleton executr together with his Mother, willing my Executrixe to disburse what is needed for my Funerall Charge & my Executor to pay

* The original at this place is so obliterated that I doubt the correctness of the words enclosed, though I can make nothing else of the text.

all my debts. And I request Mr Joshua Moodey & Mr Richd Martyn to bee overseers to this my last Will & Testam^t^.

In witnes to all & Singular ye p^r^misses I have set to my hand & seale this 9th August 1677.

Witnesses BRIAN PENDLETON. (Seal.)
Joshua Moodey
Ann Moodey

As a schedule to this my last will & Testament I give unto my beloved son James Pendleton all my land on the East of Westbrook butting on the great river of Saco six Hundred Acres more or less. My [house & lands lying?] at Cape-Porpus in all Three Hundred Acres in the occupation of Richard Palmer, all my severall Islands in or near s^d^ Cape-Porpus the one half of my stook of Cattle of what sort soever upon my farm at Winter Harbour found after mine & my wives decease with all my wearing apparell & one third of my House hold goods, except my utensels of Husbandry.

& Unto Mary & Hannah Pendleton, daughters of my s^d^ son James all my lands in Wells being three plantations or lotts, bought of Mr Fletcher Hamond & were improved by Joseph Cross. & to each of them one third part of my household goods after mine and My wives decease. It^m^. to Brian Pendleton my Grandson the remainder of my land on Great Island Piscataq. what is contayned herein is addition to My will any thing in s^d^ will notwithstanding.

This Schedule was Signed & Sealed BRIAN PENDLETON. (Seal.)
in presence of us
Joseph Dudley
Joshua Moodey

Joshua Moodey made oath y^t^ ye writeing on ye other side was signed & sealed by Maj^r^ Brian Pendleton & declared by him to bee his last will & Testament & y^t^ Mr Joseph Dudley did write & sign a witnes to the schedule annexed at ye foot of ye foreg^g^ Page.

* * * this 5th day Ap^l^. 1681
Before us
John [Wincoll?]
T * * S * * *
[Charles?] Frost
} Justices of Peace

This will within *** *** *** written ** attest above *** *** *** *** *** *** *** *** for M^r^ *** ***
23. Ap^l^ 1681. p^r^ Ed. Rishworth.

DANIEL GOOKIN.

[The following scraps are worthy of preservation, as relating to that "right good man," Major-General Daniel Gookin, of whom some account has been given in a previous number of the Register.*]

"Daniel Gookin, the last Major-General of the colony, was a stern, Puritan, republican. He was not only ready 'to serve his renowned Highness in the Lord,' but was an efficient friend and protector to his associates, Whalley and Goffe, the Regicides. After an absence of about three years in England, a portion of which was probably passed in 'his Highness' ser-

* See his letter to Secretary Thurloe, Vol. I. p. 350, of the Register.

vice,' he 'returned back,' a fellow passenger with Colonel Whalley and Colonel Goffe, in the ship ——, Pierce, commander, and arrived at Boston from London, on the 27th of July, 1660,* and on the same day they went to Cambridge, the place of residence of their chosen friend, Gookin, and there resided until the next February, when, finding themselves unsafe there from the vengeance of Charles II., aided by their friends they escaped to Connecticut. They were men of singular abilities, and had moved in an exalted sphere. Whalley had been a Lieutenant-General, and Goffe a Major-General in Cromwell's army. Their manners were elegant, and their appearance grave and dignified, commanding universal respect. Governor Endicott, and gentlemen of character in Boston and its vicinity, treated them with peculiar kindness and respect. They attempted no disguise, and publicly appeared at meetings on the Lord's day, and at occasional lectures, fasts, and thanksgivings, and were admitted to the sacrament and attended private meetings for devotion, visited many of the principal towns, and were frequently at Boston.†

The king's commissioners, who were Colonel Nichols, Cartwright, Carr, and Maverick, in their narrative about New England, 1667, speaking of these Judges, say, among other accusations, 'Colonels Whalley and Goffe were entertained by the magistrates with great solemnity, and feasted in every place, after they were told they were traitors, and ought to be apprehended. They made their abode at Cambridge, until they were furnished with horses and a guide, and sent away to New Haven for their more security. Captain Daniel Gookin is reported to have brought over and to manage their estates; and the commissioners being informed that he had many cattle at his farm in the king's province, which were supposed to be Whalley's or Goffe's, caused them to be seized for his majesty's use, till further order, but *Capt. Gookin, standing upon the privilege of their Charter, and refusing to answer before the commissioners, so that there was no more done about it.* Captain Pierce, who transported Whalley and Goffe into New England, may probably say something to their estate.'‡ The position taken by Gookin as represented by the commissioners, and the tone of his 'remonstrance' in 1680, thirteen years afterwards, render it hardly probable that *he* ever attempted or wished to vindicate his conduct in this matter."

The following vote shows the location of General Gookin's estate:—

"Billerica, 19. 9^{m}. 1661. At a Towne Meeting, The towne do grant to ffrances Wyman & John Wyman that parcell of land that lyeth betweene Woburne line & the former that they purchased of Mr. Dunster, which is by estimation four score acres, more or less and is bounded on the South or South East with Captaine Gookins farme line.

Attest Jonathan Danforth, C."

"Those Bookish Gentlemen & Ladies, who contributed so much to my well being and with whom I spent some of the *most agreeable minutes* of my whole life, those noble friends that I would here characterize are, Christopher Usher, Esq., Major Dudley, Major Gookins, and others," in America.—*John Dunton's Life and Errors*, p. 355.

* This date corresponds with that given by Gookin in his *Historical Collections*, where he incidentally remarks that he "returned back in the year 1660, *a year or more* before Major Atherton's death," which occurred Sept. 16, 1661.—*Mass. Hist. Col.*, i. 177.

† Trumbull's *Connecticut*, (8vo. New Haven. 1818) i. 251; Stiles's *Hist. of the Judges*, (12mo. Hartford. 1794) pp. 22, 23, 28, 60.

‡ See the Commissioners' Narrative, in *Hutchinson's Collection of Papers*, (8vo. Boston. 1769) pp. 419–20.—Ed.

Gookin and Danforth, for daring to favor the Praying-Indians, were openly threatened with death by placards posted up in Boston, Feb. 28, 1675–6. The following extract from one of these placards furnishes a striking exemplification of the excitement which was so prevalent at this time:—

"Some generous spirits have vowed their destruction; as Christians we warn them to prepare for death, for though they will deservedly die, yet we wish the health of their souls. By the new society,

A. B. C. D."

The following votes are an additional indication of the temporary unpopularity of Gookin and his associates:—

"The Names of eighteen Gentlemen who had most Votes for Magistrates for the year ensuing, as appears at opening the sd Votes at Boston, April 11*t*: 1676, with the number of Votes for each.

Simon Bradstreet, Esqr.	974	Wm. Hathorne, Esqr.	1052
Daniel Gookin, Esqr.	446	Edw. Ting, Esqr.	1183
Ric. Russell, Esqr.	1225	Mr. Joseph Dudley,	669
Tho. Danforth, Esqr.	840	Major Tho. Savage,	441."*

The Rev. Thomas Shepard of Charlestown, who died Dec. 22, 1677, in the 43d year of his age, bequeathed "£5 to his honored guardian Capt. Daniel Gookin, whom he chose at his fathers death when a lad of fourteen."

When Gookin, Eliot, and others were capsized in Boston harbor, in April, 1676, he lost "a large cloak of drab due berry lin'd through with fine searge, cost in London about eight pounds," "a new pair of gloves cost 2[s] and a rattan, headed with Ivory worth 18[d]. Capt. Henchman lost a good broadcloth clarge coate worth 40 shillings, & Mr. Eliot lost a good castor hat worth ten shillings."

In the Worcester Magazine, Vol. I. p. 383, it is stated that General Gookin was a Hebrew scholar.

Judge Sewall thus notices in his Diary the death of Gookin. "$168\frac{6}{7}$. March 18. Goe to see Major Gookin, who is dying. He speaks to us. March 19. Satterday, ab[t] 5 or 6 in y[e] morn Major Daniel Gookin dies, *a right good Man.*"

Inscriptions at Allyn's Point, the terminus of the Worcester and Norwich Railroad, on the east side of the river Thames, seven miles below Norwich, Ct.

In memory of Mr. Benadam Allyn† who died Sept. 6th 1781, by traitor Arnold's murdering corps in the 20th year of his age.

To future ages this shall tell
This brave youth in fort Griswold fell
For amaricas liberty he fought & bled
Alas he died.

In memory of Capt. Simeon Allyn who died Sept. 6th 1781 in fort Griswold with his Lieutenant, Ensign & 13 soldiers by traitor arnolds murdering corps in the 37th year of his age.

In memory of Belton Allyn who fell in fort Griswold by traitor Arnolds corps Sept. 6th 1781.

* See *N. H. Hist. Coll.*, iii. 99, 100.—Ed.

† This name, we believe, does not appear among those engraven on the monument at Groton Heights, while that of *Samuel* Allyn does.

RECORDS OF BOSTON.

[Copied for the Antiquarian Journal by MR. DAVID PULSIFER, member of the N. E. H. Geneal. Society.]

[Continued from page 40.]

[NOTE.—These records contain the marriages, births, and deaths of several towns, as they were returned to the recorder in Boston, and are copied in the order in which they were entered. The following are of Braintree.]

A register of Births & burialls in Braintree from the yeare 1637 vnto the first month 1644.

Mary the daught^{r} of Thomas Adams was borne 24° (5°) 1643 & dyed soone after. *Adams.*

Sarai the daught^{r} of Samuel Allen & Anne his wife was borne the 30° (1°) 1639. *Allen.*

Anne the wife of Samuel Allen dyed 29° (7°) 1641.

Miriam the daught^{r} of Georg Aldreth was buried 1639 27° (11°.) *Aldreth.*

Experience the daught^{r} of Georg Aldreth dyed 2° (12°) 1641.

Hanna the daught^{r} of Benjamin Albie was borne 16° (6°) 1641. *Albie.*

Lidia the daught^{r} of Benjamin Albie was borne 14° (2°) 1642.

Hannah the daught^{r} of William Ames was borne 12° (3°) 1641. *Ames.*

Rebecca the daught^{r} of William Ames was borne (8°) 1642.

Sarai the daught^{r} of Matthew Barnes was borne 29° (6°) 1641. *Barnes.*

Mary the daught^{r} of Samuel Basse was borne 26° (2°) 1643. *Basse.*

Samuel the sonne of Gregorie Belshar was borne 24° (6°) 1637. *Belshar.*

Mary the daught^{r} of Gregory Belshar was borne 8° (5°) 1639.

Joseph the sonne of Gregory Belshar was borne 25° (10°) 1641.

Phillip the sonne of Henry Blage was borne 24° (1°) 1643. *Blage.*

John the sonne of Peter Bracket was borne 30° (9°) 1641. *Bracket.*

Joseph the sonne of Peter Bracket was borne 13° (8°) 1642.

Mary the daughter of Richard Bracket was borne 1° (12°) 1641. *Bracket.*

ffrancis Browne servant to John Alby dyed (1°) 1640. *Browne.*

Richard the sonne of Richard Chamberlaine was borne 19° (10°) 1642 & dyed the 25° (10°) 1642. *Chamberlaine.*

Joseph the sonne of William Cheesborough was borne 18° (5°) 1640. *Cheesborough.*

Joshua the sonne of James Coney was borne (2°) 1640 & dyed the (10°) 1642. *Coney.*

Patience the daughter of James Coney was borne (6°) 1642.

Experience the daughtr of James Coney was borne (6°) 1642.

James son to James Coney dyed (10°) 1642.

Joseph the sonne of John Darset was buryed (10°) 1642. *Darset.*

Ambrose the sonne of William Dawes was borne 24° (5°) 1642. *Dawes.*

John the sonne of William Devel was borne 24° (4°) 1643 & dyed 15° (5°) 1643. *Devel.*

Mary Eliot the daughtr of ffrancis Eliot was borne 27° (11°) 1640. *Eliot.*

John the sonne of William Ellis was borne 5° (1°) 1641. *Ellis.*

Elisabeth the daughr of Thomas fflatman was borne 7° (3°) 1640. *fflatman.*

Thomas the sonne of Thomas fflatman was borne 3° (5°) 1643.

Dorothie the daughtr of Henry fflint was borne 11° (5°) 1642. *fflint.*

Susan the daughtr of Peter George was borne (12°) 1642. *George.*

John the sonne of John Hanset was borne 15° (5°) 1641. *Hansett.*

Elisabeth the daughtr of John Hastings was borne 2° (5°) 1643. *Hastings.*

John the sonne of John Hecknell was borne 3° (10°) 1638. *Hecknell.*

Nathaniel the sonne of Nathaniel Herman was borne 8° (12°) 1640. *Herman.*

Mary the daughtr of Nathaniel Herman was borne 15° (12°) 1642.

Jonathan the sonne of John Hoydon was borne 19° (3°) 1640. *Hoydon.*

Hannah the daughtr of John Hoydon was borne 7° (2°) 1642.

Joseph the sonne of Thomas Jewel & Grisell his wife was borne the 24° (2°) 1642. *Jewell.*

Lidia the daughtr of Joel Jenkins was borne 13° (8°) 1640. *Jenkins.*

Theophilus the sonne of Joel Jenkins was borne 7° (2°) 1642.

Mary the daughtr of Steven Kinsley was borne 30° (6°) 1640. *Kinsley.*

Ezechiel the sonne of Ezechiel Knight & Elisabeth his wife was borne 1° (12°) 1640 & dyed 29° (7°) 1641. *Knight.*

Elisabeth the wife of Ezechiel Knight was buried 28° (2°) 1642.

Mary the daughtr of Henry Maudsley was borne 29° (7°) 1638. *Maudsley.*

Samuel the sonne of Henry Maudsley was borne 14° (4°) 1641.

Sarah the daughtr of Thomas Mekins was borne 24° (2°) 1641. *Mekins.*

Thomas the sonne of Thomas Mekins was borne 8° (4°) 1643.

[To be continued.]

INSCRIPTIONS FROM THE BURYING-GROUNDS IN SALEM, MASS.

[CHARTER STREET BURYING-GROUND.]

Here Lyes buried the body of Mrs. Mary Andrew, wife to Mr. Nathaniel Andrew, who died October ye 3d, 1747, in ye 39th year of her age.

Here lyes buried the body of Mr. Jona. Archer, died July 16th, 1746, in the 76th year of his age.

Here lyes buried the Body of Mrs. Rachel Barnard, wife to Samuel Barnard, Esq., Aged 56 years, died Aug. ye 30th, 1743.

Here lyes buried the body of Mrs. Elizabeth Barnard, the Pious and Virtuous Consort of Samuel Barnard, Esq., who departed this Life Novr. 9th, Anno Domini 1753, Aged 46 years.

In memory of Samuel Barnard Esq., who departed this life, November 21st, 1762, in the 78th year of his age.

Here lyeth buried ye body of Elizabeth, wife to Henry Bartholmew, aged about 60 years, deceas'd ye 1st day of September, 1682.

Here lies buried the body of Mr. Edmond Batter, who departed this life, November ye 2d, 1756, aged 84 years.

Here lyes the body of Martha Batter, wife to Mr. Edmond Batter, aged 36 years, dec'd June 1st, [ ]

Here lyeth ye body of William Beckett, senr., who died ye 10th of November, 1723, in ye 55th year of his age.

Here lyes ye body of Capt. William Bowditch, merchant, deceased ye 28th of May, 1728, aged 64 years and 9 months.

Here lyes ye body of Mrs. Mary Bowditch, wife of William Bowditch, who died [ ] 1724, in ye 53d [or 55th] year of her age.

William, son of Jos^h. and Elizabeth Bowditch, died June 26th, 1729, aged 2 years and 5 months.

Here lies buried the body of Mr. Ebenezer Bowditch, who departed this life Feb^{ry}. ye 2d, 1768, in ye 65th year of his age.

Here lyes buried the body of Mr. Ebenezer Bowditch, who departed this Life August the 16th, 1771, Aged 42 years.

Here lieth buried ye body of William Browne, Esq., Aged 79 years. Departed this Life the 20th of January, 1687.

This Stone perpetuates the memory of John Cabot, Physician, who died June 3d, 1749, aged 44,

Likewise of William, son of Hannah Cabot, died Decr. 9th, 1750, Aged 1 year 2 mo.

Mary Corey, wife of Giles Corey, aged 63 years, died August 27th, 1684.

Here lies the body of Mary Cox, wife to Edward Cox, sen^r., who died Nov. y^e [ ] 1737, aged 63 years.

Here lyes ye body of Doraty Cromwell, aged 67 years, Dec^d. Sept. ye 27th, 1673.

Here lieth Buried ye body of Mrs. Mary, wife to Mr. Philip Cromall, aged 72 yeares, departed this life the 14 day of November, 1683.

Here lyeth buried y^e body of Mr. Philip Cromwell, aged 83 years, departed this life y^e 30th March, 1693.

This Stone Perpetuates the memory of Capt. John Crowninshield, mariner, Ob^t. May 25th, Anno Dom. 1761, Ætatis 65.

Here lyeth y^e body of Martha Dean, y^e wife of Thomas Dean, who died y^e 24th of $Decem^r$. 1729, in the 31st year of her age.

Here lyes y^{e} body of Edward Dean, son of Mr. Philemon Dean of Ipswich, who died Sept. y^{e} 14th, 1743, aged 21 years.

Here lyeth y^{e} body of Mary, Wife to Edmond Feveryeare & formerly wife of Joseph Hardy, Aged about 45 years, died Nov. 1705.

Here lyeth buried ye body of Sarah, wife of Ebenezer Gardner, Aged about 23 years, dyed ye 5th of September, 1682.

Here lyes Interred the body of William Gedney, Esq., who died Jany. ye 24th, 1729, aged 62 years.

In memory of Mrs. Mercy Goodhue, wife of Mr. William Goodhue, died May 22d, 1772, in the 56th year of her age.

Here lyes ye body of Mr. John Grafton, senier, died Novr. ye 24th, 1715, aged 77 years.

Here lyeth buried ye body of Joseph Hardy, Dyed April 17th, 1687.

Here lyeth ye body of Seeth Hardy, dau^{t}. of Joseph & Mary Hardy, aged about 25 years & 7 months, Died Decr. 21st, 1712.

In memory of Mr. Benjamin Herbeart, who departed this Life Jan^{ry}. the 20th, 1761, in the 52d year of his age.

Here lie buried the remains of Elizabeth, Consort of Capt. Benjamin Herbert.

In her were united the affectionate wife, the tender Parent, the Friend to the distressed, and in a Word, the Pious and good Woman.

Ob^{t}. Octr. 23d, A. D. 1772, Ætatis 55.

Francis, son of John Higginson, 3^{tius}. & Hannah his wife, born Novr. ye 29th, 1705, & died ye same day.

Henry, son of John Higginson, 3^{tius}. & Hannah his wife, aged 14 monthes & and 7 dayes, died Decr. ye 1st, 1709.

John, son of William & Mary Hirst, aged 1 year & 9 mo. Died Octob^{r}. 9th, 1687.

In Memory of George Hodges, son of Mr. Gamaliel Hodges, jr. & Priscilla Hodges, Aged 17 years. Died March ye 25th 1764.

Here lyes buried the body of Mr. Gamaliel Hodges, who departed this Life August the 27th, 1768, Aged 51 years and 11 months.

Here lyeth buried ye body of William Hollingworth, aged 33 yeares, departed this Life Novr. 7th, 1683.

Here lyeth buried ye body of Elianor Hollingworth, aged 59 yeares. Deceased ye 22d of November, 1689.

2 daut^{rs} of Jno. and Sus^{na} Holliman. Susanna died Sept. ye 27th, 1721, in the 2d year of her age. Susannah died Nov^{mr}. ye 4th, 1729, in ye 2d year of her age.

John Holliman, son to John and Susan Holliman, who died July ye 1st, 1732, in ye 10th year of his age.

Here lies the body of Mrs. Eunice Hunt, the wife of Mr. William Hunt. Died August 30th, 1764, aged 57 years and 6 months.

Here lyes buried the Body of Mr. William Hunt, who departed this Life May the 29th, 1769, Aged 25 years.

Here lie Interred the remains of Mrs. Elizabeth, wife of Mr. John Ingersoll & daut. of Captain Daniel Bray. Obt. Augt. 5th, 1768, Ætatis 56.

Happy the Virtuous & the Just,
They from their Sins and Labor rest,
Their holy works do follow them,
To the bright mansions of the blest.

Also Philip, son of Capt. & Mrs. Susanna Ingersoll, Obt. Sept. 8th, 1781, Ætatis 2.

Here lyes the body of William Jeffry, son of Mr. James and Mrs. Ruth

Jeffry, who departed this Life July the 8th, 1772, in ye 35th year of his age.

Katherine, wife to Mr. William King, died Decr. 17th, 1718, Aged 22 years.

Here lyeth buried ye body of Mr. Timothy Lindall, aged 56 years & 7 mo. Deceased January ye 6th, 1698.

Here lyes buried the body of Mrs. Mary Lindall, wife to Mr. Timothy Lindall, aged 83 years. Dec'^d^. Jan^ry^. ye 7th, 1731.

Here lies buried the body of Mr. Caleb Lindall, Merch^t^. Obi't. Novr. 13th, 1751, Ætatis 67.

Here lyes Interred ye body of James Lindall, Esq. who departed this life May ye 10th, Anno Dom'i 1753, Aged 77 years.

Here lyes buried ye body of Mrs. Sarah Lindall, wife to Mr Caleb Lindall, Merch^t^. who departed this life June ye 27th, A. D. 1764, aged 60 years.

Here lies Interred the body of Mrs. Mary Lindall, who departed this life Jan^ry^. the 22d, 1776, aged 70 years.

This Stone perpetuates the memory of Mad^m^ Sarah Marshead, who died Decr. 25th, 1750, aged 67.

Here lyeth buried ye body of John Marston, senior, aged 66 years. Dec'd December ye 19, 1681.

Here lyeth buried ye body of Mary ye wife of John Marston, Aged 43 years. dyed ye 25th of May, 1686.

Mr. Nathaniel Mather. Dec'd October ye 17th, 1688.

An aged person
that had seen
but nineteen winters
in the world.

Here lyeth ye body of Judath, Daut^r^. of Joseph & Judath Neale. Deceased February ye 25th, 1697–8, in ye 16th year of her age.

Here lyeth the Body of Ruth, wife of John Nutting, who died Novr. 22d, 1736.

Also John, their son, died June 20th, 1720, aged 4 years.

Benjamin Orne, son to Benjamin Orne & son to Elizabeth Orne, who ye 7th of September died aged 9 months and 8 days, 1736.

In memory of Mrs. Alice Orne, who died Nov. 16, 1776, in the 30th year of her age.

This Stone has something great to teach,
And what you need to learn,
For Graves my friends most loudly preach,
Man's Infinite concern.

Here lyes buried the Body of Deacon Peter Osgood, aged 90 years. died September ye 24th, 1753.

Here lies buried ye body of Mrs. Martha Osgood, the widow of Deacon Peter Osgood. She died Septr. 10th, 1760, in the 92d year of her age.

Hephzibah Packer, ye wife of Thomas Packer, aged 25 years and 5 months. departed this Life ye 22d of January, 1684.

Here lyes buried ye body of Margaret, ye wife of Deliverance Parkman, Aged 24 years. Dec'd March ye 25th, 1689.

Here lyes Buried ye body of Mr. Deliverance Parkman, Mercht. Dec'^d^. Novr. the 15th, 1715, aged 64 years, 3 mo. and 12 days.

Here lies the body of Mrs. Elizabeth Peele, wife to Mr. Robert Peele, jr. who departed this life August the 6th 1770, Aged 27 years.

Here lies ye body of Mrs. Mary Peele, wife to Mr. Robert Peele, who departed this Life, May ye 4th, 1771, aged 58 years.

Here lies buried the body of Mr. Robert Peele, who departed this life April the 29th, 1773, aged 60 years.

Here lyes Interr'd the body of Sarah Peele, who died Decem^r^. 10th, 1736, in the 32d year of her age.

A prudent wife.

Here lyes ye body of Abigall Pickman, wife to Mr. Joshua Pickman & daur. to Mr. Nehemiah Willoughby & Abigall his wife, aged 30 years. died August ye 24th, 1710.

Here lyes buried ye body of Capt. Benjamin Pickman, senior, who died April ye 26th, 1719, Aged 46 years.

Here lyeth ye body of Mrs. Elizabeth Pickman, who died Decr. 19th, 1727, Aged 77 years.

Here lyes Interred the body of Mr. Caleb Pickman, who died June 4th, 1737, (being struck with lightning,) Aged 22 years.

My times are in thy hand,
Remember my life is wind.

This stone perpetuates the memory of Mad^m^. Elizabeth Pickman (widow of Capt. Benjamin Pickman,) aged 56 years. departed this Life March ye 24th, 1737–8.

Here lyes buried ye body of Capt. Joshua Pickman, Mariner, Obt. Jan^ry^. 24th, 1750, Ætatis 69.

Here lyeth ye body of John Pratt, who died March ye 12th, 1729–30, in the 66th year of his age.

Here lies buried the body of Mrs. Maverick Pratt, who died Jan^ry^. 23d, 1763, in the 50th year of her age.

Here lyeth buried ye body of Samuell Shattock, aged 69 years, who departed this life ye 6th day of June, 1689.

Here lyeth buried ye body of Retire Shattock, aged 27 yeares departed this life ye 9th day of September, 1691.

Here lies buried ye body of Thomas Smith, son of Edward Smith, who departed this Life April the 11th, 1771, aged 4 years and 3 months.

now in my childhood i must die,
leave all my playmates and my toys,
hoping to inherit eternal joys.

Here lyeth buried ye body of Robart Stone, Junear. died [ ] 1688, Aged [ ]

Here lyes the Body of Hannah, ye wife of Robert Stone, aged 29 years deceased April 17th, 1691.

Here lyes ye Body of Capt. Benjamin Stone, aged about 38 years, died Novem^r^. 30th, 1703.

In memory of Mrs. Elizabeth Stone, wife of Mr. Robert Stone, who departed this Life July the 2d, 1763, in the 76th year of her age.

In memory of Mr. Robert Stone, who departed this Life May the 20th, 1764, in the 77th year of his age.

Here lyeth buried ye Body of John Swinnerton, Phis^ian^. deceased ye 6th of Jan^ary^. 1690, in ye 58th yeare of his age.

Here lyes ye body of Hannah Swinnerton, widdow of Dr. John Swinnerton, aged 71 years. died December 23d, 1713.

Here lyes ye body of Mrs. Mercy Swinnerton, who died Nov. 3d, 1727, in ye 44th year of her age.

Here lyes buried the body of Mr. Isaac Turner, who departed this life, August the 17th, 1754, aged 62 years.

Here lieth the body of John Turner, Aged 36 years, who departed this Life the 9th of October, in the year of our Lord, 1680.

Here lyeth buried ye body of Hilliard Verrin, aged 63 years. Dec'd. ye 20th Decr. 1683.

Here lyeth ye body of Sarah Ward, wife to Miles Ward sen^{r}. who died Nov^{mr}. ye 20th, 1728, in ye 59th year of her age.

Here lyes ye body of Dea. Miles Ward, who died August 13th, 1761, Aged 92 years.

Here lyes ye body of Elizabeth, wife of Miles Ward, jun^{r}. died 13th April, 1737, in her 28th year. Elisabeth, their dau^{t}. died April ye 11th, 1737, in her 8th year. Ebenezer, their son, died April ye 13th, 1737, aged — hours. Anne, their dautr. died May ye 2d, 1737, in her 2d year. Also Sarah, daut^{er}. of Miles & Elisabeth Ward, died Augs^{t}. ye 10th. 1729, Aged 9 mo. & 20 days. Abigail, their daug^{htr}. died ye 22d of May, 1731, aged 5 weeks.

Here lyeth ye body of Deborah Ward, wife to Benjamin Ward, who died April ye 6th, 1736, in ye 36th year of her age.

Here lies the Body of Joshua Ward, Esq., who departed this Life December 2d, 1779, in the 81st year of his age.

Here lies the body of Mrs. Ruth Ward, Relict of the late Joshua Ward, Esq. who died June 5th, 1787, in the 74th year of her age.

Here lyes ye body of Rebekah Whitford. Died April ye 14th, 1744, in her 7th year, Being willing to die.

Here lyeth ye body of Deacon Jonathan Willard, died April 7th, 1773, Aged near 49 years.

Here lyeth ye body of John Wind, who died Octo^{br}. ye 7th, 1732, in ye 80th year of his age.

[To be continued.]

LETTER TO REV. MR. ADAMS, 1737.

March 27th, 1849.

MR. EDITOR,—

During the days of the almost theocratical government of New England, there were but few changes in the poetry used in divine worship. The insertion of this original paper in your valuable pages may gratify the curiosity of some of your readers, and also serve the student who may search for the curious learning in this portion of our ecclesiastical learning. This is probably the only copy in existence, and if one historic fact perish, it is lost forever.

T.

REV. S^{R}

The New England Version of the Psalms, however usefull it may formerly have been, is now become through the natural variableness of Language, not only very uncouth, but in many Places unintelligible; whereby the mind instead of being Raised and spirited in singing The Praises of Almighty God, and thereby better prepared to attend the other Parts of Divine Service, is Damped and made spiritless in the Performance of the Duty; at least such is the Tendency of the use of That version, and it being the Duty of Christians to make use of the Best helps for the right & acceptable performance of Divine Worship and as in Regard to Psalm singing there are several versions of the Psalms much preferable to that Before mentioned, especially the version Made by Tate & Brady, which has been lately Rec^{d} by Divers of the Neighbouring Churches in the Room of the New England version.

We the subscribers (a number of your Parish) hereby Express our inclination and desire, that you would propose to the Church and Congregation under Your Care (in such manner as you Think sutable) the introducing among them of the last Mentioned version: and we would recommend that Edition (lately Published) to which is annexed a number of Hymns, suited to sacramental Occasions.

We are with Great Esteem
S[r] Your Most Humble Servants.

James Bowdoin
Ebenezer Dorr
Sam[ll] Stevens
Sam[ll] Gridley
James Mears
Sam[ll] Williams
Jonathan Hall
William Bosson
Noah Perrin
James Mears jun[r]
Benjamin Williams
Joseph Weld
Benjamin May
Ebenezer May
Isaac Winslow
Joseph Curtiss
Ebenezer Newell
John Williams
Joseph Williams
Eben[r] Pierpont

William Gridley
John Pierpoint
William Pierpont
William Heath.

To the Rev[d] M[r] Adams

The within is a True Copy of a letter Communicated to the first Congregation in Roxbury on Sep[t] 11* 1737, and agreeable to the Desire therein Expressed it was proposed by the Paster to the Congregation that they Take this version into Consideration for a considerable Time at least six or seven weeks, and it was Recommended to them to Read and acquaint themselves with this version, and if after having Carefully Read & Considered this version any find Cause to object against it the Pastor Desires that he may be Timely informed of it.

attest

AMOS ADAMS.

FIRST SETTLERS OF BARNSTABLE.

[Communicated by MR. DAVID HAMBLEN.—Continued from p. 87.]

JOSEPH HULL m. Experience Harper, Oct., 1676; child, Trustram, b. 8 Oct., 1677.

ELKANAH HAMBLEN m. Abigail Hamblen, 13 April, 1711; children, Sylvanus, b. 20 July, 1712; Reuben, 13 March, 1714; Abigail, 17 Oct., 1715; John, 2 Nov., 1717; Rachel, 7 Sept., 1720, d. 1722; Patience, 12 June, 1721; Tabitha, 14 April, 1723. Abigail, the wife of Elkanah Hamblen, d. 29 May, 1733, and he m., for his second wife, Margaret Bates of Agawam, 9 June, 1734.

* Query, 4 or 11?

James Hamblen, Jr. m. Mary, dau. of John Dunham, 20 Nov., 1662; children, Mary, b. 24 July, 1664; Elizabeth, 13 Feb., 1665; Eleazer and Experience, 12 April, 1668; James, 26 Aug., 1669; Jonathan, 3 March, 1670–1; a child, 28 March, 1672, d. 7 April, 1672; Ebenezer, 29 July, 1674; Elisha, 15 March, 1676–7, d. 30 Dec., 1677; Hope, 13 March, 1679–80; Job, 15 Jan., 1681; John, 12 Jan., 1683; Elkanah, no date; Benjamin, baptized 1685. Mrs. Mary Hamblen, wife of the above James, d. 19 Dec., 1715, æ. 73.

James Hamblen, Jr. m. Ruth Lewis, 8 Oct., 1690; children, Mary, b. 24 June, 1691; Ruth, 25 Jan., 1692; James, 17 July, 1696; Benjamin, 8 Nov., 1702, d. 23 Jan., 1732; David, June, 1708, d. 4 Nov., 1732; Hannah, 17 June, 1709, d. 7 Nov., 1735; Job, 25 June, 1711, d. 28 Sept., 1732; Deliverance, no date.

Jonathan Hamblen m. Esther Hamblen, 6 March, 1705; children, Solomon, b. 5 Dec., 1705; Content, 12 Dec., 1707; Priscilla, 13 July, 1709; Zacheus, 17 June, 1711; Jabez, baptized 13 July, 1718; Jonathan, baptized 13 July, 1718; Sarah, baptized 13 July, 1718; Josiah, b. 16 Oct., 1720, d. 1 March, 1789, æ. 69. Mr. Jonathan Hamblen d. 22 June, 1743, æ 74. His wife, Esther, d. 1 Sept., 1746, æ 69.

Dea. Ebenezer Hamblen m. Sarah Lewes, 4 April, 1698, d. in Sharon, Conn., 1755; children, Ebenezer, b. 18 March, 1698–9; Mercy, 10 Sept., 1700; Hopestill, 23 July, 1702; Cornelius, 13 June, 1705; Thomas, 6 May, 1710; Isaac, 1 July, 1714; Lewis,* 31 Jan., 1718–19.

Eleazer Hamblen m. Mehitable Jenkins, Oct., 1675; children, Isaac, b. 20 Aug., 1676; Joseph, 20 Nov., 1680, d. 27 Aug., 1766; Mehitable, 28 March, 1682; Shubal, 16 Sept., 1695; Elisha, baptized 30 July, 1685; Ichabod, baptized May, 1687.

Isaac Hamblen m. Elizabeth Howland, 14 Sept., 1698; children, Eleazer, b. 22 Aug., 1699; Isaac, no date, baptized 20 July, 1701; Joseph, 4 June, 1702, (deacon) d. in Yarmouth, 19 Jan., 1777; Elizabeth, Oct., 1705.

Joseph Hamblen m. Mercy Howland, 27 April, 1704, d. 27 Aug., 1766, æ. 86; children, Alice, b. 4 Feb., 1705; Seth, March, 1708; Sarah, 4 April, 1711; Joseph, 10 March, 1715, d. 8 Aug., 1767; Southward, 21 May, 1721, d. 13 Jan., 1766.

John Hamblen m. Sarah Bearse, Aug., 1667; children, Melatiah, b. 1 July, 1668; Priscilla, 30 April, 1670; Sarah, 1 July, 1671; Martha, 16 Feb., 1672; Experience, 16 April, 1674; Hannah, 16 Feb., 1675; Ester, 17 March, 1677; Thankful, Oct., 1679, d. Oct., 1683; John, 10 March, 1680; Ebenezer, 12 May, 1683; Abigail, 25 April, 1685; Benjamin, 11 Feb., 1686.

Benjamin Hamblen m. Hope Huckins, 29 May, 1709, d. 1718; children, Rebecca, b. 17 May, 1711; Hannah, no date, baptized July, 1714; Benjamin, no date, baptized 18 Nov., 1716; Hope, no date, baptized 31 Aug., 1718.

Shobal Hamblen m. Eleanor Winslow of Harwich, 25 March, 1719; children, Jerusha, b. 4 May, 1722; Shobal, 20 Sept., 1724; Eleanor, 18 Oct., 1726; Joshua, 21 Aug., 1728; Mehitable, 4 Dec., 1730; Elenor, 15 April, 1733; Lydia, 15 Nov., 1735.

Bartholomew Hamblen m. Susannah Dunham, 20 Jan., 1673, d. 24 April, 1704, æ. 63; children, Samuel, b. 25 Dec, 1674; Mercy, 1 June, 1677; Patience, 15 April, 1680; Susanna, 16 March, 1682; Experience,

* Grandfather of Capt. Nathaniel Hamblen of Boston, and Hon. Frederick Hamblen of Elyria, Ohio.

13 Feb., 1684; John, 19 June, 1686, d. 26 April, 1705; Ebenezer, 23 March, 1689; Mary, 23 May, 1691; Bethiah, 26 Nov., 1693; Reliance, 30 Nov., 1696.

EBENEZER HAMBLEN m. Thankful Childs, 25 Oct., 1722; child, Elizabeth, b. 1 Oct., 1723.

ISRAEL HAMBLEN m. Abigail ——; children, a child, b. 1687, d. 1687; Thankful, 24 Aug., 1689; Prudence, Oct., 1692; Israel, 15 March, 1694; Joseph, 12 Sept., 1697; Jemima, 15 Aug., 1699.

Mr. Israel Hamblen, sen., m., for his second wife, Jemima ——; children, Jacob, 28 May, 1702; Ann, 10 April, 1706.

EBENEZER HAMBLEN m. Thankful Hamblen, May 11, 1710; children, Isaac, b. Feb., 1711, d. seven weeks after; Gershom, 19 July, 1713; Thankful, 6 Aug., 1715; Nathan, 29 June, 1717; Ebenezer, 26 Nov., 1719; a daughter, Sept., 1720, d. 1720; Samuel, 7 Jan., 1722; Dorcas, 5 June, 1727; Timothy, 3 Sept., 1728; Elizabeth, 20 Nov., 1730; Daniel, 2 April, 1735.

[Tradition says that James Hamblen, one of the first settlers of Barnstable, was a brother of Hon. Giles Hamlin, one of the first settlers of Middletown, Ct., and that he first came to Barnstable with his brother before going to Middletown.—D. H.]

JOHN HINKLEY, JR. m. Thankful Trot, 1 May, 1691; children, John, b. 29 March, 1692, d. 24 Aug., 1694; Mary, 24 Feb., 1694; Abiah, 24 March, 1696; Thankful, 14 July, 1699; John, 17 Feb., 1701; James, 9 May, 1704.

EBENEZER HINKLEY m. Mary Stone, Nov., 1706, at Sudbury; child, Rachel, b. 1 Nov., 1707.

JOHN HINKLEY m. Mary Goodspeed, 24 Nov. 1697.

SAMUEL, son of Thomas Hinkley, m. Sarah Pope, 13 Nov., 1676; children, Mary, b. 22 July, 1678; Mehitable, 28 Dec., 1679; Thomas, 19 March, 1680–1; Seth, 16 April, 1683; Samuel, 24 Sept., no year; Elnathan, 8 Sept., no year; Job, 16 Feb., 1687–8; Shobal, 1 May, 1690; Mercy, 11 Jan., 1692–3; Josiah, 24 Jan., 1694–5; Elnathan, 29 Dec., 1698.

SAMUEL HINKLEY m. Mary Goodspeed, 14 Dec., 1664; children, Benjamin, b. 6 Dec., 1666. Wife Mary d. 20 Dec., 1666, and he m. second wife, Mary Fittsrandle, 15 Jan., 1668; children, Samuel, b. 6 Feb., 1669, d. 3 Jan., 1676; Joseph, 15 May, 1672; Isaac, 20 Aug., 1674; Mary, May, 1677, d. 15 June, 1679; Mercy, 9 April, 1679; Ebenezer, 2 Aug., 1685; Thomas, 1 Jan., 1688–9.

BENJAMIN HINKLEY m. Sarah Cob, 27 Dec., 1686; children, Benjamin, b. 18 July, 1694; Mary, 3 Oct., 1696; Sarah, 12 June, 1696, probably 1697; Nathaniel, 30 June, 1698; Mercy, 1 Sept., 1704.

JOSEPH HINKLEY m. Mary Gorham, 21 Sept., 1699; children, Mercy, b. 17 Aug., 1700; Joseph, 6 May, 1702; Mary, 25 Feb., 1703–4; Samuel, 24 Feb., 1705–6; Thankful, 9 June, 1708; Abigail, 30 Oct., 1710; Elizabeth, 4 Jan., 1712–13; Hannah, 10 June, 1715; John, 16 Nov., 1717; Isaac, 31 Oct., 1719.

EBENEZER HINKLEY m. Sarah Lewes, 17 June, 1711; children, Ebenezer, b. 10 Sept., 1712; Daniel, 8 July, 1714, d. 8 Aug., 1714; a son, 24 Sept., 1715, d. 27 Sept., 1715; Thomas, 27 July, 1717; Susannah, 18 April, 1720; Samuel, 7 Sept., 1727; Mary, 12 April, 1729.

JOHN HINKLEY m. Bethiah Lathrop, July, 1668, d. 7 Dec., 1709. Bethiah Lathrop d. 10 July, 1694; children, Sarah, b. May, 1669; Samuel, 2 Feb., 1670; Bethiah, March, 1673, d. 2 April, 1715; Hannah, May, 1675;

Jonathan, 15 Feb., 1677; Ichabod, 28 Aug., 1680; Gershom, 2 April, 1682.

SAMUEL, son of Ensign John Hinkley, m. —— ——; children, John, b. 28 July, 1700; Martha, 8 March, 1701.

ICHABOD HINKLEY m. Mary Goodspeed, 7 Jan., 1702; children, Mary, b. 27 March, 1704, d. 2 March, 1718; John, 4 Jan., 1710–11, d. Feb., 1710–11; Benjamin, 19 June, 1707; David, 1 March, 1709; John, 7 March, 1712; Ebenezer, 7 July, 1714; Thankful, 1 Aug., 1716; Mary, 26 Sept., 1718. Wife Mary d. 1 Oct., 1719, and he m. second wife, Mary Basset, by whom he had one child, Thankful, b. 2 Dec., 1723.

JOB HINKLEY m. Sarah Lumbart, 15 Nov., 1711; children, Hannah, b. 23 Nov., 1713; Huldah, 26 Dec., 1715.

ISAAC HOWLAND m. Ann Tayler, 27 Dec., 1686; children, Ebenezer, b. 7 Sept., 1687; Isaac, 3 July, 1689; Mary, Oct., 1691; Ann, Dec., 1694. John, 2 Feb., 1696; Joseph, 31 July, 1702.

JAMES HOWLAND m. Mary Lothrop, 8 Sept., 1697.

SHOBAL HOWLAND m. Mercy Blossom, 13 Dec., 1700; children, Jabez, b. 16 Sept., 1701; Mercy, 21 May, 1710; Zaccheus, no date.

JOHN HOWLAND, JR., m. —— ——; children, George, b. 30 Dec., 1705; Hannah, 2 Feb., 1708; Mary, 11 Aug., 1711; Joannah, 8 Jan., 1715. By his second wife, Mary Crocker, John, b. 13 Feb., 1720–1; Job, June, 1726.

JOHN HUCKENS m. Hope Chipman, 10 Aug., 1670, d. 10 Nov., 1678, æ. 29; children, Elizabeth, b. 1 Oct., 1671; Mary, 3 April, 1673; Experience, 4 June, 1675; Hope, 10 May, 1677.

THOMAS HUCKENS m. Hannah Chipman, 1 May, 1680; children, Hannah, b. 6 April, 1681, d. 29 Oct., 1698; Joseph, 6 Oct., 1682; Mary, 13 June, 1684; John, 4 May, 1686; Thomas, 15 Jan., 1687–8; Hope, 21 Sept., 1689; James, 20 Aug., 1691; Samuel, 19 Aug., 1693; Jabez, 20 July, 1696, d. June, 1699. Married second wife, Widow Sarah Hinkley, 17 Aug., 1698; Hannah, b. 22 Aug., 1699. Mrs. Hannah Chipman, first wife of Thomas, died 4 Nov., 1696, æ. 37.

JOHN HAWES m. Desire, dau. of Capt. John Gorham, 7 Oct., 1661.

JOHN JENKINS m. —— ——; children, Mehitable, b. 25 Sept., 1694; Samuel, 15 July, 1697; Phillip, 26 July, 1699; Joseph, 13 Aug., 1701; Ruth, 1704. Mr. John Jenkins died 8 July, 1736.

JOSEPH JENKINS m. Lydia Howland, Oct., 1694; children, Abigail, b. July, 1695; Bathshuah, July, 1696; Ann, May, 1701; Joseph, 29 Feb., 1703; Lydia, 30 June, 1705; Benjamin, 30 June, 1707; Reliance, 6 April, 1709.

THOMAS JENKINS m. Experience Hamblen, 24 Aug, 1687; children, Thankful, b. 19 May, 1691; Experience, 28 March, 1693; Mercy, 5 Jan., 1695; Ebenezer, 5 Dec., 1697; Samuel, 7 Jan., 1699–1700; Josiah, 16 April, 1702; Hope, 5 July, 1704; Sarah, 1 Dec., 1706.

JEDEDIAH JONES m. Hannah Davis, 18 March, 1681; children, Shobal, b. 17 July, 1683; Simon, 5 April, 1685; Isaac, April, 1690; Timothy, May, 1692; Hannah, Sept., 1694.

MATTHEW JONES m. Mercy Goodspeed, 14 Jan., 1694 [probably 1684;] children, Benjamin, b. 5 Jan., 1690; Ralph, 5 Jan., 1692; Experience, 1 March, 1697; Josiah, 14 June, 1702; Ebenezer, 6 June, 1706.

ADAM JONES m. Mary Baker, 26 Oct., 1699.

JOHN JONES m. —— ——; children, Abigail, b. 18 Jan., 1698–9; Mercy, July, 1700; John, 12 Feb., 1703.

[To be continued.]

BIOGRAPHICAL SKETCHES OF THE EARLY PHYSICIANS OF MARIETTA, OHIO.

By S. P. Hildreth, M. D., of Marietta, Member of N. E. Hist. Geneal. Soc.

[Continued from page 55.]

DOCTOR WILLIAM B. LEONARD

Was born in London, in the year 1737. Little or nothing is known of his early life. He was bred a surgeon and became an associate of Apothecaries' Hall, as appears from a diploma which he had set in a frame under glass and kept hung up in his room. When in the prime of life he served as a surgeon in the British navy, and at the time of his emigration to America, one of his sons was a lieutenant in the same service. About the year 1794, having lost his wife, he decided on removing to the United States, and be concerned in a woollen factory. For this purpose he clandestinely packed up the machinery and put it on board the vessel in which he had engaged his passage. Before he sailed it was discovered by the officers of the customs, and being a contraband article prohibited by the laws of England to be transported out of the realm, he was arrested and confined for some time in prison. Being finally discharged, he came to America about the year 1797. The following year he was practising his profession in Newburyport, Mass., where he again married; but his wife dying soon after, he moved to Marietta in 1801, and boarded in the family of Mr. William Moulton, who was a native of the former town, and one of the earliest settlers at the mouth of the Muskingum. Here he again renewed the practice, and in 1802 married Lydia Moulton, the maiden daughter of his landlord. He appears to have been a skilful surgeon, but was rough and coarse in his manners and language, retaining the habits acquired in his naval service, at a period when profanity and rudeness occupied the place of the genteel manners of the present day. He still retained and kept up the fashion of the showy dresses, such as prevailed in the days of Queen Elizabeth, which in the backwoods of Ohio excited the curiosity of a people accustomed to the most simple attire. He was thin and spare in person, with very slender legs, on the borders of old age. His favorite costume was a blue broadcloth coat trimmed with gold lace, and enormous gilt buttons, a waistcoat of crimson velvet, with large pocket flaps, and small clothes of the same material, a pair of silk or worsted stockings drawn over his slender legs, with large silver buckles at the knees and in his shoes. On his head he wore a full flowing periwig, of which he had six or eight varieties, crowned with a three cornered or cocked beaver hat. Over the whole, when he appeared in the street, unless the weather was very hot, he wore a large scarlet colored cloak. This dress, with his gold headed cane, always called forth the admiration and wonder of the boys, who followed close in his train, and were often threatened with his displeasure in not very civil language. When travelling on horseback to visit his patients, he rode a coal black steed with long flowing mane and tail, the saddle and trappings of which were as antiquated and showy as his own dress. The shop furniture, surgeon's instruments, skeletons, and books he brought out with him, were as odd and ancient as himself. The writer of this article has preserved several of them as curious relics of this singular man. Amongst them is a small quarto volume, printed at London in the old black letter, in the year 1562. It is entitled "The Secrets of Master Alexis of Piemont," and is filled with curious recipes in the arts, with odd, fanciful remedies for various diseases, such as were in use three hundred years ago. He died of a consumption, in 1806, aged 69 years. On a copper plate prepared before his death with suitable blanks, and attached to his tomb-stone, is engraved the following quaint lines:

> "Friend! for Jesus' sake forbear
> To touch the dust enclosed here;
> Blest is the man that spares this urn,
> And he's a knave that moves my bones."

DOCTOR JOHN BAPTISTE REGNIER

Was born in the city of Paris, in the year 1769. His father was "a Notaire," or writer for the courts of law, while his mother kept a small store for fancy goods, which the French are famous for exhibiting in the most tasteful manner. She was a very beautiful woman, dressing in the neatest style of fashion, to be in keeping with her employment, and the mother of nine children, seven sons and two daughters. John Baptiste was the oldest of the sons, and named for his father. He received a good education, but studied chiefly architecture and drawing, intending to follow the former as a profession. He also attended courses of lectures on various scientific subjects, but more especially that of medicine, which his fine memory stored up as a useful treasure in after life. Born and educated admidst the elegances and ease of Paris, little did he then think of the trials and vicissitudes which awaited him in after years. The convulsions which agitated France during the period of the Revolution had commenced their movements on the surface of society in the autumn of 1789. His father was a good loyalist and sided with the crown, as did all his sons who were old enough to act. In 1790 the young men were called upon to enrol themselves in the ranks of the reformers, but as this was not in accordance with their feelings, their father collected all the ready money he could command and sent his sons out of the country. The only safety for the orderly citizens was to flee, and thus were expatriated a large number of the best families of France. John Baptiste, then in his twentieth year, with his little brother Modeste, in his fourteenth year, joined the company of emigrants who had purchased lands of Joel Barlow, and embarked for the United States in February, from the port of Havre; while his brother Francis, aged 18, and Benjamin, about 16, sailed for the island of St. Domingo. After their departure the lawless Jacobins,* treating every one as enemies who were not openly on their side, plundered their father's house and shop of every thing movable, destroying what they could not carry away. His life was spared, but he was left in wretchedness and want. Some years after, when Napoleon had restored order by his iron sway, two of the brothers returned and served under that noted man in his German and Russian campaigns, and settled in Paris, where their descendants now live. Early in May, 1790, he landed in Alexandria with his little brother and the other emigrants, this port being nearer the Ohio river than any other, and reached Marietta the 16th October following, after many delays and hindrances. Doctor Lamoine was in the same ship, but settled in Washington, Pa. After a few days the emigrants again embarked in boats procured for them by Mr. Duer of New York, the agent of the Scioto Land Company, who also supplied them with one year's provisions, as stipulated in their contract for lands. They landed on the right bank of the Ohio, at a point a little below the mouth of the Big Kenawha river, supposed to be the upper end of their purchase, and founded a town which they called Gallipolis, or the French city. Here he passed the winter and built for himself and brother a small frame house, which was the first and only one erected that winter, the others being made of logs. The next summer was occupied in cutting away the forest trees which covered the site of the new city. They were of immense growth, and the whole season was busily occupied in clearing and fencing about an acre of ground; a task which a backwoodsman familiar with the use of the axe would have accomplished in four or five weeks. By this time they had ascertained that the Scioto Company could give them no title to their lands, and they were left in the wilderness without a home. The year had also expired in which they were to be supplied with provisions, and want stared them in the face. An arrangement was finally made with the directors of the Ohio Company, by which the site covered by this town was secured to them, and subsequently Congress, commiserating their losses, with a magnanimity creditable to the United States, granted them a tract of twenty-four thousand acres on the Ohio river in Scioto county, making a good farm for every family. Under these disheartening circumstances, a large portion of them having spent all their money, and the Indian war breaking out, many of them left the settlement for Kaskaskia and other towns in the west. His little brother Modeste, who looked up to him as a father, had imbibed such a dread of the Indians that he did not cease to importune him until he decided on leaving the place and going to New York. Towards the last of February, 1792, they embarked in a large perogue with a small party who joined them, and proceeded up stream for Pittsburgh. Being little acquainted with water craft, their progress was slow. Near the head of Buffington's Island, in passing round a fallen tree top, their vessel upset. All their provisions and clothing were lost, while they barely escaped with their lives to the shore. Among the other effects of the unfortunate Regnier then lost in the Ohio, was a curiously wrought octagonal cylinder, of black marble, made with mathematical accuracy, eight or ten inches long and one in diameter, manufactured in Paris. Several years after this curious stone was found on the head of a sand bar some distance below, and presented to an eastern museum as a relic of that singular but unknown race who built the mounds and earthworks in the valley of the Ohio. The spot where they were wrecked was many miles from any settlement, and no boat to be procured: the rest of their journey was performed on foot. They suffered much for food, and were all nearly poisoned by eating the seeds of decayed Papaws, which resemble a large bean. The party finally reached Pittsburgh, and after resting a few days, crossed the mountains and proceeded on to New York. Not finding employment here he went by water to Newfoundland, where there was a French settlement. How he was occupied while here is unknown. In 1794 he returned again to New York, and was employed by Benjamin Walker, the proprietor of a large body of land in the eleventh township of the military tract, lying on the Co-ne-se-wae-ta creek. It was the more agreeable as a small settlement of French families had been already commenced. Fortune, which had so long frowned on all his attempts at making a living, now seemed to relent. For three years in a land of strangers, with an imperfect knowledge of their language, destitute of all things but his head and his hands wherewith to procure a support for himself and brother, he was many times tempted to give up in despair, and cease any further struggles for existence. But his buoyant French heart enabled him to resist such thoughts, and kept him afloat in the wide sea of life. His business now was to explore the lands of that wilderness region and sell them to actual settlers. He had also to superintend the erection of mills on the creek, for which his architectural studies had well prepared him. Having many men under his care, who were often wounded with their edge tools in addition to the sickness which attends all new settlements in the summer and autumn, his medical knowledge was daily called into active service, as he was the only man in a distance of thirty or forty miles who had any skill in medicine. It was, however, a work of necessity and mercy, as he had not at that time any expectation of following this profession for a living, or even dreamed of the popularity and fame that awaited his future life, when he was to become a physician in Ohio. A store of merchandise was also placed under his care by Mr. Walker, of which he received a portion of the profits. Potash was largely manufactured in the new settlements, and taken in exchange for goods. This was sold at an advance in New York, and his gains increased rapidly in the course of two years. In 1796 he married a Miss Content Chamberlain of Unadilla, N. Y., whose father kept a public house, and with her had become acquainted in his journeys to New York. In the year 1800 he exchanged his profits in the store for a drove of horses, which was sold to a dealer in Louisburgh, N. Y., who failed to make payment. This loss, together with that of a debt in the city for five hundred dollars, made him a bankrupt, and left him as destitute of worldly goods as he was after his shipwreck on the Ohio, in 1792. He now had a wife and two children to provide for, and must make one more effort for a living. A lingering desire to see once more the beautiful shores of the Ohio, on which he had labored and suffered so much, still continued to haunt his imagination; and more especially his brother Modeste, now arrived at manhood, never ceased to importune him to return. Having now no means of commencing again in merchandise, although while he remained in Louisburgh a kind-hearted Parisian had employed him in a store, he finally concluded to enlarge his stock of knowledge in the healing art by studying a year under his friend, Doctor Lamoine of Washington, Pa. The larger portion of the year 1802 was passed in diligent application with that eccentric teacher, and witnessing his practice at the bedside. He now returned to his wife and children, whom he had left with her father at Unadilla, and soon after decided on moving to Ohio. After a wearisome journey across the mountains to Wheeling, he embarked on the river and landed at Marietta, in November, 1803. Monsieur Thiery, an honest baker of bread and one of the French emigrants, offered him for a home a hundred acres of land on Duck creek, nine miles from the Ohio, in the present township of Fearing, which he purchased on a credit and moved immediately out. The country at this time was in a manner a wilderness, with here and there a settler along the borders of the creeks, without roads or bridges; but he was young and in the vigor of manhood, determined to do all he could for the support of his family. A log cabin was soon erected by the aid of the neighbours, who were always ready to assist any one who came among them. It was soon spread through the country that the new settler was "a French doctor," and as there was no one of this calling within a circuit of twenty or thirty miles, except in Marietta, he was directly employed by the sick in all directions. Being a very active pedestrian, he for several months visited his patients who were within six or eight miles distance on foot, travelling at the rate of four or five miles an hour, the speed of an ordinary horse. This course was pursued until, in addition to other expenses, he had earned enough to purchase a horse without incurring a debt. During the first years of his settlement on the creek there was an unusual amount of sickness, especially of bilious fever, in the treatment of which he was eminently successful, rarely losing a patient. There were also many cases of surgery, wounds from axes, and fractured limbs, which he dressed in the neatest and most rapid manner. There was one case so singular that it is worth preserving, of a man who was thought to be mortally injured from a falling tree, which caught him under the extreme branches, bruising his flesh all over as if whipped with a thousand rods. So many blows parallzed the heart and rendered him as cold as a dead man. The doctor immediately ordered a large sheep to be killed and the skin stripped hastily off, wrapping the naked body of the man in the hot, moist covering of the animal. The effect was like a charm on the patient, removing all the bruises and the soreness in a few hours. So great was his success in treating diseases, that in one or two years he was often called to advise with the physicians of Marietta in difficult cases. In 1806 the profits of his business enabled him to afford pecuniary aid to his brother Francis, who had been forced to leave the island of St. Domingo, and was now living in great destitution in the city of Baltimore. So considerable was this assistance that it enabled him to establish himself again in merchandise. In 1809 his brother came out to Ohio and proposed to enter into partnership with him in a store at Marietta. As there was no opportunity for educating his children in the country, he consented to the change. In August, during the journey the doctor had to make to Wheeling on account of the goods for the store, his brother Modeste, who had been married for some time and lived on the same farm, was attacked with the epidemic fever which prevailed that summer all over the country from the falls of the Ohio to Wheeling. In many places it was very fatal, especially in Marietta. On his return he found him in the last stage of the disease, and in a day or two after he died. The shock of his death quite overwhelmed the doctor, especially as he thought had he been at home he could have saved him, and for some days he neglected all business, to mourn for his dear departed brother. In February, 1808, he gave up the farm and moved into Marietta, entering into partnership with Francis in the sale of merchandise, for which his former experience, polite, agreeable manners, and handsome person eminently fitted him. His reputation already established as a skilful physician, was well known to the inhabitants of Marietta, and he was often called on to attend them in sickness, which, with the demands made on him from his old patrons in the country, kept him constantly employed. In the autumn of 1808 his brother became dissatisfied with the amount of sales, and with the doctor's consent moved the merchandise to the town of St. Genevieve, in the newly acquired territory of Upper Louisiana. Soon after this he purchased a drug store and added the sale of medicine to his other business. Success attended all his endeavors, and his wealth increased in full ratio with his family, which finally embraced six sons and a daughter. About the year 1814, he enlarged his possessions in town by the purchase of a city square, which he immediately commenced improving by planting fruit trees and laying out a large flower garden ornamented with arbors and walks, for which his fine taste peculiarly fitted him. So long as this garden remained in his possession it far excelled all others in town. It was a model from which divers individuals highly improved their own, and ultimately implanted a permanent taste for this refining art to the citizens of Marietta. He was an original member of the first incorporated medical society of Ohio, in 1812, and remained a useful associate until the time of his death. In 1818 he was elected by the people one of the county commissioners, and assisted in drafting the model for the court house built in 1822. In May, 1819, he sold his property in town to Doctor Cotton, and purchased three hundred and twenty acres of Congress lands on Duck creek, twenty-two miles from Marietta, and moved out his family. To this change he was partly led on account of the number of his sons, whom he wished to establish on farms, together with a desire of conducting improvements on a larger scale for the benefit of the country. During the following year he built a flouring and saw mill, with a brick dwelling house, while through his influence greater improvements in roads and bridges were accomplished in that time than in ten previous years. The adjacent country was covered with a forest, but the soil was rich, and in a few years not a quarter section remained without a family, so great an impulse had his name and character given to the settlement. When he left Marietta his intention was to quit the practice of medicine and devote his time to the farm; but the inhabitants far and near ceased not to importune him to assist them with his well known skill in their sicknesses, to which his innate kindness of heart could not say nay. Worn down with the cares of his improvements and an extensive practice, he in August, 1821, was attacked with a bilious remittent, then prevailing in that vicinity, which assumed the congestive type and destroyed his life in a few days, while in his fifty-second year, and in the midst of his usefulness. In person Dr. Regnier was of a medium height with a stout, active frame, features well formed, full blue eyes, and a countenance expressive of benignity and intelligence. His head was finely formed, and becoming early bald, gave him an appearance of age beyond his years. Close observation and accurate discrimination of all the phases and shades of diseases gave him wonderful tact in prognosis, the base of all successful practice, while his knowledge of the proper remedies rendered him very successful in their application. His colloquial powers were unrivalled, and at the bedside his cheerful conversation, aided by the deep interest he actually felt in the welfare of the sick, with his kind, delicate manner of imparting his instructions, always left his patients better than he found them, and formed a lasting attachment to his person in all who fell under his care. His death was lamented as a serious calamity, and no physician in this region of country has since fully filled the place he occupied in the public estimation.

His children are yet living and rank amongst our best citizens. Two of them are physicians, and the others engaged in merchandise.

DOCTOR SAMUEL PRESCOT HILDRETH

Was the son of Doctor Samuel Hildreth, and born in the town of Methuen, Essex county, Massachusetts, the 30th of Sept., 1783. The old mansion house stands about a mile north of the present manufacturing town of Lawrence, on the river Merrimac. The great ancestor of all of this name in Massachusetts was Richard Hildreth. It is uncertain in what year he emigrated from England, but his name is found amongst a company of twenty men from the towns of Woburn and Concord, who petitioned the General Court of Massachusetts Bay, in the year 1652, "for a tract of land lying on the west side of Concord, or Mus-ke-ta-quid river," where the petitioners say "they do find a very comfortable place to accommodate a company of God's people upon." The petition was granted, and a settlement founded, which proved to be very prosperous. From the date on an old grave-stone standing a few years since in the burying-ground, it is ascertained that he was born in the year 1612. The subject of this brief sketch was of the sixth generation from Richard the progenitor. His early life, until he was fifteen years old, was passed on a farm, in the labors of which he actively engaged, thereby acquiring the habit of industry and laying the foundation of a vigorous, healthy frame of body for after life.

The amusements of the youth of that period were all of the athletic kind, such as running, leaping, and wrestling, promoting still further the development of the muscular system. When a small boy a taste for reading was imbibed from a social library established in the town at an early day, which remained a durable habit. After receiving as good an education as the schools of the town afforded, he was sent to Phillips' Academy in Andover, then under the care of that veteran teacher Mark Newman, Esq., whose name is yet venerated by hundreds in the United States who received the benefit of his sage instructions. He here commenced the study of Latin. Four seasons being spent at this and the Franklin Academy in the north parish, he was prepared in the languages and other branches for entering college. Instead of completing a college course, he, however, entered on the study of medicine under the instruction of Doctor Thomas Kittredge of Andover, who stood at the head of his profession in that part of the state as a surgeon, and had constantly a number of pupils under his care. More than a year was devoted to school teaching, chiefly in Andover and Bradford, as was common to the young men of limited means who studied a profession, and was time profitably bestowed in the improvement of their own faculties as well as those of the scholars. After the usual period of study he attended a course of medical lectures at Cambridge University, and received a diploma from the Medical Society of Massachusetts, in February, 1805. In May following he commenced the practice of medicine in Hempstead, N. H., boarding in the family of John True, Esq, whose brother, Dr. Jabez True, was living in Marietta, Ohio. Learning from him that this town afforded a good opening for a young man, he decided on leaving the land of his fathers and trying his fortune in the "far west," which from boyhood he had desired to see. He left the parental hearth, then in Haverhill, Mass., early in September, 1806, on horseback, and arrived at Marietta the 4th of October following. The State of Ohio was in its third year, and contained about eighty thousand inhabitants, amongst which there was no one with whom he was acquainted. It was a land of strangers; but he was young, and his heart buoyant with hope and expectation of good fortune. He soon obtained a share of the practice, the only physicians then being Dr. True and Dr. Hart. Dr. Leonard had recently died, and Dr. McIntosh had abandoned medicine. His rides sometimes extended to thirty miles through the wilderness, the settlements being "few and far between." Belprie, a flourishing town of New Englanders, fourteen miles below on the Ohio, being destitute of a doctor, he was invited by some of the leading inhabitants to come and be their physician. He went there on the 10th of December, the night on which the celebrated Blennerhasset left his fairy island, in sight of his boarding house, to join the utopian expedition of Aaron Burr. In the summer of 1807 an epidemic malarious fever prevailed all along the valley of the Ohio for several hundred miles, where there were any inhabitants, and scarcely a family in Belprie escaped an attack in some form. More than a hundred cases of fever came under his care, which he was so fortunate as to treat in a successful manner, as there were only three deaths in all that number. In Marietta the disease was much more fatal. Some of the worst cases nearly resembled the yellow fever. In August of that year he married Miss Rhoda Cook, from New Bedford, Mass. Late in the autumn, from over exertion in riding, he had an attack of inflammation of the hip joint, which continued for several months, and so greatly incommoded him on horseback that in March, 1808, he moved back to Marietta, where the practice was less laborious. Here he has remained until this time, a period of forty years, constantly engaged in his profession. In the spring of 1808 he wrote a history of the epidemic of the preceding year, which was published in the tenth volume of the New York Medical Repository. In 1810 and 1811 he was elected a representative of the State Legislature, and in the latter year drafted a bill for the regulation of the practice of medicine and establishing medical societies, which passed into a law, and remained in force with various modifications until the year 1819, when all laws on the subject were repealed. In 1812 a description of the American Colombo, with a drawing of the plant, appeared in the same work, Vol. XV. In 1822 two articles were published in the twenty-second volume of the same journal, from his pen, on Hydrophobia, and a curious case of Siamese twins, in his obstetric practice. In 1822 and 1823 the great western epidemic fever prevailed through the valley of the Ohio, visiting Marietta and the adjacent country with great virulence, few persons escaping its attack in a population of two thousand souls. In the summer and autumn of 1822 he visited daily from sixty to eighty patients in town and country; being constantly occupied from sixteen to eighteen hours in every twenty-four. In August, 1823, he was himself attacked with the prevailing fever, but arrested its course in a few days by taking Jesuit's bark in quarter ounce doses, every two hours, alternated with a solution of arsenic. Sulphate of Quinine had not then come into use in Ohio, or by it many valuable lives might have been saved. It was, however, a trial of medicine, to which few patients would submit. The year following a full history of this epidemic was written and published in the Journal of Medical Science at Philadelphia, and in 1825 an article on the minor diseases or sequela of the great epidemic, in the Western Journal of Medicine at Cincinnati. In 1826 a series of articles written in 1819, on the natural and civil history of Washington county, were published in Silliman's Journal of Science, with a drawing and description of the Spalularia, or Spoon-bill Sturgeon, found in the waters of the Ohio. This was followed in 1827 with descriptions and drawings of several undescribed fresh water shells found in the Muskingum river and other streams. From 1826 to the present time he has published annually a journal of the weather, amount of rain, flowering of plants, ripening of fruits, &c., in the same periodical, concentrating an amount of facts that may be useful to the future writers on the climate of Ohio. In 1830 an article on the history of the Cicada Septemdecim, or "North American Locust," with drawings of the insect; "The Saliferous rock formation," with a history of the manufacture of Salt, from the first settlement of Ohio;" "Ten days in Ohio," being a geological description of the region from Marietta to Chillicothe, by way of Zanesville; "The geology and coal formation of the valley of the Ohio," with numerous plates of fossils, and "The Diary of a Naturalist," on the same subject, all appeared in annual succession, from 1832 to 1836. The materials and facts for these articles were collected during journeys of ten or twelve days over the districts described, and by correspondence with intelligent individuals in tracts of country not personally visited. In 1832 he wrote a history of the floods in the Ohio river since the first settlement of the country, with a particular account of the disasters of the memorable flood of Feb., 1832, which was published in the first volume of the transactions of the Historical Society of Ohio. In 1837 he was engaged in examining and reporting on the geology of Ohio, in company with other geologists employed by the state. In 1839 he delivered an address to the Medical Society of Ohio, of which he was then president, at Cleveland, being a history of the diseases and climate of the southeastern portion of Ohio since its first settlement; which was printed by the society. In 1830 he commenced in earnest the collection of a cabinet of natural history from the fossils, insects, shells, and plants of his own state, and by exchanges of these for minerals, insects, and marine shells, with naturalists and collectors in the Atlantic cities. In the course of about eight years his cabinet contained more than four thousand specimens in the various departments of natural history, arranged in cases and drawers, labelled, numbered and entered in a catalogue under their respective heads. All this was accomplished while he was busily engaged in the practice of his profession, by saving the "odds and ends of time." Insects were gathered and pinned to the inside of the crown of his hat while riding in the country; and every stream crossed in low water was examined for shells, and the farmers' boys were employed to bring in all they could collect, and instructed how to take and preserve them in the best manner. In the summer of 1832, by the aid of two or three men a few days, he collected more than five thousand shells from the various streams about Marietta, embracing about sixty species. The finest of these were selected, labelled with printed tickets, and put up in neat boxes containing from two hundred to two hundred and fifty specimens, and sent to the eastern cities, where they were exchanged for other articles of natural history and books on the subject, by which course a valuable library was formed without trenching on his other resources. In this way he in a few years possessed a respectable cabinet in one of the most interesting branches of science. The room devoted to this object and a collection of curious relics from the mounds, being filled up, he in 1840 turned his attention to writing the history of the first settlement of Ohio, collecting the materials from such manuscripts as he could find, and from the lips of the few surviving pioneers. Two volumes of 550 pages each were thus accomplished by 1846, one of history and the other of biographies of the first settlers, who were many of them officers in the Revolutionary War. To these may be added numerous articles of early adventures on the Ohio for the Western Pioneer, and a history of the first settlement of Belville, written for the Hesperian, both printed at Cincinnati; a journal of the diseases of each month, with a bill of mortality since 1824, and still continued, may be reckoned among the products of his laborious life.

DOCTOR JOHN COTTON

Was the son of the Rev. Josiah Cotton of Plymouth, Mass., and born in Sept., 1792. His mother was Miss Rachel Barnes, daughter of the Rev. David Barnes of Scituate. His father was a graduate of Yale College, educated for the ministry, and settled over a church in Wareham. He afterwards left the desk and was appointed clerk of the court in Plymouth county, which post he filled for many years. Doctor Cotton was a descendant of the Rev. John Cotton, one of the early ministers of Boston, whose name he bore, as well as inherited no small share of the intellect of his pious ancestor. His boyhood was passed in the town of Plymouth, in attending the common schools. He was noted for his mild and gentle disposition, retiring habits, and greater fondness for study than the rude sports which so commonly occupy the time and thoughts of most boys. His preparation for college was completed at the academy in Sandwich, and he entered Cambridge College at the early age of fourteen years. His standing in the University, although not marked for brilliancy, was equal, on all accounts, to that of any other in the class. "His recitations were always correct, and he particularly excelled in logic and metaphysics." For strength of memory few could equal him. "His deportment was invariably correct, modest and unassuming," thereby sharing largely in the good will of the faculty. He graduated in 1810, soon after which he was the preceptor of an academy in Framingham, and while there commenced the study of medicine under Dr. John Kittredge of that town. He subsequently attended the medical lectures in Boston, and took the degree of Doctor of Medicine at Cambridge, in 1814.

Soon after taking his medical degree he commenced the practice of medicine in Andover, but left there in a short time for Salem, at the urgent request of the Rev. Dr. Worcester, who wished him to occupy the place lately vacated by Dr. Muzzy. In August, 1815, he married Miss Susan Buckminster of Framingham, Mass., whose family was nearly related to Doctor Buckminster of Portsmouth, and the gifted Joseph S. Buckminster of Boston. The harsh, chilly atmosphere and changeable climate of the sea coast of New England not agreeing with his rather delicate constitution, Dr. Cotton decided on removing to the milder region of the valley of the Ohio, and arrived in Marietta with his wife in November, 1815, in company with Dr. Jacob Kittredge of Salem, who sought a more temperate home on the same account. Directly after his arrival he commenced the practice of medicine on the west side of the Muskingum river, which soon yielded a support for his family. In the course of the following year he entered zealously into the enterprise of establishing Sabbath Schools, a mode of instructing the young in morality and religion then unknown in the valley of the Ohio. In this laudable effort he found many willing to aid and encourage him amongst the influential inhabitants. In 1816 one was opened on the west side of the river, and two on the east side. From thence onward he was a constant teacher in this valuable institution of righteousness to the time of his death, a period of thirty years. For the last few years he had a class of young ladies under his charge, the larger portion of whom became members of the Congregational church. That he might be able to explain more fully some of the darker passages of the Old Testament, he took up the study of Hebrew after he was forty years old, and was soon able to read in the original the words of eternal life His library abounded in works on divinity, equalling in number those of many preachers of the gospel, showing it to be a subject in which his heart was deeply engaged. He had studied the Scriptures from his youth, and united himself with the church before his marriage. Soon after his settlement in Ohio he became an associate of the Medical Society in this district, and was for a portion of the time its president, as well as that of the State Medical Society, after the districts were abolished. In the year 1824 he was chosen a representative in the Legislature from Washington county, which post he filled with credit to himself and the benefit of his constituents, forming while at Columbus lasting attachments between himself and many members from different portions of the state. The Legislature of Ohio in 1825 elected him an associate judge of the Court of Common Pleas, which appointment was renewed from time to time until the period of his death. To this station he was eminently adapted by his calm, considerate turn of mind, sound judgment, and thorough knowledge of the principles of law, which he had studied with great care, as well as the statutes of the State, by which he was guided. He was a man who did not live, like many others, entirely for himself, but took delight in diffusing the brilliancy of his own mind on those aronnd him. The stores of classical and scientific knowledge laid up in his collegiate course were often spread before the public in lectures delivered in the Marietta Lyceum and to the scholars in the Female Seminary. His favorite subject was Astronomy, which he elucidated in a familiar and easy manner, aided by diagrams of his own construction. It was the portion of the vast work of creation which above all others displayed the majesty of God, a theme on which he delighted to dwell. His familiarity with the classics, especially those of the Latin language, is another proof of his scholarship, as he composed and delivered in that tongue addresses on several occasions, especially at the installation of the first president of Marietta College, showing his familiarity and command over a subject that had long lain idle in the storehouse of his memory. When the college was incorporated, in 1836, he was one of the original trustees, and for some years the presiding officer of the board. Amongst his other posts of distinction was that of trustee of the Medical College of Ohio; an Institution patronized by the State. The weight of his character and influence was always given to what he thought to be the cause of truth, not only in religion, morals, and science, but also in politics, holding that all good men should exercise a jealous care over the ballot box, and not abandon it to demagogues. Embracing with zeal whatever was for the good of the country, he acted as chairman of the "Whig Central Committee of Washington county" for several years, discharging the duties of that vexatious post with energy and fidelity, having the satisfaction of seeing the measures recommended by the illustrious man whose name it bears generally triumphant. As a medical man he stood deservedly high among his brethren, being often called in council in difficult cases, not only in Marietta, but the adjacent towns. He was a skilful operator in surgery, as well as a successful practitioner of physic. When in the sick room his pleasing manner, kind address, and mild expression of face, won the entire confidence of the sick and greatly endeared him to the families in the circle of his practice. "Thinking no evil," and far from speaking any of his fellow-men, he was a friend to all and received in return their confidence and good will in no ordinary degree. He was the model of a Christian gentleman. His death was sudden and unexpected, after a brief illness of three or four days; but the solemn messenger found him ready and "watching for the coming of his Lord." He died on the 2d of April, 1847, aged 55 years.

[NOTE TO THE LIFE OF DR. WM. B. LEONARD.—In the wide range and severe search of the author of the *History of Newbury*, he was not able to discover whence came this singular individual, or what became of him. All he could learn about him was contained in an advertisement which he extracted into his work, under 1793. As the advertisement is curious as well as characteristic, we here insert it:

"He states, that he had been a physician thirty-five years, and that 'a kind Providence has enabled him to spring out of the iron chains of tyranny, horror, devastation, and murder to the only summit of liberty under the sun, and where the diadem of a despot was hurled down to the bottomless abyss.'" —ED.]

A RECORD FOR IMITATION.

Daniel Wetherell Esq. dyed on the 14th day of April, 1719, in the morning at sun about an hour high, being in the 89th year of his age. He was born Nov. 29. 1630 at the free school house in Maidston in the county of Kent in Old England.—*New London Records*, Vol. I. p. 72, furnished by MR. EDWIN HUBBARD of West Meriden, Conn.

WOBURN BURYING-GROUND.

[Communicated by MR. N. WYMAN, JR.—Continued from p. 46.]

Thompson	Ebenezer of Charlston	Apr	19 1741	58
Cotton	Here lyes the Remains of Mrs Elisabeth Cotton Daughter of the Rev[d] Roland Cotton late of Sandwich Deas[d] who Died A Virgin Octo[br] 12th 1742 Ætatis 46. if a virgin Marry she hath not sinned. Nevertheless Such shall have trouble in the flesh. But he that giveth he not in marriage doeth better. She is happier if She so abide.			
Hartwell	Dea Joseph	Nov	14 1743	63
Wyman	Ensign Samuel	Dec	28 1743	55y
Flagg	Esther Wid of Eleazer	Sept	18 1744	70
Brooks	Hepzabah w of Jabez	Jan	1 1745	75
Baldwin	Ruel s of James & Ruth	Feb	21 1745–6	3y 2m
Brooks	Jabez	Aug	30 1746	74y
Flagg	Ebenezer	July	10 1746	68y
Fox	Anna w of Jabez of Falmouth [Portland]	Aug	5 1746	43
Reed	Elisabeth d of Isreal & Hannah	Dec	9 1747	10 wanting 9 [d]
Snow	Timothy	Mar	11 1747	74y
Brooks	Sarah w of Nathan	Feb	21 1747	40–6–3
Richardson	Abigail d of Jonathan & Abigail	Oct	27 1747	25
Tay	Mary d of William & Abigail	May	5 1747	1y 10m
"	Ruth	Jan	15 1747	10–4–9
Wright	Dea Josiah	Jan	22 1747	73y
Richardson	Eunice w of Joshua	Apr	13 1748	29
Richardson	Hannah w of Jacob	Sept	7 1748	69
Thompson	Samuel	May	13 1748	43
Richardson	Joshua	Nov	5 1748	68
Cotton	Susanna d of Rev Josiah & Susanna	Aug	3 1748	10y
Salter	Thomas of Boston Merchant	Aug	2 1748	62
Walker	Mary wid of Samuel formerly w of James Foul Esq	Oct	23 1748	80
Holding	Mary w of John	Nov	21 1749	49
Hayward	Doc[t] Jonathan	Aug	13 1749	45
Richardson	Daniel	Apr	20 1749	57
Brooks	Benjamin s of Benjamin & Susanna	Sept	1 1749	8 weeks 4 ds
Richardson	John	Oct	29 1749	81–2m 5d
Wyman	Phebe w of David	Nov	24 1750	55y
Wright	Rachel wid of Joseph	June	21 1750	55y
Richardson	Bridget w of Dea Stephen	July	1750	76
Sawyer	Mary wid of Joshua	Oct	23 1751	69
Carter	Susanna w of Thomas	Aug	12 1751	57
Brooks	Nathan	Jan	6 1751	45
Wyman	Esther w of Benjamin	Sept	16 1751	44y
"	Elisabeth d of " & Esther	Aug	26 1751	4 days

[To be continued.]

SOME MATERIALS TOWARDS A GENEALOGY OF THE FAMILY OF THE NAME OF ROLFE.

Rolfe is the same name, or most probably of the same origin, as *Ralfe, Ralph, Rolph,* and other variations. According to CAMDEN* it is contracted from *Radulph,* and like *Rodulph* signified "Helpe-councell." The family of *Rolphe* extract their origin from a Saxon, who added much to the castle of Rochester.†

No persons of the name have come under our observations of any very great distinction, and but one of any extraordinary notoriety; nor was the name ever very common in England, judging from such researches as we have been able to make in the local and other histories of that country.

The armorial bearings are thus published by the Burkes:‡

ROLFE of Deptford, co. of Kent, and Hackney, co. of Middlesex. Ar. three ravens Sa.; a trefoil vert, for diff. Crest — A raven, close, sa. in the beak a trefoil, slipped, vert. — ROLFE of Chislehurst, co. of Kent, and London, same *Arms,* with a cinquefoil in chief, vert. — ROLFE of Sarum, co. Wilts. Ar. three ravens sa. *Crest* — on a staff, couped and raguly, lying fesseways, and sprouting at the dexter end, vert, a raven, close, sa. — ROLFE of Inglethorpe, co. York. Az. three water bougets or. — ROLFE of Yorkshire. Or, three water bougets sa. — ROLFE. Ar. a raven sa. — ROLFE of Heacham Hall, co. Norfolk; as borne by S. C. E. NEVILLE ROLFE, of Heacham Hall, Esq., who took the name and arms of Rolfe by royal license, 19 April, 1837, on coming into possession of the property of the late Edward Rolfe, of Heacham Hall, Esq. Quarterly, first and fourth, gyronny of eight, or and az. on a chief sa. three annulets, ar.; second and third, gu, five mascles in fesse ar. within a bordure ar. *Crests* — First, a lion's head erased; second, on a mount a crescent, therefrom issuant a rose slipped.

The following are some of the early notices of the name in England. In the will of Humphrey de Bohun, earl of Hereford, dated "on the Sunday following St. Denis, [October 10] 1361, *John Rolf* is a legatee, and also *John Ralph,* who, in the obscurity of "'venour;' à un garson pur le ferour xx *s.*;"§ may be an expected son of the former.

When the "survey of Domesday" was taken, a person of the name of *Rolf* possessed the manor then called Chenvestan, since Cheinstone in Devonshire; none of the name appear to have been there in the time of Edward the Confessor, but a person named *Algar,* abbot of Buckfastleigh. We find a *Ralph* (time of the Conquest) at Chivelstone also in the county of Devon.‖

In 1447, *William Rolph* was a bailiff of Bristol.¶

* *Remaines Concerning Britaine,* 85, ed. 4° 1637.
† MS. of H. G. Somerby, Esq.
‡ *General Armory,* ed. 1847.
§ *Testamenta Vetusta,* i. 67.
‖ Lyson's *Magna Britannia.* lx.
¶ Barrett's *Hist. Bristol,* 680.

In 1532, *Robert Rolf* was one of the executors of the will of Lord Berners, (the well known translator of Froissart.) He was then recorder of Calais.*

Robert Rolf of Hadley, co. Suffolk, m. Bridget, fifth dau. of Edward Wright of Sutton Hall in the same county. George Wright, brother of Edward, m. in 1542. *Bridget*, dau. of *Robert Rolfe*, Esq., m. Richard Champney, who d. 1653.†

There was a family of *Rolfe* at Harwich in the county of Essex, of great respectability, two centuries ago; the names of the members of which are spelt with nearly all the variations to be found at the commencement of this memoir. From some circumstances we hazard the opinion that the *Rolfs* of New England are of this family. Between 1612 and 1620, Mr. *Edward Rafe* [Rolfe] was mayor of Harwich. In 1636, *Mr. John Rolfe* was mayor of that place, and in 1643 he was again chosen to the same office. In 1674, Mr. *John Rolfe* (not the same) was mayor, and again a second time in 1685. And as late as 1728, a Mr. *George Rolf* was mayor of that borough.

In the church-yard of Harwich are some monuments to the family of Rolfe. On one of black marble we read—

Here lyes Inter'd the Body of
IOHN ROLFE Gentleman who
Departed this Life on the 2[d] day of
Octobr: 1717. in the 75 Year of
his Age who was married to his
Wife ELIZABETH 54. Years
And had issue by her six Sons
And Three Daughters
Here Lyeth also the Body of
M[rs] ELIZABETH ROLFE Wife to
M[r] IOHN ROLFE who Departed
this Life the 23[d] Day of August
1721 Aged 76 Years.

On another stone—

"Three sons of Geo: Rolfe & Martha his wife,"
viz. JOHN, GEORGE and JOHN; all in infancy 1709–11.

WILLIAM ROLFE was one of the executors of the will of the eccentric and vastly rich Henry Smyth of London, 1627.‡

There was a Captain (though oftener, perhaps, styled Major) Rolfe, of extensive notoriety in the time of the "Civil War." He was accused of attempting the life of the king (Charles I.) The matter was long under the consideration of Parliament, and at the restoration he was brought to trial, but was eventually discharged on the ground of his being *non compos mentis*.§

In the 16th of Charles II., *Abraham Rolfe*, clerk, had erected at Lusham, near Greenwich in Kent, two Free Schools and an Almshouse.‖

Of what family Mr. John Rolf was, who married the world renowned Indian princess POCAHONTAS, we are not able to state. There cannot, however, be much doubt that he was of some of the families enumerated above; and we hope at some time to be able to show the connection of all

* *Testamenta Vetusta*, ii. 659.
† Burke's *Commoners*.
‡ Dale's *History of Harwich*, 42, *et seq.*
§ In the *Parliamentary History*, Clarendon, Prince's *Worthies*, and other works of the time, are numerous and curious particulars respecting this affair.
‖ Gibson in Camden, i. 222.

these families, and those with that of New England, if any ever existed. The gentleman who married POCAHONTAS had one son, but this son left no male posterity. In the female line, however, are descended the Bollings, Randolphs, Blands, and many other distinguished families of Virginia.*

We come now to the family of Rolfe in New England. The following is the article concerning them in FARMER'S Genealogical Register:

ROLFE, BENJAMIN, Newbury, where he was b. a. 1641. BENJAMIN, the second minister of Haverhill, was son of Benj. Rolfe, and was b. 13 Sept., 1662 [Coffin.]; grad. at H. C. 1684, ordained in Jan. 1694, and was slain by the Indians in an attack on Haverhill, 29 Aug., 1708, æ. 46. DANIEL, EZRA, and THOMAS were of Ipswich in 1648, and David Rolfe died in Salem, ab. 1654. HENRY, one of the proprietors of Newbury in 1635. JOHN, one of the first settlers of Newbury, and a proprietor of Salisbury,† was admitted freeman, 1639, and d. 8 Feb., 1663. His last wife, Mary Scullard, he m. in 1656.

For much of the above, as is seen, Farmer was indebted to the since historian of Newbury. In his work Mr. Coffin has added something to Farmer's article, but he was not able to establish or define a relationship between many of the members of the family which he has given. From what he has given and several other sources,‡ the following pedigree is made out.

HONOUR ROLFE appears to have been the immediate ancestor of two or more Newbury emigrants of the name. It is not ascertained that this person came to America.

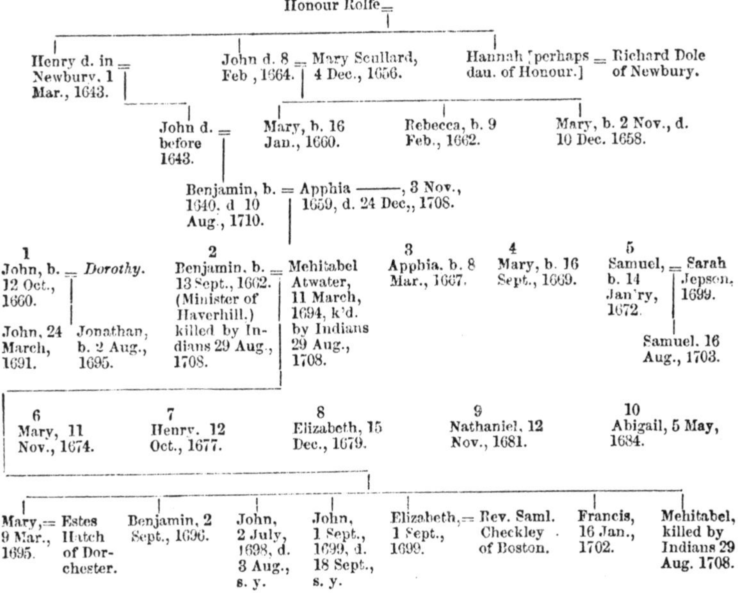

There are several items on the records at Haverhill about other branches of the Rolfe family, which we are unable at present to dispose of except by giving them an insertion in our work as we find them.

EZRA ROLFE m. *Abigail Bond*, 2 March, 1676, and had 1, *Abigail*, b.

* Nothing in Smith's *Hist. of Virginia* to throw light on the parentage of *Rolfe*.

† See pp. 55, 56, and 57 of the present number. — ED.

‡ For the facts respecting the Haverhill branch, we are indebted to MR. JAMES S. LORING of Boston, member of the N. E. Hist. Gen. Soc.

17 Sept., 1677; 2, *Ezra*, b. 24 Nov., 1680; 3, *Daniel*, b. 14 Feb., 1685; 4, *Mary*, and 5, *Martha*, b. 23 Nov., 1687. Mr. EZRA ROLFE, Sen., was wounded and taken prisoner by the Indians on the 17 October, 1689. and died on the 20th following.

DANIEL ROLFE m. *Mercy Pattee*, and had 1, *Samuel*, b. 30 June, 1718; 2, *Mary*, 11 April, 1720.

NATHANIEL ROLFE m. *Hannah Rolfe*, and had 1. *William*, b. 5 March, 1748; 2, *Benjamin*, d. 30 Oct., 1749; 3, *Judith*, b. 25 Nov., 1750; 4, *Benjamin*, b. 31 May, 1753.

EPITAPH.

Enclosed in this tomb is the body of the reverend, pious and learned man Benjamin Rolfe, who was a most faithful pastor of the Church of Christ in Haverhill. He was barbarously slain by the enemy at his own house, on the morning of the Sabbath, 29th of August in the year of Our Lord 1708, and in the 46th of his ministry.

Not having the acquaintance or knowledge of a single individual of the name of *Rolfe*, the writer of this article may be excused for his apparent dearth of information respecting the family. He hopes that what is here given may meet the eye of some descendants, and prompt them to look into the matter, and to communicate the result of their inquiries.

Since the above was in type we have received* the following additional particulars:

A daughter of *John Rolfe* m. a Ring. His grandchildren were *John*, *Joseph*, and *Esther*. A *John Saunders* m. *Esther Rolfe*, dau. of *John*.

Hester, wife of *John Rolfe*, d. 3 June, 1647.

"The *Confidence* of London, 200 Tons, John Johnson Master, sailed April, 1638, having 110 passengers. Among them were *John Sanders*, aged 25, and *Sara* his wife, from Lamford, Wilts Co. *William Cottle*, Servant. *John Rolfe*, aged 50, and *Ann* his wife and 2 Sons, *John* and *Thomas*, 4 years and under, from Melchitt Parke, Wilts Co."

It is presumable that the *John Rolfe* here mentioned is the same who d. 8 Feb., 1664, but further than that we cannot at present go.

LONGEVITY.

At one of the late anniversary meetings in Boston, Rev. Dr. Pierce, of Brookline, remarked, that when first invited to attend this Jubilee, he felt that he was *too old*, but he had since looked into the State of Connecticut, and found a clergyman born the 23d of January, 1754, who was now 94 years old. He was ordained on the 13th of March, 1782, when this white-headed man was little short of nine years of age. And what was worthy to be mentioned, he had preached ever since *without a colleague*. On his sixty-fifth anniversary, he mentioned in his sermon that he had never been detained but eleven days during the whole time, from his work. When this venerable man — Dr. Nott — was asked what was the secret of such a long life, and such health and strength, he replied that there were four rules: rise early; live temperate; work hard; keep cheerful. The chairman, when Dr. Pierce sat down, said, surely nobody can think that Dr. Pierce is an old man yet. — *Transcript*, 19*th June*, 1848.

* From Joshua Coffin, Esq.

Bramford ye 11 of October 1669

A List of the names of the Free men living in ye Towne of Bramford

Mr. John Wilford
Thomas Blackley
John Lingly
Michaell Taintor
Daniell Swayer
Michaell Pamir
Samuill Ward
John Rogers

Thomas Blackley
Mich Taintor

Joseph Dowey

March 22. 1709=10
Joseph Dowey personally appeared in Colchester before me the subscriber her majesties Justice of peace for the County of Hartford: & acknoliged the above written instrument to be his vollentary act & deed: Michaell Taintor Justice
entered on Record march 22 1709=10

Signed sealed & delivered in presents of us witnesses
Samuell pollet
William Chamberlin

EARLY RECORDS OF BRAINFORD, NOW BRANFORD, CT.

[From materials principally furnished by MR. CHARLES M. TAINTOR of Shelburne, Mass.]

In the accounts of Branford which we have seen, we do not find any reason given why that name was made choice of. It was for a time called *Brainford*, which was probably as correct as *Branford*, neither giving a very precise idea of its probable origin. It is our opinion that it was so named after *Brentford* in England; if so, its signification is perfectly apparent. Our fathers have left us much in the dark in respect to the reasons they may have had for naming many of our towns; and although we have no *Barnstaple*, or *Brentford*, there can be but little doubt that our towns of *Barnstable* and *Branford* were so named to perpetuate those.

Whether some of the early inhabitants of Branford came originally from Brentford in the county of Middlesex, England, or whether some of their friends or connections distinguished themselves on the side of the Parliament there in 1642, we have not the means within our reach to decide. However, we are told that Branford received its name in 1644. It may be interesting to our readers to note that Brentford is early mentioned in English history. There was a bloody conflict between Edmund Ironside and the Danes here, A. D. 1016, and in the time of Mary, six persons were burnt at the stake on account of their religion. The famous battle-ground of Hounslow-heath is near it. In its church is an inscription to John Horne, father to the well known John Horne Tooke. The last Duke Schomberg was Earl of Brentford. He died in 1719.

Branford was purchased by the New Haven colonists in December, 1638, a few days after they had bought New Haven of Momanquin, sachem of that place, then called Quinnipiac. In 1644, a tract of land was sold by New Haven to Mr. William Swain and others, for the accommodation of those persons in Wethersfield who wished to remove from thence. Sept. 5th, 1640, the General Court at New Haven made a grant of a tract, the Indian name of which was Totokett, to Samuel Eaton, brother of Governor Eaton, upon the condition of his procuring a number of his friends from England to make a settlement in that tract of country. Mr. Eaton failed in fulfilling the conditions. About three years after, the subject was acted upon thus: "Totokett, a place fit for a small plantation betwixt New Haven and Guilford, and purchased from the Indians, was granted to Mr. Swayne and some others in Weathersfield, they repaying the charges, which are betwixt £12 and £13, and joining in one jurisdiction with New Haven and the fornamed plantations, upon the same fundamental agreement settled in October 1643, which, they duly considering, accepted."*

The following is a verbatim copy of the "NEW PLANTATION AND CHURCH COVENANT" of Branford, with its original signers' names:—

"Jan. 20: 1667 — forasmuch as y[t] it appeares y[t] the undertaking & the settlement of this place of Brainford was secured by & for men of congregationall principles as to church orders according to y[e] platforme of disceplaine agreed on by the senate or thare abouts drane from y[e] word of God in y[e] which we y[t] remaine hear can say we have found much peace & quiatnes to our great comfort for y[e] which we desire for to bless God & that it may so remaine unto such as do continue thair abode in this place & to such as

* *New Haven Records* in BARBER'S *Hist. Cols. Ct.*, 188–9.

shall come in to fill up the roumes of those y^t are removed & that do intende for to remove from this place of Brainford = wee all do see cause now for to agree that an orthodoxe minester of y^t judgement shall be called in & settled amongste vs = The gathering of such a church shall be Incouraged — The vpholdment of such Church officears shall not want pporshanall supplye of maintainence according to Rull — We will not in any waise Incroach upon or disturbe the liberties in so walking from time to time & att all times Nor will we be any wayes Injurious vnto them in civil or Ecclesticall Respectes & this wee ffreely & volentarily Ingage ourslves vnto Joyntly & severally so long as we remayne Inhabetants in this place & this we bind ourselves unto by our subscription unto this agreement It is also agreed y^t whosoever shall come for purchise or admitted a free planter hear shall so subscribe before his admittance or his bargine vallid in law Amongst us —

Jasper Crane
John Wilford
Tho. Blachly
Samuell Plum
Mich. Taintor
John Collens
Mich. Pamer
John Ward
John Linsley
John Robins
Robart ffoott
George Page
Thomas Sutliff
Daniell Swaine
Samuell Pond
Isaac Bradley
Jonathan Rose
Georg Adames
John Whithead
Samuell Ward
Edward Frisbe
Henry Gratwick
Mathew Bickatt
Thomas Harrison
Thomas Whedon
George Seward
Edward Ball
William Hoadlie
Eleazer Stent
John Rogers
Samuel Bradfeld
John Charles
William Roswell
Edward Barker
Peter Tyler
Anthony Howd
John Adames
Thomas Sargent
Moses Blachly
Jan. Waters
John ffrisbe
John Linsley jun[r]
William Maltbie
John Rose
Bartholomew Goodrich
John Taintor
Frances Tyler."

MICHAEL TAINTOR

Was one of the principal inhabitants of Branford, drew up the "New Plantation and Church Covenant" above inserted, still preserved in the records in his hand-writing, and he was probably the author of it. A good facsimile of his autography and of the records accompany this article. The autograph of a progenitor of a highly respectable race must be viewed by his descendants with much satisfaction; and not only by his descendants, but by all true lovers of antiquarian matters.

Michael Taintor came from Wales, and in 1653 was master of a vessel trading to Virginia. He afterwards settled in Branford, and died there in 1673. In 1667 he was one of four persons "employed and empowered by the town of Branford to buy the house and lands of Richard Harrison." In 1669 he was of the number chosen by the town to settle certain difficulties between Branford and New Haven, respecting bounds. The next year he was employed upon a like matter relative to the bounds of Branford and Guilford. About the same time he was judge of a court at Branford, and he was frequently a member of the General Court or Assembly of Connecticut. At his decease his estate amounted, as per inventory, to £166 4s. 10d. His wife Elizabeth died July, 1659.

PEDIGREE OF THE TAINTOR FAMILY.

Charles Taintor was in N. England in 1643. Lost at sea 1654.=

Michael above noticed. = Elizabeth. | Charles went to Virginia, about 1656. | Joseph. | Marie = Thomas, s. of Rev. Abraham Pierson, of Branford, Nov., 1662.

John, b. May, 1650, at Branford, d. Sept., 1699, s. p. = Dorcas Swain. | Micaiell, b. Oct., 1652, at Colchester, died Feb., 1730. = 1, Mary Loomis, 2, Mabel, wid. of Daniel Butler, 1697. | Elizabeth, b. June, 1655. = Noah Rogers. | Johana, b. Apr., 1657. | Sarie, b. Oct., 1658.

Micael, deac., b. Sept., 1680, at Windsor, Ct., d. March, 1771, æ. 91. = Eunice Foote, 1712. | John, b. October, 1682. | Mary, b. Sept., 1685. = Edw'd Moore of Windsor. | Joseph, b. Nov., 1687, settled at Branford, d. 1728. = Elizabeth Foote, 1710. A | Sarie, b. Nov., 1698. = Noah Clark of Colchester.

Eunice, b. Apr., 1717. = Aaron Skinner of Colchester. | Michael, b. 31 Dec., 1719, Colchester, d. Nov., 1748. = Sarah Loomis of Colchester. B | Charles, b. Feb., 1723, Colchester, d. March, 1807. = Mary, dau. of Rev. Tho. Skinner of Westchester, d. 1822. C | John, b. July, 1725. = 1, Esther Clark, 1751; 2, Sarah, dau. Capt. Gershom Bulkley, 1758. D

Mary, b. Nov., 1727, d. Dec., 1815. = Col. David Wells of Shelburn, Ms., 1749. | Prudence, b. Dec., 1729. = Dr. John Watrous of Colchester. | Sarah, b. April, 1731. = Nathaniel Otis of Colchester. | Anne, b. Oct., 1734, d. unm. Jan., 1755.

A

Mary, b. July, 1711. = Samuel Lewis of Colchester, 1729. | Joseph, b. Nov., 1714, Branford, d. Oct., 1750. = Sarah Barker, April, 1743. E | Elizabeth, b. Oct., 1716. = ——— Moore of Windsor.

John, bap. July, 1719. = Sarah Foote, (wid.) 1746. | Michael, b. 8 June, 1723. = Sarah Foote, Sept., 1747. | Nathaniel, bap. Nov., 1725. = Submit Tyler, Jan., 1753.

B

Sarah, b. 30 Dec., [?] 1746. = Asa Strong. | Michael, deac., b. 14 March, 1748, Charleston, S. C., Orford, N. H., a soldier Rev., d. April, 1831. = Lydia Loomis of Colchester, April, 1767. F

C

Anne, b. July, 1767. = Erastus Worthington. | Charles, b. Jan., 1769, d. in infancy. | Eunice, b. Dec., 1770. = Cyrus Bill of Lebanon, Ct. | Charles, b. Dec., 1772, d. in Buffalo, N. Y., 1827. = Sarah Fox of Colc'r. Dec. 1800. | Sarah, b. July, 1775. = John C. Bulkley of Colchester

Betsey, b. Dec., 1777. = Fox of N London. | Sophia, b. Feb., 1780. = Daniels of N. York. | Newhall, b. July, 1782, has held many offices. Still living. = Ruth Smith of Haddam. | Eudocia, b. Aug., 1785. = Samuel Reid of Colchester.

D

Esther = Hon. Joseph Isham of Colchester. | Betsey = Capt. Chas. Bulkley of Colchester. | John, b. Sept., 1760, a rev. sold., settled in Windham, Ct., d. in New York, 1825. = ——— Hosford of Marlboro', Ct. | Charles, b. 17 Dec., 1762, Colchester, a rev. sold., living in Windham, 1847 = ——— Abbe of Windham. | Gurshom, b. May, 1765, d. Oct., 1775.

Roger, b. Dec., 1767. = Nabby Bulkley. | Solomon, b. Oct., 1769. = Judith Bulkley. | Sally, b. Aug., 1773. = Joshua R. Bulkley. | Polly, b. May, 1777. = Godfrey Grosvenor of Pomfret. | Jared, b. 1746. = Rebecca Linsley.

E

Sarah, b. Nov., 1743. = ——— Norton, of Durham, Ct. | Joseph, b. Sept., 1745. = Mary Wilson of Windsor, Ct. | Elizabeth, b March, 1748, d. 1751. | Benjamin, b. June, 1751.

Lydia, b.=Moses Palmer of Orford, Jan., 1768, Colc'r. N. H. | Michael, b.=Martha Harris. Apr., 1770. | Sarah, b.=Peter Moulton of Orford, Dec., 1771. N. H. | Asa, b. Sept.,=1, Damaris, 1778, Orford. 2, Elizabeth Convers of Lyme, N. H. | Mary, b. Sept., 1780, d. unm. 1813.

Alfred, b.=Anne Chamberlaine of Thetford, Vt. March, 1785. | Charles, b. 16=Phebe Hubbard Wells of Shelburne, Mass., April, 1787. 1810. She d. 5 June, [1848, æ. 62. These were the parents of Mr. Charles Micaiell Taintor, our authority before mentioned. | John R., b.=Roxa Woodruff, Apr., 1791. Wolcott, N. Y.

WILL OF RIARD HAFFEELD.

Vpon the 17th daye of y^{e} 12th month in ye yeare 1638. I Richard Hafeeld* of Ipswich in New England, being of body weake & feeble, but of mind & memory pfectly able to make this my last will & testament — as followeth —

1. To my two oldest daus. mary & Sara £30 apeece — viz. that £30 w^{h} I am to rec. of Thos. fferman for a house sold to Robt. wallis his man wch is to be paid at three paiments, £10 at a time, according to ye tenour of a bill, this £30 as it is rec^{d} to be devided eqly betxt y^{m}, also 20 acres vpland & meadow at Reedy marsh valued at 20£ to be deuided betxt y^{m} prsently after my decease: alsoe 10£ in money or my Cow Calfe to be devided betxt y^{m} & in case either of y^{m} dye before theye are posest wth y^{s} my guift then my will is y^{t} ye longer liuer to haue ye whole £60

Alsoe I giue to my 3 younger daus. Martha, Rachell & Ruth, to each of y^{m} 30£ apeece, to be p^{d} y^{m} as y^{a} shall com to y^{e} age of 16 yeares old, And my will is alsoe, y^{t} y^{f} any one of y^{m} dy before y^{a} attaine to y^{e} age of 16, y^{t} y^{n} y^{e} whole £90 to fale [fall] to y^{e} longer liuers or longer liuer, y^{s} s^{d} 90£ to be p^{d} y^{m} as $afores^{d}$. I doe enjoyne my wife to y^{e} true & just paiment of it whome I make my executrix of y^{s} my last will & testmt.

The mark of
Robert Andrews
George Giddings

Wee whose names are vnder written do witness y^{t} y^{e} testator at y^{e} same time did giue unto his 2 daus. Sara & Mary certaine debts owing to him by these men

Goodman Foster	3£ 5s
Richard Waters	2 10
William Avery	1
Thos. Dorman	1

Geo. Giddings
John Browne

Geo. Giddings & John Browne came into court held at Ipswich y^{e} 29th of Sept. 1668 & owned y^{t} y^{a} did beleeve that there names heareunto were y^{r} owne hands writing.

Robt. Lord Cleric

This is a true Copie Compared with the original on file in Salem Court $Recd^{s}$ Attests

* This name is not found in FARMER's *Register*. In Mr. FELT's *Hist. of Ipswich* he is registered among the early settlers of that town under 1635. From the will of *Richard Haffeeld* given above, it does not appear that he left any male posterity, and the name is probably extinct in New England.

THE TULLY FAMILY OF SAYBROOK, CT.

HISTORICAL AND GENEALOGICAL SKETCHES OF THE TULLY FAMILY, INCLUDING AN ACCOUNT OF THEIR FIRST SETTLEMENT IN AMERICA; COLLECTED FROM MANUSCRIPTS IN POSSESSION OF INDIVIDUALS BELONGING TO THE FAMILY.

[Communicated by SAMUEL H. PARSONS, ESQ., Member of the N. E. Historic, Genealogical Society.]

[It is stated in the following memoir, that "there were few in England of the name" of Tully, and from considerable investigation we are led to the same conclusion. We meet with *Robert Tully*, a monk, of the city of Gloucester, at a very early age. He belonged to the "famous church" of that city, "the great and stately tower" of which was built by Abbot *Seabroke*. "This is so neat and curious, that travellers have affirm'd it to be one of the best pieces of Architecture in England. Abbot *Seabroke*, the first designer of it, dying, left it to the care of *Robert Tully*, a Monk of this place; which is intimated in those verses written in black Letters, under the arch of the Tower in the Quire:

Hoc quod digestum specularis, opusque politum,
Tullii hæc ex onere, Seabroke Abbate jubente.

This Fabrick which you see, exact and neat,
The Abbot charg'd Monk Tully make compleat."*

In the pedigree of Savile of Thornhill, mention is made of *Elizabeth*, daughter of *Dr. Tully*, married to John Savile, rector of Thornhill in Yorkshire. This was in the early part of the last century. And in the pedigree of Netterville of Ireland, it is noted that *James Tully* of Dunmore, M. D., married one of that family. We meet with several eminent authors of the name. *Thomas*, a native of Carlisle, educated at Queen's College, Oxford, flourished from 1642 to 1675. He was born 1620. *George Tully*, a relative of the preceding, according to Lempriere, was also of Queen's College; a publisher of a translation of Plutarch's Morals—of Miltiades's Life of Nepos, Cæsar by Suetonius, with notes, &c. He was born 1653.

In the Heraldic Dictionary we find only

TULLY (Wetherall Abbey, co. Cumberland). Ar. on a chev. gu. three escallops or, in chief a lion pass. vert. *Crest*—A cupid with his bow and quiver, all ppr.

TULLY (Ireland). Ar. on a chev. three escallops of the second. *Crest*—On a chapeau a serpent nowed in a loveknot, all ppr.]

It appears that the family originally belonged to the parish of Horley,† in the county of Surry, England, about twenty miles from London; and that the grandfather of him who first came into New England had three children, namely, *John*, *William*, and *Martha*, but neither his age, his marriage, or christian name is known.

The father of him who first came to New England was brother to the above named William and Martha, and married Sarah, the sister of John Fenner, the first of that name who came to Saybrook, the brother of Arthur and William Fenner, who settled in Providence, R. I.

The two last mentioned were the progenitors of the present Fenner

* BISHOP GIBSON in CAMDEN.

† In the hundred of Reigate.—ED.

Family in Providence. It further appears that John Tully of the parish of Horley, who married Sarah Fenner and died while in England, had by her two children, namely, John and Sarah, the former of whom, as appears by the clergyman's certificate, was baptized Sept. 9th, 1638, and the latter, Sept. 27th, 1640.

In the year 1644, on the 11th June, John Tully, who died in England, made his will, leaving a widow Sarah, with her son John, five or six years of age, her daughter, about three or four, and herself about twenty-seven.

This John Tully of Horley, by his will, after making a donation to the poor of the parish, and after giving a legacy to his brother William, of fifty pounds sterling, to be raised from the rents of a certain piece of land in said parish known by the name of Featheridge, placed all his lands under the care of his brother and one George Kerrall as overseer, and ordered the rents of said lands to be put into his wife's hands till his daughter should come to the age of ten years; and after that the avails of the lands to continue in the overseers' hands till the rents should amount to fifty pounds, and then to return to his widow to be held and improved by her during her natural life; but in case she should die before the fifty pounds should be raised, he directed that said lands should continue in the overseers' hands for the purpose of educating his daughter. He then bestowed on his brother William a small gift, and another on his sister Martha, and a valuable present in personal estate on his son John, then about five or six years of age; after which he gave all his goods and chattels to his wife Sarah, his debts being first paid, and made his wife sole executrix, putting into her possession all his lands, houses, and other buildings, till his son should come of age. In the year 1646 or 1647, Sarah, the widow, with her two children, accompanied her two brothers, Arthur and William, to New England, and settled here. At this period, his son was in the ninth year of his age. At a proper time, one of the Fenners, in behalf of John Tully, made a voyage to England for the purpose of obtaining possession of his property, but by some means now unknown, was unsuccessful in effecting it; but neglecting to take his deeds, his uncle William and the other overseer denied his right, and in fact asserted that he was an impostor, and that they had ample proof of the death of the real heir. Therefore he was necessitated to return to America in order to procure testimonials of his descent, and possess himself of the writings of the estate. On reaching the house of his mother, who had not long before married Mr. Robert Say of Saybrook, he found the deeds, so essential to the case in question, cut into narrow slips and attached to a lace pillow; but with much difficulty the pieces were at last so nicely pasted together as to answer the purpose. When he reached England, having happily recovered the estate, he disposed of the same, which seems to have been very valuable, as the house had been used as a house of entertainment.

By one deed he sold to Peter and Anthony Leachford all that messuage or tenements, gardens, orchards and backsides, barns, stables, &c., thereto belonging, with that piece of land adjoining called Styfields, containing eight and one half acres, lying in said parish of Horley, for £120.

The recovery of the estate appears to have been about twenty years after his father's death.

In 1671, *John Tully* was married to *Mary Beamont*, daughter of William Beamont, a native of Carlisle, in the county of Cumberland, on the borders of Scotland, who came to *Connecticut* in the capacity of tailor to Sir Richard Saltonstall.

The mother of this Mary Beamont, it appears, was a Danforth, sister to him who was formerly deputy governor of Massachusetts. After this, John

Tully settled at *Potapaugh*, in that part called Denison's Point, in the now second society of Saybrook, where his first four children were born. In February, 1680, he purchased of Robert Say, his father-in-law, a house and lot on the Town Plot, about three quarters of a mile westward of a nook of salt meadow, in which house he resided till the day of his death, which happened October 5, 1701.*

As he had not been bred a farmer, and had no relish for agriculture, he disposed of his property in lands, which it seems was very considerable, and almost wholly supported his family by teaching arithmetic, navigation, and astronomy. In addition to this, he annually furnished New England with almanacs, from 1681 to 1702,† the last of which was published in Boston, after his death. The duties attached to the office of Town Clerk were also discharged a long time by him, and from the ancient mode in which writings of this nature were executed, he probably made the business lucrative. So greatly superior was this man's education to most, if not all, of his cotemporaries in America, and so superstitious and ignorant were the common people in the country, that with them he was reputed a conjurer. This strange reputation, however, was acquired, as appears, merely by exercising what at the present day would be termed common sagacity. As an instance of this we have an account of an application from a person at Long Island respecting a child that was lost in the woods several months before by a party who were gathering wild fruit; and as it appeared on enquiry that no search had been made in a neighboring village of Indians, our ancestor directed the father to enquire there, which he accordingly did with success.

From papers now in possession of the family, it may with the greatest certainty be concluded that his established principles and practices were those of true Christianity.

Sarah, the sister of said John, it appears, married a *Denison*, soon after she came to this country, and from her, we are told, sprung all the present families of that name in the towns of Stonington and Saybrook. Their mother died soon after her son removed to the Town Plat.

The children of John Tully were as follows:

John, b. Dec. 3, 1672, lost at sea.
Sarah, b. April 9, 1674, d. Dec. 30, 1692.
William, b. Jan. 5, 1676, d. July 5, 1744.
Lydia, b. March 15, 1679, d. July 12, 1740.
Mary, b. Aug. 10, 1681.
Deborah, b. Feb. 24, 1683, d. March 13, 1721.
Lucy, b. March 22, 1686, d. April 5, 1692.
Hepsibah, b. Dec. 22, 1689, d. Oct. 26, 1767.

John, the eldest, married in Boston and settled there, whence he sailed master of a vessel bound to England just before a remarkably severe storm, in which it was conjectured he was lost. It is now suspected, however, considering the little intercourse which in that day subsisted between the colonies, that the storm in which he was supposed to have perished shipwrecked him on our southern coast, where he probably made choice of another wife, for it is worthy of remark, that in the year 1775, an individual of the Tully family from Saybrook became acquainted at Roxbury, near Boston, with two young men of the same name from Pennsylvania, or one of the South-

* See Dr. Field's *Account of Middlesex, Ct.*, p. 104.—Ed.

† We have seen but one set or series of the Almanacs of Tully, and that was in the valuable library of Alfred D. Foster, Esq., of Worcester.—Ed.

ern States. They were mutually surprised on meeting, neither having known of any family in the country of their name except his own. Inquiries followed, and it appeared that the father of these young men had no brothers or sisters, but of their grandfather's name and place of nativity they were totally ignorant. The reason why it is disbelieved that there was another family is, that there were few in England of the name, and that none of them have ever been mentioned in the numerous catalogues of emigrants. It is, however, possible, that the ancestors of these young men had changed a name nearly similar into that of Tully, which had long been famous in the literary world.

Sarah, the first daughter, married John Smith of Haddam, and had one daughter, Lucy, who married Andrew Beach of Branford.

Mary married Daniel Clark of Haddam.

Deborah, fourth daughter, died unmarried in Saybrook.

Lucy died by scalding, about six years old.

Hepsibah, the youngest daughter, died in Saybrook, unmarried.

William, the second son, from whom sprung all the successive families in Saybrook, married Abigail Maverick of Boston, the daughter of a clergyman who left England in the time of persecution. The maiden name of Mr. Maverick's wife was Sherwood, and it appears that she came from Cornwall in company with a brother, who settled at Little Chaptauk, in Maryland. The children of the above named William and Abigail were ten, their births and deaths as follows:

John, b. March 18, 1702, d. Oct 29, 1776.
Margaret, b. May 23, 1704, d. Sept. 15, 1775.
Abigail, b. July 5, 1707, d. May 2, 1773.
William, b. June 13, 1709, d. March 18, 1775.
Lydia, b. July 24, 1711, d. July, 1792.
Elias, b. Jan. 17, 1713, d. July 19, 1773.
Sarah, b. Jan. 6, 1715, d. Oct. 19, 1764.
Mary, b. March 30, 1718, d. Sept. 17, 1739.
Samuel, b. April 29, 1721, d. Aug. 4, 1749.
Daniel, b. July 24, 1723, d. March 25, 1727.

Abigail, the mother of the last named family, was born Sept., 1675, and d. Dec. 9, 1750.

William, the husband of Abigail, was bred a farmer and shoemaker, which branches of business he carried on largely until his death.

Margaret, the first daughter, was once a promising child, but in early years disease deformed her person and impaired her intellect. She died in Saybrook, unmarried.

Abigail, the second daughter, married Captain John Lee of Lyme, 7th Oct., 1741, an attorney at law, and had two children, Eunice, b. 1743, and Andrew, b. 1745, the former of whom married Samuel Hall of Wallingford, and the latter having been liberally educated in Yale College and otherwise duly qualified, became a minister, and was ordained pastor of a church in Lisbon, Ct.

The above named Abigail afterwards became a widow, and married Deacon Caleb Chapman of Saybrook.

Lydia, third daughter, married Humphrey Pratt of Saybrook, by whom she had five children, namely, Humphrey, William, Lydia, Elias, and Andrew.

Sarah, fourth daughter, married Captain Joseph Buckingham of Saybrook, and had six children, namely, Sarah, Esther, Margaret, Louisa, Abigail, and Anna.

Mary died a single woman at Saybrook.

Samuel, fourth son, lived at Saybrook, unmarried. He was by occupation a farmer and shoemaker, and a person of such known and strict integrity and uprightness as to have become proverbial, being styled by his acquaintances the honest shoemaker.

Daniel, the fourth son, died in early childhood.

John, the eldest son and child, married Parnell Kirtland, by whom he had seven children:

Parnell, b. June 5, 1732, d. Sept. 1, 1796.
John, b. March 12, 1734, d. Oct. 22, 1760.
Anne, } twins, b. Nov. 24, 1736, d. Sept. 5, 1739.
Daniel, } d. Sept. 13, 1739.
Elizabeth, b. April 23, 1739.
Mary, b. July 21, 1742, d. Aug., 1793.
Sarah, b. June 25, 1745, d. Aug. 30, 1747.

The mother of the above children died July 26, 1748, aged 43 years and 8 months.

After this, John Tully married a second wife, the widow of John Russell of Branford, whose name before marriage was Mary Barker, by whom he had two children hereinafter named:

Maverick, born June 10, 1754, d. Sept. 26, 1754.
Sarah, b. Oct. 11, 1757.

Mary, the mother of the last named children, died at the birth of the last child.

Parnell, the first child, died a single woman, in Saybrook. She was carried off suddenly, with less than half an hour's illness, by Asthma.

Elizabeth, third daughter, married *Ambrose Whittlesey* of Saybrook, by whom she had nine children, namely, Mary, Ambrose, Elizabeth, Lydia, John Tully, Parnell, Sarah, Anne and Daniel, twins.

Mary, the fourth daughter, married *Richard Dickinson* of Saybrook, by whom she had eight children, namely, Richard, John, Charles, George, Mary, Samuel, William, and Anne.

Sarah, by the second wife, was married to Samuel, eldest son of Elias, brother of the father of said Sarah, whose family see hereafter.

John, the eldest son, followed the business of a merchant for a number of years, but taking the small pox in New York, died of it, by which event that branch of the family became extinct. John, the father of these children, was bred to the business of his father, but as he advanced in years, agriculture became more congenial to his taste, and he devoted to it all the time not employed in discharging the duties of Town Clerk, an office that he held a long time.

William, the next brother to said John, married two wives, the first of whom was Anne Beament of Saybrook, granddaughter to a brother of the same Mary Beament who married John Tully who came from England.

By this wife he had two children, 1, Abigail; 2, Anne, who died an infant one month old, five days after the mother expired, Aug. 5, 1748.

Said Abigail married Seth Pratt of Saybrook, by whom she had five children, Azariah, Daniel, Ezra, Elisha, and Anne.

The second wife of said *William* was Elizabeth Say of Lyme, to whom he was married August, 1750, and by whom he had the following children:

Anne, b. June, 1751.
William, b. Sept., 1752, d. aged 6 weeks.
Elizabeth, b. Nov. 6, 1753.
Hepsibah, b. Feb. 12, 1755.
Sarah, b. Jan. 5, 1757.

William, b. Feb. 10, 1759, d. Oct. 5, 1811.
Lydia, b. Feb. 5, 1761, d. Feb. 13, 1813.
The mother of these children died Sept. 8, 1793.

Elias, of second generation, married *Mercy Pratt* of the parish of Potapaugh in Saybrook, by whom he had four children, namely, Samuel, b. May 28, 1750, died Nov. 1, 1827; Mercy, b. April 14, 1755, d. Aug. 26, 1775; Charles, b. July 30, 1752; Eunice, b. Aug. 5, 1758.

Mercy, the mother of the last named children, died April 26, 1800, aged 85. The said Mercy was born July 27, O. S., 1715. Samuel, the last male of the third generation, married Sarah, the youngest daughter of his uncle, John Tully, on the 6th of February, 1783, and by her had the following children: Sarah, b. Dec. 8, 1783; Mary Barker, b. Feb. 12, 1786; John, b. Oct. 4, 1788; Samuel Maverick, b. Nov. 28, 1790; Eunice, b. Feb. 7, 1794; Sophia, b. June 6, 1798.

Elias, the second male of the third generation, married *Azubah*, the dau. of Deacon *Samuel Kirtland*, Jan. 23, 1783, and had issue, Polly, b. Oct. 21, 1783; Mercy, b. April 27, 1785; Betsey, b. March 18, 1787; Azubah, b. March 20, 1789; Lucia, b. May 15, 1791; Harriet, b. March 21, 1794; Lydia, b. June 27, 1796. The mother died June 27, 1796. The said Elias married Lydia, the daughter of Mr. Adonijah Buckingham, Dec. 24, 1797, and had issue, Jannet, b. Nov. 15, 1799; Anne, b. March 22, 1801.

William, third male of the third generation, married Eunice, second dau. of his uncle, March 13, 1785, and by her had a son, who, on the 6th of April, 1786, was baptized by the name of *William*, who, having been liberally educated in Yale College and otherwise duly qualified for the practice of physic, resided awhile in Milford, but in the winter of 1816, removed to Upper Middleton. He married Mary Potter, daughter of Elam Potter of Enfield, Ct.

Polly, the oldest daughter of Elias Tully, was married to Asa Kirtland, Jr., Feb. 18, 1807. Their son Asa, b. May 14, 1808, d. May 22; Henry, b July 4, 1809; Azubah, b. Sept. 14, 1811; Elias Tully, b. Sept. 7, 1814; Frederick, b. July 31, 1817; Ozias H., b. Sept. 24, 1819; Mary Ann, b. Dec. 26, 1821; Asa, b. Jan. 9, 1825; Emeline, b. Sept. 14, 1827.

Mercy, the second daughter, was married to Dr. Asa Miller Holt of East Haddam, Sept., 1816, and had issue, Elizabeth, b. Nov. 25, d. Dec. 26; Theodore, b. May 13, 1818; Asa, b. Nov. 24, 1819; William, b. May, 1822; Harriet, b. March 29, 1824; John, b. July, 1826, d. Dec.

Betsey, third daughter, m. Ozias Holmes of East Haddam, Jan. 21, 1808; issue, Mary Ann, b. Feb. 4, 1809; Joseph, b. Dec. 17, 1817.

Lucia, fifth daughter, married George Henry Chapman of Saybrook, Nov., 1814; issue, George Henry, b. May 15, 1817; Harriet, b. April 15, 1819; Edward, b. Dec. 2, 1820; Clarissa, b. June 12, 1824; Robert, b. Jan. 12, 1824.

George Henry Chapman, above named, owns and resides upon the place which was originally owned and occupied by his ancestor, Robert Chapman, who was born in Hull, England, came to Boston in 1635, and to Saybrook in 1636. Said Robert married Ann Bliss, April 29, 1642.

Harriet, sixth daughter, married Ezra Kertland, Oct. 6, 1821; issue, Ellen, b. Feb. 18, 1823; Harriet, b. Feb. 6, 1826; Ann; Elizabeth; George.

Lydia, seventh daughter, married William Rufus Clark of Saybrook, April 3, 1822; issue, Azubah, b. Jan. 5, 1827; Mortimer, b. Jan. 12, 1829.

Azubah, fourth daughter, married Samuel S. Warner of Lyme, Nov. 17, 1825; issue, Mary, b. Aug. 23, 1826; Samuel, b. Dec. 17, 1827.

Lydia, wife of Elias Tully, died Sept. 19, 1825, aged 60. Mr. Elias Tully is now living in Saybrook, (August, 1848,) aged 96 years, "sana mens in sano corpore."

INDIAN WAR PAPERS.

[Communicated for the Antiquarian Journal by CHARLES W. PARSONS, M. D., of Providence, R. I., Member of the N. E. H. Gen. Society.]

[Continued from page 25.]

VI.

Province of
Mayne Yorke May the 1st 1690

We whose names are under written beinge Appoynted and Commissionated by the Govern^{r} and Counscell of the Masset...sset Collony in New england to visett the Estern parts & in pertecular this province of Mayne In persuance of which we doe advise such as here are called unto and Intrusted with the Goverment of said Province for theire Majestes

Imp^{r}. That they Exert theire power to uphold and Mayntaine the Gouerment In keepeinge the peace and administring the Lawes that the end of Gouerment May be attained: to be a terror to euell doers and a prayes to them that doe well

2^{ly} In Millitary Concerns that theire be due care taken In Watchinge & wardinge that you May not be surprised by the Ennemy & suddenly destroyed as other playses have benn

3^{ly} That you draw you^{r} selves Into soe few Garrissons and those soe Conveniently situate as you may be in a good poster of defence

4^{ly} That a Convenient Number of the Inhabitance that know ye Countrey be Imployed by turns in Cnstant Scoutinge

5^{ly} That a sutable party or partyes be sent forth to disrest and Attaacqk the Ennemy at there usall fisshinge places or Els Wheare as theire may be oppertunitye: In all which: and all other your Conscerns We desire the Lord to dirict and bless you and subscribe

Yours to our power
John Hathorn
Jonathan Corwin

VII.

April: 2: 1693

Leiut Hill

Last night a Litle after sun sett Noah Emory was coming from Kittery to Sturgion Creke & by the waie sid herd som crackling of stickes: & herd a man whissell: upon which he stopt under a bush: and went an other waie: John Smith coming after him saw a man nere Sturgion Creke bridge who ran a waie down the creke: Smith being on horse back came to my Garison — this morning I sent out som men who saw the Indian track at the same place where Noah Emerey herd him whissell — Kepe out scouts about the borders of the towne: I will send out from hence: all o^{r} souldiers at the banke are drawen of those y^{t} belong to you are sent up: dispose of them to such garisons at present as you thinke fitt: I have given two of them liberty to goe home for a few dayes:

In hast I Remaine yor: Lo: freind
Charles Ffrost major

[Superscribed]
Ffor Leiut John Hill
At Newitchawoneck
Hast Post Hast

VIII.

Boston: 23 Octr. 94.

Major Hooke

By this informe you that I have receved an account sent by Coll: Pincheon that came to him by an express from Albany that by 4 Indians that are com from Canada, that they are makinge great preperations for to Atack the English in seueral places and in pertickular at the easward, and the Indiens there shewed a bagg of English scalps and ingadged forthwith to returne & send out 130 men to destroy the English; and the gouernour of Canada resolved to fall upon the English about Albany, thes Indiense cam from Canada about the 22: Septembr last yo^{u} are therefore to put y^{r} selves and neyboures in the best posture you can for theire security & for the discouery of the enemy, and to gayne any advantadg yo^{u} can upon them; if there be anythinge wantinge for yor defence and theyre Majesty's servis that there is an opertunity to suply yo^{u} with; informe by the first, and forthwith take care to give information to ye neybours at piscataqua york wells & Sacoc that soe they may not be surprysd.

y^{r} Lo: freind
William Phips

Vera copia

[Superscribed]

For Liut Abraham Preble and Liut: Anthony Brackett and from them to be conveyd forthwith to Wells to the oficers there, and from thence to be posted forthwith to Capt Hill at Sacoe

lett this be sent unto Mr Wheelwright to be remunerated

Hast post hast

for theire Majesty's service

IX.

Octob^{r}: 26 1694 Kittery

Liut Preble &
Lieut. Brackett

The last night I was at Newbery intendinge for Boston but preuented by a post letter from the governour a copy of which is underwritten * by which yo^{u} may perceive we may speedily expect the enemy to be amongst us, therefore yo^{u} are required to take efectuall care to keep a strict watch & warde to prevent a surprysall and to keep out what scouts posible yo^{u} can in york & Wells for to make a discouery of them if may be, before they com in upon us, pray post this away imeadiatly to Wells that soe it may be posted to Capt Hill thus not doubtinge of care herein

I remayn y^{r} Louinge freind
Francis Hooke

X.

Wells August 13th: 1696 —

Sonn Hill

I am now at Wells with twenty horse Intending to Com over to you but hereing of severall guns about yor parts I have sent over three men to know how it is with you I have an order from the governor to assist you in drawing of: and I have an order from the Leu^{t} gouernor to draw of & bring a waie what can be transported by Land: & to hide the rest in the ground with the great guns: but o^{r} townes are soe weake for want of men that if the enemie be about you we fere wee are to weke to com and bring you of: I was informd as I writ to you that Major Church was com

* [It is No. VIII. of this series.]

to o^{r} assistants but it is not soe but tis said he is coming with three hunderd men: & major Gidney with five hundred men to o^{r} assistants: o^{r} people are much troubled that yor fort should be Demollished: Capt Chubb gave up his fort without firing a gun against the Enemie, Let me here from you by the barer here of my Love to yor selfe and wife: I pray god to keepe you from the Rage of the Enemie:

I Remaine
Yo^{r} Loving ffather in Law
Charles Ffrost

tis said six Indians
were sen here this day

[Superscribed]
To Capt. John Hill At Saco ffort
Hast post Hast

XI.

Brother Hill my Kind Love to you with my wifes: hoping these few Lines will find you in good health as we are all at present Blessed be god for it; It hath pleased god to take a way; Major Frost—the Indens waylad him Last Sabbath day as he was cominge whom from meetting at night; and Killed him and John Heards wife and Denes Downing: and John Heard is wounded; the Good Lord santifie it to us all; it is a Great Loss to the whole Province; and Espesely to his famyley: and Last Monday the post that Cam to Wells as they went to goe whom the Indens Killed them a bout the marked tree: namly Nicholas Smith Proper; and Hennery Simson; Brother mistress Frost is very full of sory; and all her Children: Cousen Charles and John was with there Father: and Escaped wonderfuly: and seuerall others with them: Capt Brekett went with som of his Company a Monday by the way of Nechewanack and I went with them—and was there at the Major's Funerall; and I see your wife full of greef: and your Child is well; Mrs Frost and sister & all your Brothers & sisters Remembers theire loue to you; and Ernestly desires you to com over if you can possible without danger

pray doe not venter In the day to Com; Remember our Love to all our Brothers and sisters and Cousens; and the good Lord Keepe us in these perreles times and santyfie all his Awfull dispensations to us noe more at present

praying for you
your uery Louinge Brother
Joseph Storer

Wells the: 10th July 1697

XII.

Kittery ye 9th 9mo 1675

Capt ffrost.

you are desired to Expediate downe the Soldiers appertening to this garrison & pray Let them bring downe Jno Heards cattle Intended for Slaughter wch Ich wittom [?] will informe with them, and Also Jno Rosse his Cow, wch is all for present. Not doubting y^{r} punctuality. I rest

yor ffriend and serv^{t}
Richard Allexander
Ser^{t} to ye Garryson.

[This note was written on the same paper with No. I. of this series.]

EARLY RECORDS OF WEYMOUTH.

[Copied by Mr. Cyrus Orcutt, for the N. E. Genealogical and Antiquarian Register.]

[Continued from Page 72.]

Samuel son of William & Elizabeth Chard	born	Oct 1 1665
Experience of John & Mary Bicknell	"	Oct 20 1665
Samuel of Nicholas & Hannah Whitmarsh	"	Oct 27 1665
Elizabeth of Richard & Mary Philips	"	Nov 27 1665
Hannah of Samuel and Hannah Pratt	"	Dec 21 1665
Joseph of Joseph & Sarah Pratt	"	Feb 2 1665
Amy of Thomas & Jane Drake	"	Feb 3 1665
Jacob son of Andrew & Ellen Ford	"	Feb 29 1665
Lidda of John & Mary Rodgers	"	March 1 1666
Mary of John & Abigail Whitman	"	Mar 10 1666
James son of Daniel & Sarah fairfield	"	Mar 18 1666
John son of John & Phebe Taylor	"	April 10 1666
Hannah of Thomas & Rebecca Kingman	"	June 1 1666
Sarah of Holbrook Born of Sarah Holbrook		June 3 1666
Alice daughter of John & Alice Shaw	"	July 6 1666
Joseph of Joseph & Sarah Shaw	"	Oct 21 1666
Thomas of John & Elizabeth Hollis	"	Jan 7 1666
Sarah of Samuel & Experience King	"	Jan 31 1666
John, of John & Sarah Bartlett	"	Feb 11 1666
Samuel son of Thomas & Ruth Bayley	"	Feb 21 1666
James of James & Jane Lovell	"	Mar 7 1667
John son of John & Deliverance Porter	"	July 12 1667
Mary of Joseph & Elizabeth Green	"	Aug 15 1667
Joanna of William & Elizabeth Chard	"	Aug 17 1667
of Daniel & Sarah Fairfield	"	Aug 24 1667
Zechariah son of John & Sarah Whitmarsh		Sept 1 1667
Mary Daughter of Richard & Rebbecca Gurney	"	Sept 9 1667
Elizabeth of James & Mary Smith	"	Sept 14 1667
Ruth of Simeon & Sarah Whitmarsh	"	Sept 29 1667
Richard son of Richard & Mary Phillips	"	Oct 20 1667
Thomas of John & Mary Vining	"	Oct 30 1667
Elizabeth of Andrew & Ellen Ford	"	Nov 2 1667
Experience of John & Mary Rodgers	"	Nov 29 1667
Susanna of Nicholas & Hannah Whitmarsh	"	Jan 18 1667
Zachary son of John & Mary Bicknell	"	Feb 7 1667
Mary Daughter of Matthew & Sarah Pratt	"	this year 1667
Mary of Samuel & Hannah Pratt	"	March 3 1668
Hannah of John & Alice Shaw	"	Apr 7 1668
Samuel son of Stephen & Hannah French	"	May 5 1668
Henry son of John & Elizabeth Kingman	"	May 11 1668
John son of Joseph & Sarah Pratt	"	May 17 1668
Mary of John & Mercy Randall	"	May 31 1668
Edward son of Nathaniel & Susanna Blancher	"	June 7 1668
John son of John & Abigail Whitman	"	June 22 1668
Andrew son of John & Jane Lovell	"	June 28 1668
Hannah of James & Jane Lovell	"	Sept 29 1668
Patience of John & Esther King	"	Oct 4 1668

[To be continued.]

ARCHIVES OF CONNECTICUT.

[Communicated for the N. E. Gen. and Antiquarian Journal, by Rev. Wm. S. Porter.]

Besides the Records of the State, and the various manuscript volumes in the office of Secretary of State, there is a great quantity of papers which have been accumulating since the settlement of the colony of Connecticut, some of which were filed, and others in disorder. About *fifty thousand* of these have been arranged and parted into books, where they are easily accessible. This was done under direction of the Connecticut Historical Society, by Sylvester Judd of Northampton, who indexed a few volumes; for the expenses of which the General Assembly made an appropriation to the Society. To complete the work of indexing, the Assembly authorized the Secretary of State to employ a Clerk. Two or three volumes were indexed under direction of Mr. Secretary Tyler. In the fall of 1846, Mr. Secretary Bradley, who well understood the character of the work to be done, employed and gave suitable directions to William S. Porter of Farmington, to continue the indexing, who has been retained by the present Secretary, Mr. Robertson.

The papers were arranged under heads as follows:

Militia, 5 volumes.

War, 10 volumes, including Indian, French, Spanish wars, &c.

Revolutionary War, 37 volumes of great interest and importance.

Indians, 2 volumes.

Private Controversies, 6 volumes; useful in tracing family histories.

Ecclesiastical, 15 volumes, giving a history of societies and ecclesiastical affairs, as yet but little explored.

Towns and Lands, 10 volumes; of great value in compiling the histories of the several towns, their settlement, organization, &c. &c.

Susquehanna and Western Lands, 1 volume; showing our claims in Pennsylvania and the Western Reserve, &c.

Colonial Boundaries, 3 volumes, in which are copies of many valuable early historical documents.

Foreign Correspondence, 2 volumes, of great interest. The first contains original letters from Kings, Queens, Dukes, Lords, &c., and the second, letters on foreign affairs, &c., many of which relate to the charter, and rights and privileges of the colony.

Trade and Manufactures, 2 volumes.

Travel, 3 volumes; Highways, Ferries, and Bridges.

Industry, 2 volumes; Agriculture, Manufactures, Fisheries, and Mines.

Colleges and Schools, 2 volumes.

Courts, Civil Officers, Laws, &c., 3 volumes.

Court Papers, 1 volume. There are Court Papers still in files sufficient for 20 volumes.

Insolvent Debtors, 1 volume.

Lotteries and Divorces, 1 volume.

Crimes and Misdemeanors, 6 volumes.

Miscellaneous, 2 volumes. Vol. I. contains, Papers relating to Sir Edmond Andros; The Union with New Haven; Commissioners from England; Appeals to England, &c. Vol. II. contains, Papers relating to Slavery; Houses Burned; Briefs for Charitable Collections; Inquests; Small Pox, &c.

Finance and Currency, 5 volumes.

Finances, 2 volumes.

Journals of the Two Houses, Conventions, &c., 3 volumes.
Votes for State Officers, 3 volumes.
Reports of the Comptroller, 3 volumes.
Reports of Treasurer and Auditor, 2 volumes.
Grand Lists, 2 volumes.
Miscellaneous Statistics, 1 volume.

These 138 volumes, embracing about 50,000 papers, are by no means the whole. They include very few papers of a more recent date than 1790; and from that date back to 1706 are many papers still in files, most of which should be arranged in volumes and indexed.

The indexes are full and complete. Every paper is carefully read, and an analysis given, under appropriate heads, in the general index; and alphabetical lists are given of the names of all important persons and places; and on a page preceding the index of each volume is given a synopsis of the index; so that, at a single glance, the contents or subjects of the volume may be seen.

Thus facilities are rendered to any who wish to investigate any subject pertaining to the history of this commonwealth, or town or family histories; for here are many papers relating to the history of every town and almost every ancient family in the state.

LAST OF THE SIGNERS.

[The following we cut from some Boston paper nine years ago. We should like to see it beat.]

Error corrected. — We lately published a paragraph, which appeared originally in the Philadelphia Gazette, stating that only two of the sons of the SIGNERS OF THE DECLARATION OF INDEPENDENCE are now living. This is incorrect, as appears by the following lines in the above paper, from a genuine scion of one of the signers:

THE DEAD ALIVE.

What, Mr. Editor, got in your head,
So to confound the quick and dead,
And kill off, of "THE SIGNERS" true,
Each son they left, excepting "Two" —
To wit, "North Bend" and Johnny Q.?
Murder by wholesale! *I* can tell
At least a dozen, live and well,
"Besides the rest" I could set down,
If old Aunt Smith were now in town.
ELBRIDGE GERRY, he left *one*,
And so did FRANCIS HOPKINSON;
MORRIS left *two*, and RUSH left *four*:
CLYMER and WILSON, each, *one* more.
MCKEAN and PACHA, each a son,
And WALTON, LEA, and MIDDLETON —
"Alive and kicking" — every one.
These *fifteen* killed off — what a pity!
Eight murdered in this very city!
Yes, fifteen graves untimely filled!
But I, for one, will not "stay killed."
If to such wrong I said not nay,
I'd be but a poor son of a —

SIGNER.

THE PEASE FAMILY.

[By Frederick S. Pease of Albany, N. Y., Member of the N. E. Hist. Geneal. Soc.]

[Continued from page 31.]

THIRD GENERATION.

(3) III. John, [1—1.] born March 30, 1654, removed to Enfield, Ct., 1679, married Margaret Adams of Ipswich, died 1734, æ. 80. It is stated by Joseph Pease, that John and Robert, who removed to Enfield in 1679, lived, the first winter, in an excavation which they made in the side of a hill. It was about forty rods east from where the old meeting house stood. He left children,

9—1.—John, b. at Salem, 1678. (8)
10—2.—James, b. at Salem, 1679. (9)
11—3.—Joseph, b. at Enfield, 1693. (10)

Margaret, b. 1683, m. Josiah Colton, 1709, d. 1775. Had two sons and five daughters: Josiah, b. 1709; Job, b. 1711; Esther, b. 1714, m. Obadiah Hurlbut, 1745; Margaret, b. 1716, m. David Phelps, 1737; Abiah, b. 1718, m. Colonel John Bliss of Wilbraham, and d. 1803; Ann, b. 1720, m. John Parsons, 1740; Hannah, who m. Joseph Gleason, 1745.

Sarah, b. m. Timothy Root, 1710, settled in Somers, 1713, d. 1750. Had two sons and five daughters: Timothy, b. 1719; Thomas, b. 1726; Elizabeth, who m. Ebenezer Spencer, 1733; Sarah, who m. John Abbe, 1739.

Mary, b. m. Thomas Abbe, 1714, d. 1746. Had two sons and five daughters: Obadiah, b. 1728, d. young; Thomas, b. 1731, d. 1811; Mary, who m. Dennis Bement, 1737; Sarah, who m. Nathaniel Chapin; Tabitha, who m. Ephraim Pease, 1740.

Ann, b. m. Jeremiah Lord, 1719, settled in East Windsor, d. 1753. Had two sons and one daughter.

(4) III. Robert, [2—2.] born March 14, 1656, removed to Enfield, 1679, d. 1744, æ. 88. Had four sons and three daughters:

12—1.—Robert, b. 1684. (11)
13—2.—Samuel, b. 1686. (12)
14—3.—Daniel, b. 1692. (13)
15—4.—Ebenezer, b. 1698. (14)

Abigail, m. Nathan Hayward, had two sons, Thomas and Ebenezer, and five daughters.

Mary, m. Israel Phelps, 1703, had one son and three daughters.

Hannah, m. David Miller, and had one daughter. Gershom Sexton was her second husband, by whom she had five sons and four daughters.

(5) III. Jonathan, [5—5.] born Jan. 2, 1668, married Elizabeth Booth, 1693, died 1721. Had children:

16—1.—David, b. 1698, removed to the Southern States.
17—2.—Josiah, b. 1706, went to Massachusetts.
18—3.—Pelatiah, b. 1709, m. Jemima Booth, 1736, d. 1769, had four sons and one daughter. One of the sons, Jonathan, d. in Schenectady, 1760.

Rebecca, m. John Pierce, and had four sons and two daughters.
Elizabeth, m. Ebenezer Chapin and had two sons and five daughters.

(6) III. JAMES, [6—6.] born Oct. 23, 1670, removed to Enfield, when he was ten years old, m. Hannah Harman, 1695, died 1748. Had children:

Hannah, b. 1700, m. Benjamin Terry, 1721, had six sons and three daughters.
Elizabeth, b. 1703, m. Benjamin Meacham, 1722, had eight sons and three daughters.
Mary, b. 1706, m. Jacob Terry, 1730, had five sons and two daughters.
Abigail, b. 1708, m. Nathaniel Collins, 1735, had three sons and six daughters.
Sarah, b. 1710, m. Jonathan Terry, had two sons and three daughters.
19—1.—Joseph, b. 1712. (15)
Jemima, b. 1716, m. Lot Killam, 1739, had four sons and six daughters.

(7) III. ISAAC, [7—7.] born July 15, 1672, married Mindwell Osborn, 1691, died 1731, æ. 59. Had children:

20—1.—Isaac, b. 1693. (16)
21—2.—Abraham, b. 1695. (17)
22—3.—Israel, b. 1702. (18)
23—4.—Ezekiel, b. 1710. (19)
24—5.—Timothy, b. 1713. (20)
25—6.—Cummings, b. 1715. (21)
26—7.—Benjamin, b. 1717. (22)
Ann, m. Nathaniel Prior, 1725.
Abigail, history unknown.

FOURTH GENERATION.

(8) IV. JOHN, [9—1.] born at Salem, 1678, married Elizabeth Spencer of Hartford, Ct., died 1761, æ. 83. Had one son,

27—1.—John, b. 1726. (23)

(9) IV. JAMES, [10—2.] born at Salem, 1679, removed to Enfield, 1679, married Mary Abbe, dau. of Thomas Abbe, 1710, settled in Somers, 1713, and died there. Had one son,

28—1.—Richard, b. 1717. (24)

(10) IV. JOSEPH, [11—3.] born in Enfield, 1693, married Mary Spencer of Hartford, Ct., 1727, died 1757. Had three sons, who all left Enfield, and a daughter Mary, b. 5 Nov., 1734, m. Captain David Parsons of Enfield, d. at Freetown, Ms., Nov., 1783.

29—1.—Joseph, b. 1728, d. in Suffield, 16 Oct., 1794.
30—2.—Stephen, b. 5 Feb., 1731, d. Nov., 1816, at Long Meadow, Ms.
31—3.—Jonathan, b. 11 Sept., 1740, d. at Ellington, Ct., 1824.

(11) IV. ROBERT, [12—1.] born 1684, removed from Enfield to Somers, between 1713 and 1727 or 1734, and died 1766, æ. 82. His first wife was Hannah Sexton, by whom he had one daughter,

31½—1.—Mirriam, who m. Nathaniel Pease, 1730. (25)
His second wife was Elizabeth Emery,* by whom he had,

* *Will of Elizabeth Pease.*—I Elizabeth Pease of Somers, wd and Relict of Robert Pease late of Somers in the County of Hartford and Collony of Connecticut, decd, do this

32—2.—Robert, b. 1724. (26)
33—3.—Emery, b. 1727. (27)
34—4.—Abiel, b 1737, died at Somers, 1806, without male issue. He left one daughter. He was an officer in the Revolutionary army.
35—5.—Noah, b. 1740. (28)
(12) IV. SAMUEL, [13—2.] born 1686, married Elizabeth Warner, died 1770. Had children:
36—1.—Samuel, b. 1717, m. Teriah Chapin, settled and died in Enfield. They had three sons who were Shakers at Enfield, Ct., and New Lebanon, N. Y., Eli, Elias, and Peter. Peter was one of those who established the Shaker Society at a place now called Union Village, near Lebanon, Ohio, in 1806.*
37—2.—Ephraim, b. 1719. (29)
38—3.—Aaron, b. (30)
39—4.—Nathaniel, b. 1725. (31)
Mary, m. James Gains, and had one son and two daughters.
Elizabeth, m. John Allen, and had one son and two daughters.
Joanna, m. Benjamin Root, and had one son and one daughter.
Mary, m. Christopher Parsons, and had three sons and four daughters.
(13) IV. DANIEL, [14—3.] born 1692, married Abigail Fletcher, settled in Somers. Had four sons and four daughters:
40—1.—Daniel, b. 1718.
41—2.—William. 42—3.—Parker. 43—4.—Asa.
(14) IV. EBENEZER, [15—4.] born 1698, married Mindwell Sexton, died 1743, had two sons:
44—1.—Ebenezer, d. 1784. (32)

12th day of July 1768, make and publish this my last Will.—I give to son Robert Pease five shillings, son Emery P., five shillings, and two sheep, son Abiel P. fivè shillings, son Noah, five shillings, to dau. Bathsheba Hunt, five shillings, to grand-son Benjamin Jones three pounds worth of neat cattle, when he shall arrive at the age of 21 years. All the rest of my movables to be equally divided among all my daughters, and my son-in-law David Rood. Except to my dau. Mary Pease, one Cow besides the division mentioned. Son Emery my executor—but so as not to be accountable for any bad debt or debts—he to be paid all his cost and expense in executing sd trust.

This 12 day of July in the 8th year of the Reign of our Sovereign Lord George ye 3d, and in the year of our Lord, 1768.

In presence of Stephen Sexton
Joseph Sexton
ELIZABETH PEASE.

From the above instrument may be learned the method of disposing of estates in those days, namely: the real estate was divided among the heirs according to established laws, if no will by the husband, without any will of the widow, and *independently* of it, as she had no control over real estate belonging to her husband, to dispose of it, except by his will. But she was at liberty to make such disposstion of all the *personal* and *movable* property as she pleased.

* To what particular family the following persons belonged, we are unable yet to state; but that they were of this branch of the family is beyond question.

There lived in Somers, previous to 1783, *Lot* and *Sarah* Pease, who had four sons and two daughters, namely, Samuel, Caleb, Enoch, Lot, Jemima, and Elizabeth. Jemima went to the Society in Hancock, Ms., and died there a year or two since. Enoch was a preacher at Enfield, but left the Society some eighteen years ago. Samuel, the eldest son, was b. 19 Sept., 1766. He removed to Watervliet, May, 1788, at the time of the organization there, where he d. 8 Oct., 1831, highly respected. Lot, the father, was in the old French War.

45—2.—James, b. 1724. (33)
(15) IV. Joseph, [19—1.) born 1712, died 1800. Had four sons:
46—1.—Noah, b. 1736.
47—2.—Joseph, died 1758.
48—3.—Gideon, settled and died in Enfield.
49—4.—James, died in Somers, in 1830.
(16) IV. Isaac, [20—1.] born 1693, married Amie French, 1722, died 1757. Had children:
50—1.—Isaac, (34)
51—2.—Abner, (35)
52—3.—Jacob,
53—4.—Noadiah, (36)
Ann, m. Ebenezer Hall, 1753, and resided in New Marlborough, Mass.
Laurani, m. John Gaines, 1755, died in Granby, Ct.
Another dau. m. a Brooks, and d. in New Marlborough, and another m. a McGregory, and lived and died in Enfield.
(17) IV. Abraham, [21—2.] born 1695, married for his first wife, Jemima Booth, 1719. His second wife was Abigail Warren. He died 1750. Had children by his first wife:
54—1.—Abraham, b. 1721.
55—2.—John, b. 1725, settled in Suffield.
Also a daughter, who m. William Lord, 1752, and a son, who d. young. By his second wife,
56—3.—Moses, settled and died in Enfield. (37)
57—4.—Samuel, d. 1772. (38)
58—5.—Joel, b. 1737.
59—6.—Nathan, b. 1740, removed to Wilbraham.
60—7.—Gideon, b. 1741, removed to Massachusetts. (39)
61—8.—Josiah, b. 1744.
62—9.—William, b. 1746, d. at Enfield.
63—10.—Zebulon, b. 1749, d. 1829.
Also a daughter, who married Nathaniel Parsons, and a son, who d. young.
(18) IV. Israel, [22—3.] born 1702, married Sarah Booth, 1726, died 1771. Had children:
64—1.—Israel, d. in Middlefield, Ms. (40)
65—2.—David, b. 1729, d. in Enfield.
66—3.—Hezekiah, d. in Enfield.
67—4.—Jesse, b. 1739.
68—5.—Nathan, d. in Enfield.
Sarah, who m. Jeremiah Lord.
Mindwell, who m. Ebenezer Terry.
Alice, who m. Thomas Root.
Bathsheba, who m. David Wilson.
(19) IV. Ezekiel, [23—4.] born 1710, married Hannah Chandler, 1732, died 1793. Had children:
69—1.—Ezekiel, b. Aug. 18, 1734. (41)
70—2.—Henry Chandler, b. Feb. 11, 1738. (42)
71—3.—Isaac, b. June 1, 1752. (43)
Oliver, b. Sept. 6, 1754, d. young.
Hannah, b. Jan. 11, 1732, m. Job Gleason, had three sons and seven daughters.

Abiah, b. Aug. 11, 1736, m. Samuel Gowdy, 1759, had four sons and three daughters.

Jane, b. Aug. 13, 1743, m. Obadiah Hurlbut, had one son and four daughters.

Mehitabel, b. Sept. 23, 1745, m. Edward Parsons, had two sons and four daughters.

Sarah, b. Feb. 28, 1747, m. Jehiel Markham, had two sons and two daughters,

Eleanor, b. March 15, 1741.

Abigail, b. March 15, 1749.

(20) IV. TIMOTHY, [24—5.] born 1713, married Mary Chandler, 1736, died 1794. Had children:

72—1.—Timothy, b. 1737, settled in Enfield. He had three sons and two daughters, Abigail, Levi, Ruth, Jonathan, and Justin. They were Shakers at Enfield, Ct. Justin was killed by lightning, while engaged in getting in hay, some thirty years ago. Levi, the second child, b. 5 Aug., 1771, removed to Watervliet, N. Y., 15 June, 1790, and d. there in the Shaker society, highly respected, 5 Sept., 1832. Timothy, the father, was in the "Old French War."

73—2.—Edward, settled in Enfield. (44)

74—3.—James, " " "

Mary, m. Wareham Parsons; Abigail, m. David Terry; Martha, d. young; Deborah, m. Gideon Pease; Dorcas, m. Isaac Pease; Lydia, m. Ezekiel Pease; one daughter m. Benjamin King; another m. Samuel Hale, and another m. Freegrace Hancock.

(21) IV. CUMMINGS, [25—6.] born 1715, married Elizabeth Pease, dau. of John Pease, for his first wife. He married his second wife, Sarah Hale, 1755. Had by his first wife:

75—1.—Cummings, left Enfield. (45)

76—2.—Ebenezer.

77—3.—Asa, d. in Enfield. (46)

Love, who m. Jacob Hills, and Ruth, who m. David Hale.

By his second wife he had two sons.

(22) IV. BENJAMIN, [26—7.] born 1717, married Abigail Rose, died 1768. Had children:

Benjamin, m. Margaret Prior, died at Enfield. They became members of the Shaker society in Enfield.

Two daughters died young. Abigail, m. Zacheus Prior, 1759. Lucy, m. Reuben Perkins. Rose, m. Daniel Kingsbury. Damaris, m. Edward Collins.

FIFTH GENERATION.

(23) V. JOHN, [27—1.] born 1726, married for his first wife, Bathsheba, daughter of Thomas Jones, one of the early settlers of Enfield. He was a large farmer in the eastern part of Enfield. His location was part of the share which was assigned to his grandfather, in the distribution of the land at the first settlement of the town. Had children:

78—1.—John, b. 1753. (47)

79—2.—Thomas, b. 1754, m. Mercy, dau. of Josiah Hall of Somers, removed, in early life, to Ellington, where he died, about 1815, leaving four sons and three daughters. He was a farmer.

80—3.—Gideon, m. Prudence, dau. of Asahel Sexton; removed early to Vermont, where he died, about 1824, leaving a large family of sons and daughters. He has a grandson in Salem, Racine Co., Wisconsin.

81—4.—Simeon, b. 1764, m. Susan, dau. of Ebenezer McGregory, 1787, died in Hartford, 1827, æ. 63. Had nine children, most of whom died in early life. The last of them died in 1844.

82—5.—Elizabeth, b. 1756, married, for her third husband, Joshua Giddings of Hartland, Ct., who removed to Western New York, and was among the pioneers of the region. She subsequently removed to Ohio, where she died, at an advanced age. She left three sons, the youngest of whom is the Hon. Joshua R. Giddings, M. C. for the northeast district of Ohio.

83—6.—Bathsheba, m. Eli McGregory, who removed to the State of New York. She died in the northern part of the state, at an advanced age. Had three sons and three daughters.

(24) V. Richard, [28—1.] born 1717. Had a son,

84—1.—Richard. (48)

(24½) V. Joseph, [29—1.] born Aug. 10, 1728, removed to Suffield, Sept., 1750, married Mindwell, daughter of Lieut. Josiah King, July 28, 1756, died Oct. 16, 1794. He was a successful merchant, a zealous advocate for liberty, and suffered much in the struggle for Independence; stood high in the confidence of his townsmen, whom he often served in a public capacity. Children,

85—1.—Augustine, b. May 18, 1757. (49)

86—2.—Zeno, b. Feb. 2, 1759. (50)

87—3.—Oliver, b. July 27, 1760. (51)

88—4.—Royal, b. April 15, 1762. (52)

89—5.—Seth, b. Jan. 9, 1764. (53)

90—6.—Mindwell, b. March 16, 1765, d. May 20, 1765.

91—7.—Joseph, b. Sept. 11, 1766. (54)

92—8.—Calvin, b. Aug. 22, 1768, d. Aug. 27, 1775.

93—9.—Mindwell, b. Aug. 31, 1770, m. Gideon Granger, late Postmaster General, Jan. 14, 1790. Had children: Ralph, b. Nov. 22, 1790; Francis, b. Dec. 1, 1792; John A., b. Sept. 11, 1795, and a son, who died young.

94—10.—William, b. June 22, 1772. (55)

95—11.—Calvin, b. Sept. 9, 1776. (56)

(25) V. Mirriam, [31½—1.] m. Nathaniel Pease, in 1730. This Nathaniel was the eldest son of Robert Pease, who, according to tradition, came directly from England to Enfield, and was a distant relative of the original Pease family in that town. He was designated by the name of "*latter*" Robert, and admitted an inhabitant of Enfield in 1687, and settled on the lot south of the Somers road. He married Hannah Warriner, 1691, and had three sons, born in Enfield, viz:

Nathaniel, above mentioned, who was b. 1702; Joseph, b. 1707, and Benjamin. Nathaniel kept a tavern in Blandford, Ms., and afterwards removed to Ballston, or Stephentown, N. Y., where he died. Children of Mirriam and Nathaniel:

96—1.—Nathaniel, b. 1737, whose daughter, Huldah, m. Ebenezer Pease. (See No. (63) VI.) This Nathaniel is said to have been a sea-faring man, and to have died at sea. He married and settled in Enfield, Ct., and had three children, born in that town.

He subsequently left Enfield, and was gone for several years to parts unknown; during which time his wife married one Benjamin Parsons. On his return to Enfield, ascertaining what had taken place during his absence, and finding that his wife preferred her latter husband, he soon disappeared, and was never afterwards seen or heard of there.

97—2.—Levi, b. 1739. (57)
98—3.—Abel, b. 1741.
99—4.—William, (58)
100—5.—Joel,
101—6.—George.

Eleanor, who m. a Holcomb; Hannah, who m. a Wheeler; Mirriam, who m. a Jones, and another daughter, who m. an Ashmun.

(26) V. Robert, [32—2.] born 1724, died 1805, æ. 81. He resided in Blandford, about 1780, one or two years, where he lost the most of his property, by the depreciation of continental money, which he received in payment for a farm, at a time when it was made "lawful tender for the payment of debts." He spent the remainder of his days at Somers. His children were,

102—1.—Robert, d. 1827, æ. 78. (59)
103—2.—Stephen, b. about 1755. (60)
104—3.—Abner, b. Nov. 9, 1757. (61)
105—4.—Erastus, b. about 1759, married, and resided in Newport, died a few months after his marriage. He had one daughter, Ann, who m. a Coe, and resided in Newport.
106—5.—Alpheus, b. about 1762. He served in the Revolutionary war, was taken prisoner by the British, and afterwards exchanged. He removed, with his family, to Lewis Co., New York, when it was a wilderness, at that time called the "Black River Country." (62)

[To be continued.]

REGISTER OF THE DEATHS IN NORTHAMPTON, MS.,

FROM ITS FIRST SETTLEMENT IN 1653 TO 1700.

[Communicated by Mr. Samuel W. Lee, of that place.*]

1654, *March* 8, Sarah, dau. of Samuel Clark; Experience Pomroy.
1655, *January* 14, James Bridgman.
1656, *January*, Dorothy, wife of John Ingersoll; *February*, Patience, dau. of Jas. Bridgman.
1657, *July*, Joseph Elmer; Hannah Brotton; *August*, Rebekah Miller.
1659, *January*, Johannah Lyman; 30 *March*, Hezekiah Bridgman.
1660, *August* 30, David Burt, killed. [How, not stated.]
1661, *November* 30, Henry Curtis.
1662, *March* 16, John Brotton; 15 *April*, Jonathan Burt; 24 *April*, In-

* It would have added greatly to the value of this list had our correspondent been able to add the ages of the deceased. But we would by no means be understood to complain, but return Mr. Lee our grateful thanks for what he has done. We are by no means in the fashion of the age—to find fault with all that is given us, because it is not better and more in amount!—Pub.

crease Clark; 26 *April,* Mercy Hutchinson; 22 *May,* Eldad Pomeroy; 3 *June,* Richard Lyman; 15 *July,* Mercy Phelps; Edward Lewis; 4 *August,* Mary Jones; 15 *November,* Timothy Lee.

1663, *March* 7, Child of Joseph Leeds; 4 *April,* Miriam Leeds; 3 *June,* Thomas Marshall; 24 *June,* Mehitable Hutchinson; 12 *October,* Sarah Lyman.

1664, *January* 5, John Merry; 17 *February,* Joseph Pomeroy; 5 *March,* Joseph Dickerson; 17 *May,* Nehemiah Allen's child; Joshua Carter's child; 14 *August,* John Kingsley; 28 *December,* Mrs. Cornish.

1665, *January* 11, Mary Dewey; 14 *January,* James, son of James Bridgeman; 28 *April,* Matthew Cole, killed by lightning; 17 *October,* Samuel Wright died in his chair.

1666, *January* 11, Thomas Lewis; 6 *March,* Thomas Woodford; 8 *July,* Lydia Cole; 26 *August,* Ann Webb.

1667, *February* 18, Samuel, son of Judah Wright; 28 *August,* Robin, an Indian, servant to Nathaniel Clark, killed by the Indians.*

1668, *March* 23, John Searle's son; 2 *June,* Nehemiah Allen's son; 15 *July,* Mary, dau. of John Hotton; 3 *August,* Sarah, wife of James Bridgeman; 1 *November,* Ford, son of Jedediah Strong.

1669, *January* 5, dau. of William Hubbard; 17 *February,* son of John Hilliour; 16 *March,* Experience, dau. of John Lyman; 30 *March,* Nathaniel Clark; 16 *May,* son of Ralph Hutchinson; 24 *July,* Rev. Eleazer Mather; Jedediah Strong's child.

1670, *February* 20, Mary, wife of Thomas Strong; 27 *February,* child of Samuel Allen; 2 *March,* Samuel Davis's child; 19 *May,* John Webb; 1 *July,* son of John King; Israel Rust's child.

1671, *October* 23, John Hannum's child; 11 *December,* Mary, dau. Matthew Clesson; 14 *December,* Rowland Stebbins.

1672, *February* 13, Eleazar, son of Isaac Sheldon; *April,* Joseph Lead's child; 20 *November,* Ruth, wife of John Searl.

1673, *January* 4, John Bridgman's child; 10 *February,* Timothy Baker's daughter; 22 *March,* Solomon, son of Solomon Stoddard; 29, James Wright's child; 30 *May,* Sarah, wife of John Hannum; *November,* son of Jedediah Strong.

1674, *March* 15, Mindwell and Experience Hannum; 25 *March,* Hester, dau. of Judah Wright; son of Joshua Pomeroy; 29 *March,* child of James Wright; 10 *July,* Medad Pomeroy's son.

1675, *March* 1, Jeremiah James; 14 *March,* Robert Bartlett, Thomas Holton, Mary Earle, Increase Whelstone and James Mackrannels, slain by Indians;† 7 *June,* Anthony, son of Solomon Stoddard; 25 *August,* Samuel Mason, slain by Indians; 6 *September,* Sarah, wife of William Clark; 28 *September,* Praisever Turner, and Isaac Abee Shakspeare slain by Indians; 29 *October,* Joseph Baker, and son, and Thos. Salmon, slain by Indians; John Roberts; 19 *November,* Susanna Cundlief; 19 *December,* Sarah, dau. Ebenezer Strong.

[To be continued.]

* This year there is great complaint among the settlers high up on the Connecticut river, that the Eastern Indians have committed murders and other depredations.—*MS. Chronicles of the Indians.*—Pub.

† The deaths thus far recorded in this year, undoubtedly belong to 1676. See *Old Indian Chronicle,* 101, *n.*; *Hubbard,* 77; *Willard in Rowlandson,* 41.

ABSTRACTS OF THE EARLIEST WILLS UPON RECORD IN THE COUNTY OF SUFFOLK, MS.

[Continued from page 82.]

JOHN BENJAMIN.

12 (4) 1646.

I *John Benjamin* being in pfect memory, as touching my outward estate—do bequeath to sonne *John* a double portion, beloved wife two Cowes, fourty bushels of Corne out of all my lands, to be allowed her towards the bringing vp of my smale Children yearly such as growes vppon the ground, one part of fower of all my hous hold stuffe, all the rest of my lands goods & chattels shal be equally divided betwen seven other of my children. Provided that out of all my former estate my wife during her life shall enjoy the dwelling house I live in, & three Acres of the broken vp ground next the house, & two Acres of the Meddowe neere hand belonging to the house. That this will be truly pformed I do appoint my brother *John Eddie* of Watertowne & *Thomas Marrit* of Cambridge that they doe theire best Indevo[r] to see this pformed.*

JOHN BENJAMIN.

Witnes *Georg Muniage* [Muning]
the 15 (4) 45.

This was proved to be the last will & testament of *John Benjamin*, & that he did further declare (as an addition to this his will) that his wife should have liberty to take wood for her vse vppon any of his Lands dureing her life, vppon the Oath of *John Eddye* (5) 3. 1645

Before
Thomas Dudley Gov[r].
Jo: Winthrop Dep. Gov.

WILLIAM HALSTED.

13 (4) 1646.

Whereas I *William Halsted* do find by dayly experience my body to decay. *Imp.* vnto the poore of the towne fyve pound to be laid out in a Cow w[ch] I would haue so ordered by the Decaons & my executors that may be a continual help to such as are in need, God giueing a blessing therevnto. The remander of my estate, vnto brother *Henry*, & to my sister *Edna* her child or children—to brother *Henry*, at the end of two years, except he dispose of himselfe in marriage, or haue a lawfull calling to England by his friends there, to the satisfaction of my executors, & in case he should goe to England of his owne accord, then not to have it till they heare certainly of his welbeing there. And in case he should dye before this time be accomplished, then my sister *Edna* her child or children shall haue it. And I make *william Wood* & *George Heyward* executors.

WILLIAM HALSTED.

witnes
Rob[t] Miriam.
Luke Potter.

* The inventory of the estate of *John Benjamin* may be seen in Vol. II. on p. 25 (Suffolk Wills.) No footing appears to the various items, but we make the amount of the whole, £297. 3s. 2d.

"This was deliuered as a true Inuentory of the estate of *Benjamin* deceased vppon the Oath of *Symon Stowe John Eddye* & *Thomas Marret*, to the best of theire knowledge. Taken before *Thomas Dudley*, Gover: & *John Winthrop*, Dep. Gover. 3 (5) 1645.

The testimony of *Luke Potter* to this will was taken vppon oath the 13 (8) 1645 before *Thomas fflint.*

Robt Miriam sworne 15 (8) 45 before *Joh: Winthrop* dep Govr. & *Tho fflint.*

Inventory is dated 10th 8th 1645. Robt. Miriam & Georg Heward [Heyward] apprisers. Amount, £97, 10s, 7d.

Samuel Crowes.

3 (4) 1646.

I do appoint *Samuel Bitfield* to take my goods & pay my debts & take the remainder to himselfe.

This was approved to be a lawfull will by the Court & Jury in tryall of an action betweene *Thomas Skidmore* & *Samuel Bitfield* at a Court held at Boston 2 (4) 1646.

Mary Benjamin.

13 (4) 1646.

I *mary Benjamin* of Watertowne do give to *Pastor Knolls* fyve Acres of Marsh at the Rocky Meddow in Watertowne bounds. I giue to my *Aunt Wines* one Cowe, I giue to my sister *Abigail Stubbs* two Cowes my best clothes wth my best searg Peticoate. I giue to my brothers in generall one Cows worth. To my Cosin *Anne Wyes* my best wastcoate. May 16 1646.

Mary Benjamin her owne act & deede.

Witnes to this will
Jane Mahew
Elizabeth Child
both sworne in Court 4 (4) 46.

Increase Nowell Sec^r.

Richard Barber.

13 (4) 46.

I *Richard Barber* of Dedham. I haue receiued a Cow of Mr *Prichard* of Roxbury as the gift of one M^r. *Anderson* of London. I will & bequeath the said Cow to remaine to the vse & benefit of the poore in Dedham. My house & lands in Dedham, & goods & chattles vnto my Executors. My beloved friends & brethren in Christ *Henry Brock* & his sonne *John Brock* my executors.

The mark of *Richard Barber.*

Testified in Court the 21 (3) 1646.

Increase Nowell Sec^r.

Lawrence Buckmaster.

4 (5) 1646.

Seene that I am now bound for the sea, & soe for England, them smale things that I haue heare leve & thos desposed of if *Capt. Smith* doe not recover my wages againe, then thus I have ordered it if God take me away. That the piece of land I bought of *Thomas Spaul* I giue it to my sister *Elisabeth Buckmaster* & some smale things in my chest, as a great Coate to *Thomas Spaule*, & the sixe shillings due to me from *Thomas wellens* wth it. My black hatt to *Abigail Sherman*, the suite of apparell to my brother *Zachary Buckmaster*, & a shirt and band or two for my ffather, there wil be left a paire of Stockings; the best to *Matthew Coy*, the worster paire or two paire, & the Chest vnto the said *Thomas Spaule*, & a smale caske of Mackrells that *Thomas* is to send to Sea for me for to let them go to sea for his daught[r] *Mary* till they come to some thing or nothing.

LAWRENCE BUCKMASTER in
the presence of *Thomas Spaule*.

But the land she is not to make it away nor part frō, but she is not to haue it, nor haue nothing to doe wth it till the yeare of O[r] Lord 1649, & that, Mayday. If I dye at Sea, then to demand vppon inquiry, you may true wages for the time, & to giue my ffather it.

Robert Portous the 27th (9) 1645.

Deposed the 2 (5) 1646, by *Thomas Spaule* & *Robert Portous* vnter *M[r] Nowells* hand.

THOMAS MUSSELL.

This twenty seventh of July 1640. [4 (5) 1646 in margin.]

I *Thomas Mussell* seaman, doe giue full power to *John Sweete*, Carpenter of Boston to receiue or take up for my vse: the 4th part of the pinnace called the Mary, & the profits of it: the said my share or part: till such time as he the said *John Sweete* by power & vertue of this my will doe sell the same: or if one *Phillip White*, my partner in the said vessell, do sell her, he is to giue *John Sweete* before named, the money or goods, what shee is sould for. To said *John Sweete* twenty three shillings due me from *William Quick*. A hand & Seale

Nicholas Lopdell.
John Mansfield.

The said *John Mansfield* did testifie this vppon oath, 26 (1) 1646, before *John Winthrop*, Dep. Gov[r]., & *Increase Nowell.*

WILLIAM WEALE.

15 (12) 1646.

William Weale made a Nuncoupative will the 5th (8) 1646 as was testifyed by Goodwife *Milom* & *John Harwood.* See Affidavits,* p. 42.

NICHOLAS STOWER.

The last will of *Nicholas Stower* of Charlestown. 16 (3) 1646.

To beloved wife *Amy Stower* my dwelling house wth y[e] barn & all other houseing, w[th] the two Acres of ground by it, & all the ground in the necke of Charlestowne. Also a hay lot on Mistick syde near the North spring next o[r] sister *Rands*, also half of the hay of the other hay lots on Mistick syde. Likewise 4 Cowe Cōmons on the stinted Cōmon w[th]out the necke. Also 3 of the Acres of planting ground on Misticke syde that is broken vp, & it is now sowen w[th] english corne & planted w[th] Indian Corne: she

* We are informed by the very obliging and intelligent gentlemen in our Registry Office, that they know of no such book.

to haue the vse of all the aforenamed—She to haue vse of the cart & plow & its furniture: she to haue my two best working oxen—all the English Corne & Indian corne on the ground on mistick syde—except that wch my Son *Richard* is to haue of the same crop.

When wife is deceased my sonne *Joseph Stower* to haue the house, barne & other housing wth the 2 Acres of ground, to abide with his mother to do her service while she liues, or till he be twenty & one yeare old. Hee to pay his sister *Abigail* 2 Cowes, & one to his sister *Jone* at ye decease of my wife.

To daughter *ffar* a great bible, & the great brasse pan after my wifes decease, all the rest to be my wiues for euer.

To son *Richard* my two oxen next to the best, land on mistick syde, only his mother to haue the vse of 3 Acres,—To dau. *Jone Stower* one Cowe presently, & one out of *Josephs* portion.

To dau. *Abigail Stower*, after my wives decease, two good Cowes out of *Joseph's* portion.

To dau. *ffarre* a great Bible. Wife sole executrix—loued brethren *Thomas Lyne* & *Robert Hale* to be overseers of this my last will.

Witnesses

Increase Nowell
John Greene
Thomas Lyne
Robert Hale.

Thomas Williams.

25 (2) 1646.

I *Thomas Williams* doe make this my will. To *John Spoore* of Boston my part in the bote, & one pound seven shillings that *John Norman* of Jeffrey Creecke haue, & is in my master *Holgraues* hand, due to mee, & that wch he tooke order to leaue at M^r^. *Stodders* for me, & what els I haue, & my master *John Spoore* to pay Mr *Oliver* for letting me blood & to pay Mr *Ayers* & Mr *Cordll* of Salem one shilling & eight pence, that wch I did owe Mr *Holgraue* haue or ingaged himselfe to satisfy *John Norman* wch was for dyet & lines & other things axes, one at *Jeremy* the *Smith*, & another at Mr. *Holgraue*. I owed a shilling at the ferry at Salem, & *Henry Swan* I apponted to pay it. Dated, 25 (2) 1646.

Witnesses, *Bartholomew Chever* & *Edward Cowell* testifyed 5 (9) 1646. by *Bartholomew Chever* & *Edward Cowell* before the Magistrates. *Increase Nowell* Sec^r^.

Date of Inventory, 1 (3) 1646.

2 weekes wases due by Mr *Holgraue* of Salem 8s. Mr *Holgraue* debtor for a bullocke £6. Due by *Thomas Williams* to *John Norman* of Marblehead, £4.—to *John Spoore* £4. paid for him by *John Spoore* to Mr *Correll* of Salem, 1s. 8d.—p^d^. to Mr *Aires* by *John Spoore* 17s. *John Spoore* count for tendance in *Tho Williams* Sicknes, for makeing graue, coffin, & all charges, £1. 10s.

Amt of Inventory £15 10s 6^d^: debts £10 9s. 8d.

[To be continued.]

ANCIENT WILLS IN MIDDLESEX.

Cambridge, Jan. 25, 1849.

Mr. Drake,

Dear Sir: Agreeably to promise I send you, for publication in the Register, two of the oldest Wills recorded in Middlesex, Matthew Day's and Simon Stone's, with an Indian deed, not recorded, to "Elder John Stone," of Sudbury, the son-in-law of Edward How of Watertown, whose Will, from the Suffolk Records, you inserted in the last number of the Register. I intend soon to furnish you with the Will of Gregory Stone, of Cambridge, my first ancestor in this country, who was a brother of Simon, of Watertown, and the father of Elder John, whose Will, also, I should like to have published, as it throws considerable light on the first generations of the family whose genealogy, you know, I have been some time collecting and preparing for press. And I would now admonish my cousins and kindred of the *Granite* race, scattered thick and wide all over the land, as Burns once did his "brither Scots"—

"If there's a hole in a' your coats,
I rede you tent it,
For a chiel's amang you taking notes,
And, faith, he'll prent it."

Your friend and serv't,
Wm. F. Stone.

The last will & Testament of Mathew Day may 10. 1649.

1. I doe give with all my heart all that part I have in the Garden unto the fellowes of Harvard Colledge for ever.*
2. I doe give to m[r] Shepard my diaper table cloath & napkins which were not yet made up.
3. I doe give my 3 silver spoones, the one to David Dunster† the other to Doraty Dunster,† & the 3[d] that hath my owne name on it w[c] I brought out of England to my old acquaintaince little Samuel Shepard.‡
4. I doe give to my mother all the estate I have in both the houses, together with all the furniture beds & all moveables (my debts being first paid) to her for her life, & when she dies to the little childe Moyses.
5. I doe give to S[r] Brocke§ (my ould & deare friend) all the Bookes I have which he thinkes may be usefull to him, except those which may serve for the trayneing up of the childe to schoole.

* "Mr. John Buckley first Master of Arts in Harvard Colledge & Matthew Day Steward of the Colledge gave a Garden conteyning about one Acre & one Rood of Land scittuate & neer adjoyning to the Colledge & ordered the same to be for the use of the ffellows that should from time to time belong to & be resident at the said Society, the sd Garden being now commonly called & known by ye name of the ffellows Orchard."—*College Records, Book III. p.* 32.

"Mr. John Buckley" was the son of Rev. Peter Bulkley, the first minister of Concord, and was of the first class of graduates at Harvard College. Of Matthew Day and his family, some account may be given in a future number of the Register.—Ed.

† These were the children of Rev. Henry Dunster, the first President of Harvard College. David, the eldest, was born May 16, 1645. Dorothy was born Jan. 29, 1647–8.—Ed.

‡ The son of Rev. Thomas Shepard, by his second wife, Joanna, daughter of Rev. Thomas Hooker. He was born in Cambridge, in October, 1641, was ordained at Rowley, as colleague with Rev. Samuel Phillips, Nov. 15, 1665, and died April 7, 1668.—Ed.

§ Undoubtedly John Brock, a graduate at Harvard in the class of 1646, afterwards settled in the ministry at Reading. "Sir" was the title formerly given to those who had received their first collegiate degree.—Ed.

6. I doe give unto my mother that eight pound or there about which is due to me for printing, to pay for the house which is due at michalemas.
7. I would have Daniell & Mary Lemon & my moothers girle have something given them as mr Shepard & my mother shall see meet.
8. I doe give my Ivory Inkhorne in my box with a whistle in it unto Jeremy Shepard.*
9. I give 20ˢ in mony which once I had & layd out for the Colledge & is to be paid by it in mony againe unto mr. Thomas Shepard.
10. I give unto John Glover† my lookeing Glasse.
11. I give to Elder Frost‡ foure pounds.

Those before whome he spake these things were

Mr Tho: Shepard
Mrs Day.

Rec]orded 2] 9th mo. 1649. Deposed the 30th 8th mo. 1649. Increase Nowell.

This will is recorded, not in the Probate Office, but in the *Registry of Deeds*, Lib. 1, fol. 1. The testator, supposed to be a son of Stephen Day the printer, died the same day on which his Will was made, and without issue. "Mrs. Day," one of the witnesses, was probably his mother, and the other, doubtless his minister, Rev. Thomas Shepard.

Setember the 7th 1665.

I Simon Stone do give unto my two Sons Simon and John, my whole Estate which I am now possessed with all in what soever is mine unto an equall division between them, only I appoynt them to give or pay unto my two daughters Frances and Mary ten pounds apiece within twelve months after my decease, and also to pay all my debts, and discharge my buriall. And my mind is that John —— should have the land I bought of brother Hayward belong to him, and 2 Silver bowles, the lesser to Simon, and the greater to John. And My Mind is that My daughter Frances' ten pounds should be payd 5lbs to Johnana Greene her daughter and Nathaniel her Sonne, 50ˢ a peece, and the other five to the children she ha*ve* by her husband. [illegible] This writing intends nothing of any former lands & conveyances to the*m*, but only the present things wᶜh I did reserve to myself.

The marke of + Simon Stone.

This writing was Exhibited on oath as the last will of the said Simon Stone, by his brother Gregory Stone and Steeven Day§—and Simon Stone & John Stone, sonnes of the said Simon Stone dec'ed, were granted power of administration on that Estate left by him.

Octo 3, 1665.

Thomas Danforth, R.

Recorded by Tho. Danforth R.

Copied from Probate Records for Middlesex county, Book 2, p. 316.

* The youngest child of Rev. Thomas Shepard, by his third wife, Margaret Boradile. He was born Aug. 11, 1648, was ordained pastor of the church at Lynn, Oct. 6, 1680, and died June 3, 1720.—Ed.

† Second son of Rev. Josse Glover, rector of Sutton, in the county of Surrey, England, to whom New England was indebted for her first printing-press. Mrs. Glover became the first wife of Rev. Henry Dunster, under whose watchful eye John Glover received his education, at Harvard College, from which he graduated in 1650.—Ed.

‡ Edmund Frost, one of the ruling elders of Shepard's church.—Ed.

§ "The first that sett upon printing" in North America, and the father of the Matthew Day whose will is given on the preceding page. He died Dec. 22, 1668. Rebecca, his wife, died Oct. 17, 1658.

[NOTE.—Among the emigrants to New England in 1635, was Simon Stone, the testator, who, having obtained leave of government, in the spring of that year embarked, with his family, at London, "to be transported to the plantation" then just commenced in this vicinity. He settled in Watertown, on the banks of the river, at what is now called Mount Auburn, the beautiful location of our cemetery, around which a number of his descendants are now living on portions of the ancestral estate, while on the very spot where the old patriarch first pitched his tent, Mr. Winchester, of this city, is erecting the most splendid mansion that ever adorned the banks of Charles river. Of the five children brought over by Mr. Stone, (the eldest only 16,) all but one are named in the will; the daughter, Ann, had probably deceased, as had the mother, and also the father's *second wife*, who left a will, which the writer is desirous to have abridged and transferred to the pages of the Register, preparatory to his account of the family.]

INDIAN DEED TO JOHN STONE.

This witnesseth, that William Boman, Cap[t] Josiah, Roger & James and Keaquisan, Indians, now liveing at Naticke, the Indian Plantatton neare Sudbury in the Massachusetts Bay in New England, ffor and in consideration of a valluable Sum̄e of *Pease* and other goodes to us in hand payd by John Stone of Sudbury aforenamed to our full content and satisfactton before the signing and delivery hereof. Have given, granted, bargained & sould, assigned enfeoffed & confirmed, and by theis p[r]sents do give, grant, bargaine & sell, assigne, enfeoffe and confirme unto the said Jno. Stone his Heyres & assignes a parcell of Broaken up and ffenced in land, lying on the South side of Sudbury line, upon the falls of Sudbury River, and bounded with ye Com̄on land Surrounding, the said land conteyning by estimatton about ten Acres more or lesse. To Have & to Hould the said land with ye ffences, and all other the priviledges and Appurtenances thereof, be the same more or less, to him the said Jno. Stone his Heyres and Assignes for Ever to his and their only propper use & behooffe. In witness whereof wee the above named Indians have hereunto put o[r] hands & seales this 15[th] day of May 1656.

	markes of
Signed & Read	William + Boman
in p[r]sence of	Cap[t] Ω Josiah
William warde	—, Roger
his Σ marke.	Ξ James
John *Prudd*urke.	+ Kerqisan

This deed of sale was acknowledged by the Indians above named, and with their full consent the said land is passed *out* the 15[th] of: 3: mo 1656.

Daniel Gookin.

OBITUARY ON REV. DANIEL BAKER.

[From the Boston Weekly News-Letter, No. 1425, May 20, 1731.]

"Sherburne, May 14, 1731. Died here the Reverend and Worthy Mr. *Daniel Baker*, Pastor of this Church, in the 45th Year of his Age. He was born in *Dedham*, of Religious and worthy Parents; had his Education at *Harvard College* in *Cambridge*, N. E. was Ordained in the Year 1712, Assistant to the Reverend and Valuable Mr. *Daniel Gookin*, late Pastour of this Church: He married two Worthy and Virtuous Gentlewomen, the first was Mrs. *Mary Quincy* of *Braintree*, by whom he had one Daughter yet surviving; the other Mrs. *Rebecca* Smith of *Boston*, now his mournful Widow, by whom he had several Children, one of which only Survives. He was a Gentleman of bright natural Parts, much improved by acquired Knowledge, very pathetical in Prayer, Orthodox and Powerful in Preaching, tender of his Flock and Congregation, having always the Cause of GOD and Religion much at Heart: His Church increas'd greatly under His Ministry. He was Exercised with much Affliction, under which his Patience and Resignation was very signal, and notwithstanding which, he was very affable and pleasant in Conversation. In his later Years, he has been attended with uncommon Indisposition of Body, which growing upon him, frequently interrupted him in, and sometimes wholly incapacitated him for his Work, and at length had so much the Mastery of him, as entirely to deprive him of the Power of Speech some days before his Death. As he was much esteemed and beloved by his People, in his Life, so his Death is much lamented by them, and all that knew him. He was decently inter'd the 17th Instant."

PASSENGERS FOR VIRGINIA.

[Communicated by H. G. SOMERBY, ESQ., for the Antiquarian Journal.]

20th June 1635. Theis under written names are to be transported to Virginea imbarqued in the Phillip Richard Morgan Mr. the men have been examined by the minister of the towne of Gravesend of their conformitie to the orders & disipline of the Church of England: And tooke the oath of Alleg die et A° pred.

John Hart,	33	Tymothie Featlie,	23
John Coachman,	28	Wm Arundell,	32
John Reddam,	32	Alexander Leake,	22
John Shawe,	30	John Mason,	16
George Hill,	23	Willm Emson,	33
George Bonham,	31	James Habroll,	22
Wm Rogers,	35	Richard Jn°son,	19
Edward Halock,	22	John Lawters,	17
Ric: Dawson,	31	Thomas Edwards,	20
Peter Johnson,	36	Robert Davies,	28
Willm Bransby,	34	Richard Upcott,	26
Nicholas Rippen,	31	Thomas Peslett,	23
James Quarrier,	22		
Wm Taylor,	36	Women.	
James York,	21	Ellin Burgis,	45
Thomas Gorham,	19	Katherin Bowes,	20
Nathaniell Disnall,	23	Suzan Trask,	25
John Taylor,	16	Marcie Langford,	24
John Gorham,	18	Elizabeth Willerton,	18
Richard Wilson,	19	Sara Shawe,	18
Robert Morgan,	33	Marie Baker,	25
Samuel Milner,	18	Ann Barnie,	23

REV. JOSEPH FARRAR.

We beg leave to invite particular attention to the following circumstances.

There now resides in the Town of Petersham, County of Worcester, State of Massachusetts, an aged Lady, named Mrs. Mary Farrar, the widow of the Rev. Joseph Farrar, sometime Minister of Dublin, N. H., and subsequently a Chaplain in the Army of the Revolution. This venerable matron, now upwards of 91 years of age, is in indigent circumstances; but is unable to substantiate her claim to a pension from the Government, for want of the necessary evidence of her husband's services.

Information on this point is earnestly desired, as an act, no less of justice, than of charity, to one who has now arrived at that age when poverty, with all its deprivations, is most severely felt; one whose declining years and consequently increasing infirmities stand most in need of the aid which would be afforded by a pension.

We call, then, upon our brother Antiquaries, throughout New England, to lend a hand in this matter; and, to aid them in their researches, we will first state the points upon which information is desired, and will then give such facts as we have been able to collect respecting Mr. Farrar; premising, only, that such further information as may come into the possession of any of the readers of this article, may be communicated to the Editor.

Information is desired on the following points.

1. *Where* did Rev. Joseph Farrar enlist as Chaplain in the Army?
2. *When* did he enlist?
3. *In what Regiment or Regiments* did he enlist or serve as Chaplain?
4. *What were the names of the Officers* of the Regiment or Regiments in which he enlisted and served?
5. *Where did he serve* while in the Army?
6. *What was the date of his discharge?*
7. Did he ever serve in *any other capacity* than as Chaplain? and if so, *where* and *when?*

We would remark, in this connection, that the Military Rolls in the State House, Boston, have been examined, but without success, for information relative to Mr. Farrar. The Rolls give *two* persons, to be sure, of the name of "Joseph Farrar," as serving in the Continental Army. But, in the first place, neither of them appears to have been a Chaplain; and secondly, the dates of their respective periods of service do not agree with what we know of Rev. Mr. Farrar; inasmuch as *one* of them was in the Army in 1775, at the very time when Mr. F. was settled in Dublin, N. H., and the other served in 1780, at which time, as will be seen, Mr. F. was in Dummerston, Vermont.

Now for what we know respecting Rev. Joseph Farrar.

He was the son of George Farrar, of Lincoln, Mass., where he was born, June 30, 1744.* He graduated at Harvard College in 1767,† studied Divinity, and on the 17th of October, 1771, was chosen by the people of Dublin. N. H., to be "their Gospel Minister." He was ordained June 10, 1772; was suspended from his ministerial labors, by advice of an Ecclesiastical Council, (on account of difficulties proceeding from "bodily diseases, which greatly affected his mind, and not from any moral cause,") Dec. 7, 1775;

* Shattuck's *History of Concord*, p. 314; Farmer's *Genealogical Register.*
† Ibid; Records of Harvard College.

12

and was finally dismissed from his pastoral relation, for the duties of which he was incapacitated by "a singular hallucination" of mind, June 7, 1776.*

It must have been at this time that he joined the Army; as the next trace we have of him, is on the 24th of August, 1779, on which day he was ordained Pastor of the Church at Dummerston, Windham County, Vermont, where he is remembered as "a man of great eccentricities, deeply afflicted with hypochondria."†

In the year 1779 Rev. Joseph Farrar was married, in Grafton, Mass., by Rev. Daniel Grosvenor, to MARY BROOKS.‡

Mr. Farrar was dismissed from his labors in Dummerston about the year 1783,§ and here we again lose sight of him. It is supposed that he subsequently settled in the town of Eden, Lamoille County, Vermont, where a Rev. Joseph Farrar was ordained Minister of the newly-gathered Church in that place, Dec. 15, 1812, and continued in the Ministry until Dec. 15, 1815, when he was dismissed, and is said to have gone "into some part of the State of New York."‖

Rev. Joseph Farrar died at Petersham, Mass., April 5, 1816, aged 72.¶

JESSE GALE, of Petersham, testifies that Rev. Joseph Farrar "was in the Army at White Plains, New York, and Cambridge, Mass., with his father, DANIEL GALE, who said Farrar did service as Chaplain in *two* Regiments."**

This testimony is confirmed by ESTHER GALE, the widow of Daniel Gale.††

Mary Prentice, wife of Josiah S. Prentice, of Oxford, Mass., and daughter of Rev. Joseph Farrar, certifies that she "saw the Certificate of her father Joseph Farrar's discharge, in childhood, but it was lost or destroyed. Remembers her father did duty as Chaplain, *and soldier also*, and that he took care of a man named COOK, of Phillipston, a sick and wounded soldier, who died, and of the same Regiment or Army."‡‡

We have thus given all the information in our power respecting Rev. Joseph Farrar; and we sincerely hope that there will not be wanting those, who will have the charity to endeavor to enlighten us on those points where we are at a loss, and thus be the means of conferring an incalculable benefit upon a worthy woman.

* Rev. L. W. Leonard's Anniversary Discourse at Dublin, N. H., Sept. 7, 1845, p. 25.

† Complete List of the Congregational Ministers and Churches in Windham County Vt., by Rev. Charles Walker, of Brattleboro', in *Am. Quart. Register*, XIII. 29, 32. Mr Walker erroneously calls him "Thomas Farrar."

‡ MS. Letter of C. J. F. Binney.

§ Walker, as above.

‖ Shattuck's *Concord*, p. 314. Brief Survey of the Congregational Churches and Ministers in Lamoille County, Vt., by Rev. S. Robinson, of Morristown, in *Am. Quart. Register*, XIV. 129, 130.

¶ MS. Letter of C. J. F. Binney.

** Ibid.

†† Ibid.

‡‡ Ibid.

LIST OF FREEMEN.

[Communicated by Rev Lucius R. Paige of Cambridge, Member of the N. E. Hist. Geneal. Society.]

[Continued from page 96.]

22 May, 1639.

Jarvas Garfoard
Edward Breck
William Clarke
Edmond Bloise
Willi. Osborne
John Miller
George Holmes
Mathewe Boyse
James Astwood
John Rob^{r}t
Rich^{r}d Pecocke
Edward Bridge
Walter Blackborne
Joseph Jewet
Roger Porter
Thomas ffirman
Natha. Chappell
John Skot
James Buck
Hugh Laskin
John Smythe
Henry Swan

C. R., Vol. I. p. 254.

23 May, 1639.

Mr. Ezechi. Rogers
Mr. Natha. Rogers
Robert Saunders
Mr. Nathani. Sparhauke
Mr. Thom. Nelson

C. R., Vol. I. p. 254.

6 June, 1639.

Steven Paine
James Garret

C. R., Vol. I. p. 254.

6 Sep. 1639.

Mr. Thomas Ginner
Mr. Benia. Keayne
Job Swinnerton
William Lord
Laurence Southick
John Crosse
John Roffe
John Ellsley
Luke Hearde
Anthony Sadler
Thomas Masie

C. R., Vol. I. p. 254.

7 Sep. 1639.

Edmond Bridge
Rich^{r}d Mellen
Robert Tucke
Robert Saunderson

C. R., Vol. I. p. 254.

13 May, 1640.

Mr. Willi. Worcester
Henry Munday
John Saunders
Thom. Bradberry
Thom. Dumer
Thoma. Barker
Thoma. Mighill
Maxami. Jewet
ffranc. Parrat
Rich^{r}d Swan
Rob^{r}t Haseldine
John Haseldene
ffranc. Lambert
Willi. Scales
John Burbanke
Willi. Bointon
John Jarrat
Micha. Hopkinson
Geo. Kilborne
Mr. Thoma. Coytemore
Mr. Thoma. Graves
Mr. ffranc. Willoughby
Edward Larkin
Thom. Caule
John Penticus
John Martin
Willi. ffillips
Abrah. Hill
Edward Woode
Willi. Paine
John Oliver (Newb^{r})
James Standige
John Whipple
Mr. Edwa^{r} Norrice
Mr. Thom. Ruck
Mr. Willi. Stevens
John ffairefeild
John Bachilor
Robert Elwell
Thom. Watson
Mark fformais
Thom. Waterhouse
Jeremy Howchenes
Jonas Humphryes
Thom. Toleman
George Weekes
John ffarnum
Rich^{r}d Lipincote
Rich^{r}d Withington
Rich^{r}d Syckes
Clement Tapley
Gouin Anderson
John Bowelis
Edw^{r}d Passon
Willi. Chanler
John Hall
John Trumbell
Edwd Bumsted
Joseph Wheeler
Tymo. Wheeler
John Chaundler
Symon Rogers
Michaell Wood
John Merrill
George Browne
John Norwick
Edmo. Pitts
ffranc. Smyth
John Harding
Willi. Carpenter
John Holbroke
Nicho. ffillipes
Thom. Bayly
Samu. Butterworth
Rob^{r}t Marten
Mathewe Prat
Rob^{r}t Tytus
Thom. Rich^{r}ds
Henry Greene
Willi. Godfree
Thom. Arnall
Willi. Haward
Abra. Perkins
Jeffry Mingy
Arthur Clarke
James Davis
Mr. Edmond Browne
Peter Noyse
Walter Hayne
Edmond Rice
Thom. White
John Parmenter
John Bent
Edmond Goodnor
Thom. Islin
John Wood
John Ruddyk
John Howe
Mr. Willi. Hibbens
Arthur Perry
Valentine Hill
ffranc. Seyle

John Hurd
Natha. Williams
John Leveritt
Peter Oliver
John Kenerick
Antho. Stodard
Samu. Sherman
George Curtis
Cotten fflack
Mr. Willi. Tompson
George Rowes
Steven Kinseleye
John Dassette
Willi. Potter
Gregory Belchar
Thom. Place
James Copie
Thomas ffackman
Edward Spolden
Willi. Allise
Martin Saund'rs
John Read
Willi. Andrews
John Stidman
Edmond Anger
Rich'd ffrances
John Thrumball
Willi. Manning
Edward Collins
Rich'd Hogg
Nathan Aldishe
Mychall Medcalfe
ffardinando Adams
ffranc. Chickering
Willi. Bullard
John Bullard
Henry Smythe
John Mose
Daniell ffisher
Josua ffisher
Rich'd Barbore
Jn°. Scarbrow

C. R., Vol. I. p. 281.

7 Oct. 1650.

Mr. Samu. Dudley
Josias Cobbitt
Edmond Gardner
James Barcker
Henry Sands
Rob'rt Hunter
Willi. Stickney

C. R., Vol. I. p. 281.

8 Oct. 1640.

John Page
Samu. Morse
Thomas Weight

C. R., Vol. I. p. 281.

9 Oct. 1640.

Rob'rt Ringe
Isaack Buswell

C. R., Vol. I. p. 281.

12 Oct. 1640.

Willi. Hudson
James Oliver
Thomas Painter
Edward ffletcher
Mr. Willi. Bellingham
Mr. Willi. Hooke

C. R., Vol. I. p. 281.

2 June 1641.

Mr. Henry Dunster
Mr. Rich'd Russell
Mr. John Allen
John Maies
Rich'd North
John Seir
John Stevens
Mr. Adam Winthrope
William Barnes
John Harrison
John Lowell
Thom. Davies
John Emery
Samu. Plumer
Moses Payne
Daniell Weld
Samu. Bidfeild
ffrancis Eliot
Abell Kelly
Jacob Wilson
Nicho. Woode
John Harbert
Thomas Lake
Andrew Pitcher
Rob'rt Holmes
Goulden More
Rich'd Cutter
John ffossenden
Willi. Woodberry
Willi. Geares
Philemon Dickenson
Esdras Reade
John Robinson
Thom. Gardner
Thom. Marston
Rich'd Bartelmew
Thom. Gould
Thom. Wildar
Rich'd Robinson
John Marston
Rob'rt ffuller
Willi. Blanchard
Bozoun Allen
Miles Ward
Samu. Corning
Jonathan Porter
Rich'd Pattinggell
John Goodnow
Willi. Browne
Samu. Chapun
Christo. Stanley
John Harrison
Thom. Davenish
Walter Harris
Ellis Barrone
Willi. Parker
Philip Veren
John Palmer
Rich'd Parker
Edw'd Tinge
Nehemi. Bourne
ffranc. Lawes
Rob'rt Bridges
John Baker
Rob'rt Cooke
Henry Dauson
Willi. Tiff
Willi. Brisco
Rich'd Sanford
Augustine Walker
Henry Archer
Charles Glover
Rob'rt Paine
John Baker
Micha. Katherick
John Jackson
John Deane
Edward Browne
Dani. Warner
John Knoulton
Symon Tompson
Rob'rt Daye
Andrewe Hodges
Jacob Leager
George Bullard
Henry Chick'ry
Michaell Powell
Joseph Kingsberry
John Roaper
Nathani. Coalborne
John Elis
Edward Rich'ds
Beniamin Smyth
Austen Kilham
Thom. Payne
Tymo. Dwight
Henry Wilson
Samu. Bullen
Willi. ffuller
Willi. ff——
Evan Thomas
Abell Parr
Benia. Ward
Willi. Hunt
Willi. Bateman
Josias ffirman
Willi. Cop
Natha. Halsteed
Natha. Billing
Benia. Turney

Rich'd Rice
James Blood
Thom. Clarke
John Viall
Thom. Buttolph
ffranc. Douse
John Sweete
Arthur Gill
Thom. Clipton
George Merriam
John Heald
George Wheeler
Obedi. Wheeler
ffranc. Bloyce
C. R., Vol. I. p. 312.

4 June 1641.

Thom. Marshall
C. R., Vol. I. p. 312.

7 Oct. 1641.

Mr. Richard Blindman
Thomas Wheeler
C. R., Vol. I. p. 315.

18 May 1642.

Mr. ffrancis Norton
John Withman
Gawdy James
John March
Rob^r^t Button
Benia. Vermaes
Thom. Antrum
Michaell Shaflin
Thom. Putman
John Cooke
Phineas ffiske
Willia. ffiske
James ffiske
George Byam
Rich'd Bishope
Allen Kenniston
Elias Stileman
John Tomkins sen^r^
Ananias Conkling
John Neale
John Bulfinch
Joseph Boyse
Samu. Grimes
Theodo. Atkinson
Rob^r^t Bradford
Hugh Williams
Rich'd Crithley
John Guttering
John Ingoldsbey
Robert Howen
Thoma. Snowe
Thoma. ffoster
Dani. Briskow
John Search
John Baker
Rich^r^d Knight
Rich'd Tayler
Philip Tayler
John Bulkeley
Edward Okes
Thom. Okes
Edward Gooding
Sampson Shore
Willi. Torry
John Coggan juni.
John Clough
John Witherell
Samu. Thatcher
John Hill
Rich'd Wody
John Mathis
Willi. Lewes
Rich'd Taylor
Edward Carleton
Humphrey Reyn^r^
Hugh Smith
Hugh Chapline
Rich'd Lowden
John Burrage
Solomon Phips
John Greene
Isaack Comins
Allen Pearley
Thom. Thackster
Willi. Ripley
Mathewe Hawkes
Hugh Prichard
Thom. Lincolne
John Stoder
Willi. Robinson
Robert Peirce
Thom. Davenport
Rich'd Baker
Robert Pond
John Rigbey
George Right
Thom. Blisse
Benia. Albey
Roger Bancroft
Rich'd Eckels
John Cooper
John Tomkins jun^r^
Willi. Dickson
Moses Wheat
Rob^r^t Edwards
Thomas Bateman
Willi. Aline
Thom Wheller
Willi. Hartwell
John Stevens
Willi. Stevens
Antho. Somersbey
Henry Somersbey
Willi. Berry
Samu. Guil
Abell Hews
John Swett
Peter Woodward
John Brock
Natha. Whiteing
Micha. Metcalfe
Rob^r^t Page
ffranc. Pebody
Isaack Perkins
Thom. Worde
Henry Ambros
Walter Ropper
Henry Kibbey
David Zullesh
C. R., Vol. II. p. 18.

19 May 1642.

John Sadler
Walter Tybbot
Obedi. Brewer
Willi. Hilton
Willi. Walderne
C. R., Vol. II. p. 18.

22 June 1642.

Henry Palmer
Joseph Peaseley
Rich'd Pid
Willi. Titcombe
Willi. White
Thomas Dowe
C. R., Vol. II. p. 18.

2 August 1642.

Mr. Willi. Pinchen
C. R., Vol. II. p. 18.

14 Sept. 1642.

Thom. Het
C. R., Vol. II. p. 18.

21 Sept. 1642.

Will. English
C. R., Vol. II. p. 18.

27 Dec. 1642, At Salem.

Walter Price
Rob^r^t Gutch
George Gardner
Rich'd Prence
Rob^r^t Leoman
Thom. More
Thom. Tresler
Willi. Robinson
Hugh Cawkin
C. R., Vol. II. p. 18.

28 Feb. 1642–3.

Thom. Edwards
John Kitchin
Henry Harwood
C. R., Vol. II. p. 18.

28 Feb. 1642–3. At Salem.

Rich. More
Hugh Stacye

Thom. Avery
Edw^a. Beachamp
C. R., Vol. II. p. 27.

10 May, 1643.

Mr. Thom. Wallis
John Scot
Isaack Wheeler
John Ward
Andrew Lister (27)
Thom. Goodnow
Rob^r't Dants
Henry Looker
John Parmenter
Willi. Ward
John Newton
John Thurston
Christo. Smyth
John Guile
John Plunton
John Knights
John Jackson
Nathan ffiske
Geo. Parkhurst
John Pratt
Thom. Beard
John Arnol
John Hollister
James Prest
Nicho. White
Jeffry Turner
Willi. Turner
Roger Billindg
Laurence Smyth
Willi. Ware
Rich. Evans
Willi. Trescot
John Gurnell
Henry Woodworth
Nathani. How^r'd
Rich. Way
Rob. Williams
John Mansfeild
ffranc. James
Rob^r't Proctor
Willi. ffletch^r
Willi. Vincen
John Woode
Hen. Bridgham
Rob^r't Mader
Geo. Barrell
Rich. Rawlen
Strong ffurnell
John Sand^r'bant
Isa. Colimer
Willi. Blanton
Miles Tarne
Natha. Norcros
James Morgan
Rob^r't Pepper
Rich. Hildrick
Edw^a Sheopard
Dan. Stone
Tho. Danforth
Andr. Stephenson
Willi. Manning
Henry Symons
John Tydd
John Wright
Benia. Butterfeild
Edw^a. Winn
Nicho. White
John Hollister
James Prest
John Albye
Peter Bracket
Natha. Herman
Sam. Adams
John Hastings
John Whetley
Willi. Phese
John Shephard
Tho. Adams (28)
C. R., Vol. II. pp. 27, 28.

29 May, 1644.

Cap. Dan. Gookens
ffaithfull Rouse
Rob^r't Leach
ffaintnot Wines
Willi. Bachiler
Willi. Smith
Willi. Green
Rob^r't ffeild
Thom. Marshall
Roger Toule
Edw^a Witheredge
Tymo. Prout
Geo. Spere
Symon Bird
Hen. Powning
Thom. Webster
Rob^r't Gowing
John Lake
Thom. Trot
John ffrench
Rich. Haule
Nicho. Boulton
Henry Gunlithe
Natha. Partridge
Thom. Dyer
Edw^a Wilder
Jos. Phippen
John Blake
Jasper Rush
John Gay
Rich. Goard
John Smeedly
Thom. ffox
Baptize Smeedly
Ste. Streete
John Maynard
Philip Tory
Rich^r'd Wooddy
Edm^o Shefeild
James Joanes
Tho. Chamb^r'lin
John Russell
Allen Conv^r'se
Lamb^r't Sutton
John Carter
James Park^r
C. R., Vol. II. p. 53.

May, 1645.

Herb^r't Pelham
Joseph Hill
Mathewe Smith
Abraham Hawkins
Abra. Hackburne
Sam. ffellows
George Halsall
Abr. Parker
George Davies
Rich. Newberry
Natha. Bishop
John Stimson
Thom. Line
Antho. ffisher
Thom. Richards
Willi. Pardon
Thom. Holbrooke
George Allen
Willi. Davies
John Joanes *stud.*
Sam. Stowe
Edw^a Jackson
Nicho. Wise
John Watson
Hugh Griffin
John Langford
Rich. Newton
John Toll
Jeremy More
Peet^r Aspinwall
Edw^a Wyat
Rich. Leeds
James Umphryes
Rich. Blacke
James Nash
Benia. Thwinge
Samu. Davies
Rich. Bullock
Abr. Harding
Christo. Webbe
Thom. Barrill
John Morly
Henry Blacke
Edw^a Gilman
Lamb^r't Genery
John Gaye
Sam. Miles
John Daming

Ralph Day
Micha. Medcalfe
Sam. Sendall
Wm Hely
Hen. ffirnam
Thom. Roberts
Robrt Jenison
John Warren
Edwa Devotion
Hen. Chambrlin
Vincent Ruth
Thom. Barnes
Joseph Undrwood
Hen. Evance
John ffownell
Sam. Bright
Willi. Wenbane
John Bird
Harman Atwood
Natha. Greene
ffranc. Grissell
John Rydeat (78)
Wm. Parsons
Thom. Thacher
Robrt Longe
Thom. Reeves
Nicho. Chelett
Georg Dowdy
Hen. Aldridge
Willi. Patten
Eliiah Corlet (79)

C. R., Vol. II. pp. 78, 79.

6 May 1646.

Mathew Day
John Lewes
Nathani. Hadlock
John Hill
ffran. Heman
John Gingen
John Haynes
John Looker
Tho. Buckmr
Alex. Baker
Thom. Collier
Thom. Gardnr
Ben. Crispe
Wm. Pary
Wm. Dawes
Hen. Modsley
Joel Jenkins
Henry Thorpe
Geo. Woodward
Charles Sternes
John Wincoll
Willi. Duglas
Peter Place
John Collens
Rich. Everad
Josua Kent
Robrt Onion
Andrew Dewing
Antho. ffisher
Tho. Joanes
Isa. Walker

C. R., Vol. II. p. 124.

26 May 1647.

Ro. Chaulkly
James Green
Tho. Carter jr.
Mighil Smith
Manus Sally
James Pike
Richrd Harrington
Sam. Carter
John Wayte
Law. Dowse
Wm. Bridges
Edwa White
Mr. John Wilson
Wm. Harvy
Wm. Kerly
Rich. Newton
Thom. Tayer
John Nyles
John Stebben
John Whitny jr.
Moses Payne
David ffiske
David Stone
Philip Cooke
John Harris
Thom. Boyden
Mr. Samu. Danford
Willi. Ames
Dani. Kempster
Jonah Clooke
Thom. Huit
John Smith
Bartho. Cheever
John Miriam
ffranc. Kendall
Wm. Cotton
George Munioy
Rich. Hassall
Wm. Butrick
Geo. Barber
Ro. Wares
Thom. Jordan
John Metcalfe
John Bakor
Henry Wight
James Allen
Natha. Adams
Wm. Holbrooke
Thom. Dun
Thom. ffoster
Thom. Prat
Robrt Rendell
Tho. Poget
Geo. Davies
John Peirson

C. R., Vol. II. p. 163.

13 April 1648, at Springfield.

John Pynchon
Elitzur Holioak
Henry Burt
Roger Pritchard
Samu. Wright
Willi. Branch

C. R., Vol. II. p. 201.

10 May 1648.

Mr. Edwa Denison
Georg Denison
Thom. Osburne
Benia. Negus
Thom. Hartshorn
Thom. Kendall
Wm. Hooper
Edwa Tayler
Rich. Holbrooke
Willi. Daniel
Rich. Hardier
Wm. Needam
Samu. Basse
John Chickly
James Pemberton
Philem. Whale
Henry Rice
Mr. Samu. Danforth
Mr. Sam. Mather
Alex. Adams
John Staple
Benia. Negus
Henry Allen
John Peerce
Symon Tomson
Bartho. Porsune

C. R., Vol. II. p. 202.

5 April 1649.

Made free at Springfield.

Thom. Cooper
Griffin Jones
David Chapin

C. R., Vol. II. p. 227.

2 May 1649.

Mr. Willi. Browne
Joseph ffarnworth
Robrt Brick
John Maynard
Alexandr ffeild
Jona. Michell
Samu. Haward
Robrt Browne
Garret Church
Josua Stubbs
John Butler
John Turner
Thom. Saretell

Samu. Hides
Thom. Baker (227)
Josua ffisher
Corneli. ffisher
John Blanchard
John Hull
John Harwood
Will. Merriam
Nathani. Sternes
Peter Lyon (228)

C. R., Vol. II. pp. 227, 228.

3 May 1649.

John Ward

C. R., Vol. II. p. 228.

22 May 1650.

John Shepheard
Henry Prentice
Abraham Busby
Jacob Greene
Richard Stower
Thomas Welch
Wm. Pajne
David Mattocke
John Saunders
Robt Parmiter
Peeter Addams
John Jones
Joshua Edmonds
Wm. Underwood
Nathaniell Bale
Joseph Mirriam
Isacck Addington
Habbacuck Glover
Samuell foster
John Weld
Robt Harris
George Brand
Samuell Williams
Thomas Hanford
John Parker
Mr. John Knoules
John Ball
Robt Pearse
Henry Mason
Wm. Ireland
Edmond Browne

C. R., Vol. IV. p. 1.

7 May 1651.

Mr. Sam. Haugh
Rich. Whitney
Rich. Ouldam
Wm. Hamlett
John Taylor
Henry Butler
George ffry
Wm. Pratt
Wm. Blake
Aron Way
Josias Convers
John Brookes
John Mousell
Hugh Thomas
Charles Grise
Martjn Saunders
Samuel Kingsly
Wm. Owen
David Walsby
Edward Rise
Solomon Johnson
Georg Dell

C. R., Vol. IV. p. [illegible]

26 May 1652.

Joseph Rocke Bost.
James Richards "
Tho. Emans "
Henry Steevens "
Jo. Marrjon "
Robt. Sanforth "
Joshua Brooke Conc.
Joseph Knight Woob.
Hen. Baldwine "
Rich. Gardiner "
Jno Sawen Water
Ric. Norcrosse "
Niccolas Willjams Roxbur.
Isacke Heath "
Wm. Garey "
Peleg Heath "
Tho. Brewar "
Jacob ffrench Weim.
Wm. Atwood Charlst.
ffrancis Moore "
Dan. Bloget Camb.
Wm. Bordman "
Solomon Martjn And.
James Blake Dorch.
Tho. Prentice Rox.
Jno. Pier Point "
Moses Colljer Hing.
Jno. Fering "

C. R., Vol. IV. p. 75.

Feb. 1652–3.

Tho. Wisewall Dorch.
Norcross Water.
Robt. Howard Dorch.

C. R., Vol. IV. p. 75.

18 May 1653.

Mr. Wm. Hubbard I.
Symon Stone W.
Sam. Stratten "
Abra. Newell Rox.
Jos. Griggs "
Tho. Stowe C.
Wm. Martjn Read.
Wm. Eaton "
Jonas Eaton "
Tho. Marshall "
Tho. Dwight Ded.
Tho. Medcalfe "
Wm. Hilton Newb.
Tho. Skinner Mald.
Jno. Sprage "
Nath. Upham "
Rich. Boulter Weim.
Tho. Whitman "
Walter Cooke "
Jno. Guppee "
Jno. Thompson "
Jonas Humphry "
Richard Porter "
Wm. Reade "
Joshua Hubbard Hing.
Jerremiah Hubbard "
Jno. Wight Meadf.
Wm. Patridg "
Joseph Clarke "
Nath. Souther Boston.
Steeven Pajne "
Joseph Addams "

C. R., Vol. IV. p. 113.

16 Nov. 1652.

Appeared before the Commissioners at Kittery, and submitted to the Government of Massachusetts; the record of their oath does not appear.

Tho. Withers
Jno. Wincoll
Wm. Chadborn
Hugh Gunison
Tho. Spencer
Tho. Durston
Robt. Mendam
Rise Thomas
James Emery
Christian Remeth
Niccolas ffrost
Robt. Weimouth
Humphry Chadorne
Charles ffrost
Abraham Cunley
Richard Nason
Mary Bayly
Daniel Paule
Jno. Diamont
Georg Leader
Jno. Symons
Jno. Greene
Hugbert Mattoone
Gowen Wilson
Wm. Palmer
Jerre. Shrires
Jno. Hoord
Tho. Spinny
Nath. Lord

Joseph Mile
Antipas Mavericke
Niccolas Shapleigh
Antho. Emery
Reignald Jenkin
Jn°. White
Tho. Jones
Dennis Douning
Jn°. Andrewes
Daniell Davies
Phillip Babb
Wm Everett
C. R., Vol. IV. p. 116.

22 Nov. 1652.

At Accomenticus or Gorgeana.

Mr. Edward Godfry
Tho. Crocket
Jn°. Alcocke
Wm. Dixon
Ricd. Codogan
George Parker
Andrew Evered
Robt. Knight
Wm. Rogers
Sam. Alcocke
Joseph Alcocke
Peter Wjer
Phillip Addams
Mr. ffrauncis Raines
Lewis
Robt Ed—— [blotted]
Phillip Hatch
Jn° Davis
Niccolas Bond
Mr. Edw. Johnson
Hugh Gajle
Wm. Garnesey
Rich. Banckes
Edw. Wentom
George Braneen
Mary Topp: acknowledged herself subject &c. only.
Mr. Wm. Hilton
Wm. Moore
Henry Donell
Edward Stirt
Rowland Young
Jn°. Parker
Arthur Bragdon
Wm. Ellingham
Jn°. Tuisdale junr.
Tho. Courteous
Silvester Stover
Tho. Dennell
Mr. Edward Rushworth
Jn°. Harker
Niccolas Davis
Sampson Angier
Mr. Henry Norton
Robt Hetherse
Wm. ffreathy
Jn° Davis
Jn° Tuisdall senr.
Mr. Abra. Preble
Mr. Jn°. Couch
Mr. Tho. Whelewright
C. R., Vol. IV. p. 119.

4 July 1653.

Inhabitants of Wells: at Wells.

Joseph Emerson
Ezek. Knight
Jn°. Gooch
Joseph Boules
Jn°than Thing
John Barret senr.
C. R., Vol. IV. p. 142.

5 July 1653. At Wells.

Henry Boade
Jn°. Wadly
Edmond Letlefeild
Jn°. Saunders
Jn°. White
Jn° Bush
Robt Wadly
ffrauncis Litlefeild senr.
Wm. Wardell
Samuell Austin
Wm. Hamans
Jn°. Wakefeild
Tho. Milles
Antho. Litlefeild
Jn°. Barrett juni.
Tho. Litlefeild
ffrauncis Litlefeild jun.
Nicho. Cole
Wm. Cole
C. R., Vol. IV. p. 142.

5 July 1653.

Inhabitants of Saco, sworn at Wells.

Thomas Willjams
Willjam Scadlocke
Christopher Hobbs
Thomas Reading
Richard Hitchcocke
James Gibbins
Thomas Rogers
Phillip Hinckson
Robert Booth
Richard Cowman
Ralfe Tristram
George Barlow
Jn°. West
Peter Hill
Henry Maddock
Thomas Hale
C. R., Vol. IV. p. 145.

5 July 1653.

The Commissioners of Wells and Saco were empowered to give the oath of freemen to

John Smith	Saco.
Richard Ball	Wells.
Richard Moore	"
Jn°. Elson	"
Arthur Wormestall	"
Edward Clarke	"

C. R., Vol. IV. p. 145.

5 July 1653.

Inhabitants of Cape Porpus, sworn at Wells.

Morgan Howell
Christopher Spurrell
Thomas Warner
Griffin Mountague
John Baker
Wm. Renolls
Steven Batsons
Gregory Jeofferjes
Peter Turbat
Jn°. Cole
Symon Trott
Ambros Bury
C. R., Vol. IV. p. 146.

3 May 1654.

John Morse
Jacob Eliott
Jn°. Tinker
Hugh Drury
Jn°. Parker
Tho. Weld
Jn°. Rugles
Nath. Glover
Isacke Jones
Tho. Hinksman
Sam. Hunt
Caleb Brooke
Tho. Marsh
Michaell Knight
Jn°. Kent
Tho. Battle
Tho. Herring
Joseph Child
ffranc. Whitmore
Tho. Sawer
Jn°. Greene
Joseph Champney
Alex. Marsh
Jn°. fasell
Edw. Addams
Wm. Chard
James Smith

Andrew ffoored
Jn°. Smith
Wm. Marble
C. R., Vol. IV. p. 160.

23 May 1655.*

Mr. Seaborn Cotton
Abra. Newell
Joseph Griggs
Tho. Stowe
Mr. Wm. Hubbard
Wm. Martyn
Wm. Eaton
Jonas Eaton
Thomas Marshall
Tim°. Dwight
Tho. Medcalfe
Wm. Hilton
Tho. Skinner
Jn°. Sprauge
Nathan. Upham
Rich. Boulter
Thomas Whitman
Walter Cooke
Jn°. Guppee
Jn° Thompson
Jonas Humph
Rich. Porter
Wm. Reade
Symon Stone
Sam. St atten
Joshua Hubbard
Jerremy Hubbard
Jn°. Wight
Wm. Patridge
Joseph Clarke
Steeven Pajne
Joseph Addams
Wm. Johnson
C. R., Vol. IV. p. 194.

14 May, 1656.

Mr. Sam. Bradstreet
Mr. Sam. Whiting
Mr. Wm. Thompson
Job Lane
Jn°. Freary
Tho. Read
Tho. Basse
Hen. Wooddey
Abr. Jackewish
Jn°. Chadwicke
Steeven Gates
Abr. Ripley
Jn°. Ripley
C. R., Vol. IV. p. 219.

6 May 1657.

Willjam Lane
Henry Douglas
Joseph How
Wm. Dinsdale
Amiell Weekes
Roger Sumner
George Sumer
Justinian Houlden
Anthony Beers
Jer. Beales
Rich. Griffyn
Humphry Barrat
Jacob Park
Leonard Hurryman
Francis Weyman
Sam. Stone
Tho. ffaxon
Jn°. Dussett
C. R., Vol. IV. p. 241.

13 July 1658.

Inhabitants of Black Point, Blue Point, Spurwinke, and Casco Bay, sworn at Spurwinke, by Commissioners.

ffrancis Smaley
Nicho. White
Tho. Stamford
Jonas Bayly
Robert Corbyn
Nathaniell Wallis
Arthur Angur jun.
John Phillips
Rich. Martyn
Georg Lewis
Ambrose Boden
Samuell Oakeman
Andrew Brand
Mich. Madinde
Tho. Hamot
George Taylor
Henry Jocelyn
Georg Cleane
Robt Jordan
Jn°. Bonighton
Richard ffoxwell
Henry Watts
ffranc. Neale
Abra. ffellew
Ambros Boden sen^r.
Mich. Mitten
Jn°. Symes
Nico. Edgcomb
C. R., Vol. IV. p. 295.

30 May 1660.

Colonell Wm. Crowne
Augustine Lindon
Tho. Dwisdsall
Tho. Watkins
Hugh Clarke
Jn°. Majes
Sam. Majes
Jn° Elliott
Alex. Pannly
Wm. Wheeler
Jn°. Billing
Tho. Rice
Mathew Rice
Hen. Spring
Jacob Heurn
Nath Clap
Tho. Rand
Josiah Hubbard
James Whitton
John Nutting
Phillip Read
C. R., Vol. IV. p. 336.

27 May 1663.

Mr. Jn°. Croad
Charles Gott
Exercise Connant
Samuel Champneys
Jonathan Hide
Zech. Hicks
Abr. Holman
Jn°. Stratten
Robt Harrington
Nath. Holland
Robt. Twelves
Jn°. Ruggles
Jn°. Thirston
Wm. Clough
Nath. Hutchinson
Marke Batchiler
Dani. Pearse
Jos. Ellis
Wm. Toy
Laurenc. Waters
Tho. Collier
C. R., Vol. IV. p. 416.

19 Oct. 1664.

John Coldam Gloucester.
Mr. Robert Gibbs, Boston.
Mr. Abraham Browne "
Mr. Richard Price "
Arthur Mason "
Samuel Gallop "
C. R., Vol. IV. p. 458.

3 May 1665.

"The several persons underwrit returned by certificates from the several ministers and selectmen, were by public suffrage of both magistrates and Deputies admitted to

[To be continued.]

* Nearly a duplicate of the record under date of 18 May, 1653.

MARRIAGES AND DEATHS.

MARRIAGES.

ALLEN, MAJ. ROBERT, of the U. S. A., 15 Feb., in New York, to MISS MARY MEHITABLE BELCHER of Boston.

AYERS, MR. LUCIUS, to MISS ANN M. DEAN, both of Boston.

BARTON, MR., United States Chargé to Chili, 28 Dec., at St. Iago, to a lady of that country.

BLISS, LIEUT. COL. WM. WALLACE, Baton Rouge, 6 Dec., to MARY ELIZABETH, dau. Maj. Gen. Zachary Taylor.

BOLES, MR. GEORGE W., 7 Jan., to MISS AMANDA F. SMITH, both of Boston.

BOYNTON, MR. WILLIAM, 1 Feb., to MISS AUGUSTA S. MORSE, both of Boston.

BREWSTER, LIEUT. GEO., U. S. A., 27 Dec., in Brooklyn, N. Y., to FRANCES A., dau. of late E. W. Whiting of Boston.

DAGGET, MR. HANDEL N., of Attleboro', Ms., 20 Dec., in Livonia, Livingston Co., N. Y., to MISS JANE A. ADAMS, dau. of Ephraim Adams, Esq., of Livonia.

DENTON, MR. JAMES WARREN, of Cambridge, 25 Feb, to MISS SARAH ANN, dau. of Rev. Stephen Lovell of Boston.

DIMMICK, REV. LUTHER F., D. D., of Newburyport, 13 Mar., at Bradford, to MISS MARY ELIZABETH, dau. of Andrew Ellison, Esq., and late Principal of Bradford Academy.

DIXON, MR. GEO., 8 Feb., in Roxbury, to MISS ELIZABETH C. DAVENPORT of Boston.

FARRINGTON, MR. SAMUEL P., 15 Jan., to MRS. SARAH P. ELDREDGE, both of Boston.

FULLER, RICHARD R., ESQ., of Boston, 5 Feb., in Canton, to MISS SARAH K. BATCHELDER of Canton.

GANDELET, ALFRED, ESQ., of Boston, 22 Jan., to MISS HARRIET H., dau. of Col. Paul Chase of Brattleboro', Vt.

GOOKIN, MR. JAMES M., of Boston, 25 Nov., to MISS MARY ANN, dau. of H. B. Webb, Esq., of Bath.

HARTSHORN, JOHN, ESQ., 30 Jan., to MISS LOUISA F., dau. of late James Pickens, both of Boston.

HOWE, DR. ESTES, of Cambridge, 28 Dec., to MISS LOIS L., dau. of late Abijah White, Esq., of Watertown.

KNIGHT, MR. EDWARD, 1 Feb., to MISS ELIZABETH H. MORSE, both of Boston.

LAWRENCE, MR. HOEL KEATING, of Circleville, Ohio, 15 Jan., at Boston, to MISS PAMELIA WILLIAMS, dau. of Maj. D. H. Vinton of the U. S. A.

MOULTON, BENJAMIN P., 3 Jan., to MISS JULIA M. W. LEONARD, both of Boston.

OYSTER, MR. GEO., of New Jersey, 4 Feb., to MISS MARGARET, dau. of Abraham Crabb, Esq., of Oyster Bay, Long Island.

PERRY, OLIVER H., ESQ., of Lowell, 3 March, to MISS MARY ANNE, dau. of Eben Mosely, Esq., of Newburyport.

PHINNEY, MR. HENRY FREDERIC, 8 Feb, in Cooperstown, N. Y., to MISS CAROLINE MARTHA, dau. of James Fenimore Cooper.

PHIPPS, MR. BENJAMIN, JR., at Chelsea, 3 Jan., to MISS ANNE M., daughter of Abel Bowen, Esq.

PHIPPS, REV. JOSEPH H., of Framingham, 1 Jan., to MISS LAURA MATILDA, dau. of Dr. Charles Wild of Brookline.

PULSIFER, MR. SAMUEL, of Newton, 11 Jan., to MISS MARY ANN CHICKERING of South Dedham.

REYNOLDS, THOMAS CAUTE, Esq., of Richmond, Va., 28 Nov., at Gibraltar, to MISS HELOISE MARIE, dau. of late Horatio Sprague, Esq, of Gibraltar.

SAXTON, MR. H. D. S., 25 Jan., to MISS JANE ISABEL JENKINS, both of Boston.

SHERWOOD, THOMAS D., ESQ., of New York, 25 Jan., in Boston, to MISS MARY, dau. of late Hon. S. J. Hitchcock of New Haven, Ct.

SLACK, CHARLES W., editor of the Boston "Excelsior," 9 Jan., to MISS EVELINA E., dau. of Mr. Alexander Vannevar.

SMITH, MR. GEO. H., 6 Feb., in Cleveland, Ohio, to MISS MARY J. SANBORN, formerly of Salem, Ms.

SMITH, MR. J. H., of Cincinnati, 1 Mar., in Brooklyn, N. Y., to MISS MARY J., dau. Joseph Arnold, Esq., Boston.

SMITH, MR. JOHN T., of Boston, 1 Jan., at Stratham, N. H., to MISS LYDIA P., dau. of John Scammon, Esq., of Stratham.

THAYER, MR. G. FRANCIS, of Boston, 18 Jan., to MISS SARAH H., dau. of Mr. Timothy Emerson of Dover, N. H.

THOMAS, MR. JOHN N., 14 Feb., in Providence, R. I., to MISS ELIZABETH D., dau. of John H. W. Hawkins, the celebrated Temperance lecturer.

THOMPSON, MAJ. P. R., of the U. S. A., in New Orleans, to MISS HENRIETTA, dau. of H. Lockett, Esq.

TYLER, MR. JOSIAH, of East Windsor, Ct., 27 Jan., in Northampton, to MISS SUSAN W., dau. of Mr. Chester Clarke. They are attached to the South African mission.

WAINWRIGHT, LIEUT. RICHARD, of the U. S. N., in Washington, D. C., to MISS SALLY FRANKLIN, dau. of late Richard Bache, Esq., of Philadelphia.

WHELPLEY, JAMES, ESQ., editor of the American Whig Review, 3 Jan., in New York, to MISS ANN MARIA WELLS of Roxbury, Ms.

WILLIAMSON, WILLIAM RAWLINS, ESQ., Cincinnati, Ohio, 23 Nov., to MISS CAROLINE, dau. of Col. Henry Hobart of Foxborough, Ms.

YOUNG, REV. JOSHUA, of New North

Church, Boston, 14 Feb., in Cambridge, to Miss Mary Elizabeth, dau. of Sylvanus Plympton, M. D.

DEATHS.

Abbot, Miss Elizabeth, at Cambridge, 27 Feb., æ. 33. She was the youngest child of the late Rev. Abiel Abbot, D. D., (the beloved Pastor, successively, of the First Churches in Haverhill and Beverly,) by his wife Eunice, daughter of Ebenezer Wales, Esq., of Dorchester; and was born March 24, 1815. Her life was one of almost uninterrupted physical suffering; throughout which she displayed a truly Christian fortitude and resignation, and finally breathed her last at the house of her sister, Mrs. Charles Vaughan, late of Hallowell, but now of Cambridge.

Adams, Mr. John, Hartford, Pa., 27 Feb., æ. 105. He was a native of Worcester, Ms., and spent much of his early life at what is now West Cambridge.

Adams, Mr. Laban, Boston, 9 Jan., æ. 64.

Alder, Mr. Jonathan, Cincinnati, 30 Jan., æ. 75. "Mr. Alder was a native of New Jersey, but at a very early age removed with his parents to Wythe County, Va., where his father soon after died. At about the age of eight, as young Alder and his brother David were out hunting for a stray horse, they were surprised and taken prisoners by a straggling party of Indians belonging to the Mingo tribe. David they soon killed, but Jonathan was taken to their village on the waters of Mad river, near to what is now the limit of Logan County, where he remained a captive until after Wayne's treaty in 1795, a period of 24 years, never during that time receiving any intelligence of his mother, or any of his relatives. After Wayne's treaty, Mr. Alder, having accidentally learned that his relatives were still living in Virginia, paid them a visit, and was once more clasped in the arms of his aged mother, who had long since supposed him numbered with the dead. Mr. Alder returned to Ohio, married, and settled on a farm on Big Darby, where he resided until his death, respected by all."
Cincinnati Times.

Arnold, Col. Elisha, Cranston, R. I., 11 Jan., æ 87, a revolutionary soldier.

Bartlett, Rev. John, Marblehead, 3 Feb., æ. 66. Mr. B. was settled in Marblehead in 1811, and we know of few clergymen whose paternal regard for the people of his charge was more extensive, or whose loss would be more generally felt.

Bates, Capt. Bela, Cohassett, 13 Jan., æ. 77, for many years a master shipbuilder.

Bigelow, Benjamin, Esq., Cambridge, 24 Feb., æ. 83. Mr. Bigelow was one of the oldest inhabitants of Cambridge. He was born in Westminster, Worcester County, Aug. 6, 1765. His father, Jabez Bigelow, was a Lieutenant at West Point at the time of Arnold's treacherous attempt to deliver that fortress into the hands of the British, and died at the age of 90. His grandfather, Eliezur Bigelow, was the son of Joshua Bigelow, who served in King Philip's War, received a grant of land for his services, and lived to be 90 years of age. *He* was the son of John Bigelow of Watertown, who is said to have taken the Oath of Fidelity in 1636. His name in the ancient records is usually spelled *Biggely* or *Bigulah;* and the first marriage recorded in Watertown is that of "John Bigulah and Mary Warin, joyned in mariag before Mr. Nowell, the 30. 8. 1642." Bigelow's occupation appears from the following entry in the Town Records, under date of March 4, 1650–1.

"Agreed wth John Biglo y^t^ for ten trees the towne allowed him for the setting up a shop for a Smithes forge, y^t^ he shall either goe on wth y^t^ his promise of setting up *his trade, w^h^ is the trade of a Smith,* w^th^in one twelfmonth after the date hearoof, or else to pay unto the towne ten shillings for these ten trees he acknowledged to have off the townes."

John Bigelow was chosen a Surveyor of Highways in 1652 and 1660; a Constable in 1663; and one of "the seven men" (i. e. Selectmen) in 1665, 1670, and 1671. His "Homestall" consisted of six acres, and was bounded north by Richard Ambler and William Parker, east by Thomas Straight,* south by the highway, and west by Miles Ives. He died July 14, 1703, aged 86 years.

Benjamin Bigelow, the subject of this notice, was one of ten children, all of whom lived to become heads of families, and two of whom still survive, one being 86 years of age, the other 73. Mr. Bigelow was the son of religious parents, his mother, especially, being remembered as "an eminently godly woman." Brought up in his native town, he was married to Rebecca Boman, in 1790, and removed to Boston in 1802, and thence to Cambridge in 1804; from which time he was actively engaged in mercantile pursuits till 1835, when, possessed of a competence, and beginning to feel the weight of years, he closed his public business concerns, and passed the rest of his days in retirement, on his beautiful estate, well known as the "Inman Farm," of Revolutionary memory.

In early life Mr. Bigelow was honored

* This name is not to be found in Farmer's Genealogical Register.

with important military trusts; serving, also, as a volunteer in the force which was raised to suppress Shays's Rebellion. As an inhabitant of Cambridge, he enjoyed the respect and confidence of his fellow citizens. He frequently was chosen Selectman, and also an Overseer of the Poor; was repeatedly elected Representative to the General Court; and sustained the office of Assessor for a greater number of years than almost any other person in the town.

After the death of his wife, which occurred some five years since, Mr. Bigelow, whose sight had been gradually failing for some time previous. soon became totally blind. But though his hearing was also seriously affected, and he had buried nearly all of his own generation, he never appeared otherwise than cheerful. Surrounded by kind friends, he patiently awaited his end, and when it approached, sank to rest without a murmur and without a struggle.

The leading traits in Mr. Bigelow's character were, an earnest, but unostentatious, piety; a social disposition, which rendered his company agreeable to persons of all ages; an unbounded hospitality, which caused his noble mansion to be frequented by a large circle of friends; and an unbending integrity and high sense of honor in his intercourse with others. In addition to this, he was charitable to a proverb, so that it was said of him. "his heart is as large as that of an ox."

On the Sabbath but one after his decease, an affectionate tribute was paid to his memory by his Pastor, Rev. William A Stearns, in a discourse from 1 Chron. xxix. 28. *And he died in a good old age, full of days, riches, and honor.*

Boothby, Wid. Sarah, Limington, Me., 31 Jan., æ. 88 yrs., 6 mos., having had 11 children, 56 grandchildren, and 52 great-grandchildren.

Bowden, Mr. Samuel, Marblehead, 6 Feb., æ 98 yrs., 2 mos, 9 days.

Bowen, Mr. Jeremiah, Landaff, N. H., 10 March, æ., 98, a soldier of the Revolution.

Bradford, Mr. Josiah, Duxbury, 27 Jan., æ. 79 yrs., 2 mos, and 2 days. He was the youngest and last surviving of six sons of Capt. Samuel Bradford, who died in Duxbury while on a furlough, 17 Feb., 1777, æ. 47.

Brooks, Hon. Peter C., Boston, 1 Jan., æ 82.

Brown, Mr. Robert, Belchertown, 13 Feb, æ 85 A Revolutionary soldier

Browne, Capt. Thomas, Portland, Me. 2 March, æ. 81.

Carr, Miss Judith, Newbury, 31 Jan., æ. 90.

Caswell, Rev. Jesse, at Bankok, Siam, 25 Sept., æ. 39. He was an American Missionary, had been nine years on that station, and died after an illness of only one week.

Clayton, Mr. Charles M., in Havana, of consumption, 20 Jan, æ. 24; son of Hon. John M. Clayton, of United States Senate.

Colby, Lt. Thomas, Bow. N. H., 25 Dec., æ. 92; a Revolutionary soldier.

Crafts, Samuel, Esq., Hartwick, Otsego Co., N. Y., æ. 89; a native of Monson, Mass, and a Revolutionary soldier.

Crawford, Hon. Wm., Mobile, Ala., 28 Feb.; Judge of the U. S. District Court. He was born in Virginia, and removed to Alabama in 1810.

Crosby, Mrs. Kitty, in Louisville, Ky., 10 Feb, æ. 81. She was widow of the late Dr. John Crosby of Montpelier, Vt., and sister to Hon. John Locke and Hon. Joseph Locke of Lowell.

Currier, Mr. Richard, Methuen, 27 Feb., æ. 99 yrs., 11 mos., 6 days.

Cushing, Capt. John N., Newburyport, 5 Jan., æ. 69 yrs., 8 mos., father of Hon. Caleb Cushing.

Davenport, Mrs. Mary Jane, Boston, 1 Jan., æ. 36, wife of Mr. Hart Davenport.

Davenport, Rev. Robert D., Alexandria, La., 24 Dec., for many years missionary at Siam from the Baptist Board.

Dean, Prof. James, LL. D., Burlington, Vt., 20 Jan., æ. 73. Prof. Dean was son of Williard, b. 1739, son of William, b. 1712, son of William, b. 1689, son of James, b. 1647. He was formerly Professor of Mathematics and Natural Philosophy in Vermont University, an early member of the American Academy of Arts and Sciences, and contributed several very valuable articles to the publications of the Society. His contributions may also be found in the American Journal of Science and of the Franklin Institute. He graduated at Dartmouth in 1800.

Dean, Mrs. Sarah, Raynham, æ. 99, widow of late Hon. Josiah Dean.

Dix, Lieut. Col. Roger S., Hillsboro', Pa., 7 Jan., Paymaster of U. S A.

Doliber, Mrs. Sarah, Marblehead, æ. 98 yrs, 3 mos., and 21 days.

Drake, Mr. William, Middleboro', 14 Dec., æ 87, a Revolutionary pensioner. He served during nearly all the war, was in many trying scenes and conflicts, and had a knee broken in the service. He was a son of Joseph Drake of Taunton, who was son of Benjamin of Easton, who was son of Thomas of Weymouth, an original emigrant to New England.

Drake, Mr. Noah, Torrington, Ct., 3 March, æ. 91, a Revolutionary pensioner. He had taken the *Hartford Courant* above *sixty years!* He was son of Noah Drake of Windsor, Ct., who died in 1804, æ. 90, grandson of Enoch, great-grandson of Enoch who was son of John, son of John who emigrated from England and settled in Windsor, 1635 or 1636. His wife was Anna Parsons.

EMERSON, MR. JOSEPH, Newburyport, æ. 81. Mr. E. was postmaster of Newburyport during Washington's administration.

EVERETT, MR. OTIS, Boston, 4 Jan., æ. 70.

FESSENDEN, MISS SALOME, Boston, 31 Jan., æ. 80.

FISH, CAPT. LEWIS L., in the Sea of Ochotsk, master of the Bremen whale ship Alexander Barclay, and a native of Sandwich, Mass.

FORD, HEZEKIAH, E. Cleveland, Ohio, 18 Dec., æ. 91.

FOSTER, MRS. SARAH, Beverly, 22 Feb., æ. 94 yrs. 11 mo. She was widow of late Ezra T. Foster, and dau. of Deacon William Stickney of Billerica.

FOOTE, MRS. S. A., Cleveland, Ohio, 12 Jan., widow of late Gov. Foote of Connecticut.

FOX, JOEL, Dracut, 8 Feb., æ. 91, a soldier of the Revolution.

GAY, MRS. LUCY, W. Dedham, 8 Feb., æ. 84, widow of late Lemuel Gay.

GRANGER, THOMAS, Middlebury, Ohio, æ. 83, a soldier of the Revolution.

GRIMES, CAPT. ELIAB, in San Francisco, California, 7 Nov., æ. 69, a native of Fitchburg, Mass.

HALE, DAVID, Fredericksburg, Va., 20 Jan., æ. 59, editor of the New York Journal of Commerce.

HARRIS, SARAH DUNCAN, South Boston, 16 Dec., 1848, æ. 17. She was the eldest daughter and second child of Mr. John Alexander and Mrs. Harriet Miller Harris, and granddaughter of the late Rev. Thaddeus Mason Harris; and was born Dec. 30, 1831. She died of a rapid consumption, after a sickness of but a few short months.

HAVEN, MRS. ABIGAIL, Portsmouth, N. H., æ. 92. She was widow of the late Samuel Haven, Esq., who died in 1825, æ. 71, and was eldest son of Rev. Samuel Haven, D. D., for many years pastor of the South Parish in Portsmouth.

HICKS, MRS. SARAH, Warren, R. I., 1 Feb., æ. 90, widow of Capt. Samuel Hicks.

HINKLEY, SAMUEL, ESQ., Hardwick, 29 Jan., æ. 82, a soldier of the Revolution.

HOLMAN, MR. STEPHEN, Bangor, 6 Feb., æ. 88, a soldier of the Revolution.

HOLMAN, MRS. SUSANNA, Millbury, 25 Feb., æ. 89, widow of the late Col. Jonathan Holman of the Revolution.

HOWE, WIDOW LUCY, N. Salem, 2 Mar., æ. 86 years 10 mo., a Revolutionary pensioner.

JEWETT, MR. ENOCH, Hollis, N. H., æ. 91. He was a Revolutionary soldier from the battle of Bunker Hill to the end of the war.

JOHNSON, CAPT. SILAS, Amherst, 13 Mar., æ. 86. A soldier of the Revolution.

KELLOGG, MAJOR CHESTER, Amherst, 7 Jan., 61.

KNAPP, JOHN, ESQ., Boston, 9 March, æ. 70. He was a graduate of H. C. in the class of 1800.

KRAMER, MR. MELCHIOR, Boston, 23 Feb., æ. 56.

LAMB, MRS. ROSANNA, Boston, 10 March, æ. 89, widow of late Thomas Lamb.

LARKIN, SAMUEL, ESQ., Portsmouth, N. H., 10 March, æ. 76. Mr. Larkin has long been known as one of the most respected, upright, industrious, useful citizens of that town. He was faithful and exemplary in the discharge of all his duties as a citizen, a friend, and a Christian. He bore prosperity without pride, and adversity without complaint. His loss is one that will be severely felt by his friends, his townsmen, and the community at large.

LATHAM, MR. WILLIAM, Ledyard, Ct., 29 Jan., æ. 85, one of the defenders of Fort Griswold.

LEAVITT, MR. JOSEPH M., Boston, 19 Feb., æ. 44 yrs. 7 mo. Mr. L. was long a respectable member of the firm of B. & J. M. Leavitt, merchants, Boston.

LE BARON, DR. ISAAC, Plymouth, 29 Jan., æ. 71.

LEONARD, MR. DAVID, æ. 84, and Mr. Benjamin, æ. 80, brothers. Their deaths occurred about two hours apart, and they were buried in the same grave.

LEONARD, DR. JONATHAN, Sandwich, 26 Jan., æ. 86, a graduate of H. C. in the class of 1786.

LORING, MRS. ELLEN MARIA, N. Andover, 4 March, æ. 24, dau. of Hon. Daniel P. King.

LORING, MR. DAVID, Cincinnati, Ohio, 22 Jan., æ. 64. Mr. Loring removed from New York to Cincinnati thirty-five years since, and by a life of industry and perseverance has done more there towards beautifying the city with substantial structures than perhaps any other man now living. He was a devoted student of the doctrines of SWEDENBORG, scrupulously just in all his intercourse with his fellow men, upright in his course through life, and enriched by the love and respect of all who knew him.

LORING, MRS. LOVE, Cambridge, 18 Jan., æ. 74.

LYON, MISS MARY, South Hadley, 5 Mar., æ. 52, Principal of the Mount Holyoke Seminary.

MASON, GEN. JOHN, Clarmont, Va., 19 March, æ. 83. He was the personal and intimate friend and associate of Jefferson, Madison, and Monroe, and during the administrations of the two last, filled offices of trust and honor, which he accepted at their request.

MILLS, LT. THOMAS, Dunbarton, N. H., 15 Dec., æ. 90. He retained his bodily and mental faculties to the last in a remarkable degree. He was very abstemious, never drank any ardent spirit, and never was sick a day in his life. He was the first person in the town who enlisted to join Gen. Stark at Bennington in 1777, and among the first who went over the breastworks of the enemy in that battle. During the war, Lt. Mills and a man named Piper, took prisoners seven men and two boys near a bridge over the Hoosick, although Mills and Piper had each a Hessian prisoner taken just before.

MORRILL, HON. DAVID L., Concord, N. H., 28 Jan., æ. 76 yrs. 7 mo. 18 days. "Gov. Morrill was born in Epping, this State, June 10, 1772; was the oldest son of Rev. Samuel Morrill, and grandson of Rev. Isaac Morrill, of Wilmington, Ms., both graduates of Harvard College. In 1793 he settled at Epsom, as a physician, where he remained until 1800. In October, of that year, he commenced the study of divinity, was approbated as a preacher the following June, and was ordained as pastor of the Presbyterian Congregational Church in Goffstown, March 2, 1802. In 1807, he resumed the practice of physic, and continued it, when not drawn from it by public duties, until 1830. In 1811, at his own request he was dismissed from his pastoral duties to the church in Goffstown, on account of ill health. In 1808 he was elected a member of the Legislature from Goffstown, and was annually re-elected Representative until 1817; at the June session, 1816, he was elected Speaker of the House of Representatives and the same session was chosen Senator in Congress, for 6 years from the 4th of March, 1817; his term expired on the 4th of March, 1823, and at the March election, of that year, he was elected a State Senator to represent the 3d Senatorial District, and was chosen President of the Senate the following June. The next year he succeeded Governor Woodbury as Chief-Magistrate of the State, and in 1825 he received 30,167 of the 30,770 votes given for Governor in the whole State that year. In 1826, in a sharp contest, he was re elected Governor, having for a competitor for the Gubernatorial Chair, the late Gov. B. Pierce of Hillsborough.

In addition to the titles of 'Dr.,' 'Rev.,' 'Gov.,' 'Senator,' &c., Dartmouth College conferred upon him the titles, '*Master of Arts*,' and '*Doctor of Medicine*,' and the University of Vermont added, '*Doctor of Laws*.'" — *Conc. Dem.*

MORRIS, THOMAS, ESQ., New York. He was for many years U. S. Marshall, and son of the celebrated Robert Morris of Philadelphia.

MORSE, MR. LEONARD, Sherburne, æ. 57.

MUSSEY, MRS. BETSEY WOODBURY, wife of Benj. B. Mussey, Esq., of Boston, 20 March, æ. 40 years.

MUSSEY, MRS. DOLLY, N. Brighton, Me., 5 Feb., æ. 91, widow of late Theodore Mussey, Esq., of Standish.

OGIER, LEWIS, Camden, Me., 30 Jan., æ. 88, a soldier of the Revolution.

OLIVER, MRS. ELIZA, Boston, 28 Dec., æ. 71, widow of late Hubbard Oliver.

PARKER, MR. ELIAB, N. Reading, 11 Feb., æ. 80.

PETERS, AMOS, Mt. Airy, Hunterdon Co., N. J., 14 Jan., æ. 90, a sergeant in the Rev. army. "Several matrons of that period have left us within a few days, all over 90 years of age; among them Mrs. Amelia Lippincott, grandmother of Stephens, the traveller and author, who died at Shrewsbury, Monmouth county, on the 27th ult., in the 96th year of her age. She retained the possession of her faculties to the last." — *Newark Daily Adv., Feb.*, 1849.

PORTER, MRS. HANNAH, Hampton Falls, N. H., æ. 96. She was widow of late John Porter, and dau. of Hon. Meshech Weare, first Governor of New Hampshire. She is said to have entertained at her house, Washington, Lafayette, and many Revolutionary worthies.

POTTER, CAPT. JAMES, North Adams, 22 Jan., æ. 89, a soldier of the Revolution.

PRENTISS, MRS. SARAH JEWETT, Boston, 5 Jan., æ. 39, wife of Mr. Henry James Prentiss, and dau. of late Eliphalet Jewett, formerly of Salem.

PRINCE, DAVID, ESQ., Cumberland, Me., 3 Feb., æ. 95 yrs. 9 mo.

RANDALL, REUBEN, Greenville Co., N. Y., æ. 91, a Revolutionary soldier. He was a native of Connecticut, and 19 years of age when he entered the army.

REED, WILLIAM GORDON, at Paris, 13 Feb., æ. 37, eldest son of William Reed, of Boston, formerly of the house of Paine, Striker & Co., Batavia, Java.

SALMON, JOHN, ESQ., Boston, 15 March, æ. 83. Mr. Salmon has, through a long and active life, sustained the reputation of an honest man and one of the most useful citizens. When about ten years old he witnessed the battle of Bunker's Hill and the conflagration of Charlestown. This he viewed from Copps Hill, and though he was at that time a mere child, the impressions made on his mind by that tragic scene remained clear and vivid till the end of his life.

SANDERSON, MRS. SARAH, Roxbury, 14 Jan., æ. 98.

SIMPSON, MR. BENJ., Saco, Me., æ. 94, one of the immortal "Tea Party."

STACKPOLE, ABSALOM, N. Berwick, Me., 30 Jan., æ. 96, a soldier of the Revolution.

STONE, CAPT. JOHN, Worthington, 20 Feb., æ. 96. He survived his wife, with whom he had lived sixty-five years, just two weeks.

STONE, MRS. SARAH, Watertown, 27 Feb., æ. 87, widow of late Jonathan Stone.

STONE, WILLIAM, Hallowell, Me., æ 87, a Revolutionary soldier and one of the first settlers of the town.

TEN BROECK, REV. PETRUS S., Danvers, 21 Jan., æ. 57, formerly Rector of St. Paul's church in Portland.

THOMAS, MR. SIDNEY, St. Louis, 28 Jan., æ. 34, a native of Plymouth, Mass.

THOMPSON, MR. BENJ. F., of Hempstead, L. I., suddenly, in the city of New York, 22 March. Mr. Thompson is extensively known as the author of the history of Long Island, was for several years District Attorney of Queen's County, and ranked among the most respectable scholars in historic and antiquarian lore that this country affords.

WEBSTER, MRS. CYNTHIA, widow of late Charles R. Webster of Albany, N. Y., at Albion, N. Y., 22 Dec., 1848, æ. 78.

WILKINSON, MRS. BETSEY, Boston, 11 Jan., æ. 66, wife of Simon Wilkinson, Esq.

WILLIAMS, MISS DOROTHY, Hadley, 7 Jan., æ. 84, dau. of Hon. William Williams, formerly of Dalton.

WILLIAMS, WIDOW ELIZABETH, Roxbury, 31 Jan., æ. 89.

WILLIAMS, JOEL, Orange, N. J., 28 Feb., æ. 85. He was a soldier of the Revolution, and had lived with his wife, who survives him, sixty-one years in the same house where he died.

WILLIAMS, MISS JULIA, Northampton, 10 March, æ. 65, eldest dau. of late Rev. Solomon Williams, of that town.

WILLIAMS, HON. TIMOTHY S., Ithaca, N. Y., 11 March, Senator from the 26th district of that state.

WILSON, MRS. JANE, Bath, Me, 14 March, æ 99.

WINGATE, PAINE, ESQ, Hallowell, Me., æ. 61.

WITHIN, SAMUEL, Wilton, Me., æ. 91 yrs. 8 mo., a Revolutionary pensioner.

WOODBURY, MR. JOHN, Boston, 24 Dec., æ. 80.

DONATIONS TO THE SOCIETY.

HON. SAMUEL BRECK, of Philadelphia, an ancient Map of Boston, (1769)

C. M. TAINTOR, ESQ., of Shelburne, Ms., several MSS. of the Revolutionary period, and early newspapers.

REV. ERASTUS WENTWORTH, of Lebanon, Ill., catalogue of the officers and students of M'Kendree College, 1848.

MR. S. T. FARWELL, several valuable modern pamphlets.

J. WINGATE THORNTON, ESQ., do. do.

☞ The publisher would ask pardon of all persons of the name of *Frobisher*—regularly entitled to that name—in the United States, for what may be considered ignorance on the part of the author of the "Memoirs of Sir Martin Frobisher," in the last number of the Register. The writer of that article will be acquitted even of the charge of ignorance, when we assure our readers that *no such name is to be found among our subscribers!*

☞ Several valuable works sent to be noticed will receive attention in our next.

☞ Many valuable communications are unavoidably deferred at present. They shall receive early attention.

☞ Mr. A. M. Griggs, of Chaplin, Ct., desires information respecting his name and family.

Edward Rawson.

NATIS 1615 ÆTATIS SUÆ 55. 1670.

Engraved from the original Portrait in the possession of R.R. Dodge.

East Sutton, Mass.

NEW ENGLAND

HISTORICAL AND GENEALOGICAL REGISTER.

VOL. III. JULY, 1849. NO. III.

NOTICE OF EDWARD RAWSON,

SECRETARY OF THE COLONY OF MASSACHUSETTS BAY, FROM 1650 TO 1686.

EDWARD RAWSON, the reputed descendant and namesake of a certain doughty Sir Edward Rawson, of ancient memory, was born in the village of Gillingham, upon the river Stour, in the County of Dorset, Old England, April 16th,* 1615. Of his early life we know but little. He was married, in due time, to Rachael, daughter of Thomas Perne, and granddaughter of that John Hooker, whose wife was a Grindal, sister to Edmund Grindal, " the most worthily renowned Archbishop of Canterbury," in the reign of Queen Elizabeth. By this marriage he became connected with two of New England's greatest Divines, Hooker and Wilson, the latter of them, says Cotton Mather, " having for his mother a niece of Dr. Edmund Grindal;" and the same veracious chronicler makes honorable mention, in his life of Wilson, of the " good kinsman of his, who deserves to live in the same story, as he now lives in the same Heaven, with him, namely, Mr. Edward Rawson, the honored Secretary of the Massachuset Colony." †

Rawson came to New England in 1636 or 1637, and became an inhabitant of the town of Newbury, then recently settled. His name appears on the list of twenty-six persons who were admitted Freemen in " the first m° $\frac{1637,}{1638,}$" ‡ i. e. in March, 1637-8; and on the 19th of the following month, April, he was invested with the office of " publick notary and register for the towne of Newbury, and whilst he so remains to be allowed by the towne after the rate of five pounds per annum for

* The " Memorial of the Rawson Family," says, on page 5, that Rawson was born April 15, 1615. But on page 10 of the same work is a record, extracted from the Family Bible of the Secretary, in the following words:—" This may certify whome it may concerne that Edward Rawson (Secretary) was borne in Old England in the yeare of our Lord 1615, April 16th," &c &c. The original record is stated to be "in the handwriting of his [the Secretary's] son William," to whom the Bible descended on the death of his father; and if this is the case, we can have little hesitation in preferring the date here given.

† Mather's Magnalia, (fol. Lond. 1702,) Book III. pp. 41, 50.

‡ Mass. Colony Records, Lib. I. fol. 195.

his paynes." To this office was added that of a Selectman, and also that of "Commissioner for small causes;" * and he was chosen one of the Deputies to represent the town at the May and September sessions of the General Court.† Thus suddenly, in a few short months, was Edward Rawson elevated to civil office. We must suppose him to have been possessed of no ordinary talents for business, and of a large share of public spirit, thus soon to have recommended himself so favorably to the notice of his fellow townsmen, and to have taken his seat, at the age of three and twenty, among the legislators of the Colony.

In 1639 Rawson again represented Newbury in the General Court, at its three sessions; and at the May session the Colony Records ‡ inform us that he "is granted 500 acres at Pecoit so as hee go on with the busines of powder if the salt Peter come." In 1641 we again find him serving in the capacity of Commissioner for small causes in Newbury; and in 1642 he was one of the committee to which "by the generall consent of all the freemen, the stinting of the commons was referred." § In September of this year he again appears as a Deputy to the General Court. In January, 1643-4, the Town Records of Newbury recite that "in consideration of Mr. Rawson's keeping the towne book, it is ordered by us according to our power from the towne and courte granted to us, that he shall be freed and exempted from all towne rates for one whole yeare from the twenty-ninth of September last to the twenty-ninth of September next 1644." ‖ In May of this year, 1644, Rawson again took his seat in the House of Deputies; and at the session in October,

"In answer to a petition p^r^ferd by M^r^. Rawson for land in refference to his Journey to the eastward, this Court graunts him two hundred acres uppon Cochituate River above Dover bounds not graunted to any others p^r^vided that Capt. Pendleton be Joyned wth Peter Coffin in laying out the same."¶

In 1645 Newbury was represented at the three ** sessions of the

* Memorial of the Rawson Family; Coffin's History of Newbury, pp. 27, 28, 316.

† As this statement apparently conflicts with that of the laborious historian of Newbury, on page 48 of his work, it behooves us to account for the discrepancy, in self-defence. Mr. Coffin says, under date of April 1, 1647, "At the same meeting the 'selectmen,' 'one grand juryman,' a 'constable,' three 'waywardens,' and a 'deputy' to the general court were chosen. This deputy was Mr. Edward Rawson, who this year was chosen secretary of state, in room of Mr. Increase Nowell." This passage, taken in connection with the circumstance that the diligent author has not indicated, in any previous year, an election of a Deputy, has caused it to be inferred that Newbury was for the first time represented in the General Court in the year 1647. But that this was not the case will be apparent from a glance at the Colony Records, which show that the Town was represented, in May, 1636, by John Spencer; in September, of the same year, by Spencer and Edward Woodman; in December by Spencer; in 1637 by Woodman and John Woodbridge; in March, 1637-8, by Woodbridge; in May, 1638, by Woodbridge and Rawson; &c. For a corroboration of this statement we would refer to New Hampshire Hist. Coll. II. 210, 211, 212, as more accessible to the general reader than the Colony Records. With regard to the Secretaryship, we would merely remark, in this connection, that from the Colony Records it appears that Increase Nowell was chosen Secretary, for the last time, on May 2d, 1649, and was succeeded by Rawson at the next annual election, and not until then.

‡ Lib. I. fol. 252. § Coffin's Newbury, pp. 33-4, 35-6. ‖ Ibid., p. 40.

¶ Colony Records, Lib. III. fol. 442-3.

** "Att another Session of y^e^ Generall Courte of Eleccōns called by warrants by y^e^ Gou'no^r^ y^e^ 12 $\frac{6}{\text{mo:}}$ 1645: P^r^sent thereat the Gou'no^r^ Deput Gou'no^r^ & y^e^ rest of y^e^

General Court by Rawson and Richard Dummer. The first session of the Court in this year was very long, continuing from May 14th until Saturday, July 5th.* In the last week of this protracted sitting, but a day or two before their dissolution, the Deputies passed the following vote :—

"Edward Rawson is chosen & appointed Clarke to the house Depu^{t}s for one whole yeere to Enter all votes past in both houses & those alsoe y^{t} passe only by them into their booke of Records." †

In 1646 Rawson retained his seat as Deputy, and his office of Clerk of the House ; and was also, in conjunction with "Mr Woodman and Hene^{r}y Shorte," appointed and authorized, by both houses, "to end smale causes at Newbe^{r}y for the yeere ensewing aco^{r}ding to Lawe." ‡ At the same time he sustained the office of Selectman § in Newbury, and in November received a commission "to see people joyne in marriage in Newberry, during the pleasure of the Court." ‖ At this same session, in November, 1646,

"Itt is Ordered" by the Deputies "y^{t} Edward Rawson shall have twenty markes allowed him for his paines out of ye next levy as Secr^{t} to ye House of Depu^{t}s *for two yeeres past*."¶

This vote of the Deputies was passed "by both houses," and the Court, subsequently to its passage, entered the following declaration in their Records :—

"Mr. Edward Rawson having been employed to signe and transcribe all bills that passe in a booke, yet being sensible of the great expences and charge which this Court is at, and difficulty to raise small matters, not doubting of his being sensible with us thereof, to meet in that respect what was allowed him by us for one year's service, viz : twenty marks, shall be all that shall be alowed him, and paid him out of the next levy for his service done, and he shall do to the end of this Court, conceiving it to be but just in some measure to recompence labours of this kind, which we would not be backward in."**

In 1647 and 1648 Rawson continued to represent Newbury in the General Court. In the former year he seems to have been superseded in his office as Town Clerk of Newbury, by "Mr. John Lowle."†† In

Assistants *wth all the deputs of ye last generall Courte* excep^{t} Left. Atherton: who was sent out on speciall occacōn." *Col Rec.*

At the session of the Court in October the Records inform us that there were present "*all the depu^{t}s.* Capt Wyggin excepted : & ye depu^{t}s of Boston." *Ibid.*

* See Savage's Winthrop, ii. 246.

† Colony Records, Lib. III. fol. 21.—In the Memorial of the Rawson Family mention is not made of this early appointment, but of its renewal only, in 1649.

‡ Ibid. Lib. III. fol. 66. § Coffin, pp. 44. 46.

‖ Colony Records, Lib. II. fol. 244.—The passage in the text is from the Records of the General Court, properly so called, kept by the Colonial Secretary. But the Records of the House of Deputies, which are indiscriminately numbered and cited as consecutive volumes of the Colonial Records, contain the following more minute entry, by Rawson himself, of this appointment :—"In Ans^{r} to ye peticōn of ye Towne of Newbery Edward Rawson is Appointed & Authorized by this Courte to marry such as are published acording to ye order of ye Courte & during ye Courts pleasure." *Col. Rec. Lib.* III. *fol* 84. The fact that this appointment, trivial in itself, was made "*in answer to the petition of the Town of Newbury,*" evidences the consideration in which Rawson was held by his fellow townsmen.

¶ Ibid. Lib. III. fol. 84. ** Ibid. Lib. II. fol. 245. †† Coffin, p. 48.

1648 he received two grants of land, the first, at the May session of the Court, of fifteen hundred acres, jointly with Rev. John Wilson, of Boston, "next adjoining to the three thousand acres granted to Mr. John Winthrop, at Paquatuck, near the Narraganset Country, but in case Mr. John Winthrop perform not the condition with respect to the time limited, that then the fifteen hundred acres of the said Mr. Wilson and Mr. Edward Rawson shall be of the said three thousand acres granted to the said Mr. Winthrop;"* the second grant is the subject of the following vote of the Court, passed at its session in October:—

"In answer to the petition of Mr Edward Rawson for satisfaction in regard of charges he hath ben at & damages which he hath sustaynd about pvisions to make gunpowder It is ordred that in Regard of his great forwardnes & Readines to advance so hopefull a designe as the makinge of saltpeter within this Jurisdiction who for that end & purpose hath disbursed certayne moneyes to his great Losse & Damage p^rsented to us at Large in his petition Delivered into the p^rsent Court have therefore in Consideration of the p^rmises & Answer to his sd petition given and graunted unto him & his heires for ever five hundred acres of Land at Pequot to be Layd out by the appoyntment of this Court as also five pounds to be payd him out of the treasury."†

Rawson was also one of two persons (Mr. Joseph Hills, of Malden, being the other) who were this year desired by the Court "to compose the amendments of the book of laws passed and make them as one; one copy to remain in the hands of the committee for the speedy committing them to the press, and the other to remain in the hands of the Secretary sealed up till the next Court." ‡

At the General Court which convened upon the 3d of May, 1649, the election of Rawson (who had appeared as sole representative from Newbury) to the office of Clerk of the Deputies is mentioned, in the following brief paragraph at the bottom of the page § whereon are inscribed the names of those who composed the civil government for the year ensuing:—

"Edward Rawson Cleric for ye yeere."

Captain Thomas Wiggin and Rawson had been appointed by the General Court of the Colony to settle the estate of William Waldron, of Dover, "a good clerk and a subtle man, their Recorder, and also Recorder of the Province of Maine under Sir Ferdinando Gorge," who, "returning from Saco about the end of September, 1646, alone, passing over a small river at Kennebunk, was there drowned, and his body not found until near a month after." ‖ Having accomplished the duty thus imposed upon them, Wiggin and Rawson asked to be discharged from their trust, and upon the 10th of May, 1649,

"In Ans^r to the petition of Capt Tho Wiggin & Edward Rawson The Courte Judgeth it meete their accompt be accepted and they dischardged and that Mr. Rawson be allowed out of the Estate of the said Walderne for his paines in & about the matter of his petition fforty shillings and

* Rawson Memorial, p. 128.
† Colony Records, Lib. III. fol. 159.
‡ Coffin, p. 50.
§ Colony Records, Lib. III. fol. 209.
‖ Savage's Winthrop, ii. 278.

Capt Wyggin thirty shillings & that the Estate of the said Wm. Walderne consisting of lands houses & cattle are hereby Appointed to be & Remayne in the hands of Hate Evill Nutter & John Hall of Dover to dispose of as they Judge may best tend to the Impvement of the Estate & to be ready to be accomptable when the Courte shall think meete to call for it for y[e] satisfaccōn of the Creditors." *

At the Court of Elections in Boston, May 2, 1649, Increase Nowell was for the last time chosen Secretary of the Colony. At the next annual election, on the 22d of May, 1650, EDWARD RAWSON was raised to the office which Nowell had filled, without interruption, since the year 1636. With his appointment Rawson begins a new volume of the Colonial Records, on the first page of which is written, in his own hand,

"At a Generall Cou[r]t of Eleccōns held at Boston 22[th] of May 1650: Edward Rawson gent was chosen Secretary." †

The Records of the Deputies for this period, which are contained in what is numbered as the third volume of the Colony Records, give Rawson's name as Secretary, and, at the end of the list of the members of the lower house, record ‡ that

"Left. W[m]. Torrey was chosen Clarke for this next yeere,"

as successor to Rawson, who had, probably, been their Clerk ever since his first election to the office, in 1645.

Edward Johnson, in his "Wonder-working Providence of Sions Saviour in New England," published in London, in 1654, a beautiful copy of which lies before us at this moment, enumerates, among the "able instruments that were skill'd in Common-wealth work," with which, as he tells us, "the Lord was pleased to furnish these his people,"

"Mr. Edward Rawson, a young man, yet imployed in Common-wealth affaires a long time, being well beloved of the inhabitants of Newbery, having had a large hand in her Foundation; but of late he, being of a ripe capacity, a good yeoman, [penman?] and eloquent inditer, hath been chosen Secretary for the Country." §

At the meeting of the Commissioners of the United Colonies at New Haven, in September, 1651, Rawson was chosen steward or agent "for the receiving and disposing of such goods and commodities as shall be sent hither by the Corporation in England for the Propagating the Gospel amongst the Indians in New England." The record of the proceeding is as follows:—

"For the better ordering and carrying on the affayres of the Indians in respect of the gifts procured for them by the Corporacōn in England the Comissioners have made choise of Mr. Edward Rawson as a Steward to receive and dispose of the same; and have entreated the Comissioners of the Massachusets to treat with him about his Imployment and Salary and if hee accept thereof to deliver him the ensueing Comission if hee refuse the said Comissioners are desired to appoint and agree with som fitt person for that work for this yeare next ensueing." ‖

* Colony Records, Lib. III. fol. 226. † Ibid. Lib IV. fol. 1. ‡ Ibid. Lib. III. fol. 253.

§ Johnson's History of New England, (sm. 4to. Lond. 1654,) p. 109.

‖ Hazard's State Papers, II. 187–8.

This appointment was accepted by Rawson, but it has been stated that "in this office he did not give so much satisfaction as in the other," i. e. that of Secretary. "The Praying Indians complained to Ratcliffe and Randolph that they could not get cloaths, &c., which were allowed them." * The only authority which we have been able to find for this statement is the following passage in a letter † from Edward Randolph, New England's sorest enemy, dated at Boston, (in New England) Oct. 27, 1686, to the Archbishop of Canterbury. Says Randolph: —

"I have taken care to informe myself how the money sent over hither for the Company of Evangelizing Indians in New England (for soe by their Pattent from his late Majesty they are stiled) is disposed of here. Here are seven persons, called Commissioners or Trustees, who have the sole manage of it; the chief of which are Mr. Dudley, our President, a man of a base, servile, and antimonarchicall principle, Mr. Stoughton, of the old leaven, Mr. Richards, a man not to be trusted in publique business, Mr. Hinkley, Governor of New Plimouth Collony, a rigid Independant, and others like to these. The poor Indians (those who are called ministers) come and complaine to Mr. Ratclieffe, our minister, that they have nothing allowed them. We have spoken to the Commissioners to have some allowance for them; all we can gett is the promise of a coarse coat against winter, and would not suffer Aaron, an Indian teacher, to have a Bible with the Common Prayer in it, but took it away from him. This money is not less than three or four hundred pounds which is yearly returned over hither, (some say six hundred,) with which they enrich themselves, yet charge it all as layd out among the poore Indians. I humbly presume to remind your Grace of your promise to me, when in England, that a commission should be directed to some persons here, unconcerned, to audit and report their acts of this money."

In a former letter,‡ dated May 29, 1682, to the Bishop of London, Randolph writes,

"In my attendance on your Lordship I often exprest that some able ministers might bee appoynted to performe the officies of the Church with us. The maine obstacle was, how they should be mainetayned. I did formerly, and do now, propose, that a part of that money sent over hither and pretended to bee expended amongst the Indians, may be ordered to goe towards that charge. I am told by credible persons that there is nigh two thousand pounds of that money put out to interest in this country. *I know two hundred hath bin for many yeeres in the hands of Mr. Rawson, their Secretary, who is now pressed for to pay the money, to his utter ruin.*"

It is more than probable, indeed it is perfectly apparent, from other passages in Randolph's letters, that the real cause of his disinterested zeal for the proper application of the funds devoted to "Evangelizing Indians," was his desire to establish the rites and ceremonies of the Church of England on the strong Puritanical soil of New England, and to bestow thereupon the surplus funds of the country, as well as

* See Eliot's New England Biographical Dictionary, Art. Rawson.
† See it in Hutchinson's Collection of Papers, pp. 552–3. ‡ Ibid, pp. 531–4.

to aggrandize himself at the same time. Hence no great reliance is to be placed upon his statements.

At the session of the General Court in the month of October, 1651,

"Its Ordred that M[r] Edward Rawson Secreitary to the Generall Court shall henceforth be Recorder for the County of Suffolk, and that M[r] Aspinwall shall deliver him all the records belonging to the s[d] County." *

In that dark day of New England's history, the season of the persecution of the Quakers, Rawson was, unfortunately, hurried along by the torrent of popular fanaticism; and his name too frequently occurs upon the records of that gloomy period, as the "Persecutor." *De mortuis nil nisi lene.* This is the only blemish upon the fair fame of the Secretary, and we may hope that his conduct during this excitement, chargeable, perhaps, in a great measure to his peculiar position, may be counterbalanced by the virtuous deeds of an, apparently, otherwise irreproachable life.

On the 6th of May, 1657, the General Court

"Graunted to M[r] Edward Rawson Sec, in refference to his service to the Eastward 200 Acres of land to what he hath already had to be layd out not interfearing with former graunts."†

Rawson's salary as Secretary was, at first, but £20 per annum, but was subsequently increased to £60. He retained his office, by annual election, often receiving grants of land, &c., for "extraordinary services," until the arrival of Edward Randolph from England in 1686, a circumstance which, of itself, affords a strong proof of the good esteem in which he was held throughout the Colony.

On the 15th of May, 1686, arrived in Boston harbor the Rose Frigate, bringing Edward Randolph, the bearer of a Commission ‡ to Joseph Dudley as President, and sixteen others as Councillors, of New England, until a Governor in Chief should be appointed by the King. Randolph had also with him the King's Commission § to himself, bearing date, Sept. 21, 1685, as "Secretary and sole Register" of New England, including the Colonies of Massachusetts and New Plymouth, the Provinces of New Hampshire and Maine, the Narraganset Country, commonly called the King's Province, and the islands appertaining to either and all of these several Colonies and territories. The Commission for Dudley having been laid before the General Court, that body resolved upon an answer, which was drawn up and signed by Edward Rawson; and this was probably his last official act. The Court ordered the Secretary to deliver the government records to a committee which it appointed to take charge thereof, and adjourned.‡ From Rawson's petition to Andros, we learn that the Governor in Chief, who arrived in December, 1686, employed him "in the custody and remethodizing of the books, records, and papers for future use and delivering them over to Mr. Randolph," with "gracious promise of consideration for the same;" and we may also infer, from the same

* Colony Records, Lib. III. fol. 329. † Ibid. Lib. III. fol. 200.

† See an abstract thereof in Mass. Hist. Coll. V. 244–6. § See it, ibid. XXVII. 161–2.

‡ Hutchinson's History of Massachusetts, (Salem ed.,) i. 306–8.

document, that he was without the means of support, as he prays that he may receive "a satisfaction, not only for the two last years, wherein he hath actually served his Majesty, according to his former salary of sixty pounds per annum, but also some future yearly annuity or pension, out of his Majesty's Revenue here, for his sustenance." Whether his petition met with the desired reception, does not appear. He was not, as might have been supposed, reinstated in his former office upon the restoration of the old Charter Government, in April, 1689. His age probably precluded him from any active participation in the "glorious revolution," and Isaac Addington was appointed Secretary. In the year 1691 was published a little work entitled

"The Revolution in New-England Justified, and the People there Vindicated from the Aspersions cast upon them by Mr. John Palmer, in his Pretended Answer to the Declaration published by the Inhabitants of Boston, and the Country adjacent, on the Day when they secured their late Oppressors, who acted by an Illegal and Arbitrary Commission from the late King James," &c. &c.

This work is prefaced by an address of three pages "To the Reader," signed by "E. R." and S. S." I conjecture these initials to be those of Edward Rawson and Samuel Sewall, the former now in the 77th year of his age, respected for his gray hairs and past public services, the latter in the prime of life, and a member of the Board of Assistants.

Rawson's residence in Boston is said to have been on "Rawson's Lane," afterwards called Bromfield Street; and here we may presume he passed the last days of his life, meditating upon the wondrous change which had been wrought, the stirring events which had followed each other in rapid succession, since first he sought a home in the wilds of New England. And here, too, we may suppose he closed his eyes in peace, on the 27th of August, 1693, at the age of 78 years.

Secretary Rawson had by his wife Rachael twelve children, seven daughters and five sons. His eldest child, a daughter, was left in England, where she was born, and where she married an "opulent gentleman," whose name is, unfortunately, not known. His sons Edward, David, and John went to England, and there settled. Two of his daughters died young; the remaining four were married, in Boston, respectively, to William Aubray, Rev. Samuel Torrey, of Weymouth, Thomas Rumsey, and Thomas Broughton. His two sons, William and Grindal, settled in this country, and of them, as well as of some of the other members of the family, we shall speak in a future number.

Thus have we given a meagre sketch of the life of Edward Rawson. We expected to have been furnished with the materials for an extended Biographical Notice; but as our expectations were disappointed, we have been obliged to content ourselves with giving such particulars concerning him as could be gleaned from printed books, with the addition of the few passages which met our eye in an exceedingly brief and hasty glance at the Colony Records, which, alone, if subjected to a proper examination, would furnish abundant materials for a LIFE of the third Secretary of the Massachusetts Colony.

THE NEW ENGLAND PRIMER.

Yes, Readers, THE NEW ENGLAND PRIMER! Is there one of you to whom the name is not "familiar as a household word?" Can there a person be found who will not confess that that one short sentence awakens, as it were by magic, an interminable train of recollections, of commingled joy and sorrow—that it carries him back to the days of his childhood, and places before him the little square volume, with its dingy besplintered leaves and rude pictures, which was, at once, the source of childish amusement and anguish? Who does not remember the tedious moments, perhaps hours, during which he or she was doomed to con the Assembly's "Shorter Catechism," and the little comfort derived, while suffering chastisement for the non-performance of the task, from the example of Job, and the wonder caused by the patient fortitude of the persecuted patriarch, who, though he

"——feels the Rod,—
Yet blesses GOD."

Finally, whose brain has not been effectually confused by copious and involuntary draughts of John Cotton's "Spiritual Milk for Babes;" and when reminded, in a moment of despondency, that his

"——Book and Heart
Must *never* part,"

who has not felt the full force of the line,

"Our days begin with trouble here?"

But if the name of THE NEW ENGLAND PRIMER awakens some recollections of a sombre hue, there is also a bright side to the picture. With what pride did the child, after having mastered the Alphabet, both "Great Letters" and small, become deeply versed in the mysteries of "Vowels," "Consonants," "Double Letters," "Italick Letters," and "Italick Double Letters," and toiled through the columns of "Easy Syllables," proceed, by degrees, from "Saint" to "Babel," from "Jacob" to "Damnify," "Barbarous" and "beggarly" "drowsiness;" then, by the stages of "glorious" "gratitude," to "Happiness;" and so, "Benefited" by past experience, and becoming conscious of his "Ability" and "capacity" to grapple with those hitherto "formidably" "everlasting" difficulties, attain "glorifying" "beatitude," leave behind him "Abominable" "fermentation" and "beneficial" "admiration," with a "Benediction," and at last find himself, as he supposed, on the very topmost round of "The Ladder to Learning," upon terms of the most perfect "Familiarity" with "Edification" and "Gratification," having passed "Beneficially" through "Humiliation" and "Mortification," to final "Purification." Having learned "Who was the first man" and "Who was the first woman," "Who was the first Murderer" and "Who was the first Martyr," the child is rewarded for his diligence by the privilege of poring over the pictured couplets, from the mysterious and (to a child) inexplicable declaration that

"In ADAM'S Fall
We sinned all,"

to the end of the alphabet, where he exultingly reads how

"ZACCHEUS he
Did climb the Tree
Our Lord to see."

Or perhaps he turns from the mournful "Conclusion" of the "Dialogue between Christ, Youth, and the Devil," to the thrilling account of "Mr. John Rogers, the first Martyr in Queen Mary's reign," and while the eye is dimmed with tears at the portraiture of his horrid death, wearies himself in an ineffectual attempt to count the heads of the "nine small children and one at the breast."

Truly, never was a book published, with the exception of the Scriptures, whose influence has been so extended and enduring as that of THE NEW ENGLAND PRIMER; and although we are not prepared to say that, as a manual for the young, it is wholly unexceptionable, still it will readily be confessed, we think, by all, that it is infinitely preferable to nine tenths of those productions of later days, which have, in a measure, superseded it. Its aphorisms and "Choice Sentences" convey, in a few words, the sublimest lessons of Christian morality, and the very brevity of its instructions impresses them so deeply upon the mind of the child, that it is impossible ever to forget them. The hymns and prayers contained in this unpretending little volume are, many of them, unrivalled for simplicity and beauty of expression; and when associated with the earliest recollections of a mother's love, can never be effaced from the memory. There they are, those holy recollections, graven upon the heart's innermost surface, and there they remain, fresh as ever, buried, it may be, under the mass of selfish and worldly cares and troubles which every year, as it passes, helps to heap up; but still they are there, ready to pour a flood of tenderness through the soul, at the calm hour of twilight, or when the world is hushed in slumber, or when soft music dissolves the whole being into tender melancholy. Then it is that the simple petition of childhood, first learned from the PRIMER, while standing by the side of a fond mother, whose voice, perhaps, has long been hushed in death, steals upon the memory, with a gentle and holy, yet irresistible, influence, subduing the coarser passions of our imperfect nature, and making us once more as little children. Then it is that the petition of the child becomes the prayer of the man, the supplication of infancy becomes identical with that of old age.

We have spoken of the widely extended influence of the Primer. Mighty indeed was that influence upon the people of New England. Its teachings gave the first bias to their dispositions; their characters were moulded in accordance with its precepts; their religious creed was drawn from its pages. Such being the case, this little book has a large claim upon the attention of the local historian; it is intimately connected with the growth of our peculiar institutions and prejudices; its history becomes, in fact, a part of the history of New England.

Singularly enough, after a few years' comparative neglect, the Primer has once again been put in requisition as a manual of religious instruction for the young. Various religious associations throughout the country have passed resolutions in favor of its circulation; over one hundred thousand copies of a modern edition of the work have been distributed by a single Society within the last ten years; and Societies have actually been formed for the purpose of introducing it into our Sabbath and Common Schools.

A portion of the reading community has recently been highly gratified with a series of articles in The Cambridge Chronicle, by "THE ANTIQUARY," upon the origin, history, and character of the New England Primer, as it existed in the days of our ancestors, with critical remarks upon the modern editions thereof. The writer of these articles is extensively known, as an enthusiastic and profoundly learned bibliographer; and he tells us that with a single exception — the Bible — there is no work whose origin and history he is more desirous of tracing, no work of which he possesses so many copies and such a variety of editions, as the Primer. "THE ANTIQUARY," with whom, as well as with his choice Library, it is our privilege to be somewhat acquainted, appeals to his brother Antiquaries throughout the country, for their assistance in completing his collection of the early editions of the Primer. The earliest edition in his possession bears date at "PROVIDENCE, Printed and sold by JOHN WATERMAN at the Paper-Mills, 1775." Cannot some of our readers draw forth from the dust and obscurity of their garrets an early edition of this curious little book, and forward it to the Editor or Publisher of the Register, for the inspection of "THE ANTIQUARY?"

REV. JOSEPH FARRAR.

IN our last number we solicited information respecting this truly eccentric son of Harvard, whose career is, as yet, involved in no inconsiderable mystery. We are certain that no apology will be required for the publication of the following letter from Rev. LEVI WASHBURN LEONARD, the esteemed pastor of the First Congregational Church and Society in Dublin, N. H., — so well known for his zealous efforts in the cause of education, — presenting as it does a succinct view of the genealogical connection between the two branches of the Farrar family from which descended, respectively, Rev. Joseph Farrar, of Dublin, N. H., and Rev. Stephen Farrar, of New Ipswich, N. H. These two clergymen have often been confounded with each other, though with what reason it is difficult to say. They were, as will be seen from the statement in Mr. Leonard's letter, first cousins, and the present town of Lincoln, Mass., was the native place of both. Rev. Stephen Farrar, (son of Dea. Samuel, and brother to the late distinguished Judge Farrar, of New Ipswich and Hollis, N. H.,) was born in that part of Concord which is now called Lincoln, Sept. 8, 1738, graduated at Harvard College in 1755, was ordained as the first minister of New Ipswich, N. H., Oct. 22, 1760, and died, after a long and eminently successful ministry, June 23, 1809. A sermon preached at his funeral, by Rev. S. Payson, D. D., of Rindge, from Acts VIII. 2, "*Devout men carried Stephen to his burial, and made great lamentation over him,*" contains a well-merited tribute to his memory. "The capacities with which the God of nature had endowed him," says the reverend author of the discourse, "were of such a kind as eminently qualified him for usefulness in that work to which he was devoted. He had a good heart — he loved his Master — he loved his work. He had, indeed, his trials and his enemies, but they seemed to promote his sanctification.*

To return to Mr. Leonard's letter, which is as follows:

Dublin, N. H., March 23d, 1849.

C. J. F. BINNEY, ESQ.

Dear Sir, — Your letter of March 3d has been received. You inquire respecting the Rev. Mr. Farrar of New Ipswich, whether he was the same person as the Rev. J. Farrar of Dublin. He was *not* the same person.

* See N. H. Hist. Coll. I. 151, V. 165, 166–7; New Hampshire Repository, I. 182, 197–8; Shattuck's Concord, p. 314.

It is commonly said that the Rev. Mr. Farrar of Dublin, and the Rev. Mr. Farrar of New Ipswich, were cousins, the native place of both being Lincoln, Mass. The Christian name of the minister of New Ipswich was Stephen. The following genealogy of the Farrar family will show that these two clergymen *were* cousins.

(1) I. Jacob Farrar, Lancaster, killed by the Indians Aug. 22, 1675. His son

(2) II. 1—1.—Jacob had by Hannah his wife the following children:
2—1.—Jacob, b. March 29, 1669.
3—2.—George, b. Aug. 16, 1670.
4—3.—Joseph, b. Aug. 16, 1672.
5—4.—John, b.

(3) III. George, [3—2.] m. Sept. 7, 1692, Mary How, of Concord, and had sons:
6—1.—Joseph, b.
7—2.—Daniel, b.
8—3.—George, b. Feb. 16, 1705.
9—4.—Samuel, b. Sept. 28, 1708.

(4) IV. George, [8—3.] had nine children, of whom were
10—1.—Rev. George Farrar, b. Nov. 23, 1730, graduated at Harvard College in 1751.
11—2.—Rev. Joseph Farrar, b. Jan.* 30, 1744, graduated at Harvard College in 1767. This was the minister of Dublin, N H., settled 1772.

(5) IV. Samuel, [9—4.] m. Lydia Barrett, of Concord, and had seven children, of whom were
12—1.—Samuel.
13—2.—Rev. Stephen Farrar, graduated at Harvard College in 1755; (New Ipswich.)
14—3.—Hon. Timothy Farrar, graduated at Harvard College in 1767; Judge; died at Hollis, N. H., in 1848, aged 101 years.

Judge Timothy Farrar had a son Timothy, who, I believe, now resides in Boston, and may know more about his father's cousin and class-mate than any one else. I find no person in Dublin who has any recollection of Rev. Joseph Farrar's enlisting in the army, nor of residing anywhere after leaving Dublin, except in Dummerston.

It has been proposed to collect materials for a history of Dublin, and to have a celebration on the hundredth anniversary of the settlement of the town. The hundredth year will not be till 1850 or 1852, it is not determined which. We should be glad to be informed more particularly respecting Rev. Mr. Farrar, the first minister. When did he settle in Dummerston? In what year dismissed? Was he settled anywhere else? When and where did he die? Whom did he marry? In what year was he married? How many children had he? How many are now living? Any other circumstances in his history that might be deemed of any moment, we should be glad to be informed of.

Most of the first settlers of Dublin came from Sherburne, Mass., and Rev. Abner Morse is collecting materials for their genealogy, which I suppose will be published during the current year. Yours respectfully,

LEVI W. LEONARD.

* The College Records, as well as Shattuck's Concord, say *June* 30, and this we suspect to be the true date.

Thanks to the exertions of Mr. Binney, the following items of information have been obtained from the Revolutionary Rolls in the State House at Concord, N. H.

On the pay-roll of Capt. Daniel Wilkens's Company, in Col. Bedel's Regiment, mustered and paid by John Bellows, Esq., under date of 1776, JOSEPH FARRAR receives £5, 2, 6. Each private in this company was to receive one month's wages; bounty, 40s; blanket money, 15s; and 1 penny per mile.

The name of JOSEPH FARRAR appears as Sergeant to Capt. Simeon Martin's Company, in a Regiment raised by New Hampshire for the Continental service in Rhode Island, in 1778, and commanded by Stephen Peabody, Lieutenant-Colonel, which was discharged at Rhode Island, Dec. 30, 1778. and allowed one day's pay for every twenty miles' travel homeward. JOSEPH FARRAR enlisted June 10, 1778, and was discharged Sept. 16, 1778, having served three months and seven days, and receiving for said service the sum of £6.*

It will be seen, by reference to our article in the April number of the Register, p. 186, that, so far as *dates* are concerned, the JOSEPH FARRAR mentioned above may very well have been the REV. JOSEPH FARRAR whose course we are endeavoring to trace; inasmuch as the latter was dismissed from his pastoral office in Dublin, June 7, 1776, and is not again heard of until his ordination at Dummerston, Aug. 24, 1779; during which interval, if at all, he must have served in the Continental army.

SKETCHES OF THE EARLY HISTORY OF THE TOWN OF MIDDLEBOROUGH, IN THE COUNTY OF PLYMOUTH.†

THIS Town, the *Namasket* of the Indians, is, probably, of greater extent of territory than any other in the State of Massachusetts, being fifteen miles in length, and averaging about nine in breadth.‡ It is situated fifteen miles from Plymouth, twenty from New-Bedford, eleven from Taunton, and thirty-four from Boston; § and is remarkable for its large and fine ponds, which bear the names of Assowamsett, Long Pond, Quitticus, Quiticasset, Pocksha, and Pockanina. Of these the first two are the largest. Indeed, the first, Assowamsett, Assawamsett, Assawampsitt, or Sowampset, as it is variously spelt, is said to be "the largest collection of water in Massachusetts," its length from North to South being "about six miles, its breadth in some places nearly four miles; but the width is very variant. At one place, called Long Point, in the summer, the width is not more than three rods." ‖ These ponds furnish large quantities of fish.¶

The outlet of these ponds is the Namasket River, which furnishes an extensive water-power, and, with its tributary streams, "waters the Town very advantageously."

For the space of a hundred years Bog-iron-ore was extensively used in this town and the vicinity, until about the year 1747, when it was discov-

* For this last paragraph see Concord (N. H.) Rolls, Book 3, Letter N., p. 2.

† For several of the particulars contained in the following "Sketches" we are indebted to ZECHARIAH EDDY, Esq., of Middleboro', a Corresponding Member of the N. E. Hist. Gen. Society.

‡ Barber's Historical Collections of Massachusetts, (8vo. Worcester, 1844,) p. 513.

§ Ibid. ‖ Mass. Hist. Coll. III. 2, XX. 35. ¶ Ibid.

ered that " there was iron-mine in the bottom of our great pond at Assowamset; and after some years it became the main ore that was used in the Town, both at furnaces and forges, and much of it has been carried into the neighboring places for the same purpose. Men go out with boats, and make use of instruments much like those with which oysters are taken, to get up the ore from the bottom of the pond." *

This Town, although it has several pretty villages, is, by no means, densely populated. In a "numeration of the people," taken, " by authority," in the summer of 1776, there were "four thousand four hundred and seventy-nine souls" in Middleborough; and by an account taken the winter following, it appears that there were then but one thousand and sixty-six males, of sixteen years and upwards, in the Town, of whom five were Indians, and eight negroes. In the year 1791 there were but "four thousand five hundred and twenty-six souls" enumerated, shewing an increase of only *forty-seven* for fifteen years.† As the town has been uniformly healthy,‡ the cause of this apparently small increase in population must be sought in the emigration of the inhabitants; a large part of the Towns of New Salem and Shutesbury, in the County of Franklin, and of Woodstock, in the State of Vermont, having been settled by people from this place.§ The whole population, at the present time, does not much exceed five thousand.

Agriculture was formerly the principal occupation of the inhabitants, the soil being favorable to the growth of corn, rye, and grass. The Town also enjoyed, " in the days of Auld Lang Syne," a great reputation for its Cider, which is said to have been " ever unrivalled" both in quality and abundance.‖ There are now in the place a number of Cotton mills and manufactories of shovels, nails, straw bonnets, &c. &c.¶

* Mass. Hist. Coll. III. 2, 175, XX. 35. † Ibid. III., 152.

‡ Witness the following table of mortality for " the First Precinct."

Year.	Over 90.	Between 70 and 90.	Between 50 and 70.	Between 20 and 50.	Under 20.	Total.	Year.	Over 90.	Between 70 and 90.	Between 50 and 70.	Between 20 and 50.	Under 20.	Total.
1779	1	3	3	3	4	14	1795	1	8	3	1	7	20
1780		1	4	3	5	13	1796		5	2	5	10	22
1781	1	5	9	3	9	27	1797		3	1	3	9	16
1782	1	6	4	1	19	31	1798	1	2	4	3	6	16
1783		4	4	2	6	16	1799	2	2	3	4	4	15
1784	1	5	3		19	28	1800		5	6	12	8	31
1785	1	6	6	6	10	29	1801	3	3	5	4	4	19
1786		5	3	4	10	22	1802	1	5	2	3	8	19
1787		7	3	2	11	23	1803	1	6	4	4	16	31
1788	1	3	6	3	9	22	1804	1	3		1	7	12
1789	1	3	6	5	10	25	1805		5	7	2	6	20
1790	1	4	1	5	11	22	1806		6	3	14	6	29
1791		7	1	4	11	23	1807						22a
1792	2	1	3	4	9	19	1808		12	7	4	8	31
1793	1	5		2	7	15	1809		6	7	4	12	29
1794	2	7	3	4	1	17	1810						20b

— *Mass. Hist. Coll.* VIII. 79, IX. 235, X. 188, XII. 261-2.

(a) 5 upward of 80,
2 between 70 and 80,
5 between 60 and 70,
4 between 40 and 60,
2 between 20 and 40,
4 under 20.

(b) 2 between 80 and 90,
3 between 70 and 80,
3 between 60 and 70,
1 between 40 and 60,
5 between 20 and 40,
6 under 20.

§ Barber, p. 264; Mass. Hist. Coll. III. 152. ‖ Mass. Hist. Coll. XVII. 116.

¶ Barber, p. 514.

It has been already mentioned that this Town is the *Namasket* of the Indians. The spot became known to the Europeans at an early period. In the Spring of 1619 that "understanding and industrious Gentleman," Captain Thomas Dermer, was despatched from Plymouth, by Sir Ferdinando Gorges, in behalf of the Council of New-England, in a ship of two hundred tons, to carry on the fishing-business in connection with Captain Edward Rocroft, who had sailed for New-England in the spring of the preceding year, 1618. Dermer was accompanied by *Tisquantum*, or *Squanto*, one of the Natives which had been seized and carried to England by the notorious Hunt. Arriving at Monhegan, Dermer learns from some mutineers, who had been left behind, that Rocroft had sailed for Virginia, and thereupon determines to await his return. On the 26th of May, taking Tisquantum with him, he embarked in an open pinnace, of five tons, to make a voyage of discovery along the New England coast, "searching every harbor, and compassing every cape-land." He found many "ancient plantations," which had been visited by the plague, some of them "utterly void" of inhabitants. "When I arrived," says he, in his letter of Dec. 27th, 1619, to Purchas, "at my Savage's native country,* finding all dead, I travelled alongst a day's journey to *a place called Nummastaquyt*, where, finding inhabitants, I despatched a messenger a day's journey further West, to Pocanokit, which bordereth on the sea; whence came to see me two Kings, attended with a guard of 50 armed men, who being well satisfied with that my Savage and I discoursed unto them, being desirous of novelty, gave me content in whatsoever I demanded. Here I redeemed a Frenchman, and afterwards another at Masstachusit, who three years since escaped shipwreck at the North-East of Cape Cod." From a subsequent letter of Dermer, it appears that the Indians would have killed him when he was at "*Namassaket*" had not Squanto "entreated hard" for him. Returning from this expedition to Monhegan, Dermer was apprised, by a ship from Virginia, of Captain Rocroft's death; whereupon, having despatched his ship to England with a valuable cargo, he leaves Squanto at Sawahquatook, † and then sails in his pinnace, with five or six men, and the two Frenchmen whom he had liberated from captivity, for Virginia, where he arrived on the 7th of September.‡

In the Summer of 1621 "it seemed good" to the little band of Pilgrims, which had recently sought a home on "the stern and rock-bound coast" of New England, "to send some amongst them to Massasoyt, the greatest commander amongst the Savages" in their neighborhood; "partly to know where to find them, if occasion served, as also to see their strength, discover the country, prevent abuses in their disorderly coming unto us, make satisfaction for some conceived injuries to be done on our parts, and to continue the league of peace and friendship between them and us. For these and the like ends it pleased the Governor § to make choice of Steven

* Patuxet, now Plymouth.—*See Bradford's and Winslow's Journal, in Young's Chronicles of the Pilgrims, pp.* 190–1.

† "Probably Satucket, now Brewster," says Judge Davis, in his edition of Morton's Memorial, p. 60, note. "Sawahquatooke, now Saco," says Dr. Young. "Sawaquatock, Sagadahock," says the Index to the Second Series of the Massachusetts Historical Collections.

‡ The authorities are, Smith's General History of Virginia, New England, &c., (fol. Lond. 1632,) p. 229; Mass. Hist. Coll. XIX. 7–10, XXVI. 62–3; Prince's New England Chronology, (8vo. Boston, 1826,) pp. 145–6, 151, 152, 153–4; Morton's New England's Memorial, (Davis's ed., 8vo. Boston, 1826,) pp. 55–60; Drake's Book of the Indians, (8vo. Boston, 1845,) Book II. pp. 20–1; Young's Chronicles of the Pilgrims, (8vo. Boston, 1844,) pp. 190–1, note.

§ William Bradford, who had been chosen Governor soon after the death of Carver, in the month of April preceding.—*Bradford, in Prince, p.* 190; *Davis's Morton, pp.* 68, 69.

Hopkins and Edward Winsloe to go unto him; and having a fit opportunity, by reason of a Savage called Tisquantum, that could speak English, coming unto us, with all expedition provided a horseman's coat of red cotton, and laced with a slight lace, for a present, that both they and their message might be the more acceptable amongst them." Furnished with appropriate presents and a message to the Indian King, the two messengers and their attendants, with Tisquantum, or Squanto, for a guide, set out "about nine o'clock in the morning" of July 3d, intending to rest that night "at *Namaschet*, a Town under Massasoyt," which they supposed to be at no great distance from Patuxet; but "we found it" says Winslow, in his narrative of the expedition, "to be some fifteen English miles. On the way we found some ten or twelve men, women, and children, which had pestered us till we were weary of them, and now returned with us to Namaschet. Thither we came about three o'clock, afternoon, the inhabitants entertaining us with joy, in the best manner they could, giving us a kind of bread called by them *maizium*, and the spawn of shads, which then they got in abundance, insomuch as they gave us spoons to eat them. With these they boiled musty acorns; but of the shads we eat heartily." *

"After this, Tisquantum told us," continues Winslow, "we should hardly in one day reach Packanokick, moving us to go some eight miles further, where we should find more store and better victuals than there. Being willing to hasten our journey we went, and came thither at sunsetting, where we found many of the *Namascheucks* (they so calling the men of *Namaschet*) fishing upon a wear † which they had made on a river which belonged to them, where they caught abundance of bass. These welcomed us also, gave us of their fish, and we them of our victuals, not doubting but we should have enough where'er we came. There we lodged, in the open fields, for houses they had none, though they spent the most of the Summer there. The head of this river is reported to be not far from the

* The food of the Indians "is generally boiled maize, or Indian corn, mixed with kidney-beans, or sometimes without. Also they frequently boil in this pottage fish and flesh of all sorts, either new taken or dried, as shads, eels, alewives, or a kind of herring, or any other sort of fish. But they dry, mostly, those sorts before-mentioned. These they cut in pieces, bones and all, and boil them in the aforesaid pottage. Also they boil in this furmenty all sorts of flesh they take in hunting, as venison, beaver, bears flesh, moose, otters, rackoons, or any kind that they take in hunting, cutting this flesh in small pieces, and boiling it as aforesaid. Also they mix with the said pottage several sorts of roots, as Jerusalem artichokes, and ground-nuts, and other roots, and pompions, and squashes, and also several sorts of nuts or masts, as oak-acorns, chestnuts, walnuts; these, husked and dried, and powdered, they thicken their pottage therewith. Also sometimes they beat their maize into meal, and sift it through a basket, made for that purpose. With this meal they make bread, baking it in the ashes, covering the dough with leaves. Sometimes they make of their meal a small sort of cakes, and boil them. They make also a certain sort of meal of parched maize; this meal they call *nokake*. It is so sweet, toothsome, and hearty, that an Indian will travel many days with no other food but this meal, which he eateth as he needs, aud after it drinketh water. And for this end, when they travel a journey, or go a hunting, they carry this *nokake*, in a basket or bag, for their use."—*Gookin's Historical Collections of the Indians in New England*, (*printed from the original MS.*) *in Mass. Hist. Coll.* I. 150–1.

"The Indians have an Art of drying their chesnuts, and so to preserve them in their barnes for a daintie all the yeare. Akornes, also, they drie, and, in case of want of Corne, by much boiling they make a good dish of them; yea, sometimes in plentie of Corne doe they eate thes Acornes for a novelty."—*Roger Williams's Key into the Language of America, in R. I. Hist. Coll.* I. 90.

† "At Titicut, on Taunton River, in the Northwest part of Middleborough, is a noted place, which was formerly called the Old Indian Wear. Though other wears have been erected on Taunton River, yet this is, probably, the place intended."—*Mass. Hist. Coll.* VIII, 233, *note*.

place of our abode. Upon it are and have been many towns, it being a good length. The ground is very good on both sides, it being for the most part cleared. Thousands of men have lived there, which died in a great plague not long since; and pity it was and is to see so many goodly fields, and so well seated, without men to dress and manure the same. Upon this river dwelleth Massasoyt. It cometh into the sea at the Narrohigganset Bay, where the Frenchmen so much use."

Returning on the 6th of July from their mission to Massasoit, Winslow says, "that night we reached to the wear where we lay before; but the Namascheucks were returned, so that we had no hope of any thing there. One of the Savages had shot a shad in the water, and a small squirrel, as big as a rat, called a *neuxis;* the one half of either he gave us, and after went to the wear to fish. From hence we wrote to Plymouth, and sent Tokamahamon before to Namasket, willing him from thence to send another, that he might meet us with food at Namasket."* On the 7th of July, "being wet and weary, we came to Namaschet. There we refreshed ourselves, giving gifts to all such as had showed us any kindness. Fain they would have had us to lodge there all night, and wondered we would set forth again in such weather. But, God be praised, we came safe home that night, though wet, weary, and surbated."†

About a month after this expedition, the inhabitants of New Plymouth were startled by the intelligence that their friend and ally, Massasoit, had been driven from his country by the Narragansetts,‡ and that a petty Sachem, named Corbitant, one of Massasoit's tributaries, who was known to be hostile to the English, was at Namasket, taking advantage of his Sovereign's absence to act the demagogue, denouncing the league which had been solemnly made with the infant Colony, and deriding the feebleness of the settlement, and making use of every means in his power to create a faction which should contribute to his own elevation, at the same time that it involved Massasoit and his new allies in destruction.

* The messengers were so unfortunate as to visit Massasoit at a time when his larder was exhausted. Not doubting, as Winslow tells us, that they should have enough where'er they came, they had not husbanded their own little stock of provisions, but had freely dispensed thereof to the Natives on the way. Arrived at their journey's end, on Wednesday, the 4th of July, faint and weary with travel, no one but — *a hungry man* — can form any conception of their dismay when they found that they had mistaken the capability of the mighty chieftain's stores, and must chew, for want of something better, the cud of sweet and bitter recollections. "Late it grew," thus pathetically does Winslow paint their situation, "late it grew, but victuals he offered none; for, indeed, he had not any, being he came so newly home. So we desired to go to rest. He laid us on the bed with himself and his wife, they at the one end and we at the other, it being only planks laid a foot from the ground, and a thin mat upon them. Two more of his chief men, for want of room pressed by and upon us; so that we were worse weary of our lodging than of our journey." The next day, Thursday, "about one o'clock, Massasoyt brought two fishes that he had shot; they were like bream, but three times so big, and better meat. These being boiled, there were at least *forty* looked for share in them; *the most eat of them. This meal only we had in two nights and a day;* and had not one of us bought a partridge, we had taken our journey fasting. Very importunate he was to have us stay with them longer. But we desired to keep the Sabbath at home; and much fearing that, if we should stay any longer, we should not be able to recover home for want of strength, on the Friday morning, before sunrising, we took our leave and departed, Massasoyt being both grieved and ashamed that he could no better entertain us, and retaining Tisquantum to send from place to place to procure truck for us, and appointing another, called Tokamahamon, in his place."—*See Bradford's and Winslow's "Relation or Journall of the beginning and proceedings of the English Plantation at Plimoth in New England."* (*sm. 4to. Lond.* 1622,) *pp.* 45–6.

† Ibid., pp. 40–8; also, Davis's Morton, pp. 69–70, and Prince, pp. 191–2.

‡ "Governor Bradford says nothing of this, nor of Masassoit's being either seized or invaded by the Narragansetts."—*Prince, p.* 193, *note.*

Upon the arrival of this news at New Plymouth, Hobbamock and Tisquantum, probably at the suggestion of the Colonists, went forth on an expedition, to see if they could learn aught concerning their King, who had thus been expelled from his dominions, and to watch the motions of Corbitant and his faction. Proceeding to Namasket, as privately as possible, they there thought to lodge in security for the night; but were discovered by Corbitant, who beset the house, in which they were, with his followers, and seized Tisquantum, threatening him and his companion with death, for their adherence to the English; and, holdiug his knife to Tisquantum's breast, seemed about to execute his threat; for he had been accustomed to say, that, "if *he* were dead, the English had lost their tongue." He next attempted to stab Hobbamock; but this savage, being a man of great strength, shakes himself free from the grasp of his antagonist, dashes through the guards which had been placed around the wigwam, and succeeds in effecting his escape. He immediately repairs to New Plymouth, where he communicates to Governor Bradford the particulars of his capture and escape, and his fears that their trusty interpreter, Tisquantum, has, by that time, fallen a victim to the hatred and fury of Corbitant.

Upon the receipt of this intelligence, the Governor summoned a council, to deliberate on what course it was best to pursue. It was determined to send a band of chosen men on the morrow, under the command of MILES STANDISH, to avenge the supposed death of Tisquantum, and to quell the insurrection which seemed upon the point of breaking out against their friend Massasoit.

On the 14th of August, Captain Standish, with ten or fourteen* men, well armed, sallied forth, under the guidance of Hobbamock, and took up their line of march for "the Kingdom of Namaschet." The day was rainy and their journey wearisome. Having proceeded to within three or four miles of the little town of Namaschet, they turned aside from their course and waited until night, in accordance with the orders which Standish had received, when they might hope to approach the town under cover of the darkness, without being discovered. A consultation being now held, Standish communicated his instructions to his followers, and assigned to each man his position and duty. He had been directed to surprise the enemy by night; if he should ascertain that Tisquantum had actually been killed, as was feared, then to cut off Corbitant's head, but on no account to hurt any except those who had been concerned in the murder of the Interpreter; and to retain Nepeof,† a Sachem who had joined Corbitant's faction, as a hostage, until news should be received from Massasoit. It having been resolved to make their contemplated attack at midnight, the party now resumed their march. But before they had gone far, it was discovered that the guide had lost his way. This was a sore discouragement to men already drenched with rain, and wearied by the weight of their arms. But the mistake was happily rectified by one of the company, who had visited Namaschet on a previous occasion, and they started anew. "Before we came to the town," says the writer of the narrative of this expedition, "we sat down and ate such as our knapsacks afforded. That being done, we threw them aside, and all such things as might hinder us, and so went on and beset the house,‡ according to our last resolution.

* Bradford and Winslow, in their Journal, say, "we set out *ten* men, armed." But Bradford says, "Captain Standish, with fourteen men, and Hobamak, set out."

† "This is the only time the name of this Chief occurs in the annals of the Colony." — *Young's Chronicles of the Pilgrims, p.* 220, *note.*

‡ The house in which Corbitant had lodged during his stay at Namasket.

Those that entered demanded if Coubatant * were not there; but fear had bereft the Savages of speech. We charged them not to stir; for if Coubatant were not there, we would not meddle with them. If he were, we came principally for him, to be avenged on him for the supposed death of Tisquantum, and other matters; but, howsoever, we would not at all hurt their women or children. Notwithstanding, some of them pressed out at a private door and escaped, but with some wounds. At length, perceiving our principal ends, they told us Coubatant was returned [home] with all his train, and that Tisquantum was yet living, and in the town; offering some tobacco, [and] other [provision,] such as they had to eat. In this hurly-burly we discharged two pieces at random, which much terrified all the inhabitants, except Tisquantum and Tokamahamon,† who, though they knew not our end in coming, yet assured them of our honesty, that we would not hurt them. Those boys that were in the house, seeing our care of women, often cried *Neen squaes!* that is to say, I am a woman; the women also hanging upon Hobbamock, calling him *Towam*, that is, friend. But, to be short, we kept them we had, and made them make a fire, that we might see to search the house. In the mean time Hobbamock gat on the top of the house, and called Tisquantum and Tokamahamon, which came unto us, accompanied with others, some armed, and others naked. Those that had bows and arrows we took them away, promising them again when it was day. The house we took, for our better safeguard, but released those we had taken, manifesting whom we came for, and wherefore."

"On the next morning," continues our narrative, "we marched into the midst of the town, and went to the house of Tisquantum to breakfast. Thither came all whose hearts were upright towards us; but all Coubatant's faction were fled away. There, in the midst of them, we manifested again our intendment, assuring them that, although Coubatant had now escaped us, yet there was no place should secure him and his from us, if he continued his threatening us, and provoking others against us, who had kindly entertained him, and never intended evil towards him till he now so justly deserved it. Moreover, if Massasoyt did not return in safety from Narrohigganset, or if hereafter he should make any insurrection against him, or offer violence to Tisquantum, Hobbamock, or any of Massasoyt's subjects, we would revenge it upon him, to the overthrow of him and his. As for those [who] were wounded, we were sorry for it, though themselves procured it in not staying in the house, at our command: yet, if they would return home with us, our Surgeon ‡ should heal them. At this offer, one man and a woman § that were wounded went home with us; Tisquantum and many other known friends accompanying us, and offering all help that might be, by carriage of anything we had, to ease us. So that, by God's

* "Governor Bradford plainly writes him Corbitant."—*Prince, p.* 194, *note.*

† He went to Corbitant immediately upon the receipt of the intelligence of that Sachem's machinations. He had been denounced by Corbitant for his adherence to the English; and why he should thus put himself in his power is a mystery.

‡ Mr. Samuel Fuller. He died in 1633, of an infectious fever which was prevalent in Plymouth, "after he had much helped others, and was a comfort to them. He was their surgeon and physician, and did much good in his place; being not only useful in his faculty, but otherwise, as he was a godly man, and served Christ in the office of a deacon in the Church for many years; and forward to do good in his place, and was much missed after God removed him out of this world."—*Davis's Morton, p.* 173.

§ Bradford, in his History, says that "*three* are sorely wounded in trying to break away" from Corbitant's house, when it was beset by the English. And in recording the safe return of Standish and his companions, he tells us that they "bring with them the *three* wounded Savages; whom," says he, "we cure and send home."

good providence, we safely returned home the morrow night after we set forth." *

Thus terminated the first warlike expedition of the Pilgrims in New England, the events of which have been narrated with the greater particularity, as possessing peculiar interest for the inhabitants of the ancient Namasket, which became, on this occasion, the scene of the second encounter between the Indians and the English within the limits of Plymouth Colony.

[To be continued.]

MEMOIR OF REV. BENJAMIN COLMAN, D.D.

[Continued from page 122.]

The tempest of opposition to the "New Church" had but lulled for a moment, to break out with renewed violence on the first favorable opportunity. Increase Mather, in his sermon on occasion of the Fast, had taken care to insert a qualification of his text, sufficiently ample to warrant any attack which he might subsequently feel inclined to direct against the "innovators." He and his son Cotton, "with many prayers and studies, and with humble resignation of" their "names unto the Lord," had prepared "a faithful antidote" for the Churches "against the infection of the example" which they feared "this company had given them," and had actually "put it into the press; but, when the first sheet was near composed at the press," had "stopped it, with a desire to make one attempt more for the bringing of this people to reason." That object having been attained, and a formal reconciliation effected, they, probably, considered it a pity to withhold from the world an "antidote," which had cost so "many prayers and studies," and whose effects could not but be so highly beneficial to the endangered churches. Accordingly, in the month of March, 1700, was opened the battery which was to annihilate, at once, the "apostates and backsliders," those "underminers of the Gospel," and the "wandering Levite," the "raw and unstudied youth, who had not feared to mock his fathers." This battery, although its aim was apparent to all, was masked under the semblance of a general treatise, bearing the title of "The Order of the Gospel Professed and Practised by the Churches of CHRIST in *New England* Justified," &c. &c., by Increase Mather. Prefixed to the work is an Epistle Dedicatory, wherein are stated the principles of the *Manifesto*, which are afterwards controverted in answers to seventeen questions.

Not long after the publication of this work, and in the same year, appeared "Gospel Order Revived, being an Answer to a Book lately set forth by the Rev. Mr. Increase Mather, President of Harvard College, &c., by sundry Ministers of the Gospel in New England"; being an able disquisition upon the questions proposed in the former work. *Gospel Order Revived* is distinguished for its calm and candid spirit, and for the enlarged views

* "After this," writes Governor Bradford, "we have many gratulations from divers Sachems, and much firmer peace. Yea, those of the Isle of Capawak [Martha's Vineyard] send to secure our friendship, and Corbitant himself uses the mediation of Masassoit to be reconciled." On the 13th of September, 1621, nine Sachems, of whom Corbitant was one, subscribed an instrument, by which they acknowledge themselves "to be the loyal subjects of King James," &c. &c.

The authorities are, Bradford and Winslow, pp. 51, 53–6; Davis's Morton, pp. 67, 71; Prince, pp. 193–5; Young, pp. 219–23.

which it displays of religious liberty. "'Tis possible," say the authors thereof, "that some good people may blame us for carrying on the contention, wherein, as one saith, though there be but little truth gained, yet a great deal of charity may be lost. We hope the best as to both these." "We must do justice, also, to those who have first openly asserted and practised those truths among us. They deserve well of the Churches of Christ; and though at present decried as apostates and backsliders, the generations to come will bless them."*

This work was printed at New York; and prefixed to it is the following advertisement.

"The Reader is desired to take Notice, that the Press in Boston is so much under the aw of the Reverend Author whom we answer, and his Friends, that we could not obtain of the Printer there to Print the following Sheets, which is the only true Reason why we have sent the Copy so far for its Impression, and where it is Printed with some Difficulty."

The Printer in Boston above referred to, was Bartholomew Green, a highly respected member of the Old South Church. There being no Newspaper printed in Boston at this time, Green published a vindication of himself in a handbill, dated Dec. 21, 1700, to which were appended some "Remarks," attributed to Cotton Mather, and "dated in Boston, December 24th, 1700." In these "Remarks" *Gospel Order Revived* is termed a "libellous pamphlet, which no man is as yet so hardy as to own himself to be the author of," replete with "profane scoffs and scurrilities, not only on particular persons, who never deserved such treatments, but also on the holy Churches of the Lord, and on the most sacred actions performed in them, which is the spirit of their whole pamphlet;" and the advertisement prefixed to the work is denounced as containing "impudent falsehoods."

This publication was answered by another, from the office of John Allen, containing two depositions, the first, by Thomas Brattle and Zechariah Tuthill, relating to an interview between them and Green, the printer, "on Saturday, the 13th of July last," "to treat with him about printing an Answer to old Mr. Mather's book, called *The Order of the Gospel;*" at which time, they say, "he made not any objection against printing said Answer, only said he could not go about it till he had printed off the Laws, which would not be till the Tuesday following." The second deposition, by John Mico and Zechariah Tuthill, gives an account of a conversation with Green "on or about the 16th of July," when they called at his printing-office "to see if he were ready to print the Answer to old Mr. Mather's *Gospel Order;* but he was then unwilling to print it, because, as he said, it would displease some of his friends, and, to the best of their remembrance, he mentioned particularly *the Mathers.* They told him it was strange he would print *any thing* for the said Mathers, and particularly the said *Gospel Order*, and nothing in answer to it or them; by which means the world might think those principles to be approved by all, which were abhorred by sundry worthy Ministers in the land; the unfairness of which practice they labored to convince him of. Yet he still declined to print it; but at length said, if they would admit the Lieutenant Governor to be askt, to give his Approbation to it, he would Print it; which they were unwilling to for this reason: Because they conceived it a new Method, not practised heretofore, and which the said *Green* would not have required of them now,

*From a passage in Josiah Cotton's Diary it appears that *Gospel Order Revived* was generally considered to be the joint work of the Rev. Messrs. Colman, Bradstreet, (of Charlestown,) and Woodbridge, (of West Springfield?)

but to put off the Printing of this Book which answered the *Mathers*, whom he seemed loth to displease," &c. &c. Following these depositions are some sufficiently caustic remarks, from the pen of Thomas Brattle, on the "Advertisement" of "Mr. Green the Printer," and "that *Libellous Scribble* at the *tail* of said *Green's* Advertisement, *to which the Reverend Author was not yet so Hardy as to set his Name;*" the whole bearing date Dec. 27, 1700.

In a paper dated January 10, 1700–1, Green replies to this last publication, reviews the whole controversy, and states that his reluctance to print "Gospel Order Revived" was caused by his recollection of the "great disturbance the MANIFESTO had made," which he had printed "very privately at Tuthill's desire," and which, says he, "made me the more thoughtful, lest this might give more offence;" adding, in an address "*To the Candid* READER," that "considering the Lieut. Governours Eminent Qualification to judge of Books, the station God has given him in the *New English* Church, and the good Offices he has done for Mr. *Benjamin Colman* and his Church in particular, Every one that is not a Stranger in *Boston* may wonder at it, that a Book Dedicated to the Churches of Christ in *N. England*, a motion to have it first view'd by his Honour, should be rejected with so much Disdain;" and "for my own part," continues Green, "The obstinate Refusal of so fair an Arbiter made me fear some foul Play: which is the principal Aw that I remember myself to have been under."

The indignation of the Mathers was excited beyond all bounds by "Gospel Order Revived," and early in the following year, 1701, they gave vent to their wrath in "A Collection of some of the many Offensive Matters contained in a Pamphlet entitled *The Order of the* GOSPEL *Revived*," which was graced with the motto "*Recitasse est Refutasse;* In English, To recite them is enough to Refute them." This publication, consisting of twenty-four 16mo. pages, is replete with the most virulent invective, with the most flagrant abuse, which ever disgraced the pages of theological controversy. It is divided into three parts, namely, an address "To the Reader," of three pages, dated "Boston, December 31, 1700," and signed by Increase Mather; a series of remarks "on some of the Scandalous violations of the Third, Fifth, and the Ninth Commandments," contained in "Gospel Order Revived," dated Jan. 6, 1700–1, to which is appended "A Short Scheme of the PLOT against the CHURCHES of *New England*, as 't is Confessed by some of the *Plotters*, in that which the Publisher pleases to call their *Great*, and *Noble*, and *Excellent* work, Entituled *Gospel Order Revived*," both attributed to Cotton Mather. President Mather, after a tirade against Gospel Order Revived, "of which some say, that if it had been called The Order of the Gospel *Reviled*, that had been a very true and proper *Title* for such a Discourse," gives utterance to a severe rebuke, evidently intended for Colman, whom he styles "a little thing," whose "impotent *Allatrations*" are beneath his notice, accusing him of "vilifying his Superiors, unto whom he ows a special Reverence," and asserting that "at *Mocking* he has outdone *Ishmael*: For *Ishmael* Mock'd his Brother only; but this *Youth* has not feared to Mock his *Fathers*." He then makes due mention of "One that is of the same Spirit with him, [Colman,] viz. *T. B.* [i. e. Thomas Brattle,] who "has ventured to own himself to be the Publisher of that which is an heap of Rude, Unmannerly, and unmanly Reflections: who likewise in Print Scornfully styles HIS President a *Reverend Scribler*, and complains of his *Cantings*, with other Scurrilous Expressions, which shew what Conscience he makes of the fifth Commandment —A *Moral Heathen* would not have done as he has done."

We gladly turn from this unhappy controversy to the consideration of more pleasing subjects. The Church, thus established in the very face of a most violent and unchristian opposition, increased rapidly in numbers and influence. The ordinance of the Lord's Supper was first administered on the 4th of February, 1699–1700, on which occasion fifteen persons * added themselves to the number of communicants. In Mr. Colman were combined all the qualifications of an attractive and profitable preacher. In the sacred desk his air is said to have been "composed and grave, his action just and delicate, and his voice, inimitably soft and tuneful, managed with the greatest propriety and exquisite sweetness of modulation. His diction was animated and lofty, but easy and plain, like his models, the inspired Classics; and the arrangement of his style and the turn of his periods exactly adapted to the elevations and cadences of his own musical pronunciation;" and his taste in composition was so far in advance of that of his contemporaries, that he has been considered as the introducer of a new style in the preaching of the Massachusetts clergy. With such gifts, when taken in connection with his liberal views, it is no wonder that Colman should render himself peculiarly acceptable in the pastoral office, or that, after the first storm of opposition had subsided, his Church should steadily progress in numbers and influence. Within two years after the settlement of their Pastor, the Society proposed to furnish him with permanent assistance in the ministry; and in the month of June, 1701, engaged the services of Mr. Eliphalet Adams, a graduate at Harvard College in the Class of 1694, who preached for them two years and a half, and then withdrew.† The eminent Dr. John Barnard, of Marblehead, is said to have been employed, for some time, as an assistant to Mr. Colman. In the year 1715 the Society determined to obtain permanent assistance for their Pastor, and on the 16th of August invited Mr. William Cooper to a settlement as colleague. The invitation was accepted by Mr. Cooper on the condition that he should be excused "from engaging presently in a constant course of preaching, it being a very early day with him." After preaching once a fortnight for nearly a year, he was finally ordained May 23, 1716.

From this time Benjamin Colman's life forms a chapter in the history of New England. His influence was felt in every quarter; his advice was sought upon all occasions; and to him did the heads of Church and State yield that deference which his eminent talents challenged at the hands of all men. In September, 1717, he was chosen Fellow of the Corporation of Harvard College, in place of Rev. Ebenezer Pemberton, who had died in the month of February preceding; and his election was approved and allowed by the Overseers on the 14th of November following. Upon the death of President Leverett, in 1724, and the refusal of Rev. Joseph Sewall to accept the vacant chair, Colman was chosen by the Corporation, on the 18th of November, to succeed his former Tutor and constant friend as head of the Institution whose interests it had been the study and delight of both to promote; a sufficient evidence, if we had no other, of the confidence reposed in his abilities by the friends of the College. His election was approved by the Overseers on the 24th of the same month, and a committee of that body was appointed to inform Mr. Colman of their approbation of his election, and

* Thomas Bannister and Elkanah Pembroke, of the "Undertakers," with Nathaniel Oliver, John George, William Paine, John Chip, John Kilby, sen., Mary Tuthill, Rebecca Taffin, Mary Mico, Mehitabell Cooper, Lydia George, Sarah Bannister, Jane Pembroke, and Elizabeth Royall.

† Mr. Adams was subsequently settled in the ministry at New London, Conn., where he died in 1753.

to desire his acceptance, and to apply to his Church for his discharge from the pastoral office; and also to "wait on the Honorable Gen[l] Court to inform them of the Choice that is made of a President and to move for a proper Salary for his Incouragement." But, unfortunately, Colman was peculiarly obnoxious to a majority of the House of Representatives, where sectarian prejudices and political animosities now raged hand in hand; and consequently, when the memorial of the committee of the Overseers was laid before them, praying that they would "appoint a larger salary than has been usually allowed, for the honorable maintenance of the President," it was voted that, "forasmuch as at present it is uncertain whether the Church, of which the Rev. Mr. Colman is Pastor, can be persuaded to part from him, or whether Mr. Colman is inclinable to leave his Church and undertake the office of President of Harvard College, and this being a matter of great weight and importance, especially to the establishment of the Churches in the Province, as well as to the said College, the further consideration of this memorial be therefore referred until the said Mr. Colman's mind, as well as [that] of the Church of which he is Pastor, be communicated to this Court, and made certain, whether he and they are willing he should accept of the choice and undertake the office of a President of Harvard College, to which he is chosen as aforesaid." This vote, although not concurred in by the Council, indicated with sufficient clearness the disposition of the popular branch of the General Court towards Mr. Colman, and convinced him that it was useless to expect from them a permanent provision for his support, should he accept the Presidency; and the melancholy experience of his predecessors in that office was a warning to him of what he himself might expect, should he trust his fortunes to the tender mercies of the Provincial Government. He was also well acquainted with the feelings of the General Court towards him, as is evident from a letter on this subject to White Kennett, Bishop of Peterborough, in which he says, "I am not well in the opinion of our House of Representatives of late years, on whom the President depends for his subsistence, and they could not have pinched me without the Chair's suffering with me, which I could by no means consent it should do for my sake." Determined, therefore, to bring the question of his support to a speedy decision, and having privately seen a copy of the vote passed on the 3d instant by the House of Representatives, and been informed of its nonconcurrence by the Council, Mr. Colman addressed a letter, on the 10th of December, to Hon. Samuel Sewall, chairman of the committee of the Overseers, in which, after stating that, although he had always served the College to the extent of his abilities, he not only had never sought the office of President, but had rather shunned it, and expressing his disinclination to leave his Church, he declares that, "as I wish the President in all times to come may especially give himself unto sacred studies and exercises, so I would humbly supplicate the General Court for any one who shall do so, to grant him a very sufficient and honorable support; but for the honorable Court to insist on their vote of knowing my mind, whether I am willing to accept of the choice, and to undertake the office of President, to which I am chosen, and also of knowing my Church's mind, whether they can part from me, before they will fix any salary for me in the said office, must determine me to give my answer in the negative to the Honorable and Reverend the Overseers of Harvard College, which in that case I now do." This letter being read at a meeting of the Overseers, on the 17th of December, the committee was directed to "wait again on the honorable General Court, with Mr. Colman's answer and with this vote, praying that the matter of a salary may be considered by them, and so acted upon as may be most for the speedy settlement of a President in the said College, and therein for the good of the whole Province." The proceedings of the Representatives, upon the reception of this application, were as follows, as stated in the Records of the Overseers.*

"The Overseers met according to adjournment aforesaid Dec. 18, 1724, In the Council-Chamber in Boston.

The aforesaid Committee of the Overseers made report that they had waited on the General Court with Mr. Colman's answer and the Votes of the last meeting, which were read and debated in the House, the return thereto being as follows, viz.

In the House of Representatives Dec. 18, 1724.

The question was put,

Whether the Court would establish a salary or allowance for the President of Harvard College for the time being before the person chosen to that office had accepted the duty and trust thereof.

It passed in the NEGATIVE, *nemine contradicente.*

W^m. DUDLEY, Speaker.

Sent up for concurrence.

In Council, Dec. 18th, 1724.

Read and NONCONCURRED.

J. WILLARD, Secretary."

Notwithstanding the nonconcurrence of the Council, the symptoms of hostility were too strong to be mistaken, and Colman's independence of spirit would not allow him to be dependent for support upon the uncertain favors of party administration. Accordingly, upon the 26th of this month, in answer to another application from the Overseers, he transmitted his final answer to the committee of that board, in the negative, declaring that he "does not see his way clear to accept of the choice made of him to be the President of the College."

In December, 1728, Colman resigned his station as a Fellow of the Corporation, although earnestly requested by his colleagues to continue his connection with that board, as an active, faithful, and able member of which, for eleven years, he had rendered the most essential services to the College.

On the 1st of November, 1731, Mr. Colman received, through the hands of Governor Belcher, a Diploma of Doctor in Divinity from the University of Glasgow, an honor the more highly to be prized on account of its rarity in those days, when such degrees were but seldom conferred.

On the 12th of December, 1743, the faithful colleague and dear friend, who, for twenty-seven years, had shared his labors and contributed, in no small degree, to his comfort and happiness, was suddenly snatched from his side, by an attack of apoplexy, and Dr. Colman found himself once more the sole Pastor of his flock. Already sinking beneath the infirmities of three-score years and ten, his chief anxiety seems to have been lest his flock should be left without a shepherd, the great desire of his heart, to see his people united in the choice of another Pastor — "another Cooper, one like the deceased — not a novice, but one able and apt to teach, a man of understanding, prudence, and wisdom." His wish was gratified, in a year from this time, by the almost unanimous invitation of Mr. Samuel Cooper, a young man of the greatest promise, and a graduate at Harvard in 1743, to accept the office left vacant by the death of his father. The invitation being accepted, coupled, however, with a request similar to that of his father, on the like occasion, Mr. Cooper entered upon his duties, and was finally ordained as colleague Pastor, May 21, 1746.

* Book I. pp. 72–74.

His fondest hopes realized, in the acquisition of so worthy a successor to his late colleague, Dr. Colman was ready to say, with the Patriarch of old, "Now let thy servant depart in peace." Sensible, as it would seem, of approaching dissolution, he abated not his usual attention to his duties, and after receiving and entertaining his wife's children on the evening of the 28th of August, 1747, and telling them "That they were come to see him die," he expired, calmly and peacefully, about ten o'clock the next forenoon, in the 74th year of his age, and the 43th of his ministry, "in a good old age, full of days, riches, and honor," amid the lamentations of his people and of the Province.

It was the singular fortune of Dr. Colman to have been, at different periods, the youngest and the oldest minister in Boston. After the decease of Cotton Mather he stood at the head of the clergy of the Province, in respect of age, character, and influence. As the Pastor of an affectionate flock "he approved himself a wise, diligent, zealous, faithful, tender, and condescending minister of Jesus Christ, in studying, watching, visiting, counselling, earnest praying and preaching, exhorting, charging, and comforting them as a father his children. And this he did through a long and shining course." For the younger members of his flock his feelings seem to have been truly those of a parent; and his affectionate regard and anxious solicitude for their welfare and happiness ceased not with their childhood, but followed them in youth and middle age. Indeed, this parental concern for those who were just setting out on life's journey was not limited to his own immediate congregation, but extended to all who came within the circle of his acquaintance. The following letter, the original of which is in the possession of the writer, will testify to the warmth of feeling of which we have spoken.

Boston, Nov. 19, 1712.

DEAR MR. SEWAL.

Give me leave, now you are going off, to give you my best wishes and prayers, counsels and charges, in writing, as the best demonstration of that great love, respect, and friendship I profess to bear you. You are entring into a world, and going to a place, that is full of temptations and snares: be sensible of your danger, be jealous of yourself, be sober, and watch unto prayer. Watch both against a sensual spirit and a worldly one; let it be your chief care to preserve a religious one. Remember your education, your birth, your dedication to God, your nurture under the admonitions of God's Word, the prayers and charges of your pious parents, and all the awful convictions from the blessed Spirit of Grace, and all the pious resolutions you have had under the same. Remember awefully the vow and bond of your baptism, and the solemn recognition and renewal thereof which you have voluntarily made. Remember that you have solemnly given yourself up to God, to obey and serve him, and promised to make his Word the rule of your life. Therefore study the Holy Scriptures daily, pray in secret without ceasing, accustom yourself unto religious reflections and meditations, and ejaculatory prayer, frequently, on one occasion and on another; and do not fail of frequent serious self-examination in secret. Keep God's Sabbaths, and be retired thereon, and in particular preparations for it the evening before; frequent the Public Worship, and reverence God's Sanctuary, as you would preserve yourself from a profane spirit in all instances. Avoid evil company, and seek that which is good and virtuous; be cheerful with sobriety, and study to be obliging in your conversation; meek, humble, charitable, and devout. Guard against your passions, the irascible and concupiscible; keep the door of your mouth, and give not your heart to wine or women. My son, if sinners entice thee, consent thou not: Watch and pray that you enter not into temptation. Always preserve honorable and reverential thoughts of the Divine Providence; how great a thing it is to commend one's self to its favor and gracious care, especially in setting out in the world. You can't have too high thoughts of this, nor too great a solicitude about it. Let your Soul be your care, and familiarize the thoughts of death and eternity. Lay not up your treasure, set not your heart, seek not your portion, upon Earth. Live in the abiding sense of our common frailty and dying state, the vanity of this life, the necessity of an interest in Christ, and the salvation through him, with Eternal Glory.

Be just and upright in your dealings, be true and faithful to your employers: keep a good conscience, void of offence before God and toward man: prepare for crosses and losses: if the world be your idol these will be insupportable to you, and lead you into much sin.

Acknowledge God daily in praise and thanksgiving to Him, for all the mercies and favors of his Providence to you. Humble yourself before God under any remarkable frowns of it on your affairs and interests. If you should be sickly, or arrested by any distemper, let not your spirits sink, but encourage yourself in God; whose providence, power, and goodness is the same in every part of the earth. If your health grow and increase, (as I pray God it may, if He see it best for you) be not secure, and forgetful of sickness and death.

Beware of disposing yourself to love and marriage. Be sure that inclination, virtue, and wisdom do guide you, and not money. Have a care of an everlasting temptation, snare, and cross. A good portion of ingenuity, meekness, good temper, and grace is of more worth than all the millions of the Indies. Heaven guide you; seek its guidance.

I commend you to the grace and care of God: the prayers of many will follow you, and, I hope, prevail with God to bless you and prosper your way. And when you return the prayers of your friends, forget not to pray for *me* in particular, who am

my dear friend and brother,

Your affectionate and unworthy Minister,

B. Colman.

[Superscribed]
"For
Mr. Samuel Sewal,
Merchant
in Boston."

In high intellectual cultivation, Dr. Colman had but few equals. To nature as well as to art he was indebted for a most graceful and winning manner and pleasing address, which constituted one of his most distinguishing accomplishments. His colleague, in an unpublished funeral discourse, testifies "how perfectly he understood the decorum of the pulpit; and the gravity and sweetness at once expressed in his countenance, the music of his voice, the propriety of his accent, and the decency of his gesture, showed him one of the most graceful speakers of the age." Although he modestly pleads, when chosen President, his "long disuse of Academical studies and exercises," he was, in truth, a diligent student through life, and possessed a good library, for that day, a portion of which he bequeathed "for the use of the Pastors of the Church in Brattle Street, forever, to be kept in the Senior Pastor's study, on a separate shelf." * His Latin letters are highly ornate, and he read Horace not long before his death. He composed with great rapidity and elegance; and his preëminent talents in this respect were in constant requisition to draught letters and addresses from the Churches to the General Court, the King, and his Ministers, as also to distinguished personages, at home and abroad. His occasional discourses were frequently solicited for the press, and scarcely an individual of any merit or eminence departed life without receiving a tribute from his pen; and that, too, although the subjects of his praises had, in many instances, been among his most violent and acrimonious persecutors. One of the best discourses he ever published is said to have been that upon the death of Cotton Mather! This kindness of heart and exemplary charity caused his services to be much sought by Churches, as well as by individuals, in the character of a peacemaker; and the numerous letters and papers called forth by such occasions furnish a striking proof of the confidence which was reposed in his wisdom and moderation.

As would be expected from one of such world-embracing charity, Colman was deeply interested in the diffusion of Christianity among the remnants of the various Indian tribes which still lingered upon the outskirts of New England, and for the extension of the privileges of a Gospel ministry to

* See his Will, Suffolk Probate Records, Lib. 40, fol. 76.

places which had been destitute thereof, either from the poverty of the people, and their consequent inability to support a Pastor, or from other causes, as at Block Island, Nantucket, Providence, South Carolina, the Bermudas, Cape May, &c. &c. His time, talents, and influence, his pen and purse, were alike unhesitatingly and unsparingly devoted to the furtherance of this work; and in his younger days he not unfrequently went in person to preach among them. He rendered important services as a Commissioner, for many years, of the Society for the Propagation of the Gospel among the Indians in New England and the Parts Adjacent; and on the 14th of September, 1730, he was appointed a Commissioner and Corresponding Member of the Edinburgh Society for Propagating Christian Knowledge, an office which he sustained with his wonted ability until about the year 1740, when the increasing infirmities of years induced him to resign it. It was at the nomination and request of this latter Society, that the Degree of Doctor in Divinity was conferred upon him and the Rev. Joseph Sewall, Senior Pastor of the Old South Church, by the University of Glasgow. He rendered essential service to the Society for Propagating the Gospel in Foreign Parts, (an Episcopal Association,) by pointing out, from time to time, a proper field for its labors, and giving information of the false misrepresentations which had been made, in some instances, to its managers, by interested persons, in consequence whereof its funds had been shamefully misapplied. It was at Dr. Colman's suggestion that the Church of which he was Pastor, with others in the (then) town of Boston, agreed to make a contribution, twice in each year, to form an "Evangelical Treasury," the funds thereof to be appropriated to the extension of the knowledge and influence of religion. The "Proposal" for this contribution, "humbly offered to the consideration of the Ministers and Churches of Christ, through this and the neighboring Provinces," was found among his papers after his death, labelled *My own.*

Colman's official connection with Harvard College has already been incidentally noticed. As a member of the Board of Overseers for nearly half a century, and an active Fellow of the Corporation for the period of twelve years, the services rendered by him to his Alma Mater have never been equalled in extent and value by any one man before or since. To his influence the College is said to have been indebted, in a great measure, for the brilliant Presidency of Leverett. But for him the genial bounty of the Hollises and Holdens might never have gladdened New England's young University. He sacrificed his own popularity to defend the Institution against the storm of stubborn and unyielding fanaticism which threatened its existence, and withdrew not his hand until, with the coöperation and assistance of Leverett, Pemberton, Wadsworth, and the Brattles, he had placed the interests of the rising School of the Prophets upon a sure foundation. In his position as a member of the two Boards, he was continually called upon to exercise his peculiar talents, in draughting the various letters and addresses of these bodies; an office which seems to have been imposed upon him on every occasion; so that, during his life, scarcely a letter or address seems to have been put forth on any occasion, either by General Court, College, or Clergy, in Massachusetts, which was not drawn up, in part, at least, by his hand. But Colman's great and acknowledged services to the College have been set forth at large in the recent History of the University, by one of its Presidents, so that it does not become us, even were it necessary, to say more on the subject.

The liberal spirit of Dr. Colman, and his zeal in the cause of education, would not permit him to confine his good offices to the Institution at which he had received his education, and where, as he declares in a letter to the Bishop of Peterborough, he "had breathed in the catholic spirit" for which he was so remarkable. He exerted his great influence with success in the behalf of Yale College, at that time the only other Collegiate Institution in New England, and "greatly served" it, as we are informed, "by procuring for it many valuable books, whereby its Library has been enriched;" and his letters to its Rector and some of its Trustees, upon the receipt of Dean Berkley's Gift, sufficiently indicate his interest in its welfare and prosperity.

"In the estimate of impartial history," says a late writer, "Dr. Colman is entitled to the highest rank among his contemporaries for his philanthropic spirit and public services." His sphere of usefulness was not limited to the pulpit and the College, but embraced even the Council Chamber of the Province. He mingled without reserve in public affairs, and his opinions were always received with deference. His influence in the counsels of his country may in a great measure be attributed to his peculiar elegance and impressiveness of deportment; for he was, as his biographer informs us, "a good master of address, and carried all the politeness of a Court about him; and as he treated mankind of various degrees and ranks with a civility, courtesy, affability, complaisance, and candor scarce to be equalled, so all but the base and mean showed him a high degree of respect and reverence, love and affection; particularly men of figure and parts, of our own nation, and foreigners, whom he failed not to visit upon their coming among us, greatly valued and admired him." Colman did not escape censure "for intermeddling with civil and secular matters." But, as his biographer, reasonably enough, asks, "must a person who knows well the interest of his country, and is capable of serving it, and saving it too, when sinking, be silent only because he is a Minister? Is he nothing else? Is he not a subject of his Prince, and a member of the Commonwealth?" Colman thought so; and he was the very last person to allow his opinions to be influenced by carping busybodies; and we accordingly find that he was largely employed by the "Great and General Court" to prepare their addresses on occasions of importance, and also to preach before them at various times and seasons. He carried on, through life, a free correspondence with the Chief Magistrates of the Province, the leading members of the Council, and the Agents of the Colony in England, on public affairs; and as an instance of the freedom of intercourse between the heads of the Government and himself, it may be mentioned, that there is preserved, in the Library of the Massachusetts Historical Society, a letter from London, in which Governor Belcher informs him of the circumstances of his appointment to the Gubernatorial chair.

Beside his numerous letters on public affairs, Dr. Colman carried on a most extensive correspondence with eminent individuals at home and abroad. "He wrote many hundred epistles in a year, to all ranks of persons, on all occasions and businesses, and with greatest ease imaginable, to the vast pleasure and profit of his friends, the benefit of his country and the Churches in it, and the good of mankind." Among his correspondents may be mentioned the names of the Hollises and Samuel Holden, Drs. Hoadly, Watts, Calamy, Kennett, Harris, Avery, Burnet, and Wilson, Sir Richard Blackmore, Rev. Daniel Neal, the Historian of the Puritans, besides very many others, of the most distinguished civilians and divines in Great Britain, as well as most of the Governors and most eminent men in the different Colonies.

The town of Boston — the place of his nativity, for the interests of which he ever expressed the strongest regard — was indebted to the sagacious foresight and strong practical good sense of Dr. Colman for many improvements which he hazarded his popularity to effect. In 1719 he published an essay in favor of the establishment of a Market in Boston. He was very active in introducing the practice of Inoculation for the Small Pox, and published a pamphlet on the subject, in 1721, dedicated to President Leverett, which was reprinted in England, and received the warm commendation of the Secretary of the Royal Society. He also published a letter in vindication of his friend Dr. Boylston, who had been ably sustaind in his philanthropic efforts by himself and Cotton Mather, against the combined opposition of clergy and people. Among his beneficiary projects was that for the establishment of two "Charity Schools," the one for boys, the other for girls, to be located on Fort Hill. The scheme for their foundation and regulation is dated "Feb. 1713," and is said to be essentially the same with that of the present well known "Farm School." The schools in Boston were an especial object of his attention. He frequently visited them, "and encouraged the youth in piety and learning, both by word and writing," inciting them to diligence by "moving speeches," and "often giving them hymns of his own composing to translate into Latin." To the Prison and Alms House he was a frequent visiter, ministering both to the spiritual and pecuniary wants of their inmates. The poor ever found in him a wise counsellor, a faithful friend, and a liberal benefactor. His kindness of heart and exemplary charity for the opinions of others, without any attempt to conceal his own, made him, as we have before mentioned, emphatically the "peacemaker" of the Province. "He ever expressed" — such is the language of one whose privilege it was to stand in an intimate connection with him — "an utter dislike of that narrow spirit of bigotry, which he saw prevailing in too many of the greatest and best men of all sects and persuasions in past ages and the present; he was for extending his charity and holding communion with all that held the foundation. He loved and honored good men of every denomination, how much soever they differed from him in some peculiar sentiments, circumstantials, and modalities." He was wont to declare "that the Bible was his Platform," and he recognized no other.

To a large circle of relatives and friends Dr. Colman was endeared by his eminently social qualities. In him were combined the dutiful son, the tender and affectionate husband, the wise yet indulgent father, the kind, sincere, and useful friend. His extensive learning, brilliant conversation, willingness to communicate information, and his thoughtful consideration for the feelings and prejudices of those with whom he was brought in contact, contributed to render him the delight of all who were so fortunate as to enjoy his acquaintance. "His conversation was admirably polished and courtly, and all his behaviour was that of the most elegant gentleman and benevolent Christain." Such is the testimony of his contemporaries.

"If any should enquire" says his son-in-law, Turell, "concerning the person of Dr. Colman, in what kind of body this bright and holy soul was lodged, — his form was spare and slender, but of a stature tall and erect above the common height; his complexion fair and delicate; his aspect and mien benign and graceful; and his whole appearance amiable and venerable. There was a peculiar flame and dignity in his eye, which he could soften and manage with all the beauty and force of oratory, but still natural and without the least affectation. Wisdom and grace made his face to shine; and his neat and clean manner of dress, and genteel, complaisant behavior, politeness and elegance in conversation, set off his person to the best advantage."

Perhaps the best summary of Dr. Colman's character is to be found in Dr. Barnard's "Sketch of Eminent Ministers in New England," where he is described as "a most gentlemanly man, of polite aspect and conversation, very extensive erudition, great devotion of spirit and behavior, a charming and admired preacher, extensively serviceable to the College and country, whose works breathe his exalted, oratorical, devout, and benign spirit; an excellent man in spirit, in faith, in holiness, and charity."

It is certainly very surprising that the decease of such a man as Dr. Colman, who stood at the head of the clergy in respect of talents and influence, who went down to the grave while the brightness of his intellect was yet undimmed, ere a breath had sullied his fair fame, or the least shadow fallen upon his moral excellence, should have been suffered to pass almost unnoticed by his eminent brethren in the Ministry; not one of whom was found, to honor his memory in public, not one to pay a trifling tribute of respect to the exalted virtues of him whose pleasure it had always been to hold up for imitation the shining examples of departed worth! True it is that President Holyoke, in his Oration at the Commencement succeeding his death, eloquently commemorated his talents and learning, his public services and private virtues; but this was an official address, in the Latin language, and delivered upon an occasion which allowed of no extended eulogium or just delineation of character. An apology has been found for this, otherwise, unaccountable neglect, in the peculiar state of religious parties at the time, which rendered it difficult to speak of the professional career of one so liberal in his theological views as was Dr. Colman, without rekindling the then smouldering flames of sectarian controversy and religious excitement, which had but recently agitated the Province.

The neglect of others induced Dr. Colman's son-in-law, Rev. Ebenezer Turell, of Medford, to become the writer of his Life; and to this circumstance are we indebted for what has been pronounced "the best biography extant of any native of Massachusetts, written during its Provincial state, and a monument honorable to him who raised it, as well as to the individual to whose memory it was erected." Prefixed to this work is a Preface, signed by three clergymen, (Mather Byles, Ellis Gray, and Samuel Cooper,) commending the memoir to the attention of the public, and paying a just though brief tribute to the talents and virtues of Colman, the opening paragraph of which is as follows:—

"As the Rev. Dr. Colman stood among the first ornaments and benefactors to his country, it seems but a becoming gratitude to him, and honor to ourselves, to raise a monument to his memory. His polite and generous pen was always ready to do the same for others, and seized every opportunity to charm the living by the virtues and examples of the dead; though few characters and actions would bear to be transmitted down to posterity with equal advantage to his own."

Benjamin Colman was thrice married; first, by Rev. Increase Mather, to Jane, daughter of Thomas and Jane Clark, June 8, 1700. She was born in Boston, March 16, 1679–80. 2d., by Rev. William Cooper, to Mrs. Sarah Clark, May 6, 1731. This lady was the daughter of Richard and Sarah Crisp; was born in Boston, Sept. 15, 1672; and married, April 11, 1695, William Harris, Esq., a rich and influential merchant in Boston, and Treasurer of Brattle Street Church. He died Sept. 22, 1721, and his widow was married, April 5, 1722, to the Hon. and Rev. John Leverett, President of Harvard College, whose wife had died June 7, 1720. President Leverett dying suddenly, May 3, 1724, his (undoubtedly disconsolate) relict was united to her third husband, Hon. John Clark, Esq., by Rev. Mr Colman, July 15, 1725. He dying in 1728, she still possessed sufficient attractions, either of person or purse, to secure her fourth husband, in the person of Dr. Colman; but at length died, April 24, 1744, aged 71 years, 7 months, and 9 days. Dr. Colman was married, Aug. 12, 1745, by Rev. Joseph Sewall, D. D., to his third wife, Madam Mary Frost, of New Castle, N. H., widow of Hon. John Frost, and sister of Sir William Pepperell, who survived him.

Dr. Colman had issue by his first wife, only; viz Benjamin, born Sept. 1, and died Sept. 18, 1704; Jane, born Feb. 25, 1707–8; and Abigail, born Jan. 14, 1714–15. The eldest daughter, Jane, was married, by her father, to Rev. Ebenezer Turell, Aug. 11, 1726, and died March 26, 1735, leaving a son, Samuel, the only survivor of four children, who died Oct. 8, 1736.* The misconduct of his second daughter, Abigail, was the greatest affliction of the Doctor's life. He thus speaks of her: — "She gave herself to reading from her childhood, and soon to writing. She wanted not a taste for what was excellent in books, more especially of a poetical turn or relish, which soon appeared to be her favorite turn. This run her too soon and too far into the reading Novels, &c, for which God in his righteous Providence afterwards punished her, by suffering her to leave her father's house, to the grief of her friends and the surprise of the town." She was married (probably secretly, as no record thereof is to be found †) to Mr. Albert Dennie, a merchant in Boston, in September, 1737, and died May 17, 1745, leaving a son John, the only survivor of three children, whom Turell speaks of as "the only lamp the Doctor left burning in his house at his decease." In this child seem to have centered Colman's hopes and affections; he devoted himself to his instruction during his own life, and by his last will provided liberally for his education and support. But he died childless, and the Doctor's family became extinct. ‡

NEVER TOO LATE.

We hear from *Weymouth*, says the BOSTON EVENING POST for Monday, Dec. 24, 1753, that on Thursday last was married there, at the hour of 12, *Mr. Ephraim Thair* of *Braintree*, being 85 years old, to Mrs. *Mary Kingman* of that place, aged 78, it being about fifteen months since he buried his former wife (with whom he had lived 60 years in the married state) at which Time he was the Father, Grandfather, and Great-grandfather of 66 Male and 66 Female Children, since when there has been an increase of upwards of 20 more. After the ceremony was over, he returned with his wife to his House in *Braintree*, attended with a great Concourse of People, and 'tis judged, that from the Vigor and Activity which he then display'd, that were he to have married a young woman, he would have still been the Father of a numerous offspring.

* Turell's Life of Colman, p. 209, is the authority for the date of the death of Mrs. Turell, and the particulars respecting her family.

† We find neither the record of her birth or marriage, and are, therefore, indebted to Turell's Life, &c., for both, as well as for the particulars concerning her family.

‡ Circumstances have occurred, which have induced us to bring this article to a close in a much more summary manner than was anticipated when the first part of it was prepared. This will account for the apparent incompleteness of this latter portion, when compared with that in the preceding number.

THE PEASE FAMILY.

[By FREDERICK S. PEASE of Albany, N. Y., Member of the N. E. Hist. Geneal. Soc.]

[Continued from page 175.]

FIFTH GENERATION, CONTINUED.

107—6.—Charles, b. about 1764. At the age of thirteen he enlisted into the army as drummer. He m in Somers; died in 1839 Had one son Charles, who is m and is supposed to have children, and lives in Somers; also two daughters.

7.—Hannah, b. about 1751, d. 1768.

8.—Biah, b. about 1753, d. 1768.

9.—Sarah, b. about 1765, d. of small pox, 1778.

10.—Hannah, b. 1760, d. of cancer in the breast. She m. a Pelton.

11.—Mirriam, b. about 1772.

(27) V. EMERY, [33—3] was born 1727, resided in Somers, and died there in 1796. Had children:

108—1.—Emery (63)

2.—David; 3. Augustus; 4. Sylvanus; 5, Gaius; 6, Betsey; 7, Polly; 8, Matilda; 9, Peggy; 10, Independence.

(28) V. NOAH, [35—4.] was born in Somers, 1740, and died July 20, 1818. His first wife was Mary Ward, who was born 1738, and died Nov. 3, 1807. His second wife was Dorcas Arnold, widow of Samuel Arnold of Somers, and daughter of Deacon John Hubbard of Ellington, Ct., by whom he had no children. She died Nov. 1824. Children by his first wife:

111—1.—Giles, b. April 13, 1763, d. Sept. 26, 1823 — (64)

2.—Hannah, who m. Calvin Pitkin, and died many years before the death of her brother. She had several children

(29) V. EPHRAIM, [37—2] was born 1719, m. Tabitha Abbe, 1740, and d. 1801. At the commencement of his career he was a merchant, and subsequently a contractor during the French war. He acquired a large estate, and was one of the most wealthy of the colonists at the commencement of the Revolution Had children:

112—1.—Ephraim, who was a merchant, and died in his prime.

113—2.—Peter, died while a student at Yale College

114—3.—Obadiah, died soon after his graduation at Yale.

Sybil, m. Rev. Elam Potter, the third minister of Enfield She was the mother of Elam O Potter, Esq., who died in 1827.

Agnes, m. Rev. Nehemiah Prudden. She was the mother of Ephraim P. Prudden, who graduated at Yale in 1811, and died 1836.

Nancy, m. Augustus Diggins, and died young.

Tabitha, died young.

(30) V. AARON, [38—3] married Anna Geer, 1751, settled and died in Enfield. Had children:

115—1.—Aaron, (65)

116—2.—Stone, (66)

Ephraim, —— ——

Elam, —— ——

(31) V. NATHANIEL, [39—4] was born 1725, married Eunice Allen,

1754, died in Norfolk, Ct., March 28, 1818, aged 93. His wife died March 21, 1807. He was among the first settlers of the town. Had children:

117—1.—Phineas, b. in Enfield, Jan. 9, 1755. (67)
118—2.—Calvin, b. " Sept. 14, 1757. (68)
119—3.—Lovisa, b. " Dec. 1760, m. Giles Pettibone of Norfolk, d. 1835.
120—4.—Allen, b. in Enfield, Windsor, or Goshen, Ct., Oct. 12, 1762. (69)
121—5.—Nathaniel, b. in Goshen, Oct. 22, 1764. (70)
122—6.—Obadiah, b. " Nov. 21, 1766. (71)
123—7.—Dudley, b. in Norfolk, Feb. 1768, died in infancy.
124—8.—Eunice, b. June 29, 1770, m. Edmund Akin of Norfolk, d. Oct. 3, 1806.
125—9.—Electa, b. July 20, 1772, m. Abijah Pettibone of Simsbury, Ct., d. Aug. 30, 1843.
126—10.—Betsey, b July 21, 1774, m. Azias Pettibone of Granby, Ct., d. Feb., 1819.
127—11.—Flavius, b. Oct., 1776, d. young.
128—12.—Earl P., b. July 30, 1778. (72)
129—13.—Martha, b. May 5, 1781, d. March 5, 1784.

(32) V. Ebenezer, [44—1.] m. Mary Terry, 1739, died 1784. Had children:

130—1.—Ebenezer. (73)
131—2.—James. (74)
132—3.—Peter. (75)
4.—Azubah.
5.—Mary.

(33) V. James, [45—2.] was born 1724. Had five daughters:

Hannah, who m. Shubael Geer, had two sons and four daughters; Abigail, who m. George Pynchon of Springfield, Ms., had three sons and two daughters; Mindwell, who m. Amos Bull 1744, had five sons and four daughters; Catharine, who m. Benjamin Hall 1746, had three sons and five daughters; Martha, who m. Caleb Bush, had six sons and five daughters.

(34) V. Isaac, [50—1.] had a son:

133—1.—Rufus. (76)

(35) V. Abner, [51—2.] was twice married. His first wife was Elizabeth Farrington, by whom he had five sons and two daughters. His second wife was Lovicy Allen, by whom he had no children that lived.

He was a member of the religious society commonly called Shakers. He, with his second wife, Lovicy, united with that society in 1780, the first year of its opening in America. His family and others who had embraced the Shaker faith, remained at their usual places of residence until 1787, when they began to sell their possessions, and come together. He died at his residence in Stephentown, N. Y., in 1784, of small pox, aged 45, and his wife Lovicy died at the establishment in New Lebanon, N. Y., (near Stephentown,) in 1788, aged 37.

Abner came to his death by the following singular circumstance: One of his sons, who was living at home, was extremely opposed to the Shakers; so much so that he brought the small pox into the family, by which the whole family were taken ill, which resulted fatally in the death of the father.

Previously to his joining the Shakers, during the Revolutionary War, in 1777, he held the office of deputy sheriff in what was then the county of Albany. At that time, he, with two others, Sheldon and White, having been to Albany, were on their way home, and while stopping at a tavern kept by Nicholas Mickle, about four miles east of Albany, several tories came in and began to abuse them, making considerable disturbance. White, being a justice, ordered Pease to apprehend them. They surrendered, requesting that they might go up stairs after their knapsacks, and presently came down armed with muskets and cutlasses. They fired at them and wounded Pease in the thigh; at the same moment he received a horrible gash on his head from a cutlass, the scar of which he carried until his death. Unable to resist, the villains robbed them of their money and horses, and took them pinioned into the woods.

They had not gone far, when he became faint from loss of blood, and fell. They were on the point of killing him, when one of the gang, a young man named John Sloss, had compassion on him and tore a strip from his own shirt and bound up his head and left him senseless. He remained there several hours, until he was discovered by a Dutch farmer who was after his cows, who took him to his house and kept him until he was able to ride, and then lent him his horse to return to his home. These tories, with the exception of Sloss, who was liberated on condition of his becoming a witness against his comrades, were afterwards hung in Albany. One of them was named Robert Sloss. The judges before whom they were tried, were Richard Morris, Robert Yates, and John Sloss Hobart.

He was captain of a volunteer military company that was formed in the county at the time of the destruction of the tea in Boston harbor, under apprehensions that the affair would arouse the British to some severer measures.

The children by his first wife were:

134—1.—Abner. (77)
135—2.—James. (78)
136—3.—Daniel, who died in infancy.
137—4.—John. (79)
138—5.—Samuel. (80)
6.—Sally, m. Richard Hayes, and had two daughters.
7.—Sybil, who was three times married. 1st to Elisha Kibbe, in Somers. 2d to John Henry, of Norwich, N. Y. 3d to Joseph Powers, of Worcester, N. Y. She never had any children, and was living in Cooperstown, N. Y., in 1847, at the age of 80.

(36) V. Noadiah, [53—4.] was born in Enfield, Ct., about 1736; married for his first wife, Tirzah Smith of Glastenbury, Ct., about 1763, and settled in Enfield, where he lived till about 1782, when he removed to Sandisfield, Ms. He was a tanner and shoemaker. At Deerfield, Ms., he enlisted into the command under Gen. Putnam, called Putnam's rangers. He was in the expedition against Ticonderoga, under Gen. Abercrombie, in the French war in 1758. He was at Deerfield at the time the Indians were committing their depredations there. He died

March 26, 1822, aged 86. His first wife died in 1789. The children by her were:

139—1.—Roxanna, m. Ebenezer Ames of Brimfield, Mass., and died soon afterwards.

140—2.—Noadiah, m. the widow Abigail Breck of Northampton, and died there. He left two daughters: one m. Benj. Eastman, and removed to Philadelphia; the other died unmarried.

141—3.—Elihu, died young.

142—4.—Tabitha, died young.

143—5.—Philena, m. Obadiah Chapin of Enfield, and died soon afterwards.

144—6.—Tirzah, died young.

145—7.—Walter, m. Naomi Clark in Northampton, and died there.

146—8.—Asaph, resides in Winsted, Ct. (81)

147—9.—Achsah, Persis, and Erastus, all died young.

148—10.—Alvah. (82)

Noadiah married a second wife, by whom he had

Simeon, who m. Betsey Arnold of Canaan, Ct. They lived in Sandisfield until they had a numerous family. He now lives in Canandaigua, N. Y.

(37) V. Moses, [56—3.] settled and died in Enfield. His children were:

149—1.—Moses. (83)

150—2.—Lemuel. (84)

151—3.—Benjamin. (85)

(38) V. Samuel, [57—4.] who died in 1772. Had one son:

152—1.—Abiel. (86)

(39) V. Gideon, [60—7.] was born 1741, married Sybil Markham of Enfield, for his first wife, and removed to Munson, Ms. Had children:

153—1.—Gideon, who m. Hannah Rood.

154—2.—Dan. (87)

155—3.—Urbane, who m. Judith Piper, and removed to Michigan.

4.—Sybil, who m. Aaron Lamphear and removed to Ohio.

5.—Experience, m. Henry Gardner, and removed to Chatauque Co., N. Y.

6.—Jerusha, m. Ariel Lamphear, and lives in Munson, Ms.

Gideon's second wife was Deborah Meacham, by whom he had:

7.—Ira, who m. Sally Tupper.

8.—Abraham, who m. Mary Davis.

9.—Salmon, m. Roxa Howe.

10.—Samuel, m. Harriet Underwood.

11.—Deborah, m. Joseph Dwight.

12.—Achsah, m. Joshua Williams.

13.—Prudence, m. Gideon Bliss, and removed to Wisconsin.

14.—Eunice, m. Austin Bliss, and lives in Munson.

15.—Candice, m. Barney Stowell.

(40) V. Israel, [64—1.] who died in Middlefield, Ms. He had children:

156—1.—Simeon. (88)

157—2.—Israel. (89)

158—3.—Gad.

159—4.—Dan. (90)

(41) V. Ezekiel, [69—1.] was born Aug. 18, 1734, married Jemima Markham, who died Dec. 11, 1811, aged 76. He removed to

Weston, Windsor Co., Vermont, about 1770, died 1807, aged 73. Had a son:

160—1.—Ezekiel. (91)

(42) V. Henry Chandler, [70—2.] was born Feb. 11, 1738, married Ruth Chapin, about 1760, removed to Sandisfield, Ms., 1763, died there Sept. 1812. Had children:

161—1.—Oliver, b. 1777, m. in 1800, removed to Cambria, Niagara Co., N. Y., May, 1828, from there to Blissfield, Lenawee Co., Michigan, Sept. 1835. Has been twice married, had four sons and four daughters by his first wife, and one daughter by the second.

162—2.—Henry, b. 1772. (92)

3.—Ruth, m. Richard Adams; Abby;

4.—Abi, m. Mr. Atwater of Sandisfield.

5.—Eliza, m. Mr. Baker "

6—Tabitha, m. Mr. Dowd, had a family and removed to Sodus, N. Y., where she died.

7.—Mehitabel, m. and removed to Colebrook, Ct., and died there.

(43) V. Isaac, [71—3.] was born June 1, 1752, lived and died in Enfield. Had children:

163—1.—Oliver; 2, Isaac;

164—3.—Reuben, (93)

165—4.—Daniel; 5, Abel; 6, Calvin; 7, Isaac T.; 8, Theodore.

(44) V. Edward, [73—2] settled in Enfield. Had children:

1—Timothy; 2, Edward; 3, Heber.

(45) V. Cummings, [75—1.] left Enfield. Had a son:

1.—Wilder C.

(46) V. Asa, [77—3.] died in Enfield. Had a son:

1.—*Maj.* Elam.

Sixth Generation.

(47) VI. John, [78—1.] born 1753, married Charity Thompson, 1781, died 1843, æ. 90. He served in the Revolutionary War, and was a farmer. Had three sons and six daughters:

1.—John C., b. 1782, m. Naomi G. Niles of Windsor, Ct., sister of the Hon. John M. Niles, U. S. Senator. He was associated with Mr. Niles in the publication of a Gazetteer of Connecticut and Rhode Island.

This name, (Dr.) John C Pease, is entitled to the credit of having compiled the genealogy of the first settlers of Enfield, Ct, some years ago; to which the compiler of this genealogy is indebted for many of the facts which form the basis of the work. It is with pleasure that he tenders to him, on behalf of the family at large, his sincere acknowledgments.

2.—Walter, b. 1784.

4.—Lorrain T., b. April 17, 1788, m. Sarah Marshall of Windsor, 1809. Had children, Elisha M., b. 3 Jan., 1812, who removed to Texas in 1834, and is a practitioner of law at Brazoria. He was one of those who composed the first meeting which was called to consider the expediency of taking up arms against Mexico, and was for a short time engaged in active military service. Lorrain T., b. 11 Aug., 1815. He removed to Texas, and died there 31 Aug., 1836. He was in active service in the Texan war against Mexico, and one of the few who escaped the Fannin massacre. And five other children.

(48) VI. Richard, [84—1.] had children, 1, Richard; 2, Luke; 3, Walter; 4, Orrin; 5, Alpheus; 6, Austin; 7, Azariah.

(49) VI. Augustine, [85—1.] born May 18, 1757, married Mary Austin, dau. of Seth Austin, Oct., 1781. He died at Nashville, Ten., April, 1791. Had children, Mary, b. March 5, 1782; Nancy, b. March 1, 1784.

(50) VI. Zeno, [86—2.] born Feb. 2, 1759, married Hannah Leavitt, Dec. 13, 1781. He died of dropsy, at Suffield, Feb. 3, 1809. Children, 1, a son, b. March, 1782; 2, Charlotte, b. Jan. 25, 1784; 3, Hannah, b. April 9, 1785; 4, Henry, b. Jan. 14, 1787; 5, Lydia, b. June 23, 1789; 6, Cynthia, b. Nov. 28, 1790; 7, Chauncey, b. Feb. 1, 1793; 8, Adaline, b. Aug. 29, 1801.

(51) VI. (Dr.) Oliver, [87—3.] born July 27, 1760, married Cynthia Smith, dau. of Seth Smith, June 3, 1795, died in 1843. He was a highly respectable physician of Suffield for more than forty years; town clerk for twenty years or more; a justice of the peace; and for a long time judge of probate for the Suffield district. He had a daughter, Emily L., b. March 5, 1796, who m. a Mr. Clark.

(52) VI. Royal, [88—4.] born April 15, 1762, married Deborah Meacham, Dec. 10, 1798, died in Vermont, 1830. Children, 1, Delia, b. April 27, 1799; 2, Albert, b. Sept. 14, 1800.

(53) VI. Seth, [89—5.] born Jan. 9, 1764, married Bathsheba Kent, Dec. 21, 1785, died in Philadelphia, Sept. 1, 1819. His wife died June 14, 1818. Children, 1, Betsey, b. April 4, 1786; 2, James, b. April 10. 1788; 3, Gamaliel, b. June 26, 1790; 4, Alfred, b. May 28, 1793.

(54) VI. Joseph, [91—7.] born Sept. 11, 1766, married Elizabeth Pierce of Suffield, Aug. 18, 1790, died near Dayton, Ohio, in 1842. Children:

1.—Horace, b. Feb. 14, 1791, m. Ann Stilts, 1821, for his first wife, who died 1829; second wife, Sarah Bellville, in 1832. Residence, Dayton, Ohio.

2.—Edward, b. Nov. 3, 1792, m. Patsy Phifer, 1824, residence near Dayton, Ohio.

3.—Perry, b. Jan. 23, 1797, m. Catharine E. Smith, 1822, residence, Carrolton, Mont. Co., Ohio.

4.—George, b. Nov. 25, 1798, m. Ellen Wheatley, 1831, who died 1839. He m. Mary Ann Lamme, for his second wife, 1841.

(55) VI. William, [94—10.] born June 22, 1772, married Zilpah Spencer, Oct. 10, 1792, died at Suffield, 1846. Children, 1, Lucy, b. Feb. 10, 1793; 2, Don, b. May 11, 1797.

[To be continued.]

"Neither give heed to *endless genealogies*, which minister questions; but avoid foolish questions and genealogies, for they are unprofitable and vain." — *Ancient Chronicle.*

LIST OF FREEMEN.

[Communicated by Rev. Lucius R. Paige of Cambridge, Member of the N. E. Hist. Geneal. Society.]

[Continued from page 194.]

3 May 1665.

"The several persons underwrit returned by certificates from the several ministers and selectmen, were by public suffrage of both Magistrates and Deputies admitted to freedom, and took their oaths accordingly."

Capt. George Corwin	Sal.
John Endecott	"
Zerubbabl Endecott	"
Eliazer Hauthorne	"
John Corwin	"
Wm. Browne jr.	"
Jn°. Putman	"
Joseph Porter	"
Rich. Leech	"
Sam. Eburne sen.	"
Jn°. Rucke	"
James Browne	"
Phillip Cromwell	"
Rich. Hollingsworth	"
Edw. Humber	"
Joshua Rea	"
Xtopher Babridge	"
Georg May	Bo.
Joseph Belknap	"
Amos Richardson	"
Tho. Joy	"
Deane Winthrop	"
Nath. Reynolds	"
Benj. Thirston	"
John Toppan	"
ffrancis Bacon	"
Nath. Greene	"
Humphry Davy	"
James Alljn	"
Abijah Savage	"
Henry Taylor	"
Tho. Underwood	"
Wm. Hazzey	"
Benj. Muzzey	"
Tho. Hoole	"
Hen. Messenger	"
Jn°. Minot	Dor.
James Minot	"
Stephen Minot	"
Dani. Preston	"
David Jones	"
Wm. Weekes	"
Edw. Blake	"
Jn°. Blackman	Dor.
Jn°. Lewis	Lanc.
Georg Colton	Spr.
Edm°. Quinsey	Br.
Isak Sternes	Wat.
Jn°. Stone	"
Steven Willoues	Camb.
Jn°. Marret	"
Georg Cooke	"
James Trowbridge	"
Jn°. Grout	"
Joseph Esterbrooke	"
Nath. Saltonstal	Hav.
Edmo. Chamberlaine	Chelm.
Jn°. Wright	"
Jn°. Stevens	"
Jno Martin (463)	"
James Heildrick	"
Herlakenden Symons	Gloc.
Sam. Ward	Marbh.
Stephen Pajne	Mald.
Peter Tuffs	"
Rich. Cutts	Port.
Jn°. Gold	"
Tho. Baker	"
Shubal Dumer	Newb.
Tho. Steevens	Sudb.
Ri. Meade	Rox.
Edm°. Eddenden	"
Tho. Eames (464)	"

C. R., Vol. IV. pp. 463, 464.

3 May, 1665.

Mr. Phillip Nelson	Rowley
Tho. Nelson	"
Jn°. Trumble	"
Benjª. Scott	"

C. R., IV. p. 465.

11 Oct. 1665.

Thomas Merrick	Springfd.

C. R., IV. p. 557.

23 May 1666.

Mr. Joseph Cooke	Camb.
Daniel Wellow	"
Jn°. Swayne	"
Jn°. Addams	"
Tho. Browne	"
Tho. Phelabrowne	"
Tho. Cheney	"
James Hubbard	"
Rob't Ayer	Haver.
Tho. Ayer	"
Peter Ayer	Haver.
Tho. Whittier	"
James Davis	"
Jn°. Dow	"
Tho. Lillford	"
Sam. Converse	Wob.
Jn°. Benjamin	Watr.
Edw. Allen	Bost.
Jno. Bracket	"
Joseph Davis	"
Seth Perry	"
Tho. ffitch	"
Sam. Norden	"
Georg Mang	"
Edm°. Eddington	"
Tho. Matson jun.	"
Jn°. Batchelor	Red.
Edw. Burns	Hng.
Ben. Bosworth	"
Jn°. Cole senr.	Had.
Joseph Balduin	"
franc. Bernard	"
Phillip Russell	"
James Bapson	Glo.
Wm. Kerly	Marl.
Edm°. Gate	Sal.
Sam. Moody	Newb.
Caleb Moody	"
Isack Butter	Med.
Nicho. Rocket	"
Benja. Gibbs	Bost.
Abr. Willjams	Marlb.
Nath. Weare	Hampt.
Hen. Page	"
Rob'rt Vose	Milt.
Antho. Gullifer	"
Nicho. George senr.	Dorch.
Obadiah Hawes	"
Jn°. Capen jun.	"
Tho. Peirse	"
Rob'rt Spurr	"
Timo. Tileston	"
Jn°. Gill	"
Tho. Smist jun.	"
Ezra Clap	"
Wm Cheny	Rox.
Jn°. Moore	"
Tho. ffoster	"
Wm Lyon	"
Jn°. Kingman	Weym.
Sam. Pratt	"
Sam. White	"
Jn°. Vining	"

Tho. Bayly Weym.
James Nash "
Jacob Nash "
Laurenc Hamond Bost.
Robt. Coxe "
Hugh Amos "
Moses ffiske Dovr.
Peter Coffyn "
Jn°. Woodman "
Jn°. Davis "
Jn°. Martjn "
Antho. Nutter "
Tho. Roberts "
Tobias Davis "
Tho. Eaton Hav.
Jn°. Johnson "
Jn°. White ——
Elish. Huthinson
David Saywell
Eph. Turner
Jn°. Turner
Caleb Watson
Jn°. Crow
Jn°. Browne
Jn°. Samborne Hampton
Nath. Batchelor "
Wm. Marston "
Hen. Dow "
C. R., Vol. IV. p. 562.

29 April 1668.

Mr. James Russell Charlstown
Jn°. Heyman "
Nathani Rand "
Peter ffrothrington "
Jn°. Louden "
Jn° Benjamin Wattown.
Nath. Coolidge "
Jonath. Whitney "
Jonatha. Browne "
Symon Stacy Ipswich
Jn°. Whiple "
Tho. West Salem
Henry West "
Samuell Archard "
Jn°. Massey "
Wm. Downton "
Jn°. Ingersoll "
Jn°. Pease "
Jn°. Dodge senr. Bass River
Nath. Stone "
Peter Woodbury "
Ephrajm Hereck "
Wm. Peelsbury Newbery.
James Ordaway "
Nath. Clarke "
Tristram Coffin "
Henry Leonard Lynn
Nehemiah Jewet Lynn
Tho. Call jun. Malden
James Nicholls "
Tho. Hall Cambridge.
Tho. Philebrowne "
Jn°. Swan "
Nath. Handcock "
Sam. Hastings "
Jn°. Addams "
Thom. Browne "
Nath. Smith Haverill
Steven Dow "
Robert Emerson "
Ralph Holton Lancstr
Henry Kelly "
James ffowle Wooborne
Benj. Bullard Meadfeild
Sam. Gary Rocksbury
Tho. Philbrick Hampton
Sam. Wadsworth Milton
Sam. Smith North Hampton.
Jn°. ffarrington Dedham
C. R., Vol. IV. p. 600.

24 Oct. 1668.

Jn° Green Maulden
Wm Greene "
Symon Crosbee Billirrikey.
Thomas Day Springfeild
C. R., Vol. IV. p. 624.

19 May 1669.

"Persons admitted to ffreedom by this Court, and those that tooke their oaths are set down first; those that tooke it not are under the line."

Mr. Tho. Deane
James Whetcombe
Daniel Turill
Sam. Norden
Jn°. Mosse
Joseph Parsons
Jn°. Gidney
Barthol. Gidney
Sam. Cheevers
Jn°. Pickering
Joseph Grafton

Mr. Jn°. Davenport senr.
Mr. Jn°. Shearman
Mr. Sam. Torrey
Mr. Rich. Hubbard
James How
Mr. Jn°. Davenport jun.
Jn°. Prescott
Rich. Wheeler
Jn°. Moor
Jn°. Rugg
Jno°. ffletcher
Joakim Harvey
Tho. Daniel
Wm Vauhan
Rich. Cumings
Henry Deering
Jn°than Wade jun.
Jn°. Conney sworn July
Moses Bradford
Sam Mason
Jn°. Roberts
Jn°. Gorton
James Kent Newb.
Jn° Kent
Jn°. Bartlet jun.
Jn°. Wells
Abiel Somersby
Henry Jacquish
Benja. Lowell
John Bayley
Sam. Perly
Nehemiah Abbot
Georg Lyon
Ezra Clap
Ebenezar Clap
Tho. Gunn
James Cornish
Jn°. Roote
Tho. ffarnum
Jn°. Steephens
Jn°. fry
Steven Osgood
Georg Abbat
Wm. Chandler And.
Andrew ffoster
Jn°. Maxwell
Laurenc. Willis
Wm. Greenough
Benj Gage
Jn°. Bayly Newb.
Nath. Hancock
Jn°. Bayley Rowley
Mathew Edwards
Jn°. Keepe Spr.
Isack Graves sworn
Henry Jacquish
Benj. Kelly
Jn°. Hastings
Boaz Browne
Ezek. Jewet
Antho. Austin
Jn°. Kelly
Benja. Rolfe
Thomas Wiggin
C. R., Vol. IV. p. 629.

11 May 1670.

Mr. Jn°. Chickering Chars.
Daniel Edmonds "

Tho. White	Chars.
Abraham Smith	"
Sam. Peirce	"
Joseph ffrost	"
Tho. Chadwell	"
Sollomon Phipps jun.	"
Joseph Ketle	"
Sam. Ketle	"
Wm. Symonds	Woo.
Roger Kenicot	"
Tho. Green	"
Jn°. Baldin	Bill.
Samuell Maning	"
Jn° Bracket	"
Mr. Jn° Oxenbridge	Bost.
Henry Tompson	"
Adam Niccolls	"
Mr. Sam. Willard	Groton
Wm. Lakin	"
Mathyas farnworth	"
Tho. Patch	"
Henry Bayly	Bev'ly
John Black	"
John Gally	"
Jn°. Woodbery	"
Tho. West	"
Mr. Beter Bulkley	Conc.
John Haywood	"
Thomas Mason	North Hampt.
Tho. Bascome	"
Wm. Webster	Hadley
Joseph Baldwin	"
Joseph Plumer	Newb.
Benj. Rolfe	"
John Poore jun.	"
ffranc. Thurlo	"
Nicho. Batt	"
Job Pilsbury	"
John Gerrish	Dov.
Wm. Bartol	Marbhd.
Benja. Leeds	Dorc.
Henry Haggit	
Dani. Gott	
Wm. Rayner	
Jn°. Batchiler	
Wm ffiske	
John Albye	

C. R., Vol. IV. p. 651.

11 Oct. 1670.

John Sandford
John Gipson
John Warren
David Cop
Samuel Worcester
Nicholas Wallington

C. R., Vol. IV. p. 660.

31 May 1671.

Giles fyfield	Charls.
Ric. Asting	Charls.
Tho. Hale	"
Nath. ffrothingham	"
Joseph Lynd	"
Abr. Smith	"
John Call	"
Sam. ffrothingham	"
Mr. Alexandr Nowell	"
Tho. Parkes	Cambr.
Jn°. Tuttle	Lyn
Mr. Josiah flynt	Dorch.
Antho. Newton	"
Hen. Leadbetter	"
Robt. Spurr	"
James Convers	Wob.
Eljazer Jaco	"
Mr. Wm. Brinsmead	
Hen. Collins jun.	
Allin Broad	
Jn°. Penniman	Brant.
Moses Belcher	"
Caleb Hubard	Hing.
Josh. Lyncoln	"
Joseph Baldwin	Hadl.
Noah Coleman	"
ffr. Wainewright	Ips.
Wm. White	"
Isack ffoster	"
Sam. Younglove	"
Rich Waker	"
Wm. Story jun.	"
Arthur Abbot jun.	"
Robt. Allin	Dedh.
Jn°. Richards	"
Nath. Heaton	"
Jn°than ffuller	"
Medad Pumrey	North Hamp.
Jn°. Barber	"
Charls fferry	Spring.
Jn°. Riley	"
Tho. Hobbs	Topsf.
Paul White	Newb.
Tho. Noyes	"
Jn°than Morse	"
James Smith	"
John Smith	"
John Knight jun.	"
Isack Phelps	Westf.
Joseph Whiting	——
Jonothan Corwin	Salem.
Jn°. Marston	"
Eliazr. Gidney	"
Jn°. Maskor	"
Tho. Ingolls (676)	"
Jn°. Alden 3d Chh.	Boston.
ffranc. Robinson	"
Jn°. Mellowes	"
Jonathan Jackson	"
Wm. Hoare	"
James Hill 3d Chh.	Boston.
Jn°. Marshall	"
Ambrose Daws	"
Ezra Morse	"
Jn°. Lytlefeild	Ded.
Jn°. Holton	"
Sam. How	Sud.
Jn°. Roberts 1st. Ch.	Bosto[n]
Edmo. Ranger	"
Bartho. Toppn	"
Jn°. Temple	"
Jn°. farnham	"
Jn°. Moore	"
Jn°. Cotte	"
Jn°. Cleanesby	"
Robt. Wms	"
Tho. Overmore	"
Mr. Jn°. Saffyn	"
Capt. Tho. Lake	"
Josh. Holdsworth	"
Jn°. Barnard	Watr.
Sam. Livermore	"
Jn°. Bright	"
Sam. Craft	Rox.
Ephraim Hunt	Wey.
Jn°. Rogers	"
Benj. Gage	Havr.
Sam. Gage	"
Rogr Kennicot	Mald.
Sam. Lee	"
Tho. Green	"
Tho. Burnham jun.	Ips.
Tho. Beard	"
Jn°. Bickford sen.	Dorch.
Robt Burnm	"
James Coffyn	——
Tho. Bill (677)	

C. R., Vol. IV. pp. 676, 677.

15 May 1672.

Mr. Urian Oakes	Camb.
Mr. Joseph Dudley	Roxbu.
Wm. Laking	Groaton
Mathias farnworth	"
Jn°. Morse	"
Joseph Morse	"
Nath. Lawrence	"
Jn°thn Sautell	"
Jn°thn Morse	"
Mr. Jn° Winslow	Boston
Dani. Henchman	"
Ephraim Savage	"
Joseph Wheeler	"
Mannasseth Brike	"
Symon Amery	"
Tim° Thornton	"
Hen. Allin	"
Edw. Grant	"
James Townsend	"

Wm. Smith Boston.
Sam. Bridge (688) "
Wm. Griggs "
Ephraim Searl "
Abell Porter jun. "
Isack Brookes Woob.
Joseph Richardson "
Wm Ellery Gloc.
Tho. Pinney "
Georg Laines Ports.
Jn° Breuster "
Robt Purrington "
Rich. Shortridg "
Jn°. Dennet "
Jn°. Thompson "
Tho. Eggerly Dovr.
Jn°. Rand "
Jn°. Dam "
Stev. Jones "
Jn° Wingat "
Thos. Layton "
Tho. Ollivr Cambr.
Natha. ffiske "
Jn° Morse Watrt.
Wm Torrey Weym.
Micajah Torrey "
Joseph Prat "
Ric. Temple Conc.
Tho. Deane "
Gershom Brooks "
Obadiah Morse Medf.
Jn°thn Morse "
Joseph Morse "
Nath. Whiting "
Ezekiel Jewet Rowley
Abr. Haseltine "
Tho. Rimgton "
Jn°. Watson "
Jn°th. ffuller Dedh.
Edw. West Medfie.
Mr. Hope Atherton Hatfeid.
Jn° Coleman "
Thadeus Riddan Lyn
Josep Gardiner Salem
Rich. Hutton Wenh.
Joseph Rice Marlb.
Tho. Chubbuck
Tho. Lincolne
Jn° Beale
Dani. Cushin
Mathias Bridges
Joseph Bate
Benj. Bate
Samuell Bate
Wm. Hearsy
Onesepherus Marsh
Jacob Beale
Caleb Beale (689)
C. R., Vol. IV. pp. 688, 689.

8 Oct. 1672.

Mr. Solomon Stoddard North Ham.
George Lane Hing.
Dr. Leornard Hoare Bost.
Tho. Lull Ips.
Sam. Wight Medf.
Eph. Wight "
Joseph Croufot Springf.
Henry Walker Glocest.
C. R., Vol. IV. p. 705.

7 May 1673.

Mr. Peter Lydget 1st. Ch. Bost.
Mr. Samuel Shrimpton "
Mr. Elisha Cooke "
Mr. Eljakim Hutchinson "
Mr. John Usher "
Mr. Jn° ffaireweather "
Mr. John Clarke "
Mr. Isack Addington "
Mr. John Buttolph "
Samuel Bridge "
Mr. Xtopher Clarke 3d Ch. Bost.
Mr. John Joyliffe "
Mr. Edward Willis "
Mr. Nathaniel Davenport "
Tho. Bingley "
Paul Batt "
Timothy Batt "
Mr. John Woodmansey "
John Drury "
James Bracket "
Mr. Edw. Willis "
Mr. Jn°. Walley, mercht "
Lyonel Wheately "
Robert Mason "
John Walley, mariner "
Mr. John Pole "
Rich. Paddeshall "
John Wilkins "
John Osborne 21 Ch. Bo.
Hopestil foster "
ffrancis Hudson "
Wm. Greenore jun. "
Math. Barnard "
Daniel Travis "
Rich. Bennet "
Capt. Sam. Scarlet "
John Anderson senr. "
Joseph Cooke "
Obadiah Swift Dorch.
John Bird "
Eliazr Hawes "
Joseph Weekes "
Samuel Topliffe "
Jn° Wthrington "

Mr. Thomas Graves Ch.
Mr. Joseph Browne ——
Mr. Sam. Brakenbury Ch.
Humphry Bradshaw Camb.
Samuell Oldam "
Nath. Robbinson (718) "
Wm Davis Rox.
James Day Ips.
Mr. Joseph Gerrish New.
Jn° Bailey Wey.
ffrancis Browne "
Elisha Elzie Newb.
James Bayly "
Dani. Cheny "
Joshua Browne "
Sam. Poore "
Moses Pilsbury "
Benja. Morse "
Sam. Bartlet "
Hen. Ingalls And.
Jn°. Lovejoy "
John Barker "
John Baker Drch.
Ellis Wood "
Edw. West "
Jos. Heyward Conc.
Nathan. Billings "
Abra. Bryant Red.
Mr. Gershom Hobbart Hing.
James Bate "
Clement Bate "
Mr. Zecha. Whitman Hull
Benj. Bosworth "
Tho. Loring "
Jn°. Loring "
Jn°. Lobdell "
Isack Lobdell "
Benj. Loring "
Sampson Shoare "
Abra. Jones "
Jn° Cumins Tops.
Isa. Cumins "
Isack Easty "
Jn° Row Glo.
Nathan. Joseljn Lanc.
Sam. Belden Hatf.
Dani. Warner "
Wm. Gull "
Chileab Smith Hadl.
Jos. Warner "
Jn° Tucker Ports.
Nicho. Woodbery Bevrly
Peter Noyce Sudb.
John Goodenow "
Tho. Barnes Marlb.
James Vales Medf.
Mr. Charls Nicholate (719) Salem
C. R., Vol. IV. pp. 718, 719.

15 Oct. 1673.

Nathaniel Peirce B. 1 Ch.
Mathew Atkins B. 2^d Ch.
Boaz Browne Conc.
Ephraim Clarke Medf.
Wm. Coleman Glo.
Stephen Cooke Mend^n
Danel Lovet "
Abra. Staple "
Joseph Steevens "
Samuel Read "
Hope Tyler "

C. R., Vol. IV. p. 732.

20 Dec. 1673.

John Lovejoy
John Barker
Henry Ingalls

C. R., Vol. IV. p. 737.

9 January 1673–4.

Jno Noyes New.
Cutting Noyes "
John Lunt "
Abra. Addams "
John Badger "
Joseph Gerrish "
Nathaniel Brewer Rox.
Mr. Wm Addams Ded.
Sam. Capen Dorch^t.

C. R., Vol. IV. p. 737.

11 March 1673–4.

Pen Townsend B.
Mr. John Rodgers Ips.
Mr. Samuel Cobbet "
Robt. Kinsman "
Thomas Clarke "
Daniell Hovey "
Abraham ffitt "
Joseph Goodhue "
Joseph Whiple "
Philemon Dane "
Tho. ffisher Ded.
Joseph Pratt Weym.
Tho. Andrew Hing.
Nath. Cutler Ch.
James Bacon Roxb.
Josias Richardson Chelmsfo.
Eliazer Browne "
Jacob Warren "

C. R., Vol. IV. p. 738.

27 May 1674.

Mr. Daniel Epps Ips.
Tho. Jacob "
Tho. Metcalf "
Nico. Wallis "
Nathaniel Addams "
Nathan: Rust Ips.
Tho. ffrench "
Jno Lumpson "
Jno Pebody Tops.
Joseph farnum 1 Ch.
Jno. Rugles sen^r. Rox.
Elnathan Chancy [Camb^r.]
Ruben Luxford "
Andrew Boardman "
Jno. Jackson "
Daniel Markham "
Jno Buss Conc.
Jacob french Bill^r.
Wm Seavir Ports.
Obadiah Morse "
Tho. Harvie ——
Antho. Ellings
Richard Sampson
Abell Poster
Caleb Pumbrey N. Hamp.
Ebenezer White Weym.
Edw. Addams Med.
Joseph Wright "
Gershom flagg "
Samuel Walker Woob.
James Thompson "
Israel Walker "
Jno Snow "

C. R., Vol. V. p. 1.

7 Oct. 1674.

Samuel Douse Ch.
Tho. Bligh Bost.
Rich. Sharpe "
Tho. Smith ——
Wm Ingram
Dudley Bradstreet

C. R., Vol. V. p. 15.

22 July 1674.

At a Court at Pemaquid the following named persons took the oath of fidelity.

Thomas Humphreys
Robert Gamon
Willjam Waters
John Dolling
Thomas Cox
Robt Edmunds
Ambrose Hanwell
John Wriford
Eljas Trick
John Pride
George Bickford
Reynald Kelley
Jno Cole
Capt. Edmnd Pattestall
Mr. Ichabod Wisewall
Mr. Richard Olliver
Wm. Buckford
Edward Barton
Rich^d. Hill
Henry Curtis
francis Browne
Rich^d. Warren
Henry Stoakes
Wm. Denlo
Edwd. Dorr
Jno Dare
Geor. Burnet
Nicho. Osbourne
Tho. Parker
David Olliver
Emanuel Whichalls
Jno Cock
Tho. Phillips
Tho. Hilman
Nicco. Carary
Jno Parker
Nicco. Deming
Abell Hoggeridge
Edward Cole
Jno WildGoose
Tho. Parnell
Aaron Beard
Gregory Langberry
Abra. Clarke
Tho. Cox jun.
Henry Curtis jun.
Shadrick Cox
Richard Cox
Richard Pearce jun.
Robert Cauly
Tho. Adger
Richard Bradeway
Richard Bucknell
Wm. Edwards
Tho. Cox
Wm. Waters
Wm. Welcome
Jno. Bessell
Peter Collins
Richard Glass
Tho. Phillips
Henry Palmer
Jno Palmer jun.
Phillip Bry
Wm. Phillips
Jno. Stover
Jno. Palmer sen^r.
Robrt Edmnds
James Widger
Tho. Harls
Jno Gingden
Nico. Vallack
Jno Selman
Wm. Trout
Nico. Heale
Georg Bucknell
Wm. Cox

Tho. Cox
C. R., Vol. V. p. 17.

12 May 1675.

John Valentine Bost.
Joseph Webb "
Elisha Audljn "
Sam. Ware "
Jn°thⁿ Bridgham "
Peircy Clarke "
John Davis "
Joshua Gee "
Benja. Dyer "
Edw. Thwing
Sam. Gardiner Salem
Samuel Warner Ips.
Tho. Weld "
Tho. Gittings "
Symon Chapman "
Nath. Warner "
James Bracket Bev.
Andrew Boardman Camb.
Ruben Luxford "
Dani. Markeham "
John Jackson "
Ebenezr Wiswall "
C. R., Vol. V. p. 25.

21 Feb. 1675–6.

Jn° Tucker 3d Bost.
Jn° Noyes "
Natha. Willjams "
Dani. Gookin jun. Camb.
Jn° Pike Salis.
Hen. Trow Ips.
Jn°. Jewet "
Robt Pierpoint "
Jn° Atwood Bost. 2d
Joseph Knight Woo.
Georg Abbot And.
Xtopher Osgood "
Tho. Osgood "
Jacob french Bille.
Tho. Russell Charles.
Jn° Clifford Hamp.
Joseph Barret Chelms.
[illegible] Amistreale ——
Tho. Dyer Weym
C. R., Vol. V. p. 70.

3 May 1676.

Mr. Sam. Alcock Boston
Mr. Dani. Russell Charl.
Zech. Johnson "
Isaack ffowle "
Zech. fferris "
John Goodwin "
Timo. Baker Northam.
Joseph Person "
Jn° Bridgman "
Judah Wright Northam.
Sam. Smith "
Mr. Jn° Younglove Hadly
Samuel Wentworth Dov.
C. R., Vol. V. p. 73.

11 Oct. 1676.

Richard Hall Bradf.
Dani. Hazeltine "
Jn° Hardy "
Jn° Hubbard Ips.
Jn° Jewet "
Benja. Emons Bo. 3d Ch.
Sam. Davis Northam.
Nehemia Allin "
Jn° Knight "
Jn° Dowse Charls.
C. R., Vol. V. p. 112.

23 May 1677.

Mr. Jn° Price Salem
Jn° Higinson jun. "
Jn° Hauthorne "
Manasses Marston "
Henry Kirrey "
Mr. Sam. Nowel Charls.
Jn° Phillips "
Xtopher Goodin "
James Millar "
Jn° Blany "
W'm. Gibson Boston 1 Ch.
Nathani Barnes "
Edwd Ashley "
Jn° Cadwell Ips.
Jn° Wales Dorch.
James Blake "
Joseph Roads Lin.
Jn° White Rox.
Jabez ffox Camb.
Jn° Rogers Wey.
Jn° Bayly "
Nathani. Gay Dedh.
Tho. Aldridge "
Nath. Kingsbery "
Jn° Weare "
Wm. Avery "
Jn° Hollioke Spr.
Sam. Stoddar Hingh.
Andrew Lane "
Jn° Tucker "
Richd Dumer jun. Newb.
Hen. Short "
Steph. Greenleaf "
Jacob Toppan "
Rich. Bartlet jun. "
Tho. Pearly "
Wm. ffoster Rowley
Nath. Barker "
Obadiah Morse Meadf.
Edwd Addams "
Eljazr Addams Meadf.
Jn°th Morse "
Jos. Bullin "
Jn° Walker Wooburn
Jn° Carter "
Jn° Brarboun "
franc. fletcher Concord
Timo. Wheeler "
Jn° Merriam "
Sam. Jones "
Sam. Lampson Redding
Jn° Eaton "
Henry Merrow "
Sebred Taylor "
C. R., Vol. V. p. 126.

10 Oct. 1677.

John Clarke B. 3 C.
Gilbert Cole "
Robert Butcher ——
Nathaniel Patten
Jn° Wales senr. Dor.
Sam. Hix "
Henry Withengton "
Amos Woodward Camb.
Dani. Champney "
John Wells Rox.
Tho. Pierce Woob.
Jn° Smeadley Conc.
Joseph Boynton Row.
Alexandr Sessions And.
Benja. Lincolne Hing.
John Chubbuck "
John fering "
Tho. Gill jun. "
C. R., Vol. V. p. 146.

8 May 1678.

Joseph Bridgham
1 Ch. Bost.
Joshua Windsor 2 Ch.
Jonas Clarke "
Hen. Dauson "
Wm Way "
Jn° Barnard "
Tho. Barkr "
Jn° Goffe "
Wm. Sumer "
Mr. Peter Thatcher 3 Ch.
Mr. Sam. Seawall "
Mr. Elnath. Chancey Camb.
Timo. Lyndall Salem
Isack ffoot "
Roger Hill "
Wm. Barker "
Edw. Read "
Benj. Parmiter "
Richard Riff "
Francis Girdler "
Jn° Mascoll "
Walter Cloys "

Joseph fairbank Ded.
Tho. ffisher "
Sam. Guile "
Benj. Miles "
Joseph Wight "
Josia ffisher "
Robrt Weare Hamp.
Jonath. ffreeman "
Jn°. Clifford "
Wm. ffuller "
Jn° Parker Mauld.
Joseph Lynds "
Dani. Thirston Meadf.
Sam. Baker Hull
Joseph Benson "
Samuel Prince "
Jn°th. Vickree "
Tho. Toleman Dorch.
Jn°. Toleman "
Nath. Glover "
James ffoster "
Incre. Sumer "
Hope Clap "
Jn° Baker "
Wm. Ryall "
Josia Chapen Brant.
Jos. Peniman "
Sam. Penniman "
Jos. Parmiter "
Steph. Payne jun. "
Jn° Lazell Hing.
Sam. Thaxter "
Tho. Marsh "
Jos. Walker Biller.
Tho. Patten "
Sam. ffrost "
Obadia Perry "
Mr. Edw. Taylor Westf.
Jn° Maudsley "
Vickry Sike Spr.
Isa. Cakebread "
Luke Hitchcoke "
Jn° Richardson Woob.
Tho. Bankroft Red.
Jn° Townsend "
Rich. Phillips Weym.
Sam. Humphry "
Joseph Dyar "
Edmo. Grover Bevr.
Nehem. Grover "
Isa. Woodbery "
Hump. Woodbery "
Robt. Bradbuth "
Ric. Patch "
Jn° Blatt "
Jn° Richds. "
Jn° Patch "
Tho. Holman Milton
Ephr. Tucker "
Manasses Tucker "
Timo. Nash Hadl.
Tho. Hale Hadl.
Jn° Russell "

C. R., Vol. V. p. 175.

2 Oct. 1678.

Mr. Isack ffoster Charls.
Jn° Pengilley Ips.
Enock Hubbard Hing.
Sam. Man Ded.
Jn° Brewer Sud.
Jonas Prescot "
Tho. Reade jun. "
Wm. Addams "
Joseph ffreeman "
Samll Carter Woob.
Jn° Kendall "
Jos. Winge "
John Lynds Mald
Jn° Greenland "

C. R., Vol. V. p. 202.

15 Oct. 1679.

Mr. John Browne Red.
Benja. ffitch "
Hananiah Parker "
Nath. Gooding "
Peter Tuffes Mald.
francis Jones "
Mathew Cushin jun. Hing.
Jn° Smith jun. "
Dani. Cushin "
Josia Levet "
Joseph Wing Wo.
Joseph Lyon Rox.
Jn° Dole New.
Sam. Butterick Conc.
Jn° Prescot "
Ephraim Winship Camb.
Jn° Marrion "

C. R., Vol. V. p. 232.

4 Feb. 1679–80.

"Ordered, that the Honble Georg Russell Esq., now resident with us in Boston, be admitted to the freedom of this corporation, if he please to accept thereof." Marg. note. "He accepted it, and took his oath 13 ffeb. 79, before the Governor and Assistants."

C. R. Vol. V. p. 259.

19 May 1680.

Mr. Jn° Bowles Rox.
Mr. Edw. Pason "
Jn°. Grafton Salem
Resolved White "
Benja. Thwing 1 C. Bost.
Jerr. Dumer "
Jn° Thing 1 C. Bost.
Jacob Hurd "
Tho. Chard "
Jn° Cotton 2d Ch.
Cotton Mather "
Wm. Coleman "
Jabez Broune Sud.
Jn° Held Chelmsf.
Eliar Ball "
Jonathan Tyng "
Mr. Jose. Hawley North.
Davjd Burt "
Wm. Smead "
Jn°. Woodward "
Jonathan Hunt "
Joshua Pomrey "
Eliazr frary "
Joseph Dodge Bevr.
Jn° Balch "
Paul Thorndick "
Richd. Norman Marblehd
Jn° Legg "
Nathan. Walton "
Richd Mountequе "
Mr. Tho. Shephard Charls.
Mr. Neh. Hubbard Camb. Villg.
Ebenezr Wiswall " "
Sam. Robbins " "
Jn° Gardiner Wob.
Jn° Chadwick "
Mr. Wiglesworth Mald.
Peletiah Smith "
Tho. Putnam jun. [illegible.]
Wm. Stacy
Zache Marsh
Symon Booth
Israel How
Benj. Leeds
John Pason
Symon Willard Ips.
Joseph Pitty "
Nath Humphry "
Abra. Whitman Wey.
Wm. Pratt "
Mr. Edw. Taylor West.
David Ashley "
Jeddedia Dewy "
Sam. Roote "
Joseph Pomry "
Nath. Melby Hull
Jn°. Hanchet "
Benj. Bosworth "
Abr. Jones "
Robt Gold "
Jonathan Nile "
Nathani. Bosworth "
Sam. Prince "
Zach. Hund "
Jose. Bosworth "

Iseck Vickrey — Hull
Steven Lincoln — Hingh.
Mr. Jer. Shepr'd — Lynn
Tho. Layton — "
Ralph King — "
Robt. ffuller — "
Jn° felton — "
Jos. Phippen — "
Mr. Danl. D [blotted]
Japhet Chapin — Spring.
Sam. Ely — "
Tho. Shelden — Biller.

C. R., Vol. V. p. 260.

13 Oct. 1680.

Mr. Tho. Cheever — 1 C. Bost.
Nicho. Willis — "
Mr. Deodat Lawson — 3 C.
Sam. Ballard — Cha.
Mr. Edw. Pason — Rox.
Danie. Kellum jun. — Wenh.
John Knolton — "
Sam. Knolton — "
Tho. Bayly — "
Sam. Abby — "
Sam. ffiske — "
Tho. Prentice senr. — Camb. Vill.
Tho. Prentice jun. — "
Tho. Parke senr. — "
Jn° ffuller jun. — "
Jn°than ffuller — "
Joshua ffuller — "
Joseph ffuller — "
James Hawkes — Hingh.
Jos. Jacob — "
Enos. Kinsly — N. Hamp.
Peter Bracket — Biller.

C. R., Vol. V. p. 285.

11 May 1681.

Tho. Eaton — Ded.
Natha. Chickering — "
Robert Weare — "
David Hubbart — Hing.
Jerr. Beale — "
Tho. Hovey — Hadl.
Sam. Lancton — N. Hamp.
Nath. Phelph — "
Benja. Gerrish — Salem
Ezekiel Cheevers — "
John Leech — "
Ephrajm Colton — Spr.
Tho. Colton — "
Joseph Stebbing — "
Joseph Trumble — "
Georg Norton — "
Sam. Kent — Glou.
Jn° Burbank — [?]
Wm. Starlinge — "
Sam. Peirson — "
Nath. Jewett — Conc.
Allen Bread senr. — Lyn
Joseph Reads — "
Josiah Reads — "
Ephrajm Winship — Camb.
Abraham Tilton — Ips.
Isa. Esty — Tops.
Tho. Norman — "

C. R., Vol. V. p. 306.

12 Oct. 1681.

Mr. Jn° Olliver 2 Ch. — Bost.
Tho. Chard — "
James Barnes — "
Hen. Bartholmew 1 Ch. — B.
Obadiah Sajle — "
Jn° Russells — Camb.
Jn° senr. — "
Tho. Con — Ips.
Sam. Ingolls — "
Wm. Goodhue jun. — "
Jn° Pierson jun. — Row.
Jn° Sanyde (320) — "
John Whitman — Wey.
Nicholas Whilmarsh — "
Steven ffrench — "
Jn° Bayly — "
Tho. Bayly — "
Richd. Gurney — "
James Smith — "
Nathan Smith — "
Samuel Holbrooke — "
Wm. Richards jun. — "
Joseph Richards — "
Jn° Richards — "
Tho. Kingman — "
Samuel King — "
Wm. Read — "
Abijah Whitman — "
Tho. White — "
Joseph Dyer — "
Jn° Shaw jun. — "
Joseph Pitty — "
Tho. Noble — Wenh.
Eliazr Weller — "
Sam. Ball — Spr.
Tho. Spencer — Suffd.
Tho. Stuksley (321) — "

C. R., Vol. V. pp. 320, 321.

24 May 1682.

Jn° ffoster — Salem
Antho. Buxton — "
Peter Prescot — "
Mr. Jno. Apleton — Ips.
Jn° Dane — Ips.
Jn° Wardner — "
Dani. Warner — "
Tho. Boreman — "
Joseph ffellows — "
Tho. Tredwell — "
Nath. Tredwell — "
Jos. far — Lyn
Jn° ffarrington — "
Humph. Barrat — Conc.
Sam. Haur — "
Roger Chandler — "
Sam. Stone — "
Sam. Kemball — Wenh.
Jn° Gilbert — "
Charl Got — "
Jn° Harding — Meadfei.
Jn° Warfeild — "
Benj. Clark — "
Jn° fisher — "
Sam. Rockwood — "
Nath. Allin — "
Jn° Bates — Chelms.
Abra. Byam — "
Nath. Butterfeild — "
Abr. Parker — "
Isack Morrell — Chs.
Jn°than Caree — "
Sam. Bartlet — N. Hamp.
Jn° Pinor — Northfeild

C. R., Vol. V. p. 348.

11 Oct. 1682.

Mr. Sam. Gardiner jun. — Salem.
Mr. Jn° Apleton — Ips.
Jn° Dane — "
Daniel Warner — "
Tho. Boreman — "
Joseph ffellows — "
Tho. Tredwell — "
Nath. Tredwell — "
Mr. Tho. Wade — "
Joseph Giddings — "
Joseph Safford — "
Wm Butler — "
Jn° Harding — Meadf.
Jn° Warfeild — "
Benja. Clarke — "
Jn° ffisher — "
Samuel Rockwood — "
Joseph Allin — "
Jn° ffegg — Watertn
Abra. Guile — "
Nath. Marcham — "
Wm. Band — "
Sam. Jeningson — "
Jn° farwell — Conc.
Tho. Browne jun. — "

[To be continued.]

RECORDS OF BOSTON.

[Copied for the Antiquarian Journal by MR. DAVID PULSIFER, member of the N. E. H. Geneal. Society.]

[BRAINTREE.—Continued from page 127.]

Helin Mekins was drowned 3° (10°) 1638. *Mekins.*

Oliver Mellow dyed *Mellowes.*

Sarah the wife of John Merchand dyed 3° (10°) 1638. *Merchand.*

Joshua the sonne of Thomas Metson was borne 23° (5°) 1640. *Metson.*

Bridget More wife to John Moore dyed 1643. *Moore.*

Martha the daughtr of Henry Neale was borne 16° (11°) 1642. *Neale.*

Mary the daughter of ffrancis Newcom was borne 31° (1°) 1640. *Newcomb.*

Sarai the daughtr of ffrancis Newcomb was borne 24° (3°) 1643.

Matthew the sonne of John Osborne dyed (3°) 1641. *Osborne.*

Moses Paine dyed 21° (4°) 1643. *Paine.*

Joseph the sonne of James Penniman was borne 1° (6°) 1639. *Penniman.*

Sarai the daughtr of James Penniman was borne 16° (3°) 1641.

Mary the daughtr of John Perrin was borne 22° (12°) 1640. *Perrin.*

George Pocher dyed 29° (7°) 1639. *Pocher.*

John the sonne of John Reade was borne 29° (6°) 1640. *Reade.*

Thomas the sonne of John Reade was borne 20° (9°) 1641.

Symon Rey dyed 30° (7°) 1641. *Rey*

Agnes the wife of Richard Rockett dyed 9° (5°) 1643. *Rocket.*

John the sonne of Richard Rocket & Agnes his wife was borne 1° (10°) 1641.

Ruth the daughter of David Rogers was borne 3° (11°) 1640. *Rogers.*

David Rogers dyed 24° (7°) 1642.

Georg the sonne of George Ruggle borne 5° (3°) 1640, and dyed (5°) 1641. *Ruggle.*

Rachell the daughtr of Georg Ruggle was borne 15° (12°) 1642.

John the sonne of William Savell was borne 22° (2°) 1642. *Savell.*

John the sonne of Benjamin Scott was borne 25° (10°) 1640. *Scott.*

Thomas Sellein dyed 3° (10°) 1642. *Sellein.*

Mary Sergeant servant to Thomas Metson dyed (8°) 1641. *Sergeant.*

John the sonne of Robert Sharpe was borne 12° (1°) 1642. *Sharpe.*

Samuel the sonne of John Shepheard dyed 29° (6°) 1641. *Shepheard.*

Benjamin the sonne of Edward Spalden *Spalden.*
his wife was borne 7° (2°) 1643.

Grace the daughtr of Edward Spalden
his wife was buryed (3°) 1641.

Margaret the wife of Edward Spalden dyed —— 1640.

Sarah the daughtr of Robert Steevens was borne 31° (3°) 1641. *Steevens.*

John the sonne of Thomas Stowe & Mary his wife was borne the 3° (12°) 1640. *Stow.*

Mary the daughter of Thomas Stow & Mary his wife was borne 6° (12°) 1642.

Joan Symons the daughtr of Thomas Symons was borne 8° (9°) 1638. *Symons.*

Abigail Symons the daughtr of Tho: Symons was borne the 8° (9°) 1640, & dyed 30° (3°) 1642.

Thomas Symons dyed 15° (4°) 1642.

Anne the daughtr of John Symons dyed (4°) 1640. *Symons.*

Joseph the sonne of Wm Thomson & Abigail his wife was borne 1° (3°) 1640. *Thomson.*

Benjamin the sonne of Wm Thomson & Abigail his wife was borne 14° (5°) 1642.

Abigail the wife of mr William Thomson dyed (11°) 1642.

Dorcas the daughtr of Daniell Weld was borne 6° (2°) 1643, & dyed 15° (4°) 1643. *Weld.*

Isaac the sonne of Jacob Wilson was borne 28° (11°) 1640. *Wilson.*

Sarai the daughtr of Jacob Wilson was borne 28° (11°) 1641.

Elisabeth the daughtr of Alexander Winchester was borne the 28° (1°) 1640. *Winchester.*

Hannah the daughtr of Alexandr Winchestr was borne 10° (10°) 1642.

James the sonne of James Wiseman was borne 8° (8°) 1640. *Wiseman.*

Mercie the daughtr of James Wiseman was borne 28° (1°) 1643.

A register of Births & Burialls in Cambridge from the yeare 1632 vntill the first Month 1644.

Mary the wife of William Andrews dyed 19° (11°) 1639. *Andrews.*

Mary the daughtr of Joseph Baster & Mary his wife was borne the 13° (3°) 1643. *Baster.*

Jemimah the daughtr of Andrew Belchar & Elisabeth his wife was borne the 5° (2°) 1642. *Belchar.*

William Bittlestone dyed 5° (8). *Bittlestone.*

Thomas Bittlestone dyed 23° (9°) 1640. *Bittlestone.*

Susan Blogget the daughter of Thomas Blogget & Susan his wife was borne (4°) 1637. *Blogget.*

Joseph the sonne of Robt Bradish & Mary his wife was borne (3°) 1638. *Bradish.*

Mary the wife of Robt Bradish dyed (7°) 1638.

Samuel the sonne of Robt Bradish & Vashti his wife was borne 13° (12°) 1639 and dyed 6° (5°) 1642.

John the sonne of John Brewer & Anne his wife was borne the 10° (8°) 1642. *Brewer.*

Samuel the sonne of Roger Burt & Susan his wife was borne 6° (12°) 1642. *Burt.*

Thomas Blogget dyed 7° (6°) 1639. *Blogget.*

Jonathan the sonne of Christopher & Margaret Caine borne 27° (1°) 1640. *Caine.*

[To be continued.]

MEMOIR OF CHARLES FROST.

[By Usher Parsons, M. D., of Providence, R. I., Member of the N. England Historic Genealogical Society.]

[Mr. Editor: The last two numbers of your journal contained copies of ancient manuscripts relating to Richard Waldron, Charles Frost, and others, who were among the first settlers about the Pascataqua. These I have thought might serve to render a brief sketch of the life of Major Frost interesting to your readers.]

Charles Frost was born in Tiverton, England, in 1632. He accompanied his father to the Pascataqua river at the age of three or four years.

His father, *Nicholas Frost*, was also a native of Tiverton, and resided "near Lemon Green, over against Bear-Garden." He had one sister, who "married Charles Brooks, a brazier in Crown Alley, London." He was born about the year 1595, and arrived at Pascataqua about 1635 or 1636, and settled at the head of Sturgeon Creek, on the south side of Frost's Hill, where he died, July 20, 1663, and was buried in the rear of his house. He brought over a wife and two or three children. The wife is not mentioned in his will, dated 1650, from which it is to be inferred that she died before that time. This will was examined in court of probate, and, from some cause now unknown, was deemed "invalid and of none effect." The court ordered that his estate be divided among his children equally, excepting that Charles, the oldest, should have a double share, "for his care and former trouble." This amounted to £211. Charles took the homestead, with five hundred acres of land. To his second son, John, he gave three hundred acres in York, with a marsh valued at £65, the rest in money. To William Leighton, for his wife Catherine, personal property. To Elizabeth, when she should arrive of age, personal estate. To Nicholas, a house and lot adjoining Leighton's, and personal property; he being a minor, was placed under the guardianship of his brother Charles.

Catherine Leighton had a son and a daughter named John and Elizabeth. The latter died young. The son married Oner Langdon, and was the ancestor of a numerous race, among whom were a grandson, Major Samuel Leighton of Elliot, and his son, General Samuel Leighton, who died in Alfred, Sept., 1848. Catherine married again, to Joseph Hammond, who was Register and Judge of Probate, and had children by him. She died Aug. 1, 1715.

John settled in York and afterwards at the Isles of Shoals, where he carried on fisheries. He died 1718, at Star Island, leaving a widow named Sarah, and a son Samuel, who inherited the York estate, and two others, named Samuel and Ithamer, and one daughter, who married William Fox, and three grandsons, the sons of John, the eldest of whom was named John.

Elizabeth married William Smith.

Nicholas followed the sea, was bound an apprentice as sailor to Thomas Orchard. He commanded a ship that sailed between Maryland and Ireland. He died at Limerick, Ireland, August, 1673, unmarried, and left his estate to the children of his brother Charles and sister Catherine. Hammond claimed of Leighton's children a share of their uncle's legacy for his own children, and, after a lawsuit, obtained it.

Mr. Nicholas Frost was an uneducated farmer. His signature to papers was with a mark. He was, however, esteemed a trustworthy, judicious citizen, as appears from the fact of his appointment to responsible offices, as constable and selectman.

Charles Frost, who succeeded to the homestead of his father Nicholas, at the head of Sturgeon Creek, became a distinguished man, both in civil and military life. In narrating the events of his life, it will be necessary to connect them with a brief sketch of the political history of Pascataqua, comprising the present towns of Kittery, Elliot, and South Berwick. They were designated by the first settlers by local names, as Kittery Point, Spruice Creek, now Kittery, Sturgeon Creek, in Elliot, Newichewannick, extending from the mouth of the river at South Berwick to the mills at Great Works, so called, Quampegan, still known as such, and Salmon Falls. These names were applied to the villages or settlements near them, and were all included under the plantation of Pascataqua. In 1647 it was incorporated under the name of Kittery, after a town of that name in England, where several of the emigrants formerly resided. Berwick was separately incorporated in 1723, being for some time previous designated as Union Parish. Elliot was separated from Kittery in 1810, and South Berwick from Berwick in 1824. In 1636 the number of inhabitants in all these towns was two hundred, the population of Maine being one thousand four hundred. The grand highway of the inhabitants of Pascataqua was on the river, to Portsmouth, Dover, and Exeter.

The first settlement of Pascataqua followed soon after that of Plymouth. In 1622 the Council of Plymouth (England) granted to John Mason and Sir Ferdinando Gorges "all the lands situated between the rivers Merrimac and Kennebec," by the name of "the Province of Laconia." These two gentlemen, with some associates, constituting the company of Laconia, erected salt works at Little Harbor, near Portsmouth, and carried on fishing and furtrading with the Indians. In 1624 Ambrose Gibbons built a mill at Newichewannick, (South Berwick,) which was soon after managed by Humphrey Chadborne. The company appointed Walter Neal their agent, who served till 1634, when he was succeeded by Francis Williams. Failing of anticipated success, most of the company of Laconia became discouraged, and sold out to Gorges and Mason, who, in 1634, divided their lands, Mason taking New Hampshire, and Gorges taking all eastward of the Pascataqua to Kennebeck, which he called *New Somersetshire.*

Settlements were made on the eastern shore of the river, at Kittery Point, Spruce Creek, Sturgeon Creek, and Newichewannick. Gorges sold to Mason a strip of land along the whole length of the river, three miles wide, including the mills at South Berwick, but Mason soon died, and this reverted back to Gorges, and was reannexed to Somersetshire. William Gorges, nephew of Sir Ferdinando, was appointed governor, and served two years. The courts were at this time held at Saco, which was settled earlier.

The agent of Pascataqua, Williams, was directed to encourage emigration from England; and, between 1634 and 1640, a large number of persons arrived, among whom were Nicholas Frost and family. It is not known precisely what year he arrived, but, from the fact that he was appointed to an important office in 1640, it is probable he came much earlier, perhaps 1635 or 1636. The settlers were allowed to take up as much land as they could fence, by paying two shillings and two and a half per acre, for one hundred years. Nicholas Frost took four hundred acres.

In 1639 Sir Ferdinando Gorges obtained a new charter under the name of the Province or County of Maine. Another nephew of his, Thomas Gorges, was appointed deputy governor, with six councillors. The courts were held at Saco and York. In June, 1640, the governor and council held a court at Saco, where, among other officers appointed, was Nicholas Frost, as constable of Pascataqua. Sir Ferdinando caused Agamenticus (old York) to be erected into a borough, and soon after into a city, called Georgeana, with mayor and aldermen. Being involved in the civil wars now raging in England, and connected with the prostrated party, he was imprisoned during his few remaining days, and his nephew, Governor Thomas Gorges, becoming discontented, resigned his office at the end of three years, when his commission expired, and returned home to England, leaving Maine without a successor. The council appointed one of their number, a Mr. Vines, as deputy governor, in 1644.

A claim had recently been set up to the eastern part of Maine, from Kennebunk river to Kennebeck, under what was called the Plough patent, by one Rigby, of England, who appointed George Cleves as his deputy or agent. Cleves made interest with Massachusetts, and with the commissioners of plantations in England, who decided that Rigby's title was undoubtedly good, and this decision left Sir Ferdinando in possession of only the land between Kennebunk and Pascataqua rivers. He, however, died soon after.

The whole province of Maine was badly governed, and, after a time, the people became desirous of following the example of New Hampshire, whose inhabitants, a few years previous, (1642,) applied for and obtained annexation to Massachusetts. This government was very willing to receive Maine in like manner, and, "by a plausible construction of their own charter," claimed it as their property. The claimants under both Rigby and Gorges, through their agents, Cleves and Godfrey, though previously opposed to each other, united now, in resisting the claim of Massachusetts. But the inhabitants under Gorges were anxious for annexation, and it was soon effected. In 1652 four commissioners were sent from Boston to Pascataqua, or Kittery, as it was now called, where a court was held during four days, and, after much discussion and altercation, they received the concession of forty-one persons, among whom were Nicholas Frost and his son, *Charles Frost.*

The other towns west of Kennebunk river immediately followed their example, and, in process of time, the towns eastward, in Rigby's patent, submitted in like manner. In 1653 Kittery sent a representative to the general court of Massachusetts, and, in 1658, *Charles Frost*, then 26 years of age, was chosen to the office, which he held five years.

In 1660 Ferdinando Gorges, grandson of the baronet, laid claim to the province as heir at law. King Charles II. sanctioned the claim, and, in 1664, ordered it to be restored to him. Nichols, Carr, Cartwright, and Maverick were directed by the king to demand possession and to hold courts. A sharp altercation took place between them and the general court of Massachusetts, and they left for Maine without effecting a reconciliation. The king wrote a reprimand to the people of Massachusetts and Maine, and required them to restore the province to Gorges forthwith. Archdale, an appointed agent, made the demand of the Massachusetts government; but instead of complying, they ordered a county court, consisting of Thomas Danforth and others as judges, to be held at York. But on arriving at Portsmouth, the court were forbid to enter Maine. They therefore returned to Boston, followed by the king's comissioners, who were so insolent and overbearing to the government as to prevent all further conference. They were soon after recalled or dismissed from office.

The interrupted state of the courts caused by these contentions, left Maine without suitable legislation or courts of justice. In 1668 Massachusetts sent four commissioners to hold a court in York, where they met the justices appointed by the king's commissioners ready to hold a court also. After much quarrelling those of Massachusetts prevailed, and a government and court were organized in due form. The following year, 1669, the province, after a suspension of three years, again sent representatives to the general court, among whom was *Charles Frost* of Kittery.

The militia of Maine was now organized into six companies, one of which was commanded by *Charles Frost.*

The Dutch war ensued, which engrossed the attention of the king, and thus gave Massachusetts a short respite from his interferences. But after a time the claim of Gorges's heirs was again renewed, and, to obviate all further trouble from them, it was deemed the wisest policy to buy them out. This was effected through the agency of John Usher, for the sum of £1200. This procedure displeased the king, who was at the time trying to negotiate for it with Gorges's heirs, intending it as a place for one of his court favorites. He wrote a reprimanding letter to the government; but the bargain was made and completed, and Gorges's claim for ever extinguished.

Although Massachusetts had by purchase become "the assignee and proprietor of Maine, yet it was contended that she must govern it according to the stipulations in Gorges's charter," and not as a constituent part of her own colony. Accordingly it was determined to restore the form of civil administration established by Gorges, subject, however, to the general oversight and direction of her governor and assistants. They therefore appointed, in 1680, a president (Thomas Danforth) and six assistants or councillors, who were to act as judges of the courts. Among the six councillors thus appointed was *Charles Frost.* He was also appointed at the same time commander-in-chief of the Maine regiment.

Edward Randolph, the bitter enemy of the colonies, was appointed by the crown as collector and surveyor. He acted as an emissary and secret informer against Massachusetts, representing her government and people as enemies to the authorities in England, and presented grave accusations to the throne against her best men, which threatened to result in the upsetting of her charter. So imminent was the danger of this, that in order to avoid it, she would willingly have relinquished her title to Maine. At length, however, the fatal blow was struck. On the 4th of June, 1684, the charter was adjudged to be forfeited, and the liberties of the colonies were seized by the crown. Colonel Kirke, a brutal tyrant, was appointed governor, but Charles II. died the following February, 1685, which annulled the appointment before his arrival, and his successor, James II., did not incline to renew it.*

The general court was soon after annihilated by the arrival (May, 1686) of Joseph Dudley as President of New England, with the names of fifteen councillors, among whom was John Usher and the odious Randolph. In a few months Dudley was succeeded by Sir Edmond Andros, a man of despotic temper. He was subsequently commissioned (1688) as President of New England and New York, and New Jersey. His council consisted of thirty-nine members, among whom were John Usher and Joseph Dudley. His government was arbitrary and despotic. The people chafed under it until they became desperate. In the spring of 1689 a rumor was spread among them that the governor's guards were to be let loose on Boston. This produced an explosion, and early in the morning of April 8, the popu-

* Williamson.

lace rose in a mass, seized the governor and thirty of his more obnoxious partizans, and confined them, some of them twenty weeks. Andros surrendered the keys, but not without some reluctance.

As soon as Andros was deposed, a general convention was held at Boston, which appointed a council of safety, consisting of Danforth, Bradstreet, and thirty-four others. In about thirty days after this the joyful news arrived, not, however, unexpected, that James had abdicated, and that William and Mary had ascended the throne. The council recommended that delegates be chosen by towns, and, accordingly, fifty-four towns were represented at Boston, May 22d, who voted "to resume the government according to charter rights," and they appointed Bradstreet governor, and Danforth lieutenant governor.

Danforth had presided over Maine as a province, assisted by *Charles Frost*, Francis Hooke, and others, for the term of six years. But Maine, like Massachusetts, was involved in the overturning and arbitrary measures of Dudley and Andros, under whose administration courts were held at York by William Stoughton, John Usher, and others. The council of safety now reinstated the former governor and council of Maine, namely, Danforth, *Frost*, Hooke, and others. They also appointed and "commissioned *Charles Frost* to command the western regiment, and Edward Tyng the eastern regiment of Maine."

The province was soon after reannexed as a constituent part of Massachusetts, and remained so for more than a century. *Charles Frost* was appointed in 1693 one of the three councillors from Maine, which office he held till his death, in 1697.

It may serve to illustrate the customs of early times in respect to drinking, to insert an ordinance of the court in 1690, soon after Danforth was deposed, and to relieve the fatiguing detail of dates and events which we have now passed through. "July 15, 1690. In the court of sessions of the peace for the Province of Maine, held at York before Major John Davis, Deputy president, *Major Charles Frost*, Captain Francis Hooke, and John Wincoln, Justices. Whereas, there is great complaint made of several abuses taken notice of in ordinaries, by excessive drinking of rum, flip, and other strong liquor, the ill consequences of which are seen in the misbehavior of several persons in the presence of authority; for the preventing of the like in future it is therefore ordered, that if any ordinary or tavern keeper should sell any rum, flip, or other strong drink, to an inhabitant of the town, except in case of sickness or necessity, or more than one gill to a stranger, he should forfeit his licence."*

The foregoing sketch of the political history of the western part of Maine during Major Frost's life, and of the services he rendered in various responsible offices, exhibits clearly the high estimation in which he was held by his fellow citizens and the government. His military services remain to be noticed. Trained from childhood to agricultural employments and to the still more invigorating toils of the hunter, and removed from the enervating influences of polished life, he acquired the stamina of body and mind which fitted him for the arduous and perilous duties of savage warfare. The howling of wolves around his father's cabin was his evening entertainment, and, from the neighboring hill-top, his morning vision could survey the curling smoke arising from numerous Indian villages on the tributary streams of the Pascataqua. The savage yell and war whoop awakened no fearful throbbings in his youthful heart, but rather served to enkindle a

* Collections of the Maine Historical Society.

zeal for daring and heroic achievements. He early evinced a fondness for military exercises and parade, and being enrolled as a soldier at sixteen, he gradually rose, through successive grades, to be commander-in-chief of the militia of Maine.

His early fondness for the use of firearms led him, at the age of fourteen, to an accidental deed which occasioned great sorrow to himself and others. He unintentionally killed a comrade, named Warwick Heard. He submitted himself at once for trial by a jury, which took place at Wells, July 6, 1646. The jury were ordered by the court to inquire whether the killing was from malice, or accidental, or a misadventure. They reported that "they find that Charles Frost did kill Warwick Heard by misadventure, and acquit him by proclamation."

It was the practice of the militia of Maine to train in companies six times a year, and to have general musters once in two years. The county records contain the following account of a sentence passed upon a soldier in 1674 by the court, which may interest the reader. "Richard Gibson complained of for his dangerous and mutinous conduct towards his commander Captain Charles Frost, which misbehaviour appearing in court, the court order as follows, 1. that the said Gibson, for striking Captain Frost at the head of his company, is appointed to receive, by John Parker senior, twenty-five stripes on the bare skin, which were this day given him in presence of the court. And further, considering the insolence of the said Gibson's behaviour in the premises, it is further ordered that Captain Frost shall have and is empowered by warrant, to call before him the said Richard Gibson, the next training day at Kittery, and whither he is to order him to be laid neck and heels together at the head of his company for the time of two hours, or to ride the wooden horse at the head of the company, which of these punishments Captain Frost shall see meet to appoint; and, for the said Gibson's multiplying of oaths, he is fined 20 shillings; and, for being drunk is fined 10 shillings, and to pay all charges of court, and to stand committed until the sentence be performed; and further, the said Gibson is required to give bonds for his good behaviour of £20. that the said Gibson shall be of good behaviour towards all persons, and more especially towards Captain Frost, until the next county court, and that the said Gibson shall appear at Kittery, when required by Captain Frost, there to perform the order of court, and further that he pay to the county treasurer 82 shillings. James Warren, as abettor, is sentenced to ride the wooden horse."*

Military discipline was practised among the settlers, in anticipation of a war on the seaboard, rather than against savages from the interior. Perfect peace had existed with these during the first forty years of the settlement, with the exception of a short conflict with the Pequods, in the year 1636, in which the people of Maine scarcely participated. But the time was arriving when a savage war was suddenly to break out in every part of New England. Its approach was foreseen and predicted by the Indian Sagamore Knowles, who resided at Quampegan, in South Berwick, and was Sachem or governor of the tribe that previously occupied the shores of the Pascataqua. "In 1670, when Knowles was bed rid of sickness and age, he complained of the great neglect with which the English treated him. At length he sent a message to some of the principal men of Kittery to visit him. 'Being loaded with years,' as he told them, 'I had expected a visit in my infirmities, especially from those who are now tenants on the land of my fathers. Though all these plantations are of right my children's, I am forced, in this

* York County Records.

age of evils, humbly to request a few acres of land to be marked out for them, and recorded as a public act in the town books, so that when I am gone they may not be perishing beggars in the pleasant places of their birth. For I know that a great war will shortly break out between the white men and Indians over the whole country. At first the Indians will kill many and prevail, but after three years they will be great sufferers, and finally be rooted out and destroyed.' This was sworn to by Major Richard Waldron, Captain Charles Frost, and Rev. Joshua Moody, who were present and heard it."

The war of King Phillip began in 1675, five years after the date of Frost's commission as captain, and of Roger Plaisted's as his lieutenant. The former had immediate charge of the garrisons at Sturgeon Creek, (Elliot,) where he resided, and the latter of Salmon Falls and Quampegan. The first alarm of Phillip's war was in June, 1676, and spread like wildfire. In twenty days the flame broke out on the Kennebeck river. Depredations and murders were committed by numerous parties of savages in quick succession upon the scattered settlements. In September a party approached Durham, near Dover, killed two and took captive two. A few days after they attacked the house of one Tozier, at Newichewannick, (South Berwick) which contained fifteen women and children, all of whom, with the exception of two children, were saved by the intrepidity of a girl of eighteen. On seeing the Indians approach the house, she shut the door and braced herself against it till the others escaped to the next house, which was better secured. The Indians chopped the door down with hatchets, and knocking her down, left her for dead; but she recovered. They murdered several other persons, and burnt houses. The inhabitants were panic struck and fled to the garrisons, where they lived in constant fear of an attack.

On the 16th of October, 1675, they made an onset upon Salmon Falls. Lieutenant Plaisted sent out a party of seven from his garrison to reconnoitre. They fell into an ambush and three were killed, the rest retreated. The next day, Plaisted, venturing out with his team to bring in the dead for burial, was waylaid and fell into another ambush. He and his son were killed, and another son mortally wounded. In the midst of the fight he despatched messengers to his superior officers, Major Waldron of Dover, and Captain Frost, imploring their aid and their prayers, but their aid came too late.* The gallantry of Plaisted arrested the progress of the Indians for a time, and Captain Frost had an opportunity to bury the dead unmolested.

But the Indians soon returned, and, destroying other lives and dwellings, they proceeded to Sturgeon Creek and burnt a house and killed two men. The house of Captain Frost being a little remote from neighbors and unfortified, was marked out by them for destruction. "He was a short dis-

* The following letter is preserved in Hubbard's most valuable History of the Indian Wars, Part ii. p. 23, Boston edition, 4to, 1677.

"*Salmon Falls October* 16. 1675. *Mr. Richard Waldern and Lieut. Coffin*, these are to inform you, that just now the Indians are *engaging us* with at least *one hundred men*, And have *slain four of our men* already, *Richard Tozer*, *James Barny*, *Isaack Bottes*, *and Tozers Son*, and burnt *Benoni Hodsdan's house; Sir*. if ever you have any love for us, and the Country, now show *your self* with men to *help us*, or else we are all in *great danger to be slain*, unless *our God wonderfully appear for our Deliverance. They that cannot fight, let them pray;* Not else, but I Rest, Yours to serve you

Signed by *Roger Plaisted,*
George Broughton."

For more full accounts of these times of terror the reader is referred to the author above cited, to Belknap's "New Hampshire," and Williamson's "Maine" — Ed.

tance from it when attacked, and narrowly escaped the effect of ten shots aimed at him. There were only three boys with him in the house," (probably his sons) "yet he had the forethought and prudence to give out audible words of command, as if a body of Indians was with him — load quick! fire there! that's well! brave men! — a stratagem which saved themselves and the house."*

The Indians proceeded down the shore of the Pascataqua, and thence eastward through York, burning houses and killing people wherever they found them unguarded, so that in the short period of three months, eighty lives were taken, a great many houses plundered and burnt, and animals killed.

Frost wrote to his commander, Major Waldron, at Dover, for permission to garrison his house, which he was directed to do, and to keep a constant guard and watch.

As the winter approached, the Indians found themselves destitute of ammunition and provisions and in danger of starvation. All the neighboring Sagamores, from Dover to Casco, sued for peace, which, being granted by Waldron, they were quiet for seven months, till August, 1676, in which month the war at the west terminated by the death of King Phillip. Some of his adherents fled from the conquered tribe to the eastward, and mixed with their brethren of Penacook, (Concord, N. H.,) Ossipee, Pickwacket, (Fryeburg,) and Saco. Others mixed with the Kennebeck and Amoriscogen tribes, which were ravaging all the eastern settlements of Maine.

Waldron and Frost received orders this same month to kill and destroy all hostile Indians, and two companies, commanded by Captains Hawthorn and Sill, were sent from Boston to Maine with like orders. On their way thither they came to Dover, September 6th, 1676, where four hundred mixed Indians were assembled at the garrison of Major Waldron, with whom they had made peace, and whom they considered their friend and father. Hawthorn and Sill were for attacking them at once, but Waldron objected to it, and contrived to take them by stratagem. He proposed to the Indians to have a sham-fight, and, on the following day, summoned his men with Captain Frost and his men, who were at Pascataqua. They, in conjunction, formed one party, and the Indians another. Having diverted them a while in this manner with manœuvres, and induced the Indians to fire the first volley, they surrounded and seized the whole of them with peculiar dexterity, excepting two or three, before they could form a suspicion of what they intended, and disarmed them without the loss of a man on either side. They then separated those known to be friendly, and dismissed them. The strangers from the south and west, amounting to three hundred, were sent to Boston to be dealt with judicially, seven or eight of whom being known to have killed Englishmen, were hanged; the remainder were sold into foreign slavery. Public opinion has ever been divided as to the propriety of the whole affair. Be that as it may, the two leading officers concerned in it, Waldron and Frost, after a lapse of many years, paid the forfeit of their lives at the hands of savages, who always spoke of the stratagem as a base yankee trick.†

Two days after this surprisal the forces proceeded eastward, but they found the settlements all deserted or destroyed, and they soon returned and made an excursion to Ossipy ponds, which proved alike fruitless.

After a time an Indian named Mogg came in and proposed peace; but it was soon violated, and no alternative was left but to renew hostilities.

* Williamson's History of Maine.

† Belknap.

Accordingly in February following, 1677, Waldron and Frost, with one hundred and fifty men, sailed from Boston eastward. Public prayers were offered on the day of their departure. They landed at Brunswick, where they held a parley with Indians, who promised to bring in captives that afternoon. But no more was heard of them till the next day, when there was seen a flotilla of canoes approaching, who menaced a scouting party sent towards the place of landing. But Captain Frost attacked them from an unexpected quarter, killing and wounding several. This led to another parley, which resulted in the recovery of none of the promised captives. They then sailed to the mouth of the Kennebeck, and held a parley with an assemblage of Indians on shore. "It was mutually agreed to lay aside arms, and to negotiate for the ransom of prisoners. The Indians demanded twelve beaver skins for each, with some good liquor, but only three captives could be obtained. Another parley was proposed, when Waldron, *Frost*, and three others landed under a mutual promise that no weapons should be worn on either side. But Waldron espied the point of a lance under a board, and searching further, found other weapons, and taking and brandishing one towards them exclaimed, *Perfidious wretches!* you intended to get our goods and then kill us, did you? They were thunder struck. Yet one more daring than the rest seized the weapon and strove to wrest it from Waldron's hand. A tumult ensued, in which his life was much endangered. Captain Frost laid hold of Megunnaway, one of the barbarous murderers of Thomas Bracket and neighbors, and dragged him into his vessel. Meanwhile an athletic squaw caught up a bundle of guns and ran for the woods. At that instant a reinforcement arrived from the vessels, when the Indians scattered in all directions, pursued by the soldiers. In this affray Sagamore Maltahouse and an old powow and five other Indians were killed, five were capsized in a canoe and drowned, and five others were captured. One thousand pounds of beef were taken, and some other booty. Megunnaway, grown hoary in crimes, was shot."*

They left a garrison of forty men near the mouth of the Kennebeck, under Captain Davis, and returned to Boston, March 11, without the loss of a man.

A few days after they sailed from the Kennebeck, eleven of the forty men they left there were cut off in an ambush, and the others were ordered to other forts at Casco and Saco. Seventy men were now ordered eastward from Pascataqua, under Captain Swaine, to afford relief. On the 7th of April, seven men were killed in the fields near York, and six in Wells, three at Black Point, and in May, another attack was made on York, in which four were killed and two taken prisoners. In June, (1677,) two hundred and forty men were sent to Black Point, under Major Swett, sixty of whom, with their commander, fell in an encounter with the enemy. The Indians next tried their fortune upon fishing vessels along the shore, between Wells and Casco, (Portland,) and succeeded in capturing twenty. During all this spring and summer Captain Frost was constantly engaged in superintending the garrisons of the county of York.

In April he received the following, from General Dennison, the commander-in-chief.

To Captain Charles Frost —

You are hereby authorised to take under your command and conduct fifty foot soldiers herewith sent you of the county of Essex and Norfold — commanding them to obey you as their captain, whom you are to lead and conduct against the common Enemy now in-

* Williamson's History of Maine.

festing Yorkshire, whom you are with all diligence to pursue and destroy as also to succor and assist the English of Wells, York Neechiwannick or elsewhere, as you shall have opportunity. And the said soldiers are hereby required to attend your orders and commands for the prosecution of the enemy as abovesaid, according to the rules and orders of military discipline, and you are to attend such orders & instructions as from time to time you shall receive from myself or other superior authority and for so doing this shall be your warrant.

Dated April 12 1677. Daniel Dennison Major General.

Instructions accompanying the above are contained in page 23 of the January number of this volume, being paper No. II.

Such were the calamities and distresses in the spring and summer of 1677, when an unexpected relief came, by the arrival of a force at Kennebeck, sent by Sir Edmond Andros, from New York, acting under a claim to the territory from the Duke of York. Finding the Indians pacific, the commander obtained the release of fifteen captives and some vessels. During the autumn and winter following, no further ravages were committed. In the spring (April) a treaty was negotiated by Major Shapleigh, (who succeeded Major Frost as commander,) at Portsmouth, in which it was stipulated that all captives should be released without ransom; former inhabitants to return to their homes and live unmolested, but were to pay a peck of corn yearly, each family. Thus ended King Phillip's war in Maine; a war in which two hundred and sixty were killed or taken captive east of the Pascataqua, a vast number of houses burnt, animals slaughtered, and property plundered.

The next year, 1678, Charles Frost, with two others, represented Maine in the general court, from which time he continued in the office and in attending to his private affairs, until he was appointed by the governor and council of Massachusetts one of the eight members of the provincial council of Maine, to act under Gorges's charter, which Massachusetts had assumed. The council consisted of Bryant Pendleton, Charles Frost, Francis Hooke, John Davis, Samuel Wheelwright, Edward Tyng, and John Wincoln.

The arrival of Dudley and Andros, in 1688, as Presidents of New England, superseded the provincial government of Maine, which had lasted six years. Danforth and his council were proscribed, and very little is heard of Frost until Andros was overthrown, April 18th, 1689, after a reign of one or two years. It was during the last year of this reign, 1689, that another Indian war broke out, which went by the name of King William's war, and lasted ten years. No sooner was Andros deposed than the provincial government of Maine, consisting of Danforth, Frost, and others, who had been proscribed by Andros, were reinstated, and the times being perilous as in the former war, led to the appointment of *Charles Frost* as commander of the military forces in Maine.

The war of King William began in August, 1688, in North Yarmouth and Kennebeck. In April following, Dover was taken by stratagem and mostly destroyed. Major Waldron was inhumanly tortured in a savage manner. Twenty-three persons were killed and twenty-nine carried into captivity. The seizure of four hundred Indians in that place "more than twelve years before was a transaction never to be forgotten, never to be forgiven by savages." Some of those sold in Boston as slaves and sent into distant lands had probably returned, and were bent on revenge. It was unfortunate for Major Frost that he was obliged to aid Waldron in the capture of the four hundred, as it cost him his life ere the present war terminated.

Being in command of the western regiment, and having the forts and garrisons under his special care, Frost was not ordered eastward, that section of Maine being placed under the more immediate command of Dudley Tyng. Major Swaine was sent, with six hundred militia, to the eastward, accompanied by Colonel Church, who had signalized himself in King Phillip's war at the west. He was appointed by Andros to lead the forces against the Indians at Brunswick and Kennebeck, and was continued in the same service after Andros was deposed. But Church's success in his five eastern expeditions fell short of public expectation.

Major Frost's presence was greatly needed at the western part of Maine. Only a few days before the date of his commission, August, 1689, the Indians entered at Salmon Falls, (Berwick) under the command of Hartel, a Frenchman, with a force of Indians and French, killed thirty-four brave men and carried away captive fifty-four persons, mostly women and children, and plundered and burnt the houses and mills. In the following spring they revisited Brunswick and Dover, killing and destroying what was left, and extending their ravages to Sturgeon Creek, where Frost resided, and to many places on the opposite shore of the Pascataqua.

When Colonel Church left Boston for Casco, with two hundred and fifty men, to join Colonel Swaine, he took with him a mandatory letter to the military commanders in Maine, from President Danforth, (then in Boston, as president of the board of commissioners of the united colonies,) requiring them to supply him with men and means, which Major Frost promptly obeyed; and the following May, 1690, he received orders to detach one hundred men for Port Royal, near Portland, to serve under Captain Willard, many of whom were drawn into an ambush and slain by savages. It would seem, in fact, that Major Frost, residing as he did in the town nearest to Boston, was employed as a sort of general agent, or secretary of war for the province of Maine, all orders being transmitted through him. The following is his commission as commander of the Maine forces, which he continued to hold till his death.

The President of the Province of Mayne in New England.
To Major Charles Frost.

Whereas you are appointed Sergt. Major of the military fforces in the Province. These are in their Majesties names to authorise and require you to take into your care and conduct the said military forces, and diligently to intend that service as Sergent Major, by Governing and exercising the military forces of said Province as the Law directeth. Commanding the Militia of said Province that they observe and obey all such orders and directions as from time to time you shall receive from the president or other superior authority.

In Testimony whereof I have hereunto put my hand and seal the 23d day of August in the year 1689, Annoque R. R. et Regina Willielmi et Mariæ Anglica primo.

Thomas Danforth President.

Particular instructions accompanying the above are published in the January number, page 24, paper No. IV.

By constant vigilance on the part of Major Frost, the east shore of the Pascataqua was preserved from savage incursions. His soldiers were constantly on the alert, scouting about the borders of the towns. The eastern towns were deserted. Some removed to Salem, others to the fort at Wells, but a great many were butchered or carried into captivity, so that before the war ended, the number killed eastward of Pascataqua amounted to four hundred and fifty, and two hundred and fifty were made captives. All the towns and settlements except Wells and Pascataqua were overrun, the former commanded by Major Converse, and the latter by Major Frost.

In 1693 the war raged with increased barbarity. Spies were usually sent by the Indians to reconnoitre, before the enemy approached places intended for destruction, who lurked about the woods, and required a constant ward and watch. The following letter to Lieutenant Hill gives an idea of the vigilance and circumspection necessary to be observed in these trying times.

April: 2: 1693

Leiut Hill

Last night a Litle after sun sett Noah Emory was coming from Kittery to Sturgion Creke & by the waie sid herd som crackling of stickes: & herd a man whissell: upon which he stopt under a bush: and went an other waie: John Smith coming after him saw a man nere Sturgion Creke bridge who ran a waie down the creke: Smith being on horse back came to my Garison — this morning I sent out som men who saw the Indian track at the same place where Noah Emerey herd him whissell — Kepe out scouts about the borders of the towne: I will send out from hence: all or souldiers at the banke are drawen of those yt belong to you are sent up: dispose of them to such garisons at present as you thinke fitt: I have given two of them liberty to goe home for a few dayes:

In hast I Remaine yor: Lo: freind
Charles Ffrost major

[Superscribed]
Ffor Leiut John Hill
At Newitchawoneck
Hast Post Hast

This Lieutenant Hill was soon after stationed at Fort Mary, in Saco, as commander. The letter designated as No. X., on p. 164 of the April number, was addressed to him while there, and was written soon after the cowardly surrender of Fort Pemaquid, on the Kennebeck, and when the combined force of French and Indians had devastated the whole province of Maine, with the exception of Wells, York, and Pascataqua, and when it was feared by the government in Boston that even these would be destroyed by a merciless foe.

The fort at Saco was not surrendered by Hill, although all the inhabitants of the town were driven away or killed, and many of Hill's soldiers were waylaid and murdered while venturing out of the fort.

In June following a party of Indians placed themselves near the town of Exeter, and would have destroyed it but for the firing of a gun by some one who wished to frighten some women and children who had gone out to gather strawberries. It however alarmed and brought together the people, with arms. The Indians, supposing they were discovered, after killing one and taking another, made a hasty retreat and were seen no more until the 4th of July, when they waylaid Captain Frost.

It would require a volume to describe the many ambuscades, encounters, murders, conflagrations, and captivities that occurred during the ten years' war of King William, and it would exceed our limits even to name them in the brief manner we have those in King Phillip's war, which lasted only three or four years. Major Frost was constantly and actively engaged in military service till 1693, when he was chosen one of the governor's council. After this he was employed between sessions in guarding the forts and garrisons about Kittery, and in ordering out scouts and in transmitting the orders of government to the various military stations throughout the province. But the hour was approaching when his own life was to be offered a sacrifice to appease the long stifled and festering revenge of merciless savages, for aiding in the Dover stratagem. He was always attentive to his duties as a Christian professor, as well as those of the soldier and statesman, and was constant in his attendance on public worship when other duties permitted. On Sabbath morning, July 4, 1697, he expressed an unusually strong desire to go with his family to his wonted place of worship at Newichewannick, a distance of five miles. His wife and two sons, Charles and John, with some friends, accompanied him. On their return homeward, and within a mile of his dwelling, a volley of musketry was suddenly discharged at them, which brought several of them to the ground. It was the work of a party of Indians hid by the wayside under a large log, in which they had stuck a row of green boughs. The sons had passed ahead and escaped.

Several versions are given by historians of this closing scene in Major Frost's life. One states that the Major, his wife, and two footmen were killed; another that nearly the whole party were killed; and another that three were killed and several wounded. A recent discovery of a letter written by a relative, Lieutenant Storer, immediately after the funeral, which he attended, gives a particular account of the whole tragedy, which can be relied on. It was written to Major Frost's son-in-law, Capt. Hill, who commanded the fort at Saco, and was found in an old chest of papers that had lain seventy years in a garret in South Berwick. It states that the Major, John Heard's wife, and Danes Downing were killed, and John Heard wounded, and they next day killed the messengers who were sent to Wells.*

Such was the death of Major Charles Frost, after a career of distinguished activity and usefulness, both civil and military. The incidents of his life are gathered from scanty records, authentic traditions, and from descriptions of scenes and events in history, in which he is casually mentioned as having participated. To correct and arrange these materials in chronological order, after a lapse of nearly two centuries, was a laborious undertaking; and to present them free from errors, both of omission and commission, is neither pretended nor practicable. We have done the best our limited means would permit — to relate facts, in order to rescue from oblivion the name of a prominent pioneer of the wilderness, whose memory deserves the veneration of his numerous descendants.

It remains to speak of his family and descendants. He married, at the age of forty-four, Mary, daughter of Joseph Bolles of Wells, who survived him seven years, and bore him three sons and six daughters. He followed the example of his father in naming his sons Charles, John, and Nicholas. His daughters, named Sarah, Abigail, Mehitable, Lydia, Mary, and Elizabeth, all settled and were prosperous in life.

Charles, the oldest son, married Sarah Wainwright, and had nine children. By a second wife, who was Jane E. Pepperrell, widow of Sir William's brother Andrew, he had one child. He was deacon of a church, Register and Judge of Probate, and commander of a regiment of militia. He resided on the homestead of his father, Major Frost, whose remains repose in the rear of his house, and the premises continue still in possession of the name.

Hon. John Frost, second son of Major Charles, married Mary, sister of Sir William Pepperrell, and had sixteen children. He died 1732. She married again, the Rev. Dr. Colman of Boston, and afterwards Judge Prescott of Danvers. Mr. Frost commanded a British ship of war, afterwards became a merchant at Newcastle, and was in political life, being one of the governor's council. His son John was Register of Deeds for York county, (Me.) and the office continued in the family nearly fifty years. He was commissary in the Revolutionary War, during which no less than four or five of his family held offices on land and sea, among whom was his son John, usually called Brigadier, who was a colonel in the army, and who left a numerous family, John Frost, LL. D., of Philadelphia, being a grandson. Two other sons of Hon. John Frost (William and Joseph) were merchants at New Castle. Their descendants in Portsmouth and elsewhere are highly respectable. Another son, named George, settled in Durham, and was a judge and member of Congress. Another, named Charles, was a prominent man in Portland; died while a representative. One daughter, Sarah, mar-

* See page 165, of the last number.

ried Rev. John Blunt of New Castle, and after his decease, Major John Hill of South Berwick, a judge of the court and member of the governor's council.

The descendants of the Rev. John Blunt are numerous; many of them reside in Portsmouth. One branch, consisting of Joseph and Nathaniel, lawyers, and Edmond and George, merchants, resides in New York. A daughter of Rev. John, named Abigail, married William Parsons, Esq., of Alfred, whose youngest son prepared this account of the Frosts.

Nicholas Frost, the youngest son of Major Charles, died early in life and left a widow, but no children.

Major Charles Frost left a large estate by will to his widow and children, dated 1690.

WOBURN BURYING-GROUND.

[Communicated by Mr. N. Wyman, Jr.—Continued from p. 148.]

Winn	Timothy	Jan 5 1752 65y
Wyman	Susanna wid. of Ensign Samuel	Nov 24 1752 65
Boardman	Martha wid. of Andrew, of Boston,	Aug 25 1752 54
Richardson	Deac. Stephen	Feb 4 1752 79
"	Asa	Mar 17 1752 39
Thompson	Jonathan, of Medford,	June 9 1752 62
Carter	Thomas	Mar 17 1753 66
Holding	John, Jr.,	Jan 23 1753 21y 28 days
Pierce	Mary w. of Josiah, Jr.,	Nov 11 1753 36
"	Mary d. of Josiah & Mary	Dec 28 1753 2m 2d
Snow	Mary, d. of Isaac & Phebe	Dec 8 1753 7y
Brooks	Benjamin s. of Benjamin & Susanna	May 17 1753 3y
Wyman	Jesse	Nov 2 1754 23y 6m
Thompson	Hannah	June 16 1754 37y
Richardson	Sussanna w. of Elazer	Oct 7 1754 39y
Snow	Zachariah s. of Timothy & Lydia	Sept 21 1754 36y
Richardson	Samuel	Sept 3 1754 84y
Thompson	Benjamin	Nov 7 1755 25
Pierce	Hannah d. of Josiah & Hannah	Oct 23 1755 27
Brooks	Elisalett d. of Nathan & Elisalett	Feb 12 1755 8 mos
"	" " "	June 8 1755 10 weeks
Pool	Jonathan, Esq.,	Feb 8 1755 63
Richardson	Eleazer	Apr 17 1755 38
Thompson	Mary w. of Ebenezer	Mar 11 1755 72y
Tyng	Judeth wid. of Col. Jonathan, formerly wife to the Rev. Jabez Fox,	June 5 1756 99y
	"A woman of most exalted vertue & Piety, Rich in Grace & Ripe for Glory."	
Richardson	Esther d. of Noah & Phebe	Mar 15 1756 17y
"	Noah	June 23 1756 54y
Hartwel	Ruhamah wid. of Joseph	July 11 1756 78y
Reed	Deac. George	Jan 20 1756 96y
Symmes	Ruth w. of William	Mar 16 1758 ——
Brooks	Nathan	Jan 26 1758 30y
Richardson	Jonathan	July 16 1759 63y
Thompson	Esther w. of Abijah "died of Small pox,"	Jan 3 1761 21

"Oh, now behold yᵉ blooming young & fair
Se your sad picture & your peried here,
How soon your beauties vanish from your forme
Fall into dust & mingle with yᵉ wormes."

Walker	Esther w. of Edward	Sept 23 1761 65y
Giles	John	Jan 20 1761 70y
Richardson	Noah	Jan 6 1761 33y
"	Lucy d. of Noah & Phebe	July 21 1761 24
"	Doctʳ. Edmund	May 30 1761 29

"Behold all ye that do pass by,
As you are now, so once was I,
And as you see that here I be,
Prepare for death & follow me."

Pierce	Hannah d. of Josiah & Hannah	Dec 24 1762 6ᵗʰ y
Symmes	Abigail w. of John	Mar 28 1762 28y
Gardner	Henry	Dec 16 1763 66y
Kendall	Lieut. Samuel	Dec 13 1764 83y
Symmes	William	May 24 1764 86
Brooks	Betty w. of Josiah	July 3 1764 20y
Snow	Lydia Wid. of Timothy	Apr 27 1764 81y
Richardson	Zebidiah s. of Zebidiah & Esther	Jan 4 1764 5 mo
Converse	Ebenezer	Sept 6 1765 56y
Eames	Judeth w. of Deac. Samuel	Jan 10 1766 71y
Winn	Sarah w. of Timothy	Jan 17 1767 25y
Richardson	Sarah d. of Noah & Phebe	Dec 9 1767 22y
Fowle	Sussanna wid. to Lieut. Samuel	Sept 21 1768 35y
Richardson	Abigail d. of Noah & Phebe	July 23 1768 26y
Wyman	Huldah w. of Nathan	May 28 1768 68y
Brooks	Isaac	Mar 23 1768 38y
Richardson	Ichabod	May 12 1768 63y
Kendall	Samuel s. of Obidiah & Elisalett	Feb 22 1768 4ᵈ
Carter	Margaret w. of Capt. Samuel	Sept 27 1769 71y
Brooks	Benjamin	Jan 6ᵗʰ 1769 52y

"A loving husband to his wife,
A Tender Parent, two,
Greatly lamented was his death
By friend & kindred two,
The Lord was Pleased to Coll him home,
And by a suding blow,
'Twas by the falling of a tree
To His Long Home did go,
And now he slumbers in the Dust,
And will not rise before
The Lord the Judge Descends, from Heaven
And time shall be no more."

Skinner	Sussanna w. of Abraham	Jan 8 1769 23y

"Behold all ye that do pass by me
In silence hear I ly
And as you see that hear I be,
So certain yu must dy,
This call then heare for death prepare,
Now in your Youthful day.
the Lord doeth call upon you all
How dangres is delay."

Richardson	Jeduthan d. of Thoˢ & Mary	Feb 29 1769 26 days

Carter Lieut. Jabez July 10 1771 71y
Fox Abigail w. of William, & d. of Deac. Sam[l]. Wyman, Oct 26 1771 28y

"Ah behold how dos die
being young and full in bloom,
another dis being very old,
whom age commands to remine home,
O cruel death.
Ah what awaits thy rage.
thou shoest respect, to
vertue, now to age."

Richardson Rebeckah w. to Thomas Apr 11 1771 79y
Wyman Abigail w. of Deac. Samuel Aug 31 1772 53

"Here ye wife of my Youth ye delight
of my eyes."

Carter Abigail wid. of Lieut. Jabez Feb 3 1772 73y
Richardson Thomas June 13 1773 67y
Wyman Nathan Feb 4 1773 78y

"He was a kind husband, A Tender Parent,
A Good master, a Faithful Friend.
A Generous neighbour charitable to
the Poor, Prudent & diligent in his worldly
affairs, a premoter of peace in the Church
& State, upright & honest in his dealings
with man, constant senciere & devoted in the
Worship of God, useful in life peaceful &
happy in death."

Eames Nathaniel, s. of Jacob & Racheal July 21 1773 21st
Wyman Elisalett w. of Benjamin July 6 1773 30y
" Capt. Benjamin May 26 1774 68y
Brooks Jemima w. of Ebenezer Nov 5 1774 57y
Richardson Thomas Jan 12 1774 93y
Brooks Nathan (only son) of Nathan & Elisalett Apr 24 1774 20y

"As man perhaps the moment of his birth
Recieves the lurking principle of death,
The Young desees that must subdue at length
Grows with his growth & strengthens with his
strength."

Eames Deac. Samuel Jan 20 1775 84y
Thompson Daniel (slain at Concord Battle) Apr 19 1775 40y

"Here Passenger confined, reduced to dust,
Lies what was once Religious, wise & Just,
The cause he engaged did animate him high,
Namely Religion & dear Liberty,
Steady & warm in Liberties defence,
True to his Country loyal to his Prince,
Though in his breast a thirst for glory fired,
Couragous in his Countrys' cause expired.
Although hes gone his name embalmed shall be.
And had in everlasting Memory."

Carter Sibyl d. of Jonathan & Sibyl Aug 27 1775 2y 6m
Snow Timothy Sept 19 1775 69y
Carter Joseph Johnson, s. of Jonathan & Sibyl Sept 15 1775 7 mos
Richardson Deac. Nathan Oct 21 1775 74y

[To be continued.]

ABSTRACTS OF THE EARLIEST WILLS UPON RECORD IN THE COUNTY OF SUFFOLK, MS.

[Continued from page 180.]

THOMAS RUGGLES.

The 9 (9) 1644.

I *Thomas Ruggles* of Roxbury. To Sonne *Iohn* my lott w[ch] lyeth behind the great pound contains my sixteene Acres more or lesse. To sonne *Samuell* my lott butting vppon the left of *Philip Eliot* on the east, & one *A[r]thur Ga[r]is* north—7 A[c]res more or lesse. Also my land at Dedham, containing 12 Acres more or lesse. To dau. *Sarah* three pound in such pay as my wife can best spare, to be paid her at the age of one & twenty yeere. At decease of wife effects to be divided betweene my 3 children.

Witnesses THOMAS RUGGLES.
Phill: Eliot
John Ruggles
Testyfied before
the Court
Increase Nowell.

IOHN GRAVE.

November (1) 1644.

John Grave late of Roxbury. Vnto sonne *John* the ten Acre lott containing six Acres more or lesse. Also my two Oxen & the vse of halfe the barne during the time of his mothers life & then the barne to be divided as his mothers land is, one halfe vnto him. Also my best suite & the bed that he lyeth vppon. *John* shall pay vnto dau. *Mary* sixe pounds at the age of twenty-one years—but in case she dye before, *John* to pay his brother *Samuell* & *Jonathan* fourty shillings apiece.

Also vnto sonne *Samuell* my lot called the four acre lott, the lott of goodman *Lewis* between the land of *Robert Seaver* & the land of goodman *Lewis*, vnto him, &c.

vnto *Jonathan* my son that lott lying on the great hill of 5 Acres—if my two frends, *Phillip Eliot* & *Will[m]* *Heath* exchange it for land more convenient & vsefull for my son, I give them full power so to doe.

Also my lot of Co̅mon w[ch] was last divided vnto me by the towne, I give to my foresaid three sonns equally to be divided—wife to haue free liberty to fetch fyre wood.

To dau. *Mary* the bed & all that belongeth thereto w[ch] her grandmother now lyeth vppon.

If wife liue fyve years after the death of my mother, then she shall pay vnto my daughter *Hanna* six pound—if she dye before, then *Iohn* & *Samuell* & *Jonathan* to pay vnto her fyve pound.

Phillip Eliot.
Testifyed before the Court *William Heath.*
Increase Nowell sec[r].

IOHN GRAVE.

26 (9) 1645.

John Grave late of Roxbury. My land to be sould.—Vnto my brother *Samuell* Sixe pound, to brother *Jonathan* four pounds.—to sister *Sarah* three pound — to my sister *Hanna* three pound — to sister *Marah* sixe pound w[ch] I was to giue vnto her by my ffathers will — to be paid her at the age of one & twenty — vnto *Georg Brand* what he doth owe vnto mee — vnto my Mother all my wearing apparell — vnto *Phillip Eliot* what he doth owe mee, whom I doe make mine Executor. What is left to be divided between my Executor & my mother. What I was to haue by my ffathers will, after the death of my mother my two brethren, *Samuell* & *Jonathan* shall enjoy it equally. They to pay sister *Sarah* five pound, & to sister *Marah* three pound, & to sister *Hanna* three pound. The testimonies of *Robert Pepper, Widdowe Grave* & *John Hansett.* See in the book of affidavits,* fol. 43.

John Oliver.

25 (6) 1641.

This is my last will except any befoure beareing date after it concerning the disposall of estate w[ch] the Lord hath carved out vnto mee in this world, those many ingagements that lye vppon mee being by the good hand of God discharged, w[ch] may be done ptly by those ingagements whereby others stand indebted vnto mee, as also by the sale of my house at Boston & of my bookes & geometricall instruments, the remaining pt being divided into three equall parts at the discretion of my deere & reverend ffathers M[r] *Tho: Oliver* M[r] *Iohn Newgate*, one third vnto my deare & faithful yoake fellowe, the other two thirds vnto my deare children at theire (viz[t] my ffat:) discretion, and whereas my ffather M[r] *Thomas Oliver* hath according to his faithfull care, & prudence promised mee that if I should dye before him, I should have power by my will to dispose of such part of his estate, as should have fallen vnto me if I had survived, my will is that it be in like manner divided & disposed of as my owne estate. If my deare brother *James Oliver* surviue me I desire him to discharge my many ingagements wth that part of my estate foremencioned for that end. all w[ch] promises I doe in hast confirme by my own hand witnes my hand

John Oliver.

Deposed by *James Johnson*
& *James Oliver* the 11 (7) 1647 before
the court by me
Increase Nowell, Sec.

William Brinsmeade.

10 (10) 1647.

This testifyeth that I *W[m]* *Brinsmead* being in health (this 10th of the 10th month 1647) do make & ordaine that my estate be divided into fyve equal parts — two of these fyve I giue vnto *W[m]* my sonne, the other three parts I giue to my three children *Alexander Ebbet* & *Mary*, to each one part, ffurther if sonne *w[m]* Dye before he come to the age of one & twenty, *Alexander* shall haue a double part, but if either of the other die before they come of age, then it is equally to be divided to the rest. Sonne *W[m]* to be kept to schoole; also if my other sonne be capable & willing he haue so much bestowed as may fitt him to write well & cast accounts, fit for a Navigator. My daughter to be so imployed as that there may be so much saved for theire future portions as may conveniently bee

* See note, page 179, ante.

ffor the good incouragement that I haue of my sonne *W^{nj}* concerning his learning. I therefore giue to him all my bookes, only a Bible wch I had of my ffather, that I giue to *Alexander.* I giue to *W^{nj}* my *Negro Symon.* to my daughters I giue my wives cloathes. I appoint Mr *Nathaniell Patten* of Dorchester to be my childrens guardians. I assigne him to receiue what is due to mee for the vse of my children.

W^{NJ} BRINSMEADE

This will was p^{r}sented to the Court 15 (3) 1648. by *Nathaniell Patten* & *David Sellocke* written in a booke of Mr *Brinsmeads* & subscribed wth his hand as to the Court it did appeare, who ordered Mr *Patten* to bring in an Inuentory of Mr *Brinsmeads* estate.

AGNES BENT.

7 (9) 1648.

Thomas Blancher testifieth that *Agnes Bent* made her will & gaue her estate to *Richard Barnes* & *Elisabeth Plimton,* & to pay fyve pound to *Elisabeth Plimton* & twenty pounds to *Richard Barnes,* & gaue ten pounds to *John Bent* & fyve pound to *Thomas Plimton,* the rest to be divided betweene *Richard Barnes* & *Elisabeth Plimton.* Deposed the first of the 9th month 1648. before me *Increase Nowell.*

Peter Noyce testifyeth the same, all but the two debts, the same day before me *Increase Nowell.*

THOMAS NELSON.

I *Thomas Nelson* of Rowley in the County of Essex (in N. England) being called now to make a voyadge into Ould England, giue to beloved wife *Joan,* my Mill & Millshouse in Rowley, & all the ground neere vnto the said mill, wch was lately in the occupation of *Joseph Wormahill,* all my land betwene Rowley oxe pasture & the Com̄on & the mill River. Two acres in the Pond field next Mr *Rogers* leaving out the Pound to build her a house on. The remainder or reversion I giue to my children, as well that child wch my wife is w^{th}all as the rest. To oldest son *Phillip* a double portion, to son *Thomas* & to daughter *Mercy,* & the child or children shee is w^{th}all theire equall parts: If any of them dye before they come to the age of twenty & one yeares, then their part to be equally divided among the other children.

My will is that *Ri: Bellingham,* Esq., & my honoured vncle *Richard Dumer,* gent. shall haue the education of my son *Phillip Nelson* & *Thomas Nelson.* Wife & vncle *Richard Dumer* shall have the education of my dau. *Mercy* & the other child my wife is w^{th}all. To wife (*Joane*) foure choice Cowes, one choise mare & ten pounds to build her a house. To son *Phillip* ten pound wch was giuen him by my Aunt *Katherine Witham,* & his plate marked with his own name P. N: & to my second son *Thomas,* a wine bowle & one spoone. Mr *Richard Billingham* & my vncle *Richard Dumer* my executors. Mr *Ezechiell Rogers* of Rowley & Mr *John Norton* of Ipwich to bee mine overseers. To wife all her apparell, her chest boxe & bed & furniture & a silver beaker

THOMAS NELSON.
& a seale

December 24. 1645.
sealed signed & deliuered
in the presence of *Jeremie Houtchin*
Ezechiel Northend.

A schedule to be annexed to the Will of *T. Nelson.* These are to certifie all whom it any waies may concerne, that I *Thomas Nelson*, about to returne to Rowlowe in New England, being at present sick, confirm my last will made in New England wch my wiues vncle Mr *Richard Dumer*, only wth the addition of these provisions that my youngest child *Samuel Nelson*, being borne since that will was made, if my wife be now wth child, & shall bring forth a child, that *Samuel*, & this may enjoy each a childs portion proportionable to the rest of my children. I earnestly desire of our Reverend Pastor & Elder Mr *Rogers*, & of that whole Church at Rowley that they may not mistake themsels concerning the eleven pounds & seventeene pounds wch I payd to goodman Seatchwell for his fferme, & I did not giue these in wth other moneyes that I laid out for the plantation least this being a wrong to mee, bee to theire griefe at the day of Jesus Christ: as also fifteene pounds payd to Mr. *Carltons* hundred pound wch I ought not to pay. This I intreat them seriously to lay to hart, & righting mee in all these particulars. Witness my hand the sixt day of Sextiles here called August, 1648. THO: NELSON.

Testifyed as his Act & deed, &
subscribed by him in the p^rsence of vs witnesses
Henry Jacie alias *Jesse*
Daniel Elly his marke
Sarah Appleyard her marke

NICHOLAS TAILOR.

19 (11) 48.

I *Nicholas Tailor* of the p^rcincts of st Katherins neere vnto the tower London, mariner, bound to sea to New castle in the good shipp called the pilgrime of London. — To the poore of the parish twelve pence, loueing wife *Elisabeth* all my lands house or houses, being in Kingshire in the County of Norfolk or any other Country. Wife sole executrix. This 26th day of July, Anno Dni 1637. Anno Regni Regis Caroli Anglie xiii^o.

p me signum dicti
Nichol^s + *Tailor* & a seal

Sealed & D D in
the p̄nce of vs.
& on the back side.
Sealed & D D published & really declared in the presence of vs
Richard ffairefield.

THOMAS CROMWELL.

3 (9) 1649.

I *Thomas Cromwell* of Boston doe by these p^rsents make my last will & Testament. Deere wife *Anne* sole executrix. To dau. *Elisabeth Cromwell* fyue pounds sterling at marriage, or at one & twenty. To wife all the remainder of my estate, excepting the ship Anne — to pay to goodwife *Sherman* ten pounds sterling, & to goodwife *Spaule* fyve pound sterl. I giue my six bells being in the Custody of *Henry Walton* vnto the towne of Boston, This 29th of August, 1649.

THOMAS CROMWELL & a seale

Sealed signed & D D in p̄nce of
John Clark
Henry Walton

Deposed that this was the will 26 (8) 1649
Increase Nowel, Sec:

[To be continued.]

EARLY RECORDS OF WEYMOUTH.

[Copied by Mr. Cyrus Orcutt, for the N. E. Genealogical and Antiquarian Register.]

[Continued from Page 166.]

John son of Samuel & Mary Bayley	born	Dec 12	1668
James son of Joshua & Ruth Smith	"	Dec 14	1668
James son of Simeon & Sarah Whitmarsh	"	Feb 8	1668
John son of Joseph & Sarah Shaw	"	Nov 9	1668
Mary Daughter of Samuel & Mercy Pool	"	Nov 20	1668
Mary of Philip & Hannah Reed	"	March 21	1669
Hannah of John & Hannah Gregory	"	April 9	1669
Sarah of James & Sarah Nash	"	April 21	1669
Susanna of James & Anna Stewart	"	May 23	1669
Margret of Isaac & Elishama Pool	"	Aug 24	1669
Judith of John & Sarah Whitmarsh	"	Sept 2	1669
Joseph son of Jacob & Abigail Nash	"	Oct 11	1669
Elisabeth of John & Elisabeth Hollis	"	Nov 18	1669
Sarah of Nicholas & Hannah Whitmarsh	"	Nov 26	1669
Samuel son of John & Mary Vining	"	Feb 2	1669
Hannah of James & Mary Smith	"	March 1	1670
Hannah of Stephen & Hannah French	"	April 19	1670
Samuel son of Richard & Mary Phillips	"	May 7	1670
Joseph son of Ephraim & Ebbot Hunt	"	May 18	1670
Samuel son of John & Elizabeth Kingman	"	May 28	1670
Israel son of Andrew & Eleanor Ford	"	June 7	1670
Benjamin son of John & Alice Shaw	"	June 16	1670
Jane Daughter of John & Jane Lovell	"	July 28	1670
Elizabeth of Jonathan & Elizabeth Sprague	"	July 21	1670
Hannah of John & Mary Rodgers	"	July 23	1670
Sarah of Daniel & Sarah Fairfield	"	Aug 25	1670
Thomas of John & Mary Bicknell	"	Aug 27	1670
John son of Thomas & Mary King	"	Aug 29	1670
William son of William & Deborah Torrey	"	Sept 14	1670
Ezra son of John & Sarah Whitmarsh	"	Oct 13	1670
Hannah of Matthew & Sarah Pratt	"	Nov 4	1670
Samuel son of Samuel & Hannah Pratt	"	Nov 15	1670
of John & Abigail Whitman	"	Dec 4	1670
son of James & Jane Lovell	"	Dec 29	1670
Mary of Thomas & Ruth Bayley	"	Feb 10	1670
Thomas son of Thomas & Rebbeca Kingman	"	Feb 11	1670
Elizabeth of Simeon & Sarah Whitmarsh	"	Feb 15	1670
Samuel son of Samuel & Experience King	"	March 1	1671
Zachary of Joseph & Elizabeth Green	"	April 7	1671
Patience of William & Elizabeth Chard	"	April 21	1671
Susanna of	"	Aug 12	1671
Thomas son of Thomas & Sarah Reed	"	Sept 12	1671
John son of Jacob & Abigail Nash	"	Oct 8	1671
Isricum son of Ephraim & Hannah Pearce	"	Jan 4	1671
Thomas son of John & Abigail Holbrook	"	Jan 15	1671
Experience of Thomas & Hannah Bolter	"	Jan 19	1671
Hannah of Philip & Hannah Reed	"	Feb 18	1671
John son of John & Mary Dyar	"	Feb 29	1671

of John & Deliverance Porter	born	April 11 1672
Sarah of James & Mary	"	May 25 1672
Sarah of Andrew & Eleanor Ford	"	May 28 1672
Sarah of John & Sarah Richard	"	June 20 1672
James of James & Anna Stewart	"	June 26 1672
Jane of John & Mary Vining	"	July 7 1672
Abigail of John & Alice Shaw	"	July 15 1672
John son of John & Staples	"	Nov 3 1672
Joseph son of Samuel & Mary Bayley	"	Dec 18 1672
Mary of Joseph & Sarah Pittey	"	Dec 27 1672
Experience of Samuel & Hannah Pratt	"	Jan 8 1672
Thomas Porter son of Thomas Porter deceased	"	Feb 3 1672
Experience of John & Abigail Whitman	"	April 1 1673
John of Job & Mercy Randall	"	April 16 1673
Anna of Timothy & Naomy Yeals	"	April 25 1673
Elizabeth of John & Bicknell	"	April 29 1673
William of Matthew & Sarah Pratt	"	May 5 1673
Mary of Thomas & Mary King	"	June 12 1673
John son of William & Deborah Torrey	"	June 23 1673
Elizabeth of John & Elizabeth Kingman	"	July 9 1673
Micajah son of Micajah & Susanna Torrey	"	July 27 1673
Abigail of Jacob & Abigail Nash	"	Aug 7 1673
Nicholas son of Nicholas & Hannah Whitmarsh	"	Aug 21 1673
Ann of Henery Turbefield	"	Sept 8 1673
Mary of James & Jane Lovell	"	Jan 5 1673
Mercy of Nathaniel & Susanna Blancher	"	April 14 1674
Thomas son of John & Sarah Staples	"	April 19 1674
Ebenezer son of John & Alice Shaw	"	April 24 1674
Elizabeth of Stephen & Hannah French	"	April 29 1674
John son of John & Beshua Reed	"	June 5 1674
Joseph of Joseph & Elizabeth Nash	"	June 8 1674
Sarah of Joseph & Sarah Pittey	"	June 11 1674
Mary of Simeon & Sarah Whitmarsh	"	June 12 1674
Sarah of Thomas & Ruth Bayley	"	Sept 29 1674
Philip son of Philip & Hannah Reed	"	Nov 2 1674
Bathsheba of John & Sarah Richard	"	Nov 16 1674
Elizabeth of Joseph & Elizabeth Pool	"	Dec 6 1674
Hugh son of William & Elizabeth Chard	"	Jan 4 1674
John son of James & Anna Stewart	"	Jan 22 1674
Mercy of John & Elizabeth Hollis	"	Feb 5 1674
Deliverance of John & Elizabeth Kingman	"	March 12 1675
John son of James & Jane Lovell	"	April 19 1675
Joseph son of Joseph & Susan Richard	"	May 7 1675
John son of John & Sarah Vinson	"	July 28 1675
Martha of Samuel &	"	Aug 8 1675
John son of Philip	"	Aug 16 1675
Jane of John & Sarah Whitmarsh	"	Sept 8 1675
Ruth of John & Deliverance Porter	"	Sept 18 1675
Mary of Jonathan & Ruth Torrey	"	Sept 25 1675
Sarah of William & Rebecca Manly	"	Oct 5 1675
Persis of Samuel & Mary Holbrook	"	Oct 11 1675
Benjamin son of Thomas & Jane Drake	"	Jan 15 1676

[To be continued.]

FIRST SETTLERS OF BARNSTABLE.

[Communicated by Mr. David Hamblen.—Continued from p. 136.]

Ralph Jones m. —— ——; children, Deborah, b. March, 1696; Elizabeth, 25 Nov., 1698; Thankful, 12 April, 1701; Bethiah, 9 April, 1706; Cornelius, 30 July, 1709.

Samuel Jones m. Mary Blish, 26 June, 1718; children, Joseph, b. 9 June, 1719; Benjamin, 14 June, 1721.

James Lewes m. Sarah Lane, Oct., 1655; children, John, b. October, 1656; Samuel, 10 April, 1659; Sarah, 4 March, 1660; James, 3 June, 1664, d. 18 June, 1748. James Lewes, senior, d. 4 Oct., 1713, æ. 82.

Samuel Lewes m. Prudence Leonard, 10 Dec., 1690; children, Samuel, b. 22 June, 1700; Joseph and David, gemini, 10 Aug., 1702; David d. 3 Jan., 1706; Ebenezer, 9 Aug., 1706; Thankful, 27 Jan., 1708; Hannah, 1 July, 1710.

George Lewes m. Alice Crocker, 14 June, 1711; children, Sarah, b. 5 April, 1712, d. 13 June, 1713; Mary, 9 March, 1713–14; Anna, 3 Feb., 1715–16; Josiah, 19 Feb., 1717. Mrs. Alice Lewes d. 23 Feb. 1718.

James Lewes m. Elizabeth Lothrop, Nov., 1698; children, Mary, b. 16 Aug., 1700; Elizabeth, 8 May, 1702; James, 9 July, 1704; Barnabas, 17 March, 1706; Solomon, 26 June, 1708.

Ebenezer Lewes m. Anna Lothrop, April, 1691; children, Sarah, b. 13 Jan., 1691–2; Susannah, 17 April, 1694; James, 4 Aug., 1696; Ebenezer, 9 May, 1699; Hannah, 14 Feb., 1701; Lothrop, 13 June, 1702; George, 5 April, 1704; Nathaniel, 12 Jan., 1707–8; John, 15 July, 1709; David and Abigail, gemini, 8 Nov., 1711.

Edward Lewes* m. Hannah Cob, 9 May, 1661; children, Hannah, b. 24 April, 1662; Eleazer, 26 June, 1664; John, 1 Jan., 1666; Thomas, March, 1669.

John Lewes m. Elizabeth Huckins, 4 June, 1695.

John, son of Edward Lewes, m. —— ——; children, Edward, b. 6 Sept., 1697; Thankful, 6 Dec., 1698; John, 28 April, 1700; Elizabeth, 28 Aug., 1701; James, 4 June, 1703; Gershom, 30 Dec., 1704; Shobal, 29 Sept., 1705.

Thomas, son of Edward Lewes, m. Experience Huckins, 28 Sept., 1698; children, Experience, b. 15 Aug., 1699; Thomas, 1 Aug., 1702; Jesse, 11 March, 1705; Desire, 14 May, 1707; Ephraim, 8 April, 1710.

Thomas Lewes m. Mary Davis, 15 June, 1653; children, James, b. March, 1654; Thomas, July, 1656; Mary, 2 Nov., 1659; Samuel, 14 May 1662.

Benjamin Lewes m. Margaret Folland, 10 Feb., 1696–7; children, Mary, 5 July, 1698; a son, d. 22 April, 1701; Seth, 1 Aug., 1704; Elizabeth, 17 Jan., 1711; Mercy, 3 March, 1712; Benjamin, 14 July, 1716.

Jabez Lewes m. Experience Hamblen, 20 Feb., 1695; child, John, b. 27 Aug., 1696.

George Lewes, Jr., m. Mary Lumbart, 1 Dec., 1654; children, George, b. Sept., 1655; Mary, 9 May, 1657; Sarah, 12 Jan., 1659; Hannah, July, 1662, d. 1667; Melatiah, 13 Jan., 1664; Bathshua, Oct., 1667; Jabez, 10 June, 1670; Benjamin, 22 Nov., 1671; Jonathan, 25 July, 1674; John, 1 Dec., 1676; Nathan, 26 July, 1678. Mr. George Lewes d. 20 March, 1709–10.

* I think that this Edward is a son of George Lewes, senior, and is recorded as Ephraim. See page 195 in Vol. II.

JONATHAN LEWES m. Patience Looke, 25 Oct., 1703; children, Thankful, b. 22 Nov., 1704; Jane, 28 April, 1713; Lot, 6 March, 1715; Levi, 22 Sept., 1718; Melatiah, 6 Feb., 1720.

NATHAN LEWES m. Sarah Arey, 24 May, 1705; children, Hannah, b. 13 Feb., 1706; David, 24 June, 1708; Mary, 11 Sept., 1710; Sarah, 24 June, 1713; Nathan, 29 Oct., 1715; George, 18 March, 1718–19.

DEA. JOHN LEWES d. 5 March, 1738.

JOSEPH LORD m. Abigail Hinkley, 2 June, 1698.

JABEZ LUMBART m. Sarah Derby, 1 Dec., 1660; children, a son, b. 18 Feb., 1661, d. same day; Elizabeth, June, 1663; Mary, April, 1666; Bernard, April, 1668; John, April, 1670; Matthew, 28 Aug., 1672; Mehitable, Sept., 1674; Abigail, April, 1677; Nathaniel, 1 Aug., 1679; Hepthsibah, Dec., 1681.

BERNARD LUMBART m. —— ——; children, Joanna, b. Dec., 1692; Mehitable, 18 March, 1693; Matthew, 15 Jan., 1698; Mariah, Oct., 1700; Bethiah, Sept., 1702; John, April, 1704; Solomon, 1 March, 1706.

JOSHUA LUMBART m. Abigail Linnel, May, 1650; children, Abigail, b. 6 April, 1652; Mercy, 15 June, 1655; Jonathan, 28 April, 1657; Joshua, 16 Jan., 1660.

NATHANIEL LUMBART m. —— ——; Sarah, b. 2 Aug., 1710.

THOMAS LUMBART m. Elizabeth Darby, 23 Dec., 1665; children, Sarah, b. Dec., 1666; Thomas, March, 1667; Elizabeth, Sept., 1668; Mary, April, 1669; Hannah, Dec., 1671; Jabez, Feb., 1673, d. 8 days after; Rebecca, May, 1676; Jabez, June, 1678; Bethiah, July, 1680; Bathshua, August, 1682; Patience, Sept., 1684.

THOMAS LUMBART, JR., m. —— ——; children, Mehitable, b. 27 Sept., 1690; Elizabeth, 2 Sept., 1692; John, 19 July, 1694, d. October, 1694; Thankful, 19 April, 1696; Jabez, 11 Feb., 1698; Gershom, 4 July, 1700; Elisha, 20 May, 1702; Zaccheus, 9 April, 1704; Hezekiah, 18 July, 1708; Mercy, 30 July, 1706; Abigail, 3 April, 1710; Patience, 9 April, 1712.

JEDEDIAH LUMBART m. Hannah Wing, 20 May, 1668; children, Jedediah, b. 25 Dec., 1669; Thomas, 22 June, 1671; Hannah, August, 1673; Experience, April, 1675.

JEDEDIAH LUMBART m. Hannah Lewes, 8 Nov., 1699.

BENJAMIN LUMBART, JR., m. Hannah Treddeway, 23 May, 1711; children, Jonathan, b. 29 March, 1712, d. 22 May, 1712; Hannah, 8 Sept., 1714. Mrs. Hannah Lumbart d. 19 Sept., 1714.

BENJAMIN LUMBART m. Jane Warren, 19 Sept., 1672, who d. 27 Feb., 1682; children, Mercy, b. 2 Nov., 1673; Benjamin, 27 Sept., 1675; Hope, 26 March, 1679. Married for his second wife, Sarah Walker, 19 Nov., 1685, who d. 6 Nov., 1693; children, Sarah, b. 29 Oct., 1686; Bathshua, 4 May, 1687; Mary, 17 June, 1686, [probably 1688]; Samuel, 15 Sept., 1691. Married for his third wife, Widow Hannah Whetstone, 24 May, 1694; children, Temperance, b. 25 May, 1695; Martha, 28 Dec., 1704.

JONATHAN LUMBART m. Elizabeth Eddy, 11 Dec., 1683; children, Jonathan, b. 20 Nov., 1684; Alice, 19 Oct., 1686; Ebenezer, 4 Feb., 1688; Abigail, 12 July, 1691, at the Vineyard.

THOMAS LUMBART m. Mary Newcom, 4 Oct., 1694; children, John, b. 5 Jan., 1694; Jedediah, 16 Feb., 1696; Thomas, 3 Aug., 1698.

JOSHUA LUMBART m. Hopestill Bullock, 6 Nov., 1682; children, Mercy, b. 16 March, 1684; Hopestill, 15 Nov., 1686; Joshua, 5 Aug., 1688; Samuel, 1 June, 1690; Abigail, 20 Jan., 1692; Mary, 22 Nov., 1697; Elizabeth, 22 April, 1700; Jonathan, 16 April, 1703.

JOSHUA LUMBART m. Sarah Parker, 14 Dec., 1715; children, Sarah, b. 28 Sept., 1716; Parker, 24 Dec., 1718. Mrs. Sarah Lumbart d. 16 Jan., 1718.

MELATIAH LATHROP m. Sarah Farrar, 20 May, 1667, and d. 6 Feb., 1711–12, æ. 66. She d. 23 May, 1712, æ. 64. Children, Thomas, b. 22 Aug., 1668; Tabitha, 3 April, 1671; Isaac, 23 June, 1673; Joseph, 15 Dec., 1675; Elizabeth, 23 Nov., 1677; Ichabod, 20 June, 1680; Shobal, 20 April, 1682; Sarah, 5 March, 1683–4.

LIEUT. JOSEPH LOTHROP m. —— ——; child, Mehitable, b. 22 Oct., 1701.

JOSEPH LOTHROP m. Abigail Child, 14 June, 1695.

SAMUEL LOTHROP m. Hannah Crocker, 1 July, 1686; children, Mary, b. 19 Oct., 1688; Hannah, 11 Nov., 1690; Abigail, 10 Aug,, 1693; Benjamin, 16 April, 1696; Joseph, 10 Nov., 1698; Samuel, 28 April, 1700.

THOMAS LOTHROP m. Experience Gorham, 23 April, 1697; children, a son, b. 10 Jan., 1697, d. 3 Feb., 1697; Deborah, 21 April, 1699; Mary, 4 April, 1701; James, 9 Aug., 1703; Thomas, 8 July, 1705; Ansel, no date; Joseph, 8 Dec., 1709; Seth, March, 1711–12.

HOPE LOTHROP m. Elizabeth Lothrop, 17 Dec., 1696; children, Benjamin, b. 18 Dec., 1697; John, 3 Oct., 1699.

BARNABAS LOTHROP, JR., m. Elizabeth Hedge, 14 Nov., 1687; children, Mercy, b. 1 March, 1689; Elizabeth, 15 Sept., 1690; Barnabas, 10 Nov., 1692, d. 6 April, 1693; Nathaniel, Feb., 1693–4; Lemuel, 26 Dec., 1695; Barnabas, 8 Feb., 1697–8; Susannah, 8 Oct., 1699; Thankful, 24 Sept., 1701; Sarah, 22 April, 1703; Mary, 15 July, 1705; Kembel, 21 June, 1708.

JOHN, son of Barnabas Lothrop, m. —— ——, and d. 23 Oct., 1695; children, Barnabas, b. 23 Nov., 1694; Elizabeth, 3 Sept., 1692, d. 9 Nov., 1694.

NATHANIEL LOTHROP m. Bethiah ——; child, John, b. 28 Oct., 1696.

JOHN LOTHROP m. Mary Cob, 3 Jan., 1671; children, John, b. 5 Aug., 1673; Mary, 27 Oct., 1675; Martha, 11 Nov., 1677; Elizabeth, 16 Sept., 1679; James, 3 July, 1681; Hannah, 13 March, 1682; Jonathan, 14 Nov., 1684; Barnabas, 22 Oct., 1686; Abigail, 23 April, 1689; Experience, 7 Jan., 1692.

JOHN LOTHROP m. Hannah, widow of Dr. John Fuller, 9 Dec., 1695; children, Bathshua, b. 19 Dec., 1696; Phebe, Sept., 1701; Benjamin, 8 April, 1704.

BARNABAS, son of John Lothrop, m. Bethiah Fuller, 20 Feb., 1706; children, John, b. 25 Aug., 1709; Hannah, 6 July, 1712. Mrs. Bethiah Lothrop d. Oct., 1714.

MR. JOHN LOTHROP d. 27 Sept., 1727, æ. 85.

WILLIAM LOVEL* m. Mehitable Lumbart, 24 Sept., 1693, and died 21 April, 1753, æ. 90; children, Eli, b. Aug., 1694; Jerusha, Sept., 1696; Elenor, 10 Sept., 1698; Abia, 12 Sept., 1700; Beulah, 7 Feb., 1704; Eleanor, 17 May, 1707.

ANDREW LOVEL m. —— ——; children, Deborah, b. 6 May, 1689, at Scituate; Mary, 17 Nov., 1693; Jonathan, 27 March, 1697; Thankful, 6 Oct., 1699; Joseph, 10 Oct., 1707; Jane, 14 May, 1715; Silas, 16 May, 1690.

JOHN LINNEL m. Ruth Davis; children, Thankful, b. 12 Nov., 1696;

* Probably son of John and Jane Lovel, of Weymouth, Mass., born 24 Feb., 1664.

Samuel, 16 Nov., 1699; John, 15 June, 1702; Bethiah, 14 May, 1704; Joseph, 12 June, 1707; Hannah, 10 July, 1709; Jabez, 30 July, 1711.

Experience Mayhew m. Thankful Hinkley, 12 Nov., 1695.

[In Vol. II. page 196, the Records read John Manton, and I thought it should be Marston, but I am now sure it should be John Martin. D. H.]

Benjamin Marston m. Lydia Goodspeed, April 26, 1716; children, John, b. 25 Feb., 1716–17; Patience, 1 Jan., 1720; Benjamin, 2 January, 1725; Nymphas, 12 Feb., 1727; Lydia, March, 1731; Prince, 24 March, 1735–6; John, 3 Dec., 1738, d. 22 Feb., 1817. Benjamin Marston, senior, probably came from Salem, and is the first one of the name that came to Barnstable.

Samuel Norman m. Widow Casley, 24 Nov., 1697.

John Otis, Jr., m. Grace Hayman of Bristol, 13 Dec., 1711; child, John, b. 27 April, 1713.

Nathaniel Otis m. Abigail Russell, 21 Dec., 1710; children, Abigail, b. 19 Aug., 1712, at Barnstable, d. 3 Nov., 1712, at Sandwich; Abigail, 10 Dec., 1713, at Sandwich; Nathaniel, 16 April, 1716, at Sandwich, died 6 Sept., 1716; Martha, 11 Dec., 1717, at Sandwich; Nathaniel, 8 Sept., 1720; Jonathan, 30 April, 1723.

Col. John Otis d. 23 Sept., 1727, æ. 70.

[In Vol. II. page 196 of the Register, the Records read John Otis, son of Goodman John Otis, probably d. in Weymouth, 1657. This is the old man, father of Goodman John Otis and grandfather of John Otis, that m. Mrs. Mercy Bacon, 1683. D. H.]

Elisha Parker m. Elizabeth Hinckley, 15 July, 1657; children, Thomas, b. 15 May, 1658; Elisha, Nov., 1660; Sarah, May, 1662.

Samuel Parker m. Hannah Bumps, 12 Dec., 1695; children, Sarah, b. Dec., 1696; Mary, May, 1698; Peace, 28 Dec., 1699; James, 13 Nov., 1701; Prescilla, 4 Sept., 1704; Prudence, 6 Aug., 1705.

Benjamin Parker m. Rebekah Lumbart, 8 Dec., 1698.

Daniel Parker m. Mary Lumbart, 11 Dec., 1689; children, Patience, b. 1690; Abigail, 27 May, 1692; Experience, 7 Feb., 1693–4, d. 24 March, 1694; Daniel, 20 Feb., 1694–5, d. 23 Dec., 1715; Rebecca, 1 April, 1698; David, 17 Feb., 1699–1700; Hannah, 5 April, 1702, d. 14 Oct., 1715; Samuel, 5 Feb., 1703–4; Jonathan, Jan., 1706; Nehemiah, Oct., 1708; Mary, 15 Aug., 1710. Daniel Parker, Esq., d. 23 Dec., 1728, æ. 59.

Joseph Parker m. Mercy Whetstone, 30 June, 1698.

John Phinney, Jr., m. Mary Rogers, 10 Aug., 1664; children, John, b. 5 May, 1665; Melatiah, Oct., 1666, d. Nov., 1667; Joseph, 28 Jan., 1667; Thomas, Jan., 1671; Ebenezer, 18 Feb., 1673; Samuel, 4 Nov., 1676; Mary, 3 Sept., 1678; Mercy, 10 July, 1679; Reliance, 27 August, 1681; Benjamin, 18 June, 1682; Jonathan, 30 July, 1684; Hannah, 28 March, 1687, d. 10 Feb., 1689.

Samuel Phinney m. Bethiah Phinney; child, Bethiah, b. 9 July, 1715.

John Phinney m. Sarah Lumbart, 30 May, 1689; children, Elizabeth, b. 11 April, 1690; Mary, 20 Jan., 1692, d. Jan., 1694; John, 8 April, 1696; Thomas, 25 May, 1697; Hannah, 8 April, 1700; Sarah, 8 October, 1702; Patience, 12 Sept., 1704; Martha, 12 July, 1706; Jabez, 16 July, 1708.

Ebenezer Phinney m. Susannah Linnel, 14 Nov., 1695; children, Mehitable, b. 14 Aug., 1696; Mary, 23 March, 1698; Martha, 22 April, 1700; Samuel, 1 April, 1702; Ebenezer, 26 May, 1708; David, 10 June, 1710.

Benjamin Phinney m. Martha Crocker, June, 1709; children, Temperance, b. 28 March, 1710; Melatiah, 26 July, 1712; Barnabas, 28 March, 1715; Silas, 16 June, 1718, d. May, 1720; Zacchus, 4 Aug., 1720; Seth, 27 June, 1723.

Jonathan Phinney m. Elizabeth ——; children, Thankful, b. 24 Dec., 1713; Joseph, 24 Jan., 1716; Jonathan, 22 Sept., 1718.

Thomas Phinney m. Widow Sarah Beettley, 25 Aug., 1698; children, Gershom, b. 25 March, 1699–1700; Thomas, 17 Feb., 1702–3; Abigail, 8 June, 1704; James, 15 April, 1706; Mercy, 24 Aug., 1708.

Rev. Jonathan Russel m. Mary Otis, 1725; child, John, b. 30 June, 1730.

John Russel m. Elizabeth Bridgelain, 1754; child, Jonathan, b. 17 May, 1756.

John Rogers m. Elizabeth Williams, 24 June, 1696.

Benjamin Shelly m. Alice Goodspeed, 8 Aug., 1705; children, Joseph, b. 29 July, 1706; Thankful, Dec., 1707; Lydia, 8 May, 1713.

Joseph Stacy, b. 22 Sept., 1706.

Joseph Smith m. Reliance Crocker, 5 Oct., 1713; children, Lydia, b. 17 Aug., 1714; Abigail, 21 July, 1716; Joseph, 31 July, 1718.

Samuel Smith m. Mary ——; child, Mary, b. 3 Sept., 1716.

Joseph Smith m. Anna Fuller, 29 April, 1689, who d. 2 July, 1722; children, Susannah, b. 12 Jan., 1689–90; Joseph, 28 Oct., 1691; James, 18 Dec., 1693; Ann, 8 Nov., 1695; Matthias, 10 July, 1697; Ebenezer, 21 March, 1698–9, d. 27 May, 1699; Daniel, 11 April, 1700; David, 24 May, 1702; Elizabeth, 19 April, 1704; Thomas, 6 Feb., 1705–6; Mary, 22 Dec., 1707, d. 16 Sept., 1728; Jemima, 9 Nov., 1709; Benjamin, 5 Dec., 1711; Ebenezer, 26 Sept., 1714.

Jonathan Sparrow m. Sarah Cob, 23 Nov., 1698.

Nathaniel Stone m. Reliance Hinckley, 15 Dec., 1698.

Edward Sturgis m. —— ——; children, Susannah, b. 10 May, 1709; Abigail, 9 Sept., 1712.

Thomas Sturgis m. Mrs. Martha Russel, 26 Dec., 1717; children, Martha, b. 19 Nov., 1718; Elizabeth, 12 June, 1721, d. 22 August, 1721; Thomas, 22 July, 1722; Elizabeth, 26 Aug., 1725; Rebecca, 9 Oct., 1727; Jonathan, 17 June, 1730; Abigail, 22 July, 1732; Hannah, 24 Aug., 1735.

Isaac Tayler m. —— ——; children, Mary, b. 23 July, 1711; Isaac, 28 June, 1715; Josiah, 17 Dec., 1717; Experience, 20 Aug., 1720; Thankful, 13 March, 1722; Ebenezer, 13 May, 1724; Mercy, 3 March, 1727.

Jasper Tayler m. Hannah Fittsrandle, 6 Nov., 1668; children, John, b. 28 Jan., 1670, d. 9 Feb., 1670; Mercy, 6 Nov., 1671; Hope, 24 Oct., 1674; Seth, 5 Sept., 1677; John, 21 March, 1680; Elenor, 6 April, 1682, d. 26 April, 1682; Jasper, 29 April, 1684.

Jacob Tayler m. Rebecca Weeks, 29 May, 1693; children, Hannah, b. 18 Jan., 1694–5; Rebecca, 27 May, 1697.

[Page 84 reads Lozaia, dau. of Isaac Chapman, but should be Lydia. Same page, Lozaia, dau. of Joseph Davis, should be Lydia.]

INSCRIPTIONS FROM THE BURYING-GROUNDS IN SALEM, MASS.

[FROM THE BURYING-GROUND ON THE HILL.]

Here lyes buried the Body of Mrs. Elizabeth Bacon, wife to Mr. Samuel Bacon, aged 59 years, she died June ye 17th, 1753.

Here lyes buried the Body of Mrs. Anne Bacon, wife to Mr. Samuel Bacon, who departed this Life May ye 10th, 1761, in ye 43d year of her age.

Here lies buried the Body of Mr. Samuel Bacon, who departed this Life July 29th, 1765, in ye 56th year of his age.

Susanna, Daw^t^. to Mr. George and Mrs. Elizabeth Bickford, who died Novem^r^. the 5th 1738 in [ ]

Here lyes Buried the Body of Mr. George Bickford, who departed this Life on May the 30th, 1760, aged 61 years.

Here lies Buried the Body of Mrs. Elizabeth Bickford, wife of Deacon John Bickford, who died October the 22d 1760, aged 61 years.

Mary Brewer, Dau^t^. of Mr. Thomas & Mrs. Mary Brewer, Died Jany. 18th, 1754, aged 13 years.

Here lie Interred the Bodies of Mrs. Mary Cabot, the wife of Mr. Francis Cabot, who died June 18, 1756, aged 32 years.

Hear lies the body of Gibson Clough, son to Ebene^r^. and Ann Clough, who departed this life August the 1 Day, aged 12 years, 1736.

Here lies the body of John Clough, son of Ebenezer and Ann Clough, how died Aprel the 13 day, aged six years, 1750. And Also Susanna Clough, dafter to William & Susanna Clough, aged Five months; died Novembr the 24th, 1750.

Here Lies Buried the Body of Mr. Joseph Clough, who Departed this Life April the 13th, 1766, aged 57 years and 8 months.

Here lyes the Body of Capt. Thomas Eden, who departed this Life, July the 1st, 1768, in the 45th year of his age.

William Eppes, Esq. died Oct. ye 1st 1756, aged 39 years.

Jonathan son to Joseph & Experience Flint, aged 5 weeks, died Feb. 17th, 1702.

Here Lyes the Body of Benjamin Flint, who died ye 28th of Decr. 1732 in ye 54th year of his age.

Here lyes buried ye body of Mrs. Elizabeth Foster, wife to Capt. John Foster, who departed this Life March ye 6th, 1752, aged 26 years.

Here lyes the Body of Mrs. Eliz^a^. Gardner, Dau^t^. to Capt. John Gardner & Elizabeth his wife, she died April 20th, 1754, in the 21st year of her age.

Here lies buried the Body of Mrs. Elizabeth Gardner, the wife of Mr. John Gardner, she died May 24th, 1755, in the 27th year of her age.

Here lies buried the body of Mrs. Mary Gavet, wife to Mr Joseph Gavet, aged 43 years, Dec'^d^. June the 11th, 1743.

Here lies the Body of Martha, the wife of Benjamin Goodhue, who died 9th Septr. 1769, Aged 58 years.

Here lies ye body of Mrs. Elizabeth Hayward, wife of Mr. Josiah Hayward, who died Jany. 1st, 1767 in ye 34th year of her age.

Here lyes ye body of Mr. Gabriel Holman, who departed this Life July the 9th, 1756, in the 42d year of his age.

Here Lyes the Body of Mr. John Holman, son of Mr. Gabriel & Mrs.

Elizabeth Holman, who departed this Life August y[e] 13th, 1767, In the 24th year of his age.

Here lies Interred the Body of Mrs. Sarah Holman, the Virtuous Consort of Mr. Gabriel Holman, who departed this Life April the 21st, 1773, aged 31 years.

Judith, wife of E. A. Holyoke, Esq. died Nov[r]. y[e] 19th, 1756, aged 19 years.

Here lies y[e] body of Francis Joseph, son of Mr. Francis & Mrs. Mary Joseph, died Jan[ry]. 17th, 1767, aged 4 years 11 mo.

Tabitha King, daug[r]. of Mr. Dan[l]. & Eliza'th King, born Octobr 18th, 1732, Died Sept[ber]. 5th, 1737.

Here lies Interred the Remains of Elizabeth King, wife of Daniel King, who departed this Life August the 13th 1766, Aged 60 years.

Here lyes inter'd ye body of Mr. Robert Kitchen, who departed this Life Oct[r]. y[e] 28th, 1712, Ætatis 56.

Here lyes interr'd the Body of Robert Kitchen, son Mr. Robert & Mrs. Bethia Kitchen, and student of Harvard College in Cambridge, aged 17 years. departed this Life, Septr. the 20th, 1716.

Robt. Kitchen, born Octo[br]. y[e] 1st, 1735. Dec'[d]. Dec[r]. y[e] 20th, 1736.

Mary Kitchen, born Oct[r]. y[e] 2d, 1731, Dec[d]. Oct. y[e] 28th, 1738.

Here lyeth Interred the body of Mrs. Freek Kitchen, wife to Edward Kitchen, Esq. And Daughter To the Honorable Josiah Wolcott, Esq. who departed this Life January 17th, 1746–7, aged 34 years.

Here lies buried the body of Edward Kitchen, Esq. who departed this Life August the 17th, 1766, aged 66 years.

Mary Lambert, Aged 3 years and 7 mo. Died Sept. y[e] 4th, 1702.

Ebenezer Lambert, aged 1 year & 10 mo. Died Sept. y[e] 21st, 1702.

Here lyeth y[e] Body of Martha Lee, Dau'r of Thomas & Mrs. Deborah Lee, aged 20 years, who died October y[e] 20th, 1721.

Here lye the Bodies of Timothy Lindall, Esq. Aged 82 years. Deceased October 25th, Anno Dommini 1760.

Bethia, his wife, aged 31 years. Deceased June 20th, Anno Domini 1720.

Mary, wife of Timothy Lindall, aged 80 years. Deceased February 8th, Anno Domini 1767.

Here lies buried the Body of Mrs. Elizabeth Mackey, wife of Capt. Daniel Mackey, Died July 20, 1701, Aged 36 years.

Here lyes Interred y[e] Body of Mrs. Mehetable Marston, wife to Benjamin Marston, Esq. and Daur. to y[e] late Rev'[d] Mr. Henry Gibbs of Watertown, who departed this Life August y[e] 21st, 1727, in y[e] 22d year of her age.

Here lyes Interred the body of Mrs. Patience Marston, Relict of Mr. Benjamin Marston, late of Salem, Merch[t] Dec'd. she departed this life the 22d day of May, 1731, Aged 55 years and 9 days.

Here lies y[e] Body of Winslow Marston, son of Col[nl]. Benjamin Marston, Esq. & and Mrs. Elizabeth his wife Died Sept. y[e] 6th, 1755, aged 6 years.

In memory of John Marston, the second son of Benj[a]. Marston, Esq. & Mrs. Elizabeth Marston. He died April 22d, 1761, in his 21st year, and is here buried.

Here lie reposited in hope of a ressurrection to an Immortal Life, the Remains of Madam Elizabeth Marston, the wife of the hon'b[le]. Benjamin Marston, Esq. once of this place, and daughter of the hon[ble]. Isaac Winslow, Esq. of Marshfield. she died September 20th, 1761, in her 53d year.

Here lies the Body of David Neeal, son of Mr. David & Mrs. Hannah Neeal, aged 1 year & 10 mo. Died August ye 1st, 1754.

Here lyes the Body of John Norman, who died May ye 6th, 1713, in ye 77th year of his Age.

Here lyes ye Body of Mary Norman, who died Octo^{br}. 24th, 1713, Aged 68.

Here lyeth buried ye body of Leut. John Pickering. Dec'd. ye 5th of May, 1694, in ye 57th year of his age.

Here lies buried ye body of Mrs Sarah Pickering, widow of Mr. John Pickering. Died Decr. ye 27th, 1714.

Here's interr'd ye body of Mr. John Pickering, who died June 9th, A. Dom. 1732, Ætatisq; 64.

Elizabeth, wife of Saml. Pickman, Esq. died Decem^{r} ye 16th, 1761, Aged 47.

Samuel Porter, son of ye Rev^{d}. Mr. Aaron Porter & Susannah his wife, died Octob^{r}. ye 16th, 1728, Aged 7 years.

Here lyes inter'd ye remains of Mr. Thomas Robie, born at Boston, Educated in Harvard College, of which for severall years he was a Fellow. Practised Physick in this town, where he died on ye 28th of August, 1729, in the 41st year of his age.

Also William Robie, ye son of Thomas and Mehitabel Robie, who died Nov^{ber}. ye 22d, 1730, in ye 6th year of his age.

Here lyes Buried the Body of Mr. Nathaniel Ropes, who Departed this Life Octob^{r}. ye 22d, Anno Dom'i. 1752, Ætatis 60.

Here lies buried the Body of Mr. Nathaniel Swasey, who died Novem^{r}. ye 11th, 1762, in the 45th year of his age.

Here lyeth ye body of Daniel Weld, aged 11 months. died March [ ] 1701.

Here lyeth buried ye Body of Dr. Edward Weld, Aged 36 years. Dec'd October ye 3d, 1702.

Here lyes ye body of Bethyah Weld. Died October ye 24th, 1719, in ye 70th year of her age.

Here Lyes ye Body of Elizabeth West, wife to Henry West, aged 50 years. dyed 26th August, 1691.

Here lyes Buried ye Body of Mrs. Esther West, wife to Mr. Samuel West, who Departed this Life, Feby. 14th, Anno Dom. 1743–4, Aged 41 years, 7 months & 9 D's.

SURNAMES.

Many of the inhabitants of this country being descended from the early Dutch settlers, a few remarks concerning their surnames may not be without interest.

A common prefix to Dutch family names is the word "*de*," which is here generally supposed to mean *of*, and to denote a French extraction. This is, however, incorrect, it being in the former language the article "*the*," as, for example, — de Wit, the White; de Bruyn, the Brown; de Kock, the Cook; de Jong, the Young; de Koster, the Sexton; de Vries, the Frisian; de Waal, the Walloon, etc., synonymous with our English names White, Brown, Cook, Young, &c.

It is also prefixed, in its different genders and cases, as, — 't Hooft, (het Hoofd) the Head; J. in 't Veld (in het Veld) J. in the Field; F. L. der

Kinderen, F. L. of the Children; van der Hegge, of the Hedge; van den Berg, of the Hill; uit den Boogaard, out or from the Orchard; equivalent to our Head, Field, etc.

Te, ten, and ter, meaning at or to, are also often used as,—te Water, at the Water; ten Heugel, at the Hill; ter Winkel, at the Shop.

The Dutch preposition *van* before family names answers to the *French* "*de*," "*of*," and was in early times seldom borne but by nobles, being placed before the names of their castles or estates.

In later days, however, when family names came more generally into use, many added to their Christian names their places of birth or residence, which were retained as family names; as van Gent, of Ghent; van Bern, of Berne; van den Haag, of the Hague; van Cleef, of Cleves; van Buren, of Buren. This latter is derived from the village of Buren, in Gelderland. It was formerly a domain of the Princes of Orange-Nassau, and many of them bore the title of Counts of Buren. Our Ex-President's family is, however, in no wise related to them; his name probably originated from his ancestor having hailed from that town. B. H. D.

SPIRIT OF '76.

[Communicated by Mr. Thomas Watirman, of Boston.]

The following document contains "Instructions" to a Representative in the Massachusetts General Court previous to the national declaration of Independence. The Representative thus instructed was Capt. Ebenezer Harnden, who died in 1786. The author of the "Instructions" is said to have been Rev. Peter Thatcher, who settled in Malden in 1770, was dismissed in 1784, became pastor of Brattle Street Church in Boston, Jan. 12, 1785, and died Dec. 16, 1802.

INSTRUCTIONS OF THE TOWN OF MALDEN TO THEIR REPRESENTATIVE, PASSED MAY 27TH. 1776.

Sir

A resolution of the late Honorable House of Representatives, calling upon the several Towns in this Colony to express their minds, with respect to the important question of **American Independence,** is the occasion of our now instructing you.

The time was, Sir, when we loved the King and the People of Great Britain with an affection truly filial, we felt ourselves interested in their glory, we shared in their joys and sorrows, we cheerfully poured the fruit of all our labours into the lap of our Mother Country, and without reluctance expended our blood and our treasure in their cause. These were our sentiments towards Great Britain: while she continued to act the part of a parent State we felt ourselves happy in our connection with her, nor wished it to be dissolved. But our sentiments are altered, it is now the ardent wish of ourselves, that America may become FREE AND INDEPENDENT STATES. A sense of unprovoked injuries will arouse the resentment of the most peaceful, such injuries these Colonies have received from Britain. Unjustifiable claims have been made by the King and his minions, to tax us without our consent These claims have been prosecuted in a manner cruel and unjust to the highest degree; the frantic policy of Administration hath induced them to send Fleets and Armies to America, that by depriving us of our trade and cutting the throats of our brethren they might awe us into submission and erect a system of despotism which should so far enlarge the influence of the Crown as to enable it to rivet their shackles upon the people of Great Britain. This was brought to a crisis upon the ever memorable nineteenth of April, we remember the fatal day —the expiring groans of our murdered Countrymen yet vibrate on our ears!! we now behold the flames of their peaceful dwellings ascending to heaven, we hear their blood crying to us from the ground *VENGEANCE*, and charging us as we value the peace of their manes, to have no further connection with a King, who can unfeelingly hear of the slaughter of his subjects, and composedly sleep with their blood upon his soul. The manner in which the War has been prosecuted has confirmed us in these sentiments; Piracy and Murder,—robbery and breach of faith have been conspicuous in the conduct of the K ng's Troops, defenceless Towns have been attacked and destroyed,—the ruins of Charlestown which are daily in our view, daily remind us of this. The cries of the Widow and the Orphan demand our attention, they demand that the hand of pity should wipe the tears from their eyes and that the sword of their Country should avenge their wrongs. We long entertained hopes that the spirit of the British Nation would once more induce them to assert their own and our rights, and bring to condign punishment, the elevated villains who have trampled upon the sacred rights of men, and affronted the majesty of the People. We hoped in vain. They have lost their love to freedom; they have lost their spirit of just resentment. We therefore renounce with disdain our connection with a kingdom of Slaves; we bid a final adieu to Britain. Could an accommodation be now effected, we have reason to think that it would be fatal to the liberties of America,—we should soon catch the contagion of venality and dissipation, which has subjected Britain to lawless domination: Were we placed in the situation we were in in the year 1773; were the powers of appointing to office and commanding the Militia, in the hands of Governors, our arts, trade, and manufactures would be cramped; nay, more than this, the life of every man who has been active in the cause of his Country would be endangered. For these reasons, as well as many others which might be produced, we are confirmed in the opinion that the present age will be deficient in their duty to GOD, their posterity, and themselves, if they do not establish an AMERICAN REPUBLIC: This is the only form of Government which we wish to see established, for we can never willingly be subject to any other King, than He, who being possessed of infinite wisdom, goodness and rectitude, is alone fit to possess unlimited power.

We have freely spoken our sentiments upon this important subject; but we mean not to dictate.—we have unbounded confidence in the wisdom and uprightness of the Continental Congress; with pleasure we recollect that this affair is under their direction:—and we now instruct you, Sir, to give them the strongest assurance that if they should declare America to be a Free and Independent Republic, your constituents will support and defend the measure, to the

LAST DROP OF THEIR BLOOD AND THE LAST FARTHING OF THEIR TREASURE.

NOTICES OF NEW PUBLICATIONS.

The Year's Remembrances. A Discourse delivered in the Meeting-House of the First Parish in Cambridge, on Sunday, December 31, 1848. By WILLIAM NEWELL, Pastor of the First Church in Cambridge. Cambridge: Metcalf & Co., Printers to the University. 1849. 8vo. pp. 16.

This is another of those "occasional discourses," full of soul-subduing eloquence, for which Mr. Newell is so remarkable.

The past year was one of uncommon mortality in Cambridge, especially among children and youth, nearly two thirds of the deaths that occurred in Mr. Newell's Society being from their number; "a proportion much greater," says the Reverend Pastor, "than in any former year, except one, of my ministry. It has closed as it began, with the tears of parental bereavement. As it passes away I again hear a funeral voice, saying, 'Man that is born of woman is of few days and full of trouble. He cometh forth like a flower and is cut down. As for man, his days are as grass. As a flower of the field, so he flourisheth. For the wind passeth over it and it is gone; and the place thereof shall know it no more.' But I hear also another voice, — a voice from Heaven, — saying, 'Suffer the children to come unto me, and forbid them not; for of such is the Kingdom of Heaven. The flowers that were cut down shall bloom again in my presence with a fresh and eternal beauty, and they shall die no more.'

'There is a Reaper, whose name is Death,
And with his sickle keen,
He reaps the bearded grain at a breath,
And the flowers that grow between.

'He gazed at the flowers with tearful eyes,
He kissed their drooping leaves;
It was for the Lord of Paradise
He bound them in his sheaves.

'My Lord has need of these flowerets gay,
The Reaper said, and smiled;
Dear tokens of the earth are they,
Where He was once a child.

'They shall all bloom in fields of light,
Transplanted by my care,
And Saints upon their garments white
These sacred blossoms wear.'"

"In our own congregation," says Mr. Newell, "although the number of deaths has not been much greater than usual, there have been some very severe and affecting cases of domestic bereavement. Eight out of the eighteen who have been taken from us were from four families, who have thus been taught by double and quick-succeeding afflictions the lesson which is usually repeated only at long intervals."

We give the names, date of decease, and ages, of those whose deaths are commemorated in this elegant obituary.

Joseph Stacey, son of Josiah N. Marshall,	March 10,	aged	19,	of typhus fever.
John, } children of John Brewster,	June 1,	"	5,	} scarlet fever.
Frank, }	" 7,	"	3,	
Samuel Stedman,	" 18,	"	53,	typhus fever.
Charles Gordon, son of Samuel Hutchins,	" 30,	"	6,	disease of the brain.
Mary Frances, daughter of James Kent,	Aug. 21,	"	16 mo.,	dysentery.
*Mary Emilia Elizabeth, widow of the late Timothy L. Jennison, M. D.,	" 23,	"	88,	"

* This lady was the daughter of HON. JONATHAN BELCHER, who was born in Boston, July 23, 1710, graduated at Harvard College in 1728, studied Law at the Temple, in London, attained some eminence at the English bar, married, in Boston, in 1756, the sister of Jeremiah Allen, Sheriff of Suffolk, and subsequently removed to Chebucto, now Halifax, where, in 1760, he was appointed Lieutenant-Governor of Nova Scotia, and in 1761 Chief-Justice of the same Province, and where he died, March 29, 1776, aged 65. *He* was the second son of Hon. Jonathan Belcher, who was born Jan. 8, 1682, graduated at Harvard College in 1699, spent six years in travel in Europe, returned to Boston, married Mary, daughter of Lieut. Gov. William Partridge, (who died Oct. 6, 1736,) was a member of the Provincial Assembly and, afterwards, of the Council, was sent to England as agent of the Province in 1729, was appointed, by the King, Governor of Massachusetts and New Hampshire, Nov. 29, 1729, arrived at Boston with his Commission, Aug. 10, 1730, was superseded in office, after a stormy administration, by Benning Wentworth, in New Hampshire, and William Shirley, in Massachusetts, in the year 1741, was appointed Governor of New Jersey, on the death of Hamilton, in 1747, in which office he continued until his death, which occurred at Elizabethtown, Aug. 31, 1757. His remains were brought to Cambridge, and deposited in a tomb, which is not only entirely destitute of an *inscription*, but, what is yet more surprising and lamentable, has not even a *stone* to show that

John, son of John Davenport, Jr.,	Sept. 4,	"	21 mo., dysentery.
John Atkins, son of John Read,	" 18,	"	2, "
Margaret P., wife of John A. Fulton,	" 19,	"	38, typhus fever.
*Eliza N., wife of Nathan Rice,	Oct. 3,	"	52, disease of the brain.
Rebecca L., } children of William J. Coye,	" 13,	"	5, } dysentery.
Georgiana F., }	" 21,	"	11 mo., }
Lizzie Brown, daughter of E. A. Chapman,	" 16,	"	11 mo., "
† Samuel Sheafe Willard,	" 18,	"	67.
John Davenport,	Nov. 28,	"	82.
Sarah Peirce, daughter of George Nichols,	Dec. 16,	"	11.
Jonathan Derby Robins,	" 21,	"	90.

The Journal of the Pilgrims at Plymouth, in New England, in 1620: *Reprinted from the Original Volume.* With Historical and Local Illustrations of Providences, Principles, and Persons: By GEORGE B. CHEEVER, D. D. New York: Published by John Wiley, 161 Broadway, and 13 Paternoster Row, London. 12mo. 1848. pp. ix, 369.

The above title, as has been justly observed by a writer in the Evening Transcript, is calculated greatly to mislead the casual observer, and to convey the impression that a new discovery has been made in the fields of historical literature, a new treasure brought forth from amid the accumulated dust and rubbish of two centuries. Indeed, it may reasonably be doubted whether any one would ever imagine, that in this imposing volume he beheld merely a new version of what is usually, but erroneously, called "MOURT'S RELATION," a work well known to every student of New England history. Yet such is the indubitable fact; and we here have a handsomely executed reprint of the earliest publication respecting Plymouth Colony, containing a minute detail of the events attending its first settlement, from the arrival of the May Flower at Cape Cod, Nov. 9, 1620, to Dec. 11, 1621, penned by the actors themselves. The manuscript of this journal, or relation, was probably sent to England by Mr. Cushman, who sailed from Plymouth, in the Fortune, Dec. 13, 1621, and was printed in London, in a small quarto volume, of some eighty pages, in 1622, with an introductory address "to the reader," signed by "G Mourt," a manifest corruption for *G. Morton.* An abridgment of the original work was published by Purchas, in his Pilgrims, in 1625. This abridgment was printed many years since in the Massachusetts Historical Collections; and at a much more recent date, the omitted portions were also printed in the same work. The first complete reprint of the original tract was given by Rev. Dr. Young, in his "CHRONICLES OF THE PILGRIM FATHERS," published at Boston, in 1844. To the rich stores of information contained in Dr. Young's able annotations upon the early narratives of the Pilgrims, Dr. Cheever readily acknowledges his indebtedness. Indeed, but little is to be gleaned in any field over which Dr. Young has once passed; it is well nigh a hopeless task for any subsequent explorer to endeavor to pick up a single grain wherewith to grace his own basket — he finds nothing but chaff.

We have spoken of Dr. Cheever's edition of the "RELATION" as a handsomely executed reprint. It is, truly, a beautiful book, so far as regards mechanical execution highly creditable to the taste both of editor and publisher. The "Historical and Local Illustrations," too, which occupy more than two thirds of the work, abound — we are willing and

there is any tomb there; the very existence of which is now known to but few persons. Gov. Belcher was the only son of Hon. Andrew Belcher, who was born in Cambridge, Jan. 19, 1647, removed to Boston, where he became the most opulent merchant of his time, "an ornament and blessing to his country," was a Captain, an Assistant, one of the Council of Safety in 1689, and a Counsellor from 1702 till his death, Oct. 31, 1717, at the age of 70. This last was the son of Andrew Belcher, of Sudbury, in 1640, and of Cambridge in 1646, a member of the Church and the Artillery Company, who married Elizabeth, daughter of Nicholas Danforth, and was the first to whom leave was granted by the "Townsmen to sell beer and bread, for entertainment of strangers, and the good of the Town." Nothing remains to designate his last resting-place but a foot-stone, by the side of that of his wife Elizabeth, (who died June 26, 1680, aged 62 years,) bearing the initials "A. B."

* Sept. 18, 1848, died Caroline P., wife of the Rev. John F. W. Ware, of this City, and daughter of Nathan Rice, aged 28. Sept. 26th, died, at the residence of Nathan Rice, of this City, Mrs. Desire Lincoln, relict of Dr. Levi Lincoln, of Hingham, aged 78. Oct. 3d, died, at Hingham, at the residence of Mrs. Jairus Leavitt, Mrs. Eliza N. Rice, wife of Nathan Rice, of this City, and daughter of the late Dr. Levi Lincoln, of Hingham, aged 52.

"Lovely and pleasant in their lives, in their death they were not divided."

See Cambridge Chronicle, for Thursday, Oct. 12, 1848.

† He was a son of Rev. JOSEPH WILLARD, President of Harvard College from Dec. 19, 1781, till his death, Sept. 25, 1804; who was son of Rev. Samuel Willard, of Biddeford, Maine; who was son of John Willard, a merchant at Kingston, Jamaica; who was the fourth child and second son of Rev. Samuel Willard, Vice-President of Harvard College from Sept. 6, 1701, to Aug. 14, 1707; which last was the second son of Major Simon Willard, successively of Cambridge, Concord, and Groton, who died at Charlestown, April 24, 1676.

ready to acknowledge — in beautiful passages, in eloquent expressions of vigorous thought, in vivid pictures of a glowing fancy. But here our praise must stop; and we must confess that, as a whole, the work is very far from receiving our unqualified approval. We are confident, moreover, that our opinion thereof is that of nearly every person, in New England, who has seen and examined the work. The objections against it are twofold, having reference both to its manner and matter. And first, of its manner, or method, of internal arrangement.

The original work may be considered as divided into three parts, namely, the introductory portion, the Journal proper, and the appendix or conclusion. And each of these natural divisions is again subdivided into smaller ones. Thus, the introductory portion is composed of the address "To the Reader," signed by "G. Mourt," a letter from Mr. Cushman "to his much respected friend" Mr. John Pierce, and John Robinson's parting letter of advice to the Pilgrims. The Journal proper is divided into several parts, each of which forms a distinct and complete narrative of some period or event in the early history of the Colonists, as, for instance, the annals of the settlement from the arrival at Cape Cod to March 23, 1621; then an account of "A Journey to Packanokik," in July, 1621; then the narrative of "A Voyage to the Kingdome of Nauset," which is followed by the account of "A Journey to the Kingdome of Namaschet," in the month of August; and the Journal concludes with "a Relation of our Voyage to the Massachusetts," in September. Next comes a letter from Edward Winslow to some friend (perhaps George Morton) in England, and the volume closes with Robert Cushman's "Reasons & considerations touching the lawfulnesse of removing out of England into the parts of America." Now what course has Dr. Cheever pursued with regard to these several divisions? He has preserved them, it is true, exactly as in the original; but he has inserted between every two of them a summary argument, an introductory and explanatory chapter, relative to the subject of the next following division of the work! Is this, we would ask, preserving the integrity of the original? Is this giving us a *faithful* reprint of a historical work? No one will *dare* to answer in the affirmative. No! it is a scandalous way to reprint any book, more especially a historical treatise, whose great value must always depend upon the faithfulness with which the original is followed. It is a style of reproduction against which we most strenuously protest. It is but second-rate Vandalism. Give us any exact reprint of the original, with no addition save that of notes at the bottom of the page, or at the end of the work, in the shape of an appendix; and let the authorship of these be distinctly made known, that no doubts may arise in the mind of the reader on the subject. Dr. Cheever's explanatory pages might and should have been reduced to the form of notes, or have been placed at the end of the book; but never, never, should they have been foisted in between the natural divisions of the text. It is altogether too much the fashion, now-a-days, for a certain class of editors, (who, we are sorry to say it, are usually clergymen,) to remodel their originals after their own fancies. We openly and loudly denounce all such editors, we utterly condemn such pretended reprints, as a fraud upon the community. Not even the works of Dr. Young, who deservedly ranks so high as an editor and annotator, are entirely free from censure on this point. We consider it a sad mistake, and one greatly to be regretted, that he should have seen fit to divide his valuable and interesting "Chronicles" into chapters, when no such divisions existed, generally, in the original documents from which they were compiled.

Having spoken of the internal arrangement of Dr. Cheever's work, we will now say a few words respecting the matter of which his "Illustrations" are composed. And here we would remark, that we have not *read* this edition of the "Journal," but have merely examined it, cursorily; and therefore, according to Sidney Smith, we are the better qualified to express our views on the subject under consideration. It has been hinted that there are errors of fact in Dr. Cheever's annotations, and we ourselves observed one remarkable instance thereof, in the course of our hasty examination; but of such we take no note in the present case; our criticism has regard to another point. We wish to speak of the frequency and prolixity with which the reverend editor dwells upon the *special providences*, so conspicuous in the early establishment and progress of the Colony at Plymouth. They are brought forth upon every and any occasion, in season and out of season, to account for Gosnold's visit to Cape Cod in 1602 — for Squanto's captivity and subsequent residence in England — and for the putting back of the Speedwell, to give additional zest to the detail of Pierce's disasters, and to enhance the beautiful simplicity of the narrative of the first Fast. Has any one had the impiety to doubt the all-powerful and all-wise agency of God, in the planting this little band of pilgrims upon "the stern and rockbound coast" of New England, that Dr. Cheever should think it necessary to devote some two hundred pages to expository arguments on the subject? Nay, even allowing that there was such a necessity, is a work of this character — a purely historical narrative — a proper medium for the publication of an editor's peculiar religious views, with which the world has not the least concern, and for which it cares nothing? We contend that it is not — we maintain that a historical work should be solely and strictly a historical work, and not a depository for dogmatic theology. If Dr. Cheever thought that the public needed instruction on this point, that it would be benefited by an elucidation of the remarkable providences upon which he dilates with such satisfaction, why did he not put forth a separate treatise upon the subject, which might have been bought and read by any one who chose to do so, and not convert the pages of a historical tract into the means whereby to administer to each and every involuntary reader the same unwelcome dose of Pharisaical flummery. It is this prodigiously strong savor of a whining and obtrusive sanctity, very pleasant to a few, but inexpressibly disgusting to most persons, which renders this book so repulsive to the lovers of New England history. The New Englanders of the nineteenth century, although eminently remarkable for their thoughtful seriousness of deportment, and comparatively elevated standard of morality, are not by any means a cant-loving people. The day for the collection and treasuring up of marvellous providences passed away with that learned fanatic, Cotton Mather. Such things will not go down now; they are alike uncongenial to the tastes of the people, and unsuitable to the age in which we live.

Let it not be said that our remarks are dictated by sectarian prejudice. Sectarian prejudice! What is it? The concentrated essence of unchristian intolerance — a burning, blighting, withering, scathing curse to the hearts of all within its influence — the diabolical embodiment of the most ungenerous passions of human nature, animated by a spirit of which the Archfiend himself need not be ashamed! Thank God, we harbor it not! We abhor it, loathe it, despise it, as the foulest disgrace of the age, as the damnable invention of accursed spirits, seeking to vitiate and corrupt, by the virulent infection of their own pestilential breath, the souls of frail and erring mortals! Thank God that we can shake hands with an Episcopalian, that we can call a Baptist, *brother*, that we can exchange the offices of friendship with a Universalist, that we can listen with equal satisfaction to the words of truth which fall from the lips of Calvinist or Unitarian! Thank God that the obscurity of our intellectual vision is so great as to render it impossible for us to perceive that a man's soul is white or black, his heart large or small, according to the *sect* with which he may be classed; that we are in habits of close intimacy and daily intercourse with individuals of each and every of these *sects*, and never yet so much as felt the necessity or propriety of washing our hand after it had been clasped by a Congregationalist, before we could extend it to an "Orthodox!" We are ready and willing to declare, with that superlatively good man, Benjamin Colman, of Brattle Street, — the most perfect model of what a Christian *should* be — that we acknowledge no platform but THE BIBLE, that we will be bound by no creed save that of universal charity and toleration.

With such sentiments we have freely given utterance to our candid opinion concerning the new edition of "THE JOURNAL OF THE PILGRIMS," unbiassed, as we hope and believe, by any unworthy motive, and seeking only to present our views of the good and bad qualities of the work in question; setting it down as our firm conviction, that Dr. Cheever's edition of "Mourt's Relation" is not a book suited to the taste of the majority of the reading community in New England.

Catalogue of the Officers and Students of Lawrence Academy, [at Groton,] *from the time of its incorporation.* 8vo. Groton. 1848. pp. 84.

This is, certainly, the most capital work of the kind which we ever saw. Not to mention the neatness and beauty of its typographical execution, but looking at it with the eye of an Antiquary alone, it is superior we think, to any "Triennial" or "Annual" Catalogue, which has ever been published in New England. Prefaced by a brief sketch of the foundation of the "Groton Academy," and of the noble benefactions which induced the assumption of the name of the "Lawrence Academy," this Catalogue presents us with brief notices of the persons, twenty in number, who have filled the office of Preceptor since the incorporation of the Institution, lists of the Trustees, Preceptresses, Assistants, and teachers of music, drawing, and writing, together with the names of all those who have been its pupils, arranged in two distinct alphabets, the one for males, the other for females. It is in this latter portion of the work — the list of pupils — that the Catalogue of Lawrence Academy deserves to be taken as a pattern for all similar publications. The name of each male pupil is preceded by the date of his admission to the School, and followed by his place of residence while a pupil, and by such particulars as could be obtained respecting his subsequent career, together with the date of decease, when known. Most Catalogues would have stopped here; or, if they gave the names of the female pupils at all, would merely append thereto their then places of residence. But here we find the names of very many of the female pupils actually followed by the names and residences of those to whom they were eventually joined in marriage! This would appear incredible, were it not that the circumstance is accounted for by the fact, stated in the Introduction, that the compilation of the Catalogue was the work of *a lady*. To *a lady*, then, are we indebted for the preservation of facts which will be of inestimable value, in future times, in the compilation of the genealogies of the mothers and daughters of the present generation! What would we poor Antiquaries of the present day not give, were we but in possession of such information respecting our great-great-grandmothers! Melancholy, indeed, is it, that we are able to learn so little concerning the ancient matrons of New England. Honored be her memory, therefore, who has done her part towards transmitting to posterity a legacy the like of which *we should have received* from our fathers! Her name deserves to be blazoned forth in letters of gold; but as we are unable to do that, we will print it in CAPITALS, and declare to all the world that the name of MISS CLARISSA BUTLER, of Groton, is one of those which will be held in everlasting remembrance among the children of men. — May she live a thousand years!

The International Art-Union Journal. Number 1. February, 1849. Goupil, Vibert, & Co., Publishers and Proprietors, 289 Broadway, N. Y. 16mo. pp. 39.

"Our objects," say the Publishers, "are simply to diffuse among all classes, in a cheap form, knowledge of the Fine Arts, and those who have produced them; to present monthly a biographical sketch of some distinguished artist, with such notices of the goings-on in general in the world of art as we may be enabled to collect. It will be to Painting and Painters that we shall mostly devote our pages; yet the congenial and analogous subjects of Sculpture, Music, the Drama, and Architecture will engage our attention."

"Contributions will be gladly received from any whose leisure and taste lead them to desire to express themselves in print on the topics to which our publication is devoted."

"The Journal is sold for 6 1-4 cts. per copy, or 75 cents per annum, in advance."

MARRIAGES AND DEATHS.

MARRIAGES.

ARKLAY, PATRICK, ESQ., 9 April, at Trinity Church, Boston, by Rt. Rev. Bishop Eastburn, to MISS JULIA CORNELIA, dau. of William Parker, Esq.

ATKINS, MR. BENJAMIN F., of Boston, a graduate at Harvard College in the Class of 1838, 26 April, at Trinity Church, Boston, to MISS HARRIET LOUISA CUTTER, of West Cambridge.

AUBIN, MR. PHILIP J., of Boston, 17 April, at Christ Church, to MISS MARGARET P., dau. of the late Theodore J. Harris, of Portsmouth, N. H.

BAKER, MR. NATHAN W., of Brooklyn, Ct., 11 April, in Boston, to MISS EMILY, dau. of the late Edward Holbrook, Esq.

BARBOUR, JOSEPH, ESQ., of Gorham, Me., to MRS. AGNES T. D. PREBLE, widow of the late Eben P. of Gorham.

BARTON, WILLIAM SUMNER, JR., ESQ., 4 April, to MISS ANN ELIZABETH, dau. of Samuel Jennison, Esq., all of Worcester, Mass.

BENNETT, MR. JOHN C. F., of Charleston, S. C., formerly of Springfield, Mass., in April, at Richmond, Va., to MARY CAROLINE PHILLIPS, dau. of the late Dr. James Gardner, of Lynn, Mass.

CHAMBERLAIN, MELLEN, ESQ., of Boston, 6 June, in North Danvers, to MISS MARTHA A. PUTNAM, of that place.

CLAPP, MR. HIRAM, to MISS REBECCA JENKINS, 13 May, both of Dorchester.

DRAKE, MR. JOSEPH N., of Dedham, to MISS ELVIRA D. SHEPHERD, of Boston, 23 April, at Boston.

FERNALD, REV. O. J., Thomaston, Me., to MISS S. M. B., dau. of Dr. M. R. Ludwig, 30 April, all of Thomaston.

GREIG, MR. GEORGE, of Boston, 26 March, to LUCY HAYES, dau. of Robert Waterston, Esq.

HAMMOND, MR. WILLIAM, 7 June, to MISS MARY I. MASON, both of Boston.

HERSEY, CAPT. JACOB, of New York, 8 April, in Pembroke, Mass., to FRANCES G., dau. of Judge Kilborn Whitman, late of P.

HOLDEN, MR. EDWARD, late of Dorchester, now of Roxbury, 17 June, at St. Mary's Church, Dorchester, to MISS EMILY, dau. of Daniel Alden, Esq., of Belchertown.

JACKSON, ALEXANDER, M. D., of Plymouth, 14 June, in Cambridge, to MISS CORDELIA ANN, youngest dau. of the late Nathaniel Reeves, Esq., of Wayland.

JONES, EDWARD J., ESQ., of Boston, 3 May, to MISS EMILY D., dau. of Mr. James Campbell of Milton, Mass.

Knowles, Capt. Allen H., of Brewster, Mass., 4 April, in Connecticut, to Miss Caroline, dau. of John Doane, Esq., of Orleans, Mass.

Livermore, Mr. Edward M., of Cambridge, to Miss Julia Cabot, dau. of S. P. White, M. D., of New York, 18 April, at New York.

Means, Rev. James H., (Harv. Coll. 1843.) Pastor of the Second Church in Dorchester, 6 June, in Boston, to Miss Charlotte A. Johnson, of B.

Parkman, Samuel, M. D., of Boston, (Harv. Coll. 1834,) 7 May, to Miss Mary Eliot, dau. of the late Hon. Edmund Dwight.

Pease, Mr. David, of Bath, Me., to Elizabeth A., dau. of F. A. Van Dyke, M. D., of Philadelphia, 5 April, at P.

Poore, Benjamin Perley, Editor of the Bee, to Miss Virginia Dodge, of Georgetown, 12 June, at Georgetown.

Porter, Rev. G. W., Rector of St. Mary's Church, Dorchester, 9 April, in Boston, to Miss Elizabeth Eustis Langdon, of Portsmouth, N. H.

Preble, Abram, Esq., of Bowdoinham, Me., to Miss Jerusha Polley of Bangor, 6 May, in Topsham.

Raymond, Mr. Curtis B., 29 Mar., at St. Thomas's Church, New York, to Miss Lydia N. Osgood, both of Boston, Mass.

Ritchie, Harrison, Esq., of Boston, (Harv. Coll. 1845,) in New York, 3 May, to Miss Mary, dau. of Frederick Sheldon.

Rives, William C., Jr., to Miss Grace W. Sears, 15 May, in Boston.

Robinson, John H., M. D., of Charlestown, 18 April, to Miss Mary E. Waite, of Leicester, Mass.

Rogers, William B., Esq., of the University of Virginia, to Miss Emma, eldest dau. of Hon. James Savage, LL.D., of Boston, 20 June.

Sargent, Henry, M. D., of Worcester, 30 April, in Cambridge, to Miss Catharine Dean, dau. of the late Asa Whitney, Esq., of Boston.

Sears, Mr. David, Jr., of Boston, to Miss Emily E., dau. of the late Goold Hoyt of New York, 29 May, at N. Y.

Swett, Mr. H. W. to Miss Maria Louisa Kent, 22 March, at New York, both of Boston.

Thatcher, Mr. Peter, Jr., to Miss Sarah Adams Estabrook, 6 May, at West Cambridge.

Twitchell, George B., M. D., of Keene, N. H., 11 April, in Boston, to Miss Susan E., only dau. of Gideon F. Thayer, Esq., of Boston.

Vinton, Mr. C. M., of Jamaica Plains, Roxbury, 29 March, in Boston, to Miss Anne Bell, dau. of the late Stephen Badlam, Esq., of Boston.

Wainwright, Lt. Richard, U. S. N., to Sally Franklin, dau. of the late Richard Bache, Esq., of Philadelphia, 7 March, at Washington, D. C.

Washburn, Alexander C., Esq., (Harv. Coll. 1839.) in Roxbury, 7 May, to Miss Ellen M., dau. of the late Hon. John Bailey.

Whitcomb, Mr. John D., to Miss Mary Gibson, 8 March, both of Boston.

Willard, Paul, Jr., Esq., of Charlestown, (Harv. Coll. 1845.) 9 April, in Boston, to Miss Maria Louisa, dau. of Samuel F. McCleary, Esq., City Clerk of Boston.

Woodman, Mr. George, Dorchester, to Miss Lucy A. R., dau. of Joseph Howe, Esq., of Dorchester, 2 May.

DEATHS.

Adams, Mr. John, Hartford, Susquehannah Co., Pa., 27 Feb., æ. 105; a native of Worcester, Mass., and for some time a resident of *Menotomy*, now West Cambridge.

Adams, Mr. John, in New Orleans, 5 March, æ. 35. He was a native of West Cambridge; and his death was caused by injuries received at a fire, in the discharge of his duties as First Assistant Foreman of Perseverance Fire Company, No. 13.

Adams, Mrs. Persis, Cambridgeport, 8 March, æ. 78, formerly of Medway.

Adams, Mrs. Rebecca, Medford, 24 Feb., æ. 79.

Almy, Mrs. Mary, Aurora, Cayuga Co., N. Y., in June, æ. 97; formerly of Westport, Ms., widow of William Almy.

Appling, Capt. John, Carver, 29 May, æ. 92; a soldier of the Revolution, and oldest inhabitant of Carver.

Apthorp, John Trecothick, Esq., Boston, 8 April, æ. 79.

Ashley, Maj. William, Sheffield, æ. 76.

The Berkshire Courier thus notices the death of the late Maj. William Ashley, of Sheffield:

Major Ashley is descended from a long line of distinguished ancestors. The grandfather of Major Ashley, the late Col. John Ashley, was a son of David Ashley, of Westfield. Col. Ashley came to this town as early as 1725, and located himself in the beautiful valley of the Housatonic, where he continued to reside until his death. His son, the late Major-General John Ashley, was the father of the deceased, and died in 1799. Col. Ashley was the first lawyer that settled in the county, and both the father and grandfather were distinguished by many offices of trust, civil and military, which they discharged with great satisfaction to the public. Major Ashley graduated at Harvard College, 1793; married a daughter of the late Judge Hillyer, of Connecticut, who still survives, and settled upon the estate of his grandfather, where, by his liberality and patriotic spirit, he has contributed largely to build up and sustain a flourishing village, now known, in honor to himself, as Ashleyville. The deceased was extensively engaged, during a long life, in various branches of business; as farming, milling, and manufacturing, requiring the aid of many operatives and dependents, who have shared largely in his extensive means, and felt the cheering influence of his sound practical judgment. In these various and extended concerns, he has sustained a character of irreproachable integrity and uprightness.

Ashton, Mrs. Sarah, Boston, 10 May, æ. 76, widow of the late John Ashton.

Barbour, Miss Mary, Newburyport, 14 June, æ. 90.

Barker, Hon Stephen, Andover, 18 March, æ. 77.

Barnes, Mr. Thomas B., Boylston, 8 May, æ. 93 yrs., 8 mo.

Barnard, Mr. Jonathan, North Bridgton, Me., æ. 78; formerly of Harvard, Mass.

Barnard, Hon. Hezekiah, Nantucket, 25 May, æ. 80. He had been a Representative, Senator, and Treasurer of Massachusetts.

Belknap, Gen. Sewall F., Windsor, Vt., 19 June, æ. 38. Gen. B. has been very extensively known of late for his great railroad enterprises.

Billings, Mr. Jesse, South Deerfield, 19 March, æ. 84, a Revolutionary Pensioner.

Boardman, Mrs. Nancy, Cambridge, 14 June, æ. 70; widow of the late Darius B., of Boston.

Bond, Joseph, Esq., Wilmington, 21 May, æ. 65.

Bond, Mrs. Nancy, Marblehead, 10 June, æ. 78; widow of the late John Bond, Esq.

Borland, James Lloyd, Boston, 29 March, æ. 29, eldest son of John Borland, Esq.

Bowen, Mr. Jeremiah, Landaff, N. H., 10 March, æ. 98; a soldier of the Revolution.

Bowman, Mrs. Susannah, Boston, 31 May, æ. 100. 2 mo., 5 days; formerly of Amherst, Mass.

Bridge, William S., Esq., Milford, Me., 29 May, æ. 69; formerly a prominent merchant of Boston.

Bussey, Mrs. Judith, Roxbury, 1 May, æ. 86, widow of the late Benjamin Bussey.

Cassell, Mr. James, Truro, 18 June, æ. 93; for many years a shipmaster out of Boston.

Chamberlain, Mr. John, Southboro', 9 May, æ. 75.

Child, Mr. Josiah, Waltham, 9 May, æ. 78.

Child, Mrs. Lucy, Cambridge, 9 June, æ. 87 yrs., 9 mo., widow of the late Samuel Child.

Chipman, Mr. William, Oxford, Me., 30 March, æ. 86; a Revolutionary soldier. He was born in Kingston, Mass., 14 Aug., 1763.

Church, Mrs. Mary, Barrington, N. H., 14 March, æ. 92; widow of Mr. James C.

Clift, Dea. Joseph. See *Hatch, Dea. Joel.*

Comins, Capt. Josiah, Thompson, Conn., 3 May, æ. 86.

Coolidge, Mrs. Mary Carman, Watertown, 29 April, æ. 84; pensioned widow of the late Samuel Coolidge.

Cowell, Mrs., Brookfield, N. H., 14 Mar., æ. 87, widow of Dr. Samuel C., formerly of Lebanon.

Cram, Mrs. Anna, Exeter, N. H., 29 March, æ. 94. ☞ A sister of the deceased died within a few weeks, æ. 92, and three brothers are living, whose average ages are about 80.

Cumings, Mr. Joseph, Sharon, 5 June, æ. 94; a Revolutionary Pensioner.

Dame, Mrs. Hannah, Kittery, Me., in June, æ. 95.

Dana, Rev. Sylvester, Concord, N. H., 9 June, æ. 79 yrs., 8 mos., nearly. He was born at Ashford, Ct., 14 Oct., 1769; his great-grandfather, Richard Dana, was a French Protestant, who, by way of England, came to America about 1640, and for some time resided in what is now Brighton, (then Cambridge,) Mass. He had a son and grandson whose names were Jacob. Jacob, Jr., lived in Ashford, and was the grandfather of the subject of this obituary. His father was Anderson Dana, a lawyer of Ashford, who, in 1772, took up his residence in the celebrated Valley of Wyoming. Though but three years old, Sylvester always remembered the journey thence; he rode on horseback behind his mother, who carried in her arms another child, an infant. In this manner, a country chiefly wilderness of near three hundred miles was passed, about fifty of which "spotted trees" were their only guide. This pioneer mother was Susannah, dau. of Dea. Caleb Huntington, of Lebanon, Ct.

When the terrible massacre of 1778 was perpetrated by the Tories and Indians, Mr. Dana's family consisted of seven children. In that massacre, the father and a son-in-law, Stephen White, were slain. The mother and her seven children found shelter in the wilderness, and after great sufferings found their way back to Ashford on foot.

In 1786, Sylvester and his older brother, Anderson Dana, returned to Wyoming. Here he applied himself to manual labor, by which he acquired the means of obtaining a college education, and was a graduate of Yale of the class of 1797. Becoming a preacher, he officiated in that capacity in a great many places in New England, at Wilkesbarre, Pa., and as a missionary in the interior of New York in 1799–1800. About 1801 he married Hannah, third daughter of Dea. John Kimball of Concord, N. H., who died in 1846; having been the mother of six sons and three daughters. Of these children four sons and one daughter died in infancy. The oldest son, Charles Backus Dana, Dart. Coll. 1828, Rector of Christ's Church, Alexandria, Va. Sylvester, the second son, Dart. Coll. 1839, is in the practice of the law at Concord, N. H. The oldest daughter, Anne Kimball, is the wife of Reuel Barrows, M. D., of Fryeburg, Me.

Among the manuscripts prepared by Mr. Dana, was a history of Wyoming, which was consumed in the fire that destroyed the house of his son-in-law, in Oct., 1848, at Fryeburg — the work of an incendiary. — *Day & Murdock's Mems. of the Class of* 1797.

Davenport, Mr. Joseph, Cambridgeport, 28 May, æ. 76.

Davis, Samuel H., Springfield, 17 April, æ. 22, son of Rev. Emerson Davis, D. D., and Associate Editor of the Springfield Republican.

Such is the brief announcement of the sudden departure of one whose loss is deeply felt and mourned by the wide circle of friends which his estimable qualities of mind and heart had drawn about him. He has been snatched away, in the flush of early manhood, even at the very moment when his prospects of usefulness were the brightest, when the future was rich in promise of an honorable position in the affections and esteem of his fellow-citizens.

Samuel H. Davis was born in Westfield, June 27, 1826. In youth he was noted for his industry. Having nearly completed his preparatory studies in 1839, and learning his father's intention not to allow him to enter College until he should attain the age of 17 years, he was very solicitous to find some occupation wherewith to fill up the intervening period. Having procured a quantity of type from a printing-office, and learned to *set* them, he spent some time in fitting up an office for himself, and collecting materials, and began to print names, labels, &c., &c., on a small home-made press. At length, in the summer of 1840, he issued proposals for a miniature newspaper, entitled the "Westfield Courier," which he continued to edit, print, and publish, at first in connection with a young friend, afterwards alone, throughout the Presidential campaign. He thus imbibed a strong taste for the office of a newspaper editor, which continued undiminished through life; and he took especial pains to cultivate such a style of composition as he deemed most suitable for one in that station.

In his Senior year in College young Davis published, in connection with his Classmate D. A. Wells, (now a member of the Law School at Cambridge,) an interesting work of one hundred octavo pages, entitled "Sketches of Williams College," which deserves to be more extensively known to the public. He graduated with distinction at this Institution, in August, 1847; and the next week entered the office of the Westfield News Letter, where he continued, as Associate Editor of that paper, until his removal to Springfield. From April to December, 1848, in addition to his editorial duties, he discharged those of an assistant teacher in Westfield Academy. In the month of December, he became Associate Editor of the Springfield Republican, and was connected with the editorial management of that journal until his death. It has been said that "there has never appeared in this Commonwealth a person who united so many and such eminent qualifications for an Editor. He was prepared to receive, to understand, and dispose in their proper proportions the innumerable details which demand the constant attention of an Editor, and which form the daily history of society and parties. Experience would soon have enabled him to see clearly through their mazes, and to extract from their contradictions the portion of truth which they contain. He was, besides, from early practice, perfectly acquainted with the whole art of printing." His mind was very active, and his nervous system easily excited. "His intellect was of a high order. He had a sound understanding, a cautious judgment, a quick penetration of human character, a pleasant fancy, a genial wit, a cultivated and delicate taste. As a writer, his style was clear, terse, and vigorous, and often sententious and epigrammatical. He had remarkable versatileness of thought and expression. Some of his productions were grave and argumentative, and others brilliant with wit, and overflowing with genuine humor. As a public speaker he was forcible and impressive, and sometimes eloquent. As a friend he was noble, generous, and sincere. The buoyancy of his spirit was irrepressible, even by intense suffering. His conversation, though sparkling with wit and humor, was untinctured by a particle of venom. No malice embittered, no selfishness chilled, 'the genial current of his soul.' Seldom has death taken away so noble a mind, so true a friend, so esteemed a man."

Mr. Davis was a collector of coins and autographs, and gave strong indications of an antiquarian taste; and had his life been spared, it is not unreasonable to suppose that he might have lent his brilliant talents to the preservation of some portion of our early history.

DENISON, MRS. JANE, New London, Ct., 12 April, æ. 100 years.

DOLIBER, MRS. SARAH, Marblehead, 4 March, æ. 98 yrs., 3 mos., 21 days.

DWIGHT, HON. EDMUND, Boston, 1 April, æ. 68.

DWIGHT, MRS. LOUISA H., in Boston, 6 April, æ. 41, wife of Rev. Louis Dwight.

EASTMAN, CAPT. JOEL, Salisbury, N. H., 23 May, æ. 88, father of Hon. Joel E., of Conway, N. H.

EDWARDS, MR. JOHN, Cambridge, 3 April, æ. 64. "Mr. Edwards was an Englishman by birth. He has resided in this City about 32 years, during which period he sustained an unspotted character, and secured the esteem and respect of all with whom he had intercourse."—*Cambridge Chronicle, April* 5, 1849.

ELLIOTT, MR. RICHARD, North Danvers, 9 May, æ. 87; a soldier of the Revolution.

EPES, MRS. BETSEY, Boston, 4 May, æ. 82, formerly of Lyndeboro', N. H.

FARNUM, MRS. LYDIA, Smithfield, R. I., 13 June, æ. 94; widow of Mr. Noah Farnum.

FARRAR, HON. TIMOTHY, Hollis, N. H., 21 Feb., æ. 101.

The materials for the following sketch of the life of this eminent man, which has been prepared for the Register at our particular request, were principally derived from the discourse delivered at his funeral, by Rev. Samuel Lee, of New Ipswich.

Hon. Timothy Farrar was born at Lincoln, then part of Concord, Mass., 28 June, 1747, O. S.; consequently his age would have been 102 the 9th day of July, 1849. He was graduated at Cambridge, in the class of 1767. He had considered himself devoted to the Christian ministry, and made some preparation for pursuing his studies in that profession; but the death of his elder brother at New Ipswich rendered it necessary for him to take charge of the farm left vacant by that event. In the care of his farm, and in the instruction of youth, his time was spent till the commencement of the Revolutionary War. In the first attempt to organize a government by the people, he was appointed a Judge of the Court of Common Pleas for Hillsborough County. He was promoted to the Bench of the Superior Court of the State in 1791, and appointed Chief-Justice of that Court in 1802. This last office he did not accept, having determined to leave that Bench, which he did in the following year. He however accepted the Chief-Justiceship of the Court of Common Pleas for Hillsborough County, and also, on the new organization of the Judiciary in 1813, the Chief-Justiceship of that Court for the Eastern Circuit, embracing the Counties of Rockingham, Strafford, and Hillsborough. In 1816 he retired from public life, having served his country as a Judge in her Courts forty years, with the utmost fidelity, and with the highest honor to himself. The following year the death of his lamented wife occurred, leaving him thus alone.

Although he was now an old man, yet there were before him more than thirty years. This period was a most emphatic commentary on the preceding portion of his life. What he had before sown, it was his privilege now to reap, in the peaceful fruit of a happy and heavenly old age. By the death of their parents, a large circle of his grandchildren were thrown upon his special care. This care he bestowed not only with the affection of a father, but with the utmost accuracy of attention to their minutest wants. It was his privilege, on the sabbath next succeeding his one hundredth birthday, to listen to a sermon from one of them, having reference to the occasion. In 1841, in consequence of the removal of the daughter who could most conveniently take the care of him, he became a resident of Hollis.

The ordinary accompaniments of old age seem hardly to have belonged to his. He retained his mental faculties, scarcely at all impaired, to the last. His memory, after he was one hundred years of age, was scarcely less perfect than at any period of his life. He remembered not only the incidents of his early life, but also those of the passing day and year. He read much while his sight permitted, and then listened to the reading of others. Up to the last he had his own independent opinions on all the important questions of the day, political and other.

He retained the use of his bodily powers in a degree equally remarkable. In his one hundredth year he rode on horseback; and it is only within the last three or four years that his sight has been so seriously impaired as to prevent his reading the scriptures in large print.

The closing scene was in keeping with his life. He seemed ripe for the change. His death was in the highest sense a *natural* death. With very little disease the operation of the animal functions was rendered feeble, and the wheels seemed as if about to stop. But a short time before his death he fell into a quiet sleep, from which it was hoped he would awake refreshed. These hopes were not to be realized. His respiration soon became feeble, and more and more so, till, without a pang or the distortion of a feature, he ceased to breathe. Upon his countenance was left, after the spirit was gone, the impress of his character, and an expression of that peace of God which marked his end.

In attempting to delineate the character of Judge Farrar, we are embarrassed by its completeness. No one excellence stands out to arrest attention and invite description. Every element is there, and in its just proportion. All is symmetry.

As implied in this, he was a man of *principle.* He seemed to act on the assumption that "whatsoever is not of faith is sin." He had on all subjects his principles settled, and every thing, not only in religion, but also in the ordinary affairs of life, must be conformed to them. Every thing must be done *right.* There are some good sort of people, whose spirit is that of Christian benevolence, but who are loose in their ideas of the mode of acting it out. Hence they often, in specific instances, sacrifice principle in the cause of love. Such was not his practice. RIGHT was to him infinitely sacred; and he never would, for the sake of some temporary advantage either to himself or others, violate its dictates. But the uniform kindness of his disposition prevented this firmness, which was the inevitable effect of his veneration for the right, from ever assuming even the appearance of a harsh or unaccommodating temper.

Candor was a prominent trait in his character. His earnest love for the right led to a careful and honest search after *truth* — and he acted in its light; and only when he could thus act did he act at all. So far as those who knew him best could discern, the description of his mind in this particular was perfect. Prejudice was entirely excluded. Any feelings of interest he might be supposed to have, in favor of the result of an investigation, seemed to have no influence. His "ruling passion" in such a case was love of truth, as a means of judging of the right. Although of an ardent temperament, his ardor was laid aside, and all evidence was laid in the just balances of a cool and discriminating intellect.

This suggests another trait in his character; namely, an accurate intellectual discrimination. Possessed of strong native powers of mind, and these cultivated by a thorough course of study in his youth, it must follow that, with his ardent love of truth, and his candor and impartiality in the search for it, he would make distinctions when there were differences, and only then. With premises thus obtained, and with a logic of corresponding accuracy, the processes of his reasoning were scarcely less unerring than those of a mathematical demonstration.

He had a sound common sense. By common sense we mean the application of knowledge and good judgment to the common and immediately practical affairs of life. We often find great men deficient in this particular. They are familiar with abstract ideas and general principles, but not with the application of them to the purposes of ordinary utility. Not so with the remarkable man of whom we speak. While familiar with those general principles which lie at the basis of science and of all correct opinion and practice, he was equally familiar with their application. His profession was fitted especially to give this practical quality to the treasures of his mind. This trait of character rendered its possessor eminently useful, not only on the Bench, but during the long period subsequent to his professional life — useful not only to his family, but to others who needed and received his advice.

He was *temperate* — not only in the modern technical sense, applicable to the use of stimulating drinks, but in eating. He lived in this, as in every other particular, by rule. To leave the table with an appetite as good as when he came to it, was a rule he always observed. Not long before his death, in reply to the question to what he ascribed his long life, he replied, "to temperance in eating."

His equanimity deserves notice. This was not constitutional, but the result of a rigid self-discipline. Though naturally not of easy self-control, such was the power of his will, such the authority of his self-behests, that under whatsoever severity of trial, he neither spoke nor acted till reason bade and sanctioned.

He was the subject of strong domestic affections. During his public life he was much from home, and deeply engrossed in the duties of his profession. Yet he loved his family and devoted a careful attention to its wants. After retiring from public life, he became the centre of dependence to many of his grandchildren, and to the last day of his life, he kept under his notice the minutest particulars of the condition of every one of them. He was indeed a patriarch. His children, his children's children, and their children, gathered around him, to love, and revere, and almost adore, and received from him the lessons of wisdom.

He was cheerful. His natural temperament and his religion both conspired to render him so. His cheerfulness went with him through all the infirmities and privations of age. As one source of enjoyment after another was dried up, it left no trace of gloom. Heaven more than supplied an equivalent for what was withheld.

Kindness was the law of his life. It was evinced in all his domestic relations. He sought the happiness of all, and made the least possible demands upon the attention and care of others — a trait that went with him to the last. The same spirit guided him in all his intercourse with society.

His modesty was a striking characteristic. He was always brought forward — he never obtruded himself. Office was conferred, not sought by him. His deportment in all the relations of life was eminently respectful, howmuchsoever his inferiors the persons concerned.

He was a patriot. Every thing in his history was fitted to inspire him with love to his country. He had attained the age of maturity before the war of the Revolution. He was a witness of the events and a participator in the feelings that led to and attended upon that eventful period. He was placed upon the Bench at the first organization of a government by the people. In that position and at that period of his life, and with a heart like his, the events of the struggle for independence, the organization of national and state governments, the adoption of the federal constitution, in short, all the facts implied in our becoming a great and mighty nation, enlisted the deepest interest of his heart, and made his country the object of his warmest affections. It is difficult for us, who were born in other times, to appreciate the love of country, of which such a man, in such circumstances, would be the subject. The ardor of his patriotism never abated. He had an intimate knowledge of all the incidents in his country's history, up to the last week of his life, and an independent opinion on all the important measures of the national government. His opinions on the last presidential canvass were formed and defended on the same principles and by the same course of reasoning, as would have led him to the same result, under similar circumstances, at any earlier period of his life.

The religious character of Judge Farrar deserves special notice. It commenced in early life. At the age of thirteen, he listened to a sermon from Whitfield, preached at Concord, his native town. He had taken a seat in the gallery directly in front of the speaker, that he might have the best opportunity to observe his manner, and obtain a correct impression of the man. But as the preacher uttered his message, curiosity soon gave place to a conviction of the sacred importance of the truths uttered. He was deeply impressed. That sermon was never forgotten. The conviction of its truths was practical and permanent — and although he did not for several years make a public profession of religion, yet he dated the dawn of his Christian life from that sermon. His theology was of the Puritan school, and his life was in correspondence, and partook largely of the Puritan element. His religion was the religion of principle, and had his application to his whole life — yet not of mere principle; his heart and warm affections were in it. He *enjoyed* religion, and especially in the later period of his life. But a short time before his death, he remarked to a friend that his last days had been his best days — that he had never seen the time when he could say, "My soul hath no pleasure in them." He was familiar with the Bible, and quoted it with rare appositeness. He studied it as he studied Blackstone; and his religious opinions were the result of the same careful investigation of the one, as were his professional opinions of the other. His was "the full assurance of hope" — not in his youth, but in his riper years. His opinions in relation to himself were based on the same accuracy of *knowledge*, as were those on other subjects. Death was to him deprived of his sting. He had no fear of dying. "I feel just as ready," said he to a friend a few months since, "to lie down to die, as to lie down to sleep." And as the event proved, the two were to be united. He lay down to sleep. He slept, and it was death. We may add, he awoke, and it was Heaven.

Such, imperfectly sketched, was the life, such the death, and such the character of the venerable man, who, after standing so long a patriarch in our midst, has at length gone to his grave in a "full age like as a shock of corn cometh in in his season."

FAXON, ELISHA, ESQ., Stonington, Conn., 2 April, æ. 78, a native of Braintree, Mass., but for nearly 60 years a resident in S.

FENNO, MRS. NANCY, Boston, 17 June, æ. 74; widow of the late William Fenno.

FESSENDEN, MR. JOHN, Townsend, 16 Jan., æ. 74.

FISHER, MRS. JANE, Newark, N. J., suddenly, 31 March, æ. 28, wife of Oscar Fisher, Esq., and adopted daughter of Phineas Bemis, of Dudley, Mass.

FLINT, MRS. PRISCILLA, North Reading, 4 June, æ. 87; relict of the late Col. Daniel Flint.

FOSTER, MR. JOSIAH, Beverly, 29 April, æ. 90.

FOWLER, MR. MEDAD, Westfield, 26 April, æ. 89.

FRENCH, MRS. SARAH, Northampton, 9 May, æ. 90; widow of Asa French, of Williamsburg, who came from Braintree, and was son of Samuel French of that town. She was the daughter of Ezekiel White, of Weymouth, a son of Samuel White of that town, and a descendant of Peregrine White, the first Englishman born in New England, (born Nov., 1620, in Cape Cod harbor.) She was born at Weymouth, Feb. 25, 1759, her father removed to Goshen in 1777, and she was married at Williamsburg, Feb. 14, 1784. The mother of Samuel White, and grandmother of Ezekiel, was Anna Pratt, the daughter of deaf and dumb parents.

Mrs. French was well acquainted with the ancestral history of her kindred and neighbors, the exercise of her mental powers were continued in a remarkable degree to the last, and her recollections of past events were fresh and accurate.

FURBER, MRS. MARY, Farmington, N. H., March, æ. 92; widow of Gen. Richard F.

GARDNER, MRS. ELIZABETH, Nantucket, 6 March, æ. 72, widow of Mr. Shubael G.

GERRY, MRS. ANN, New Haven, 17 March, æ. 85; widow of Elbridge Gerry, one of the Signers of the Declaration of Independence.

GOOCH, MRS. ABIGAIL, North Yarmouth, Me., May, æ. 94, relict of Mr. John Gooch.

GORDON, MR. JOSEPH, Searsport, Me., 9 May, æ 90; a Revolutionary Pensioner.

GORHAM, MR. JOSIAH, Richmond, Me., 20 April, æ. 83, a soldier in the Revolution and the War of 1812.

HAILE, MR. COOMER, Bristol, R. I., 22 April, æ. 84; a Revolutionary Pensioner.

HALL, MRS. ELEANOR, Tamworth, N. H., æ. 32; wife of Mr. Obed Hall, and youngest dau. of the late John Carroll, Esq., of Pittsfield.

HAMMOND, CAPT. GIDEON, Mattapoiset, 21 March, æ. 95, a soldier of the Revolution.

HARDING, MR. URIAH, East Medway, 1 May, æ. 89.

HARRIS, MRS. EUNICE G., Boston, 11 April, æ. 68; wife of Mr. Isaac Harris.

HARVEY, HON. JOHN, Northwood, N. H., 2 May, æ. 75; formerly Judge of Probate for Rockingham Co. He was son of Major John H., an original settler in the town, and a soldier of the Revolution. Judge H. had been a Representative and Senator, and was extensively known in Rockingham county.

HATCH, DEA. JOEL, 5 April, æ. 79; CLIFT, DEA. JOSEPH, 6 April, æ. 81; both at Marshfield. They were elected Deacons of the Congregational Church in North Marshfield, in 1810, and they were both found dead, the one in his bed, and the other in his yard.

HAVEN, DEA. MOSES, Framingham, 26 April, æ. 82.

HENDERSON, MR. JAMES, Feltonville, 11 May, æ. 80, formerly of Boston.

HILDRETH, MISS HANNAH Z., at the Columbia Female Institute, Wheeling, Va., 27 Nov. 1848, of consumption.

HINMAN, MR. DAVID C., New Haven, 9 March; an engraver of much skill. Mr. H., has done great service to his country by his excellent taste in producing many excellent portraits never before engraved in this country. He had just completed some which do him great credit, and had he lived to carry out his intention, our history would not have gone without many of the portraits so necessary to illustrate it, and which he felt had been shamefully neglected.

HOBBS, MR. DAVID, North Hampton, N. H., 4 May, æ. 88 yrs. 10 mo., a soldier of the Revolution; formerly of Effingham.

HOLMES, MISS ELIZABETH, in Leicester, 29 Mar., æ. 35, dau. of the late Dr. Jacob Holmes, and for many years an Instructress in Leicester Academy.

HOUSELEY, MRS. ANNA MARIA, Boston, 18 April, æ. 85.

HOWES, CAPT. SAML. H., Cambridgeport, 22 Mar., a well known steamboat commander.

HOWLAND, MR. JOHN H., of N. Bedford, at Bloomingdale, N. Y., 13 March, æ. 76.

HUBBARD, MRS. HANNAH, Boston, 6 April, æ. 90 yrs. 1 mo.; wid. of the late Peter Hubbard of Holden, and former widow of Mr. John Dodd of H.

HUBBARD, DR. JOSHUA, Cincinnati, O., 13 May, æ. 66; a printer, published a paper for a season, at Kennebunk, Me.

JENKINS, SAMUEL — "The last of Braddock's men" — Lancaster, O., 4 Jan., æ. 115 years. He was the (colored) slave of Capt. Broadwater, of Fairfax Co., Va., in 1734, and drove his master's provision wagon over the Alleghany Mountains in the memorable campaign of Gen. Braddock. He retained his faculties to the last.

JOHNSON, MR. NATHANIEL, Acton, 9 May, æ. 87; a patriot of the Revolution.

JONES, MR. ELNATHAN, Lunenburg, 16 Mar., æ. 74.

KIDNEY, JONATHAN. — This venerable citizen, known and respected here through several generations, revered for his worth, his exemplary life, and his laborious diligence, has gone to his rest full of years, at the advanced age of nearly four score years and ten.

JONATHAN KIDNEY (says the Eve. Journal,) was born in this City, where he has resided for *eighty-eight years*. He was consequently one of the oldest connecting links between the past and the present. He has sustained through life a blameless reputation, and died, as he lived, greatly beloved by his descendants and universally respected by all who knew him. Mr. KIDNEY served his time as a Blacksmith and followed the business always.

To the just tribute of the Eve. Journal to his private character, we add briefly some of the principal incidents of his life:

At the age of 17, Mr. KIDNEY was drafted as a militia-man, under Gen. Schuyler, in 1777. His division was at first ordered to Fort Edward; but soon fell back upon Saratoga. Afterwards we hear of him at Bennington, in both engagements at that place. Again, upon the intelligence reaching that place of the expected battle with Burgoyne, he was ordered back to Saratoga, but did not arrive there until after the battle.

The most eventful period of his life was that which followed. He was one of a party who embarked at New Haven, Conn., in a privateer vessel. With the entire party he was taken prisoner by the British, and placed on board the Jersey Prison ship at the Wallabout. He was confined there some six months, at the expiration of which he was released, but in a weak state, from the tyrannical and barbarous treatment he received. He travelled on foot from Jersey City to Newburgh, where General Washington had his head-quarters, not being able to accomplish more than five miles a day. He there received assistance, by order of the Commanding General, and took passage in a sloop for Albany.

Mr. KIDNEY took an active part with the friends of George Clinton, Robert Yates, Samuel Jones, Abm. Ten Eyck, Gen. Peter Gansevoort, Chancellor Lansing, and other prominent anti-federalists, against the adoption of the U. S. Constitution in 1788; and he participated in the high scene of excitement and collision which in this City followed the attempt of the federalists of that day to celebrate the event. To the day of his death, as we are informed, he held in possession the cannon which on that occasion was planted in Green street, to dispute the passage through it of the procession headed by Gen. Schuyler, Stephen Van Rensselaer, and their friends. The venerable Isaac Denniston is now the only survivor of those who witnessed that conflict.

A patriot of the Revolution, he was ever earnest in what he regarded as synonymous with the principles and duties of that great epoch, and throughout his life was a decided and consistent democrat. — *Albany Argus*, 29 *March*, 1849.

KINSMAN, MRS. ANNA, Ipswich, 25 April, æ. 92; widow of the late William Kinsman.

LAVENDER, CAPT. ROBERT, in Portsmouth, Va., at the residence of Capt. John M. Foster, 8 April, æ. 32, a native of Provincetown, Mass.

LEWIS, MRS. REBECCA C., Dorchester, 18 April, æ. 82, wife of Mr. Thomas Lewis.

LINCOLN, CAPT. JAMES, Machiasport, Me., 16 May, æ. 73; formerly of Scituate.

LIVINGSTON, MR. GEORGE, Worcester County, Md., 1 April, æ. 93; a soldier of the Revolution.

LORING, MRS. ELLEN M., N. Andover, 4 March, æ. 24; dau. of Hon. D. P. King.

MANDRAKE, MRS. ELIZABETH, Boston, 3 June, æ. 92.

MARSHALL, MRS. ABIGAIL, Hampton Falls, N. H., March, æ. 100 years.

McCOY, MR. JONATHAN, Bow, N. H., 1 June, æ. 97, a soldier of the Revolution.

McLELLAN, CAPT. JOHN, Portland, 19 Feb., æ. 82 yrs. and 7 mo.

McMILLAN, MRS. ANNE, Bellefontaine, Logan Co., O., 24 March, æ. 124.

MERIAM, MRS. MARTHA, Lexington, 7 May, æ. 83; widow of the late Rufus M.

MERRILL, MR. SAMUEL, Kennebunk, 11 June, æ. 70; he fell dead while walking in the street.

MILES, REV. JOHN, Shrewsbury, 20 March, æ. 83 yrs., 4 mos.; he had been pastor of the Congregational Society in Grafton, nearly 30 years.

MILLER, JAMES, ESQ., E. Greenwich, R. I., 17 May, æ. 95.

MONTAGUE, JOSEPH, Esq., Remsen, N. Y., 30 April, æ. 86; a Revolutionary soldier, grad. D. C., class 1788. He was the youngest of five children, whose united ages at their decease were 425 years.

MOORE, MR. URIAH, Stow, 31 Mar., æ. 78.

MORRIS, THOMAS, ESQ., N. York, March. He was a son of Robert Morris of Philadelphia (so well known in our history,) and for many years U. S. Marshal of N. Y.

MORTON, MRS. ABIGAIL, Bristol, Me., 14 May, æ. 100 yrs. 11 mo. 12 d.; relict of Mr. James Morton; they removed from Roxbury, Mass., to B., towards the close of the Revolutionary War.

MULLIKEN, MR. BENJAMIN, in Mechanicsville, Saratoga Co., N. Y., at the residence of his son-in-law, Mr. W. B. Harris, æ. 86. The deceased was a native of Massachusetts, and was in the War of the Revolution, for which he drew a pension under the Act of 1832. He left Massachusetts in the year 1800, and settled in the town of Stillwater, Saratoga Co., in which town he continued to reside to the time of his death.—*Cambridge Chronicle.*

MUNRO, MR. JOSEPH, Bristol, R. I., 29 April, æ. 89, a Revolutionary Pensioner.

NICHOLS, MR. JOHN, Salem, 1 May, æ. 72.

NICKERSON, CAPT. SAMUEL, Boston, 13 June, æ. 83, lately one of the Port-Wardens of the City.

OAKES, ALBERT P., at Staten Island Hospital, of Small Pox, 17 Mar., æ. 25, son of the late Capt. Thomas Oakes, of Malden, Mass.

OLIVER, MRS. MARY W. T., Plymouth, 1 Apl., æ. 31; wife of Henry J. Oliver, Esq.

OSGOOD, MRS. LUCY, Andover, 10 June, æ. 80; she was the widow of the late Jacob Osgood, and died in the same house in which JAMES OTIS was killed by lightning.

OWEN, PHILIP, ESQ., Brunswick, Me. 28 May, æ. 94; a Revolutionary Pensioner.

PACKARD, REV. HEZEKIAH, D. D., Salem, 25 April, æ. 87 yrs. 4 mo.; a grad. at Harv. Coll. in the class of 1787, and a soldier in the Revolution.

PARK, MRS. LUCY, in Boston, 27 Mar. æ. 79, widow of the late John Park, of Framingham.

PARKER, MR. WILLIAM, Roxbury, 28 Mar., æ. 86.

PARMENTER, MR. LEVI, Sudbury, 11 April, æ. 86, a soldier of the Revolution.

PARSONS, MRS. SARAH, Skaneateles, N. Y., 19 April, æ. 92; widow of the late Noah P. of Westhampton.

PEARCE, HON. DUTEE J., Newport, R. I., 5 May, æ. 69. We learn from the Newport News that he died at his residence at that town, yesterday morning, at half past nine o'clock, of erysipelas. He was born in April, 1780, on the island of Prudence, and was therefore sixty-nine years of age at the time of his death. He graduated with much honor at Brown University, and after completing his study of the law, he commenced his practice of the legal profession in Newport, where he remained till the time of his death. Mr. Pearce became early interested in political affairs, and in 1819 he was elected Attorney-General of the State, which office he filled until 1825. He was then appointed United States District Attorney for the Rhode Island district, and in November, 1835, he was elected representative to Congress, in which capacity he continued to serve the people of Rhode Island until 1837, when he was succeeded by the Hon. Robert B. Cranston.

PEASE, MRS. ELIZABETH, N. Haven, Ct., 28 Mar., æ. 26; wife of Thomas Huntington Pease, and dau. of the late W. H. P. Graham of N. York.

PEAVEY, MRS. ABIGAIL, Tuftonboro', N. H., Mar., æ. 85; widow of Joseph P.

PERRY, WIDOW REBECCA, West Cambridge, 11 April, æ. 71.

PIERCE, AUGUSTUS, M. D., Tyngsboro', 20 May, æ. 47. Dr. Pierce was a native of New Salem, graduated at Harvard College in 1820, and was the author of the far-famed Poem, called "THE REBELLIAD," so well known to every son of the University.

PLUMER, MR. DANIEL, JR., Epping, N. H., 21 June, æ. 46 yrs. 7 mo. and 9 days, of fever—a most valuable citizen; and of a highly respectable family. He was grandson of Samuel Plumer, Esq., one of the first settlers in the town.

PLUMER, MR. JOHN J., Epping, N. H., 1 March, æ. 49; youngest son of Ex-Governor Hon. William Plumer, grandson of Samuel P., Esq., an early settler in that town, from Newbury, who d. in 1803, at the advanced age of 81. The venerable Ex-Governor still survives, aged 90 years.

REEVES, MRS. ELIZABETH, Wayland, 26 Mar., æ. 91, widow of the late Jacob Reeves, Esq.

RICHARDSON, MR. JOEL, Billerica, 3 May, æ. 72; formerly of Boston.

RICHARDSON, MRS. —— Saco, Me., 7 May, æ. 101 yrs. 11 mo.; widow of Mr. Nathaniel Richardson.

ROBINSON, ALEXANDER, in Pensacola, Fa., in March, æ. 26, Assistant Surgeon U. S. Navy.

SACKETT, MR. JONATHAN, Milford, 9 May, æ. 89., a soldier of the Revolution.

SAMPSON, DEA. NATHANIEL, West Brattleboro', Vt., 25 March, æ. 95; formerly of Pelham, Ms. He was born in Middleborough, Ms., July 10, 1754. He entered the army after the battle of Bunker Hill, and was present at the action in Brooklyn and the evacuation of New York. He enlisted several times for short periods, and his military life—a part of which was spent on board a privateer at sea—occupied about three years. In 1780 he settled in Pelham, Ms., where he lived till 1806, when he removed to Brattleboro'. In Pelham he appears to have first made a profession of religion, and he was early chosen a deacon of the church. He was chosen to the same office by the church in Brattleboro', soon after his settlement here. He ever maintained the character of a meek, consistent, exemplary Christian, and in society he was much respected for his integrity and his unassuming virtues.—The "memory of the just is blessed."—COM.

SEARL, MR. NATHAN, Southampton, 16 Mar., æ. 89.

SEARLE, DANIEL, ESQ., Temple, N. H., 6 April, æ. 85.

SIBLEY, MR. CHARLES, Calais, Me., 1 April, æ. 78; a native of Sutton, Ms.

SIMPSON, MR. BENJAMIN, Saco, Me., 23 March, æ. 94; "one of the immortal 'Tea Party.'"

SLAUGHTER, CAPT. PHILIP, Richmond,

Va., 24 April, æ. 90; an officer in the Revolutionary army.

SMITH, MRS. MARY, Portsmouth, N. H. 26 March, æ. 89, wife of James Smith, Esq. She was the great grand-daughter of Joseph Adams of Braintree, (grandson of Henry Adams, an early settler at Mount Wollaston, now Quincy,) by his second wife Hannah, who was the daughter of John Bass, and Ruth, his wife, the daughter of the famous JOHN ALDEN, who came to New England in the MAY FLOWER, in 1620.

SMITH, MRS. SARAH, in Boston, 23 April, æ. 76, widow of the late Ammi R. Smith, Esq., of Ipswich.

SOMERBY, MR. AUGUSTUS W., of Boston, of Cholera at Chagres, 21 May, æ. 36. He was son of Mr. Ebenezer S. of Boston, and cousin of H. G. Somerby, Esq., now of London, Eng., a young man much beloved and respected.

STARKEY, CAPT. TIMOTHY, Essex, 4 May, æ. 84; a soldier of the Revolution.

STARK, JOHN, ESQ., Washington, D. C., 14 May; very suddenly; he was grandson of Gen. John Stark, of N. H.

STEARNES, MR. DANIEL, Newport, N. H., 4 May, æ. 93, a soldier of the Revolution.

STEARNS, MRS. NANCY C., Milford, N. H., 28 March, æ. 35.

This lady was the daughter of Mr. Elijah F. Valentine, the present worthy Assistant Steward and Patron of the University at Cambridge, and was born in Northborough, Mass,, Nov. 20. 1813. Having filled the responsible situation of a school teacher, in Cambridge, for several years, with ability and success, she was married, Sept. 14, 1837, to Rev. O. O. Stearns. Naturally of a retiring disposition, she was most happy in the bosom of her family, occupied in the discharge of the duties of a wife and mother, for which relations she was admirably fitted by her mild and cheerful temperament, her truly Christian meekness and patience. Suddenly and unexpectedly prostrated upon a bed of sickness, she endured with exemplary resignation the suffering with which she was visited; and, after a few days of pain and anguish, calmly breathed her last, in the full assurance of a happy resurrection beyond the grave.

STONE, Capt. John, Dublin, N. H., 13 April æ 84.

SUMNER, MISS DEBORAH, Dedham, 20 April, æ. 70.

TAPPAN, REV. WILLIAM B., of Boston, æ. 55. We are pained to announce (says the Traveller) that our excellent friend and fellow citizen, Rev. Wm. B. Tappan, departed this life, at his residence in Grantville, [in Needham, 13 miles from the city,] yesterday morning at 3 o'clock, after a sickness of about 11 hours. He preached last Sabbath at Mattapoisett, returned to the city Monday morning, and spent the forenoon at his office, and returned home in the cars at 2 P. M. At 4 o'clock, he complained of slight indisposition, and took some medicine. Soon after he was seized with spasms, accompanied with clammy sweat, cold extremities and feeble pulse, which continued with increasing violence, baffling all remedies, till at 3 yesterday morning, his frame, constitutionally feeble, sunk under it. He was sensible of his situation from the first, and expressed quiet resignation. During the spasms, his sufferings were very great; but, when an involuntary groan escaped him, he would say, "understand, I don't complain, it's all right." His sight and hearing were affected, and he complained of burning thirst, and when his attendants touched his flesh, cold as marble, he would say, "*O you burn me.*" His end was peace; and "the memory of the just shall be blessed." The attending physicians pronounced the case one of spasmodic cholera.

[We have reason heartily to respond to the sentiments above expressed, but our friend needs no eulogy from us — his works are alike his monument and his eulogy. To know him was to admire him. Modesty, benevolence, and indeed every virtue found an abiding place in his bosom. Nothing can be purer than the sentiments which flowed from his pen — they give evidence of the purity of their fountain, and they have gone forth in his poems like the innumerable rays from the sun, and must have a benign effect upon the rising world.

Mr. Tappan was son of Mr. Samuel Tappan, who died in Portsmouth, N. H. in 1806, by Aurelia, dau. of —— Bingham of Canterbury, Ct., who died in 1846, æ. 77. — PUB.]

TEMPLE, MRS. HANNAH B., Natick, 9 June, æ. 39; wife of Mr. Jason Temple.

THAYER, MRS. CHARLOTTE, in Worcester, at the house of her son-in-law, Clarendon Harris, Esq., with whom she has lived for some years past, 14 May, suddenly, æ. 79; relict of the late Capt. Nathaniel Thayer, of Boston.

THAYER, MISS REBECCA, Boston, 2 May, æ. 70; formerly of Braintree.

TIBBETTS, MRS. MARGARET, Brookfield, N. H., 14 Mar. æ. 94; widow of Edmund T.

TIRRELL, MRS. MARY TAYLOR, Boston, suddenly, 3 Mar., æ. 70, widow of the late Capt. Thomas Tirrell.

TOWNSLEY, MR. JACOB, Steuben, Me., 14 May, æ 90, a native of Springfield, Mass., and a soldier of the Revolution.

TRASK, MRS. SARAH, Danvers, 17 Dec., 1848., æ. 81; the eldest dau. of Mr. William Trask, who died 22 Nov. 1806, aged

62. She was a lineal descendant of "Capt. William Traske" of Salem, and inherited a portion of the original homestead, where her lengthened life was spent in kind assiduities, sympathies and toils in behalf of others — these in their effects will remain an abiding "memorial of her."

TUFTS, MRS. MERCY, Weymouth, 6 May, æ. 85, relict of the late Cotton Tufts, Esq.

TURNER, MR. CALVIN, Medford, 17 June, æ. 73.

TURNER, MRS. LYDIA, Antwerp, Jefferson Co., N. Y., 25 March, æ. 86, the relict of Capt. Joshua Turner, and a pensioner for a number of years prior to her death. She was the eldest daughter and third child of Col. Luke Drury of Grafton and Marlboro', and long since the last of his family of nine children. A numerous progeny, in children, grand-children, and great-grand-children, are scattered throughout the United States, to revere her memory. T. S. T.

TURNER, MRS. MARY, Auburn, Me., 19 April, æ. 86, a Revolutionary Pensioner.

TYRRELL, MR. JACOB, Orange, 15 Feb., æ. 89, a Revolutionary Pensioner.

VARNEY, EUNICE, Dover, N. H., 1 June, æ. 99; a member of the society of Friends.

VOSE, MRS. MERCY, at Concord, Ms., 20 May, æ. 86; widow of the late Deac. John Vose of that town.

WAKEFIELD, TIMOTHY, ESQ., Reading, 19 April, æ. 93, a Revolutionary Pensioner.

WARE, MRS. MARY LOVELL, Milton, 4 April, æ. 50.

This lady, whose memory will long be cherished by a most extensive circle of friends, was daughter of Mark Pickard, Esq., formerly a merchant in Boston, by his wife Mary Lovell; and was born in Boston, Oct. 2, 1798. In June, 1827, she became the second wife of the late lamented Rev. Henry Ware, Jr., D. D.; since whose death (at Framingham, Sept. 22, 1843,) she has resided principally on Milton Hill, where her peaceful, though not uneventful, life was finally brought to a close, amid the affectionate attentions and sorrowing regrets of her children and friends.

WARE, MR. MICHAEL, Buckland, 7 May, æ. 84.

WARNER, MR. PHINEAS, Belchertown, 9 April, æ. 86.

WARREN, MR. SILAS, Upton, 10 Nov. 1848, æ. 95. He was among the soldiers over whom General Washington received command at Cambridge; he was also present at Dorchester Heights when the Americans compelled the British to evacuate Boston. After the establishment of his country's independence, he lived upon his farm in Upton to the time of his death, where it was his delight, in his hours of rest from agricultural pursuits, to entertain his friends with revolutionary tales and incidents of the "times that tried men's souls."

He had been a subscriber *for*, and constant reader *of* "The Massachusetts Spy," ever since it was published, being *seventy-seven years.* — *Worcester Spy.*

WAYLAND, REV. FRANCIS, SEN., Saratoga Springs, 9 April, æ. 76.

WEED, CAPT. ALEXANDER, Rochester, N. Y., 30 Mar., æ. 79, a soldier of the Revolution.

WEST, MRS. ABIGAIL, Taunton, 1 March, æ. 79; relict of John West, Esq., of that place.

WHEELER, MR. SAMUEL, Rockport, 21 Feb., æ. 90.

WHITCOMB, CAPT. EPHRAIM, Boxboro', 17 April, suddenly, of apoplexy, æ. 76, a kind and amiable man, and exemplary Christian. He was one of seven brothers and sisters, all of whom have attained the age of 70 years and upwards.

WHITNEY, MRS. HANNAH, 10 March, æ. 87.

WHITNEY, MRS. MARY, Hingham, 4 March, æ. 79; formerly of Northboro'.

WILKINSON, ABRAHAM, ESQ., Pawtucket, R. I., recently, æ. 83; one of the founders of that town. In connection with his brothers and the well known Mr. Samuel Slater, the manufacturing business was there established.

WILLCUTT, MRS. SUSANNAH, Cohasset, 12 June, æ. 86 yrs. 7 mo. widow of the late Thos. Willcutt.

WILLIAMS, MRS. ABIGAIL, Newburyport, 2 April, æ. 96; widow of the late Joseph Williams, Esq.

WILLIAMS, HON. TIMOTHY S., Ithaca, N. Y., 11 Mar., Senator of the 26th District of that State.

WILSON, MR. FRANCIS T., New York, 12 April, æ. 83, son of the late William Wilson, of Boston.

WINGATE, MRS. MARY, (widow,) Rochester, N. H., 19 May, æ. 95.

WINSLOW, MRS. MARY, Vassalboro', Me., 25 Feb., æ. 89; widow of Nathan W., late of Westboro'.

WITHIN, MR. SAMUEL, Wilton, Me., 21 Feb., æ. 91 yrs., 8 mos.; a Revolutionary Pensioner.

WOOD, REV. BENJAMIN, Pastor of the Congregational Church in Upton, 24 April, æ. 76. He was a native of Lebanon, N. H., and was born in 1772, graduated at Dartmouth in 1793, and was ordained at Upton, as the successor of Rev. Elisha Fisk, June 1, 1796.

WOODBURY, MR. WILLIAM, Boston, 19 April, æ. 70, formerly of Salem.

WOODWARD, DEA. JACOB, Marlboro', N. H., 9 April, æ. 87, a Revolutionary Pensioner.

WORTH, MRS. VELINA, Edgartown, 7 June, æ. 82, widow of Jethro Worth, Esq.

Æt. Suæ 1670

REBECCA RAWSON.

Born in Boston 1656 Died at Port-Royal (Jamaica) 1692

Engraved from the original Portrait in the Possession of h. R. Dodge, East Sutton, Mass

NEW ENGLAND

HISTORICAL AND GENEALOGICAL REGISTER.

VOL. III. OCTOBER, 1849. NO. IV.

GENEALOGICAL NOTICES OF THE DESCENDANTS OF SECRETARY RAWSON.

[*Note.*—In our last number we gave a brief outline of the public employments and services of Secretary Rawson. We now present our readers with a genealogical sketch of his posterity, principally condensed from the "MEMORIAL OF THE RAWSON FAMILY," recently published. A word of explanation may be necessary, with regard to the system of references which we have adopted, it being, in some respects, different from that employed in the "Memorial." The Roman numeral prefixed to a name, indicates the generation, counting from the first progenitor in this country. Beside this character, but one series of numbers is made use of, and the same number is always found attached to the same individual; thereby preventing all possibility of confusion, and affording the greatest facility for reference, backwards or forwards.]

We have mentioned, in the preceding number, that, of the five sons of Secretary Rawson, three settled in England. Respecting two of them, DAVID (born May 6, 1644,) and JOHN, we know nothing. EDWARD, the eldest son of the Secretary, graduated at Harvard College in 1653, and entered the Ministry. Of his subsequent career our only knowledge is derived from Dr. Walker's "Attempt towards recovering an Account of the Numbers and Sufferings of the Clergy of the Church of England," * where his name occurs in the following passage, relative to the Rectory of Horsmanden, in the County of Kent.

"Good old Dr. Anherst had been Sequestred and forced from this Living about the beginning of the Troubles; at which Time one *Elleston* succeeded in it; but the Doctor dying about Five or Six Years after, the Patroness presented this Mr. *Couch*, who made a shift some way or other to get Possession of it, and kept it till about the Year

* "An Attempt Towards Recovering an Account of the Numbers and Sufferings of the Clergy of the Church of England, who were Sequester'd, Harrass'd, &c., in the late Times of the Grand Rebellion: Occasion'd by the Ninth Chapter (now the Second Volume) of Dr. Calamy's Abridgment of the Life of Mr. Baxter. Together with an Examination of That Chapter. By John Walker, M. A., Rector of St. Mary's the More in Exeter, and some time Fellow of Exeter-College in Oxford." Fol. Lond. 1714. Part. II. pp. 220.

1653; at which time he was also Sequestred from it, and so makes a Second Sufferer here. Mr. Couch outlived the Usurpation, and demanded his Living again of the Intruder, one *Edward Rawson*, [presented to it in 1655,] a *New-England*-Man, and a violent *Presbyterian*. This *Rawson*, as he had immediately succeeded Mr. *Couch*, so he was resolved to have continued in the Living if he could, and therefore gave him a great deal of Trouble to Dispossess him."

Dr. Calamy, after referring to the above passage, in the third volume of his Account of the Ejected Ministers,* and citing Dr. Walker's assertion that Rawson was "a violent Presbyterian," remarks that this, "if true, was a little peculiar;" and adds, "Mr. *Rawson* was accounted a good holy Man."

Rebecca Rawson, the sixth daughter and ninth child of the Secretary, whose portrait accompanies our present number, is the heroine of as romantic a tale as can be found upon the pages of New England history. She was born May 23, 1656, was tenderly nurtured and carefully educated, and was pronounced by her contemporaries "one of the most beautiful, polite, and accomplished young ladies in Boston." As such she became the object of the attentions of one Thomas Rumsey, a young man from England, of respectable appearance and pleasing address, who pretended to be Sir Thomas Hale, Jr., the nephew of Lord Chief-Justice Hale. The young lady being of one of the first families in Boston, "had the vanity," says a document preserved among our public archives, "to think herself suitable to make the young Lord a wife." They were accordingly married, July 1, 1679, "by a Minister of the Gospel, in the presence of near forty witnesses," and being "handsomely furnished, sailed for England, and safely arrived. She went on shore in a dishabille, leaving her trunks on board the vessel, and went to lodge with a relation of hers. In the morning early he arose, took the keys, and told her he would send her trunks on shore that she might be dressed before dinner. He sent the trunks up, and she waited impatiently for the keys till one or two o'clock; but he not coming, she broke open the trunks, and to her inexpressible surprise she found herself stript of everything, and her trunks filled with combustible matter; on which her kinsman ordered his carriage, and they went to a place where she stopt with her husband the night before. She enquired for Sir Thomas Hale, Jr.; they said he had not been there for some days. She said she was sure he was there the night before. They said Thomas Rumsey had been there with a young Lady, but was gone to his wife in Canterbury; and she saw him no more." We are informed that during a residence of thirteen years in England, after her abandonment, she "learned many curious works, such as painting on glass, &c.," and by her ingenuity and industry procured a genteel subsistence for herself and child, her pride not allowing her to be dependent upon her friends for support. Determining to return to New England, she left her child in the care of her sister, in England, who had no children of her own, and embarked for Boston, by way of Ja-

* "A Continuation of the Account of the Ejected Ministers, &c. &c. By Edmund Calamy, D. D." 8vo. Lond. 1727. i. 543–4.

maica, in a vessel which belonged to one of her uncles. But her eventful life was destined to a tragical end. The ship in which she had embarked, being just ready to sail from Port Royal, in Jamaica, for Boston, was swallowed up, with its passengers and crew, upon the morning of the great earthquake, June 9, 1692, her uncle alone, (who happened to be on shore, completing the settlement of his accounts,) of the whole ship's company, escaping to tell the sad tale.

Rebecca Rawson and her father are prominent characters in the highly entertaining little work entitled "Leaves from Margaret Smith's Journal in the Province of Massachusetts Bay," which has recently been submitted to the public.

Having thus disposed of those members of Edward Rawson's family who left this country, we will now speak of those who remained in New England. And first of his third son,

William Rawson, who was born May 21, 1651,* and married July 11, 1673, as appears from the following record in the ancient Family Bible. "This may certify all whomsoever it may concern, that on ye 11th day of July, 1673, on a certificate I received that William Rawson and Ann Glover, ye daughter of ye late Mr. Nathaniel Glover, had been duly and legally published, I joined them in marriage at the house and in presence of Mr. Habackuk Glover, his wife, Mr. Edward Rawson, father of ye sd William Rawson, and other friends, as witness my hand this 31st of July, 1673. — Edward Tyng, Ass't." The mother of Ann Glover, as we learn from a memorandum of Rev. Thomas Prince, "was ye only child of Mr Quarter-master Smith by his 1st wife, formerly of Lancashire in England and afterward of Dorchester in New England," and "was born in Lancashire in 1630. Her Parents living und^{r} ye ministry of ye Rev. Mr Richard Mather at Toxteth in that shire, they came up and brought Her wth them to Bristol in order for N. E. in April, 1635. Her Father and others settling at Dorchester and a new Chh gath^{d} There Aug. 23, 1636 ye sd Mr Richard Mather became y^{r} Teacher; under w^{os} ministry she liv'd, unless w^{n} sent to school at Boston. She married to Mr Nathan^{l} Glover a son of ye Hon^{b} John Glover Esq of sd Dorchester by w^{m} she had Nathanael and Ann. And then this Husband Dying, she remained a widdow till w^{n} she married ye Hon^{bl} Thomas Hinckley Esq. of Barnstable," the last Governor of Plymouth Colony. "Her sd D^{tr} Ann married to Mr Wm Rawson a son of M^{r} secretary Rawson secretary of ye Massachusetts colony."† William Rawson resided in Boston for some years after his marriage, and then removed to Dorchester, and thence, finally, to Braintree, now Quincy, where he purchased a tract of land from the descendants of his great uncle, Rev. John Wilson, being a portion of the grant made to that eminent Divine by the General Court of the Colony. This farm, which is situated near Neponset Village, adjoining the homestead of Hon. Josiah Quincy, late President of Harvard College, is still occupied by his descendants.

His children were as follows: —

* All dates are presumed to be according to Old Style.

† See Vol. I. p. 95 of this work.

Ann,	born in Boston,	April	11, 1674;	died in infancy.
Wilson,	" " "		1675;	" " "
Margaret,	" " "	Aug.	1, 1676;	" " "
Edward,	" " "	Sept.	6, 1677;	" " "
Edward,	" " "	Aug.	29, 1678;	" " "
Rachael,	" " "	Oct.	16, 1679;	" " "
Dorothy,	" " "	Aug.	8, 1681;	" " "
William,	" " "	Dec. 2 or	8, 1682.	(1)
David,	" " "	Dec.	13, 1683.	(2)
Dorothy,	" " "	June	19, 1686;	died young.
Ebenezer,	" " Dorchester,		1687;	" Aug. 28, 1691.
Thankful,	" " "	Aug.	6, 1688;	" Aug. 21, 1688.
Nathaniel,	" " Braintree,		1689.	(3)
Ebenezer,	" " "	July	24, 1691;	died young.
Edward,	" " "	Jan.	27, 1692.	(4)
Ann,	" " "	Aug.	28, 1693;	died in infancy.
Patience,	" " "	Nov.	8, 1694;	" Novr. 14, 1694.
Pelatiah,	" " "	July	2, 1696.	(5)
Grindal,	" " "	Aug.	24, 1697;	died in infancy.
Mary,	" " "		1698;	" " "

The names of the above twenty children are found recorded in the ancient Family Bible.

GRINDAL RAWSON, the fifth son and youngest child of Secretary Rawson, was born Jan 23, 1659, and graduated, with three others, at Harvard College, in 1678. After taking his first degree, "he was invited," so writes his wife, in a letter to Cotton Mather, "by his brother-in-law, the Rev. Mr. Samuel Torrey, to come to his house and study Divinity there, which he did, with such proficiency, that he was advised to enter upon preaching. He preached his first sermon at Medfield, with great acceptation, and after two months' occasional performances at other places, he received an invitation [Oct 4, 1680,] to Mendon," in the County of Worcester, whither about twenty families had recently returned, the town having been abandoned by its inhabitants during King Philip's War. The invitation being accepted, Mr. Rawson entered upon the duties of the pastoral office, and continued to preach until April 7, 1684, when he was permanently settled. After an eminently successful ministry of thirty-four years, he died "on the Lord's Day, about sunset," Feb. 6, 1715, aged 56 years. A sermon was preached at his decease, by his friend and classmate Cotton Mather, in the preface to which he favors us with an extract from President Oakes's Latin address, at the Commencement of 1678, wherein the Reverend orator was pleased to notice three of the four members of the graduating Class, viz. John Cotton, Cotton Mather, and Grindal Rawson, making honorable mention of the progenitors of the latter, and expressing his hope that God would endue him with the learning, sanctity, and moral virtues of a WILSON and a GRINDAL. Mather thus draws the character of his "well accomplished and industrious" friend, in the sermon just alluded to. "We generally esteemed him a truly pious man, and a very prudent one, and a person of *temper*, and every way qualified for a friend that might be delighted in. We honored him for his industrious oversight of the *Flock in the wilderness* which had been committed unto him, and the variety of successful *pains* which he took for the good of those to whom God had therefore exceedingly endeared him. We honored him for his *Intellectual Abilities*, which procured frequent applications to him, and brought him sometimes upon our most conspicuous theatres; and we usually took it for granted that things would be fairly done, where he had an hand in the doing of them. We honored him for his doing the work of an *Evangelist* among our Indians, of whose language he was a *master* that had scarce an *equal*, and for whose welfare his projections and performances were such as render our loss herein hardly to be repaired." He used to preach the Gospel regularly to the Indians in his neighborhood, in their own language; and published a work entitled "Confession of Faith," in English and Indian. In the spring of 1698 he was joined with Rev. Samuel Danforth, of Taunton, in a commission to visit the several plantations of Indians within the Province of Massachusetts Bay, in pursuance of orders and instructions from the Commissioners for the Propagation of the Gospel among the Indians in New England and the parts adjacent. These two gentlemen accordingly spent from May 30th to June 24th, 1698, in this visitation. Their highly interesting and valuable report thereof may be seen in the tenth volume of the Collections of the Massachusetts Historical Society.

Mr. Rawson married Susanna, daughter of Rev. John Wilson, first minister of Medfield, and granddaughter of Rev. John Wilson of Boston. She died July 8, 1748, in the 84th year of her age, having been the mother of eleven children, as follows: —

Edmund, born			1684.	(6)
John,	"	April	26, 1685;	died May 26, 1685.
Susanna,	"	Oct.	3, 1686.	(7)
Edmon,	"	July	8, 1689.	
Wilson,	"	June	23, 1692.	(8)
John	"	Oct.	1, 1695.	(9)
Mary,	"	June	22, 1699.	(10)
Rachael,	"	Sept.	6, 1701.	(11)
David,	"	Oct.	25, 1703;	died Jan. 18, 1704.
Grindal,	"	Sept.	6, 1707.	(12)
Elizabeth,	"	April	21, 1710.	(13)

THIRD GENERATION.

1. III. CAPT. WILLIAM RAWSON, eighth child and eldest surviving son of William Rawson, was born* Dec. 2 or 8, 1682, and is supposed

* On page 13 of the "Memorial of the Rawson Family" it is stated that William Rawson "resided in Boston a number of years after his marriage," that "the births of *ten* of his children are recorded there," and that "he removed to Dorchester, where, according to the records of that town, *two* of his children were born, and from thence to Braintree, now Quincy, to the ancient Rawson farm," &c. &c. Now according to this statement, Capt. William Rawson, the *eighth* child of William, would seem to have been born in *Boston*. How, then, shall we account for the fact, that on page 22 of this same work, he is said to have been born in *Braintree?*

Again, on page 14 of the "Memorial" we are informed that this said troublesome Captain William was born Dec. 8, 1682, and on page 22 his birth is recorded as having occurred Dec. 2, 1682.

to have been the graduate of that name at Harvard, in 1703. He married Sarah Crosby, of Billerica, and settled in Mendon, as a farmer, where he died in October,* 1769. His children were,

William, born Feb. 20, 1711. (14)
Perne, " Oct. 3, 1713; Anna;
Sarah. (15)
Rachael, born Sept. 19, 1716; married a Captain Torrey, and had four sons and one daughter.
Anna, married Isaac Holten, and had four daughters.
Perne, a daughter, born Jan. 1, 1727; died April 19, 1741.

2. III. David Rawson, son of William Rawson, born Dec. 13, 1683, married Mary, daughter of Capt. John Gulliver, of Milton, and lived on his father's farm, near the Neponset Bridge in Quincy. He is said to have been a persevering business man, and distinguished for energy of character. He died April 20, 1752, leaving a valuable estate. His wife survived him, and her personal property at her decease is stated to have been valued at £212–12–4. Their children were as follows: —

David, born Sept. 14, 1714. (16)
Jonathan, " Dec. 26, 1715. (17)
Elijah, " Feb. 5, 1717. (18)
Mary, " May 20, 1718; married a Winchester, and had two children.
Hannah, " April 2, 1720; died July 24, 1726.
Silence, " June 12, 1721; " Aug. 17, 1721.
Ann, " July 30, 1722. (19)
Elizabeth, " Nov. 30, 1723. (20)
Josiah, " Jan. 31, 1727. (21)
Jerusha, " Dec. 21, 1729. (22)
Lydia, " Jan. 17, 1731; married Samuel Baxter.
Ebenezer, " May 31, 1734. (23)

3. III. Nathaniel Rawson, son of William, born in 1689, married Hannah, daughter of Samuel Thompson, of Braintree, and had six children, viz. —

Samuel,
Nathaniel, born May 27, 1716. (24)
Barnabas, " Aug. 11, 1721. (25)
Edward, " April 19, 1724. (26)
Rachael, " May 20, 1741.

4. III. Edward Rawson, son of William, born Jan. 27, 1692, was a mariner in early life, and lived awhile in Boston; but subsequently settled as a farmer in Braintree. He married Preserved Bailey, of Boston, had two children, Preserved and Ann, neither of whom lived to be married, and died in 1721, aged 29.

5. III. Pelatiah Rawson, eighteenth child of William Rawson, born July 2, 1696, married Hannah Hall, of Dorchester, and died in

* Thus is it stated on page 22 of the "Memorial;" but on page 14 we are informed that he "died Sept. 20, 1726"!

1769, aged 73. His wife died Aug. 1, 1775, aged 83. Their children were nine in number, namely,

Grindal. (27)
Edward.
Elliot. (28)
Elizabeth, died in 1780, aged 24; Sarah; Jonathan; Experience; Jonathan; and Lydia, who married Dr. John Cleverly, and had one child.

6. III. EDMUND RAWSON, eldest son and child of Rev. Grindal Rawson, was born in 1684, was a farmer, and settled in Uxbridge, where he sustained the office of Deacon in the Church. He married Elizabeth Howard, of Bridgewater, and had three sons,

Edmund, born Aug. 15, 1718. (29)
Abner, " April 24, 1721. (30)
Nathan, " Aug, 4, 1724. (31)

7. III. SUSANNA RAWSON, eldest daughter of Rev. Grindal Rawson, born Oct. 3, 1686, was married, in 1719, to Benjamin Reynolds, of Bristol, R. I., and had children,

John. (32)
Benjamin, removed to Nova Scotia; Grindal, removed to Putney, Vt.; Anna; Priscilla, married a Morse, and had one daughter, Mary (35); Sarah, married Seth Chapin.

8. III. WILSON RAWSON, son of Rev. Grindal Rawson, born June 23, 1692, was a farmer, and settled in Mendon. He married Margaret Arthur, of Nantucket, May 4, 1712, and died* Nov. 14, 1757, having had eight children, namely,

Wilson, born Aug. 13, 1713. (33)
Priscilla, " Dec. 17, 1715; Mary, born May 12, 1717;
Grindal, " July 13, 1719. (34)
Edward, " April 2, 1721. (35)
Stephen, " April 2, 1722. (36)
Paul, " April 9, 1725. (37)
Thomas, " May 2, 1733. (38)

9. III. JOHN RAWSON, son of Rev. Grindal Rawson, born Oct. 1, 1695, was a farmer, and settled in Uxbridge. He married Mercy Hayward,† of Bridgewater, Jan. 23, 1719, and had children,

John, born Nov. 9, 1720; Joseph, born March 2, 1722–3, killed at Winchester in the Indian War; Mercy, born Sept. 8, 1725, died Feb., 1725–6; Rhoda, born Nov. 22, 1730; Mercy, born June 3, 1732.

10. III. MARY RAWSON, second daughter of Rev. Grindal Rawson, born June 22, 1699, was married, April 9, 1724, to Rev. Joseph Dorr, her father's successor in the ministry at Mendon. He graduated at

*On page 21 of the "Memorial" it is stated that he died Dec. 1, 1726, more than six years previous to the date assigned for the birth of his youngest child, which looks rather suspicious, to say the least. We have, therefore, adopted the more consistent date given on page 26.

†An unaccountable discrepancy here occurs in the "Memorial," inasmuch as it is stated on page 21 that John Rawson "married Mercy Virgon, Feb. 19, 1730;" and on page 26 the same person is made to marry and have children as in the text.

Harvard College in 1711, was settled in Mendon in 1716, and died March 9, 1768, in the 79th year of his age. His epitaph informs us that "he was endued with good sense. His temper was mild and placid. He excell'd in the virtues of meekness, patience, temperance, sobriety, gravity, benevolence, and charity—was a good scholar, a learned Divine and exemplary Christian." Mrs. Dorr survived her husband, and died April 9, 1776. Their children were as follows:—

Mary, born June 6, 1725. (39)
Joseph, " May 24, 1730. (40)
Katherine, " March 8, 1732. (41)
Susanna, " Sept. 4, 1734; married Rev. Amariah Frost, May 23, 1779.

11. III. RACHAEL RAWSON, third daughter of Rev. Grindal Rawson, born Sept. 6, 1701, was married to Samuel Wood, of that part of Mendon since called Upton. He was born in 1696, and died in 1790. His widow died in 1802. They had one daughter,

Priscilla, born in 1718. (42)

12. III. GRINDAL RAWSON, youngest son of Rev. Grindal Rawson, was born Sept. 6, 1707, graduated at Harvard College in 1728, studied Theology, and was the first Pastor of the Church in South Hadley, where he was settled Oct. 3, 1733, and continued in the exercise of his ministry for about eight years, when, dissatisfaction having arisen among his people, he was dismissed. He removed to Connecticut, and was installed first pastor of the newly-formed Church at Hadlyme, in Middlesex County, Sept. 18, 1745, and there remained until his death, which occurred March 29, 1777. It is said of him that "he was remarkable for pleasantry in conversation, and had an uncommon talent in reconciling parties at variance."* His wife was Dorothy, daughter of Rev. Charles Chauncy, D. D.,† the eminent Pastor of the First Church in Boston, and great-great-granddaughter of President Chauncy, of Harvard College. She died in 1780, aged 70. Their children were:—

Edmund Grindal. (43)
Charles, a Physician, died in Rhode Island, aged 23; Wilson, died young; Hooker; Chauncy, and Dorothy, both died aged 23.

13. III. ELIZABETH RAWSON, youngest child of Rev. Grindal Rawson, of Mendon, born April 21, 1710, married, 1st, Abner Hazeltine, of Sutton, Feb. 11, 1730–1, by whom she had one son, born a few months after the death of his father, viz.—

Abner, born Nov. 5, 1731. (44)

The widow Hazeltine married, for her 2nd husband, March 8, 1737–8, James Wood, of Mendon, by whom she had seven children, namely,

* Edwards's Complete List of the Congregational Ministers in the Old County of Hampshire, Ms., in Amer. Quart. Register, X. 382, 395; Field's Statistical Account of the County of Middlesex, Conn., pp. 80, 138.

† Not "Rev. Isaac Chauncy, D. D., of Boston," as erroneously stated in the "Memorial." No such clergyman as "Rev. Isaac Chauncy, D. D.," was ever settled in Boston.

Edward; Thomas; Elizabeth; Grindal;
Joseph. (45)
Hezekiah; and Stephen.

FOURTH GENERATION.

14. IV. WILLIAM RAWSON, eldest son and child of Capt. William Rawson, born Feb. 20, 1711, married, May 13, 1731, Margaret, daughter of Thomas Cook, of Uxbridge, settled in Mendon, as a Lawyer, and was considered a man of learning in his day. He died in 1790. His children were,

Thomas. (46)
William was Sutler for the Rhode Island Forces, at Crown Point, in the French War, where he died.
John. (47)
Perne, born Oct. 24, 1741. (48)
Edward, " July 25, 1744. (49)
Margaret, " May 14, 1745.
Jonathan, " March 15, 1749. (50)
Margaret.

15. IV. SARAH RAWSON, daughter of Capt. William Rawson, married a Saunders, of Upton or Mendon, and had four children, two sons, Elijah and William, who both married and left children; and two daughters, one of whom married Capt. William French, of Mendon, and had Royal, Sally, Nancy, Eunice, Louisa, and Kate.

16. IV. DAVID RAWSON, eldest son and child of David Rawson, born Sept. 14, 1714, married Mary, daughter of Benjamin Dyer, Esq., of Weymouth, was a farmer, and settled in Milton. His wife died March 19, 1780, and he himself June 7, 1790. Their children were,

Hannah, born March 28, 1742, married John Ruggles, and died Nov. 10, 1819; Eunice, born Dec. 3, 1743, married Abner Packard, and died in Albany, N. Y.; Sarah, born Sept. 25, 1745, married James Blake, and died at Milton, Feb. 19, 1827; Dyer, born March 17, 1747, married, 1st, Susanna Webb, 2d, Abigail Pope, and died Aug. 21, 1817; Rebecca, born May 6, 1749, died March 28, 1802; Mary, born Feb. 1, 1754, married Daniel French, and died Sept. 19, 1843; Nathaniel, born Feb. 7, 1757, died in New York, Dec. 11, 1780;
Anna, born May 21, 1758. (51)
Esther, " May 6, 1761; died Oct. 27, 1792.

17. IV. JONATHAN RAWSON, second son of David Rawson, Sen., born Dec. 26, 1715, married Susanna Stone, of Roxbury, Jan. 10, 1760.* He lived on the homestead in Braintree, where he died in November, 1782. His wife died in 1773. Their children were,

Jonathan, born Aug. 7, 1762. (52)
Stephen, " Aug. 26, 1766, died in Gibraltar; Susanna, died Sept. 11, 1840;
Mary. (53)
Hannah, married Israel Cook, and died in Watertown.

* The "Memorial" says that he was married "Jan. 10, 1786." But this date being utterly inconsistent with those assigned for his death, and the births of his children, we have ventured to substitute what we supposed might be the true date.

18. IV. ELIJAH RAWSON, son of David Rawson, Sen., born Feb. 5, 1717, married Mary Paddock, of Swansey, lived a number of years in Warren, R. I., and removed thence to Pittstown, N. Y., in 1789, where he died in 1798, having had eight children,

Jonathan; Ann, married a Stone, and had four children; James; Samuel. (54)

Edward, lived in Pittstown; David; Elijah; Mary, married a Smith, had four children, and died at Lonsburge, N. Y.

19. IV. ANN RAWSON, daughter of David Rawson, Sen., born July 30, 1722, was married to Samuel Bass, of Braintree, Oct. 30, 1746, and had four children:—

Samuel, born Aug. 22, 1747. (55)
Edward, " 1749. (56)
Mary, " Oct. 21, 1750. (57)
William, " July 19, 1755; died Aug. 21, 1755.

20. IV. ELIZABETH RAWSON, daughter of David Rawson, Sen., born Nov. 30, 1723, was married to Peter Adams, of Braintree, brother of Rev. Jedediah Adams, of Stoughton, in 1756, and had two sons,

Peter, born July 20, 1760.
Jedediah, " April 13, 1766. (58)

21. IV. JOSIAH RAWSON, son of David Rawson, Sen., born Jan. 31, 1727, married Hannah Bass, of Braintree, Aug. 28, 1750, resided in Grafton for some time, and removed thence to Warwick, Mass., where he died in 1811. He is said to have been "a man of sterling good sense, and lived and died a respectable citizen." His children were,

Josiah, lived in Richmond, Mass.; Simeon, died in New York, leaving ten children; Jonathan B., settled in Alstead, N. H., and has four children, Orren, Elmon, Jonathan, and Alanson, the last of whom is settled in the ministry at Southboro', Mass.; Lemuel, settled in Richfield, Summit Co., Ohio; Anna B., married Thomas Leland, and settled in Guilford, Ohio; Abigail, married Joshua Garfield, settled in Royalston, and died April 15, 1831;

Mary, born in 1759. (59)

Lydia, died aged 18; Betsy; Hannah, died in Warwick; Amelia, married an Ellis, and settled in Orange, Mass.;

Secretary, born Sept. 19, 1773. (60)

22. IV. JERUSHA RAWSON, daughter of David Rawson, Sen., born Dec. 21, 1729, married an Eaton, of Boston, and had two daughters, Jerusha, and Mary, the latter of whom married a Glover, of Dorchester, and had seven children.

23. IV. EBENEZER RAWSON, youngest son and child of David Rawson, Sen., born May 31, 1734, married Sarah, daughter of Hon. Samuel Chase, of Cheshire, N. H., was a farmer, and settled in Sutton. He was a man of genius and extensive historical attainments. One who knew him well thus writes concerning him. "In stature he was, I think, full six feet, slender built, though with considerable breadth of

shoulders. His countenance was open, his nose aquiline, and his forehead projecting and high. His perceptive faculties must have been acute, from the very configuration of his frontal region. His step was elastic, and all his motions rapid and easy. I have rarely ever known a man gifted with higher powers of conversation. This made him the delight of every circle. His mind was rich in reading, and his own reflections were oftentimes astonishingly brilliant. His memory was a vast storehouse of facts, always at his command, and I have heard him for hours delight a small circle with sketches of early Colonial or Indian History. In his composition there was a vein of good humored irony, which never missed his mark when let off. The peculiar bias of his mind was antiquarian, and nothing delighted him more than the company of the clergy. With them he was sure to plunge into old Biblical History, with the whole of which he was perfectly familiar. His word was as good as his own or any other man's bond in Worcester County. Altogether he was a remarkable man, and as emphatically a *Genius* as any person I ever knew." In the latter years of his life Mr. Rawson became strongly attached to the Quakers, adopted their costume, attended their worship, and, in token of his regard for the sect, named a son for Marmaduke Stephenson, who was tried and imprisoned for heresy, in the early days of the Colony. His children were,

Prudence,	born	Dec.	24, 1758.	(61)
Lydia,	"	April	23, 1760.	(62)
Ebenezer,	"	Dec.	22, 1761.	(63)
Sarah,	"	March	16, 1763.	(64)
Abner,	"	March	2, 1765.	(65)
John,	"	June	1, 1767;	died young.
Jerusha,	"	Oct.	13, 1769.	(66)
Samuel,	"	Sept.	4, 1771.	(67)
Elizabeth,	"	June	5, 1774.	(68)
Marmaduke, } Nizaula, }	"	April	18, 1777.	(69)
Mary,	"	July	5, 1779.	(70)
Clarissa,	"	Feb.	26, 1782.	
Abigail,	"	May	11, 1786	(71)

24. IV. NATHANIEL RAWSON, second son and child of Nathaniel Rawson, born May 27, 1716, married, 1st, Mary Thwing, March 21, 1737–8, and had one son; 2d, Rachael Daniels, by whom he had eleven children; and died in West Stockbridge, in 1803, aged 88 years. His children were,

Silas, born Nov. 17, 1739, settled in Palmyra, N. Y.; Rachael, born May 20, 1741, settled in Conway, Mass.; Elias, born March 1, 1743; Nathaniel, Jr., born Feb. 19, 1745, married Miss Woodruff, Baker, N. Y.; Mary, born Jan. 18, 1749, married a Thwing, Conway; Jonathan, born March 17, 1751, married Miss Baldwin, Victor, Ontario Co., N. Y.; Moses, born April 26, 1753, married Miss Bussey; Anna, born Aug. 21, 1755, married a Parmely, West Stockbridge, Mass.; Mary, born Aug. 13, 1757, married J. Wheeler, Grafton, Mass.; Elias, born Sept. 4, 1760; Grindal, born Jan. 22, 1762, married Miss Grover, Windsor, Mass.; Abner, born Nov. 11, 1764, married Mrs. Jeffords, died in Wayne County, Michigan,

July 29, 1846, leaving three daughters and three sons, of whom Amariah Rawson, of Rawsonville, in that State, is one.

25. IV. Barnabas Rawson, third son of Nathaniel Rawson, Sen., born in Mendon, Aug. 11, 1721, and continued to reside there until after the birth of his fourth child, when he removed to Woodstock, Conn. His wife's name was Mary, by whom he had,

Lois, born Aug. 24, 1744;
David, " Dec. 18, 1745. (72)
Asa, " Nov. 10, 1748; Josiah, born Dec. 18, 1753;
Ruth. (73)
Elizabeth; Lois; Elizabeth.

26. IV. Edward Rawson, fourth son of Nathaniel Rawson, Sen., born April 19, 1724, married Deborah Warren, of Upton, and settled in Mendon. His wife died Feb. 11, 1802. His children were,

Levi, born March 27, 1748. (74)
Olive, " Aug. 13, 1749, died Oct. 9, 1774; Hannah, born June 22, 1751; Eunice, born July 25, 1753; Mark, born Jan. 31, 1757, died Oct. 26, 1761; Luke and Oliver, twins, born July 6, 1759, the former died Nov. 9, 1759, the latter Oct. 26, 1759;
Thompson, born Feb. 22, 1764. (75)

27. IV. Grindal Rawson, eldest son and child of Pelatiah Rawson, of Milton, was born July 29, 1721,* graduated at Harvard College in 1741, was installed as first Pastor of the Church in Ware, Mass., May 9, 1751, was dismissed from his charge June 19, 1754,† was installed at Yarmouth, as the successor of Rev. Thomas Smith, in 1755, where he continued until 1760, when, in consequence of a general disaffection among his people, he was advised by a Council to ask a dismission.‡ He died at the house of Ebenezer Rawson, in Sutton, Mass., in 1795. His wife was Desire, daughter of Colonel Joseph Thacher,§ of Yarmouth, by whom he had,

Ruth, baptized Aug. 14, 1757, died in infancy; Jonathan, born in 1759, was Aid-de-camp to Gov. John Sullivan, married a Gage, of Dover, N. H., had one son, Jonathan Augustus, and died May 17, 1794; and
Hannah, born May 25, 1761. (76)

28. IV. Elliot Rawson, third son of Pelatiah Rawson, was twice married; 1st, to Sarah, daughter of Rev. William Russel, of Middletown, Conn., by whom he had one child, Sarah; 2d, to Ann, daughter of Benjamin Cushing, Esq., of Providence, R. I., by whom he had, Ann, Elizabeth, Elliot, Cushing, Mary, Edward Wilson, and Thomas Hooker.

* Records of Harvard College.
† Edwards's Complete List of the Congregational Ministers in the Old County of Hampshire, Ms., in Amer. Quart. Register, X. 383.
‡ Pratt's Complete List of the Congregational Ministers in the County of Barnstable, Ms., ibid., XV. 61, 70; Mass. Hist. Coll. V. 60.
§ For a notice of this gentleman, his ancestors and family, see Alden's Collection of American Epitaphs, i. 124, *et seq.*

29. IV. Edmund Rawson, eldest son and child of Edmund Rawson, born Aug. 15, 1718, was a farmer in Uxbridge, and married Martha Allen, of Medway, by whom he had,

Samuel. (77)
Edmund; Rachael; Joseph, who married and left a family in Medway;
Seth. (78)

30. IV. Abner Rawson, second son of Edmund Rawson, Sen., born April 24, 1721, was a farmer, settled in Uxbridge, married Mary Allen, sister to his brother Edmund's wife, and had three children,

Silas, born in 1740. (79)
Timothy. (80)
Rhoda, born Oct. 15, 174–.* (81)

31. IV. Nathan Rawson, third son and youngest child of Edmund Rawson, Sen., born Aug. 4, 1724, married, 1st, Mary White, by whom he had one son: 2d, Mary Chase, of Sutton, by whom he had six children: —

Nathan, enlisted in the Army of the Revolution, and died at Ticonderoga.
Betsy. (82)
Isaac. (83)
John. (84)
Mary.
Edward, born in June, 1773. (85)
James. (86)

32. IV. John Reynolds, eldest son and child of Benjamin Reynolds, by his wife Susanna Rawson, was first of Bristol, afterwards of Providence, R. I., and finally of Boston, Mass. He had no issue by his first marriage; but by his second wife, Dorothy Weld, of Roxbury, he had seven sons, four of whom attained a great age, while one other still survives. These seven sons were,

Samuel, who served in the Revolutionary War, married, and died young;
Grindal. (87)
Benjamin, removed to Norfolk, Va.; John, removed to Strafford, Vt;
Edward. (88)
William, died childless; Thomas Capering, died young.

33. IV. Wilson Rawson, eldest son and child of Wilson Rawson, born Aug. 13, 1713, married, and settled in Upton. His children were,

Joshua, born April 1, 1755. (89)
Wilson. (90)
Artemas, settled in Maine, and left issue; Abigail, married a Whitney, of Milford.

34. IV. Grindal Rawson, second son of Wilson Rawson, Sen., born July 13, 1719, "was a carpenter and cabinet-maker, and was much distinguished for his mechanical genius, as well as for his general intel-

* In the "Memorial" this date is Oct. 15, 1740. But this cannot possibly be correct, if the date assigned for the birth of Silas is the true one.

ligence. During the War of the Revolution he was employed by the U. S. Government in the manufacture of utensils of war." He settled in Providence, about 1741, and died in December, 1803. He was four times married. His first wife, Hannah Leavens, of Killingly, Conn., by whom he had two children, died Dec. 21, 1750, and he married, 2d, Elizabeth Boyd, of Newport, R. I., who had six children, and died May 31, 1761, (?)* aged 34; 3d, Zeruiah Harris, who had one son, and died May 10, 1765, aged 34; 4th, Mrs. Nancy Freeman, of Providence, (sister to Colonel Atwell, of that place,) who died in 1771, within a year after her marriage, leaving one daughter. His children, by these several marriages, were,

Joseph, born in 1745, died Jan. 14, 1750; Hannah, died young; Anna, born in 1754, died Jan. 5, 1757; Mary, born in 1755, died Feb. 9, 1759;
Margaret, born in 1757. (91)
Joseph, " Dec. 24, 1760. (92)
Elizabeth, died young; Benjamin, died young; Grindal, born in 1763;
Hannah, born Aug. 18, 1771. (?)† (93)

35. IV. Dea. Edward Rawson, son of Wilson Rawson, Sen., born April 2, 1721, married Mary Morse, granddaughter of Benjamin Reynolds, by his wife Susanna Rawson, (7. III.) and settled in Mendon, where he was Deacon of the Church. "Nature did much for him, and he was a leading man in the affairs of the town. Being a staunch opposer of British rule, he was generally a member of the various committees, and was frequently a member of the Legislature previous to and during the Revolutionary War. He was also a member of the Convention to form a Constitution for the State in 1780. In the latter part of his life, he removed to Leicester, where he died at an advanced age, having lost his eye-sight several years previous to his death." His children were,

Hooker, born April 21, 1749; Edward, born June 19, 1754, was a Physician, and died young; Anna, born Sept. 22, 1756; Arthur, born Nov. 17, 1758, a Physician in Hardwick; Mephibosheth, born Aug. 7, 1763, died Aug. 9, 1763; Elizabeth, married Dea. Seth Chapin, of Mendon, Oct. 27, 1767; Mary, married Dr. Levi Willard, of Mendon, April 28, 1774; Nancy.

36. IV. Dea. Stephen Rawson, son of Wilson Rawson, Sen., born April 2, 1722, settled in Providence, R. I., and was a Deacon of the 2d Congregational Church in that town. From him was derived the right, now vested in the Rawson Fountain Company, of drawing from a certain fountain, for 999 years, the water wherewith that part of the City of Providence on the west side of the river is at present supplied. He was twice elected a member of the Legislature of Rhode

* May 31, 1760, says the "Memorial," which must be a mistake, if the preceding dates are correct.

† Of several inconsistencies in the notice of the family of Grindal Rawson, this is one. It is stated in the "Memorial," pp 41–2, that Mrs. Nancy Rawson "died the year of her marriage, 1771, leaving one daughter;" and yet, on the same page, the birth of this "one daughter" is said to have taken place "Aug. 18, 1773," i. e. two years after the death of her mother!

Island in 1760. His funeral sermon, preached by his Pastor, Rev. Joseph Snow, Jr., was from the text, "*And devout men carried Stephen to his burial, and made great lamentation over him;** a (seemingly) very appropriate text, inasmuch as the Deacons of the several religious societies in Providence officiated as pall-bearers. The inscription on his gravestone is as follows;

"Stephen Rawson, Esq., died March 14, 1773, in the 50 year of his age." He was of a noted family of great reputation."

His wife Elizabeth died March 15, 1786, aged 66. Their children, four in number, were,

Simeon and Elliot, who both joined the Revolutionary Army, and died in the service;
Elizabeth. (94)
Lucilla, married Seth Barton, brother of Gen. William Bartôn, and died in 1760, aged 21.

37. IV. PAUL RAWSON, son of Wilson Rawson, Sen., born April 9, 1725, married Phebe, daughter of Abel Gardner, of Nantucket, and settled in that town. He was master of a vessel, and was lost at sea, with all his crew, in 1772. His wife died in 1793, aged 63. His children were,

Stephen, born Sept. 29, 1761. (95)
Abel, " 1764. (96)
Deborah, " 1766. (97)
Phebe, died in 1783; Margaret, died in 1799;
Wilson, born in May, 1774. (98)

38. IV. THOMAS RAWSON, youngest son and child of Wilson Rawson, Sen., married,† 1st. Anna Waldron, about 1737, who died July 29, 1783; 2d. Hannah Nelson, March 29, 1785. He settled in Mendon, but passed the last years of his life in Milford, where he died July 10, 1802, having had issue as follows:—

William, born Nov. 11, 1738, married Mary Aldrich; Priscilla, born May 22, 1740, married Ephraim Walker; Stephen, born March 2, 1743, married Silence Wood, settled in Townsend, Vt., was Deacon of the Church there, and died in 1827.
Nathaniel, born July 9, 1745. (99)
Rachael, " March 6, 1747. (100)
Anna, " May 8, 1749. (101)
Persis, " May 6, 1751, married Joseph Carpenter, of Uxbridge; Catharine, born May 20, 1757, died Oct. 1761; Pernal, (a daughter) born July 12, 1760, died Oct. 1761; Frances, born July 8, 1763.

39. IV. MARY DORR, eldest child of Rev. Joseph Dorr, by his wife Mary Rawson, born June 6, 1725, married Rev. Moses Taft, Aug. 15, 1753. Mr. Taft, a native of Mendon, was born July 20, 1722,‡ graduated at Harvard College in 1751, was ordained Pastor of

* Acts VIII. 2.
† "The date of his birth in the records of Mendon," (as given, *ante*, 8. III,) "is probably incorrect," says the "Memorial," p. 45.
‡ Records of Harvard College.

the Church in Randolph, as successor to Rev. Elisha Eaton, Aug. 26, 1752, and continued in the ministry until his death, Nov. 12, 1791.* He had four sons,

Moses, born June 10, 1754, graduated at Harvard College in 1774, was a Physician, and settled in Sudbury, Mass.; Eleazer, born Oct. 11, 1755, graduated at Harvard in 1783, died at Exeter, N. H., in 1834; Joseph, born Aug. 15, 1756, graduated at Harvard in 1783; Phineas, born Aug. 11, 1762, graduated at Harvard in 1789; and also four daughters, one of whom married an Allen, one a French, one a Henshaw, and one Samuel Stetson, of Boston.

40. IV. HON. JOSEPH DORR, eldest son of Rev. Joseph Dorr, born May 24, 1730, graduated at Harvard College in 1752, studied Divinity, and preached occasionally for several years. His exertions in the cause of liberty were great and unceasing. He was one of the Commissioners chosen to wait upon the Mandamus Councillors of the County of Worcester, and to demand a surrender of their Commissions. Three hundred days of each year from 1773 to 1780 were devoted by him to the public service without compensation. He was Town Clerk, Justice of the Peace, a member of the Secret Committee, of the Committee of Safety, and of the Committee of Correspondence, a member of the Legislature, &c. After the War which resulted in our Independence, he was appointed a Justice of the Court of Common Pleas, and Judge of Probate, which offices were held by him until near the close of his life. He died Oct. 31, 1808. By his wife, Catherine Bucknam, whom he married Dec. 6, 1768, he had eight children, namely,

Joseph, born March 10, 1769, died March 25, 1769; Catherine, born Aug. 17, 1770, died young;
Joseph Hawley, born July 20, 1772. (102)
Samuel, " June 23, 1774. (103)
Sarah, " Aug. 10, 1776, married Jonas Newell, of New Braintree, and died in 1823; Thomas Shepard, born Nov. 11, 1778, married a Parsons, and died Oct. 1816; Mary, born Jan. 7, 1784, married Oliver Fox, Esq., of Fitchburg; Edward, born Oct. 20, 1786, went South in 1815, and settled in Nova Iberia, Louisiana. He owned an Island at the mouth of Trinity River, Texas, called Dorr's Island, where he was extensively engaged in the breeding of horses and cattle. He died in April, 1847.

41. IV. CATHERINE DORR, second daughter of Rev. Joseph Dorr, born March 8, 1732, married Rev. Ezekiel Emerson, March 27, 1760. Mr. Emerson was a native of Uxbridge, Mass., and in the summer of 1764 preached in Georgetown, Lincoln County, Maine, as a candidate for settlement. Soon receiving a call, he accepted thereof, was ordained July 3, 1765, and "remained happily and peacefully with the people for about fourteen years. At that period the Revolutionary War rendered his situation unpleasant. The settlements on the coast, and especially at the mouth of large rivers, were considered unsafe, the expenses of the war lay heavy on the people, and the depreciation of

*Noyes's Complete List of the Congregational Ministers in the County of Norfolk, Mass., in Amer. Quart. Register, VIII. 45, 54.

the paper currency of the country made Mr. Emerson's nominal salary to be of little value. All these circumstances induced him to remove for a season. He accordingly suspended his ministrations at Georgetown, and, taking his family, removed up the river to Norridgewock, where he remained until May 1st, 1783. The country was then at peace, and taking the advice of a Council, he returned, resumed his ministerial labors in Georgetown, and continued to discharge them steadily and faithfully until the year 1810. At this time his mental powers became impaired to a considerable degree, and he found it necessary to retire from the ministry. He died Nov. 9th, 1815, at the age of 79 years," and is spoken of with marked respect, as an "*excellent man.*"* His children were

Phebe, born July 20, 1762. (104)
Ezekiel, " July 6, 1765. (105)
Hawley, " Dec. 7, 1766. (106)
Calvin, " Jan. 9, 1769. (107)
Luther, " Sept. 26, 1772, graduated at Dartmouth College in 1799, married a Holden, practised Law in Sedgwick, Me., for some years, and removed to Ohio; Eusebius, born Aug. 24, 1774, married Mary Linen;
Susannah, born Dec. 13, 1776. (108)
Mary, " July, 1778. (109)
Elizabeth, " in May, 1780; died in July, 1789.

42. IV. Priscilla Wood, only child of Samuel Wood, of Upton, by his wife Rachael Rawson, born in 1718, married a Davis, who lived in that part of the town of Mendon which is now Milford. She died in December, 1802, having had ten children, as follows:

Phineas, married and settled in Mendon; Ebenezer, who was mortally wounded at the battle of White Plains;
Samuel, born April 1, 1752. (110)
Aaron, served in the Continental Army in his youth, settled first in Surry, N. H., and afterwards in Wardsboro', Vt., and was a millwright; Jane, married and settled in Springfield, Oswego County, N. Y.;
Paul. (111)
Lois;
Eunice. (112)
Eleanor, married Daniel Hayward; Dinah.

43. IV. Edmund Grindal Rawson, eldest son and child of Rev. Grindal Rawson, Jr., graduated at Yale College in 1759, studied Divinity, and preached occasionally. He married, in 1768, Sarah, daughter of Christopher Holmes, a Deacon in his father's Church, and lived in the house which was owned and occupied by his father. He died in the 85th year of his age, having had issue,

Charles Chauncy, died in Bermuda, aged 19; John Wilson, died aged 9 years; Thomas Hooker, married Melinda Bingham, was a Physician, and practised in New Haven a few years, whence he removed to Geneva Co., N. Y., where his descendants reside; Edmund Grindal, born Jan. 26, 1772, married Maria Van Buren, of Kinderhook, N. Y., May 11, 1794, was a

* Greenleaf's Ecclesiastical History of the State of Maine, pp. 79—81; Williamson's History of Maine, (new impression, 8vo. Hallowell, 1839,) ii., 89, note.

Physician, settled in Broadalbin, N. Y., and died Nov. 28, 1847; Dorothy Blanchard, died aged 2 years; Ozias Holmes, a Physician in New York, died aged 24; Joseph Perne, died aged 26; Sarah Andrews, married Oliver Usher, of Hartford, Conn., and removed to Macon, Georgia; Dorothy Nichols, lives at Macon, Ga.; Catharine Chauncy, married George Palmer, in 1815, and died in 1826; Charles Wilson, married Mary Shackleford, of Gwinett County, Georgia, and died leaving five children, Mary, Charles, Edward, Floyd, and Grindal.

44. IV. ABNER HAZELTINE, only child of Abner Hazeltine, of Sutton, by his wife Elizabeth Rawson, born Nov. 5, 1731, married Widow Martha (Robbins) Goss, of Mendon, removed to Wardsboro', Vt., about 1795, and died in February, 1816. His wife died in May, 1806. Their children were,

Susanna, married John Belcher, of Wrentham, Mass., and had seven children; Martha, married Oliver Carpenter, of Mendon, and had four children; Daniel, married Susanna Jones, removed from Vermont to New York, had ten children, and died in June, 1828; Chloe, married Phineas Wood, of Mendon; Betsy, married Whitney Jones, of Dover, N. H., and had nine children; Rhoda, married Asa Phillips, of Milford, Mass., and had ten children; Polly, married Levi Jones, of Bunti, N. Y., and had eight children; Abigail, married Benjamin Gould, of Dover, and had three children; Hannah, married Joseph White, of Uxbridge, and had nine children.

45. IV. JOSEPH WOOD, son of James Wood, of Mendon, by his wife Elizabeth, widow of Abner Hazeltine, married and had six children, named Hezekiah, James, Susan, Benjamin, Sarah, and Amos.

FIFTH GENERATION.

46. V. THOMAS RAWSON, eldest son and child of William Rawson, Jun., married Miss Read, daughter of Samuel Read, Esq., of Uxbridge, was a farmer, settled in Uxbridge, and was an active whig in the time of the Revolution. He died or was killed, in the service of his country, in New York or on York Island, when New York was evacuated, as nothing was heard of him afterwards. He had eight children, viz:

Bailey, settled in Townsend, Vt., and is Deacon of the Church in that town; Gardner, married Susan Wilkinson, settled in the same place, and had fourteen children, of whom Rev. Thomas Read Rawson, of Albany, N. Y., born in 1803, a graduate at Amherst College in 1830, is one; Samuel, also settled in Townsend: Lyman, settled in the same town, died in Caroline, N. Y.; Nabby, married George Parsons, of Uxbridge, and settled in Northbridge; Lydia and Eunice, both settled in Townsend; Olive, born in 1789, married Capt. J. Hazelton, of Townsend.

47. V. JOHN RAWSON, son of William Rawson, Jun., married Elizabeth Bruce, of Mendon, May 26, 1761, and settled in that place. Their children were,

Margaret, born Dec. 14, 1761; Catherine, born Aug. 27, 1763; Turner, born Sept. 3, 1767; Abigail, born Aug. 21, 1770; John Cook, born March 1, 1774; Betsy, born Feb. 7, 1778.

48. V. PERNE RAWSON, son of William Rawson, Jun., born Oct.

24, 1741, married Mary Aldrich, of Mendon, Feb. 4, 1762, settled in Mendon, and had,

William, born Aug. 26, 1762, killed in the Revolutionary War, while quite a young man; Margery, born Dec. 26, 1764; Secretary, born Dec. 28, 1768, married Lucy Maynard, Oct. 6, 1794; Mary, born July 21, 1771; Andrew, born March 10, 1773, graduated at Brown University in 1800, married Jerusha Skinner, Jan. 21, 1807, died March 28, 1835, at Barre, Orleans County, N. Y., leaving four children, (namely, Mary A., born July 31, 1809, married Alvah Lewis in 1827, settled at Elyra, Ohio; Rev. Samuel Andrew, of Rushford, N. Y., born Aug. 23, 1811, married Susan L. Hubbard; Lydia Everett, born Sept. 28, 1813, Oberlin, Ohio; Martha W., born April 16, 1826); Thomas, born Dec. 4, 1776; Lucy, born March 7, 1779; Jane, born Sept. 14, 1781; Margaret, born Jan. 15, 1784; William, born Dec. 18, 1786, married Polly Harvey, in 1813.

49. V. Edward Rawson, son of William Rawson, Jun., born July 25, 1744, married, in 1764, Sarah, daughter of Joseph Sadler, of Upton, settled in Mendon, was a farmer, and highly useful as a farrier, and died in 1806, having had children as follows, viz.

Cyrenius, of Mendon, born Dec. 12, 1764, died Jan. 27, 1806; Sarah, of Mendon, born Aug. 4, 1766, died Sept. 24, 1848; Joseph, born Aug. 16, 1768, graduated at Brown University in 1794, married Rebecca Bullock, settled at Bristol, R. I., afterwards at Barrington, in the same State, was Justice of the Peace, member of the General Assembly, and Chief-Justice of the Court of Common Pleas, and died Dec. 14, 1843, having had five children, namely, Ethan Allen, born Oct. 22, 1798, served in the U. S. Navy a number of years, Julia Moreau, born Aug. 17, 1801, married J. B. Allen, of Providence, Mary Ann, born Oct. 6, 1804, married George S. Brown, Providence, William Bullock, born Aug. 17, 1807, died May 10, 1810, and Joseph W., born June 2, 1810, died Aug. 24, 1843; Leonard, of Pittsford, Vt., born Aug. 23, 1771, married Lydia Hitchcock, had seven children, of whom Professor Leonard Rawson, of Middlebury College, Vt., was one, and died Dec. 27, 1820; Orson, born in 1772, died Oct., 1775; Liberty, born April 13, 1775, graduated at Brown University in 1800, of Mendon, died June 15, 1819; Mary born Dec. 30, 1777, married Jared Thayer, of Mendon, had a daughter Mary, and died June 25, 1803; Simon or Simeon, of Mendon, born June 24, 1780, married Abigail Wood, had ten children, and died July, 1847; Abigail Ellis, born June 19, 1784.

50. V. Jonathan Rawson, youngest son of William Rawson, Jun., born March 15, 1749, married Bathsheba Tracy, of Preston, Conn., was a sadler, and removed to Wyoming, Penn., where he was sent out, at the time of the memorable massacre, with twenty others, on a scouting expedition, on which occasion the party of which he was one, fell in with some few Indians, belonging to a scout of the enemy, whom they killed. He did not return to Wyoming until after the battle. He died in Rushford, N. Y., in 1827, having had,

Isaac, born June 25, 1773, married Rhoda Culver in 1796; Margaret; Hannah; Zeyphena; Solomon, born in 1786, married Mehitable Tracy, of Angelica, N. Y.; William, married, first, Susanna Swift, second, Betsy Osborn, and died at Lynden, N. Y.

51. V. Anna Rawson, daughter of David Rawson, Jun., born

May 21, 1758, married John Younge, of Milton, Mass., and had one son, John Rawson,* born Sept. 18, 1798, married Submit Holbrook, settled in Milton, and had four children. For her second husband she married Nicholas Frothingham, and died Sept. 15, 1837, aged 79.

52. V. Jonathan Rawson, eldest son and child of Jonathan Rawson, born Aug. 7, 1762, married Widow Mary Houghton, daughter of Ebenezer Pope, Esq., of Dorchester, Jan. 10, 1786, and died July 31, 1819. His wife was born Jan. 18, 1756, and died March 2, 1831, having had, by her second husband,

Ebenezer, born July 6, 1787, married Leah Davis in 1827, and settled at Townsend, Mass.; Jonathan, born Nov. 1, 1789, resides in Boston; Mary, born Sept. 12, 1791, married Beza Soule, Sept. 17, 1815, settled in Quincy, Mass., and has had five children, one of whom, George, graduated at Amherst College in 1847; Abigail, born Jan. 12, 1793; Samuel, born Feb. 22, 1794, resides on the ancient Rawson farm in Quincy; William, born Aug. 22, 1796, died Jan. 1, 1824; Henry, born Jan. 7, 1798, died Sept. 7, 1798; Clarissa, born July 7, 1800.

53. V. Mary Rawson, daughter of Jonathan Rawson, married Lemuel† Billings, May 8, 1783, and lived in Quincy, where she died March 19, 1795. Her husband died Oct. 14, 1797. Their children were,

Mary, born Oct. 20, 1783, married William Glover, June 14, 1804; Eunice, born Dec. 11, 1784, died Aug. 10, 1802; Hannah, born Jan. 13, 1788, married Thomas Adams, and died Feb. 6, ——; John, born Aug. 27, 1792, married Lydia Faxon, Oct. 10, 1813, settled in Quincy, Mass., and had seven children.

54. V. Samuel Rawson, son of Elijah Rawson, married, and removed from Shrewsbury, Mass., 1793, to Pittstown, N. Y. His children were,

Eleanor, lives in Pittstown; Lois, married Henry Manderville, and had nine children; Parmy, married a Stearns, and had four children; Samuel, married, and settled in Adams, Jefferson County, N. Y., had twelve children; Sally, married Phillip Mitchell, settled in Pittstown, and had eight children; Mary, married William Wellington, had two children, and died in Pittstown; Lydia, born Dec. 3, 1788, married Charles W. Harbach, of Sutton, Mass., settled at Pontiac, Michigan, and has had six children; James, married, settled in Belfast, N. Y., and had seven children; Alice, married James Knapp, settled in the same place, and had six children.

55. V. Dea. Samuel Bass, eldest son and child of Samuel Bass, by his wife Ann Rawson, born Aug. 22, 1747, married, 1st, Sept. 29, 1772, Elizabeth Brackett, who had seven children, and died Jan 15, 1828; 2d, Nancy Battles, by whom he had two daughters, and died Feb. 23, 1840. His children were:—

* Thus on page 54 of the "Memorial;" but on page 109, where his children are given, he is called "*David* R. Younge."

† *Samuel* Billings, on page 31, and *Lemuel* Billings on page 55, of the "Memorial." The latter reading being accompanied by the date of his marriage, we have thought best to adopt it, on that account, in preference to the former.

William, born Oct. 3, 1773, married Abigail Neff; Samuel, born June 2, 1775, married Polly Belcher, settled at Randolph, Vt., and had eight children; Moses, married Mehitable Herrick, settled in Randolph, and had six children; Peter, married Hannah Hardy; Seth, married Polly Whiting; Hiram, married Rebekah Herrick; Elizabeth, married Samuel Harwood; Sarah, married Micah Mann; Anna, married Joseph Flint.

56. V. Edward Bass, second son of Samuel Bass, Sen., born in 1749, married Bathsheba, daughter of Abiah Keith, of Bridgewater, Nov. 9, 1771, had children,

Isaac, born Nov. 5, 1772; Ziba, born May 28, 1774, studied Medicine with Dr. Ebenezer Alden, of Randolph, and commenced the practice of his profession in the North Parish of Bridgewater, under the most favorable auspices, but died Sept. 23, 1804, universally lamented.*

57. V. Mary Bass, only daughter of Samuel Bass, Sen., by his wife Ann Rawson, born Oct. 21, 1750, married Samuel Howard, of Quincy, and had four children,

Elsey; William, died young; Solomon, died young; Betsy.

58. V. Jedediah Adams, second son and child of Peter Adams, by his wife Elizabeth Rawson, born April 13, 1766, married Esther Field, in 1787, lived in Quincy, and had issue,

Peter, born Jan. 5, 1789, married Elizabeth S. Field; Mary, born Dec. 30, 1790, died May, 1791; Jedediah, Jr., born March 16, 1792, married Mary P. Brackett, died Oct. 21, 1825; Samuel B., born Aug. 2, 1794, died Aug. 31, 1795; Jerusha E., born June 14, 1796, married David Battles; Ebenezer, born July 22, 1800, died Aug. 12, 1818; Elizabeth, born Sept. 12, 1802, married Joshua Veazie, died June 12, 1832; Thomas, born Aug. 13, 1813, died Oct. 2, 1813.

59. V. Mary Rawson, third daughter of Josiah Rawson, born in 1759, married David W. Leland. She is said to have been endowed with considerable poetical taste, and sketched very neatly with the pencil. She and her husband lived and died at Grafton, Mass., and had children as follows, viz.

Hannah, born in 1779, married Benjamin Heywood, settled in Grafton, and had six children; Mary, born in 1782, married John Page, settled in Salem, and had ten children; Sally, born in 1783, married Joseph Merriam, and settled in Grafton; Joseph, born in 1786, married Charlotte Merriam, is a Merchant in Charleston, S. C., of the firm of Leland, Brothers & Co., and has two children; Sabra, born in 1789, resides in Grafton; Mehalea, born in 1791, married John Wyman, and settled in Suffield, Conn.; Betsy, born in 1793, died in infancy; David Warren, born in 1795, married Maria Howe, is one of the firm of Leland, Brothers & Co.; Gardner Secretary, born in 1797, died at Nice, Italy, in 1822; Phineas Washington, born in 1798, was a graduate of the Maine Medical School in 1826, married Parmelia Wood, of Mendon, settled at Fall River, where he was for several years Collector of the Customs, and member of the State Legislature, had five children.

Mrs. Mary Leland died Jan. 14, 1825.

* See a more extended notice of Dr. Bass in Thayer's Family Memorial, pp. 58–9.

60. V. DR. SECRETARY RAWSON, youngest child of Josiah Rawson, born Sept. 19, 1773, married Lucy Russell, and died in 1842, at Jericho, Vt., leaving five children,

Eleanor D., Solon B., Oran, Lucy, and Homer, most of whom reside in Jericho.

61. V. PRUDENCE RAWSON, eldest child of Ebenezer Rawson, born Dec. 24, 1758, married Stephen March, of Sutton, Aug. 24, 1783, and had,

Daniel, who died young; Daniel, graduated at Brown University in 1806; Hannah, married George Robinson (64. V.); George; Prudence, died young; Oliver, settled in Illinois.

62. V. LYDIA RAWSON, second child of Ebenezer Rawson, born April 23, 1760, married Daniel Bullen, in June, 1784, who was a farmer, and lived in Hebron, now Oxford, Maine. Their children were,

Daniel, born in 1784, died in 1788; John Rawson, born March 19, 1787, married Sally Wright, settled at Oxford, Maine, had five children, and died July, 1846; Sally, born April 2, 1789, married Eliab Richmond, settled at Rumford, Maine, and had eight children; Lydia, born in 1791, married Robert Hilburn, settled in Oxford, and had four children; Daniel, born April 18, 1793, married Mary Lombard, and had five children; Julia, born April 1, 1796, married Amos Merriam; Clarissa, born June 27, 1799, married Giles Shurtleff, settled in Oxford, and had two children; Mary, born March 20, 1801, married Luther Perkins, settled in Oxford, and had seven children.

63. V. COL. EBENEZER RAWSON, eldest son of Ebenezer Rawson, born Dec. 22, 1761, married Elizabeth Tailor, of Cornish, N. H., settled in Cornish, where he lived several years, removed thence to Paris, Maine, and in various capacities contributed to the advancement of the interests and prosperity of that town. He died June 26, 1839, and his wife died in 1841. Their children were,

Eliza, born Dec. 6, 1792, married Asa Robinson, settled in Paris, and had two children; Celinda, born April 22, 1795, married John Deming; Sarah, born Oct. 24, 1797, died Aug. 18, 1821; Harriet, born April 20, 1800, married James F. Carter, Esq., of Bethel, Maine, had one child, Harriet Octavia, who died Nov. 28, 1844; Ebenezer Gilman, born Oct. 16, 1802, graduated at Union College in 1827, is a Lawyer in Bangor, and the present Judge of Probate for Penobscot County; Sullivan Sumner, born Oct. 3, 1806, graduated at Waterville College in 1828, is a Lawyer in Eastport, and has been County Attorney, Collector of the Port of Passamaquoddy, Senator in the State Legislature, and Aide-de-Camp to the Governor.

64. V. SARAH RAWSON, daughter of Ebenezer Rawson, Sen., born March 16, 1763, married Samuel Robinson, a farmer, settled in Hebron, now Oxford, Maine, and had issue, three sons,

Prescott, a West Point Cadet in 1816; George, married Hannah March (61. V.), settled in Oxford, and had three children; Samuel, married Mary Williams.

65. V. ABNER RAWSON, second son of Ebenezer Rawson, Sen.,

born March 2, 1765, married, 1st, Abigail Fuller, of Hebron, Maine, 2d, Widow Poor, of East Andover, was a farmer, and had children,

Evander Fuller, graduated at Brown University in 1819, settled as a Lawyer in Lynchburg, Virginia; Orissa, married Thomas Clark, for some years Clerk of Courts, at Oxford, Maine; Sabra; Lyman, graduated at Waterville College in 1827, married Jerusha Holmes (66. V.), several years a Representative in the State Legislature from Rumford, late Judge of Probate for Oxford County, Maine; Louisa Abigail Fuller, married Ebenezer Rawson Holmes (66. V.); Diantha Jane Angeline, married Dr. Pidgin, son of Rev. William Pidgin, former Pastor of the Second Church in Minot, Maine; George Burrill, M. D., married a Mellen, and lives in New Portland, Maine.

66. V. Jerusha Rawson, daughter of Ebenezer Rawson, Sen., born Oct. 13, 1769, married Capt. James Holmes, a farmer, in Hebron, and had nine children, namely,

James Stewart, graduated at Brown University in 1819, married Jane Shaw Patten, settled in Foxcroft, Maine, and had seven children; Salmon, married Abigail Blake, settled in Foxcroft, and had six children; Cyrus, married Fidelia Blake, settled in Foxcroft, and had eight children; Job, married Vesta Hamlin, settled in Calais, Maine, and had five children; Eleazer Austin; Ebenezer Rawson, married Louisa A. F. Rawson, (65. V.); Jerusha, married Lyman Rawson, (65. V.); John Sullivan; Freeland.

67. V. Capt. Samuel Rawson, son of Ebenezer Rawson, Sen., born Sept. 4, 1771, married Polly, daughter of Dr. Freeland of Sutton, was a sadler in early life, subsequently an affluent farmer in Paris, Maine, where he settled. He died in 1829, his wife surviving him. His children were six in number,

Mary Ann, married Simeon Fuller, M. D., settled in Rumford, Maine; Arabella, married Hon. Timothy J. Carter, Sept. 11, 1828, who settled in Paris, and died at Washington, a member of Congress, in 1837, leaving one son, Samuel Rawson, now in Bowdoin College; Abigail A., married Henry E. Prentiss, Sept. 30, 1836, settled at Bangor, and had four children; Columbia, married Dec. 30, 1833, Hon. Virgil D. Parris, formerly member of Congress from Oxford District, Maine, now United States Marshal for Maine, and has had three children; Frances F., married, June 29, 1842, William H. Kimball, County Attorney for Oxford, settled at Paris, and had three children; James Freeland, a partner in the practice of the Law with Henry E. Prentiss, Bangor.

68. V. Elizabeth Rawson, daughter of Ebenezer Rawson, Sen., born June 5, 1774, married Jacob Dodge, a farmer, of East Sutton, Mass., and settled in that town, where they had children as follows, viz.

Sarah, born Sept. 4, 1801; Mary, born Oct. 14, 1803, married Silas Rawson, of Northbridge; Harvey, born March 23, 1807, married Catherine, daughter of Elijah Thayer, Esq., of Mendon, and has one child; Clara R., born May 1, 1809; Ebenezer R., born March 3, 1811, married Mercy M. Comstock, of Blackstone, lives in Grafton, and has one child; Reuben Rawson, born April 3, 1819, settled at East Sutton; Gardner Hubbard, born June 17, 1821, married Charlotte, daughter of Dr. Benjamin Hubbard, of Rome, N. Y.

69. V. Nizaula Rawson, daughter of Ebenezer Rawson, Sen., born April 18, 1777, married Timothy Hutchinson, (born in 1776,) in 1796, who settled finally in Albany, Maine, as a farmer. Their children,

Lewis, born Oct. 3, 1797, married a Merrill, in March, 1819, settled at Milan, N. H., and had four children; Galen, born Jan. 8, 1798, married and settled in Milan, and had four children; Nizaula, born Feb. 13, 1801, married Herman Town, and had two daughters; Marmaduke Rawson, born in 1802, married in 1826, settled in Albany, Maine, and had five children; James Sullivan, died young; Charlotte, died young; Liberty Haven, born in 1808, married in 1835; Timothy Harding, born in 1810; Arvilla, born in 1812, married William Evans, settled in Milan, and had five children; Clarissa, born in 1813, married William Pingree, settled in Riley, Maine, and had four children; Edwin F., born in 1815, married in 1843, has three children; Freeman; Mary, born in 1817, married Dustin P. Ordway, in 1839, had one child; Diantha, born in 1819, married Prescott Loverin in 1841, and has two children; Ebenezer Sumner, born in 1821, married in 1845, and has one child.

70. V. Mary Rawson, daughter of Ebenezer Rawson, Sen., born July 5, 1779, married, 1st, Sullivan Bridgham, who settled in Charleston, Maine, and there died, having had one son; 2d, Thomas Brown, settled in Hebron or Minot, Maine, and had two children: —

Sullivan; Thomas Huntington, M. D., a Physician in Paris, Maine; Sarah Chase, died Nov. 14, 1836, aged 22.

71. V. Abigail Rawson, youngest child of Ebenezer Rawson, Sen., born May 11, 1786, married Daniel Adams, of Northbridge, Mass., and died March 2, 1844, having had issue two daughters,

Sarah, born July 8, 1816, married Albert Burr, and has two children; Clarissa, died young.

72. V. David Rawson, eldest son and second child of Barnabas Rawson, born Dec. 18, 1745, married and settled in Woodstock, Conn., and had six children,

Asa; Asa; Lois; Josiah; Luther, married and settled in Woodstock, and had eight children; Calvin, married and settled in Woodstock, and had six children.

73. V. Ruth Rawson, daughter of Barnabas Rawson, married Andrew Brown, and had five children.

74. V. Levi Rawson, eldest son and child of Edward Rawson, born March 27, 1748, was twice married. His first wife's name was Thankful, by whom he had six children:

Warren, born Dec. 15, 1777, married 1st, Mary Adams, 2d, Martha Bullen, was a Lawyer, settled for many years in Mendon, Mass., a member of the State Legislature, &c., and died at Mendon, June 17, 1848, having had six children; Olive, born March 7, 1780; Hannah, born May 5, 1782; Levi, born Jan. 4, 1785; Edward, born Aug. 23, 1787; Daniel, born Sept. 6, 1790, married and settled at Oakham, Mass., and had nine children.

For his second wife Levi Rawson married Widow Nancy (Wheelock) Fairbanks, by whom he had three children;

Levi, born July 2, 1808, married Mary F., daughter of Capt. Mayhew Folger, formerly of Nantucket, Mass., engaged in mercantile business, and settled at Akron, Ohio, and has four children; Hannah, born Aug. 5, 1811, married Ezra Leland, lives in Massillon, Ohio; Silas, born Feb. 27, 1814, married, 1st, Augusta, and 2d, Dorothy, daughters of Ferdinand Hurxthall, Esq., of Baltimore, Md., settled at Massillon, Ohio, where he is extensively engaged in mercantile business, and has two children.

Levi Rawson died at Mendon, his place of residence, April 17, 1819. His widow Nancy, born Nov. 14, 1767, died Oct. 9, 1843.

75. V. Thompson Rawson, youngest child of Edward Rawson, born Feb. 22, 1764, was a soldier in the Revolution, married Lucy Baker Fisher, Oct. 6, 1785, and settled in Brookfield, Mass., where he continued to reside until 1814. After the death of his wife he lived with his son Fisher in New Orleans, La., where he died March 24, 1848. His children were,

Hiram, born July 18, 1786, married Nancy Hamilton, March 1, 1808, settled in Montgomery, Vt., and had ten children; Betsy, born March 22, 1788, married Charles Bruce, April 3, 1806, died at Waldoboro', Maine, Sept. 12, 1818; Avery, born Nov. 25, 1789, married Harriet Barnard, June 11, 1816, had two children, and died Feb. 22, 1827; Lucy Fisher, born Dec. 26, 1791, died March 10, 1815; Nancy, born Jan. 6, 1794, died Oct. 24, 1814; Horace, born Sept. 30, 1795, married Mary Low Barnard, Nov. 21, 1820, had one son, a merchant in Waldoboro', and died April 3, 1835; Eunice, born Dec. 18, 1797, died Dec. 25, 1816; Fisher, born Feb. 15, 1800, married Mary R. Berry in 1834, and died at New Orleans, July 23, 1848; Warren, born June 21, 1802, married Lucy H. Gould, of Camden, Maine, Oct. 6, 1825, had six children; Harriet, born Jan. 9, 1805, married Daniel Ide Felt, Dec. 25, 1844; Thompson Baxter, born May 21, 1807, died at Waldoboro', Dec. 20, 1827; Hannah, born March 16, 1810, married Edward Curtis, of New Orleans, June 3, 1832, died Jan. 2, 1845.

76. V. Hannah Rawson, youngest child of Rev. Grindal Rawson, of Ware and Yarmouth, born May 25, 1761, married Paul Thurston, of Medway, Sept. 13, 1781, settled in Ward, Mass., where she died March 31, 1816, having had issue,

Jonathan Grindal, baptized July 8, 1782, died in infancy; Elihu Cleverly, died in November, 1809; Dianthe Thatcher, born Dec. 23, 1790, married Benjamin Putnam, of Sutton, Mass., Aug. 25, 1812, and lives in East Eddington, Maine.

77. V. Samuel Rawson, eldest son and child of Edmund Rawson, Jun., married a Thwing, of Uxbridge, settled in Montague, and had several children, two of whom, Elias and Reuel, went to Michigan.

78. V. Seth Rawson, son of Edmund Rawson, Jun., married Sarah Torrey, of Mendon, settled in Uxbridge, and had two children,

Warren, who resides in Mendon; and Martha, who married a Brown, of Uxbridge.

79. V. Silas Rawson, eldest son and child of Abner Rawson,

born in 1740, was a farmer, and settled in Uxbridge, married Sarah Draper, of that town, sustained town offices for many years, and died March 6, 1825, having had children,

Charles, born Oct. 21, 1768, married Sarah Hale, had five children, and died Dec. 11, 1808; Mercy, born Nov. 10, 1770, married Josiah G. White, and had two children, who both died; Milley, born Dec. 23, 1772; Simon, or Simeon, born April 9, 1775, married, 1st, Lavina Brown, 2d, Nabby Putnam, settled in Uxbridge, and had four children.

80. V. Timothy Rawson, second son of Abner Rawson, was a farmer, settled first in Uxbridge, and afterwards removed to Newport, N. Y. He was twice married. His first wife was a Miss Fish, and his second an English lady, with whom he removed to Canada. It is said of him that "he could manage a cause in a Court of Justice with ability, and could preach a good sermon." He lived to be nearly eighty years of age, and had eight children, named Dolly, Chauncy, Perly, Lucy, Sally, Luther, Calvin, and Perlina.

81. V. Rhoda Rawson, youngest child of Abner Rawson, born Oct. 15, 1740, married Aaron Taft, a farmer of Uxbridge, about the year 1768, lived in Uxbridge until March, 1799, when they removed to Townsend, Vt., where her husband died in March, 1808, and she herself June 9, 1827. She is described as "a woman of superior ability," and a "devoted Christian," and was a member of the Congregational Church in Uxbridge and Townsend for more than forty years. Her children were,

Milley, born July 29, 1769, married Ezekiel Clark in 1792, settled in Utica, N. Y., had five children; Selina, born Feb. 20, 1771, married Jesse Murdock in 1793, settled in Townsend, Vt., had three children; Cynthia, born Aug. 17, 1773, married Nathaniel Butler in 1798, settled in Mexico, N. Y., and had four children; Rawson, born Oct. 15, 1775, died Oct. 26, 1776; Nancy, born Aug. 20, 1777, married Rev. David R. Dixon, of Utica, N. Y., in 1810, left one son, who received a Collegiate education, and is a Congregational Minister in Michigan; Zeruiah, born Nov. 21, 1779, married Maj. Willard Lovell, of Grafton, Mass., afterwards removed to Climax, Michigan, had four children; Mary, born July 12, 1783, married Nathaniel Stiles, a farmer, of Rockingham, Vt., and resides in that place; Peter Rawson, born April 14, 1785, married Sylvia Howard, in 1810, settled in Townsend, Vt., was Judge of the Court of Common Pleas, and a member of the Legislature for many years, emigrated to Cincinnati, Ohio, in 1841, and has one son, Alphonso, born Nov. 5, 1810, who graduated at Yale College in 1833, and is a Lawyer in Cincinnati; Sophia, born Dec. 3, 1787, died Nov. 27, 1843; Judson, born Nov. 6, 1791, died March 20, 1794; Samuel Judson, born Oct. 4, 1794, married Lucy Hayward, in 1825, resides in Boston, and has one child, Sophia.

82. V. Betsy Rawson, eldest daughter and second child of Nathan Rawson, married Abel Aldrich, and died about 1840, having had issue,

Abel, married a Comstock, settled in Mendon, and died in 1846; Maranda, married James Howard, and resides at Woonsocket Falls; Ira, lives in Uxbridge; Welcome, married Maria, daughter of Caleb Rawson, of Northbridge; George W., died young; Julia, married a Morse; Thomas J., married, and is a farmer in Uxbridge.

83. V. Isaac Rawson, second son of Nathan Rawson, married Mary Ward, of Sutton, settled in Sullivan, N. H., is a farmer, and has had children named Ira F., Ira M., Chauncy W., James, Charles, and George.

84. V. John Rawson, third son of Nathan Rawson, married Lydia Chase, of Sutton, and settled in Croydon, N. H. Their children were,

Daniel; Cynthia; Seth W.; Hepsabath; Polly, who married Daniel Ward; Jenny; Anna; and Cynthia.

85. V. Edward Rawson, son of Nathan Rawson, born in June, 1773, married Lucy Jones, of Chesterfield, N. H., (who yet survives,) and died in August, 1833, having had seven children, namely,

Abner, born May 15, 1796, married Martha Johnson, and had five children; Deering Jones, born Aug. 8, 1798, married, 1st, Thankful F. Sherman, 2d, Abigail F. Gleason,* lives in Worcester, Mass, and has had five children; Nathan, died in April, 1824; George W., married Mary Cartwright, and had four children; Mary, married Schuyler Fisher, in 1827, and had two children; Hannah J., married Benona B. Rogers, and had two children; Sally W., born May 15, 1810, married Phineas M. Gleason,† and had six children.

86. V. James Rawson, youngest son and child of Nathan Rawson, married Polly Seagreaves, of Uxbridge, settled in that place, and had,

Merritt, died in 1827; Sally; Mary Ann, married John Newell Rawson, (90. V.); James Augustus, married Louisa Scott, and has two children.

87. V. Grindal Reynolds, of Boston, second son of John Reynolds, had issue, by a third wife, two sons and a daughter, viz.

Rev. Grindal Reynolds, a Unitarian Clergyman, ordained at Jamaica Plains, Roxbury, Mass., in 1847; Cynthia; and Henry Russell.

88. V. Edward Reynolds, son of John Reynolds, married, 1st, Deborah Belcher, of Boston, 2d, Ann, daughter of Dr. Isaac Foster, of Charlestown, Mass., and had six children, by his first wife,

Jane Belcher, married Ephraim Hall, of Boston; Edward, M. D., graduated at Harvard College in 1811, married, 1st, Adaline Ellen, daughter of William Pratt, Esq., of Liverpool, England, 2d, Margaret Wendell, daughter of Hon. John Phillips, of Boston; William Belcher, married Elizabeth Margaret Carter, of Newburyport; Frances Mackay, married William Turrell Andrews, of Boston; Emily Augusta, married Thomas Dimmock, of Boston; Charles Green, married Charlotte Staniford, of Roxbury.

89. V. Joshua Rawson, eldest son and child of Wilson Rawson, Jun., born April 1, 1755, married Rebecca Griffith, settled in Upton, and died June 24, 1804, having had issue,

Polly, born Sept. 11, 1778, married Jonathan Vail, and had eleven children; Rebecca, born June 14, 1780, died Dec. 25, 1839; Chloe, born Nov. 7, 1782, died March 30, 1804; Wilson, born Oct. 9, 1784, married, 1st,

* Thus on page 92 of the "Memorial;" but on page 70 Deering J. Rawson is made to marry Thankful *T.* Sherman, and *Abigail P. B.* Gleason.

† Thus on page 70 of the "Memorial." On page 92 we read *Phineas* Gleason, without a middle initial letter, as the name of the same man.

Elizabeth Vail,* 2d, Phila, daughter of Israel Adams, of Sutton, and had nine children; Joshua, born Oct. 27, 1786, married Hopestill Aldrich, had one son, Joshua L.; Abigail, born March 24, 1789, married Freeman White,† had seven children; Stephen, born April 14, 1791, graduated at Brown University in 1817, married Joanna B. Aldrich, and lives in Upton; Daniel, born July 12, 1793, married and settled in Ohio; John; Levi, M. D., born March 17, 1800, graduated at Brown University in 1825, married a Temple, settled at Farnumsville, Grafton, as a Physician, and has one daughter.

90. V. Wilson Rawson, second son and child of Wilson Rawson, Jun., married, lived in Upton, and had five children,

Caleb; Rana; Caleb, born June 9, 1780, married Mary Aldrich, and had ten children, of whom the third, John Newell, born Dec. 17, 1807, married Mary Ann Rawson, (86. V.); Hannah; Rhoda, married James Viall.

91. V. Margaret Rawson, daughter of Grindal Rawson, born in 1757, married Capt. Isaiah Cahoone. "He followed the seas, was a bold and enterprising man, and took an active part in the American Revolutionary struggle. He was once taken prisoner, and confined in the 'Old Jersey Prison Ship.' With one or two others he effected his escape, and reached home after various hardships and sufferings." He died in Providence, June 1, 1798, aged 44. Mrs. Cahoone died April 11, 1801, having been the mother of five children, viz.

Asa Rawson, died at sea, aged 30; Mary, married Ephraim Horsewell, and died in 1825; Elizabeth Rawson, married Thomas Brownell, died in 1825; Matilda, married John Jepson, died in 1818; Maria, died in December, 1841, aged 51.

92. V. Joseph Rawson, son of Grindal Rawson, born Dec. 24, 1760, joined the Revolutionary Army at the age of 16, and served during the war, part of the time as a Lieutenant; married Elizabeth, daughter of Samuel Rhodes, in 1785, and died in Providence, R. I., July 19, 1835. His wife, born in 1776, died May 9, 1843. Their children were ten in number,

Samuel, born Aug. 19, 1786, married, 1st, Rosalie Gremont, 2d, Eliza Richmond, resides in Providence, and has had eight children; Joseph, born Jan. 27, 1788, a Cabinet maker in Providence; William Rhodes, born in 1790, married Eliza Peckham, had three children; Abby, died young; Abby Reynolds; Edward Dickens, born in 1800, died in 1822; Grindal, died young; Hannah Ruden; Grindal, born Aug. 12, 1803, married, March 30, 1823, Lucretia, daughter of James Cornell, and granddaughter of Christopher Leffingwell, Esq., of Norwich, settled at South Woodstock, Conn., and had four children; George Burrill, born in 1805, married Sarah Cook, in 1832, and had six children.

93. V. Hannah Rawson, daughter of Grindal Rawson, born Aug. 18, 1773, married, 1st, Silas Mitchell, Nov. 15, 1795, who died in Buenos Ayres, in 1798, 2d, Capt. John Glazier, of East Greenwich,

*Elizabeth *Viall*, on page 71 of the "Memorial"; but we have followed the reading given on page 93.

† *Freeborn* White, on page 71 of the "Memorial."

R. I., 3d, Col. John S. Eddy, Sept. 10, 1844. Colonel Eddy, now or late an officer of the Customs in Providence, R. I., was formerly a noted ship-builder. His wife had by her first two husbands three sons,

Thomas, born Oct. 17, 1796, a Physician in South America; James, born Dec. 25, 1798, died in 1807; Edward Rawson, born Oct. 20, 1800, now member of the Town Council in Cranston, R. I., married Elizabeth, daughter of Chester Clark, of Providence, and has one son, Thomas Burroughs.

94. V. Elizabeth Rawson, eldest daughter of Dea. Stephen Rawson, married, June 12, 1768, James Burrill, (who had removed from Lynn, Mass., and settled in Providence, R. I.,) and died March 1, 1811, having had children,

George Rawson, born Feb. 8, 1770, married Amelia Smith, had two children, and died Feb. 19, ——; James, born April 25, 1772, graduated at Brown University in 1788, and immediately entered upon the study of the Law, in the office of Hon. Theodore Foster. He was admitted an Attorney and Counsellor at Law in all the Courts of the State, at the September Term of the Supreme Judicial Court, in the year 1791. In October, 1797, at the age of twenty-five years, he was appointed Attorney-General, as successor to Hon. R. Green, who had been transferred to the United States Senate; and retained this office till May, 1813, when, his health being greatly impaired by professional labor, he resigned it, and the practice of the Law, together. In June following he was elected a member of the General Assembly for the town of Providence. In May, 1814, he was chosen Speaker of the House of Representatives, and at the May session, 1816, was elected Chief-Justice of the Supreme Judicial Court of Rhode Island. This office he held until the following February, when he was elected United States Senator. He attended four sessions of Congress, and died Dec. 25, 1820, after a few days illness, of a pulmonary complaint, universally regretted. By his wife Sally Arnold, whom he married Oct. 8, 1797, he had six children.

95. V. Stephen Rawson, son of Paul Rawson, born Sept. 29, 1761, for many years commanded a ship in the Whaling business, from the United States and Havre, France. During the last five years of his life he commanded a vessel in the merchant service; and was lost at sea, with his whole ship's company, within a few hours' sail of his home, April 2, 1807. His wife Abigail, daughter of Joseph Heath, of Boston, whom he married in 1787, died in December, 1832, having been the mother of seven children, viz.

Avis, born in 1788, married Capt. Timothy Bunker, of Nantucket, in 1807, and died in 1812, leaving one daughter, Avis R., born in 1808; Priscilla, born in 1790, married William Stubbs, of Nantucket, died in 1822; Charles, born in 1794, married, 1st, in 1817, Mary, daughter of Thomas Nickerson, of Warwick, who died in January, 1833, 2d, Mary, daughter of Samuel L. Valentine, formerly of Boston, was taken prisoner by the British four times during the War of 1812, and was a successful shipmaster in the Whaling business from 1820 to 1839, seven years from New Bedford, four years from Havre, France, and eight years from Hudson, N. Y.; Joseph, drowned in the English Channel, in 1827; William, born in 1798, married Susan Chase, of Nantucket, at present commands the whaleship

John Adams, of Nantucket; Margaret, born in 1802, married Shubael Clark, in 1824, and had four children; Lydia, born in 1804, married Dr. Nathaniel Ruggles, died in 1829, leaving one son, Charles.

96. V. ABEL RAWSON, son of Paul Rawson, born in 1764, was a successful shipmaster, for many years, from New York, subsequently settled at Princes Bay, Staten Island, N. Y., where he was several years keeper of the beacon-light, and where he died in 1840. He married in 1785, Lydia Briggs, of Nantucket, who now lives in Brooklyn, N. Y., having had children as follows:

Susan, married Charles Coffin, and had two children; Valina, married Rev. Seth F. Swift, lives at Oswego, N. Y., and has had three children; Edward B., born in 1795, married Sarah Joy, had two sons, and died in 1840; Deborah, married Charles F. Briggs, has one child; Charlotte, married a Puffer, a Merchant of Brooklyn, New York.

97. V. DEBORAH RAWSON, daughter of Paul Rawson, born in 1766, married Edmund Crocker, a farmer, of West Barnstable, and had one son,

Stephen B, born in 1807, married* in 1831, and had four children.

98. V. WILSON RAWSON, eldest son and child of Paul Rawson, born in May, 1774, settled in Nantucket, where he was Deacon of the First Congregational Church from 1802 until his death, in 1836. He married twice, 1st, Ursula, daughter of Caleb Gardner, of Nantucket, who died in 1795, having had six children, and 2d, Phebe, daughter of Solomon Folger, of the same place, who died in 1846, leaving no issue. The names of his children were,

Paul, died in New York, a Merchant, in 1804, aged 24; George, died in 1803; Valentine, drowned at sea, in 1806; Phebe, born in 1785, married Capt. Jesse Coffin, in 1801; Asa, born in 1791, married Mary Fish, in 1822, and had six children; Buell, born in 1794, married, 1st, Mary Coffin, 2d, Mrs. Mercy Jones, and died in 1845, having had three children.

99. V. DEA. NATHANIEL RAWSON, son of Thomas Rawson, born in Mendon, July 9, 1745, was a farmer, and Deacon of the Congregational Church in Mendon, whence he removed to Milford, April 1, 1793. By his wife Elizabeth Nelson, whom he married March 26, 1768, he had,

Sophonisba, born Dec. 14, 1768, married Elijah Stone, Dec. 5, 1794, and had six children; Ruth, born Oct. 25, 1770, married Nathan Parkhurst, and had six children; Catherine, born Jan. 7, 1773, married Ithiel Parkhurst, March 6, 1794, and had eight children; Elizabeth, born Feb. 9, 1775, married Rev. Gordon Johnson, of Killingly, Conn., a Congregational Minister, and had two sons, of whom one died, and the other is Rev. J. R. Johnson, a Congregational Clergyman; Hammond, born April 22, 1777, died July 7, 1846; Silence, born March 16, 1779, died March 7, 1797;

* This is an instance in which the unaccountable discrepancies in the "Memorial of the Rawson Family" is a source of much perplexity. On page 79 of the "Memorial" it is stated that Stephen B. Crocker "married Lydia Crocker, 1831;" while on page 97 we are informed that the same Stephen B. Crocker's wife's name was "Deborah Rawson," with nothing added to this bare statement, to shew that the former was erroneous, or that "Deborah Rawson" was a second wife.

Nathaniel, born Feb. 26, 1780, settled as a Congregational Minister in Hardwick, Vt., subsequently in Hampton, Conn., married, 1st, Betsey Fitch, 2d, Sarah Piper, and had six children; Jared, born Jan. 2, 1782, married Anna T. Waldron, Nov. 5, 1820, and had six children; Anna, born March 21, 1785, married Luther Clafton,* June 8, 1809, and had seven children; Roxa, born June 30, 1788, married Dea. Peter Rockwood, of Milford.

100. V. RACHAEL RAWSON, daughter of Thomas Rawson, born March 6, 1747, married Stephen Chapin, Jan. 22,† 1768, lived in that part of Mendon since incorporated as Milford, and died Dec. 2, 1797. Her husband died in 1816, having had issue,

Calvin, born in 1769, a farmer, married, and settled in Pelham, Mass.; Rachael, born in 1771, married Elijah Albee, a farmer, of Milford; Luther, married Polly Wedge, of Milford, settled in Pelham, where he now resides; Cynthia, born in 1773, married Nahum Wedge, of Milford, a farmer, who settled in Pelham; Stephen, born in 1777, graduated at Harvard College in 1804, was settled as a Congregational Minister in Hillsborough, N. H., where he married, was afterwards installed at Mount Vernon, N. H., where he became a Baptist, was Professor of Theology in Waterville College, Maine, from 1822 to 1828, was elected President of Columbia College, Washington, D. C., where he died in 1846; Seth, born in 1783, married Polly Wood, of Mendon; Otis, born in 1785, married Abigail Haywood, of Milford, settled in Monson, as a manufacturer.

101. V. ANNA RAWSON, daughter of Thomas Rawson, born May 8, 1749, married Col. Benjamin Hoppin, of Providence, "a worthy man and an honorable merchant," and had children,

Davis W.; Candace; Benjamin; George Washington; and Thomas Cole; born, respectively, in 1771, 1773, 1777, 1779, and 1785; Levi, born in 1789, died in 1804, while a member of Brown University; Henry; Lorania, married Gen. Edward Carrington, of Providence, and had one son, Edward, who graduated at Middlebury College in 1832.

102. V. JOSEPH HAWLEY DORR, second son of Hon. Joseph Dorr, born July 20, 1772, married Lucy Penniman, of New Braintree, and settled in Boston, as a Merchant, where he has sustained numerous offices of trust under the Town and City Governments. Of seven children the following survived infancy, namely,

Joseph H., graduated at Bowdoin College in 1827, spent two years at the University of Gottingen, Germany, and some time in Paris, at a French School, is settled as a Physician in Philadelphia; Thomas Edward, was a scholar of high rank in the Boston High School; Lucy Penniman, married David Whiton, and died soon after.

103. V. SAMUEL DORR, son of Hon. Joseph Dorr, born June 23, 1774, married, 1st, Lucy, daughter of Joseph Fox, Esq., of Fitchburg, by whom he had five sons, 2d, a Brown, by whom he had two children, was President of the New England Bank for ten years, a member of the House of Representatives and Senate at different times, and died in Boston, in December, 1844. His children were,

* Thus on page 80 of the "Memorial;" but on page 106 we read "Luther *Cloflen*" as the name of the husband of Anna Rawson.

† Thus on page 80 of the "Memorial;" but on page 45 the date of the marriage is given as "Jan. 3, 1768."

Samuel F., died leaving a wife and two children; George B.; Albert H., settled in Ramsford, N. Y.; Francis F.; Martha Ann, married Henry Edwards; James Augustus, graduated at Harvard College in 1832, is a Lawyer in New York; Susan; Charles H.

104. V. PHEBE EMERSON, eldest child of Rev. Ezekiel Emerson, born July 20, 1762, married Josiah Hale, of Norridgewock, Maine, and died June 19, 1829, having had children as follows:

Josiah, born Sept. 7, 1782, married Mercy Baker, in 1801, and had three daughters; Ezekiel, born May 24, 1784, married, 1st, Susan Kidder, in 1810, 2d, Sarah Tazier, and had five children; Ebenezer, born Feb. 1, 1786, married Ann Dinsmore, in 1807, and had ten children; Charles, born Feb. 19, 1788, married Nancy Holman, formerly of Milbury, Mass., and had four sons; Calvin, born Dec. 3, 1789, married Maria Gould, settled in Norridgewock, Maine, and had six children; Lutker, born Dec. 15, 1791, married Phebe Kidder, settled in Norridgewock, and had ten children; Thurston, born Jan., 1793, married Lydia Gould, had ten children, and died April 14, 1839; Lucinda, died aged 18 months; Diantha, born Feb. 19, 1798, married Samuel G. Tuck, and had three children; Sumner, born in 1800, died in 1805; Simon, born in 1802, died in 1826; Eusebius, born Dec. 18, 1805, a Clergyman, married Philena Dinsmore, settled at Waterville, and afterwards at Foxcroft, Maine, and had four children; Sumner, born March 9, 1808, graduated at Waterville College, has been settled as Pastor of a Baptist Church at Beverly Farms, now resides in Fitchburg, Mass., married a daughter of Deacon Farwell, of Chelmsford.

105. V. EZEKIEL EMERSON, eldest son of Rev. Ezekiel Emerson, born in Mendon, July 6, 1765, married a Mrs. Fish, settled in Norridgewock, Maine, and died suddenly, in the woods, near Moosehead Lake, in the year 1809, having had,

Ezekiel, lives in Bangor, has several children; Mary, married Augustus Taylor, and had issue; Isabella, married Melvin Lincoln, lives in Madison, Maine; Betsey, married a Merrill, of Dexter, Maine; Lucina, married a Thurston, and lives in Solon, Maine; Luther, married D. H. Dennett, has nine children; Jotham, married, lives in Dover, and has children.

106. V. HAWLEY EMERSON, son of Rev. Ezekiel Emerson, born Dec. 7, 1766, in Georgetown, Maine, where he married Rachael Linen, and there settled, had children named

Catherine; Mary; Rachael; Julia; Rebecca; Theodosia; Diantha; Margaret; Betsey; Nancy; and Luther;

and died Jan. 6, 1844.

107. V. CALVIN EMERSON, son of Rev. Ezekiel Emerson, born Jan. 9, 1769, in Georgetown, married Elizabeth Petty, of that place, settled in Fairfield, Maine, and died in November, 1827, having had issue,

Catherine, born Nov. 14, 1793, married Benjamin Harriman; John, born Jan. 20, 1796, married Mary, daughter of Stephen Holbrook, of Grafton, Mass., April 13, 1831, lives at Norridgewock, Maine, and has had two children; Ezekiel, born March 15, 1798, married and has a family; Gillette, born in March, 1800; Jeremiah, born Feb. 29, 1804; Miranda, born April 5, 1810, married John Fogg, had two sons and one daughter; Nancy; Collins, born in April, 1802.

108. V. SUSANNAH EMERSON, daughter of Rev. Ezekiel Emerson, born Dec. 13, 1776, married Charles Witherell, March 5, 1795, settled in Norridgewock, Maine, and had the following children:

Sarah, born Feb. 7, 1796, married David H. Tuck, Feb. 7, 1820, and had three children; Leah, born May 3, 1798, married Rufus J. Woodman, Dec., 1820, settled in Waterboro', Maine, and had seven children; Betsey, born April 29, 1800, married Amos Richards, March, 1824, settled at Milo, Maine, and had eight children; Susan, born May 13, 1803, married G. N. Edes, May, 1826, settled in Norridgewock, and had eight children; Phebe H., born Aug. 21, 1806, married J. M. Bartlett, Sept. 24, 1846, and resides in Harmony, Maine; Sumner; Samuel B., born April, 1813, married A. Keane, settled at Norridgewock, and had five sons; George W., born March, 1816, married Sarah Savage, Sept., 1843, resides in Fairfield, Maine, and has had three children; Mary Ann, born Dec. 21, 1820.

109. V. MARY EMERSON, daughter of Rev. Ezekiel Emerson, born July, 1778, married John Tazier or Tozier, settled in Fairfield, Maine, and died in Norridgewock, May 17, 1838, having had,

Adaline, married Dr. Gontharie, a German, and has children in Ohio; Almiran, married Lydia Dunlap, who is a farmer, resident at Stark, Maine; Benjamin F., born Feb. 3, 1807, a printer, married Sybil L. Russell, lives in Dexter, Maine, and has one son, Frank Dorr; Loring, a school teacher in Massachusetts; Theodosia, married a Jones, and lives in Waltham, Mass.; Elizabeth D., married a Beard, and lives in the same place; Thurston, married, and also lives in the same town.

110. V. SAMUEL DAVIS, third son and child of Priscilla (Wood) Davis, born in Mendon, Mass., April 1, 1752, and died in Wardsboro', Vt., in 1836. By his wife Deborah Chapin, who was born in Milford, Mass., June 10, 1757, and died in Wardsboro', Oct. 1, 1811, he had children as follows:—

Lydia, born March 7, 1777, died in 1780, (?) at Busti, Chautauque Co., N. Y.; Ebenezer, born May 18, 1779, married Lydia Hall, and had ten children; Simon, born April 9, 1731, married Clarissa Daniels, of Westmoreland, N. H.; Susanna, born Oct. 31, 1783, married Samuel Hall, and had seven children; Olive, born Sept. 16, 1786, married Joseph Wait, and had three sons; Diana, born May 20, 1789, married Eli Hoskins, and had five children; Emery, born Oct. 20, 1791, married Amy Aikin, and had eight children; Lucinda, born Dec. 14, 1794, married Davis Read, settled in Wardsboro', and had nine children; Elisha, born Sept. 14, 1797, died in Eliott, Chautauque Co., N. Y., Dec. 16, 1818; Adams Chapin, born April 11, 1800, married Abby Alexander, March 10, 1831, settled in Flemington, New Jersey, where he has been Judge of Probate, member of the Legislature, and clerk of the Assembly, of that State, and has had eight children.

111. V. PAUL DAVIS, son of Priscilla (Wood) Davis, in early life served three years in the Continental Army, and then settled at Wardsboro', Vt., where he became a Baptist Minister, removed to New Salem, Mass., and was the Pastor of a Baptist Church in that place, removed thence to Carroll, N. Y., where he died in December, 1826, having had issue, by his wife Rachael Chapin, of Milford, Mass., as follows:—

21

Joseph, married Dorothy Maynard, settled first in Leicester, Vt., and subsequently in Orleans Co., N. Y.; Abigail, married Jeremiah Brown, settled, successively, in the same places; Grindal, married Zeruiah Corbin, of Wardsboro', and settled in Orleans Co.; Simeon Chapin, married, 1st, Lydia Tobey, 2d, Betsy Rawson, settled in Carroll, N. Y.; Deborah, married Elias Woodcock, of Carroll, where he settled; Priscilla; Levi, married Lorana Hunt, settled first in Carroll, and then in Orleans Co.; Paul Wheeler, married Mary Jones, settled first in Carroll, removed to Ohio; Ora, married Mary Jones, and settled in Busti, N. Y.; Roba, married Hiram Brown, settled in Carroll; Shepherd E., married, and settled in Busti; Marvel Chapin, married, and settled in Ohio; Seraphine, married David Jones, of Carroll, and there settled.

112. V. Eunice Davis, daughter of Priscilla (Wood) Davis, married a Sanger, settled in Rochester, Vt., and had children named

Ebenezer; Isaac; and Susan.

SKETCHES OF THE EARLY HISTORY OF THE TOWN OF MIDDLEBOROUGH, IN THE COUNTY OF PLYMOUTH.

[Continued from page 220.]

In the beginning of April, 1622, Captain Standish set out in a shallop, with ten of the principal men of the Colony, and Hobbamock and Tisquantum, on a second* voyage to "the Massachusetts." They had not proceeded far, however, before the discharge of a piece of ordnance from their little fort warned them of impending danger, and that their return was desired. The shallop is, accordingly, put about, and soon arrives again at Patuxit. They found the town in a posture of defence, and the whole military force of the Colony mustered under arms; and are informed that immediately after their departure, those who remained at home were alarmed by the appearance of a wounded Savage, a member of Tisquantum's family, who announced that "at Namaschet† there were many of the Nanohiggansets, Massassowat, their supposed friend, and Conbatant, their feared enemy,‡ with many others, with a resolution to take advantage on the present opportunity to assault the town in the Captain's absence." The Savage affirmed that he received his wound for speaking in behalf of the Colonists, and that he had escaped by artifice, to give warning of the danger. Hobbamock was highly indignant at this aspersion upon the good faith of his Sovereign, and declared the whole story to be a fabrication. The Governor, who was also loth to mistrust the faithfulness of his ally, directed Hobbamock to send his wife privately to Pokanoket, the residence of Massasoit, with instructions to take note of what she should hear or see there, and to bring back information of the "right state of things." Finding all things quiet, the woman "told Massassowat§ what had happened at Plymouth; which, when he

* The Pilgrims first visited "the Massachusetts" in September, 1621. For an account of their adventures the reader is referred to Bradford and Winslow, pp. 57–9; or to Young's Chronicles of the Pilgrims, pp. 224–9.

† "A town some fifteen miles from us," adds Winslow, in a parenthesis.

‡ From this expression of Winslow, it is evident that Corbitant was still regarded with distrust, notwithstanding his formal submission to King James, and apparent reconciliation with the English.

§ This is the way Winslow, in his Good News from New England, from which the pas-

understood, he was much offended at the carriage of Tisquantum,* returning many thanks to the Governor for his good thoughts of him, and assuring him that, according to their first Articles of Peace,† he would send word and give warning when any such business was towards." In short, their alarm had been groundless, and as soon as it was ascertained that such was the case, the shallop was again despatched on its voyage to "the Massachusetts."‡

The next notice which we have of Namaschet is in the month of January, 1622–3, when we read that Governor Bradford went on an expedition "to two inland towns, and bought corn of them; the one called Namasket, the other Manomet.§ That from Namasket was brought home partly by In-

sage in the text is taken, uniformly spells the name of the Chieftain who is generally known, nowadays, as Massasoit. Prince says, "the printed accounts generally spell him Massasoit; Governor Bradford writes him Massasoyt and Massasoyet; but I find the ancient people, from their fathers, in Plymouth Colony, pronounce his name Ma-sas-so-it." And this is the orthography which the distinguished Annalist has adopted throughout his "Chronological History of New England." — *See Prince, p.* 187, *note.*

* This simple son of the forest appears to have been dazzled by the favor and confidence exhibited towards him by the English, and to have begun "to feel his oats." Winslow, in his Good News, seems to be unnecessarily severe in his language on this point. He says, after relating the particulars of the alarm at Plymouth, "thus by degrees we began to discover Tisquantum, whose ends were only to make himself great in the eyes of his countrymen, by means of his nearness and favor with us; not caring who fell, so he stood. In the general, his course was to persuade them he could lead us to peace or war, at his pleasure, and would oft threaten the Indians, sending them word in a private manner we were intended shortly to kill them, that thereby he might get gifts to himself, to work their peace; insomuch as they had him in greater esteem than many of their Sachims; yea, they themselves sought to him, who promised them peace in respect of us, yea, and protection also, so as they would resort to him; so that whereas divers were wont to rely on Massassowat for protection, and resort to his abode, now they began to leave him and seek after Tisquantum. Now, though he could not make good these his large promises, especially because of the continued peace between Massassowat and us, he therefore raised this false alarm; hoping, whilst things were hot in the heat of blood, to provoke us to march into his country against him, whereby he hoped to kindle such a flame as would not easily be quenched; and hoping if that block were once removed, there were no other between him and honor, which he loved as his life, and preferred before his peace. For these and the like abuses the Governor sharply reproved him; yet was he so necessary and profitable an instrument, as at that time we could not miss him. But when we understood his dealings, we certified all the Indians of our ignorance and innocency therein; assuring them, till they begun with us, they should have no cause to fear; and if any hereafter should raise any such reports, they should punish them as liars and seekers of their and our disturbance; which gave the Indians good satisfaction on all sides." — *Winslow, in Young, pp.* 289–90.

Tisquantum, or Squanto, did not survive long after this. His last service was to pilot an expedition, by water, to Manamoic, now Chatham, in search of provisions. This was in the month of November, 1622. "Here Squanto falls sick of a fever," writes Governor Bradford, who conducted the expedition, (Standish, who had been appointed to the command, having been taken sick of a fever,) "bleeding much at the nose, which the Indians reckon a fatal symptom, and here in a few days dies; desiring the Governor to pray that he might go to the Englishman's God in Heaven, bequeathing his things to sundry of his English friends, as remembrances of his love; of whom we have a great loss." Judge Davis remarks that "Governor Bradford's pen was worthily employed in the tender notice taken of the death of this child of nature. With some aberrations, his conduct was generally irreproachable, and his useful services to the infant settlement entitle him to grateful remembrance." A beautiful promontory in Quincy perpetuates the name of this friend of the Pilgrims. — *Winslow, in Young, p.* 301; *Prince, pp.* 206–7; *Davis's Morton, pp.* 85–6.

† Ratified at Plymouth, March 22, 1620–1, and religiously observed by Massasoit as long as he lived. — *See Bradford and Winslow, pp.* 35—8; *Prince, pp.* 186—8; *Davis's Morton, pp.* 53—5.

‡ Winslow, in Young, pp. 286—9; Prince, pp. 201–2; Davis's Morton, pp. 76–7.

§ "The part of Sandwich which lies on Manomet River." — *Mass. Hist. Coll.* VIII. 252, *note.*

dian women; but a great sickness arising amongst them,* our own men were enforced to fetch home the rest."†

In March, 1622–3, "news came to Plymouth," says Edward Winslow, "that Massassowat was like to die. Now it being a commendable manner of the Indians, when any, especially of note, are dangerously sick, for all that profess friendship to them to visit them in their extremity, either in their persons, or else to send some acceptable persons to them; therefore it was thought meet, being a good and warrantable action, that as we had ever professed friendship, so we should now maintain the same, by observing this their laudable custom. The Governor laid this service upon myself, and fitted me with some cordials to administer to him; having one Master John Hamden,‡ a gentleman of London, who then wintered with us, and desired much to see the country, for my consort, and Hobbamock for our guide. So we set forward, and lodged the first night at Namasket, where we had friendly entertainment." Winslow and his companions, having visited Massasoit, and spent one night with Corbitant, at Mattapuyst,§ passed the last night of their journey, as they had the first, at Namasket, whence they returned home the next day.‖

At the villages of Namasket and Titicut, within the present bounds of Middleborough, were, in former times, the favorite summer residences of the principal Chiefs of the New England tribes. Hither they were accustomed to resort, with their chosen followers, to pass a portion of the fishing and hunting season on the borders of the beautiful ponds in this neighborhood. Here was the royal hunting-house of the good King Massasoit, and also, at a later day, of his sons and successors, the short-lived Wamsutta, or Alexander, and the warlike Pometacom, or Philip. Tehticut, Teightaquid, Tettiquet, Teticut, or Titicut, on Namasket River, within the present bounds of Middleborough, is said to have been one of the favorite resorts of *Chikataubut*, the Chieftain of the Massachusetts Indians, and "the greatest Sagamore in the country." His territory in this part of New England "did extend from Nishamagoguanett, near Duxbury mill, to Titicut, near Taunton, and to Nunckatateset,¶ and from thence in a straight line to Wanamampuke,** which is the head of Charles River." Although Chikataubut was one of the nine Sachems who subscribed the Articles of Submission to King James, on the 13th of September, 1621, Dudley remarks of him, in 1631, that he "least favoreth the English of any Sagamore we are acquainted with, by reason of the old quarrel between him and those of Plymouth, wherein he lost seven of his best men." However this may be, it is certain that, on the 23d of March, 1630–1, but a few days after Dudley had penned the above passage in his famous Letter to the Countess of Lincoln, Chikataubut visited Boston, "with his Sannops and Squaws, and presented the Governor with a hogshead of Indian corn." Indeed, the whole intercourse of this Chief with the Massachusetts Colonists seems to

* I. e. the Indians at Namasket. † Winslow, in Young, p. 305; Prince, p. 208.

‡ Not, as has been often asserted, the distinguished English patriot of that name.— *See Young's Chronicles of the Pilgrims, pp.* 314–15, *note.*

§ A neck of land in the township of Swanzey, commonly pronounced Mattapoiset; now Gardner's Neck, situated between the Showamet and Towooset Necks. — *Belknap's American Biography*, (*8vo. Boston*, 1794 & 1798,) ii. 292, *note; Baylies's Memoir of Plymouth Colony*, (*8vo. Boston*, 1830,) *Part* II. *pp.* 232, 234.

‖ For an account of this expedition, and the visit to Massasoit, see Winslow, in Young, pp 313—26.

¶ A pond of considerable size, in the southwest part of Bridgewater, adjoining Raynham. It was sometimes called by the Indians *Neapnuncket.* Its modern name is *Nippenicket.*

** Whiting's Pond, in Wrentham.

have been of a uniformly friendly character. His principal residence was "upon the River of Naponset, near to the Mattachusetts Fields, three miles to the north of Wessaguscus." He, with many of his people, died of the Small Pox, in the month of November, 1633. His favorite domain at Tehticut, comprising "three miles on each side of the River," was granted by his son, Josiah Wampatuck, to the Titicut Indians, so called, before August, 1644; as, by an order of that date, the General Court at Plymouth, "upon the petition of Duxbury men, thought good that there be a view taken of the lands described by them, namely, twelve miles up into the woods from Plymouth bounds at Jones' River, and if it prove not prejudicial to *the Plantation to be erected at Teightaquid,*" &c. &c., "it may be confirmed unto them."*

In all grants of lands in this part of the Colony, the General Court was always very careful to insert a proviso with regard to the "Titicut Purchase," cautioning the grantees against encroachments upon this Indian settlement, the bounds and limits of which seem not to have been very accurately defined, and warning them not to locate themselves "too near to Titicut," or to "molest the Indians." So much, however, of this reserve, as was situated on the north side of the river, was included within "the additional grant" to Bridgewater, in 1668; and the inhabitants of that town obtained permission to purchase the tract, and William Brett, Nicholas Byram, and Samuel Edson were appointed by the Court to negotiate with the Indians for it. A deed was, accordingly, obtained from "Pomponoho, alias Peter, an Indian, living at Titicut, in the Colony of New Plymouth," bearing date Nov. 20, 1672, wherein it is recited that "I, Pomponoho, have sold for the full sum of sixteen pounds, viz., six pounds of current money of New England, and ten pounds in good merchantable corn, all the lands lying on the north side of Titicut River within the bounds of Bridgewater, what lands were mine, or were either my father's or grandfather's, or any otherwise conferred on me, excepting those lands expressed as follows," &c. &c., "unto Nicholas Byram, sen., Samuel Edson, sen., and William Brett, sen., in and for the use of the townsmen of Bridgewater, joint purchasers with them," &c. &c.†

For many years the settlements of the English in Plymouth Colony were confined to the seacoast, and to such portions of the interior as had been depopulated by the fearful pestilence, which had swept through the country shortly before their arrival on the New England shores. Hence it was that the territory of Namasket, comprising the Indian villages of Namasket and Titicut, which seem to have escaped the almost universal desolation, notwithstanding its proximity to Plymouth, did not begin to be settled by the English until about the year 1660, forty years after its first exploration by Winslow and Hopkins. The natives, comparatively inconsiderable in numbers, readily sold the larger portion of their ancestral domains to the English.‡ The first considerable purchase of lands occurred in the year 1662, when a large portion of territory was obtained from Josiah Wampatuck, for the sum of £70, bounded on one side by the Namasket

* Drake's Book of the Indians, Book II. pp. 19, 42—4, III. p. 7, *note;* Hutchinson's History of Massachusetts, (Salem ed., 8vo. 1795,) i. 262, *note;* Mitchell's History of Bridgewater, (8vo. Boston, 1840,) pp. 9–10, 17–18; Davis's Morton, p. 67; Dudley's Letter to the Countess of Lincoln, in Young's Chronicles of Massachusetts, (8vo. Boston, 1846,) p. 305; Winthrop's History of New England, (Savage's ed., 8vo. Boston, 1825–6,) i. 48, 53, 56, 61, 72, 87, 115–16; Mass. Hist. Coll. XVII. 142–3.

† Mitchell, pp. 17, 18—19; Mass. Hist. Coll. XVII. 142–3.

‡ Baylies, Part II. pp. 229–30; Part III. p. 2.

River, and on the other by Tippacunucut Brook.* Purchases were also effected at different times, of Watuspequin, or Tispacan, the "Black Sachem," the distinguished Chieftain of "Assowampsett;" until at length the whole territory, now comprised within the limits of the town, had been fairly acquired of the rightful lords of the soil.†

The names of the first purchasers were as follows.

F. John Adams,	M. Thomas Dotey,	George Partridge,
F. William Bassett,	Samuel Eddy,	William *Pontus* (?)
M. Francis Billington,	Lt. Matthew Fuller,	Andrew Ring,
Thomas Bordman,	M. Samuel Fuller,	John Shaw,
M. William Brewster,	Edward Gray,	F. Moses Simmons,
M. Peter Brown,	William Hodskins,	M. George Soule,
F. Edward Bumpus,	M. John Howland,	A. Francis Sprague,
M. Francis Cook,	M. William Mullins,	M. Resolved White.‡
F. Philip Delanoy,	William Nelson,	

* Eddy, MS. Letter. † Ibid; Drake's Book of the Indians, Book II. p. 45; III. pp. 57–8.

‡ For this list we are indebted to Mr. Eddy. The letters prefixed to some of the names indicate that the individual himself, or his immediate ancestor, came over either in the May Flower, in 1620, the Fortune, in 1621, or the Ann, in 1623. JOHN ADAMS was, perhaps, the person of that name mentioned by Deane, (History of Scituate, p. 211,) as being of Marshfield, and marrying Jane James in 1654. *He* may have been the son of John, who came over in the Fortune, in 1621, whose widow, Eleanor, married Kenelm Winslow in 1634. BASSETT was probably the son of the passenger of that name in the Fortune, who settled, first, in Plymouth, then in Duxbury, and finally in West Bridgewater, of which town he was an original proprietor, and died in 1667. BILLINGTON was the son of John Billington, one of the passengers in the May Flower, in 1620, who was executed at Plymouth, for murder, in 1630. The name of this his son will be transmitted to posterity, as the discoverer, in 1621, of the beautiful pond, called, after him, Billington Sea. BORDMAN may have been he of Lynn in 1637, who removed to Sandwich. BREWSTER was probably the son of Jonathan, and grandson of Elder William Brewster. BROWN may have been the passenger in the May Flower of that name. BUMPUS (said to have been originally *Bon passe*,) seems to have been of Marshfield in 1640, and of Duxbury soon after its settlement. The name of FRANCIS COOKE is found among the passengers of the May Flower, of whose wife Edward Winslow, in his "Briefe Narration," makes mention, as "being a Walloon." Of DELANO, originally De la Noye, Winslow tells us that he was "born of French parents," and that he "came from Leyden to New Plymouth;" and "coming to age of discerning, demanded communion with us; and proving himself to be come of such parents as were in full communion with the French Churches, was hereupon admitted by the Church of Plymouth; and after, upon his removal of habitation to Duxburrow, where Mr. Ralph Partridge is Pastor of the Church, and upon letters of recommendation from the Church at Plymouth, he was also admitted into fellowship with the Church at Duxburrow." He was early at Duxbury, and was one of the original proprietors of Bridgewater. He married Hester Dewsberry in 1634, and Mary, widow of James Glass, of Duxbury, and daughter of James Churchill, in 1657. DOTEY was, without doubt, the son of Edward Dotey, that chivalrous esquire of Stephen Hopkins, who signalized himself by being a party to "the first duel fought in New England, upon a challenge of single combat with sword and dagger," at Plymouth, June 18, 1621. The *doughty* hero seems to have subsequently exchanged the weapons of Mars for those of Cupid, as we find him, at a later date, besieging, nay, carrying by storm, one Faith Clarke, undoubtedly a notable virgin of Plymouth Colony. SAMUEL EDDY was the son of Rev. William Eddy, of Cranbrook, in the County of Kent, England, and arrived at Plymouth, with his brother John, in the Handmaid, Captain Grant master, Oct. 29, 1630. He settled at Plymouth, and had four sons and several daughters. "His son OBADIAH," (writes his lineal descendant, ZECHARIAH EDDY, ESQ.,) "inherited the Middleborough lands; whose son, SAMUEL, had some of the farms by inheritance from him; whose son ZECHARIAH, inherited the same. JOSHUA, the son of ZECHARIAH, was the next inheritor; and the writer now owns and occupies the same lands which the first Samuel purchased, and which were set off to him in the division made of that purchase by the twenty-six men among themselves." Of MATTHEW FULLER we have been able to find only a brief notice, which states that he was "first of Plymouth, about 1640, removed to Barnstable in 1652, where he died, 1678. He was appointed Surgeon-General of the Provincial forces raised in Plymouth Colony in 1673, and he is also styled Captain in 1675." Of SAMUEL FULLER, supposing him to be identical with the first Minister of the town, we shall have something to say

The settlement of the whites was followed by its usual consequence, the gradual disappearance of the red race. The native inhabitants of the territory of Namasket, having alienated their possessions, sought other hunting-

anon. GRAY married Mary, (born in 1630, died in 1663,) daughter of Mr. John Winslow, (a brother of Gov. Edward,) Jan. 16, 1650–1. He was a respectable merchant and ship owner, and resided in that part of the town of Plymouth which borders upon Kingston, and which was called, by the first planters, "*Plain Dealing*." In 1678 he hired Clarke's Island, "for seven years, to keep 16 neat cattle, free of rate; townsmen to have liberty to bring wood for building, fencing, and firing." His daughter Desire married Lieut. Nathaniel Southworth, Jan. 10, 1671–2. From Mass. Hist. Coll. XIII. 167, note, it appears that he died in 1681. There was a WILLIAM HOSKINS in Scituate, a freeman in 1634. JOHN HOWLAND, the first of the name, came to Plymouth in the May Flower, in 1620, as a member of the family of Governor Carver, whose daughter Elizabeth he afterwards married. After a long life of usefulness, he died at his residence, at Rocky Nook, Feb. 24, 1672–3, aged 80. Plymouth Colony Records, taking notice of his decease, add that he was "a godly man and an ancient professor in the ways of Christ, and proved a useful instrument of good in his place, and was the last of the male survivors of those who came over in the May Flower in 1620, *whose place of abode was Plymouth*." Of his four sons, JOHN resided a short time in Marshfield, and then settled in Barnstable; Jabez settled, finally, in Bristol, R. I.; ISAAC in Middleborough; and Joseph, the youngest, remained in Plymouth. Of MULLINS it can only be conjectured that he was a son of the tenth signer of the celebrated COMPACT, "a man pious and well deserving, endowed also with a considerable outward estate," who died at Plymouth, Feb. 21, 1620–1. There was a person of the name in Duxbury, about 1642. Of NELSON we have not been able to obtain any information. A *John* Nelson, of *Middleborough*, married Lydia, (daughter of Robert Bartlett, of Plymouth; born June 8, 1647,) the widow of James Barnaby. GEORGE PARTRIDGE may have been the brother of Rev. Ralph Partridge, whose tedious and distressing voyage, and safe arrival, with "many good people," at Boston, Nov. 17, 1636, are recorded by Winthrop. The "godly minister, Mr. Partridge," was soon called to a pastoral office in the Church at Duxbury; and simultaneously appears the name of George Partridge as an inhabitant of that town. They were both, also, original proprietors of Bridgewater. Sarah, the daughter of George, born in 1639, married Samuel Allen, of Bridgewater, about 1658. The next name upon our list is evidently a misnomer; but what it *should* be, we are unable to say. Of ANDREW RING we know nothing with certainty. A person of that name married Deborah, a daughter of Stephen Hopkins, the Pilgrim, in 1646, and died in 1692, aged 75. SHAW is said to have "arrived at Plymouth about 1627." His residence was at "*Plain Dealing;*" and his name, with those of Francis Billington, Samuel Eddy, and William *Hodgkinson*, appears on the list of those "townsmen of New Plymouth" among whom was divided, in July, 1638, the live stock remaining from Mr. James Shirley's donation, in 1624, of "an heifer to the Plantation, to begin a stock for the poor." MOSES SYMONSON, (as his name was originally, but now corrupted into *Simmons*,) came to Plymouth in the Fortune; and being, says Winslow, "a child of one that was in communion with the Dutch Church at Leyden, is admitted into Church fellowship at Plymouth in New England, and his children also to baptism, as well as our own." He was one of the first settlers of Duxbury, and an original proprietor of Bridgewater. His sons Moses and Thomas settled, the former in Duxbury, where he died in 1689, and the latter in Scituate, where he was a householder before 1647. GEORGE SOULE, the thirty-fifth signer of the Compact at Cape Cod, and a member of Edward Winslow's family, sold his lands in Plymouth, and removed to Duxbury before 1645, in which year he was one of the deputies from that town to the General Court at Plymouth; and was an original proprietor of Bridgewater. In 1668 he gave his lands in Middleborough to his sons-in-law John Haskell and Francis Walker, both of that town, and their wives (his daughters) Patience and Elizabeth. His wife, Mary, died in 1677; he himself in 1680, "very aged." SPRAGUE settled in Duxbury, and is spoken of as having been "a man of influence and property." He was an original proprietor of Bridgewater, but neither removed thither himself, nor did any of his family. RESOLVED WHITE was the eldest son of "Mr. William White," the eleventh signer to the Compact, who died Feb. 21, 1620–1. He was one of the early settlers of Scituate, whence he removed to Marshfield in 1662. He married, in 1640, Judith, the eldest daughter of William Vassall, of Scituate. He remained in Marshfield until 1670, about which time his wife died, and then disappears. He was living in 1675, as is evident from a bequest to him, in the will of Josiah Winslow, of that date.

See Farmer's Genealogical Register; Baylies's Historical Memoir of Plymouth Colony; Deane's History of Scituate; Shurtleff's "Passengers of the May Flower," in N. E. Hist. and Gen. Register, I. 47—53; *Mitchell's Hist. Bridgewater; Prince's Annals; Davis's Morton; Massachusetts Historical Collections; Russell's Guide to Plymouth; Winslow's "Briefe Narration," in Young's Chronicles of the Pilgrims; Ward's History of Shrewsbury.*

grounds; and the forests, through which they had roamed in savage dignity, vanished before the axe of the sturdy pioneer. But though the red man retreats, he leaves traces behind him, which perpetuate his remembrance for ages after the last miserable remnant of his tribe shall have passed away forever. The ploughshare not unfrequently exposes to view the Indian sepulchre, where, close beside the bones of the deceased, are found the various articles which the pious care of friends had provided, in anticipation of the long journey to the land of spirits; while the bow and arrows, the knife and pipe, shew what was to be the nature of the warrior's pursuits upon his arrival at the happy hunting-grounds of the blessed. Here and there the field thickly sown with arrow-heads, and the mouldering skulls, upturned by the careless husbandman, evidence the mighty harvest which Death once reaped there, and call to mind the race which in former days peopled the country, stalking through its majestic forests, or sauntering on the borders of its beautiful ponds and streams. On the Eastern shore of Assowamsett Pond there were, some few years since, two rocks, whereon were to be seen sundry "curious marks," which the wise are fain to suppose to have been "done by the Indians," and in some of which they trace a resemblance to "the steppings of a person with naked feet, which settled into the rocks;" while others are as evidently "the prints of a hand." On a high hill, too, a little to the eastward of "the old stone fishing-wear," * there is a venerable rock, bearing the veritable impress of a man's hand upon its flinty surface.†

The following document is not without interest at this stage of our history. It was found among the rich collection of manuscripts in the Library of the Massachusetts Historical Society; ‡ and we will give a complete transcript of it, *verbatim et literatim*, even at the risk of being thought somewhat tedious, inasmuch as it has never before been printed, to our knowledge.

"PRENCE GOVr.

The Several Lotts laid forth & bounded lying and being upon Pochade neck near unto Namasket Granted unto Several Persons afternamed, are as followeth

Imprs. The Majr. Winslow.	1 Lot beginneth at a White Oak tree marked on four Sides near the Brook where the three Brooks meet & it runs up a Southwest line and is bounded on the other Side with two red Oaks marked
Mr. Thos Prence.	2 Lott is bounded with a Pine tree and red Oak tree marked
Mr John Alden.	3 Lot is bounded with two red Oak trees marked
Lt Peregrine White	4 Lot is bounded with a white Oak & a red Oak tree marked
Nathl. Warren	5 Lot is bounded with a white Oak marked Standing alone in a plain
Wm. Basset	6 Lot is bounded with two walnot trees marked
Mr John Winslow.	7 Lot is bounded with two red Oak trees marked & with ye River
Capt Bradford.	8 Lot lyeth across the Ends of the other Lots next unto Namasket & is bounded with a red Oak & a pine tree marked next unto the sd. Lotts. and on the other side with a white Oak marked near unto the bounds of the purchase.

The bounds of Several Lotts granted unto Sundry Persons besides those above named lying near unto Namaskett are as followeth

Francis Sprague.	1 Lot is bounded with a red Oak at the River side that Comes from Winnatuxet & Bridgwater, & on the other side running Cross the Neck, it is bounded with a red Oak & a white Oak marked, this is the first Lot lying on the Northwest side of the sd. neck
John Adams.	2 Lott is bounded with a Stooping maple tree in a little Swamp & a red Oak marked

* See *ante*. † Mass. Hist. Coll. III. 2; Drake's Indian Wars. (12mo. Boston, 1727,) p. 99.
‡ In a volume entitled "Letters & Papers, 1632—1678," p. 75.

George Patridge	3 Lot is bounded with two red Oak trees marked
Francis Cooke	4 Lot is bounded with two red Oaks marked
Thos Barman	5 Lot is bounded with a red Oak and a pine tree marked
Wm Parkes	6 Lot is bounded with two red Oak trees marked
Saml ffuller	7 Lot is bounded on the Side next the foregoing Lot with two red Oaks marked & on the other side with a pine & a White Oak marked, there being a parcel of Barren Land betwixt this & the foregoing Lot
	8 The Eighth Lot lyeth Vacant
	no 9 on list
Edwd Bumpus	10 Lot is bounded with a red Oak & a Walnut marked
Mr. Wm. Brewster	11 Lot is bounded with two red Oaks marked
John Shaw.	12 Lot is bounded with a White Oak & a red Oak marked.
Edwd Gray	13 Lot is bounded with a maple tree & a pine tree marked.
Edwd. Gray	14 Lot is bounded [with] a Rock & a red Oak marked
Mr Resolved White	15 Lot is at the wading place & is bounded with the path & the Beaver Damm & lyeth in half the length of the former Lotts
Wm Hoskins.	16 Lot abutteth on the path wth two white Oaks marked
Andr Ring	17 Lot is bounded with two red Oaks marked
Moses Simons	18 Lot is bounded with a red Oak & a Walnut tree marked
Wm. Nelson	19 Lot is bounded with a White Oak & a walnut tree marked
Mr Jno. Howland	20 Lot is bounded with two red Oaks marked
George Soule.	21 Lot is bounded with two red Oak trees marked
Philip Delanoy	22 Lot is bounded with two white Oaks marked
Wm. Mullins	23 Lot is bounded with two white Oaks marked
Petr. Browne	24 Lot is bounded with a White Oak & a red Oak marked
Saml. Eddys	25 Lot is bounded with a red Oak & a white Oak marked
Lt. Fuller	26 Lot is bounded with a white Oak & a Red Oak marked.
Thos Dogget	27 Being the first at Whetstones Vineyard, the bounds of it are two White Oaks on the Northwest side marked, & on the other side with two white Oaks
The Ministers Lot.	28 Lot lyeth at Wahuckett Brook next the Path & runneth half the length of the other Lotts

A true Copy as appears of Record
Examd pr Josiah Cotton Cler
& Regr.
Recorded in or about the year 1664
A true Copy
Examd pr Josiah Cotton Cler
A True Copy
Examd pr Samll. Tyley Cler"*

Superscribed
"Namaskett Props Names."

* "The Major" JOSIAH WINSLOW, whose name stands at the head of our list, was the son of Gov. EDWARD WINSLOW, (by his second wife, Susanna, the widow of Mr. William White, whom he married May 12, 1621,) and was born at Marshfield, in 1628. He married Penelope, a daughter of Herbert Pelham, Esq., in 1657; was many years an Assistant, was Commander-in-chief of the forces employed during PHILIP'S WAR, sustained the office of Governor from 1673 to 1679, inclusive, being the first Chief Magistrate who was born in the country, and died at Marshfield, Dec. 18, 1680, and was buried on the 23d. His wife died in 1703, aged 73. "MR. JOHN WINSLOW" was probably JOHN, JR., the son of John the brother of Gov. Edward, who came over in the Fortune, and married, before 1627, MARY CHILTON, the daughter of James Chilton, one of the passengers in the May Flower, and had nine children, the eldest of which was John, who died in 1683. One of the daughters of John, Sen., married, as has been already mentioned, EDWARD GRAY. THOMAS PRENCE came from Leachlade, in Gloucestershire, to Plymouth, in the Fortune, married Patience, daughter of Elder William Brewster, Aug. 5, 1624, was chosen Governor in 1634, and served one year. In 1635, his wife having died in the course of the preceding year, he married Mary, daughter of Mr. William Collier, and about this time took up his residence at Duxbury. He was an Assistant in 1635, 1636, and 1637, and was again chosen Governor in 1638, for one year, during which he continued to reside in Duxbury. From 1639 to 1656, inclusive, he was an Assistant. In 1644 he had removed to Eastham, where his wife died. In 1657 he was, for the third time, elected Governor, and retained the office until his death. He married, in 1662, Mrs. Mary, widow of Samuel Freeman; and in 1665 removed to Plymouth, where he passed the remainder of his days, in a house provided for him by the Government, at "*Plain Dealing.*" He

In the year 1668 the General Court of Plymouth Colony, in answer to a petition of July 5, 1667, from the town of Bridgewater, "desiring their enlargement may extend to where the six miles extends that they purchased of the Indians by order from the Court," passed an act confirming to the petitioners the lands in question, with the proviso, however, "that grants of lands formerly made by the Court be not molested," and ordered that "as to those lands that are between Bridgewater and Namasket, already granted, it shall be determined by the Court unto what town they shall belong; and that the Indians be not molested, notwithstanding this enlargement."*

The various purchases of territory which had been made of the natives in Namasket, having been duly authorized and confirmed† by the General

died March 29, 1673, in the 73d year of his age, "having been a worthy, pious gentleman, and very capable of the office of Governor, being therein a terror to evil doers, and an encourager of those that did well; and was honorably interred at Plymouth, April 8, 1673." His wife survived him. The name of JOHN ALDEN is familiar as a household word. He married Priscilla, daughter of Mr. William Mullins; was one of the first settlers of Duxbury, one of its Deputies to the General Court, an original proprietor of Bridgewater, and many years an Assistant; and after a long life of eminent usefulness, died — the last of that little band of PILGRIMS which first stepped upon Plymouth Rock— on the 12th of September, 1687, aged 88. His wife appears to have survived him. His descendants have been remarkable for longevity. Of his children, JOSEPH, of Bridgewater, died Feb. 8, 1697, aged about 73; JONATHAN died in February, 1697, aged about 70; Elizabeth, the wife of William Paybody, died May 31, 1717, aged 93; JOHN, the third son of JOSEPH, sold his father's homestead in Bridgewater, about 1700, and removed to Titicut, in Middleborough. His son JOHN lived in Middleborough, where he died in April, 1821, aged 102, having been twice married, and had 19 children, 62 grandchildren, 134 great-grandchildren, and 7 great-great-grandchildren, 172 of whom were living at the time of his decease. "Three of his children," says a late writer, "two daughters and one son, are now [1845] living, and dwell under the same roof in Middleborough, whose average age is 84 1-3 years." PEREGRINE WHITE, the first-born of English parents in New England, was born on board the May Flower, in Cape Cod Harbor, in November, 1620. His mother, upon the decease of her husband, married Gov. Edward Winslow, May 12, 1621; and her sons by her first husband were, consequently, bred in the town of Marshfield, where the Governor resided. Peregrine married Sarah, daughter of William Basset, and passed his days in Marshfield, where he died July 20, 1704, "vigorous and of a comely aspect to the last." His wife died in 1711. NATHANIEL WARREN was the son of "Mr. Richard Warren," one of the passengers of the May Flower, whose death, in 1628, is commemorated in New England's Memorial. His family arrived in the Ann, in 1623. Nathaniel married Sarah Walker, in 1645. Captain (afterwards Major) WILLIAM BRADFORD, son of Gov. William Bradford, (by his second wife, Mrs. Alice, widow of Constant Southworth, whom he married Aug. 14, 1623,) was born June 17, 1624, sustained many offices, both military and civil, and died Feb. 20, 1703-4. He lived in Kingston, near Duxbury, and was one of the original proprietors of Bridgewater. He was thrice married, and left a numerous posterity. Of WILLIAM PARKES we *know* nothing. He *may* have been he of Roxbury, who died May 11, 1685. But we are inclined to think that WILLIAM PARKER, of Scituate and Barnstable, is the person intended. THOMAS DOGGET we presume to have been he of Marshfield, who married Mary Chillingworth, in 1654, according to Deane. Of the other persons, whose names are upon this list, we have already spoken.

* Mitchell's Bridgewater, p. 16.

† In 1643 it was enacted by the General Court of the Colony "that if any person or persons hereafter purchase rent or hyre any lands herbage wood or tymber of any of the Natives in any place within this Govern^t without the consent and assent of this Court every such person or persons shall forfait five pounds for every acree which shal be so purchased hyred rented and taken and for wood and tymber to pay five times the value thereof to be levyed to the Colonies use." In 1660, "in reference unto the law prohibiting buying or hiering land of the Indians directly or indirectly bearing date 1643 the Court interpretts those words alsoe to comprehend under the same penaltie a prohibition of any mans receiving any lands under pretence of any gift from the Indians without the approbation of the Court." And in the edition of "The General Laws" published in 1672, the same provision is inserted.— *See Plymouth Colony Laws, (Brigham's ed., 8vo. Boston,* 1836,) *pp.* 74, 129, 289.

Court, the town was finally incorporated, by the name of Middleborough, (or Middleberry, as it is uniformly spelt on the Colony Records,) in June, 1669.*

In the course of this same year died Josiah Wampatuck, of whom, as we have seen, a portion of Middleborough was purchased. He was the son of Chikataubut, of whom we have before spoken, and was the Sachem of Mattakeesett, or Pembroke. He was a minor in 1641, and "was bred up," says Gookin, "by his uncle Kuchamakin," or Cutshamekin, a Sachem who resided at Neponset, within the bounds of Dorchester. On the 5th of February, 1643–4, Cutshamekin, Agawam, and "Josias, Chikatabot's heir," writes Winthrop, "came to the Governor, and in their own name and the names of all the Sachems of Watchusett, and all the Indians from Merrimack to Tecticutt, tendered themselves to our [the Massachusetts] government, and gave the Governor [Winthrop himself] a present of thirty fathom of Wampom, and offered to come to the next Court to make their acknowledgment, &c. The Governor received their present to keep it till the Court, &c., and if the Court and they did agree, then to accept it." According to his promise, Cutshamekin presented himself at the Court in March following, accompanied by the Squaw Sachem of Massachusetts, (widow of the mighty Nanepashemet,) and three other Chiefs, and "according to their former tender to the Governor," says Winthrop, "desired to be received under our protection and government upon the same terms that Pumham and Sacononoco were." This application, coinciding as it did with the policy of the Massachusetts Government, could not but meet with a favorable reception; and the chiefs, having first listened to an explanation of the Articles of Agreement and "*all the ten commandments of God,*" were taken under the protection of the Government; and after an exchange of presents, and an entertainment, "went away very joyful." Cutshamekin, we are told, was the first *Sachem* to whom Eliot preached, and it was in his wigwam, "near Dorchester mill," that the Apostle's stated Lecture at Neponset was established, in 1646, and kept, once a fortnight. But notwithstanding Cutshamekin's profession of Christianity, he united with his neighbor Chieftains, in the year 1650, in their opposition to Mr. Eliot's project of establishing a regular town of Praying Indians; and he avowed the cause of his opposition to be, the decrease in his revenues since the conversion of his subjects, which gave him reason to apprehend that, eventually, all tribute would be withheld. Upon close investigation, however, it was satisfactorily ascertained that it was not the loss of tribute which chafed the irascible Chieftain, but the diminution of the despotic power which he had formerly exercised over his subjects, consequent upon their advance in civilization. Thanks to the firmness and patience of Eliot, the irritation of Cutshamekin was soothed, and he ceased, for the present, at least, to trouble the Apostle and his converts. But he was a man of ardent feelings, alike hasty in his resentments, and impassioned in his sorrow for his actions during his outbursts of violence, unstable as water, and veering with every wind. He died before 1655. Nurtured amid such influences, it is no wonder if the youthful Josiah should have evinced something of the impetuosity and fickleness of character for which his uncle was distinguished. "He had," says Gookin, "considerable knowledge in the Chris-

* Heretofore it has been usually stated that the town was incorporated in 1660. But see the statement in the Collections of the American Statistical Association, I. 42, which is confirmed by Mr. Eddy.

tian religion, and sometime, when he was younger, seemed to profess it for a time, and was a catechized Indian, and kept the Sabbath several years; but after turned apostate, and separated from the Praying Indians." Notwithstanding his "apostacy," Josiah is said to have been a faithful friend to the English, to whom he made numerous and extensive grants of land; as, for instance, in 1653 and 1668, in Scituate and the vicinity; in 1662, at Middleborough, and other places in its neighborhood. Aug. 5, 1665, he gave a deed of Braintree, in which he describes himself as "Wampatuck, alias Josiah Sagamore, the son of Chikataubut deceased." After his father's death Wampatuck was not unfrequently, and perhaps generally, called Josias Chikataubut; under which name he sold to Dorchester the "New Grant," so called, in 1666, promising a full and ample deed thereof in 1669; but his death prevented its delivery. The Dorchester people, however, obtained, in 1670, a deed from his brother, Squamaug, who acted as Sachem during the minority of Jeremy, the son of Josiah, which was confirmed by Jeremy himself in 1671. In 1659 we find John Eliot memorializing the General Court on "The case of the Nipmuk Indians," stating that "Uncas his men, at unawares, set upon an unarmed poor people, and slew eight persons, and carried captive twenty-four women and children. Some of them," he adds, "were subjects to [the] Massachusetts Government, *by being the subjects of Josias.*" In the summer of 1669, during the war between the Indians of New England and the Mohawks, the Massachusetts Chieftains united in raising an army of some six or seven hundred men to invade the country of the enemy. This enterprise was strongly discountenanced by the English; and the Praying Indians were so influenced by the arguments of Eliot and Gookin, that "not above five of them" could be induced to take part therein. "The chiefest General in this expedition," says Gookin, "was the principal Sachem of Massachusetts, named Josiah, alias Chekatabutt, a wise and stout man of middle age, but a very vitious person. This man was the chief, but there were divers other Sagamores and stout men that assisted." After a tedious march of about two hundred miles, the allied forces, composed of the bravest warriors of New England, arrived in the Mohawk Country, and sitting down before one of the forts of the enemy, besieged it for some days. But having been weakened by an assault of the Mohawks, who sallied from their fort, and attacked them with great fury; and finding that the strongholds of the enemy, the strength of which precluded the possibility of carrying them by assault, were well prepared to sustain a siege, while, in the meantime, their own provisions were exhausted, their ammunition well nigh spent, and sickness had made its appearance in their camp, they reluctantly abandoned the siege, and turned their faces homeward. But before they had marched fifty miles, they were pursued and intercepted by the Mohawks, and a severe conflict ensued. The New Englanders fought bravely, and many of the enemy fell before them; but they were worn out by the fatigue of the journey and siege, and had to contend with a superior force. Their leader, Josiah, with most of his chief Captains and Sagamores, to the number of fifty, were slain, fighting valiantly. The approach of night put an end to the battle, — which was the last and most fatal in the war, — and the Mohawks withdrew, well satisfied with their victory; while the remnant of the Massachusetts force made the best of its way home, overwhelmed with sorrow, shame, and confusion at the disastrous result of their enterprise, and mourning the loss of their principal Chiefs and bravest warriors.

Josiah, as we have seen, left a son Jeremy, who became Sachem upon the attainment of his majority, in 1671. Charles Josiah, the son of Jeremy, is said to have been the last of his race.*

In the year 1670 John Morton, of Plymouth, bought into the "26 men's purchase," as it was called, and took up his residence in Middleborough; and was chosen to represent the town — for the first time — in the General Court of the Colony, at Plymouth, in the month of June.† In 1671 the town does not appear to have been represented at all. In 1672 Morton again served as Deputy.‡

This year, 1672, we find it recorded that "the Island of Quetequas was let by the Colony to a Mr. Palmer, to plant and to sow." This island was in one of the great ponds in Middleborough, and probably in that one which bears the same name, Quetequas, with its variations, Quittaquas, Quitiquos, Quittiquash, and Quitticus.§

In June, 1673, the town was represented by Morton for the last time. He died before the close of the year, at Middleborough, "much lamented by sundry of the inhabitants of that place." He was the son of Mr. George Morton, of Austerfield, Yorkshire, who married Sarah, the sister of Governor Bradford, came over in the Ann, in 1623, and died at Plymouth, in the month of June, 1624, leaving three sons, of whom the subject of this notice was the second, and two daughters. The Colony Records inform us that Mr. John Morton was "a godly man," and the estimation in which he was held by the people of Middleborough is evidenced by their selecting him for their first Deputy to the General Court. He left a numerous family. His son John was "the first town schoolmaster in Plymouth, his native place"; and among his descendants may be mentioned the name of the Honorable Marcus Morton, LL. D.‖

* Drake's Book of the Indians, Book II. pp. 44–5, 80–1, 113–14; Deane's History of Scituate, (8vo. Boston, 1831,) pp. 144–5; Mass. Hist. Coll. I. 166–7, 169, IX. 160; Savage's Winthrop, ii. 153–4, 156–7, 303; Francis's Life of John Eliot, in Sparks's American Biography, V. 71, *et seq.*, 181; Blake's Annals of Dorchester, (12mo. Boston, 1846,) p. 25.

† In June, 1638, the General Court of Plymouth Colony, taking into consideration the complaint "that the freemen were put to many inconveniences and great expences by their continuall attendance at the Courts," ENACTS, "for the ease of the severall Colonies and Townes within the Government, that every Towne shall make choyce of two of their freemen and the Towne of Plymouth of foure, to be Committees or deputies to joyne with the Bench to enact and make all such lawes and ordinances as shall be judged to be good and wholesome for the whole," &c. &c.

In accordance with this Order of the Court, the first representative Legislative Assembly of the Colony convened at Plymouth, on the 4th of June, 1639, when Deputies from six towns made their appearance.

Plymouth was represented by William Paddy, Manasseh Kempton, Jr., John Cooke, Jr., and John Dunham.

Duxbury, by Jonathan Brewster and Edmund Chandler.

Scituate, by Anthony Annable and Edward Foster.

Cohannet (which received the name of Taunton at the Court which met on the 3d of March, 1639–40,) by Mr. John Gilbert and Henry Andrews.

Sandwich, by Richard Bourne and John Vincent.

Yarmouth, by Thomas Payne and Philip Tabor.

Barnstable was not represented until December, when Mr. Joseph Hall and Mr. Thomas Dimmack appeared as its Deputies.

—*See Brigham's Plymouth Colony Laws, pp.* 63, 66; *Baylies, Part* I. *pp.* 304–5.

The first Assembly of Representatives in Massachusetts, convened at Boston, on the 14th of May, 1634.—*See Savage's Winthrop*, i. 128–30.

‡ Eddy; Baylies, Part II. pp. 66, 67.

§ Mass. Hist. Coll. III. 2, XIV. 253, 254, 265–6. XX. 34–5.

‖ Baylies, Part II. p. 71; Eddy; Mass. Hist. Coll. XIV. 91; Davis's Morton, pp. iii, 100–1, 379, 385; Russell's Guide to Plymouth, (12mo. Boston, 1846,) p. 252; Mitchell's Bridgewater.

In this year, 1673, John Dunham bought into "the purchase," and became an inhabitant; * and represented the Town at the Court holden at Plymouth in the month of September. †

On the 3d of July, 1673, Watuspaquin, the "Black Sachem," and his son William, had sold, for the sum of £15, to Benjamin Church, of Duxbury, house carpenter, and John Tompson, of Barnstable, a tract of land "lying att and neare the township of Middleberry." Thompson seems to have taken up his residence in the town soon after, and in the years 1674 and 1675 represented Middleborough in the General Court.‡

1675. May 14. Watuspaquin and his son William "make over to John Tompson, Constant Southworth," and others, of Middleborough, "all that tract of land which we now have in possession, called commonly Assowamset neck or necks, and places adjacent," as security for other lands, deeded at the same time, against the claims of other persons thereupon; upon the condition that, if the purchasers of said lands are not disturbed in their possession, then the Indians "are not to be outed of Assawamsett neck."§

June. The General Court sitting at Plymouth in this month, "ordered and impowered Mr. Constant Southworth and Willam Paybody to run the line between Bridgwater and Middlebery. In case of the Treasurers [Southworth's] neglect, that then Nathaniell Thomas, Leiftenant Morton, and John Thompson to supply." ‖

As we have gradually approached that eventful period in our history, called King Philip's War, we have deviated in some instances from our chronological arrangement, in order that we might present an unbroken view of "the grounds, beginning, and progress" of this, "The Great Indian War" of New England, so far as connected with the history of the town of Middleborough.

About the year 1656 the two sons of the good King Massasoit (who had, in the year 1632, assumed the name of Ousamequin) presented themselves before the Court, at Plymouth, and requested that English names might be given to them. Wamsutta, the eldest, was accordingly complimented with the name of Alexander, and Pometacom, his brother, with that of Philip; and they departed highly gratified, without doubt, by these imposing titles.¶ The Treaty which had been made at Plymouth, by their father, on the 22d of March, 1620–1, and which had been renewed and confirmed by the Chieftain and his eldest son Mooanam, (subsequently called Wamsutta, and finally, by the English, as we have seen, named Alexander,) on the 25th of September, 1639, "being honestly intended," says Belknap, "on both sides, was kept with fidelity as long as Massasoit lived." Not long before his death, as we are informed by Hubbard, the aged Chief "came to Mr. Brown's, that lived not far from Mount Hope, bringing his two sons, Alexander and Philip, with him, desiring that there might be love and amity after his death, between his sons and them, as there had been betwixt himself and them in former times." **

* Eddy. — We presume him to have been the son of Deacon John Downham, or Dunham, who died March 2, 1668–9, aged 80. If this supposition is correct, he died in the year 1692, aged 79. — *See Russell's Guide, p.* 254; *and also Davis's Morton, pp.* 227, 384, *note.*

† Baylies, Part II. p. 71.

‡ Drake's Book of the Indians, Book III. p. 58; Eddy; Baylies, Part II. pp. 71–2.

§ Drake, Book III. p. 58.

‖ Brigham's Plymouth Colony Laws, p. 176.

¶ Davis's Morton, p. 287, note; Drake's Book of the Indians, Book III pp. 3, 6.

** Bradford and Winslow, pp. 35–7; Davis's Morton, pp. 53–5, 210–11; Prince, pp. 186–8; Drake, Book III. p. 3; Belknap's American Biography, ii. 214; Hubbard's Narrative of the Troubles with the Indians, (sm. 4to. Boston, 1677,) p. 8.

Ousamequin died between the 13th of September and the 13th of December, 1661, and was succeeded by Alexander, who, says Mather, "was not so faithful and friendly to the English as his father had been," but, if we may believe Hubbard, "had neither affection to their persons nor yet to their religion." In this last particular the new Sachem but followed the example of his father, who, although a firm friend to the English, was strongly opposed to the introduction of Christianity among his subjects; and even attempted, in or about the year 1653, when a negotiation was pending for the sale of the lands now included within the town of Swansea (vulgarly called *Swansey*) to extort from his civilized neighbors a promise "never to attempt to draw away any of his people to the Christian religion." Scarcely was Alexander invested with the power of Sachem, as successor to his father, when he was suspected — whether with reason, or not, is exceedingly doubtful — of entertaining hostile designs against the English. "For some of Boston," writes Mather, "having been occasionally at Narraganset, wrote to Mr. Prince, who was then Governor of Plymouth, that Alexander was contriving mischief against the English, and that he had solicited the Narragansets to engage with him in his designed rebellion." Upon the receipt of this intelligence, Alexander was forthwith summoned "to attend the next Court in Plymouth, for their satisfaction and his own vindication." The Sachem not appearing on the appointed day, the Governor and magistrates ordered Major Josiah Winslow to bring him before them. Major Winslow, accompanied by Major William Bradford and some eight or ten armed men, immediately proceeded towards Mount Hope, where he expected to find the Chieftain; "but by a good Providence," says Hubbard, "he found him whom he went to seek at an Hunting-house," situated midway between Plymouth and Bridgewater, on Munponset Pond,* and surprised him at breakfast with a party of his followers. Irreconcilable as are the accounts of Winslow's reception, we will merely state that Alexander accompanied the Major to Duxbury, to the house of Mr. William Collier, where he was met by a number of the magistrates, and after a conference, according to Mather, was consigned to the care of Major Winslow, until Governor Prince should arrive from Eastham, where he resided. All accounts agree that the Chief was taken sick at the house of Major Winslow, at Marshfield; and that, being sent home to his own residence, he there died within a few days. His death was ascribed by many, at the time, to the treatment which he received at the hands of the English, as we may gather from some remarks of Hubbard; and such always has been, and still is, a very general belief. Mather tells us that "proud Alexander, vexing and fretting in his spirit, such a check was given him, that he suddenly fell sick of a fever." And here we probably find the true cause of his illness; namely, his exquisite sensitiveness to what he had a right to consider a most grievous affront, an indelible stain upon his honor as a Sovereign Prince.†

On the death of Alexander, which occurred in the summer, probably in the month of July, of 1662, Philip became Chief Sachem of the Wampan-

* In the north part of the town of Halifax. The road from Plymouth to Bridgewater passes along the southwest margin of this pond. See Mass. Hist. Coll. XIV. 280-1.

† Hazard's State Papers, (4to. Phil. 1792,-4) ii. 449-51, compared with Knowles's Memoir of Roger Williams, (12mo. Boston, 1834,) p. 406; Drake's Book of the Indians, Book II. pp. 27-8, 100, III. pp. 6-9, 17; Old Indian Chronicle, (12mo. Boston, 1836,) p. 160; Hubbard's Narrative, pp. 8, 9-10; Francis's Life of Eliot, in Sparks's Am. Biog. V. 138; Baylies, Part II. pp. 233-4; Davis's Morton, pp. 287-8, *note*, 426-7; Hutchinson's Massachusetts, i. 252, *note*.

oags; and as he was aware of the suspicions which had been entertained of his brother, his first act was to repair to Plymouth with John Sausaman, his Secretary, and several of his friends and counsellors, and to present himself before the Court, upon the 6th of August, earnestly requesting, as we are told, "the continuance of that amity and friendship that hath formerly been between the Governor of Plymouth and his deceased father and brother," promising to observe the covenants which had been made by his predecessors, and to "endeavor in all things to carry peaceably and inoffensively towards the English." Hereupon the ancient league was again renewed and confirmed, and subscribed by Philip, his uncle and chief captain Uncompoin, and by Sausaman, and Francis, the Sachem of Nauset, with three others of his chief men, as witnesses.*

By this act of the young Sachem the awakened suspicions of the English were effectually quieted, confidence was again restored, and nothing farther occurred to disturb the tranquillity of the Colony until the year 1671.

A GENEALOGICAL PROBLEM.

To the Editors of the National Intelligencer. — In looking over a file of the Old Virginia Gazette for the year 1748, (No. 642,) I have stumbled upon the following curious epitaph, which is said to have been copied from a tombstone at Arlington, near Paris. Your Lady readers may be pleased to study out the meaning:

Here lies
Two Grandmothers, with their two Granddaughters;
Two Husbands, with their two Wives;
Two Fathers, with their two Daughters;
Two Mothers, with their two Sons;
Two Maidens, with their two Mothers;
Two Sisters, with their two Brothers;
Yet but six Corpses in all lie buried here,
All born legitimate, from incest clear.

From the National Intelligencer for Jan. 16, 1849.

EPITAPHS FROM THE BURYING-GROUND ON COPP'S HILL, BOSTON.

Capt. Thomas Lake, aged 61 years, an eminently faithful son of God, & one of a publick Spirit, was perfidiously slain by the Indians at Kennibeck Aug. 14th, 1676, here interred the 13th March following.

He was made Freeman June 2, 1641. Says Cotton Mather, "if I should particularly relate how barbarously they murdered my dear friend, that exemplarily *good* man, Captain *Thomas Lake*, at *Arowsick-Island* in *Kennebeck*-River, I should but unto myself, *Infandum renovare dolorem.* — *Mather's Magnalia,* (*8vo. New Haven,* 1820,) *Book* VII. *Chap.* VI., *Vol.* 2, *p.* 500. *See also Hubbard's Indian Wars,* (*ed.* 1677,) *Second Part, pp.* 39–42.

Here lyeth the body of John Lake, son to Capt. Thomas Lake, aged about 24 [27] years, deceased 27 of June, 1692.

He was born "22 (2) 1665." — *Boston Records.*

* Davis's Morton, pp. 286–8; Hubbard's Narrative, p. 10; Hutchinson, i. 253; Baylies, Part III. p. 17.

LIST OF FREEMEN.

[Communicated by Rev. Lucius R. Paige of Cambridge, Member of the N. E. Hist. Geneal. Society.]

[Continued from page 246.]

11 Oct. 1682.

Xtopher Walley	Conc.
James Parsons	Gloc.
Jn° Hitchcock	Spr.
Josiah Gage	—
Joseph Kingsbery	
Sam. Hasseltine	
Sam. Stickney	
Jn° Bojnton	
Wm. Hutchins	
Benj. Kimball	
Robert Hasseltine	
Bozoun Allen	

C. R., Vol. V. p. 381

7 Feb. 1682–3.

Mr. Sam. Parris	1 Ch. Bost.
Mr. Adam Winthrop	"
Mr. Robrt Howard	"
James Bill	"
John Olliver	"
Samuel Ruck	"
Obadia Wakfeild	"
Theoph. Rodes	"
Ebenezr Wms	Dorch.
Nehemi. Clap	"
Jn° Triscot	"
Jn° Marshall	Biller.
David Meads	"
Dani. Lunt	Newb.
Daniel Merril	"
Wm. Moody	"
Jn° Vyol	2 Ch. Bost.
Tho. Townsend	"
Samuel Townsend	"
James Green	"
John Green	"
Rich. Jincks	"
Timo. Pratt	"
Jn° Andrews	Ips.
Josep. Browne	"
Sam. Pitcher	Milton.

C. R., Vol. V. p. 383.

16 May 1683.

Jn° Ingram	Hadley.
Mark Warner	"
Nathan. Warner	"
Jn° Gardiner	"
Jn°than Metcalfe	Dedh.
James feild	"
Georg March	Newb.
Humphry Horrel	Bevry.
Edwd Ashber	"
Jn° Rayment	"
Wm. Raiment jun.	"
Andrew Elljot jun.	Bevry.
Jn° Dodge jun.	"
Wm. Dodg jun.	"
Tho. Woodbury	"
Edwd Dodge	"
Henry Herricke	"
Mr. Jn° Cobbitt	Ips.
Jose. Ewelle	"
Nath. Knolton	"
Mr. Grindall Rawson	Medfei.
Josiah Torrey	"
Dani. ffairfeild	1 Ch. Bost.
Samuell Ayres	Havll.
Jn° Pickard jun.	Rowl.
Humph. Hobson	"
Sam. Allyn	N. Hamp.
Ebener Strong	"
Sam. Wright	"
John Taylor	"
Jn° Devereux	Marblehd.
Tho. Pitman senr.	"
Jn° Peach jun.	"
Joseph Dallabar senr.	"
Wating James	"
Nicholas Andrew	"
Robert Bartlet	"

C. R., Vol. V. p. 401.

13 Feb. 1683–4.

Mr. Edward Willis	Bost.
Tho. Ray	"
Henry Eames	"
Joseph Souther	"
Joseph Knight	New.
Tymothy Noys	"
James Jackman	"
Wm. Elsly	"
Josiah ffisher	Dedh.
Jn°than ffreeman	"
Jonathan MedCalfe	"
James Vales	"
Joseph ffairbanks	"
John Colbrun	"
Peter Hansitt	"
Ralfe Dixe	Red.

C. R., Vol. V. p. 427.

7 May 1684.

Chrispus Bruer	Lynn.
Henry Collins	"
Allen Bread	"
Joseph Roads	"
Jn° Newhall	"
John Luise	"
Wm. Smith	"
Jonth Selsbe	"
John Roads	Lynn.
Sam. Senden	Marblehead
Jn° Merrit	"
Jose. Roote	N. Hamp.
Jona Parsons	"
Wm. Holton	"
Robt Lymon	"
Jn° Hubbard	"
Jn° Shelden	"
Benony Stebbins	"
Samll Judd	"
Jacob Root	"
Hen. Burt	"
Alexdr Atwood	"
Symon Burr	Hing.
francs James	"
Jn° Mansfeild	"
Ephrm Nicholls	"
Increas Sykes	Sprd.
Dani. Cooly	"
Danel Merrill	Newb.
Jn° Bartlet	"
Josia Browne	Red.
Corneli. Browne	"
Tho. Nichols	"
Jn° Hall	Rox.
Jn° Whitney	"
Jn° Dresser	Row.
Samll Palmer	"
Samll Peirce	Woob.
Samll Waters	"
Georg Read	"
Edwd Johnson	"
Ebenezr Johnson	"

C. R., Vol. V. p. 436.

9 July 1684.

John Boynton	No. Hamp.
Tho. Hunt	"
John Dressar	Rowl.
James Dickinson	"
Richd. Swan	"
Sam. Broclebank	"
James Seajles	"
Joseph Chaplin	"
Sam. Palmer	"
Samuel Platt	"
Sam. Spoffard	"
Jn° Clarke	"
Joseph Jewet	"
Caleb Boynton	"
Nath. Jacob	"
Edwd Walker	Woob.
Jn° Holden	"
Joseph Peirce	"
Sam. Nogget	"

Phineas Upham Woob.
Jn° Savil "
Sam. Savil "
Theoph. Curtis "
C. R., Vol. V. p. 447.

10 Sept. 1684.

Sam. Porter Hadley
Israel Porter jun. "
Jn° Hall "
C. R., Vol. V. p. 453.

31 Oct. 1684.

Mr. James Lewis 1 Ch. B.
David ffiske Camb.
Henry Prentice "
Ephrai. ffrost "
Math. Peirse Woob.
Sam. Wilson "
Joseph Broune Ips.
Wm. Hascall ——
Joseph Hascall
Isaacke Eveleigh
C. R., Vol. V. p. 458.

7 May 1685.

Urjah Clarke Rox.
Thomas Mory "
Benja. Darse Rox.
Peter Scott Brant.
Sam. Basse "
Nath. Wade Mauld.
Ralfe Dixie "
Dani. Eaton Redd.
Jn°. Avesson "
ffrans Hutchinson "
Josh. Eaton "
Jn° Abby senr. "
Jn° ffiske Wenh.
Zackeus Goldsmith "
C. R., Vol. V. p. 476.

21 July 1685.

Mr. Jn° Apleton jun. Ips.
Mr. Robrt Pajne jun. "
Abra. Purkins "
Jn° Harris (498) "
Jn° Graves "
Nath. Browne "
Jn° Maynard senr. Marlb.
Jn°thn Johnson senr. "
Josep. Newton "
Jn° Bowker "
Tho. Braman "
Jose. Millar "
Noah Wiswall Camb. Vill.
Edwd Jackson Camb. Vill.
Wm. Robinson "
Joseph Wilson "
Jn° Mirock "
Sam. Truesdale "
Isack Willjams "
Jn° Ward "
Wm. Pebody Topsf.
Tho Perkins jun. "
Dani. Reddington "
Tobyah Perkins "
Jocob ffoster "
Jn° How "
Edwd Converse Woob.
Ephraj. Pason Dover
Tho. Sticknee Bradfd.
Rich. Kemball (499)
C. R., Vol. V. p. 498, 499.

16 Feb. 1685–6.

Jacob Tounr Tops.
Ephraim Curtis "
John Pritchet "
Mr. Sam. Checkley 2 Ch.
John Squire 1 Ch.
Jacob Nash Weym.
Jn° Burril Lyn
C. R., Vol. V. p. 514.

[During the usurpation by Andros, 1686–1689, the practice of admitting Freemen was discontinued: it was resumed after the Revolution, but with some modifications.]

12 Feb. 1689–90. "It is ordered by this Court, that the clause in the Law, title ffreemen, referring to Ministers giving certificate to persons desiring their ffreedom, be and hereby is repealed; and the sum of ten shillings is reduced to four shillings in a single Country Rate, (without heads of persons,) or that the person to be made free have houses or lands of the clear yearly value of six pounds, freehold, which value is to be returned to the Court by the Selectmen of the place or the major part of them, who also are to certify that such person is not vicious in life. And the additional Law, title ffreemen, made Oct. 15, 1673, is hereby likewise repealed."
C. R., Vol. VI. p. 114.

22 March 1689–90. "Sir William Phipps, Knt., Maj. General Wait Winthrop, Lt. William Bond, Daniel Andrews, Peter King, and Ebenr Prout, admitted to be ffreemen, were sworn." *C. R., Vol. VI. p.* 130.

22 Mar. 1689–90. "Whereas divers returns are presented unto this Court of persons to be made free, the time being short before the nomination, Ordered, that all such persons allowed the privilege of freedom by this Court, may have the ffreeman's Oath administered unto them by any one Magistrate, and return thereof to be made to the Secretary."
C. R., Vol. VI. p. 130.

22 Mar. 1689–90. "Lists of the names of sundry persons from several Towns, qualified to be ffreemen, were presented and allowed of."
C. R., Vol. VI. p. 131.

[The Lists above-mentioned, and others which were subsequently presented, are contained in the volumes of the Massachusetts Archives, entitled Intercharter.]

22 March 1689-90.

Nathanael Wade Medford.
Stephen Francis "
Jonathan Tuffts "
John Tuffts "
John Whittimore "
Intercharter, Vol. I. p. 295.

(Cert.*) 11 March 1689-90.

Jn° Perrum Chelmsford.
Joseph Perkis "
Nath[ll] Butterfield "
Edward Spaulden "
Joshuah ffletcher "
Sam[ll]. ffletcher "
Will. ffletcher "
John Spaulden "
Ely ffoster "
Sam[ll] Cleavland "
Abrah. Parker "
Abraham Byam "
Sam[ll] ffoster "
John Bates "
Inter., Vol. I. p. 349.

22 March 1689-90.

Thomas Skinner jun. Malden
Phinias Upam "
Nathaniell Upam "
Phillip Atwood "
William Bordman "
John Green "
Samuell Sprague jun. "
Thomas Green "
Nathaniell Dunnam "
Obadia Jenkins "
John Chamberlen "
Joseph Sargent "
William Tell "
Thomas Grover "
John Sargent sen[r]. "
Joseph Wayte "
Edward Marshell "
Samuell Green "
John Sprague jun. "
Thomas Newall "
Left.—Willson "
Isak Hill "
Jonathan Sprague "
James Chadwick "
Joseph floyd "
John floyd "
Nathaniell Howard "
Phinias Sprague "
Sargent — fosdick "
Jacob Winslad "
Benjamin Whitamore "
Jonathan Knohre "
Jacob Parker Malden
Simon Grover "
William Bucknam "
Thomas Burthen "
Joses Bucknam "
Left. Samuell Sprague "
William Lerebe "
Thomas Oaks "
Lazurus Grover "
Joseph Lamson "
Inter., Vol. I. p. 349.

15 May 1690.

Jon[a] ffairbank Dedham.
Jams Thorp "
John Pidg "
John Everit "
Sam[ll]. Everitt "
John Hunting "
Timot. Whiting "
Dan[ll] Aullice "
Asahail Smith "
Eleazer Kingsbury "
Michael Metcalf "
Thom. ffuller "
Dan[ll] Pond "
John Gay "
Nath. Bullard "
John Alldis "
Dan[ll] ffisher "
Nath. Richards "
Dan[ll] Wight "
Amos ffisher "
Ralph Day "
Robert Awry "
Jon[a] Gay "
John ffuller "
Inter., Vol. I. p. 350.

16 May 1690.

William Stevens Gloucester.
Timothy Day "
Jephrey Passens "
John Passens "
Edward Huse "
Thomas Kent "
Joseph Mason Watertown
John Warren jun. "
Thomas Straite "
Samuel Biggilo "
Inter., Vol. I. p. 350.

[No date.]

Lt. John Burrill sen[r]. Lynn
Jn° Burrill jun[r]. "
Jn°. Hawcks sen[r]. "
Henry Collins sen[r]. "
Wm. Smith "
Moses Haven "
Joseph Collins sen[r] Lynn
Jonaathan Selsbee "
Crispus Brewer "
Jn°. Lynzey "
Sam[l]. Edmonds "
Allen Brade sen[r]. "
Josiah Rhoads "
Joseph Burrill "
Joseph Rhoades "
Joseph Newhall "
Joseph ffarr "
John Ballard "
Cornelius Browne "
Thomas ffarrar "
Inter., Vol. I. p. 351.

22 March 1689-90.

Abiah Sherman Watertown
Caleb Church "
Sam[ll] Edey "
Nick[s] Withe "
Tho. Rider "
Samuell Marshall Charlestown
Sam[ll]. Homan "
Eleaz[r]. Phillips "
Inter., Vol. I. p. 351.

21 March 1689-90.

Jams Minerd Concord
Danell Dane "
Thomas Gobile "
Robord Blood "
John Wheler "
Nemiah Hunt "
Samuell Davis "
John Shaperd "
Abraham Tempel "
Recherd Tempel "
Isaac Tempel "
Simon Davis "
Roberd Blood "
Simon Blood "
Josiah Blood "
Judath Poter "
John Jones "
Nathanell Stow "
Nathaell Harwood "
Eliphelet fox "
John Ball "
Samuell flecher "
Timithy Ries "
Samuell Stratten "
Johnethen Habord "
Joshua Wheler "
James Smally "
Nathanell Brise "
John Wood "

* Certified by Selectmen, as entitled to Freedom.

Abraham Wood Concord
Obadiah Wheler "
John Haward "
Thomas Wheler "
Steven Hosmer "
John Hartwill "
Inter., Vol. I. p. 352.

22 March 1689–90.

Lt. Simon Davis Concord
Lt. Jonathan Prescot "
Joseph ffrench "
Thomas Pellet "
Samuel Hunt "
Eliezer fflag "
Samuel Hartwell "
Samuel Myriam "
John Wheeler "
Samuel How "
Abraham Tayler "
John Hayward "
Nathaniel Ball "
Samuel Wheate "
Timothy Wheeler "
John Myriam "
Daniel Pellet "
John Pearly Boxford
Thomas Redington "
Joseph Byxbe "
Samuell Symonds "
Daniell Wood "
Abraham Redington "
John Kimball "
Thomas Andrew "
Joseph Andrew "
Thomas Hazzen "
Mr. William Perkins Topsfield
Mr. Timothy Perkins "
Corp^r^. Samuel Standley Topsfield
Sarg^t^. John Henry "
Corp^r^. John Curtiss "
Joseph Townes sen^r^. (353) Topsfield
Nathanael Ingersoll Salem Village
Abraham Walcott "
Zechariah Goodale sen^r^. Salem Village
Edward Putman "
Tho. Wilkins sen^r^. "
John Putman secundus Salem Village
Henry Wilkins "
Aaron Way "
Benj^a^ Wilkins "
James Putman "
Sam : Sibly "
John Tarbell "
Benj^a^. Putman "
Jonathan Putman Salem Village
Samuel Nurse "
William Way "
Samuel Abbie "
Mr. Daniel Andrew "
Henry Bowen Roxbury
Joshua Sever "
Samuel Gore "
Samuel Payson "
Isaac How "
John Scott "
Mr. Neh. Walter "
Tho. Moore (360) "
Inter., Vol. I. pp. 353, 360.

18 April 1690.

Capt. Jonathan Walcott Salem Village
Ensign Thomas fflint Salem Village
Serg^t^. Job Swinaton "
Serg^t^. John Buxton "
Mr. Joseph Hutchinson sen^r^. Salem Village
Joseph Holton sen^r^. "
Joseph Holton jun^r^. "
Joseph Pope "
John fflint "
William Sibley "
William Osburn "
Thomas Haines "
Thomas ffuller jun^r^. "
Jacob ffuller "
Edward Bishop sen^r^. Salem Village
Thomas Rayment "
Joshua Rea jun^r^. "
Walter Phillips sen^r^. Salem Village
ffrances Nurs sen^r^. "
Thomas Preston "
Joseph fflint "
Benjamine ffuller (12) Salem Village
Mr. Israell Porter "
Robt. Gibbs "
Joseph Herrick "
Capt.Nath^ll^.Norden "
Capt. Jno. Pitman "
Mr. Benj. Gale "
Wm. Woods (13) "
Peter Gardner Roxbury
Mr. John Howard "
Edmund Weld "
John Hemmingway "
John Newel "
Benjamin Gamblin "
Jacob Newel "
Josiah Holland "
Jams ffrissel "
John Griggs Rox.
Samuel Perry "
Jams Draper sen^r^. "
Thomas Cheiny "
John Holbrook "
Samuel Weld "
Isaac How "
John Ruggles 2^d^ "
William Heath "
Jonathan Peake "
John May "
John Perram "
Isaac Morriss "
Jacob Chamberlain "
John Bugbey "
Mr. William Denison "
Bengamin Dowse "
John Davis "
John Lyon (14) "
Inter., Vol. II. pp. 12–14.

(Cert.) 26 March 1690.

John ffuller sen^r^. NewCambridge
Nathaniell Willson sen^r^. NewCambridge
James Prentis sen^r^. "
John Mason "
John Kennarick "
John Hide "
Seabis Jackson "
Abraham Jackson "
Nathaniel Hamond "
Thomas Greenwood "
Nathaniell Helie "
John Ward "
William Ward "
Jacob Bacon "
Ebenezer Stone "
William Hide "
Eliezer Hide "
Edward Jakson "
Steeven Cook "
Inter., Vol. II. p. 20.

18 April 1690.

Beniamin Weeb Malden
Tryall Newbery "
Samuell Wayt "
John Mudg "
Samuell Oldum Cambridge
Nathaniell Robbins "
Samuell Robbins (20) Cambridge
Josiah Jons Watertown
John Livermore "
Thomas Woolson "
Joseph Gearfield "
Josiah Treadway "
John Woodward "
Benjamin Willington "

John Bond Watertown
John ffisske "
Joseph Herington "
Thomas Hammon "
Mihell Barsto "
Joseph Peirce senr. "
John Begolo senr. "
John Wright "
Daniel Herington "
Rodger Willington "
William Shattuck "
John Genery "
John Parkhust "
Nathaniel Bright "
Samuel Hager "
Palsgrave Willington "
Thomas Herington "
Nathaniel Bond "
John Kimboll "
Jonathan Smith (21) "
Mr. John Bisco "
Mr. Willyam Godard "
Samuell Thatcher "
John Bacon "
Thomas Whitny "
Richard Chilld junr. "
Beniamin Pearse "
Joseph Undurwoode "
Thomas Kidur "
Richard Cuttin senr. "
Henary Spring junr. "
Jonathan Stimson "
Samuell Begaloo "
Beniamin ffleg "
Beniamin Garfilld "
Richard Chilld "
Dannill Warrin (22) "

Inter., Vol. II. pp. 20–22.

[No date.]

Mr Samuell Gookin Cambridge
Nicholas ffesenden "
Peter Town "
William Munroe "
John Squire "
John Oldam "
Jacob Hill "
Samll Gibson "
John Wieth "
William Wieth "
Henry Smith "
Tho. Andrew "
Samuell Sparhawke "
Nathaniell Sparhawk Cambridge

Inter., Vol. II. p. 22.

18 April 1690.

Capt. Ralph Hill Billerica
John Starns "
Nath. Page Billerica
John Trull senr. "
Daniel Shead juni. "
Samel frost "
Jonath. Danforth juni. "
John Wilson senr. "
Cornet John Lane "
James Pattison "
John Baldwin "
Caleb farle senr. "
John Marshall "
Joseph foster "
Jonath. Hill "
Henry Jefts juni. "
Jno. Rogers "
Joshua Sawyer Woburn
Nathll Richardson "
Will. Wyman "
Jacob Wyman "
Steven Richardson "
Josiah Wood "
Benj. Simonds "
Caleb Symonds "
Sam. Blogget "
Georg Reed "
Henry Sumers "
John Peirce "
Georg Brush "
Jonathan Wyman "
Seth Wyman (22) "
Eleazer Bateman "
Joseph Right junr. (24) Woburn

Inter., Vol. II. pp. 22–24.

18 April 1690.

Mr. Will. Hooke Salisbury
Mr. Tho. Mudget "
Will. Osgood "
Danell Mondy "
Philip Grele "
Joseph Eaton "
Simon ffrench "
Isaac Buswell "
Ephraim Severanc "
Samll ffelows junr. "
Samll Estman "
Joseph fflecther "
Benjn Allin "
Samll Gill "
Andrew Grele "
Isaac Grene "
Philip fflanders "
Will. Allin "
Richard Hubard "
L: John Stevens "
E: Nathll Brown "
Joshua Bayle "
John fflanders "
Samll ffowlerer "
Ephraim Brown Salisbury
James Carre "
Solomon Shepard "
Nathll Whitcher "
Abraham Brown "
John Clough sr. "
John Clough jr. "
Richard Smith "
Meros Tucker "
Jereme Allin "
Nathll Eastman "
Jacob Morrell "
Jarvis Ringe "
John Allin "
Mr. Robt Pike jr. "
Joseph True "
Benjamin Estman (25) Salisbury
Charls Davenport Dorchester
Samuel Pason "
Henry Garnsy "
John Blacke "
John Breeck "
Ebenezer Billings "
Thomas Trott junr. "
Peeter Lion "
Standfast foster "
Daved Joans "
Daniel Preston "
Noah Beman "
Ephraim Pason "
Thomas Andrews "
James Backer "
Thomas Bird "
James Bird "
Richerd Butt "
John Blackman "
Hopstill Humphry "
Samuel Hall "
Richerd Evins "
Isack Humphry "
John Minot "
Gorg Minot "
William Rossen "
Samuel Robinson "
James Robinson "
Isack Riall "
Samuel Sumner "
Ebenezer Withington Dorchester
Phillep Withington "
Samuel Wals (26) "
Obediah Ward Marlborough
Thomas How "
Increas Ward "
John Newtten "
John Mainerd senr. "
Isace How "

Thomas Brigham Marlb.
John fay "
James Woods "
John Brigham "
John Barnes "
John Jonson "
Samuell Brigham "
Richard Barns "
Thomas Rice "
Johnathan Jonson "
Isace Amsden "
John Barritte "
Samuell Goodenew "
Nathanell Josline "
Nathanell Jonson "
Eliazer How "
Thomas Martine "
Joshua Rice "
Moses Newtten(27) "
Inter., *Vol. II. pp.* 25–27.

22 March 1689–90.

S^r^. William Phipps [not stated.]
Major Genl. Winthrop [not stated.]
Mr. Charles Morton "
Lt. William Bond "
Dan. Andrew "
Abraham Jones "
Samuel Symonds "
Phinehas Sprague "
Ebenezar Prout "
John Foster "
Peter Sergeant "
Mr. John Aires "
Mr. Nathaniel Oliver [not stated.]
Mr Pyam Blower "
Tim. Philips "
Peter King "
Mr. Edwd. Brumfeild "
Mr. Simeon Stoddard "
Mr. Joseph Parsons "
Capt. Thomas Savage "
Mr. Sam^u^. Linde (60) "
John Comes "
Thomas Savage, goldsmith [not stated.]
John Clow "
Ezek. Clesby "
Joseph Belknap "
Capt. Sam^u^. Legg "
Capt. Wm. Clarke "
Capt. Peter Buteler "
Mr. Joseph Prout "
Mr. Samson Stoddard [not stated.]
Mr. Wm. Clutterbucke [not stated.]
Mr. Robt. Bronsdon "
Mr. Rich^d^. Middlecott [not stated.]
Mr. Benj^a^. Alford "
Mr. Benj^a^. Davis(61) "
Inter., *Vol. II. pp.* 60, 61.

15 May 1690.

Mr. John Eyers Boston
Jeremiah Bumsted "
Roger Judd "
Mr. James Olliver "
Mr. William Brattle "
Joseph Squire "
Mr. Benja. Davis "
Mr. Nath^a^. Olliver "
Mr. Sam^ll^ Chicklie "
John Nicholes "
Richard Draper "
John Eastmond "
Robert Hussey "
Will. Downinge "
Mr. Joseph Bosset "
Joseph Holmes "
James Dunny "
Joseph Belknap "
Mr. Daniell Quinsey "
George Elistone "
Robt. Hawkins "
Sam^ll^ Oake "
Josiah Grise "
Sam^ll^ Grise "
John Marshall "
Mr. Peter Sergeant "
Ebenez^r^ Hayden "
Eleazer Moody "
Daniell Olliver "
John Conniball "
William Manley "
John Proctor "
Jeremiah Belchar "
James Halsey "
John Carthew "
Thomas Walker "
Tymothy Wadsworth "
Major Tho. Savage "
Thomas Cushan "
Richard Procter "
Capt. William White "
Mr. Rich^d^. Middlecott "
Mr. Benj^a^ Alford "
James Greene "
Thomas Atkins "
Nathan^ll^. Thayer "
Sam^ll^. Townsend (61) "
Thomas Harwood "
Joseph Briscoe "
Sam^ll^ Townsend jun. "
Joseph Ustice "
Jeremiah ffitch "
Roger Kilcup "
Samuell Rucke sen^r^. "
John Greene Boston
Henery Dawson "
Hezechiah Hinksman "
Nathaniell Hinksman "
Michaell Shaller "
George Hallet sen^r^. "
John Addams "
Isaac Goose "
Mr. Thomas Brattle "
Richard Wilkins "
Benjamen Pemberton "
Phillip Squire "
Ellis Calender "
Thomas Skiner "
Grimstone Bond "
Samuell Jackline "
William Clough "
Jarvis Ballard "
John Wiswall "
Joseph Bill "
John Tuttle "
Edward Tuttle "
Elisha Tuttle "
Jonathan Tuttle "
Isack Lewis "
Elias Mavericke "
Joseph Hasey "
Thomas Jackson (62) "
Inter., *Vol. II. pp.* 61, 62.

30 May 1690.

Capt. Jno. Allice Hatfield
Ens. Dan^ll^ White "
Sam^ll^ Marsh "
John Wells "
John ffeild "
Stephen Genings "
John Cowels "
Nath^ll^ Dickenson sen^r^. "
Richd Morton sen^r^. "
Sam^ll^ Dickenson sen^r^. "
John White "
John Porter Hadley
John John Smith "
Saml Philip Smith "
Joseph Smith "
Saml. Chiliab Smith "
Hezekiah Porter "
Danl. Hubbard "
John Philip Smith "
Nehemiah Dickenson "
Jonathan Marsh "
Peter Montague "
Daniall Marsh "
Nathill White "
John Goodman "
Jacob Warner "
Inter., *Vol. II. p.* 91.

30 May 1690.

Serg^t^ Joseph Coker Newb.

Joseph Bayley Newbury
Isack Bayley "
Cornet Jonathan Moores Newbury
John Worth "
Steaphen Jeques "
Silvanus Plumr "
John Emery junr. "
Serg.t Jno. Hall "
Jno. Webster junr. "
Richard Dodg Wenham
James ffreind "
Thos. ffiske junr. "
John Dodg junr. "
Wm. ffairefield "
Ephraim Kemball "
Zecheas Gooldsmith "
John Edwards "
Walter ffairfield "
John Porter (103) "
John Person Northampton
Thomas Limon "
Hezekiah Root "
Abell Jones "
Richerd Limon "
William Miller senr. "
Israell Rust "
Samll. Holton "
Samll. Marshal "
Noah Cook "
Joseph Edwords "
Samll Edwords "
Jedediah Strong "
Ensigne Prr Clap "
John Seorls "
Isack Shelden junr. "
Jonathan Root "
John Limon, weavr. "
John Limon, shoemaker Northampton
Ebnezer Allord "
Ebenezer Wright "
Nathaniel Edwards "
Mathew Clefton "
William Clarke jr. "
William Phelps "
Samuel Smith "
Samuel Parsons "
John Alexander "
William Southwell "
Samuel Curtis "
Philip Pain "
Samuel Wright "
Thomas Sheilden "
Mr. Wareham Mather Northampton
Nathaniel Alexander Northampton
John King junr. "
Joseph Wright "
Joseph Crosbey Braintree
John Adams "
Samuel Payn "
Robert feild "
John Bass junr. "
Wiliam Nightingall junr. (104) Braintree

Inter., Vol. II. pp. 103,104.

— October 1690.

Mosis Tiler Boxford
Nathaniel Browen "
Daniel Wood "
John Stiels "
John Pearly "
Joseph Pebody "
John Andrus "

Inter., Vol. II. p. 179.

19 December 1690.

Thomas Cooper Springfield
Abel Wright senr. "
Nathanll. Burt senr. "
Jno. Blisse "
John Dorchester "
James Dorchester "
Eliakim Cooley "
Benja. Cooley "
Joseph Cooley "
Joseph Leonard "
Joseph Bedortha "
Edward ffoster "
Samuel Stebbins "
Joseph Thomas "
Thomas Day junr. "
John Mirricke "
Samll Bliss junr. "
Nathanll. Blisse "
Jonatha. Morgan "
David Morgan "
James Barker "
Samll Bedortha "
Benja. Leonard "
Jonathan Ball "
John Harman "
Joseph Ely "
John Burt "
Samuell Lamb "
Josias Marshfield "
Thomas Stebbins "
Edward Stebbins "
Benjamin Stebbins "
Jonathan Burt junr. "
David Lumbard "
Isaac Colton "
John Colton "
Samll Blisse 3tius "
Samuel Miller "
John Miller "
Tho. Swetnam "
Charles fferrey Springfield
Daniel Lamb "

Inter., Vol. II. p. 255.

24 December 1690.

Capt. Tho. Harvy Amesbury
John Barnard "
John foot "
Thomas Sarjant "
Thomas Barnard senr. "
Thomas Curriar "
Nathan Gould "
Thomas Colby senr. "
Thomas Steevens "
Thomas fowlar "
Joseph Lankestar senr. Amesbury
Henry Blazdell senr. "
Henry Tuksbery senr. Amesbury
Jno. Kimball "
Moses Morrel "
Orlando Bagley "

Inter., Vol. II. p. 257.

6 February 1690–1.

John Emerson junr. Gloucester

C. R., Vol. VI. p. 174.

18 April 1691.

John Maston senr. Andover
William Blunt "
John Abbute "
William Lovioy "
Hopstill Tyler "
John Tyler "
Steven Porter "
Gorge Abbute "
Joseph Lovioy "
Samuel Hoult "
Robberd Russell "
Thomas Johnson "
ffranses Deane "
John Bridges "
James ffrie "
William Johnson "
Walltar Witt "
Andruw ffoster "
Joseph Robinson "
Edward Phelps "
John Osgood junr. "
John Russe "
Timothy Osgood "
Mr. Jonathan Woodman [Newbu. ?]
Thomas Hull "
Jonathan Emery "

Inter., Vol. III. p. 9.

(Cert.) 6 April 1691.

Samuell Johnson sen^{r}. Boston
John Bull sen^{r}. "
Jabes Neges "
Sam^{ll} Marshall "
James English "
David Jenner "

Inter., Vol. III. p. 9.

18 April 1691.

John Whitmarsh Weymouth
Joseph Drake "
Incres Bates "
Thomas Randol "
John Randol "
John Blanchar "
Joseph Shawe "
Epharem Borell "

Inter., Vol. III. p. 10.

(Cert.) 26 March 1691.

Ens. John Woods Marlborough
Samuel Ward "
Joseph Newton sen^{r}. Marlborough
John Bouker "

Inter., Vol. III. p. 10.

18 April 1691.

Joshuah Eaton Reading
Jonathan Eaton "
Thomas Damman "
John Nickols "
James Nickols "
Nathanell Parker "
Samuell Damman "
John Burnap "
John Boutwell "
Richard Harden "
Jonas Eaton "
Josepth Hartshorne "
John Woodward "
Thomas Nickols "
Beniamin Hartshorne Reading
Nathanell Gouen "
Samuell Smith "
David Hartshorne Reading
John Parker "
Timothy Hartshorne "
Jerimiah Swaine "
John Browne "
Cornelius Browne "
William Eaton "
Thomas Burnap "
John Wesson "
William Arnall "
ffrances Huchison "
Timothy Wilely "
Josepth Burnap "
John Eaton "
William Robbins "
Samuel Lilly "
Robbart Burnap "
John Uptan sen^{r}. "
Gorge fflint "
David Bacheller "
John Dunton "
John Dix "
ffrances Smith (10) "
Lieu^{tt}. Lewis Lynn
Mr. Habersfeild "
Thomas ffarrar jun^{r}. "
Joseph Meriam "
Willm. Merriam "
Ebenezer Hathorn "
John Edmunds "
Rich^{d}. Hood sen^{r}. "
John Ingols sen^{r}. "
Robt. Ingolls "
Benjam^{n}. ffar "
Henry Collins jun^{r}. "
Daniell Hithins sen^{r}. "
John Burrill 2^{d} "
Ebenezer Stocker "
Moses Hawks "
Thomas Baker "
Benjam^{n} Rednap "
Thomas Jovory "
Joseph Mansfeild jun^{r}. "
Robt. Potter jun^{r}. "
Eleazer Lynzy "
Willm ffarrington "
John Newhall sen^{r}. "
Aquilla Ramsdell "
Theophilus Bayley "
Cornet Johnson Lynn
Daniell Mansfeild "
Thomas Graves, sen^{r}. "
Samu^{ll}. Graves "
Robt. Rand jun^{r}. "
Samuell Moors "
Nathaniell Ballard "
John Bread "
Daniell Needham "
Thomas Chadwell "
Joseph Bread "
Allin Bread 3^{tius} "
Timothy Bread "
Mathew ffarrington jun^{r}. Lynn
Nathaniell Newhall sen^{r} Lynn
Sam^{ll}. Hort "
Joseph Hort "
Richard Haven sen^{r}. "
Robert Paffer sen^{r}. "
Jonathan Hudson "
Moses Hudson "
John Moor "
Edward ffuller "
Samu^{ll} Rhodes "
Ensign John Newhall "
Andrew Townsend "
Andrew Mansfeild "
Willm. Bassett sen^{r}. "
Willa^{m}. Bassett jun^{r}. "
John Lewis jun^{r}. "
Sam^{ll}. Jynks "
Nathan Newhall jun^{r}. "
Benjam^{n}. Collins "
John Richards "
John Diven "
Ens. Edwd. Baker "
Thomas Lewis "
Samuell Ingolls "
Henry Collins jun^{r}. "
John Jynks (11) "
Joseph Mansfeild jun^{r}. "
Josiah Rhodes "
Richard Hood "
Theophilus ffarrington "
Samuel Bligh (12) "

Inter., Vol. III. pp. 10–12.

ERRATA IN THE PRECEDING LIST.

Page 188,	column 1,	line 44,	for 7 *Oct.* 1650,	read 7 *Oct.* 1640.
" 245,	" 3,	" 36,	" *Zache*	" *Zacke.*
" "	" "	" 47,	" *Ashley*	" *Ashly*
" 246,	" 1,	" 5,	" *Ralph*	" *Ralp*
" "	" "	" 37,	" *Enos.*	" *Enos*
" "	" 2,	" 28,	" *Whitmarsh*	" *Whitmarsh*
" "	" "	" 34,	" *Nathan*	" *Nathani*
" "	" "	" 42,	" *Abijah*	" *Abjah*

SOME ACCOUNT OF DEACON JOHN BUTLER OF PELHAM, N. H., AND OF HIS DESCENDANTS.

BY CALEB BUTLER OF GROTON.

[Continued from p. 76.]

(I. 3. II. 3. III. 2.)

IV. *MIRIAM BUTLER m. *JOHN CUTTER.

1	Kezia,	b. Jan. 17, 1794,	m. Frye Gage.
2	*Rebekah,	b. Feb. 3, 1796,	m. Ebenezer Hall of West Cambridge.
3	*Lucinda,	b. Jan. 31, 1798,	m. Isaac Hill of West Cambridge.
4	John,	b. March 28, 1800,	m. Charlotte Varnum of Dracut.
5	Benjamin F.,	b. Aug. 27, 1802,	m. { *Esther Russell. *Sarah Russell. Julia F. Howe.
6	Clarissa,	b. Jan. 2, 1805,	m. Adna Coburn.
7	Hannah,	b. Aug. 2, 1807,	m. Rev. Robert Breeze.
8	*Joanna,	b. April 29, 1810,	m. Rev. Daniel Kittridge.
9	Sarah,	b. Sept. 3, 1811.	
10	Charles,	b. June 18, 1814,	m. Olive Noyes.

(I. 3. II. 3. III. 3.)

IV. *SAMUEL BUTLER m. { *CLARISSA BUCK. *HANNAH LUND.

{ 1	Amasa,	b. Jan. 18, 1800,	m. Roxa White. At Niagara, N. Y.
2	Caleb,	b. Sept. 4, 1801,	m. Hannah Smith of Sandwich, Ms.
3	Luther,	b. March 7, 1803,	m. Abigail Chamberlin, Haverhill, N. H.
4	*Clarissa,	b. Sept. 8, 1806,	d. young.
5	Almira,	b. Jan. 2, 1808,	m. Nathaniel Currier.
6	Calvin,	b. April 25, 1810,	m. Eliza Peck of Salem, N. Y.
7	Charlotte,	b. March 1, 1812.	
8	Jonathan L.,	b. Oct. 7, 1816.	
9	David C.,	b. Jan. 14, 1819.	

(I. 3. II. 3. III. 5.)

IV. CALEB BUTLER m. CLARISSA VARNUM. Reside at Groton.

1	Henrietta,	b. May 28, 1805,	m. { *Nathaniel Littlefield of New York. Rev. Timothy Atkinson of Lowell.
2	*Charles V.,	b. Dec. 2, 1806,	d. unm.
3	*George,	b. Feb. 14, 1808,	d. unm.
4	*Susan,	b. Sept. 19, 1809,	d. unm.
5	*Rebekah,	b. May 28, 1811,	m. Peter Anderson of Lowell.
6	*William,	b. Aug. 21, 1812,	d. unm.
7	Clarissa,	b. July 14, 1814.	
8	Frances,	b. Oct. 12, 1822,	m. Francis A. Brooks of Boston.

(I. 3. II. 3. III. 11.)

IV. PHINEHAS BUTLER m. { SARAH BARKER. BETSEY WYMAN.

1	Benjamin,	b. Aug. 23, 1819,	m. Cornelia Little of Boston.
2	Sarah,	b. Feb. 14, 1821.	
3	Ascenath,	b. Nov. 23, 1823.	
4	Justin E.,	b. Jan. 30, 1825.	
5	Reuben M.,	b. March 24, 1827.	
6	John M.,	b. July 26, 1829.	
7	Henry F.,	b. June 4, 1831.	
8	William W.,	b. Sept. 30, 1838,	by 2nd wife.

(I. 5. II. 2. III. 2.)

IV. LYDIA BUTLER m. *ELIJAH TRULL of { Billerica. Townsend. N. Boston, N. H.

1 Samuel, b. Oct. 24, 1794.
2 Lydia, b. Aug. 1, 1798.
3 Delia, b. Dec. 15, 1800.
4 Butler, b. Aug. 10, 1803.
5 Almira, b. Feb. 24, 1805.
6 Loiza, b. April 19, 1807.
7 Clarissa, b. April 6, 1809.
8 Elijah, b. June 2, 1810.
9 Cynthia, b. Dec. 9, 1811.
10 Nehemiah, b. May 6, 1815.

(I. 5. II. 2. III. 3.)

IV. Nehemiah Butler m. *Olive Davis.

1 *Elizabeth, b. Feb. 20, 1804, d. unm.
2 Asa D., b. May 13, 1806, m. Mary Gregg.
3 *Achsah A., b. Dec. 7, 1809, d. young.
4 *Josiah, b. Dec. 25, 1810, d. unm.
5 Olive J., b. April 29, 1814, m. Henry H. Peters.
6 Lydia M., b. Jan. 16, 1818.
7 Nehemiah, b. Feb. 22, 1824.

(I. 5. II. 2. III. 4.)

IV. Phebe Butler m. Eliphalet Parker of Bucksport, Me.

1 Loiza, m. —— Hinckley.
2 Lydia, m. —— Hinckley.
3 Phebe, m. —— Pollard.
4 Eliphalet.
5 Caroline, m. —— Hill.
6 Edwin.

(I. 5. II. 2. III. 5.)

IV. Josiah Butler m. Hannah Jenness of Deerfield, N. H.

1 De Witt C., b. Feb. 1, 1812, m. Mary A. Tucker.
2 Horace, b. June 5, 1814, m. Caroline Crane.
3 Josiah W., b. May 7, 1816.
4 Elizabeth H. B., b. July 9, 1819.
5 *Lydia J., b. June 15, 1821, d. unm.
6 Franklin I., b. Dec. 21, 1823.
7 Wentworth S., b. Sept. 30, 1826.
8 Caroline L., b. Aug. 23, 1830.
9 Mary J., b. Aug. 24, 1832.

(I. 5. II. 2. III. 6, and I. 8. II. 2. III. 1.)

IV. Delilah Butler m. Dole Butler of N. Boston, N. H., and ——, Ill.

1 Dole, b. June 27, 1800, m. Edner Dodge of N. Boston, N. H.
2 Daniel T., b. Oct. 27, 1801, m. Sabrina Perkins of Pottsdam, Wis.
3 Delia, b. Nov. 13, 1803, m. Jonathan Brown of N. Boston, N. H.
4 Loiza, m. John McQuestion of Galena, Ill.
5 Joseph B. V., m. Elizabeth Ingalls of Pittsfield, Ill.
6 Betsey, m. Warren Corning of Galena, Ill.
7 Hannah, m. Daniel Smith of Galena, Ill.
8 Mary J., m. Franklin Brayley of Wisconsin.
9 Lydia A., m. James Barnard of Griggsville, Ill.

(I. 5. II. 3. III. 2, and I. 5. II. 5. III. 5.)

IV. Joseph Butler m. Hannah Butler.

1 Mary, m. Reuben Melvin.
2 Daniel.
3 Ira.
4 Catharine.
5 Moses.
6 Martha, m. Abijah W. Keyes.
7 Josiah.
8 Abigail.
9 Henry.
10 Jesse.
11 Calvin.

(I. 5. II. 5 III. 1.)

IV. Polly Butler m. Jacob Stiles.

1 Fanny, m. Kendall Gray.
2 Mary, m. —— Woodward.
3 Moody.
4 Harriet, m. Sylvester Wyman.
5 Sabra, m. Nehemiah Low.
6 Amanda, m. Eppes Wyman.
7 Ambrose.

(I. 5. II. 5. III. 3.)

IV. Moody Butler m. { *Sally Dustin. / Lydia Burt. }

1 Roxana, b. Aug., 1805, m. Emerson Favour.
2 Mary D., b. March, 1807, m. Ebenezer Ranney.
3 John D., b. Feb., 1809, m. Mary Burnham.

4 Sally D., b. Oct., 1811, m. James Ramsey.
5 William D., b. Jan., 1813, m. Emeline Stone.
6 Elizabeth R., b. April, 1815, m. Gilbert P. Hall.
7 Lucinda, b. May, 1817, m. Jonathan W. Goodhue.
8 Abigail C., b. Sept., 1819, m. Eliphalet Jones.
9 Moody, b. 1821.
10 Hyman, b. 1827, by 2nd wife.

(I. 8. II. 1. III. 1.)

IV. SARAH BUTLER m. { *NATHANIEL GAGE. / ASA CARLETON. }

1 Sally, b. Jan. 8, 1795, m. —— Coburn.
2 Nathaniel, b. Feb. 25, 1796.
3 Lavina, b. Dec. 12, 1797, m. { *—— Dudley. / Life Richardson. }
4 Jacob B., b. Dec. 9, 1800.
5 Mary, b. m. George Carleton. (All by 1st husband.)

(I. 8. II. 1. III. 2.)

IV. POLLY BUTLER m. THEODORE WYMAN.

1 Jacob B.
2 Polly, m. Moses Glynn.
3 Eliza, m. John Colby.

(I. 8. II. 1. III. 3.)

IV. BETSEY BUTLER m. *SOLOMON BARKER.

1 Sophia, b. Feb. 22, 1798, m. Dudley Hardy, Jr.
2 *Betsey, b. Oct. 8, 1800, d. unm.
3 Laura, b. July 11, 1802, m. James Riddle.
4 Solomon, b. April 1, 1803, m. Sarah Simonds.
5 Jacob B., b. Aug. 14, 1804, m. Anna Marden.
6 *Clarissa, b. April 2, 1806, d. young.
7 Julia A., b. May 22, 1807.
8 Clarissa, b. Sept. 22, 1808.
9 Sarah A., b. May 17, 1810, m. William Brown.
10 Hannah, b. Nov. 22, 1811, m. { *John Gill. / James Cutter. }
11 Mary, b. Dec. 22, 1814, m. Benjamin Ames.
12 Harriet A., b. June 5, 1818, m. Rev. Titus Briggs of Ohio.

(I. 8. II. 1. III. 5, and I. 8. II. 2. III. 4.)

IV. JACOB BUTLER m. NABBY BUTLER of New Boston, N. H.

1 Isaac, b. May 18, 1815, m. —— ——, wid., of New York.
2 *Mary B., b. March 24, 1817, d. young.
3 *Eliza H., b. Jan. 27, 1819, d. young.
4 Olivia.
5 Clarissa, m. —— Knowlton.
6 *Elizabeth, d. young.

(I. 8. II. 2. III. 7.)

IV. MANLY BUTLER m. SARAH HAMBLET.

1 Manly O., b. July 19, 1812, m. Elizabeth Howe.
2 *Sarah, b. Aug. 28, 1813, d. young.
3 David H., b. Sept. 12, 1814, m. Eliza Trull.
4 *Daniel J., b. Feb. 17, 1817, d. young.
5 *George W., b. Dec. 22, 1818, d. young.
6 Charles V., b. June 28, 1820, m. Laura Jewett.
7 Sarah C., b. Feb. 21, 1822.
8 Louisa M., b. July 3, 1823, m. Stephen Sawyer, Jr.
9 Mary T., b. July 14, 1828.
10 Catharine A., b. July 17, 1830.
11 *Daniel G., b. Dec. 15, 1831, d. young.
12 Phebe A., b. Feb. 10, 1833.
13 *Henry C., b. Dec. 28, 1835, d. young.

(I. 8. II. 2. III. 8.)

IV. BELINDA BUTLER m. SAMUEL P. HADLEY of Chelmsford.

1 Belinda P., b. April 21, 1823, m. Paul Hill of Lowell.
2 Samuel P., b. Oct. 22, 1831.

Three of the fifth generation in the foregoing lists have received the honors of College, viz.:

CALVIN, son of Samuel, at Dartmouth College, 1834. He studied theology, and is settled in the ministry at Salem, N. Y.

BENJAMIN, son of Phinehas, at Dartmouth College, 1842. He read law, and is a practitioner in Boston.

HORACE, son of Josiah, at Dartmouth College, 1836.

(I. 2. II. 2. III. 1. IV. I.)

V. ASA BUTLER, Jr., m. PHEBE ROBY.

1 Araminta P., b. April 13, 1838.
2 *Eliphalet A., b. April 8, 1841, d. y.
3 James E., b. March 12, 1843.
4 David R., b. Jan. 16, 1845.

(I. 2. II. 2. III. 6. IV. 2.)

V. HENRY BUTLER m. —— TEMPLE of Pottsdam, N. Y.

1 Mary.
2 Lucy.
3 Betsey.
4 William.
5 Joel.

(I. 2. II. 4. III. 3. IV. 3.)

V. DAVID BUTLER m. MARY ANN RUSSELL.

1 Rockwood D., b. Nov. 5, 1834.
2 *Orlando R., b. Aug. 10, 1839, d. y.
3 Annette E., b. June 17, 1842.
4 Frances E., b. Jan. 30, 1844.

(I. 2. II. 4. III. 5. IV. 1.)

V. WARREN A. BUTLER m. ELIZA ——.

1 Charles W., b. June 16, 1837.
2 Susan E., b. March 10, 1843.

(I. 2. II. 4. III. 5. IV. 3.)

V. REBECCA BUTLER m. ELI HAMBLET.

1 Lovina, b. Aug. 20, 1845.

(I. 2. II. 4. III. 6. IV. 2.)

V. HANNAH BUTLER m. WILLIAM CADY.

1 David W., b. May 19, 1839.
2 Joseph L., b. April 23, 1840.
3 Eliza A., b. Aug. 2, 1842.
4 *Olive J., b. April 16, 1844, d. young.
5 *John B., b. Aug. 8, 1846, d. young.

(I. 2. II. 4. III. 6. IV. 3.)

V. SARAH J. BUTLER m. TRUMAN PARKER.

Have six or seven children.

(I. 3. II. 3. III. 1. IV. 3.)

V. BENJAMIN P. BUTLER m. CYRENE S. BRETT.

1 *Cyrene M., b. Sept. 11, 1829, d. young.

(I. 3. II. 3. III. 1. IV. 4.

V. BETSEY P. BUTLER m. NATHANIEL TRUE of N. Yarmouth, Me.

1 Betsey A. H., b. Feb. 16, 1832.
2 Lydia, b. May 7, 1835.
3 Nathaniel O., b. Feb. 9, 1838.
4 *Benjamin B., b. Nov. 22, 1841, d. young.

(I. 3. II. 3. III. 1. IV. 5.)

V. CALEB P. BUTLER m. SARAH N. LORD, Me.

1 Sarah M., b. Nov. 6, 1837.
2 Elbridge O., b. June 2, 1840.
3 Benjamin P., b. Aug. 20, 1842.
4 Martha L., b. Aug. 26, 1844.
5 Mary E., b. Sept. 22, 1847.

(I. 3. II. 3. III. 3. IV. 3.)

V. LUTHER BUTLER m. ABIGAIL CHAMBERLIN, Haverhill, N. H.

1 Almira, b. Oct. 6, 1836.
2 *Sybil, b. Dec. 25, 1837, d. young.
3 Mary, b. Jan. 13, 1840.
4 George, b. Feb. 11, 1842.
5 *Alice, b. 1844, d. young.

(I. 3. II. 3. III. 3. IV. 5.)

V. ALMIRA BUTLER m. NATHANIEL CURRIER.

1 Grenville B., b. May 16, 1841.
2 *Sabra B., b. April 11, 1846, d. young.

(I. 3. II. 3. III. 3. IV. 6.)

V. CALVIN BUTLER m. ELIZA T. PECK, Salem, N. Y.

1 *Lathrop B., b. Dec. 23, 1842, d. young.

(I. 3. II. 3. III. 5. IV. 5.)

V. *REBEKAH BUTLER m. PETER ANDERSON, Lowell.

1 *Herman M., b. Aug. 24, 1844, d. young.

(I. 3. II. 3. III. 5. IV. 8.)

V. FRANCES BUTLER m. FRANCIS A. BROOKS, Boston.

1 Frederic, b. July 17, 1848.

(I. 5. II. 2. III. 3. IV. 2.)

V. ASA D. BUTLER m. MARY GREGG.

1 Achsah, b. July 11, 1829.
2 William G., b. Jan. 30, 1832.
3 Josiah, b. March 6, 1836.
4 Mary J., b. Feb. 24, 1843.
5 George D., b. Feb. 6, 1846.

(I. 5. II. 2. III. 3. IV. 4.)

V. OLIVE J. BUTLER m. HENRY H. PETERS.

1 Horace L., b. Sept. 1845.

(I. 5. II. 2. III. 5. IV. 1.)

V. DE WITT C. BUTLER m. MARY A. TUCKER.

1 James C., b. May 6, 1838.
2 Lydia J., b. March 20, 1842.
3 Harriett L., b. April 4, 1847.

(I. 5. II. 2. III. 5. IV. 2.)

V. HORACE BUTLER m. CAROLINE CRANE.

1 Caroline I., b. July 13, 1844.
2 Ann E., b. March 27, 1846.

(I. 5. II. 2. III. 6. IV. 1.)

V. *DOLE BUTLER m. EDNER DODGE, New Boston, N. H.

1 Daniel T., b. April 21, 1826.
2 Delia, b. July 19, 1827.
3 *William, b. d. young.

(I. 5. II. 2. III. 6. IV. 2.)

V. DANIEL T. BUTLER m. SABRINA PERKINS, Plattsville, Wis.

1 A son.

(I. 5. II. 2. III. 6. IV. 3.)

V. DELIA BUTLER m. JONATHAN BROWN, New Boston, N. H.

1 Hannah m. Ezra Heath.
2 *Butler E., d. unm.
3 * d. young.
4 * d. young.

(I. 5. II. 2. III. 6. IV. 4.)

V. LOUIZA BUTLER m. JOHN McQUESTION, Galena, Ill.

Varnum,
Clinton.
John.
LeRoy.
(Several more.)

(I. 5. II. 2. III. 6. IV. 5.)

V. JOSEPH B. V. BUTLER m. ELIZABETH INGALLS, Pittsfield, Ill.

1 Orville.
Nehemiah.
(Two others.)

(I. 5. II. 2. III. 6. IV. 6.)

V. BETSY BUTLER m. WARREN CORNING, Galena, Ill.

Hannah J.
Warren.
(Two others.)

(I. 5. II. 2. III. 6. IV. 7.)

V. HANNAH BUTLER m. DANIEL SMITH, Galena, Ill.

Warren.
Jane.
Daniel.
DeWitt.
(Two others.)

(I. 5. II. 2. III. 6. IV. 8.)

V. MARY JANE BUTLER m. FRANKLIN BRAYLEY, Plattsville, Wis.

1 A son.

(I. 5. II. 2. III. 6. IV. 9.)

V. LYDIA A. BUTLER m. JAMES BARNARD, Griggsville, Ill.

Two children.

(I. 5. II. 3. III. 2. IV. 6.)

V. MARTHA BUTLER m. ABIJAH W. KEYES.

Calvin.
Charles.

(I. 5. II. 5. III. 3. IV. 5.)

V. WILLIAM D. BUTLER m. EMELINE STONE, Lowell.

1 William F. H., b. Feb. 3, 1841.
2 Charles M., b. Jan. 26, 1845.
3 Lydia E., b. July 18, 1847.

(I. 8. II. 2. III. 7. IV. 1.)

V. MANLY ORVILLE BUTLER m. ELIZABETH HOWE.

1 Orville W.
2 George H.
3 Arthur C.
4 Charles H.

(I. 8. II. 2. III. 7. IV. 3.)

V. DAVID HAMBLET BUTLER m. ELIZA TRULL.

1 George.

EXPLANATIONS.

No register of a family in the foregoing lists is made unless one of the parents' names is Butler, the female lines being omitted.

Where no place of residence is stated, Pelham, N. H., is to be understood, except in a few instances of the later generations, the residence not being known.

The Roman capitals at the left hand, and over the parents, denote the generation; the figures, the numerical order of the children.

To trace the descent of any one through all the generations from I. to V., begin with the first, I. John Butler; the figure will show from which of his children the descent is to be traced; find that child's name as a parent in the second generation, and the figure on the right hand of II. shows from which of his or her children the descent proceeds; and so proceed through all the capitals and figures over the names of the parents of the child whose descent is to be traced. For example, to trace the descent of George, the son of David H. Butler, the last in the foregoing list, the parent is of the fifth generation, denoted by V. at the left hand. I. 8 over the name denotes the 8th child of John, found to be Jacob; find Jacob in the second generation, and II. 2 denotes his 2nd child, Daniel; then III. 7 is found to be Manley; IV. 3, David K., the father of George.

To the descendants of DEACON JOHN BUTLER, the foregoing list of families and notices is respectfully inscribed, with a desire that into whosesoever hands of them it may fall, they will correct, amend, enlarge, and preserve it, preparatory to some future more perfect edition, by

C. BUTLER.

WOBURN BURYING-GROUND.

[Communicated by MR. N. WYMAN, JR.—Continued from p. 264.]

Richardson　Lydia wid. of Dea. Nathan　May 17 1776 85thy
"　Phebe wid. of Noah　April 2 1776 68
Wyman　Elisalett w. of Zebediah　Aug 12 1776 42y
Rhodes　Jacob, of Charleston,　Mar 11 1776 61y
Lamson　John, of Charleston,　Jan 12 1776 43y
Frothingham　Thomas, of Charleston,　Jan 1 1776 64
Snow　Isaac　Mar 31 1776 67y
Pool　Eleazer Flagg　Mar 17 1776 42y

"These deaths are much to be observed
Such instances are scarce heard off.
Six weeping children in eight days.
followed Father and Mother to thier graves
My chrildren dear behold and see
no age nor sex from death is free.
Soon death may come and nip your bud,
And you must stand before your God."

"　Mary w. of Eleazer Flagg　Mar 24 1776 43

"My children now behold & vew,
these Bodies once took care of you,
But now we are leveld in the dust,
In a short time you' follow us.
My loving friends that are arround,
our bodies now are in the Ground.
Our chrildren young, we leave behind,
deal you with them justly & kind."

Tay　Abigail, w. of Lieut. William　Sept 26 1778 71y
Richardson　Jerusha, d. of Josiah & Jerusha　Aug 27 1778 15m 25d
Brooks　Abigail, d. of John & Abigail　Aug 1 1778 13mo
Evens　Andrew　Dec 18 1778 70y

"Death is a debt to Nature due,
I have paid it so must you."

Skinner　Martha wid. of John　Mar 7 1781 61y
Evens　Mary wid. of Andrew　Aug 31 1781 72

"Saints at thier death do go to rest,
In the blessed Boosom of thier Fathers love
Thier happy spirits fully blest,
To worship with the church above."

Skiner　Joanna d. of John & Susanna　June 5 1782 3y 6m
Richardson　Jerusha w. of Edward　Apr 10 1782 75y

Richardson	Mary w. of Stephen	Nov 22 1783 78y
"	Lieut. Stephen	July 18 1783 39y
"	Ebenezer	Sept 8 1783 61
Simonds	Benjamin	Dec 10 1783 59
	"A Tender Parent. Charitable to the Poor. The memory of the just shall flourish when they sleep in Death."	
Richardson	Sarah w. of Thomas	June 12 1784 71
Wyman	Lucy w. of Daniel	Dec 24 1785 34
Kendall	Elisalett d. of Dea Obidiah & Elisolett	Dec 11 1787 18
Richardson	Deac. Stephen	Mar 6 1787 81
Gardner	Dorothy w. of Samuel	Feb 11 1787 43
Thompson	Lydia 2d w. of Samuel, Esq.,	Oct 19 1788 54
Gardner	Samuel, of Charleston,	May 6 1790 50y
Symmes	Zachariah	Apr 19 1793 86
Richardson	Edward	June 22 1797 88y

THE PEABODY FAMILY.

[Continued from page 372, Vol. II.]

"One generation passeth away, and another generation cometh: but the earth abideth for ever."
Ecclesiastes, i: 4.

In addition to the particulars given at the commencement of this genealogy (pages 154 and 155, Vol. II.) of Francis Pabody, the patriarch of this large family, facts have recently come to my knowledge which prove as conclusively as any *indirect* or presumptive evidence *can* prove, that the father of Francis was John Pabody, Paybody, or Pabodie, (*the spelling of this name, like many others, having been in rather a transition state at that early period,*) who came to this country, probably, about the same time with his son Francis, and settled in Plymouth Colony, where he was made a freeman in 1637. His family consisted of his wife, Isabel, three sons, and one daughter. The names of the sons in the order of their ages were, Thomas, *Francis*, and William; the name of the daughter was Annis. She married John Rouse. John's will is dated July, 1649, and proved April 27, 1667. Of the oldest son Thomas or his descendants, we know nothing; perhaps he did not follow his father to New England. The youngest son, William, is believed to be the ancestor of all the "*Pabodies*" in this country, as is our patriarch *Francis* of the "*Peabodys.*" The difference in the orthography of the name is the line of demarcation between the descendants of the two brothers.

ERRATA IN THE PRECEDING ACCOUNT.

Doct. Jacob Peabody (58) IV. on p. 372, is stated to have married for 2d wife, Dorothy Foster, of Lunenburg. It was his son Jacob (400—2) who thus married, and *not* the father. The doctor had but one wife, Susanna Rogers. An omission in some records of the name of Jacob among the heirs of the Doctor, led to this error.

Against 72—7 p. 157, read *Lucy* for *Louisa*.
Against 397—6 p. 372, read *Ezra* for *Eben* Perkins.
Against 318—5 p. 368, read *Kiff* for *Keith*.

FIFTH GENERATION.

The descendants of Francis's eldest son John. (1—1)

V. Lieut. Ebenezer Peabody, (170—3) b. Dec. 7, 1742, lived in Boxford, m. Elizabeth Pearl, Feb. 9, 1764. She died March 11, 1776, a. 32. M. Sarah Pearl, March 18, 1780, d. 1829, a. 87. He was a lieutenant in the Army of the Revolution, and a man of determined bravery; was at the battle of Bunker Hill, where he went the night before, and was one of the last to leave the field, yielding the ground inch by inch and disdaining to turn his back upon the enemy. He was also with Col. Alden at the burning of Cherry Valley by the Indians; with Col. Brooks at the taking of Burgoyne; with Gen. Sullivan when he went through the Indian country. His widow, who died March, 1847, received a pension in consideration of his services, of some four hundred dollars annually. Children by Elizabeth,

Lois, b. May 6, 1764, m. Dr. Kendell Osgood, April 22, 1790, d. previous to 1801, left two children; Ebenezer, b. Feb. 16, 1767, lived at one time in Gorham, Me., m. Sarah Lewis of Gorham, dau. of George Lewis, March 9, 1792, and had six children and perhaps more, namely, Kendell Osgood, Ebenezer, Louisa, Caroline, William Henry, and James Lewis, d. in Franklin, N. H.; Thomas, b. Feb. 4, 1769, lived in Boston, m. and had one daughter; Stephen, b. Aug. 24, 1771, lived in Boston and had one daughter; Sarah, b. Aug. 20, 1773, d. young.

Children by Sarah,

Seth, b. Feb. 21, 1782, d. 1803, left one son; Sarah, b. Sept. 11, 1783; Hannah, b. Dec. 8, 1785; Betsy, b. Oct. 7, 1787; Benjamin, b. Nov. 2, 1789, m. Rachael Hunting in Boston, March 26, 1815, living in Boxford, Mass.; Isaac, b. March 14, 1791, died in West Indies, 1817, no children; Daraxa, b. Dec. 2, 1794, m. and lived in Boxford, Mass.

V. Nathan Peabody, (176—9) b. Aug. 31, 1756, lived first in Bradford, where he married Polly Baker, July 30, 1786, removed, after his marriage, to Boston, where his children were born. Children,

Betsy, b. Oct. 21, 1787, m. an Eaton and lived in Boston; John, b. Dec. 13, 1790, lived in Boston; Susanna, b. Dec. 18, 1792.

V. David Peabody, (177—1) b. June 27, 1736, lived in Nottingham West, N. H., now Hudson, N. H., Hillsboro' Co., married Phebe Andrews. I have not been able to obtain a particular account of this family. The children, as far as can be ascertained, were,

David, m. Eunice ——; John; Esther.

V. Asa Peabody, (180—4) b. July 1, 1741, lived first in Londonderry, N. H., then in Boxford, m. Susanna Perley, Sept. 5, 1765, died Oct., 1807, a. 66 years. Will dated March 18, 1807, proved Nov. 3, 1807.

Allen, b. June 2, 1770, settled in Meredith and had one son, Asa; Ezra, b. Aug. 7, 1772, m. Christina Rose of Sandwich, July 2, 1795, and had six children, d. Aug. 27, 1811; Oliver, b. Dec. 19, 1774, m. Abby Pratt of Reading; Susanna, b. Jan. 20, 1777, m. Enoch Foster of Lynn; Lois, b. April 12, 1779, m. a Towne; Asa, b. April 13, 1781, died without family; Enoch, b. Aug. 20, 1783, died without family; Artemas, b. Sept. 2, 1785, m. Mary Perley, Dec. 29, 1807, two daughters; Polly, b. March 14, 1788, m. a Parker.

V. Jedediah Peabody, (181—5) b. April 11, 1743, married Alice Howlet, Oct. 9, 1766, lived first in the State of Maine, then in several towns in New Hampshire, and died at East Lebanon, N. H., *about* 1825. Children,

Lydia, b. Sept. 17, 1767, m. David Bowman, d. at Centre Harbor; Ammi Howlet, b. July 4, 1769, m. 1st, Margaret Rice, Feb. 22, 1797; m. 2d,

Sarah Johnson, Dec. 12, 1802, d. Jan. 30, 1845; Mary, b. July 6, 1771, m. Daniel Marshall of Tunbridge, Vt.; Moses, b. Nov. 29, 1773, m. Hannah Ward of Henniker, N. H.; Susanna, b. Sept. 29, 1775, m. Richard Thompson of Tunbridge, Vt.; Thomas, b. Aug. 11, 1777, m. Betsey Willis, Nov., 1804, living in East Lebanon, N. H.; Alice, b. June 1, 1779, m. Eleazer Whitney of Henniker, N. H., where he is now living; Andrew, b. July 13, 1782; Frederick, b. March 20, 1785, m. Rebecca E Carter of Boston, June 7, 1812, resided in Charlestown, Ms., d. Dec. 2, 1833, leaving two sons and one daughter; John, b. March 1, 1787, never married, was a purveyor in the army, and died at Buffalo; Betsey, b. June 2, 1789, m. a Blount of Danville, Vt.

V. Dea. Moses Peabody, (182—6) b. Nov. 1, 1744, lived in Boxford, m. Hannah Foster, May 26, 1767, d. Jan. 6, 1826, a. 81. His wife died Dec. 3, 1825, a. 81. Children,

John, b. June 30, 1768, m. Edith Beaman, d. in Tunbridge, Vt., July, 1835, had seven children, two sons and five daughters; Nathan, b. April 12, 1770, m. Hannah Stickney, Nov. 12, 1794, had seven children; Samuel, b. May 28, 1772, m. 1st, Huldah Gould, no children, 2d, Mrs. Elizabeth Massey of Lynn, and had three children; Hannah, b. April 25, 1774, d. unmarried in Salem, Aug., 1812; Jeremiah, b. May 23, 1776, m. Catharine Kimball of Bradford, and had three children, d. Aug., 1839; Jacob, b. May 14, 1778, m. 1st, Lucy Manning, dau. of Thomas Manning, Oct. 22, 1804, 2d, Lydia Manning, Oct. 26, 1814, had five children; Sarah, b. June 24, 1780, m. Rev. J. W. Dow of Tyringham, and d. childless, Feb., 1813; Lucy, b. June 2, 1784, unmarried, lives in Boxford; Charles, b. March 29, 1787, m. Sarah Wood of Boxford, d. without children in Illinois, Sept., 1840; Nancy, b. Oct. 31, 1790, m. Samuel Perley, Jr., of Boxford.

V. Andrew Peabody, (184—8) b. Jan. 20, 1748, lived in Bradford, m. 1st, Mary Morse; 2d, Hannah Kimball. Children by Mary,

Molly; Mehitable; Charles, m. Sophronia Carlton; Charlotte; Eliza.

V. Thomas Peabody, (192—6) b. Sept. 7, 1762, lived in Haverhill and Danvers, m. Judith Dodge of Rowley, Dec., 1788, d. May 13, 1811, a. 49. His widow died at Lockport, N. Y., June 22, 1830, a. 60. Children,

David, b. April 23, 1790, m. 1st, Sarah Caldwell, Jan. 20, 1814, 2d, Phebe Delemaster Reynolds, d. at New York, July, 1841, had two children; Achsah Spofford, b. Nov. 14, 1791, d. at South Danvers, Feb. 7, 1821; an infant son, d. immediately; George, b. Feb. 18, 1795, resided for many years in Baltimore, Md., is now a banker in London, Eng.; Judith Dodge, b. April 5, 1799, m. J. Russell, Esq., of Georgetown, Ms., Sept. 22, 1831, has one child; Thomas, b. April 17, 1801, d. in Buffalo, N. Y., April 16, 1835; an infant dau., d. immediately; Jeremiah Dodge, b. Jan. 26, 1805, m. Ellen Murry Hanna of Baltimore, Dec. 22, 1829, lives in Zanesville, O., nine children; Mary Gaines, b. Sept. 7, 1807, m. Caleb Marsh of Lockport, and d. there, Aug. 28, 1834, had three children; Sophronia Phelps, b. Nov. 4, 1809, m. Elbridge Little, had six children.

V. John Peabody, (195—9) b. Feb. 22, 1768, m. Anna Little of Newbury, March 30, 1791, lived first in Newburyport, was a representative to the Massachusetts Legislature, a General of militia, removed to Washington, D. C., about 1812, and died there Feb. 25, 1827. His wife died Oct. 20, 1826. Children,

Sophronia, b. Jan. 3, 1792; Philadelphia, b. April 13, 1794, d. Aug. 28, 1799; Adeline, b. Nov. 6, 1797, d. at Washington, D. C., Oct. 9, 1817; John, b. Sept. 11, 1799, m. Amelia H. Cathcart, lived in Washington, had six children; a son, b. Dec. 2, 1801, d. immediately; Sophila, b. Dec. 29, 1802, m. Joseph L. Smith of Boston, had five children; Joseph Little, b. Oct. 15, 1806, m. Ann Ward of Washington, one child; Edward Gaines, b. Oct. 22, 1808, m. Jane Criosey of Philadelphia, where he resides, had four children; Adolphus Wm., b. Oct. 13, 1814, resides in Baltimore, Md.

V. Josiah Gaines Peabody, (196—10) b. Sept. 18, 1769, lived in Portsmouth, N. H., m. Edna Greenough of Atkinson, N. H., Feb. 2, 1796, d. suddenly in New York, in 1832. His widow is now living (1848) in Atkinson, N. H. Children,

Leonard, b. Feb. 23, 1798, m. Mary Dame of Portsmouth, July 18, 1822, d. at St. Domingo, Aug. 16, 1824, one son; Elizabeth, b. Sept. 21, 1801, m. Henry Noyes of Atkinson, had five children, d. Aug. 1, 1837; Lavinia, b. Sept. 17, 1804, m. Robert Jones of Lowell, d. June 23, 1834; Josiah Greenough, b. Dec. 21, 1808, m. Susan Pousland of Beverly, six children.

The Descendants of Francis's 2d son, Joseph. (2—2)

V. Andrew Peabody, (204—4) b. July 21, 1745, m. Ruth Curtis, Dec. 13, 1769, lived in Middleton, Ms., died Oct. 14, 1813, a. 68. His wife died Jan. 27, 1810, a. 65. Children,

Lucy, b. Sept. 28, 1770; Andrew, b. Feb. 29, 1772, m. Mary Rantoul, at Salem, Dec. 4, 1808, lived in Beverly, Ms., kept the Grammar School, d. Dec., 1813, father of Andrew S. Peabody of Portsmouth, N. H.; Hannah, b. Aug, 22, 1783, m. Benjamin Averill, June 2, 1808.

V. Joseph Peabody, (205—5) b. Aug. 11, 1747, lived in Middleton, married Mary Symonds, Jan. 24, 1775, died Dec. 16, 1834, a. 87. Children,

Mary Symonds, b. Dec. 30, 1775; Betsey, b. Jan. 9, 1781.

V. Thomas Peabody, (207—1) b. Oct. 28, 1738, lived in Middleton, m. his cousin, Bethiah Peabody, (200—1) Nov. 12, 1760, was killed accidentally in 1787. Children,

David, b. Sept. 30, 1762, m. Eunice Peabody, (346—6) Oct. 5, 1784, had five children, administered upon his grandfather's estate, (27) IV., Nov. 9, 1796, d. Aug. 18, 1840; Ruth, b. April 21, 1766; Huldah, b. Sept. 26, 1768; Lydia, b. Feb. 9, 1770, m. Simeon Knight, Jr., July 23, 1797; Moses, b. Sept. 8, 1772; Samuel, b. Nov. 20, 1775.

V. Joseph Peabody, (208—2) b. April 4, 1741, lived in Middleton, Ms., married Mary ——, 1760. Children,

Mary, b. March 7, 1761, m. Edmund Perkins, Oct. 7, 1787; Rebecca, b. March 24, 1763; Nathaniel, b. March 20, 1772, m. Ruth ——, had eleven children.

V. Daniel Peabody, (214—3) b. May 4, 1739, lived in Boxford, married Anna Stickney, dau. of Joseph Stickney, Sept. 15, 1761. Children,

Anna, b. Jan. 8, 1762; Hitty, b. Nov. 11, 1763; Daniel, b. Feb. 3,

1766; John, b. April 12, 1768; Relief, b. April 13, 1770; Lettice, (?) b. July 6, 1772; Rebecca, b. Jan., 1775.

V. Jonathan Peabody, (215—4) b. April 24, 1744, lived in Boxford, married Mercy Kimball of Andover, 1767. Children,

Sarah, b. June 8, 1768; Oliver, b. March 3, 1770; Amos, b. Sept. 15, 1772.

V. Aaron Peabody, (216—5) b. April 30, 1747, m. Susanna Hobbs of Topsfield, May 4, 1769, and settled in Milford, N. H., about the time of his marriage. The following children were born in Milford.

Aaron, b. Jan. 15, 1774; Samuel, b. June 20, 1776, m. Hannah ——; Betsey, b. Sept. 29, 1778; Humphrey, b. Nov. 18, 1779, m. Kesiah ——, and had children; John, b. Feb. 3, 1782; Joseph, b. July 13, 1784; Amos, b. July 28, 1786, m. Sarah Wright, April 9, 1812.

V. Henry Peabody, (218—2) b. May 25, 1749, married Lydia Rea, April 27, 1769, lived in Boxford, d. 1776, administration granted to his widow March 5, 1776. Children,

Joseph, b. Sept. 17, 1770; James Rea, b. 1773.

V. Samuel Peabody, (227—4) b. Sept. 1, 1741, married Elizabeth Wilkins, lived in Middleton or its vicinity. My account of this family is imperfect. Children,

Moses, settled in Amherst, N. H.; Samuel, d. without issue; Joseph, settled in Middleton and was deacon of the church there; John, settled in New Boston, N. H., had nine sons and two daughters; Aaron, d. without children; Jacob, settled in New Boston, N. H., two sons and two daughters, and perhaps more; Joel, m. Betsy Wilkins, Feb. 8, 1807, settled in Middleton, Ms., had five children.

The Descendants of Francis's 3d son, William. (3—3)

V. Colonel Stephen Peabody, (229—1) b. Sept. 3, 1742, lived in Mount Vernon, N. H., was a colonel in the Army of the Revolution, selectman of the town several times, and represented it also in the State Legislature in 1779, married Hannah Chandler, Dec., 1763, who was born Dec., 1746, died Sept., 1780, a. 38. His widow died Aug., 1826, in her 80th year. Children,

Thomas, was in the Army of the Revolution, m. 1st, Sarah Perkins, 2d, Mrs. James Bird, sister of Gen. James Miller, of Lundy Lane notoriety, had seven children, was a Physician; John, b. May, 1766, m. 1794, Kesia Hubbard, had five sons, was a Physician, d. 1804; Hannah, b. July 2, 1768, m. Enoch Carlton of Amherst, had four sons and one daughter; Rebecca, b. July 17, 1770, like her brother, studied and practised surgery, m. Gen. Parley Davis of Montpelier, Vt., Nov. 4, 1794, who was born at Oxford, Ms., March 31, 1766, had seven children; Stephen, b. Aug. 23, 1772, m. Martha Trow, had one son, Franklin, now of Orange, Vt., was a Physician; Asenath, d. three days old; Sarah, b. Dec. 2, 1774, d. very suddenly on the day she was to have been married; Asenath, b. Dec. 14, 1777, m. Lewis Parker of Cambridge, d. childless, March, 1846.

V. William Peabody, (231—3) b. Feb. 3, 1746, lived in Milford, N. H., m. Jan., 1771, Abigail Wilkins, the only daughter of the Rev. Daniel Wilkins, first minister of Amherst, born Aug. 6, 1745. Mr. Peabody was a highly esteemed citizen, an upright magistrate, a wealthy farmer, for several years represented his native town in the State Legislature, and died Aug. 24, 1822, a. 76. His widow died Feb. 11, 1827, a. 82. Children,

Clarissa, b. Oct. 29, 1771, living (1848) on the homestead in Milford, in the house built and first occupied by her grandfather, Capt. William Peabody, (32) IV.; Abigail, b. Oct. 20, 1773, d. Sept., 1777; Hannah, b. Jan. 23, 1775, d. Sept., 1777; William, b. May 22, 1776, d. Sept., 1777; Abigail, b. Oct. 7, 1777, d. unmarried, April 28, 1827; Hannah, b. March 11, 1779, m. Rev. Humphrey Moor of Milford, April 5, 1803, had three children; William, b. July 14, 1780, d. Jan. 9, 1794; Stephen, b. Oct. 4, 1782, m. Sept. 20, 1824, Jemimi P. Bolles, dau. of Rev. Matthew Bolles of Milford, N. H., formerly of Ashford, Ct., d. Jan. 19, 1847, leaving an unsullied reputation as a lawyer, and as a citizen much lamented, had four children; Anna, b. March 30, 1784, m. Rev. Elijah Dunbar of Peterboro', N. H., Dec. 15, 1803, d. July 25, 1828, nine children.

V. Stephen Peabody, (244—3) b. April 27, 1760, lived in Boxford, was a justice of the peace, married Ann Killum, Dec. 13, 1785, died Jan. 22, 1830, a. 70. Children,

Stephen, b. Oct. 17, 1787; Samuel, b. Nov. 6, 1788, m. Mary Porter, 1819, who died Jan. 1, 1836, had six children; Nancy, b. Aug. 28, 1796.

V. John Peabody, (245—4) b. July 24, 1762, living (1849) in Lunenburg, Worcester Co., married Mary Tyler, Dec. 2, 1788, in Boxford. Children,

John and a daughter, gemini, b Oct. 8, 1789, the first of whom m. Abigail Spalding, and the latter d. in infancy; Mary, b. Feb. 8, 1791, d. young and unmarried; Oliver and William, gemini, b. Jan. 2, 1792, the first of whom m. Lydia Howard, Dec. 18, 1817, and the latter m. Mary Stevens, July 31, 1817; Sarah, b. May 23, 1794, d. about 1810; Samuel, b. Aug. 6, 1796, m. Betsy Jones, April, 1819; Joseph, b. Feb. 20, 1802, m. Mary Lawrence, May 7, 1826.

V. Richard Peabody, (246—5) b. April 16, 1764, lived in Canton, Me., m. Dolly Kimball of Bradford, May 9, 1789, died Nov. 29, 1836, a. 72. Children,

Polly, b. Dec. 31, 1788; Betsey, b. Sept. 8, 1793, m. David G. Merrill, d. Aug. 16, 1819; Jesse, b. May 22, 1796, m. Mary Elliott; Dolly, b. Jan. 22, 1798; Hannah, b. June 5, 1801, d. June 28, 1831; Samuel, b. Feb. 8, 1805, m. Susanna Reynolds.

V. Deacon Oliver Peabody, (247—6) b. May 6, 1766, lived in New Portland, Me., was deacon of the Baptist Church, m. Peggy Stickney, July 26, 1792, d. Nov. 14, 1847. Children,

Oliver, b. June 6, 1793, m. Catharine Dolliver, July 15, 1827; Richard, b. Sept. 1, 1794, m. Margarett Elliott, Feb. 6, 1816; John, b. Feb. 8, 1796, d. Sept. 2, 1802; Rebecca, b. Jan. 16, 1798, m Abner Lander, Dec. 26, 1822; Hepsibah, b. Nov. 28, 1798, d. May 26, 1815; Hannah and Nathan, gemini, b. Sept. 15, 1801, the first of whom m. Israel Haskell, and the latter m. Betsy Knapp, July 11, 1830; John, b. June 16, 1803, d. Sept. 18, 1816; Samuel, b. June 17, 1805, m. Betsy Pomroy, March 24, 1831; David Wood, b. Oct. 30, 1807, m. Judith W. Bray, June 17, 1830; Temperance D., b. May 28, 1810, m. Levi Lane, Nov. 29, 1832.

V. Doctor William Peabody, (248—7) b. Jan. 10, 1768, was a

practising Physician in Frankfort, Me., several years, married Sally Bean, resided also in Corinth, Me. Children,

Sally, m. 1st, Timothy Miller, 2d, a Briggs; Hannah; Nancy, m. Philbrick B. Tay; Lorinzo.

V. Francis Peabody, (250—9) b. June 7, 1771, lived in Pother, in the province of Lower Canada, m. Fanny Stickney, May 25, 1801. Children,

Fanny, b. June 5, 1802, m. William Manson; Betsy, b. Aug. 16, 1804, d. Jan. 22, 1806; Francis S., b. Aug. 19, 1806; Betsy, b. Dec. 22, 1808, d. April 8, 1810; Rachael S., b. June 6, 1811, m. David Nelson Brill; Nathan S., b. Feb. 27, 1813, d. an infant; Nathan S., b. Sept. 22, 1814, d. Sept. 19, 1819; Samuel, b. Aug. 28, 1817, d. Oct. 5, 1817; Sophronia, b. Aug. 26, 1818; William, b. Dec. 25, 1820, m. Esther Hildreth, 1842; Oliver, b. April 11, 1823; Albert Samuel, b. May 2, 1825; John Ide, b. Nov. 6, 1828.

V. Samuel Peabody, (252—11) b. Jan. 3, 1775, attorney and counsellor at law, D. C. 1803, resided at one time in Epsom, N. H., latterly in Andover, Ms., married Abigail Wood, Oct. 7, 1813. She was daughter of Jonathan Wood, a descendant of Ruth (Peabody) Wood. (23—9) Thus unite in this family the descendants of Francis's eldest son John (1—1) and his third son William. (3—3). Children,

Charles Augustus, b. July 10, 1814, m. Julia Livingston of New York, July 15, 1846, an attorney and counsellor at law in the city of New York; Abby Hale, b. Dec. 18, 1815; William Frederick, b. Nov. 24, 1817, physician in Baltimore, Md.; George Samuel, b. March 1, 1820, m. Anne Hammond of Liverpool, Eng., July 5, 1846, master mariner by profession; Enoch Wood, b. July 25, 1822; Sarah Jane, b. April 16, 1824; David Wood, b. June 11, 1826, d. Oct. 22, 1846; John Tyler, b. June 13, 1828; Mary Spofford, b. May 1, 1831; Ellen Eliza, b. Aug. 8, 1835.

V. Joseph Spofford Peabody, (253—12) b. Jan. 30, 1779, resided first in Boxford, Ms., then in New Portland, Me., married Hannah Foster, Dec. 25, 1800, died May 17, 1846. Children,

Lavinia, b. Sept. 20, 1801, m. Peter Johnson, lived in Orono, Me.; Lucy, b. Sept. 27, 1802, m. Aaron Richardson, d. Aug. 27, 1826, no children; Dorothy, b. June 15, 1804, m. Joseph Browne, lived in Lynnfield, Mass.; John, b. Sept. 19, 1806, m. Henrietta S. Baker, Sept. 27, 1830, lived in Boxford, Ms; Eliza, b. July 5, 1808, d. unmarried, April 12, 1826; Salome, b. July 24, 1810, m. Stephen Small, lived in New Portland, Me.; Clarissa, b. June 20, 1812; Joseph, b. Feb. 4, 1815, m. Lydia Hilton, no children.

V. Jonathan Peabody, (254—1) b. Nov. 16, 1739. All the information I possess of this family is, that "Jonathan lived in Brattleborough, Vt., some sixty years since, had a wife and three sons."

V. Ephraim Peabody, (256—3) b. in 1742, lived in Wilton, N. H., m. Sarah Hutchinson, d. 1803, a. 61. His widow died in 1816, a. 66. Children,

Sarah, m. Amos Eaton; Samuel, b. Feb. 20, 1774, m. Lucinda Pease, July, 1802, lived in Weston, Vt, had twelve children; Ephraim, m. Rhoda Abbot, lived in Wilton, N. H., had two children, d. July 15, 1816, father of the Rev. Ephraim Peabody of Boston; Betsey, m. John Appleton of New Ipswich; John, b. Feb. 25, 1780, m. Sarah Bates, d. 1824, had six children; Lydia, unmarried; Dorcas, m. Isaac Lovejoy; Hannah, m. Isaac Lovejoy, 2d wife.

V. Thomas Peabody, (258—5) b. in 1746. The only information I have obtained of him is, that "he married Mrs. Hannah Ritter, June 20, 1771, had several children, and died before his father." He lived in Shirley.

V. Phineas Peabody, (260—7) b. in 1751, lived in Lunenburg, Worcester Co., then in Petersham, Ms., married 1st, Rebecca ——; 2d, Lois Clapp of Lunenburg, Feb. 14, 1799. My account of his children is very imperfect, there being something quite irreconcilable in the Records. Children by Rebecca,

Stephen, b. Nov. 12, 1784; John, b. April 10, 1788; Sylvester, b. Sept. 12, 1794.

Children by Lois,

Jonas Humphrey, b. May 12, 1799; Mary, b. Sept. 21, 1800; Susan, b. Jan. 23, 1803; Maria, b. Feb. 18, 1805; John, b. Oct. 6, 1806; Rebecca, b. April 9, 1809.

V. Amos Peabody, (261—8) b. April 13, 1753, lived in Northfield, Vt. All I have learnt of him is, that "he had a wife and some children."

V. Moses Peabody, (262—9) b. Jan. 28, 1755, married Betty Jackman, at Lunenburg, Nov. 26, 1778, lived in Jaffry, N. H., at one time, then in Weathersfield, Vt., d. about 1842. My account of his children is very imperfect.

Thomas, m. and had several children, died before his father; and three daughters.

V. Amasa Peabody (268—1) b. May 23, 1755, lived first in Boxford, then in Dracut. Married 1st, Rhoda Runnels, 2d, Lois Runnels, Dec. 28, 1806. Children by Rhoda,

Sally, m. Clark Parsons; Jonathan; Amasa; Tryphena, m. Daniel Goodhue; Rufus; Frederic; Eliza, m. Charles Bancroft; Rhoda, m. Joseph O. Fox; Amanda M., m. Alvin Flint.

V. Ephraim Peabody (269—2) b. Nov. 16, 1787. Lived first in Boxford, then in Methuen. Married Betsy Gage of Pelham in 1783; d. 1804. Will dated April 4, 1804; proved May 7, 1804; Executor, Nathaniel Peabody, his brother, (271—4.) Children at the time of his death,

Hepsibah, b. Feb. 28, 1784, m. Alexander Graham; John, b. July 13 1786; Ephraim.

V. John Peabody, (270—3) b. Aug. 18, 1743. Lived in Bradford, married Alice Carlton, Sept. 10, 1788. Children,

Sally, b. June 20, 1789, m. Capt. Benjamin Carlton; Charlotte, b. May 19, 1791, m. James C. Tenney; Roxanna, b. March 4, 1793; John, b. May 24, 1795, m. 1st, Elizabeth B. How of Dover, N. H., 2d, Elizabeth Allen; Nathaniel, b. July 7, 1797, m. Mary Foot; Leonard, b. Feb. 7, 1800, m. Hannah Welch; Eliza, b. Feb. 10, 1802, m. an Allen; Martha, b. Aug.

16, 1804, d. unmarried in 1821; Mary, b. Oct. 16, 1806, d. unmarried July 5, 1825.

V. Nathaniel Peabody, (271—4) b. 1767. Lived first in Boxford, then in Dracut. Married Betsey Cole, April 1, 1789. Was Executor of his brother Ephraim's estate (269—2) in 1804. Children,

Hepsibah, b. Aug. 29, 1789, m. Russell Fox; Nathaniel, b. Feb. 26, 1792, m. Mary Gilchrist; Betsy, b. 1799, d. young; Ephraim, b. Aug. 25, 1804, m. Sarah P. Davis; Moses, b. Dec. 12, 1806, m. Hannah F. Gray.

V. Capt. Nathaniel Prentice Peabody, (273—2) b. Dec. 25, 1746. Lived in Norwich, Ct., married Mary Glover, May 12, 1782, d. Jan. 12, 1845, a. 59. His widow died Sept. 3, 1822, a. 64. Children,

William, b. April 5, 1783, m. Cornelia Maria Hillard, July 14, 1814, d. Sept. 23, 1822; Fanny, b. Dec. 13, 1784, m. James M. Brown, Oct. 22, 1826; Nancy, b. May 26, 1786, m. a Buswell; Betsy, b. Dec. 23, 1788, d. July 19, 1809; Nathaniel Prentice, b. June 11, 1790, d. at Oswego, Lake Ontario, Nov. 5, 1833; Asa, b. Sept. 29, 1792, lives in Syracuse, N. Y.; Mary, b. Aug. 17, 1794, m. James Perkins of Norwich, Ct.

V. John Ting Peabody, (277—6) b. Oct. 27, 1756, married twice. By his 1st wife, Elizabeth ——, he had children,

Asa, b. Jan. 6, 1782, d. Aug. 19, 1782; Sophia.

By his 2d wife,

John, lived in Nashville, Tenn.; Nancy, lived in Nashville, Tenn.; two other children.

V. William Henry Peabody, b. 1769, son of Asa Peabody (40) IV. (His name was not found in the Norwich Records of Births, and was therefore omitted among the children of Asa Peabody.) Married Ruth Bulkley of Fairfield, Ct., Feb. 19, 1795. His widow is now living in Bridgeport, Ct. Children,

Catharine Maria, b. Aug. 17, 1796; Henry Bulkley, b. Dec. 19, 1797; Charlotte, b. June 25, 1799; Mary, b. April 7, 1801; Lucy, b. March 13, 1803; William, b. May 20, 1805; George M., b. Jan. 29, 1807; Charles Alfred, b. July 29, 1810; John B., b. March 7, 1812; Augustus, b. July 3, 1814; Frederic Gideon, b. May 6, 1818.

V. Adriel Peabody, (282—4) b. May 1, 1771. Lived in Plattsburg, N. Y. Was a lawyer. Married Phebe Pennoyer of Amenia, Duchess Co., N. Y., moved to Plattsburg in 1796. Died April 20, 1810. Children,

Richard H, b. April 8, 1795, lives in Keeseville, N. Y.; William A., b. June 1, 1797, d. Jan. 30, 1820; Maria, b. Sept. 9, 1799, d. March 16, 1829; Frederick Augustus, b. April 9, 1801; James A., b. Feb. 21, 1803, d. Oct. 12, 1839; Oliver D., b. March 19, 1805, lives in Keeseville, N. Y.; Horatio N., b. April 11, 1807; Helen E., b. May 22, 1809.

V. Richard Peabody, (283—5) b. Feb. 4, 1773. Lived in Littleton, N. H. Married Elizabeth Goodhall, dau. of Rev. David Goodhall, in 1804. Children,

Clementina, b. Dec., 1805, d. April, 1806; Maria, b. Feb. 14, 1807, m. Timothy Hazelton of Barnet, Vt.; Clementina, b. Jan. 27, 1809, m. David Hibbard of Concord, Vt.; Richard W., b. July 7, 1811, m. Hannah Parker of Littleton, N. H.; Amanda, b. Nov. 18, 1812, d. Dec. 25, 1812; David G.,

b. Feb. 1, 1814, d. Sept. 1, 1822; Elizabeth O., b. July 30, 1816, m. Russell Armington of Waterford, Vt.; Persis, b. Aug. 15, 1819, d. Aug. 22, 1822; Hannah G., b. Oct. 21, 1821; David G., b. Feb. 11, 1825.

V. Judge Oliver Peabody, (286—1) b. Sept. 2, 1753. H. C. 1773. Lived in Exeter, N. H. Counsellor at Law, Sheriff of Rockingham County, Justice of Court of Common Pleas, President of the Senate. Married Frances Bourn, dau. of Hon. William Bourn of Marblehead, 1781. Died Aug. 3, 1831, a. 78. His widow died Dec. 28, 1844, a. 81. Children,

Sarah Hazard, b. Aug. 23, 1783, m. Stephen Pearse of Portsmouth, N. H., Sept. 23, 1804; Lucretia Orne, b. July 4, 1786, m. Oct. 21, 1816, Hon. Alexander H. Everett, late U. S. Envoy to China, where he died; William Bourn Oliver and Oliver William Bourn, gemini, b July 7, 1799, H. C. 1816, the former settled in the ministry at Springfield, Ms., D. D. 1842, m. Elizabeth Amelia White, Sept. 8, 1824, d. May 28, 1847, the latter was first a lawyer, then settled in the ministry at Burlington, Vt., where he died unmarried, July 5, 1848; Edward Bass, b. May 19, 1802, d. unmarried at 28 years of age. Beside the above there were seven other children, who died in infancy or early childhood.

V. Asa Peabody, (288—3) b. April 10, 1758. Lived in Bucksport, Me., then in Gloucester, Ms. Married Elizabeth Harper of Portland, dau. of Capt. William Harper, born July 20, 1765, still living, 1849. He died Jan. 24, 1839, a. 81. Children,

Oliver, b. Oct. 21, 1797; Caroline E., b. Aug. 16, 1800; Elizabeth H., b. June 20, 1802; Mary L., b. Oct. 21, 1806; Clarissa M., b. May 24, 1809.

V. John Peabody, (291—2) b. Nov. 2, 1766, married and lived in Bridgeton, Maine. Was a farmer. Children,

Mary, m. a Martin, of Bridgeton; Edward, a Physician in Hollis, Me.; Israel, a farmer in Bridgeton; Charles C., lives in Calais, Maine; Aaron, lives in Calais, Maine.

V. Thomas Peabody, (292—3) b. Oct. 31, 1768, married and lived in Gilead, Maine. Was a farmer there. Children,

Thomas; John Tarbell; Parmenio; Asa; Caleb; and several daughters. They all settled in Maine and New Hampshire.

V. William Peabody, (293—4) b. Aug. 12, 1770, married and lived in Bridgeton, Maine. Was a farmer there. Children,

A daughter, m. Ansel Smith, lived in Wisconsin; a daughter, m. a Fitch, a farmer in Bridgeton.

V. Augustus Peabody, (297—8) b. May 19, 1779, D. C. 1803, a. 1809. Counsellor at Law, Boston, Ms. Married Miranda Goddard, dau. of Dr. Thatcher Goddard, of Boston, Oct. 28, 1815. Children,

Augustus Goddard, b. Feb. 4, 1818, a Physician in Machias, Maine; Owen Glendour, b. April 23, 1822, Counsellor at Law, in Boston; Edward Thatcher, b. June 6, 1825, Professor in the College at Legrange, Ky.; Lucia Maria, b. Feb. 6, 1828; Francis, b. Jan. 22, 1833.

V. Stephen Peabody, (300—1) b. Oct. 6, 1773, H. C. 1794, Judge of the Court of Common Pleas, for Hancock Co., Maine; served also as a Captain in the Oxford army. Married Nancy Leonard Smith, April 8, 1810. Lives in Bucksport, Maine. Children,

Stephen, b. Dec. 1811, d. a member of Bowdoin College, 1831; George Augustus, b. Dec. 1813, a Merchant at Eastport, Maine; Barney Smith, b. Dec. 1815, d. an infant; William Smith, b. Dec. 1819, lives in Boston; Leonard, b. Feb. 22, 1821, a Merchant at Eastport, Maine.

The Descendants of Francis's 4th son, Isaac. (4–4)

V. Col. Benjamin Peabody, (302—1) b. Aug. 9, 1741. Lived in Middleton, Mass. Married Hannah Black, Sept. 23, 1765. Died Sept. 10, 1829, a. 88 years. His wife died Jan. 25, 1821, a. 76 years. Children,

Hepsibah, b. July 6, 1766; Sarah, b. Sept. 18, 1769, m. Joseph Symonds, April 5, 1791; Benjamin, b. Aug. 29, 1771, d. Sept. 1775; Hannah, b. Oct. 8, 1773; Benjamin, b. Oct. 8, 1776, d. 1778; Lydia, b. Aug. 14, 1779, d. Feb. 3, 1793; Olive, b. Aug. 28, 1781, m. Benj. Dole, Nov. 26, 1799; Stephen, b. Feb 25, 1784, d. 1788; Anna, b. Sept. 28, 1787, m. Jesse Esty, June 19, 1808; Peggy, b. Dec. 14, 1791, m. Jesse Wilkins, Oct. 10, 1810.

V. Francis Peabody, (305—4) b. March 4, 1745. Lived in Middleton, Mass., married Sarah Cummings, Aug. 15, 1774. Died Jan. 11, 1817, a. 72. His widow died Oct. 6, 1817, a. 58 years.

Betsey, b. Nov. 13, 1774, m. Peter Cross, Nov. 27, 1798; Sarah, b. March 8, 1777; Eunice, b. Aug. 13, 1781; Benjamin, b. Aug. 14, 1784, d. unmarried; Stephen, b. Sept. 20, 1788, living in Middleton; Samuel, b. May 9, 1799, went to New York.

V. Asa Peabody, (307—6) b. March 5, 1751. Lived in Middleton, Mass., married Anna Gould, June 4, 1771. Died in Londonderry, N. H. Children,

John, b. March 16, 1773, d. Aug. 26, 1787; Lucretia, b. April 30, 1779; Andrew, b. Sept. 17, 1781; Joseph W., b. May 18, 1787, m. Harriet French, of Milford, N. H., d. 1842 — no children; John Gould, b. Dec. 26, 1791.

V. Joseph Peabody, (310—9) b. Dec. 12, 1757. Lived in early life in Boxford and Middleton. At the commencement of the Revolution, he quit the occupation of an agriculturist to participate in the more stirring scenes of a sea life on board our private armed vessels, where he distinguished himself as a brave and skilful officer. After the Revolution he commenced business as a Ship owner and Merchant. His enterprises in this department, conceived with great ability and judgment, were rewarded with almost unprecedented success. Married first, Catharine Smith, Aug. 28, 1791, 2nd, Elizabeth Smith, Oct. 24, 1795, both daughters of the Rev. Elias Smith, of Middleton, Mass., died Jan. 5, 1844, a. 86. Children,

Joseph Augustus, b. Aug. 7, 1796, H. C., 1816, m. Louisa Putnam, dau. of Judge Samuel Putnam, Sept. 3, 1821, d. June 18, 1828; Charles, b. Dec. 8, 1797, drowned Aug. 10, 1805; Francis, b. July 14, 1799, died in infancy; Francis, b. Dec. 7, 1801, m. Martha Endicott, July 7, 1823. She was of the 7th generation from Gov. Endicott, and dau. of Samuel Endicott, Esq.; George, b. Jan. 10, 1804, H. C., 1823, m. Clara Endicott, Sept. 5, 1827, dau. of Samuel Endicott, Esq.; Charles Frederick, b. March 4, 1806, d. April 5, 1807; Catharine Elizabeth, b. June 23, 1808, m. John Lowell Gardner, of Boston, Oct. 1826.

V. Samuel Peabody, (321—8) b. 1773. Lived in Dixmont, Maine. Married Elizabeth Martin, of Bristol, Maine, daughter of Wm. Martin, 1799. Children,

Charles, b. 1800, m. and lives in Dixmont; Letitia, b. 1801, unmarried; Stitson, b. 1805, m. and lives in Dixmont; Jane, b. 1807, m. David Morrison, and lives in Dixmont; Aphia, b. 1809, m. Josiah Thomas, of Frankfort, Maine; John, b. 1811, unmarried; Joel, b. 1813, m. and lives in Troy, Maine; Abigail, b. 1815, unmarried.

V. William Peabody, (322—9) b. 1775. Lived in Hampden, Maine, married Melinda Woodcock, of Union, Maine. Died ——. Children,

Jason, lives in Union, Maine; Hannah, m. 1st, Elijah Brown, 2nd, a Smart, lives in Hampden, Maine; Almond, lives in Union, Maine; Emeline, lives in Hampden, Maine, m. a Walker; Nancy, m. a Lyon of Union, Maine; Roxanna, m. a Howes.

V. Andrew Peabody, (345—5) b. Feb. 17, 1760. Lived in Middleton, married Mary Beadle, June 2, 1791. Children,

Elias Putnam, b. Nov. 1, 1791; Daniel, b. Dec. 19, 1793.

V. Samuel Peabody, (354—3) b. Jan. 7, 1759. Lived in Salem, married Abigail Trask, Sept. 21, 1782. Died Jan. 26, 1839, a. 80 years.

Samuel, b. May 27, 1783, pressed on board a British man of War in 1801, and never returned; Thomas, b. Oct. 21, 1784, d. Jan., 1792; Bimsley, b. May 25, 1786, m. Lucy Herrick, June 29, 1809, was lost at sea; Abigail, b. Oct. 5, 1788; Oliver, b. Sept. 22, 1790; Elizabeth, b. Sept. 8, 1792; Thomas, b. Jan. 4, 1802; Nathaniel, b. Sept. 30, 1808, dead; Ruth Marston, b. Oct. 24, 18—; Mary, b. Dec. 10, 18—.

V. Francis Peabody, (355—4) b. Jan. 5, 1761. Lived in Middleton, married Lucy Masury. She died Sept. 15, 1806, a. 43 years. Children,

Allen, b. Nov. 22, 1781, m. Rebecca ———; Warren, b. Aug. 10, 1783, m. Lydia Dale, Sept. 8, 1805; Lucy, b. April 9, 1785; Joseph, b. July 5, 1787, m. Abigail Wilkins, Sept. 10, 1812; John, b. July 13, 1789, died young; Hannah, b. May 19, 1791; Francis, b. Feb. 12, 1793; John, b. Nov. 20, 1794, died young; Susan, b. Oct. 2, 1796; Huldah, b. Sept. 21, 1798; John, b. Sept. 14, 1800, lives in Chelsea; Jesse, b. Oct. 31, 1802; Ruth, b. Nov. 8, 1804.

V. Jonathan Peabody, (356—5) b. Jan. 27, 1763. Lived in Salem, married Lucy Morgan, March 14, 1784. Died May, 1849, a. 86 years. Children,

Israel, b. Nov. 11, 1786, d. 1811, never married; Susan, b. Dec. 16, 1788, d. 1789; John, b. June 3, 1790, lost at sea, in 1806; Susan, b. Aug. 14, 1792, m a Very, d. Sept. 13, 1828; Lucy, b. Jan. 19, 1797, m. Archelaus Newhall, of Lynn, d. Dec. 7, 1821; Oliver, b. Aug. 30, 1799, m. Mrs. Mercy Williams, d. Jan. 19, 1828; Charlotte, b. Feb. 19, 1802, d. Feb. 22, 1810; Ruth, b. Aug. 16, 1804, d. Sept. 8, 1804; William, b. April 8, 1806.

V. Amos Peabody (357—6) b. Feb. 7, 1765. Lived in Middleton, married Rachael Berry, Jan. 1, 1789. Died Aug. 27, 1835, a. 70. Children,

Abijah, b. March 29, 1790, died young; Fanny, b. Sept. 15, 1792; Amos, b. June 30, 1793; James, b. May 24, 1795; John, b. June 17, 1797; Betsey, b. Feb. 21, 1799; Anna, b. Nov. 6, 1801; Eunice, b. Feb. 3, 1803; Sarah, b. Feb. 4, 1805; Rachael Louisa, b. Nov. 1, 1807, d. in infancy; Rachael Louisa, b. Nov. 15, 1809; Almira, b. May 19, 1812; Abijah, b. April 9, 1814.

V. Dudley Peabody, (358—7) b. Oct. 7, 1766, married Rebecca Towne of Andover, Oct. 10, 1791. Lived first, in Boxford, then in Rindge, N. H., and lastly in Albany, N. Y. The following children were born in Boxford — others were born elsewhere, but of them there is no account.

Allen; Rebecca, m. in Boston; a daughter.

V. Benjamin Peabody, (360—9) b. 1771, married in Roxbury in 1794, Mary, dau. of John Bancroft, of Reading. Lived first, in Londonderry, N. H., removed from thence to Norway, Maine, about 1806. Is now living. Children,

Ruth, b. 1795, d. in 1822; Mary, b. 1797, m. a Lombard, of Otisfield, Maine; Charlotte b. 1799, m. a Johnson, of Albany, Maine; Lydia, b. 1801, d. in 1810; Benjamin, b. 1803, lives in Norway, Maine; Washington, b. 1805, lives in Boxford, Mass.; Oliver, b. 1807, lives in Salem, Mass., m. Abigail Morse, July 3, 1834; William, b. 1809, lives in Middleton, Mass.; Betsey and Eliza, twins, b. 1811, the former m. an Edwards, the latter a Herriman; Eunice, b. 1813, m. a Metcalf; Olive, b. 1815, m. a Herriman.

V. Oliver Peabody, (361—10) b. about 1774. Lived in Boxford, married 1st, Sarah Estes, of Topsfield, Nov. 27, 1800, 2nd, —— Chapman. Is now living. Children,

Hannah; Lucy, m. Porter Gould, of Middleton, Mass.; Sarah, m. Charles Bracket, of Topsfield.

V. Deacon Stephen Peabody, (366—4) b. July 16, 1763. Lived in Warren, Maine, was deacon of the church there, married Mercy Webber, Dec. 22, 1789. She was born Oct. 12, 1765. Children,

Ruth, b. May 9, 1791, died young; Mehitable, b. Aug. 31, 1793; Stephen, b. July 30, 1795; Jonathan, b. Nov. 16, 1797; Ruth, b. Dec. 16, 1798; Hannah, b. Feb. 1, 1801; Mary, b. April 6, 1802; Belcher, b. Sept. 5, 1803; John, b. Oct. 7, 1806; Cornelius, b. April 25, 1809; Rebecca, b. Sept. 23, 1811.

V. Solomon Peabody, (368—6) b. Sept. 4, 1768. Lived in St. George, Maine; married Lydia Alley, and had three sons, and six daughters. Their names are not known.

V. John Peabody, (374—4) b. July, 1762. Lived in Topsfield, married, 1st, Lydia Balch, March 6, 1781; 2nd, Lydia Symonds, Jan. 9, 1810. Died June 22, 1836, a. 74. Children by Lydia Balch,

John, b. Oct. 30, 1784, m. Margaret Brown of Hamilton, d. 1840, left two sons; Aaron B., b. April 12, 1788, d. 1814, unmarried; Hannah Smith, b. Dec. 28, 1792, m. Sewall Lake, June 19, 1811; Daniel and Lydia, twins, b. Jan. 12, 1797, the former d. unmarried, in 1833, the latter m. Francis Peabody, (391—8) Dec. 23, 1819; Joel Rogers, b. Nov. 29, 1800, lives in Topsfield, Deacon of the church; David, b. April 16, 1805,

D. C., 1828. Settled in the Ministry in Lynn, 1832, then in Worcester, m. Maria Brigham, of Cambridgeport, d. 1839, no children.

V. Capt. Ebenezer Peabody, (379—9) b. Sept. 14, 1778. Lived in Topsfield, married Mercy Perkins, Dec. 28, 1802, died July 16, 1825. Children,

Ebenezer, b. Nov. 7, 1803, m. Abigail Perkins, Oct. 15, 1833; Mercy, b. June 11, 1805, m. Amos Fish, Dec. 16, 1834; Josiah, b. June 7, 1807. Embarked on a Mission, April 27, 1841; Elizabeth, b. Dec. 9, 1808; Ezra, b. July 2, 1810; Lucy, b. Aug. 21, 1812, m. Benj. C. Perkins, March 10, 1835; Mary Ann, b. May 31, 1815, m. Wm. Henry Means, June, 1835; John, b. April 12, 1817; Ephraim, b. Jan. 14, 1820.

V. James Peabody, (380—1) b. in Alfred, Maine, 1772. Lived in Kennebunk, married Miriam Mitchell, of that place, Aug. 8, 1794. Children,

Betsey; John; James; Jotham; Richard; Alpheus; Abigail; Miriam.

V. Isaac Peabody, (381—2) b. Aug. 8, 1774. Lived in Kennebunk. Married Sarah Shackley of that place, Aug. 11, 1810. Is now living. Children,

Lavinia, dead; Sarah; Joseph, dead; John; Olive; Mary; Susan, dead.

V. Dr. Nathaniel Peabody, (385—2) b. March 30, 1774. D. C. 1800. Was a dentist in Salem and Boston. Married Elizabeth Palmer, Nov. 2, 1802. Is now living. Children,

Elizabeth Palmer, b. May 16, 1804; Mary Tyler, b. Nov. 16, 1806, m. Horace Mann; Sophia Amelia, b. Sept. 21, 1809, m. Nathaniel Hawthorne; Nathaniel Cranch, b. Dec. 11, 1811, m. Mary Elizabeth Hibbard; George Francis, b. Oct. 10, 1813, d. Nov., 1839; Wellington, b. Dec. 16, 1815, d. Oct., 1836; Catharine, b. April 26, 1819, d. in infancy.

V. Isaac Peabody, (386—3) b. Nov. 21, 1775. Lived in New Boston, N. H. Was a farmer. Married Mary Dodge. Died 1832, a. 47. Children,

John, lives in Antrim, N. H., married and has a family; Hannah B., m. Nathaniel Coggin, lives in Milford, N. H.; Daniel H., lives in Hooksett, N. H., married and has a family; Elizabeth, m. a Hersey, lives in Hopkinton, N. H.; Isaac and Jacob, gemini, the former lives in Lowell, Ms.; Lydia, lives in Milford, N. H., unmarried; Ezra, lives in New Boston, N. H., married and has a family.

V. Moses Peabody, (387—4) b. Dec. 22, 1778. Lives in New Boston, N. H. Is a farmer. Married Elizabeth Cochran. Children,

Ezekiel Cummings, lives in Lynn, Ms.; Horace, lives in Boston, Maine freight depot; William Watson, lives in Salem, Ms.; Harriet Newhall, m. a Fitz, lives in Lowell, Ms.

V. John Peabody, (388—5) b. Jan. 16, 1781. Lived in Salem. Was a ship-master in the East India trade. Married Elizabeth Manning, daughter of Thomas Manning, Jan. 25, 1807. Died in Batavia, E. I., in 1821, a. 40. Had three daughters.

V. Deacon Francis Peabody, (391—8) b. Feb. 6, 1793. Lives in Amherst, N. H. Married in Salem, Dec. 23, 1819, Lydia, daughter of his cousin John (374—4) Peabody. Children,

Aaron Francis, b. Jan. 2, 1821; John, b. Jan. 17, 1822, d. Nov. 30, 1824; Ann Maria, b. May 22, 1824; John, b. Nov. 9, 1827; Lydia Esty, b. Sept. 7, 1829; David, b. Dec. 17, 1831; Margaret Brigham, b. April 23, 1837; George Willington, b. Oct. 11, 1838; Daniel Augustine, b. June 29, 1842.

V. Jacob Peabody, (392—1,) b. May 10, 1764. Lived in Topsfield, Ms. Married, 1st, Huldah Wildes, Nov. 18, 1785; 2d, Betsey Perkins, Feb., 1816. Died Oct. 6, 1845, a. 81. Children by Huldah Wildes,

Thomas, b. April 20, 1786; Priscilla, b. Nov. 24, 1787; Alice, b. Nov. 3, 1790; Anna, b. Nov. 15, 1792; Huldah, b. Feb. 21, 1794; Eunice, b. July 19, 1795; Polly, b. May 3, 1797; Sarah, b. May 7, 1799; Lucy, b. April 14, 1801, m. Stephen B. Foster, June 5, 1823; Cynthia, b. April 16, 1804; Lois, b. May 2, 1806; Lydia, b. April 8, 1808.

Children by Betsey Perkins,

Francis Dana, b. Dec. 12, 1816; Elizabeth Ann, b. April 30, 1818; Henrietta, b. Dec. 14, 1819, d. Sept. 29, 1820; Joseph Emerson, b. May 21, 1822; Emeline, b. Aug. 28, 1824; Julia Jane, b. Jan. 27, 1826; Maria Louisa, May 11, 1828; Rachael Almira, June 10, 1830.

V. John Potter Peabody, (396—5) b. Dec. 8, 1780. Lived in Topsfield, married Esther Perkins, July 20, 1807. She died Aug. 11, 1842. He died Nov. 5, 1846, a. 66 years. Children,

Hannah, b. Nov. 16, 1807; Cyrus, b. March 16, 1810, d. Sept. 24, 1824; Esther, b. Sept. 12, 1812; Harriet Newhall, b. April 23, 1816, m. Alfred P. Towne; Mercy Perkins, b. Sept. 26, 1818; Mehitable, b. Oct. 23, 1825; Sarah, b. March 19, 1829.

V. Ezekiel Peabody, (398—7) b. June 13, 1788. Lives in Ipswich, married Mary Goodhue, July 6, 1815. Children,

Moses, b. April 9, 1816, m. Eunice Jewett, May 18, 1843, lives in Ipswich; Mary, b. Aug. 8, 1817, m. Woodbridge Adams, Aug. 19, 1841; Wm. Goodhue, b. Oct. 15, 1823; John Quincy, b. July 28, 1825, A. C. 1843.

The Descendants of Francis's 5th son, Jacob. (12—12)

V. Doct. Jacob Peabody, (400—2) b. Nov., 1736, (*erroneously stated to have died young, on page* 372, *Vol. II.*) Removed with his father to Leominster, Worcester County. Married Dorothy Foster of Lunenburg, March 4, 1756. Was first a physician, then a Lieutenant in the Provincial Army, and fell with Wolfe on the plains of Abraham. Child,

Eunice, m. Phineas Carter of Lunenburg, and had nine children. Thomas Carter, son of Eunice Peabody, is said to possess the identical Bible which his maternal ancestor, John Rogers, carried to the stake in Smythfield, England. It is much burnt.

V. Thomas Peabody, (405—7) b. 1746. Lived in Brentwood, N. H., married Elizabeth ———, and died in 1780. Had one child, Elizabeth.

The male descendants of Francis's son Jacob here become extinct.

END OF THE FIFTH GENERATION.

REV. SAMUEL BROWN, OF ABINGTON.

[Communicated by MR. CYRUS ORCUTT.]

The following was copied from an ancient manuscript volume, which belonged to Rev. Samuel Brown, the first minister in Abington, Plymouth County, Mass.

A Memoranda of the remarkables of my life.

I Samuel Brown — Borne at Newbury Sept 5th Anno 1687.

I went first to the Grammar School in October 1701.

I Samuel Brown was admited into Harvard College, at Cambridge on the third day of July, in the year 1705 in the eighteenth year of my age,

And took my first degree on the second day of July Anno 1709, and made entrance upon the ministry preaching my first sermon at Haverhill, on the 22ond of July Anno 1710.

Item. I came to Abington, with a unanimous call from ye people there, in order to settle on the 8th of December Anno 1711.

Item. I was married to Miss Dorothy Woodbridge on the 24th October Anno 1712, and I brought her home to Abington on the 14th December following.

My son Woodbridge Brown was borne Sept 28th Anno Domini 1714.

I was ordained Pastor of the Church of Christ in Abington Nov 17th 1714.

My daughter Dorothy was borne on the Lords day night on the 2d day of September Anno 1716, and she died September 26th living but three weeks and three days.

My son Samuel was borne July 17th 1717, and deceased 29 days after same month.

My dearly beloved and dutiful wife Dorothy deceased, on the fifth day of April Anno 1718, The Will of the Lord is done — Amen — ! But oh ! —

I was married unto Miss Mary Pratt Feb 10th 1718–19.

My daughter Sarah was borne Novr 17th 1719.

My son Matthew Brown was borne July 21st 1722, baptised Aug 5th 1722, and deceased Aug 29th 1722.

My son Matthew the second of that name was borne December 16th 1723, and was baptised on the 22ond day of the same month.

My son Matthew second deceased Jan 3d 1724–25.

My daughter Sarah aforesaid deceased, Nov 23d 1733, living fourteen years 6 days and about 6 hours.

My daughter Mary was borne Nov 8th 1734.

My said daughter Mary departed this life April 25th 1745 aged ten years five months and 17 days." *

* REV. SAMUEL BROWN, youngest son and child of Joshua and Sarah (Sawyer) Brown, and grandson of Richard, Sen., and Edith Browne, of "Ould Newberry," was born in that ancient town, if we may venture to believe his own statement, Sept. 5, 1687, though the able historian of Newbury assigns the 4th, and not the 5th, of September, for his natal day. He is supposed to have been descended from one "Sir Walston Brown, a young knight of King Henry 8th Household." Combining in his own person the vocations of Lawyer, Physician, and Clergyman, Mr. Brown's services seem to have been eminently useful and acceptable for the greater part of thirty-five years. But the latter years of his ministry were embittered by a tedious controversy, originating in the disaffection caused among a number of his parishioners, by his opposition to Whitfield; a controversy, which was only terminated by his voluntary resignation of his pastoral charge, in the month of August, 1749. He survived his dismission but a few days, and died of a fever, Sept. 12, 1749. His widow, the daughter of Matthew Pratt, of Weymouth, became the wife of Josiah Torrey, Esq. — *See Coffin's Newbury, pp.* 296–7, 352*; Hobart's Abington, pp.* 39—44, 68—71*; Am. Quarterly Register*, VIII. 144, 149. — ED.

THE DEANE FAMILY.*

In the following pages we propose to give an account of John and Walter Deane, two brothers, who emigrated from England, and were among the first settlers of Taunton, Mass. We shall also present genealogical notices of the early generations of their descendants. These accounts we shall preface with some facts concerning the origin and history of the name, though the limits of an article like this will allow us to draw but sparingly from the materials which we possess. Many of the facts withheld have, to persons bearing the name, quite as high a degree of interest as those here presented.

The name Den, or Dene, which is the ancient way of spelling what is now written Deane, makes its appearance in England soon after the introduction of surnames. It was apparently derived from the Saxon word *den*, or *dene*, a valley,† which word is not yet quite obsolete, being preserved in the proper names of certain valleys in England, as Taunton Dean, Castle Eden Dean, &c. The name was perhaps first given to estates that were situated in, or contiguous to, certain *denes*, and from the estates, the name would easily pass to their possessors. From *Dene* or *Den*, at first but different modes of spelling the same word, have arisen two surnames, which at the present time are entirely distinct, viz. *Deane* and *Denne*. Though the *name* is of Saxon origin, it is by no means certain that all the families that bear it are so. The first person of the name that we have met with is Robert de Den or de Dene, who was "pincerna, butler or sewer" to Edward the Confessor.‡ He held estates in Normandy, as well as in England, and may have been one of the Norman favorites, whom this monarch called around him. From him, he may have received estates in England of sufficiently greater importance than his Norman heritage to induce him to assume their appellation. Confirmatory of this conjecture it may be remarked that this family was not deprived of their estates at the Conquest. Another person of the name, early met with, is Sir William of Dene, who "was at the time of the Conquest owner of Throwly" in Kent, the seat of an ancient "priory of Priors Aliens" suppressed 2 Hen. V (1415).§ The name is found in Hampshire,

* The materials from which these notices are prepared, were furnished by Mr. William Reed Deane of Boston, who also aided in their compilation. Mr. Deane has, during the last few years, acquired a vast amount of valuable information relative to the name in this country and in England; and by an extensive correspondence has accumulated very many valuable letters, all tending to illustrate the object of his inquiry. — Ed.

† "The Saxon word *den* or *dene*, signifies a valley or woody place; but is very different from *glen*, which signifies a valley between hills. A den or dean sinks suddenly from the common level of the country, and cannot be seen, till the spectator is close upon its borders."—*Beauties of England and Wales*, V. 125, *note*.

‡ Berry's Genealogies, Kent; Collins's Peerage, art. Sackville, II, 263, (ed. 1768); and Kilbourn's Survey of Kent, 209.

§ Kilbourn's Survey of Kent, 273.

6 Rich. I., (1194) being mentioned in "a suit at law between Ralph de la Dene and Robert de Anvilliers, respecting two virgates of land in East Dene, a village of Hampshire bordering on Wilts, towards Salisbury."* In Staffordshire there was a John de Dene who was sheriff. 34 and 35 Edw. I. (1306, 1307.)† In Bucks, "the name occurs very early in the *Rotuli Hundredorum.* A William de Dene represented High Wycombe in Parliament in the reigns of Edward the 2d and Edward the 3d, and one of the same christian and surname was party to a suit at law respecting land in Bucks, 1 *John.* Again Hugh de la Dene (9 John) pays a fine for certain tenements at *Cestresham* (Cesterham) in that County."‡ "A member of the knightly family of Deane or Dene of Huntingdonshire, was present in the army of Edward the Second at the battle of Broughbridge;§ and in the reign of Edward I. and Edward II. "there were many distinguished knights of the name Dene, who, though it is impossible to identify them with any particular families, are fixed to Counties by the valuable Roll of Knights, 8 Edward II. of which copies are to be seen in the Harleian Collection in the British Museum. In that roll there are five knights of the name, *viz:*

1. Sir Wm. de Dene, of Essex: Arms, *Argent a fesse double dancetté gules.*
2. Sir Henry de Dene, of Dene, Northamptonshire: *The same arms with three red crescents in chief.*
3. Sir John de Dene, of Huntingdonshire: *Argent two bars sable, on each bar three crosses paté or.*
4. Sir John de Dyne, (or Deyne,) Oxfordshire: *Or a fesse sable.*
5. Sir John de Dene, Leicestershire: *Argent a lion rampant purpure.*

The Gloucestershire (Forest of Dene) family is not mentioned in this roll, because Wm de Dene of St. Briavels Castle was bound only to bear arms against the Welsh, and in the counties of Gloster, Hereford and Worcester, whereas the above named Knights were called out against the Scots."||

In the preceding names, the prevalence of the Norman prefix *de* will be noticed. This particle, at first, was generally used in conjunction with the name Dene, but as the Saxon element became more prominent in English society, it was gradually abandoned for the Saxon *at* and its variations, which finally became the prevailing prefix. Rev. J. B. Deane, F. S. A., furnishes us with the following excellent remarks upon the subject: "The prefix *atte*, *at* or *a'*, is common to many old English names, and was chiefly affected by those who prided themselves upon their Saxon descent. The name Deane is reckoned by Verstegan among the Saxon families, and accordingly the prefix *at* is frequently found in conjunction with it in the 13th and 14th centuries. In the reign of Henry the Eighth the territorial prefix vanishes altogether, and the ancient name puts on the more plebeian form of "Dene" without the distinctive particle, which, after the abolition of Feudalities by Henry the Seventh, had fallen into general desuetude. For when the ancient Nobility and Gentry were permitted to alienate their estates or to sell them, they, with proper regard to their altered circumstance, discarded the terri-

* We here quote from MSS. letters of Rev. John Bathurst Deane, F. S. A., of London, Esq., an eminent antiquary, who is, perhaps, better acquainted with the history and genealogy of the various families of Deanes in England than any other person. We are largely indebted to him for several communications and documents of great interest; and hope that we may eventually see from him a complete history of the different English families of the name. He is the author of "The Worship of the Serpent traced," and of several valuable papers published in the Transactions of the Antiquarian Society.

† Fuller's Worthies, i. 144. ‡ Rev. J. B. Deane, MSS. Letters. § Ibid. || Ibid.

torial designation, which was but a mockery after their estates were gone. What at first was a prudent necessity with many noble families, became, by degrees, a general fashion, even among those who had not alienated their property; and thus generally, throughout the kingdom, the Norman prefix *de* vanished, and the Saxon *at* was absorbed into the family name. A few however retained the latter, as A'Court, A'Becket, A'Deane, &c. The letter *a* was introduced into the name in the reign of Elizabeth, and *Dene* became Deane."* "From this prefix is derived the comparatively modern name of Adeane, which is now borne by some highly respectable families."† There are in England at least four distinct families of Deanes, from which all the others are offshoots or branches.‡

In more modern times, several eminent persons of the name have flourished in England. The four following are said to have been from Gloucestershire, and may have belonged to the family of "Dene of Dene in the Forest of Dene," namely: Henry Dene, Archbishop of Canterbury and Lord Chancellor under Henry VII.; Sir Richard Deane, Mayor of London, 1629; Admiral and Major-General Richard Deane, the Regicide, who fell in an engagement with the Dutch fleet under Van Tromp, June, 1653; and Sir Anthony Deane, Comptroller of the Navy, 1666–1688. Of a different family — Dene of Denelands — was Sir James Deane, a merchant of great wealth, who died 1603. "He left the bulk of his property in Charities, founded Almshouses at Basingstoke which still bear his name, and are supported solely by estates bequeathed by him to trustees for the purpose. He gave legacies to all the Hospitals of London, and to every parish in which he had either lived or owned property." § John Deane, who commanded a ship of war in the service of Peter the Great of Russia, perhaps belonged to Wilford, County Nottingham, England, as he appears to have been buried there.‖ He is the person who was shipwrecked in December, 1710, on Boon Island, on the coast of Maine, of which shipwreck he published, in 1711, at Boston, a narrative that has been several times reprinted. "A letter from Moscow to the Marquis of Caermarthen, relating to the Czar of Muscovy's forwardness in his Navy since his return home," published in London, 1699, was probably written by him. Edmund Deane, the author, and his brother Richard Deane, Bishop of Ossory in Ireland, were from Yorkshire, England.¶

Moses Deane, the ancestor of the present Lord Muskerry of Springfield Castle, County Limerick, Ireland, resided in the beginning of the 17th century "in the vicinity of Taunton," Somersetshire, England, "where the Deanes had lived for centuries."** His son, Matthew Deane, settled in Ireland, "near the time of Cromwell,"†† which would be soon after John and Walter Deane, also from the vicinity of Taunton, came to this country. He purchased large estates in Dromore, County Cork, and was created a Baronet by Queen Anne. He died Jan. 10, 1710, aged 84. The Hon. Sir Matthew Fitzmaurice Deane, the present Lord Muskerry, is his great-great-great-grandson.‡‡ There are now in the possession of Lord Muskerry at Springfield Castle the portraits of his ancestors, Moses Deane and his wife, "dressed in the style of covenanters." §§

* Rev. J. B. Deane, MSS. Letters. † Ibid. ‡ Ibid. § Ibid.

‖ Thoroton's Not., I. 117. ¶ Rev. J. B. Deane, MSS. Letters.

** MSS. Letters of the late Lady Muskerry, who, as well as her husband, was a descendant of Moses Deane.

†† Ibid., and Burke's Peerage. ‡‡ Rev. J. B. Deane, MSS. Letters.

§§ The late Lady Muskerry, MSS. Letters.

Previous to the arrival of the brothers John and Walter Deane, two persons by the name had emigrated to New England, namely, Stephen and Rachel of Plymouth. The latter, who must have been a widow, since she left a daughter, Martha Deane, came in 1635, and was married at Plymouth, Oct. 28, 1636, to Joseph Beedle. The former (Stephen) was one of the "pilgrims" or "first comers." He arrived November, 1621, in the second vessel—the Fortune.* The passengers in this vessel are said to have been principally composed of persons who had embarked for America the previous year in the Mayflower and Speedwell, but remained in England after the latter vessel was abandoned. Whether Mr. Deane was one of these, or even whether he had been a sojourner in Holland, we have no means of ascertaining; as he may have joined the Pilgrims in England. He appears to have been a man of enterprise, having set up the first corn mill in the Colony. For this he had exclusive right granted him in 1632 by the Colony Court, as appears by the following record:—

> "Stephen Deane desiring to set up a water worke to beate Corne uppon the brooke adjoining to the towne of Plymouth for the benefit of the Comonwealth was referred to the Govr & Council for answer who agreed with him uppon these following termes I That provided the place he made choyce of were no hinderance to a grinding mill intended heereafter he might bring the worke neere the towne II That he should receive one pottle oute of every bushell for toul and no more III That in case the said Stephen can beate all the Corne that is or shall be used in the Colony it shall not be lawful for any other to set up a worke of the kind, except it be for his owne use, or freely without toll or any other consideracion whatsoever to give leave to others to make use of the same."†

"Afterwards he was allowed to erect a grinding mill, but was to surrender his beating mill."‡ Jany 2, 1633-4, The Court ordered that he "have a sufficient water wheele set up at the charge of the Colony, consisting of one foot more depth than that he now useth, at or before 27 March—the said Stephen finding the Yron worke thereunto belonging."§ Rev. Samuel Deane remarks:—"The mill was on the town brook, where a mill now stands, and on the first dam above the town bridge."‖

Stephen Deane appears to have been unmarried when he arrived, and to have remained so as late as 1627.¶ He was probably married soon after, and it was perhaps for the purpose of erecting a house upon it, that he bought, in 1627, of Philip Delanoy, one acre of land.** His wife was Elizabeth, daughter of widow Mary Ring, but whether by Mr. Ring or by a former husband, is not known. Mrs. Ring's will is on record at Plymouth, dated 1633, in which she makes bequests, among others, to her daughter Elizabeth, wife of Stephen Deane, and to a child of Stephen Deane. On the 10th March, 1633-4, Mr. Deane purchased for £20 of "Wm Bradford, Gent, the deputed adm^r of Godbert Godbertson," the dwelling house and land of the latter in the centre of Plymouth village.†† Stephen Deane died Sept., 1634. The appraisal of his estate, amounting to £87 19s. 6d., is on record, viz.: Personal estate £45 19s. 6d., Dwelling House and Garden £20, Corn Mill £20, Land at Fresh Lake £2.‡‡ His wife Elizabeth survived him and was married Sept. 16, 1635, to Josiah Cooke, afterwards one of the first settlers of Eastham. In 1638 Mr. Cooke was granted 25 acres of land for Stephen Deane's children. These children, whose names we elsewhere learn were Elizabeth, Miriam, and Susannah, appear to have been of age in 1653, as in that year Josiah Cooke "came into Court and

* Plymouth Court Orders, I.
† Ibid.
‡ Thacher's Plymouth, 86.
§ Plymouth Court Orders, I.
‖ Rev. S. Deane, MSS. Papers.
¶ See Plymouth Court Orders, I. 56.
** Ibid, I. 30.
†† Ibid, I.
‡‡ Ibid, I. 168.

did make it appear unto the said Court that he had truthfully cleared payed & satisfied whatsoever was due unto the children of Steven Deane or any of them."* Mrs. Elizabeth Cooke died about 1687. Her husband died Oct. 17, 1673. Elizabeth Deane, daughter of Stephen D., married William Twining, of Eastham. Her sister Susannah, married 1st, at Eastham, April 4, 1660, Joseph Rogers, Jr., born at Sandwich, July 19, 1635, son of Lt. Joseph R., one of the passengers in the Mayflower. He died at Eastham, Dec. 27, 1660, and she married 2d, at Eastham, Oct. 28, 1663, Stephen Snow. Stephen and Elizabeth Snow had children, 1, Bathshua, born 1664, 2d, Hannah, born 1666, 3d, Micajah, born 1669, 4th, Bethiah, born 1672.† Miriam Deane, the remaining daughter of Stephen, was probably never married.‡

John and Walter Deane, who are the progenitors of many of those now bearing the names Deane and Dean in the United States, came to this country about 1637. "They arrived," says the late Rev. Samuel Deane of Scituate, Mass., "at Boston first, stopped a year, or nearly, at Dorchester, and then came with others to Taunton."§ It is known that a large portion of the early settlers of Taunton, Mass., were originally from Taunton, County Somerset, Eng., and its vicinity. Miss Elizabeth Poole, who has been called the "Virgin Mother" of Taunton, was from Taunton, Eng., and so, we know, were several others; and in a document signed, among others, by Walter Deane, it is stated, that the place was called Taunton "in honor and love to our dear native country."‖ It had been the tradition in the family that John and Walter Deane came from Taunton, Eng., and this tradition has even found its way into print;¶ but the late Rev. Samuel Deane of Scituate states** that they were "from Chard, near Taunton."†† We know not his authority for this statement, nor for the one that they stopped a year or nearly at Dorchester, but we think them both correct. We know that several of the early settlers of Taunton were first at Dorchester, and that there are Deanes still residing at Chard as well as Taunton, Eng. The connection of John and Walter Deane with several families who are known to have been from Taunton, and other circumstances, leave little room for doubt that they were from that vicinity. Taunton and Chard, Somersetshire, Eng., are situate in an extensive and fertile valley called Taunton Dean, on the river Tone. This "dean" or valley comprehends a region about Taunton, very pleasant and populous, of some thirty miles in extent, and has been represented as exceedingly productive. The following proverb, which, according to Fuller's Worthies, is current with the inhabitants, implies, and is meant by them to express, a pride in the place of their birth, namely, "Where should I be born else than in Taunton Dean." In Campbell's Survey of Great Britain is the following description. "The vale of Taunton Dean in respect to its amazing fertility is only surpassed by the industry of its inhabitants, which is a point that we may affirm to be extremely worthy of notice, since it very rarely happens in

* Plymouth Court Orders, III. 35.

† We are indebted to Dr. N. B. Shurtleff for most of the facts relative to S. Deane's children.

‡ There is a possibility that Miriam Deane may have been a daughter-in-law of Stephen, instead of an own daughter, as here represented.

§ MSS. Papers.

‖ Baylies's Plymouth, II. 276.

¶ Columbian Reporter, 1825, and Baylies's Plymouth, II. 282, note.

** In his MSS. Papers, in a letter to William Willis, Esq., and in Baylies's Plymouth, IV., appendix, 170.

†† Chard is about ten miles from Taunton.

this kingdom or in any other, that when, from the natural fecundity of the soil, a plentiful subsistence may be had with very little labour, the people should nevertheless apply themselves vigorously and steadily to the manual arts."

We have not yet been able to trace with positiveness the ancestry of the brothers in England. Rev. John B. Deane, F. S. A., whom we have before quoted, inclines to the opinion that John and Walter Deane belonged to the family of "Dene of Denelands," whose coat of arms we have placed at the head of this article. One of this family, Thomas Deane, son of James Deane of Deanelands, was a resident in New England for a while. He was a merchant at Boston as early as 1664, and appears to have been a man of wealth and consideration. He was a large owner of real estate in Boston, Wrentham, and perhaps other places in this vicinity. He appears to have belonged to the party who desired to see the Colony brought more directly under the authority of the king; and when the Commissioners appointed by Charles II. to regulate the affairs of New England, arrived, Mr. Deane brought a complaint before them of some injustice done him when the Charles of Oleron came into the port of Boston, in 1661.* The Commissioners prepared to hear his complaint, when the General Court of Massachusetts "sent forth a herald to sound a trumpet and read a proclamation with great solemnity in three several places in Boston, that in accordance with their duty to God, the king, and their constituents, the General Court will suffer no one to abet his Majesty's Commissioners in their proceedings." † The spirit manifested by Massachusetts at this time was much the same as that which eventually brought forth the Declaration of Independence. In 1678, Mr. Deane was appointed by the English Government one of the Commissioners to administer an oath to the Governor of Massachusetts, "faithfully to execute the duty required by the act of trade." ‡ Mr. Deane married, 1st, Sarah, dau. of William Browne, Sen.,§ of Salem, and 2d, Anne, dau. of William Farr of London. The children of Mr. Deane by his first wife were, 1. Sarah, born 1666, married Rev. Dr. Robert Woodward, Dean of Sarum, whom she survived; 2. Elizabeth, born 1667, probably died early. By his wife Anne he had, 3. Thomas, born 1673, married, 1698, Jane ——, by whom he had an only daughter Jane, married to Sir John Cullum of Norfolk, Bart.‖; 4. Rebecca, born 1677 ¶; 5. James; 6. Samuel, who was living at London, 1730.** Thomas Deane, the father, returned to England about 1678. In 1681, he was a merchant at London, after which he retired to Freefolk, Hants, where he died April 27, 1686, in his 46th year. There is a mural tablet to his memory and that of his wife Anne, in Freefolk Chapel.††

John and Walter Deane "took up their farms on the west bank of the river, about one mile from the centre of the present village" of Taunton.‡‡ Houses occupying the same lots as those erected by them, and nearly the

* Mass. Hist. Coll., XVIII. 88. † Bancroft's History of the United States.

‡ Hutchinson's Hist. Mass., I. 297.

§ Mr. Browne was one of the benefactors of Harvard College, to which he gave largely.

‖ Betham's Baronetage, II. 55, and Rev. J. B. Deane, MSS. Letters.

¶ Rebecca and the children preceding her were born at Boston, N. E. See Boston Records.

** Suffolk Registry of Deeds, Book 77, p. 65.

†† We are under many obligations to Rev. R. Fitzgerald, officiating clergyman at Freefolk Chapel, for a fine drawing of this tablet, sent us by the hands of Rev. J. B. Deane of London.

‡‡ Rev. S. Deane, MSS. Papers.

exact sites, are at this day owned and occupied by descendants of each. The road which passed their dwellings has been called Dean Street to this day. Both took the freeman's oath at Plymouth, Dec. 4, 1638. By a list of the proprietors of Taunton, 1659, made for a division of lands, we find that the families of John and Walter Deane consisted of eight persons each.*

There is a tradition among the descendants of John and Walter Deane, that a younger brother of theirs came to this country after them and settled in Connecticut, and that from him was descended Hon. Silas Deane, Commissioner to France in the time of the Revolution. This tradition is confirmed by one in the family to which Hon. Silas D. belonged, that their first ancestor in this country was a brother to the two who settled at Taunton. We are aware that traditions, especially concerning relationship, should be received with great caution; but one like this seems to be entitled to some consideration, the more so as well authenticated facts appear to indicate friendly intercourse, at least, between these widely separated families. There was a Thomas Deane in Connecticut, 1643,† who possibly may have been the brother referred to. The earliest ancestor of Hon. Silas Deane that we can with certainty ascertain, is his great-grandfather, James of Stonington, Ct., born 1647, who may have been a son of the emigrant, and thus a nephew of John and Walter.‡

Hon. Silas Deane § was a native of Groton, Conn., and graduated with distinguished honors at Yale College in 1758. He was one of the delegates from the state of Connecticut to the first Congress in 1774, and one of the most influential, able, and efficient members of that assembly. He was in 1775 solely and exclusively employed by the Marine Committee, with extensive power and authority, to procure, by purchase or otherwise, and to equip and fit out, a large naval force; and may be said to be the "father of the revolutionary marine." ‖ He received on the 2d of March, 1776, a commission from the Committee of Secret Correspondence as Political and Commercial Agent to France, where he arrived in June of that year. The instructions of the Committee conferred upon him great and exclusive powers, and authorized him not only to operate in France, but in Holland and Great Britain, and to procure clothing, arms, and military accoutrements and munitions of war sufficient for an army of twenty-five thousand men, as also one hundred field pieces — in which he was very successful.

So entirely satisfactory had been the conduct of Mr. Deane in the discharge of his confidential, complicated, important, and delicate duties in Europe, that he was, on the 26th of September, 1776, chosen by Congress to be one of their ambassadors in conjunction with Dr. Franklin and Mr. Jefferson, to transact the business of the United States at the court of

* Baylies's Plymouth, II. 271. † Hinman's First Puritan Settlers of Connecticut, p. 21.

‡ There was a family of Deans in Stamford, Ct., at an early day, to which James of Stonington may have belonged. Judge Joseph Dean of Brooklyn, N. Y., who traces his ancestry to the western part of Connecticut, may be of this family. There was also a family who settled in Westchester County, N. Y., who, though they were probably from Connecticut, could not have been descendants of James of Stonington. Nicholas Dean, Esq., of New York, a gentleman well known in that city for his taste in the fine arts, &c., is of this family. His son, George F. Dean, Esq., is a writer in the American Whig and other periodicals. There was a Samuel Dean, Sen., at Jamaica, L. I., in 1660, as appears from Thompson's History of Long Island, and a Christopher Dene in 1685 at Hempstead, L. I., who may have been from Stamford, Ct., as many of the first settlers of those places were from that vicinity.

§ We are indebted to Horatio Alden, Esq., of Hartford, Conn., for several copies of Mr. Deane's address to his countrymen in 1784, and other documents connected with his mission and life.

‖ Memorial to Congress, 1835.

France. Mr. Jefferson declining, Congress appointed Arthur Lee, Esq., at that time in England. Dr. Franklin and Arthur Lee, Esq., joined Mr. Deane at Paris on the 22d of December of that year, and commenced the discharge of their duties on the 28th of that month, when they had their first audience with the Count de Vergennes, the prime minister of France.*

The Commissioners, with an ability and zeal which were probably never exceeded under similar circumstances, accomplished the leading object of their appointment, and succeeded in negotiating treaties with France which were signed at Paris on the 6th of February, 1778.

It is believed, without detracting from the merits of his great and distinguished colleagues, that Mr. Deane, from his previous confidential intercourse with the French ministry, the marked confidence which they reposed in him individually, and the knowledge he had thereby attained, is entitled to his full share of credit in negotiating this important treaty.†

It was by Mr. Deane that the services of the great Lafayette were engaged in the cause of the colonies, and his name is thus connected with one of the most brilliant incidents in our history.‡

Mr. Deane was recalled by an order passed by Congress in December, 1777; he arrived in Philadelphia in July, 1778. He found that he was not in favor with Congress, and various charges were made against him which were never substantiated. He had a large and just claim upon our government, which was not allowed during his lifetime, and not until 1835 was the claim allowed to his heirs. Mr. Deane died at Deal in England, August 23, 1789.

Silas Deane

James Deane of Stonington, Ct., was also the ancestor of Rev. Barzillai Deane, (grad. Yale College, 1737,) who preached awhile at New Milford, Ct., and afterwards went to England for Episcopal Orders, but died on the voyage; Rev. Seth Deane, (grad. Yale College, 1738,) of Rindge, N. H., and afterwards of Killingly, Ct., where he died; Judge James Dean, (grad. Dartmouth College, 1773, died 1823,) of Westmoreland, N. Y.; Prof. James Dean, LL.D. (grad. Dartmouth College, 1800, died 1849,) of Burlington, Vt.;§ Hon. Ezra Dean of Wooster, Ohio, M. C., 1841–1845; Rev. David Smith, D.D., of Durham, Ct., and Dr. James Deane,‖ of Greenfield, Mass., a geologist, who has made valuable additions to our scientific knowledge, especially concerning the foot prints of birds in the red sandstone formation of the Connecticut valley. There were many thrilling events in the life of Judge Dean of Westmoreland. Being intended by his parents as a missionary to the Indians, he was placed by them in his youth in the family of an Oneida chief in order to learn the language and habits of that people. At a proper age he entered Dartmouth College, and after leaving it prepared himself for the ministry, and preached one or two sermons; but the revolutionary war opened to him another field of labor. "At the time

* Diplomatic Correspondence, Vol. I. p. 250. † See Memorial to Congress in 1835.

‡ See Diplomatic Correspondence, and North American Review, Oct., 1831, pp. 472, '3.

§ See N. E. Hist. and Gen. Reg., III. 197.

‖ We are under obligations to Dr. Deane for copies of valuable early records relating to the family of James Deane of Stonington, Ct.

that the troubles thickened between England and her American colonies, he was employed by the Colony of New Hampshire to visit the Canadian Indians, and win them to the side of the colonies. He was in Canada when the battle of Lexington was fought, and soon after left, traversing the length of Lake Champlain in a bark canoe, with an Indian blanket for a sail. Soon after he entered the service of the United States as Agent of Indian Affairs, and so remained through the revolutionary war, and at its close was Interpreter in the negotiation of many Indian treaties, with the tribes residing along the upper lakes."* An incident in his life "which furnishes a parallel to the rescue of Captain Smith by Pocahontas, in the early days of Virginia," is graphically described by Wm. Tracy, Esq., in his Lectures.†

The following facts are known concerning John and Walter Deane, respectively, and their descendants.

($\frac{1}{2}$) I. JOHN,[1] was born about 1600, having died between April 25 and June 7, 1660, "aged sixty years or thereabouts."‡ His wife, who was named Alice, survived him, and was probably living as late as 1668, as she is mentioned in a grant of the Plymouth Court, June 1st, of that year.§ Mr. Deane was "of the grand inquest, from Taunton, 1640."‖ The following extract from his will shows that he possessed the Puritan feeling in regard to Religion:

"Item, My will is that these my Overseers with the Consent of my Wife shall in Case heer be no Settled Ministry in Taunton; they shall have full power to sell either the whole or a parte of these my Housings and Lands, soe as my Children and Posteritie may remove elsewhere, where they may enjoy God in his Ordinances."¶ The inventory of his Estate amounted to £334, 18s.**

An anecdote has been preserved by tradition concerning Mr. Deane, that at one time he came near losing his life, while out on a hunting excursion alone. Perceiving through the bushes some Indians cautiously approach, evidently with the purpose of capturing or killing him, and that they were but a short distance from him, the thought suddenly struck him of making it appear as though he were in the company of a number of others. This he did by exclaiming loudly, "Rush on boys, and we'll have them," at the same time firing his gun and rushing forward. The stratagem succeeded, and the wild men of the woods scattered, permitting him to return home unmolested. No autograph of John Deane is known to be in existence.

($\frac{2}{8}$) II. WALTER,[1] was born, according to Rev. S. Deane, "in Chard, Eng. between 1615 and 1620.†† If he was 21 years old, as is probable. when he took the freeman's oath, he could not have been born later than 1617. Rev. Wm. Cogswell, D. D., has ascertained that he married a daughter of Richard Strong, of Taunton, England, who came to New England with her brother, Elder John Strong, afterwards of Northampton, in the Mary and John, 1630.‡‡ We were before aware that Walter Deane and John Strong were brothers-in-law, as the former in two different deeds, dated 1691, calls the latter his "brother."§§ His wife in 1693, was named Eleanor. She joins with him in making a conveyance, August 20th of that year,‖‖ which is the latest date at which we can learn that either was living. Mr. Deane was a tanner by trade.¶¶ No will or settlement of his estate is on record. We know the names of but three of his children, though from the document before quoted it is probable that in 1659 he had six. The remaining three may have been daughters. If they were sons they must have died early or removed from Taunton. We have met with no persons by the name more likely to have been his sons than John, (d. 1727,) and William, (married 1677,) of Dedham, Mass.; and perhaps Jonas, (d. 1697.) of Scituate, Mass. James, of Stonington, Ct., before referred to, if not a nephew, may have been a son. From John, of Dedham, is descended Rev. William Dean, now Baptist Missionary in China, and Dr. Oliver Dean, of Boston. There is probably a connection between the Taunton and Dedham Deans, though the exact relationship is not known.

Walter Deane was deputy to the Plymouth Court, 1640,*** and selectman of Taunton, 1679 to 1686, inclusive.††† He was a prominent man in the Town Affairs. When the Cape Towns invited the inhabitants of Taunton to come to them with their movable

*MSS. Letter of Hon. J. A. Spencer, of Utica, N. Y., whose wife, Electa, is a daughter of Judge Dean.
†Tracy's Lectures, p. 16, where will be found a very full account of Judge Dean. The anecdote is copied by Stone into his Life of Brant. Did space allow we would copy it here.
‡ Will Plym. Pr. Rec. II. 61. § Baylies's Plym. II. 273, ‖ Rev. S Deane, MSS. Papers.
¶ Plym. Prob. Rec. II. 61. ** Ibid. †† Rev. S. Deane, MSS. Papers.
‡‡ Appendix to Hitchcock's Sermon at the funeral of Mrs. Joanna Strong, 9.
§§ Bristol Reg. Deeds, I. 152, and III. 390. ‖‖ Ibid, VII. 351. ¶¶ Ibid, I. 152.
*** Plym. Court Orders, I., and Baylies's Plym., I. 307. ††† Plymouth Court Orders, VI.

property for protection during Philip's War, Mr. Deane was one of the persons appointed to decline their invitation, and return thanks for their kindness. The original of their letter, with the signatures in good preservation, is in the Library of the Massachusetts Historical Society, Hinckley Papers, Vol. I. No. 3. There is another autograph of Walter Deane preserved, attached to an Inventory of the estate of William Crewe, June 14, 1672. A fac-simile of this will be found below. It will be noticed that he spells his name with a final *e*. This, as we observe in all the records of instruments signed by them, was the invariable way in which he and his brother John wrote their names. The majority of their descendants, however, have omitted the *e*.*

Walter Deane

JOHN,[1] (1) who m. Alice ——, had

($\frac{3}{11}$) I. JOHN.[2] Settled at Taunton. He was b. about 1639, having d. at Taunton Feb. 18, 1716–17, a. 77.† He is buried in the graveyard on Summer (or Neck-of-Land) Street, Taunton. Tradition asserts that he was the first white child born in Taunton.‡ He m. Nov. 7, 1663, Sarah, dau. of Dea. Samuel Edson of Bridgewater. She probably survived him. He died during the "Great Snow," as it is called. The snow was so deep that it prevented travelling, and there is a tradition that Mr. Deane lay dead in his house for a long time before his death was known to his neighbors.

($\frac{4}{20}$) II. THOMAS.[2] Settled at Taunton. He m. Jan. 5, 1669, Katharine Stephens. His will was proved July 15, 1697. His widow, Katharine, survived him. Her will was proved June 12, 1726–7. A book which belonged to Katharine Stephens is now in the possession of one of her descendants.

(5) III. ISRAEL,[2] "was a lieutenant in Philip's War, and was in the great Narragansett Fight."§ He d. unmarried. Will dated Aug. 7, 1677.

($\frac{6}{28}$) IV. ISAAC.[2] Settled at Taunton. He m. Jan. 24, 1677, Hannah, dau. of James Leonard. His will was proved April 11, 1710. Wife Hannah, executrix. Being a relative of the wife of Sergeant Thomas Jeffrey of New Haven, he dwelt in his youth in their family. Sergeant Jeffrey was the "highest" military officer in New Haven, and "appears to have had the defence of the town under his charge. All questions in regard to fortifying, &c., were referred to him."‖ Sergeant Jeffrey, at his death, left Isaac Deane a legacy of ten pounds, which, from the following curious record, appears to have been paid to him before he was of age, by Mr. Thomas Trowbridge, who had the settlement of Sergeant Jeffrey's estate:

"Lieftenant James Wyate, together with the widdow Allice Deane of Taunton Doe both of them joyntly and severally stand bound unto the Govr and Court of New Plymouth in the summe of twenty pounds; to save the Court harmless and undamnifyed by their p'mitting of a Legacye of Ten Pounds to be payed by Thomas Trowbridge of New Haven unto Isaac Deane of Taunton the said Isaac Deane being under age."¶

(7) V. NATHANIEL,[2] died without issue, between 1660 and 1677.

(8) VI. ELIZABETH,[2] b. about 1650, having d. 1734, a 84. She married Josiah Edson, Esq., of Bridgewater, son of Dea. Samuel E. He died 1734, a. 83, leaving a large estate. He "gave lands to the town, and to the south parish, where he lived, for the maintenance of schools, commonly called the school lands."** "They left no children."††

WALTER,[1] (2) of Taunton, had

($\frac{9}{35}$) I. JOSEPH,[2] "cordwainer;"‡‡ of Taunton, 1684,‡‡ of Dighton, 1728§§. He died between Dec. 3, 1728, and Feb. 11, 1728–9, leaving a widow Mary.§§ In 1688, Bartholomew Tipping is called his "brother-in-law."‖‖

($\frac{10}{39}$) II. EZRA.[2] Settled at Taunton. He married Dec. 17, 1676, Bethiah, daughter of Dea. Samuel Edson, of Bridgewater. He died between Oct. 28, 1727, and Feb. 15, 1732.¶¶

($\frac{11}{45}$) III. BENJAMIN.[2] Settled at Taunton. He married Jan. 6, 1680–1, Sarah Williams. He died between Feb. 2, 1722–3, and April 14, 1725.***

JOHN,[2] (3) of Taunton, son of John,[1] had

(12) I. SAMUEL.[3] Settled at Taunton, of the church at which place he was deacon.

* The name DEAN (without the final *e*) is generally thought to be derived from the title of the church dignitary, and possibly in some families this may have been the origin. Lower, in his English Surnames, derives it from both the church dignitary and the valley.

† Gravestone. ‡ Rev. S. Deane, MSS. Papers. § Ibid.

‖ Thomas R. Trowbridge, Esq., MSS. Letters. He derives his information from the New Haven Records.

¶ Plym. Records. ** Mitchell's Bridgewater, 151. †† Ibid. ‡‡ Bristol Reg. Deeds, I., 63.

§§ Bristol Prob. Rec., V. 202. ‖‖ Bristol Reg. Deeds, I. 60. ¶¶ Bristol Prob. Rec., VII. 286.

*** Bristol Prob. Rec. V. 62, 72.

He was born Jan. 24, 1666–7, and died Oct. 1, 1731, in his 65th year. His widow Sarah died at Norton, "before midnight," Oct. 15, 1741, in her 74th year. Their children were, 1, Sarah,[4] b. Oct. 15, 1694, died early; 2, Bethiah,[4] b. Jan. 7, 1697, d. Oct. 12, 1778, m. Samuel Clapp, who d. June 13, 1772, in his 80th year. They were the grandparents of Hon. Asa Clapp, (d. 1848,) of Portland, Maine, whose daughter, Eliza W., is the wife of Hon. Levi Woodbury, one of the Justices of the U. S. Supreme Court; 3, Samuel,[4] b. Oct. 17, 1700, m. 1st, Mary Avery, 2d, Rachel Dwight, 3d, widow Margaret King. By Rachel, he was the father of the late Rev. Samuel Deane,[5] S. T. D., of Portland, Maine, who was born at Dedham, Aug. 30, 1733, graduated at Harvard College, 1760, and in 1763, became a tutor there, which situation he retained till 1764, when he was settled at Falmouth, (now Portland,) Maine.* While at Cambridge, he composed an English poem, which, with other complimentary effusions from those connected with the University, was printed and presented to George III., on his accession to the throne. "He also published several other poems, the longest of which was Pitchwood Hill," evidently suggested by Dyer's Grongar Hill. "His largest work, and one to which he was most devoted, and which will longest preserve his memory, is his 'Georgical Dictionary, or New England Farmer,' first published in 1790. Besides the foregoing works, the Dr. published an Oration delivered July 4, 1793, an election sermon, delivered in 1794, two discourses to the young men of his parish, and some other sermons. He was a man of good personal appearance, and of grave and dignified deportment, but in hours of relaxation he was fond of indulging in social conversation, which he enlivened with pleasantry and wit."† He married in 1766, Eunice Pearson, who died Oct. 14, 1812, aged 87, without issue. He died Nov. 12, 1814, aged 81. The following is the autograph of Dr. Deane, as written in 1774.

Samuel Deane

4, William,[4] b. Aug. 19, 1702, m. Dec. 17, 1730, Esther Avery, b. Aug. 7, 1704, d. May 9, 1773, aged 68. He d. Oct. 26, 1773, aged 71. His wife was a daughter of William Avery, who resided in the "Avery House," of which an engraving is to be seen in Barber's Hist. Coll. of Mass. Mr. Deane had, in 1728, built him a house at Mansfield, then called Norton, and originally a part of Taunton, which house is now standing and occupied by his descendants; but at his marriage, it probably needed some preparation before it was deemed ready to receive his bride, and he returned to Norton without her. A letter written by him to her, dated, "Norton January ye 25 1730–31" is now in the hands of one of his descendants, couched in very affectionate language, in which he says, "there has been long absence and great distance betwixt us and I shall mind you with a return to you on Thursday, the second day of February next." The absence of four weeks was undoubtedly long to him under those circumstances, and to us moderns it would be equally so; but the "great distance" of which he speaks, and which was then undoubtedly a very hard day's journey, and perhaps more than one, is now traversed by the rail road cars in less than forty minutes, there being a stopping-place within a stone's throw of each of the houses. It has been said that he brought her home, with her fitting out, on an ox-sled. A fac simile of his signature to this letter is here appended.

William Dean

A pair of spectacles made in 1749, which were worn by him, is preserved. His son John,[5] married Abigail White, Sept. 19, 1769. They were the parents of Rev. Samuel Deane,[6] of Scituate, Mass., who graduated at Brown University, in 1805. He died Aug. 9th, 1834, aged 50, after having been the pastor of the second church in that town twenty-four years, the early part of which period as colleague with Rev. Dr. Barnes. He married Stella, daughter of the late Hon. Seth Washburn, of Raynham, Mass., and left one son, now a resident of St. Louis, Mo., and two daughters.

"In the mind of Mr. Deane the qualities of strength and beauty were happily united. His genius was essentially poetical. An imagination exceedingly productive; a sensibility thrilling at a touch; a cultivated taste; a susceptibility to the pleasures of music rarely excelled; a true sympathy with Nature and with Man; these were all properties which were obvious in him upon even a moderate degree of intimacy."‡ His attempts at poetical composition were not numerous. He delivered a Poem entitled, "The Populous Village,"

* William Willis, Esq., of Portland, author of the History of that town, has in preparation and will soon publish, a new edition of Rev. Mr. Smith's journal, to which will be appended notes and extracts from the diary of Doctor Deane, with notices of both Dr. Deane and Mr. Smith, with engraved portraits of both. It will be an octavo volume, of about 500 pages, and will be well worthy the attention of the public, and especially of those who may have known these ministers, or are interested in the history of that town.

† Willis's Hist. of Portland, II. 232.

‡ From obituary in Chr. Reg. Aug. 23, 1834.

before the Philermenian Society of Brown University, in 1826, which was published, and also a satirical Poem on " Some Literary Errors of the age," before another literary society connected with that institution. "For History he had a decided predilection, and he indulged it. There were not many better versed than he in the Colonial History of Plymouth and Massachusetts. His History of Scituate affords evidence of research and talent highly respectable."* Mr. Deane had gathered much of the early genealogy of this family, and from his manuscript notes were we first induced to look further into its history, and to make more complete what he had thus begun. All the ancestors of Rev. Samuel Deane in this country, were deacons, excepting, perhaps, John, the first, and all of their wills, including his, are on record.

Samuel Deane

A brother of Rev. Samuel Deane, Mr Jacob Deane,[6] of Mansfield, now living in the house built by his grandfather William, in 1728, married Mehitable, dau. of Rev. William Reed, of Easton, and is the father of William Reed Deane,[7] of Boston, one of the compilers of these notices. John Deane, another brother of the Rev. Samuel, settled in Norton, and was the father of John Deane, who resides in Dedham, and is master of transportation in Boston, for the Taunton Branch Rail Road. 5, Nathan,[4] m. Elizabeth Nicholson, who d. July 17, 1741, in her 23d year. He d. July 11, 1741, in his 37th year. 6, Isaac,[4] d. April 27, 1734, in his 28th year, unmarried.

(13) II. Sarah,[3] b. Nov. 9, 1668, m. Maj. Jonathan Howard, of Bridgewater.

(14) III. John,[3] b. July 26, 1670, d. Aug. 6, 1670.

(15) IV. Mehitable,[3] b. Oct. 9, 1671, m. Joseph Wilbore.

(16) V. John,[3] b. Sept. 18, 1674, d. July 31, 1724, in his 50th year. His widow Hannah, d. July 15, 1748, in her 71st year.

(17) VI. Elizabeth,[3] b. March 15, 1676, d. unmarried, March 15, 1749, aged 73.

(18) VII. Mary,[3] b. July 15, 1680, m. Seth Williams.

(19) VIII. Susannah,[3] b. Aug. 13, 1683, d. unmarried, about 1716.

(20) IX. Israel,[3] b. Aug. 4, 1685, m. March 20, 1704–5, Katharine Bird, of Dorchester. He died July 14, 1719, in his 34th year. His wife survived him.

Thomas,[2] (4) son of John,[1] had

(21) I. Thomas,[3] b. Feb. 1, 1670–1, d. Feb. 26, 1670–1.

(22) II. Hannah,[3] b. Jan. 14, 1671–2, d. unmarried, about 1750.

(23) III. Thomas,[3] b. about 1673, having d. Sept. 10, 1747, in his 74th year. He was married Jan. 7, 1696, by Rev. Peter Thacher, to Mary, daughter of John Kingsley, of Milton, Mass. She d. Feb. 1, 1749–50, in her 74th year. From them was descended Hon. Josiah Dean,[5] (d. 1818,) of Raynham, Mass., M. C. 1807–9.

(24) IV. Deborah,[3] m. John Tisdale.

(25) V. Katharine,[3] m. April 17, 1710, Dea. Samuel Leonard. Their daughter, Hazadiah, m. Rev. John Wales, the first pastor of the church at Raynham; *their* daughter Prudence, m. Rev. Peres Fobes, LL.D., its second pastor, and *their* daughter Nancy, m. Rev. Simeon Doggett, who has also been settled at Raynham. There seems to have been a kind of hereditary charm in the daughters of this family, by whose wand the several ministers of the town of Raynham have been enchanted for three generations. Rev. Samuel Wales, D.D., Professor of Divinity in Yale College, was a son of the above Rev. John.† Hon. John Wales, who was recently chosen by the Legislature of Delaware a member of the U. S. Senate, in place of Hon. Mr. Clayton, appointed Secretary of State, is a son of Prof. Samuel, and thus the 6th generation in descent from John Deane.

(26) VI. Lydia,[3] m. George Hall.

(27) VII. Mercy,[3] m. Daniel Williams.

(28) VIII. Elizabeth,[3] b. about 1688, having d. March 18, 1758, aged 70. She m. Dec. 4, 1707, Dea. Benjamin Williams, who d. Jan. 10, 1757, aged 71.

Isaac,[2] (6) son of John,[1] had

(29) I. Alice,[3] b. Nov. 20, 1678. m Feb. 1, 1699–1700, John King of Raynham.

(30) II. Abigail,[3] b. Nov. 16, 1680. m. —— Torry.

(31) III. Hannah,[3] b. April 24, 1683, m. —— Hodges.

(32) IV. Nathaniel,[3] b. April 25, 1685.

(33) V. Jonathan.[3]

(34) VI. Abiah.[3]

(35) VII. Deborah.[3]

Joseph,[2] (9) son of Walter,[1] had

(36) I. Joseph.[3] From him was descended John G. Deane,[6] Esq., (d. 1839,) of Ellsworth and Portland, a prominent writer on the N. E. Boundary Question.

* From obituary in Chr. Reg. Aug. 23, 1834.

† See Rev. Dr. Fobes's account of the Leonard Family, Mass. Hist. Coll. 1st ser. III. 174.

(37) II. SAMUEL,[3] died without issue.

(38) III. JAMES,[3] died about 1750. Wife Mary.

(39) IV. Sarah,[3] m. —— Reed.

EZRA,[2] (10) son of Walter,[1] had

(40) I. BETHIAH,[3] b. Oct. 14, 1677, d. Nov. 27, 1679.

(41) II. EZRA,[3] b. Oct. 14, 1680, was twice married. His wife Abigail, survived. He was a physician, and resided in Taunton. His family was remarkable for its longevity. The following is an extract from a communication published in the Columbian Reporter, a newspaper printed in Taunton, 1825. We know not the name of the writer. "Dr. Ezra Dean's children were: 1, Ezra, died at the age of 89 years; 2, Theodora, 100; 3, Abijah, [Abigail ?] 95; 4, Bethiah, 96; 5, Nehemiah, 90; 6, James, 90; 7, Seth, 88; 8, Solomon, 61; 9, Elkanah, 87; 10, William, now (1825) living, aged 94; 11, George, 86; 12, Elisha, 83; 13, Nathaniel, 25; 14, Esther, now (1825,) living, aged 92; 15, Prudence, 80; 16, Stephen, 51; united ages, 1307. Eleven of the family lived more than 1000 years, two of whom are now, (1825,) living. Theodora Dean lived to see her children to the fifth generation, and was the mother of the late Dr. Job Godfrey,* of Taunton, who was eminent in his profession for more than half a century."

(42) III. SAMUEL,[3] b. April 11, 1681, d. Feb. 16, 1682–3.

(43) IV. SETH,[3] b. June 3, 1683. Settled at Taunton. From him is descended Rev. Paul Dean,[6] formerly of Boston, now of Easton, Mass., who has published a course of Lectures on the Final Restoration of all men, and various occasional sermons; also, Amos Dean,[6] Esq., of Albany, N. Y., author of the Philosophy of Human Life, Lectures on Phrenology, &c.

(44) V. MARGARET,[3] m.—— Shaw.

(45) VI. EPHRAIM,[3] m. Mary Allen, of Rehoboth. Their son Ezra,[4] m. Jemima, dau. of David Allen, and was the father of Dr. Ezra,[5] late of Biddeford, Maine, now of Cambridge, Mass., who m. 1st, Sarah, dau. of Rev. Paul Coffin, D. D., of Buxton, Maine, 2d, Mary, dau. of Rev. Silas Moody, of Kennebunkport, Maine, and by the latter, the father of Mr. Charles[6] Deane † of Boston, Mass., firm of Waterston, Pray, & Co., who m. Helen, dau. of Robert Waterston, Esq.

BENJAMIN,[2] (11) son of Walter,[1] had

(46) I. NAOMI,[3] b. Nov. 1, 1681, d. Jan. 6, 1681–2.

(47) II. HANNAH,[3] b. Dec. 26, 1682, m. —— Richmond.

(48) III. ISRAEL,[3] b. Feb. 2, 1684–5, d. March 27, 1760, in his 76th year. His widow Ruth, d. April 18, 1769, in her 80th year.

(49) IV. MARY,[3] b. June 15, 1687, m. —— Edson.

(50) V. DAMARIS,[3] b. Sept. 4, 1689, m. Matthew White.

(51) VI. SARAH,[3] b. Aug. 30, 1692, m. —— Danforth.

(52) VII. ELIZABETH,[3] b. March 26, 1694–5, m. —— Richmond.

(53) VIII. MEHITABLE,[3] b. June 9, 1697, m. —— Richmond.

(54) IX. BENJAMIN,[3] b. July 31, 1699, d. Jan. 6, 1785, in his 86th year. He m. Zipporah Dean, dau. of John D. [(16) V.] She died Sept. 27, 1778, in her 75th year.

(55) X. EBENEZER,[3] b. Feb. 24, 1701–2, d. July 30, 1774. He married Rachel Allen, who d. March 3, 1768, in her 75th year. He and his son Joshua,[4] "marched in the same army in defence of their country in the old French war." ‡ Joshua,[4] had a son Joseph,[5] who "was frequently out during the Revolutionary war, and had the command of a company that was called out to support the Courts during Shay's rebellion." § This Joseph[5] was the father of Rev. Artemas Dean,[6] (grad. U. C. 1803.) of New Windsor, N. Y., now living, and his brother, the late Rev. Joshua Dean,[6] (grad. B. U. 1809,) of Groton, N. Y.

(56) XI. LYDIA,[3] b. Dec. 11, 1704.

(57) XII. JOSIAH,[3] b. Oct. 23, 1707, d. March 23, 1709–10.

Note. — We have here given the first three generations of this family. Our notes upon the later generations are very full, comprehending several thousand descendants. We mention this for the benefit of those who may be interested.

* The Proprietors' Records of Taunton are now in the possession of a son of this person, Mr Job Godfrey, of Taunton, to whom we would return thanks for his kindness in permitting us to avail ourselves of the assistance of these valuable records. A daughter of Mr. G. married Mr. Henry A Dean, of this city, a descendant of Walter.

† We would acknowledge our obligations to this gentleman for important suggestions and aid in preparing this article.

‡ Rev. Artemas Dean, MSS. Letters. § Ibid.

PASSENGERS FOR VIRGINIA.

[Communicated by Mr. H. G. Somerby.]

23rd June 1635. Theis under-written names are to be transported to Virginea imbarqued in the America Willm Barker M^{r}; pr. cert: from the Minister of the Towne of Gravesend of their conformity to the orders & disipline of the Church of England.

Name	Age
Richard Sadd	23
Thomas Wakefield	17
Thomas Bennett	22
Steeven Read	24
Willm Stanbridge	27
Henry Barker	18
James Foster	21
Thomas Talbott	20
Richard Young	31
Robert Thomas	20
John Farepoynt	20
Robert Askyn	22
Samuel Awde	24
Miles Fletcher	27
William Evans	23
Lawrence Farebern	23
Mathew Robinson	24
Isack Bull	27
Phillipp Remington	29
Radulph Spragmy	37
George Chaundler	29
Richard Hersey	22
John Robinson	32
Edmond Chipps	19
Tho: Prichard	32
Jonathan Bronsford	21
Willm Cowley	20
John Shawe	16
Richard Gummy	21
Bartholomew Holton	25
John White	21
Thomas Chappell	33
Hugh Fox	24
David Morris	32
Rowland Cotton	22
William Thomas	22
John Yates	20
Richard Wood	36
James Somers	22
David Bromley	15
Walter Brookes	15
Symon Richardson	23
Thomas Jno.son	19
Jo: Averie	20
John Croftes	20
Thomas Broughton	19
Benjamin Wragg	24
Henry Embrie	20
Robert Sabyn	40
George Brookes	35
Thomas Holland	34
Humfrey Belt	20
John Mace	20
Walter Jewell	19
Willm Bucland	19
Launcelot Jackson	18
John Williamson	12
Phillipp Parsons	10
Henry Parsons	14
Andrew Morgan	26
Willm Brookes	17
Richard Harrison	15
Thomas Pratt	17
John Ecles	16
Richard Miller	12
Robert Lamb	16
Thomas Boomer	13
George Dulmare	8
John Underwood	19
Willm Bernard	27
Charles Wallinger	24
Thomas Dymett	23
Ryce Hooe	36
John Carter	54

Women.

Name	Age
Elizabeth Remington	20
Katherin Hibbotts	20
Elizabeth Willis	18
Joan Jobe	18
Ann Nash	22
Elizabeth Phillips	22
Dorothy Standich	22
Susan Death	22
Elizabeth Death	3
Alice Remington	26
Dorothy Baker	18
Elizabeth Baker	18
Sara Colebank	20
Mary Thurrogood	19

4th July 1635. Theis under-written names are to be transported Virginea imbarqued in the Transport of London Edward Walker M^{r} p. Certificate from the Minister of Gravesend of their conformitie to the orders & disipline of the Church of England.

	yeres		
Olliver Van Heck	35	Henry Porter	30
uxor Katherin Van Heck	34	Patrick Woddall	20
Peter Van Heck	7	John Gee	18
Richard Maton	23	Richard Cooper	28
Wm Page	18	Richard Eggleston	24
Robert Kevyn	19	Wm Harbert	15
Peter Smith	25	John Wise	18
Brian McGawyn	3	Thomas Coles	32
Daniell Symson	17	Tho: Williams	18
Patrick Breddy	21	George Ashon	22
Henry Castell	22	Peter Sexton	20
Steeven Block	18	Tho: Johnson	23
Gowen Lancaster	28	Thomas Saunders	20
Robert Farrar	24	John Lee	16
Bryan Glynn	20	Robert Farest	20
Humfrey Hadnet	22	Richard Bick	18
Jo: Woddall	18	Willm Hardisse	22
Willm Wallington	32	Daniell Rose	25
Richard Sharp	15	Richard Anderson	17
Marmaduke Kidson	18	James Phillips	26
Jo: Godfrey	21	Robert Tynman	21
Richard Critch	27	Peter Waller	24
Ellis Baker	21	Richard Petley	22
Jonathan Neale	12	Roger Hollidge	19
Jo: Bush	17	Wm Reddman	18
Wm Nesse	23	Robert Greene	20
Jo: Spreate	20	Henry Meddowes	20
Tho: Steevens	25	George Johnson	19
Jo: Waters	29	John Voss	22
Robt. Fossett	26	Andrew Adams	18
Walter Downes	24	John Wilson	32
Symon Jones	40	Nathan Anley	28
Robert Jenkinson	18	Anthony Grimston	20
Francis Clark	28	Tho: Hatchet	19
Francis Bick	23	Robert Honniborn	21
Thomas Cranfield	14	Jo: Parson	18
Tho: Payne	23	Alexander Burlie	18
Phillip Jones	22	Wm Hart	26
John Goodson	21	Nathaniell Patient	16
Steeven Beane	20	Henry Armstrong	22
Geo: Barber	20	Women.	
Richard Wheatlie	32		
Richard Lloyd	28	Katherin Long	34
Henrie Barnes	22	Elizabeth Sames	19
Tho: Moore	21	Joan Hardiss	18
John Harrison	30	Elizabeth Riley	18
Wm Hudson	20	Ellin Rogerson	20
Wm Mason	30	Elizabeth Lincoln	23
Mark Briggoll	21	Elizabeth Corker	19

Ann Wandall	18	John Drue	26
Sibbell Lakeland	25	John Horne	21
Ellin White	26	Robert Medley	16
Wm White	7 weeks old	Richard Atkinson	21
Ellener Rogers	19	Jo: Pownd	20
Dorothie Charles	20	Edward Rede	17
Hester Brotherton	18	Francis Webster	27
Margaret Watson	18	Jo: Syard	38
Oliff Sprawe	21	Geo: Midland	19
Ann Bristo	22	Wm Watson	24
Ann Gudderidge	23	Harbert Judd	16
Rabecca Lane	22	John Fox	33
Elizabeth Yore	23	Henry Burkett	34
Ralph Golthorp	20	Bennet Freeman	20
Edward Thompson	24	Edward Salter	19
Wm White	37	Robert Covett	25
Robert Lewes	38	Tho: Moore	18
Barnabie Barnes	35	Jo: Russell	16
Edward Ison	20	Edward Hunt	19
John Somerton	24	Robert Beckwith	21
Jo: Russell	14	Jo: Witton	16
Robert Bateman	20	John Harris	28
Wm Cooke	20	Jo: Baylie	42
Henry Bannister	22	Jo: Hathorn	20
Tho: Richardson	26	Edward Drue	18
Jo: Waller	19	Jo: Arp	19
Richard Weaver	27	Edmond Pryme	16

THE PEASE FAMILY.

[By FREDERICK S. PEASE of Albany, N. Y., Member of the N. E. Hist. Geneal. Soc.]

[Continued from page 238.]

The following autograph of (31) V. Nathaniel Pease, [39—4] having been overlooked in the printing office, did not have its appropriate place in the preceding number, and is here subjoined.

Nathl Pease

SIXTH GENERATION, CONTINUED.

(56) VI. (Judge) CALVIN, [95—11] was born Sept. 9, 1776, and died at Warren, Ohio, Sept. 17, 1840. The following obituary notice of him appeared in The Western Reserve Chronicle, published at Warren, O.

"It becomes our painful duty to announce the death of our respected fellow-citizen, the Hon. Calvin Pease. He died at his residence in this village, (Warren, Ohio,) on Tuesday, (17 Sept., 1840,) after an illness of several weeks, during the most of which his pain and sufferings were intense.

"In the early part of his sickness, he became impressed with the belief that he should not recover; but he saw and met the approach of death, the "termination of man's earthly hopes and prospects," with firmness and resignation. For several hours before he expired, he was apparently free from pain, and perfectly composed and tranquil, and his spirit escaped from its frail tenement without a struggle or a groan.

"Judge Pease was born in Suffield, Hartford county, Connecticut, on the 9th day of September, A. D. 1776, and on arriving at manhood, made choice of the legal profession, of which he afterward became so distinguished an ornament. He read law in the office of the Hon. Gideon Granger, late Postmaster-General; and after being admitted to the bar, and practising a short time in his native state, he emigrated to this county in the year 1800, where he has ever since resided. He was, of course, compelled, in common with his associates, to endure the hardships and privations incident to a pioneer in a new country, and it may with truth be said that no individual ever bore them with more manly fortitude.

"He was extensively known throughout the state, and possessed in an eminent degree the confidence and respect of his friends and acquaintances. He has filled various offices for the last forty years of his life, the duties of which he always discharged with great ability, and to the satisfaction of the public.

"He was appointed Prothonotary of the Court of Common Pleas and Quarter Sessions for this county, under the Territorial Government in the year 1800, which office he held for two or three years; and on the admission of the state of Ohio into the Union in 1803, he was appointed President Judge of this Circuit, at that time embracing in its territorial limits a large section of the eastern portion of the state.

"In 1810, he resigned this office, and continued in the practice of the law till after the year 1816. During this interval, in the fall of 1812, he was elected a Senator to the State Legislature. In 1816 he was elected Judge of the Supreme Court, and having been reëlected in 1823, continued in this office till 1830, being a period of fourteen years, during a part of which time he was Chief-Judge of the Supreme Court.

"After leaving the bench, he resumed the practice of the law; and at the bar was distinguished for the same unbending integrity, and vigor and energy of intellect, that marked his career on the bench.

"In 1831 he was elected a representative to the legislature from the county of Trumbull. This was the last office which he was called upon to fill by his fellow-citizens; and for a few of the last years of his life, he felt admonished, by the increasing infirmities of age, to retire from active business to the enjoyment of private life, always so grateful to those who have spent many years in the laborious duties of the legal profession.

"From this brief and imperfect sketch, it will be seen that his life has been one of unusual labor and activity. He possessed a powerful and well disciplined mind, a memory remarkably tenacious, and great facility in the transaction of business.

"To his professional brethren of the bench and the bar, who cherished for him the highest respect and regard, he has left an unsullied reputation, of which they may justly be proud; and an example which all may be ambitious to follow. At the bar he was an honorable practitioner; on the bench an able and upright judge; a useful citizen, a kind and affectionate husband, father, and friend, and an honest man. But he has now gone from us forever, and his death has shed a deep gloom over this community, of which he was so long a member. His memory, however, will be held in grateful recollection by his friends, who loved and respected him, and to whom his death will be a severe bereavement; and to his afflicted family, to whom his life was eminently precious, his death will be an irreparable loss."

On the 2d June, 1804, Mr. Pease married, at Washington, D. C., Laura Grant Risley, daughter of Benjamin and Eunice Risley, who was born at Rutland, Vt., Nov. 30, 1786. Children,

Calvin, b. June 4, 1805, now residing at Warren, Ohio; Laura Maria, b. Feb. 28, 1807, m. George W. Tallmadge, youngest son of Col. Benjamin Tallmadge of Litchfield, Ct., Sept. 13, 1824; Benjamin R., b. Feb. 22, 1809, d. Aug. 3, 1815; Charles, b. Feb. 7, 1811, m. in Boardman, Ohio, to Mary E. Kirtland, dau. of Jared P. Kirtland, July 24, 1832, and resides in Warren, Ohio; Lawrence, b. May 15, 1814, d. July 19, 1815; Nancy, b. June 29, 1816, m. in Warren, June 29, 1836, John Erwin, son of Capt. Samuel Erwin of Painted Post, Steuben Co., N. Y.; Cornelia G., b. May 11, 1820, m. Frederick Kinsman of Kinsman, Ohio, March 25, 1840.

(57) VI. Levi, [97—2.] was born in 1739. He was familiarly known as Captain Levi Pease. Whether he held the office in the Revolutionary Army, in which he served for a time, or was a captain of militia after the war, is unknown. At the commencement of the war he lived in Blandford, Ms. He, with his wife Hannah, removed from Somers, Ct., to Shrewsbury, Ms., about 1794. Having outlived all his children, he died, Jan. 28, 1824, aged 84. His widow died June 14, 1832, aged 93. He was by trade a blacksmith. He was extensively engaged in running stages; and established a line between Shrewsbury and Boston, which was the first in Massachusetts, and probably in America. He procured the first charter for a turnpike road that was granted in Massachusetts. He had a faithful negro, who, when his health declined, took charge of his stage affairs to good advantage.

He was actively and efficiently employed in the war in various ways. Wadsworth of Hartford, who was commissary-general, employed him to purchase beeves and horses for the army. General Thomas, who was then on the frontier, entrusted him to be bearer of despatches. On account of the hazardous nature of this employment, he was obliged to use extreme caution, in order to preserve his papers and his life. Having frequent occasion to travel on the lakes, he lay concealed in secluded places in the daytime, and pursued his journey in the night. When the moon shone bright, he would pull far out into the lake, and, lying nearly flat on his back, with his feet towards the bow of his boat, propelled it by using his hands as paddles, thus concealing himself from the view of the shore. He foraged for the French army in its march to Yorktown. It is related of him that he had a fine span of horses, which he desired to sell to General Washington, at the time when he had the command near Boston, and that the General made an appointment to meet him at a certain time and place; but Pease being a few minutes too late, lost the opportunity of seeing him at that time, for the General had been there and gone. He was a gainer, however, by the hint which he took relative to punctuality.

Some of the foregoing facts are recorded in Ward's History of Shrewsbury. His children are,

Hannah, who married Thomas Henry Kemble of Boston, in 1796; Levi, who married Mary Gill, and settled in Northborough, where he died, June 20, 1808, aged 40; Lemuel, who died in Shrewsbury, Sept. 3, 1816, aged

45; Lorey, or Loring, who married Rebecca Bruce of Northborough, March 18, 1798, and died in Shrewsbury, 1811, aged 37; Mary, who married Perry Chapin of Worcester, in 1807, and died there.

(58) VI. WILLIAM, [99—4.] About the year 1787, he, with his family, lived in the north part of New Hartford, Ct. One of his sons, Elijah, lived with Col. Moses Kellogg, in that town, 1791–2. He had four sons, viz.: William, Walter, Elijah, and George. William served an apprenticeship at blacksmithing, and established himself in the business at Lanesborough, Mass., where Elijah and George came and learned the trade of him. The three then removed to Charlotte, Vermont, and carried on their business there. Walter removed to Windsor, Ct., and engaged in the manufacture of hats. It is related of the father, that he assisted in the removal of the family of Mr. Jesse Goodwin, who lived near him, to Canada. "While on the lake," (probably Champlain,) they discovered a bear swimming some distance off the shore; and wanting a little sport, gave him so close a chase with their boat, that in self-defence, he turned upon them, got into the boat, and seized Mr. Pease; he was, however, beaten off, without much injury on either side. Issue,

William, m. Stala Hickok, of Lanesborough, Mass.; Walter, removed to Windsor, Ct.; Elijah, m. Abi Baker, of Lanesborough; George, m. a Sheldon, of Charlotte, Vt.; Ann, m. Lyman Wooster, of Litchfield, Ct.; Polly, m. James Walling, of Canaan, Ct.; Minerva, m. John Sherman, of Charlotte, Vt.

(59) VI. ROBERT, [102—1.] was born about 1749, and died 1827, aged 78. Issue,

Oliver, who has children, and is supposed to live in Somers; Anna; Eunice; Roxana. One of the daughters married the Rev. Luke Wood.

(60) VI. STEPHEN, [103—2.] was born about 1755, lived in Somers, and died there, in 1838. Had two or three wives. Children,

Erastus; Enos; Azel.

(61) VI. ABNER, [104—3.] was born Nov. 9, 1757, married Chloe Viets, of Becket, Mass., May 25, 1785. He removed from Somers to Blandford, when he was about 25 years old, where he was living in 1847. Children,

Levi, b. 29 May, 1787, d. 5 June, 1806; Eli, b. Jan. 23, 1793, m. Cynthia White, of Longmeadow, Dec. 3, 1819, resides at the homestead, in Blandford; Ruth, b. 22 Sept., 1789, m. Orrin Sage, of Blandford, 1817; Chloe, b. Nov. 30, 1796, died 17 Sept., 1802.

(62) VI. ALPHEUS, [106—5.] was born about 1762, married 1st, Olive Anderson, 1787, who died June, 1799; 2nd, Dorothy Spenen, April, 1801. He removed to Lewis County, N. Y., in 1803, and died in Loyden, Lewis Co., April, 1816. He served in the revolutionary war, was taken prisoner by the British, and afterwards exchanged. Children by first wife,

Lucy; Jabez, m. 1st, Fanny Dewey, 2nd, Almira Spinning; Lyman; Olive; Hannah.

Children by second wife,

Alpheus, b. 11 Sept., 1803; Charles, b. 16 June, 1804; Jonathan A. S., b. 8 March, 1810, m. Emily Terry, March, 1840.

(63) VI. EMERY, [108—1.] had children,

Emery; Luman; Sybil; Marcia; Mary.

(64) VI. GILES, [111—1.] was born April 13, 1763, and died Sept. 26, 1823. He married Jerusha Pitkin, daughter of Thomas Pitkin, Sept. 7, 1786, who was born Jan. 27, 1767, and was living in 1847. Their children are,

Theodore, b. Jan. 30, 1789, d. in Hartford, Ct., July 26, 1819. He m. Sarah, dau. of John Russell, of Somers, about 1810, and removed to Hartford, in 1812, or 1813. Was a merchant; Noah, b. July 1, 1792, m. Lucinda, dau. of John Russell, of Somers, about

1812; Augustus, b. Oct. 3, 1793, d. in Arcadia, Madison Co., Missouri, in 1844. He m. Elizabeth McKinstry, of Ellington, Ct. Was a merchant. He removed to Colchester, Ct., about 1818; thence, after the death of his brother Theodore, to Hartford; thence, about 1830, to Utica; thence, after some years, to Watertown; thence, back to Hartford; and thence, to Missouri, where he died; Jerusha, b. July 20, 1796, m. Israel Kellogg, of Somers. She has lived in West Springfield, Mass., and in 1847, she lived at Rockville, Ct.; Rebecca, b. Jan. 27, 1798, m Cyrus, son of John Russell, of Somers, and removed to Missouri, about 1838; Henry, b. April 12, 1800, m. Mary Warburton, of Vernon, Ct., dau. of the Mr. Warburton who introduced into this country machinery for the manufacture of Cotton. He removed with his brother Theodore to Hartford, in 1812, or 1813; thence, to Missouri, in 1828, or 1830; thence to Rushville, Schuyler Co., Ill., about 1843, where he now resides; Martin, b. 1 June, 1802, d. in Arcadia, Madison Co., Missouri, Sept. 1846, m. Flavia, dau. of Dea. Solomon Billings, of Somers. He removed to Hartford, about 1825, and in a few years to Ohio, and about 1839, to Missouri; Giles, b. Dec. 28, 1804, d. Feb. 7, 1805; Giles, b. Dec. 2, 1805, m. Mabel R., dau. of William Moseley, of Wilbraham, Mass. He is a Congregationalist minister of the Gospel. After his ordination as an Evangelist, he labored several years in Connecticut, Massachusetts, and Rhode Island; was installed over a Church in Lowell, Mass., in 1833, and on account of failure of health, received a dismission in 1835. In 1842, he settled in Sandwich, Mass.; Mary, b. April 5, 1808, m. Edwin W., son of Col. Oliver Collins, of Somers, Ct. After her marriage, she removed to Rochester, N. Y., where she has since resided; Sanford, b. June 10, 1810, d. in Greenville, Bond Co., Ill., while on his way to Missouri. He m. a Hitchcock, who died soon afterwards.

(65) VI. Aaron, [115—1.] had children,

Hannah, m. two or three times, had children by each marriage, and is now, (1848,) the widow Benjamin; Huldah, m. Pliny Cadwell, of Wilbraham, Mass., and is now a widow. Had children; Tabitha, m. Dudley Summers, of Chatham, Ct., and is now a widow. Had children; Aurelia, m. —— Gilbut, of Tolland, Ct., and had children; Ruth, d. when a young lady; Jerusha, m. Joseph Sheldon, of Hartford, died, and left children; Aaron, resides in Middletown, Ct.; Agift, resides in Middletown, Ct.; Randolph, resides in Middletown, Ct.; Levi, died about 1843.

(66) VI. Stone, [116—2.] had a son, Chauncey.

(67) VI. Phineas, [117—1.] was born in Enfield, Ct., Jan. 9, 1755, married Betsey Lawrence, daughter of Nehemiah Lawrence, of Canaan, Ct., Nov. 25, 1799. He died at Stockbridge, Mass., the place of his residence, July 11, 1836. His widow died April 10, 1837, aged 74. He was a tanner and shoemaker. He served as a musician in the revolutionary war. Children,

Flavius, b. Nov. 23, 1780, m. Eleanor Day, Sept. 22, 1804, d. March 6, 1845. His widow died Feb. 2, 1847, aged 63; Sarah B., b. Jan. 30, 1783, m. Minories Day, Aug. 21, 1804; Pelea, b. Feb. 6, 1785, m. Asahel Byington, Sept. 10, 1807, d. at Carlton, N. Y., Sept. 4, 1828; Martha A., b. Dec. 19, 1786, d. Sept. 29, 1847; Elizabeth L., b. Oct. 16, 1788, m. Alfred Avery, Oct. 15, 1816; Electa, b. Feb. 22, 1791, m. Henry Lincoln, Nov. 10, 1815; Phineas, b. Dec. 19, 1792, d. at Rochester, N. Y., Sept. 3, 1818; Peter P., b. April 12, 1795, m. Ruth Crocker, July 12, 1821, and lives at Oberlin, Ohio; Hiram A., b. April 19, 1797, m. Lydia Remile, May 3, 1819, lives in Oberlin, Ohio; Alonzo, b. Aug. 4, 1799, was drowned, 1802; Aurelia, b. Aug. 7, 1801, m. Daniel F. Milliken, Jan. 6, 1820; Amanda S., b. April 18, 1804, m. Ira Patterson, Aug. 28, 1837.

(68) VI. Calvin Pease [118—2.] was born in Enfield, Ct., Sept. 14, 1757, married Sally, daughter of Titus Ives, of Norfolk, Ct., for his first wife, who was the mother of all his children. His second wife, who still survives him, was Susan, widow of Joseph Benjamin, of Sheffield, or Egremont, Mass. He was a farmer, and for many years an Inn-keeper in Canaan, Ct., where he died. He was in the revolutionary war, as drummer. Children,

Salmon,* b. June 14, 1783, m. June 14, 1803, Matilda, dau. of Doct. Thomas Huntington, of Canaan, Ct., who was a native of Norwich, Ct., and for some time resided in Ashford,

* The compiler is his first born.

Ct. He lived in Canaan, Ct., until the fall of 1826, when he removed to Charlotte, Vermont; Prudden. b. May 1, 1789, d. Dec. 1, 1838, m. 5th March, 1816, Lucy Williams, of Canaan, Ct.; Sally, b. May 1, 1792, d. young.

(69) VI. Allen, [120—4.] was born in Enfield, Windsor, or Goshen, Ct., Oct. 12, 1762, and died in Sheffield, Mass., April 8, 1843. His first wife was Rachel Tibballs, of Norfolk, Ct., who was born Oct. 6, 1767, and died Oct. 4, 1798. His second wife was Tamsin Sears, of Sharon, Ct., who was born Dec. 1775. He was a clothier. Children,

Artemesia, b. Oct. 11, 1787, d. Jan. 21, 1789; Electa, b. Sept. 6, 1793, m. James Collar; Uri, b. Feb. 20, 1794, d. Oct. 11, 1798; Sarah, b. Sept. 15, 1795, m. Henry Sardam; Harlow, b. April 17, 1798, m. Ann Jane Clark, of Sheffield, Mass., Jan. 30, 1826; Eunice, b. March 13, 1806, m. Philo C. Howland; John S., b. July 17, 1807, m. Emily Ingram.

(70) VI. Nathaniel, [121—5.] was born in Goshen, Ct., Oct. 22, 1764, died at Poughkeepsie, N. Y., Nov. 6, 1815, married Jerusha, daughter of Deacon —— Hall, of Norfolk, Ct. He was a blacksmith. Children,

Dudley S., b. March 5, 1785, m. 1st, Leurilly Loomis, Nov. 14, 1805; 2nd, Maria Sears, Nov. 1810; 3d, Sarah Kelley, 1814; Grove A., b. in Norfolk, Litchfield Co., Ct., Aug. 4, 1789, m. Harriett S., dau. of Joshua R. Jewett, of Granby, Ct., May 2, 1814; Almira, b. 1792, m. Oliver Dubois, 1817, and removed to New Orleans; Elizabeth, b. 1795, m. a Mr. Anthony, of Zanesville, Ohio.

(71) VI. Obadiah, [122—6.] was born in Goshen, Ct., Nov. 21, 1766, died in Norfolk, Feb. 10, 1809, married Daziah Pettibone, of Norfolk. He was a tanner and shoemaker. Children,

Augustus P., b. June 8, 1792, m. Almira Holt, dau. of Stephen Holt, of Norfolk, Ct., Jan. 1, 1818, d. 11 July, 1848; Obadia, b. Dec. 1, 1798, m. Mary E., eldest dau. of James Brewster, New Haven, Ct., April 28, 1830; Daziah, b. Oct. 10, 1789, m. Abel Camp, of Litchfield, Ct., Feb. 22, 1808; Harriet Maria, b. Feb. 6, 1795, m. Jedediah Phelps, of Norfolk, Ct., April 16, 1818; Agnes, b. July 13, 1800, d. in infancy; Emily Agnes, b. Nov. 20, 1804, m. Marshall H. Weed, of Litchfield, April 2, 1834.

(72) VI. Earl P. Pease [128—12.] was born in Norfolk, Ct., July 30, 1778, married Mary, daughter of Joseph Ives, of New Haven, Ct., who at the time of her marriage, lived with her father, in Canaan, Ct. A manufacturer of Woollens. Children.

Joseph I., b. Aug. 9, 1809, m. Mary Spencer, of Baltimore, Md., Dec. 8, 1841; Richard H., b. Feb. 19, 1813, m. Mary E. Dawes, of Philadelphia, June 10, 1835: Roger M. S., b. Jan. 13, 1822, m. Abby E. Slack, of Albany, Jan. 26, 1841; Mary Eliza, b. March 19, 1803, m. Enoch Noyes, at Hartford, March 19, 1828, d. at Albany, Nov. 21, 1829.

(73) VI. Ebenezer, [130—1.] married Huldah, daughter of Nathaniel Pease, who was the eldest son of Mirriam and Nathaniel, [(25) V.] Children,

John B. b. Sep. 9, 1774, at Enfield, Ct., m. Freelove Frink, of Preston, Ct., 1799. Resides in Whitesborough, N. Y. Children, Harman, b. 1800, m. Hannah S. Moyston, of Schenectady; Henry H., b. July 25, 1804, m. Lydia Harris, of Rhode Island; removed to Mississippi, in 1836. His wife died there the same year, and in 1840, he was thrown from his carriage and instantly killed; Lewis S., b. Oct. 13, 1806, removed to Mississippi in 1835, and died of fever, 14 April, 1837; John, b. Jan. 28, 1809, m. Elizabeth Debrill, of Nashville, removed to Miss., and died of fever, Aug. 1842; James M., b. Sept. 14, 1811, m. Louisa Van Antwerp, of Brooklyn, N. Y., and removed to Miss. He was shot by an enemy and killed on his plantation, Oct. 24, 1842; William I., was b. Sept. 5, 1813, removed to Miss., and died of fever, April 21, 1837; Charles E., was b. Feb. 2, 1816, went to Miss. in the fall of 1842, and died there March 24, 1843. George, m. Esther Thompson, of Goshen, Ct., and removed to Ohio. Ebenezer, removed to Ohio, married there, and died in 1813; Nathaniel, m. Miss Buell, of Galway, N. Y.; Huldah, m. Charles Terry, of Enfield, Ct.; Lucretia, m. Truman Barnard, of Whitestown, N. Y.; Ann, m. Shelburn Ives, of Litchfield, Ct.; Hepsibah; Martha.

(74) VI. James, [131—2] married Lucy Meacham. Issue,

Jabez, James; Erastus; Lucy; Nancy; Aurelia.

(75) VI. Peter, [132—3.] married Huldah Stebbins, of Springfield, Ms. Issue,

Francis, m. a Pease of Enfield; William, b. 1790, m. Electa Crittenden, of Seneca, Ontario Co., N. Y., 1814, and resides in Buffalo; Peter P., died in South Carolina; Horatio N., b. 1795, m. a Chapin of Mackinaw; Margaret, b. 1797, m. Horace Hawkins; Mary, b. 1799, m. Cherry Allen, of Enfield; Huldah, b. 1804, m. Solomon Silsbee, of Reading, Steuben Co., N. Y.

(76) VI. Rufus, [133—1.] had children,

Alpheus; Enos; Augustus; Rufus; Cooley.

(77) VI. Abner, [134—1.] married Polly Blackman, daughter of Maj. Blackman, of Middletown, Ct. Had children,

James; John; Samuel, who is a lawyer at Massillon, Ohio; Alden; Elizabeth; Sally; Polly; Fanny.

(78) VI. James, [135—2.] married Lucy Day, of Chester, Mass. Issue,

Dexter; Channing D., m. Melinda Flint, of Worcester. Otsego Co., N. Y.; Erastus; John F.; Joshua I.; Ira; James; Lucy; Sybil; Clarissa A.

(79) VI. John, [137—4.] married Belinda Hayes, of Brattleboro', Vt., died Sept., 1804. Had a son, John.

(80) VI. Samuel, [138—5.] married Clarissa Horton, of Vermont, and had two sons, Harry G., and John, who died young.

(81) VI. Asaph, [146—8.] married Clotilda Hoyt, of Guilford, Ct., 1805. Children,

Lumas, d. young; Mary Clotilda; Lumas H., graduated at Williams College, 1815, and was ordained a minister of the Gospel, by the Presbytery of Albany; Julius W., m. Mary Hotchkiss, of Burlington, Ct., 1844; Laura P.

(82) VI. Alvah, [148—10.] married Abigail Severance, of Hartford, Ct. He lived in Colebrook, Ct., during the birth of his children, and at the death of his wife; but has since removed to Worcester, Mass., and married a second wife. Children,

Caroline M., m. Levi Pease, of Sandisfield, 2d son of Oliver Pease of Blissfield, Michigan; Erastus C., m. Lucy Rice, of Southbridge, Mass.; Richard S., m. Eliza Nichols, of Willimantic, Ct.; Warren W.

(83) VI. Moses, [149—1.] Children,

Moses; Barnabas; Julius; Frederick.

(84) VI. Lemuel, [150—2.] Children,

Walter, 2nd.; Erastus.

(85) VI. Benjamin, [151—3.] Children,

Benjamin; Alfred.

(86) VI. Abiel, [152—1.] One son, Abiel.

(87) VI. Dan, [154—2.] married 1st, Nabby Johnson; 2nd, Harriet Bartlett, of Munson, by whom he had,

Reuben; Truman; James; Harriet; Julia; Adalaide; Abigail.

(88) VI. Simeon, [156—1.] had children,

Wells; Loren; Kellogg; and three sons in Tompkins Co., N. Y.

(89) VI. Israel, [157—2.] married Mary Pease, granddaughter of Jonathan Pease, of Ellington, Ct., in 1789, removed to Middlefield, Mass., and resided there until his death, about 1846. Children,

Mary; Israel; Daniel; Harvey; Nancy; Horace; Nial; Oliver; Austin; Abial.

(90) VI. Dan, [159—4.] was born in Enfield, Ct., April 25, 1773. He removed to Middlefield, Mass., 1794, married Sally Wright, of Middlefield, 1799, who died March 5, 1848, aged 66. They had five sons and six

daughters, all of whom but Mary, the third child, are still living. The sons are all married, and settled in Middlefield; and the daughters are all married, and settled in that, and the adjoining towns. The father and all the sons are farmers, and the daughters all married farmers. Names of children,

Dan, b. Oct. 21, 1802, m. Polly Root, of Middlefield; Sally, b. Dec. 19, 1803, m. Harvey Root. of Middlefield; Mary, b. Nov. 19, 1805, d. Jan. 20, 1837; Walter, b. Sept. 12, 1807, m. Mary Ingham, of Middlefield; Sybil, b. Jan. 27, 1810, m. Ebenezer Smith of Middlefield; Eldridge, b. March 14 1812, m. Persis Bull, of Peru; Morgan, b. Sept. 25, 1814, m. Harriet Metcalf, of Middlefield; Amanda, b. Feb. 10, 1817, m George Cram, of Washington; Arnold, b. April 18, 1819, m. Charlotte B. Stevens, of Chester, June 15, 1848; Harriet, b. March 26, 1822, m. Hezekiah Taylor, of Westfield; Laura Ann, b. April 3, 1824, m. William Stevens, of Chester.

(91) VI. EZEKIEL, [160—1.] married about 1756. Had children,

Hannah, b. Dec. 22, 1757; Susannah, Jan. 7, 1760; Jemima, b. Jan. 20, 1762; Robica, b. May 11, 1764; Obadiah, b. Sept. 3, 1766; Eleanor, b. July 10, 1768; Elijah, b. July 13, 1770; Ambrose, b. July 21, 1772; Abigail, b. April 5, 1774; Lydia, b. Dec. 5, 1777.

(92) VI. HENRY, [162—2.] was born in Sandisfield, Mass., —— 1772, married Huldah Tilden, 1793, removed to Livonia, Livingston Co., N. Y., Sept. 1805, where he died Jan. 8, 1827, aged 55. His widow married Silas Whitney, of Geneseo, N. Y., Aug. 6, 1836, and died Oct. 4, 1846, aged 72. Children.

Born in Sandisfield:—Henry, b. March, 1794, m. Polly Gould, March 19, 1817, who d. Aug. 7, 1837. His second wife was Rowena Spafford, whom he m. Jan. 16, 1838. A farmer; William C., b. Aug. 18, 1795, m. Mrs. Hannah Lee, of Livonia, March 10, 1825. A farmer; Huldah, b. Oct. 24, 1796, m. Turner Chappell, of Avon, March 16, 1815, who d. Aug. 13, 1826. She d. Sept. 5, 1826; Thomas, b. July 13, 1798, m. 1st, Rebecca Rull, of Lima, Sept. 19, 1824, who d. March 25, 1831, 2d, Jane Trimble, of Phelps, May 10, 1832; Elizabeth, b. Jan. 13, 1800, m. Doct. Justin Gates, of Mendon, Jan. 20, 1819, who d. in Rochester, Jan. 30, 1848; Robert, b. Oct. 23, 1801; Hannah, b. May 22, 1803, m. Giles B. Bliss, Feb. 22, 1825. She d. Feb. 4, 1841. He d. March 4, 1841.

Born in Livonia, Livingston Co., N. Y.:—Belinda, b. Dec. 3, 1807; Harvey, b. March 17, 1808, m. Mary Hicks of Avon, March 6, 1834; Austin, b. Nov. 22, 1809. m. Martha Osborn, of Rochester, Dec. 21, 1834; Chandler, b. Nov. 25, 1811, m. Laurena Gale, of Rochester, Dec. 24, 1835, who d. Feb. 22, 1836, 2d wife, Mary Patrick, of Palmyra, m. June 15, 1839; Jane, b. March 31, 1814, m. A. M. Chapin, of Livonia, July 16, 1835; James H., b. June 17, 1817; Emery T., and Emily, twins, b. Sept. 20, 1820; former, m. Mary B. Whaley, of Avon, Feb. 8, 1848.

(93) VI. REUBEN, [164—3.] had a son, Ashmun.

Issue of 18—3, *Pelatiah, Generation IV., who was born in Enfield, in* 1709, *viz.:*

Pelatiah, who removed to Alstead, N. H.; Jonathan, d. in Schenectady, 1760, aged 18; Samuel, who settled on the North East part of the homestead. He was three times married, his first wife was Hannah Booth, of East Windsor, the second was a Sexton. Two of his sons were Samuel and Jonathan; John, b. Jan. 14, 1749, d. Dec. 15, 1820, settled on the West part of the homestead, m. a Booth, of East Windsor (*); Jemima, m. Eldad Phelps.

Issue of John. (*)

John, b. Aug. 23, 1777 (**); Asher, m. a Chaffee, and lives in Conway, Mass.; Lyman m. a Chaffee, and lives in Jackson, Michigan.

Issue of John. (**)

He married Patty Allen, (who was born in East Windsor, May 11, 1778,) on the 25th of April, 1799; removed to Conway, Mass., 2 May, 1800, thence to Ashfield, Mass., Feb. 20, 1811.

Patty, b. March 19, 1800, m. Sumner Graves; John, b. Nov. 24. 1801, m. Louisa Bartlett, and lives in Utica; Mirriam, b. March 14, 1804, m. Lovell H. Okes; David A., b. Dec. 9, 1805, m. Sophia Wilcox, of Utica, resides in Cincinnati, Ohio, is a physician; Luman, b. Aug. 26, 1808, m. Gratia Hawkes, removed to Vernon, Richland Co., Ohio; Diantha, b. Feb. 11, 1810, m. Daniel Clark; Hart F., b. Dec. 27, 1811, m. an Ives, of New Haven, Ct., is a clergyman; Maronett, b. Nov. 21, 1813, m. James Childs; Reuel, b. Oct. 6, 1815, m. Sarah Macumber, lives in Ashfield; George, b. March 20, 1817, m. Almira Griffin, of

New Haven, Ct., d. at Kinderhook, (Valatie,) N. Y., Aug. 8, 1848, was a physician; Liberty, b. Dec. 19, 1822, m. Emeline Paine, removed to Wisconsin, thence back to Ashfield.

Issue of 38—3, *Aaron, Generation V., who died* 1806, *aged* 82. *Additional.*

ELAM, was born in Enfield, 1771, married Jemima Bush, 1791, by whom he had two sons and eight daughters. The eldest son, Augustus Elam, was born 1805, and died 1820; the second, Henry Granville, was born 1815, and died 1823. Three of the daughters have died, and three are unmarried, and live at home. He has one son living, aged 13, by a second marriage. He removed to Charlton, Saratoga Co., N. Y., 1798, thence to Lee, Oneida Co., in 1800, thence to Denmark, Lewis Co., in 1822, thence to Copenhagen, Lewis Co., in 1834–5, where he now resides.

EPHRAIM, was born in Enfield. In 1804, he removed to Lee, Oneida Co., N. Y., where he resided until his death, in 1844. He had six children, the two eldest of whom were daughters, who died young. The four remaining were sons, two only of whom are living.

Wyllys, d. in February, 1848; Arvin B., resides in Lee, Oneida Co.; Orrin, lives in Wisconsin.

In Dugdale's History of Old St. Paul's Cathedral, London, there is mentioned the name of John Pease, LL.D., Prebendary of Coddington Manor, collated Aug 15, 1471.

In "Fuller's Worthies," or landed gentry of England, in the County of Derby, is John *Peese*, about 1520.

James and Jabez Pease, who were probably great-grandsons of Ebenezer, born 1698, — who married Mindwell Sexton, and had a son Ebenezer, who died in 1784, who had a son James, who married Lucy Meacham, and had children, Jabez, James, Erastus, Lucy, Nancy, and Aurelia, — appear to have been residents of Albany, in 1813 and 1814, and dealers in leather, at 61 Lion Street.

In 1814, Benjamin F. Pease, whose parentage cannot be traced, appears to have lived at 56 South Market Street, Albany.

Mr. Richard L. Pease, of Edgartown, is preparing a History of Martha's Vineyard, which is designed to embrace a genealogy of the Pease families which have originated on that island. Any facts relative to the subject will be thankfully received, and ably disposed of by him.

To those who may fail to find their names within the scope of this publication, the compiler would most respectfully state, that to some of his letters no responses have been made.

Some interesting facts for the extension of this memoir, which could not practicably be carried beyond its present limit, will be in due time deposited in the archives of the Genealogical Society, for the use of a future compiler.

REGISTER OF THE DEATHS IN NORTHAMPTON, MS.,

FROM ITS FIRST SETTLEMENT IN 1653 TO 1700.

[Communicated by MR. SAMUEL W. LEE, of that place.]

[Continued from page 176.]

1676, *February* 3, Thomas Bascom's wife; 19 *May*, Jones Benst, John Miller, Peter Jerrin, Thomas Roberts, John Lanberow, Samuel Ransford, Will Howard, John Foster, John Whitrig, Jacob Burton, Joseph Fowler, George Bugle, Thomas Lyon, John Walker, and

Capt. William Turner, all slain by Indians;* 22 *May*, Elizabeth, wife of Joshua Pomeroy, Mary, dau. of Samuel Marshall; 27 *May*, Sarah Bartlett; wife of Alexander Bartlett; 31 *May*, Grace, wife of Timothy Baker; 3 *July*, Robert Bartlett's widow; 6 *July*, Thomas, son of Nehemiah Allen; 23 *July*, Eliakim Pomeroy; 23 *August*, son of Solomon Stoddard; 30 *October*, son of John Woodward; 9 *November*, Thomas Ford; 29 *December*, Joye Lanckton.

1677, *June* 1, William Hannum.

1678, *March* 7, John Stebbins; 17 *March*, James Hubbard; 8 *May*, Rebeckah, wife of John Clark; 30 *August*, Rebeckah Nims; 16 *September*, Experience, dau. of Jed. Strong; 1 *December*, Thomas Mason.

1679, *March* 24, John Brotton's son; 29 *April*, Joan Whitton.

1680, *June* 27, John Bushrod; 11 *August*, Preserved, son of Ebenezer Strong; 11 *September*, Hannah Davis; Samuel Curtis; Two children of Joseph Edwards; 27 *October*, Hannah Alexander.

1681, *February* 24, M. Sheldon; 17 *May*, Freedom, wife of Jedediah Strong; 3 *June*, Joseph Stebbins; 30 *June*, Elizabeth, dau. of John Taylor; 24 *July*, Widow Wright; 2 *August*, Jonathan Lanckton.

1682, *August* 23, Dorothy Hawley; 25 *August*, son of Thomas Alvord; 26 *August*, Elizabeth Davis.

1683, *May* 8, Samuel Parsons; Sarah King; 19 *June*, John Bushrod; 11 *August*, Samuel Lanckton; *August*, Richard Ingraham; 8 *September*, Samuel French; 16 *September*, Joan Ingraham; 22 *November*, Mehitable Root; 16 *December*, Thankful Wright.

1684, *April* 17, Mary Sheldon; *May*, Susanna Alexander; 27 *June*, Nehemiah Allen, Jonathan Parsons; 31 *August*, Mary, dau. of Thomas Strong.

1685, *January* 23, John Pomeroy; 14 *March*, Ruth Wright; 7 *April*, Henry Woodward, killed at corn mill.

1686, *June* 7, Dorcas Wright; 24 June, Jacob Edwards; ——— Weller; 14 *November*, Bethiah Lyman; child of John Pomroy; 24 *December*, Keziah Lyman.

1687, *April* 12, Thomas Hosmer; John Hunt; 15 *April*, Mary Clesson; 2 *May*, Abigail Clark; 6 *May*, Elizabeth Burt; 21 *May*, William Gurley, drowned; 4 *June*, Esther Lyman; 3 *September*, Elizabeth Cook; 3 *October*, Alexander Alvord; 13 *November*, Goodwife Hulberd.

1688, *May* 8, Sarah, wife of William Clark; 6 *July*, Abigail, wife of Elder John Strong; 22 *July*, Thomas Alvord.

1689, *March* 7, Hannah Hannum; 16 *April*, John Holton; 3 *May*, Hannah Burt; 14 *May*, Sarah Porter; 16 *May*, John Porter; James Wright; 8 *July*, Clemence Hunt; Silence Allen; 15 *July*, Abigail Strong; 25 *July*, James North; Abigail King; 26 *July*, Freedom French; Haines Kingsley; 12 *August*, Seth Paine; 11 *September*, Thomas Bascom; 20 *September*, Experience Pope; 21 *September*, Jonathan Kingsley; 29 *September*, Hewet Strong; 2 *October*, Mary Sheldon; Thomas Stebbins; 3 *October*, Thomas Strong; Ebenezer Strong's twin children; John Parsons; 30 *October*, Azariah Strong.

* These men were slain in what is called "The Fall Fight." Dr. I. Mather says (Brief Hist. 30,) the English under Capts. Turner and Holioke, finding the Indians there (at the Falls,) "secure indeed, yea, all asleep, without having any scouts abroad. so that our souldiers came and put their Guns into their Wigwams, before the Indians were aware of them, and made a great and notable slaughter amongst them." See also Hubbard, Nar. 87—8, and Williams's Life of Williams, 88, where will be found a most valuable paper, giving the names of the descendants of many engaged in the "Fall Fight."—Pub.

1690, 13 *April*, Samuel Lyman; Caleb Pomeroy; 1 *May*, Nathaniel Phelps; 5 *May*, Elizabeth Bushrod; 19 *May*, Mary Mason; 26 *May*, Samuel Wright; 15 *July*, William Miller; 18 *July*, Lieut. Wm. Clark; 26 *July*, Samuel Davis; 13 *August*, Elizabeth Woodward; 20 *August*, Ensign John Lyman; 2 *September*, Elizabeth Parsons; 4 *September*, Alexander Edwards; 5 *September*, Maj. Aaron Cook; 9 *September*, David Burt; 16 *September*, Ruth Bridgman; 20 *September*, Hepzibah Lyman; William Janes; 21 *September*, Joseph Edwards; 29 *September*, Hezekiah Root, 3 *October*, Goodwife Edwards: 7 *October*, Mary Brotton; 21 *October*, Peter Bushrod; 23 *October*, Joseph Root; *December*, Elizabeth Clark.

1691, *January* 22, Sarah Wait; 26 *January*, Esther Stebbins; 28 *January*, Hannah Root; 8 *February*, Joseph Lyman; 12 *February*, Ebenezer Wright's child; 14 *February*, Thomas Root's child; 17 *February*, Elizabeth Wright; 28 *February*, Moses Lyman; 12 *August*, Deacon Holton; *September*, Hannah Wright; 30 *September*, Deacon Jonathan Hunt; 2 *November*, Mary Clapp; 9 *November*, Hepzibah Edwards; 16 *November*, Mary Holton; 18 *November*, Caleb Pomeroy; 25 *November*, Abigail Root; 29 *November*, Hannah Pomeroy; 1 *December*, Ann Webb; 7 *December*, Sarah Kingsley; 8 *December*, Sarah Baker; 3 *December*, Josiah Alvord; 15 *December*, Noah Marshall; *December*, Elizabeth Danks; Nathaniel Bartlett.

1692, 13 *February*, Christopher Smith; 18 *February*, Joseph Lyman; 24 *February*, Robert Danks; 4 *March*, Jeremiah Alvord; 8 *March*, Daniel Edwards; 9 *March*, John Kingsley; 16 *March*, Thankful Webb; 9 *March*, John Taylor; 12 *June*, Ruth Hulberd; 8 *September*, Ebenezer Brotton; *September*, Experience Wright; Wait Taylor.

1693, *February* 11, Hannah Clark; *June*, Hepzibah Wright; 4 *October*, Mary Brotton; 5 *October*, Martha Root; 28 *October*, Nathaniel Edwards; 11 *November*, Stephen Wright.

1694, *March* 25, Hewet Strong; 3 *March*, Jonathan Webb; 7 *April*, William Hulberd; 17 *June*, Thomas Root, Sen.; 17 *July*, Sarah Lyman; 12 *August*, Martha Lyman; 19 *August*, Hannah Pomroy; *December*, Mary Burt; Joseph Sheldon; Jonathan Parsons.

1695, *February* 26, Joseph Janes.

1696, *April* 5, Abigail Lyman; 9 *May*, Thankful Clark; *June*, Jonathan Wait; 19 *September*, John Kingsley; 4 *October*, Richard Webb; 23 *October*, John Miller; 22 *November*, Clemence Judd; 5 *December*, Miriam Keet.

1697, *January* 26, Mary Stebbins; 28 *January*, Caleb Pomeroy; 31 *January*, Richard Frary; 1 *February*, John French; 5 *February*, Jonathan French; 16 *February*. Joseph Wright; *April*, Joseph Edwards; 24 *April*, Eleazer Hannum; 8 *May*, Rebeckah Allen; 17 *May*, Wait Lyman; 22 *December*, Mehitable Dwight.

1698, *January* 26, Esther Strong; 14 *February*, Hannah Parsons; 11 *November*, Elizabeth Holton; 12 *December*, Benjamin Clark.

1699, *April* 14, Elder John Strong; 5 *May*, Lydia Lee; 21 *May*, John Strong; 23 *May*, Mary Hutchinson; 1 *June*, Noah Cook; 5 *June*, two children of Samuel King; 17 *June*, Abigail Root; 24 *August*, Noah Strong; 22 *September*, Ebenezer Pomeroy; 24 *October*, Hepzibah Wright; 26 *October*, Elizur King.

1700, *February* 6, Elnathan Clark; 20 *February*, Sarah Lyman; 11 *April*, Nathan Lyman.

NAMES OF PERSONS WHO TOOK THE OATH OF FIDELITY IN THE YEAR 1652.

[Copied from the Middlesex County Court Records, and communicated by CAPT. BICKFORD PULSIFER.]

Ralph Houghton
John Prescott
John Shaw
Sam[ll]. Rainer
Jonathan Danforth
Zackery Wickes
John Hall

Watertown.

Sam[ll]. Stratton Sen:
Sam[ll]. Stratton Junior
John Stratton
John Knapp
W[m]. Perse
Joseph Child
John Bourden
Stephen Paine
John Cloise
Sam[ll]. Ward
Mathew Smith
Daniell Warren
John Page
Sam[ll]. Daniel.
Richard Child
W[m]. Sanderson
Jonathan Whitney
Jn[o] Perse
Richard Smith
John Cooledge
Henry Spring
Richard Bloice
John Coller
Anthony Bevrs
Francis Bowman
Sam[ll]. Benjamin
Abra. Williams
Isacke Mixsure
Sam[ll]. Barnard
John Spring.
James Knap
Richa: Cady
Jn[o]. Barnard
Thomas Pratt
Robert Harington
Tho. Leson
Jn[o]. Traine
Tho. Straite
Jn[o]. Bush
John ffiske
John Bigolouh

10 of february 1664. Ri: Ward of Marlboroy took ye oath of ffidelity.
Before Tho: Danforth.

NOTICES OF NEW PUBLICATIONS.

God with the Aged: A Sermon preached to the First Church, Jan. 7. 1849, the Sunday after the death of HON. PETER C. BROOKS. By N. L. FROTHINGHAM, Pastor of the Church. PRIVATE. Boston: Printed by John Wilson, 21 School Street. 1849. 8vo. pp. 15.

Such is the title of an affectionate tribute to the memory of the aged parishioner and honored father-in-law, by one whose singular good fortune it was to stand in the two-fold relation of Pastor and son to the deceased.

The HON. PETER CHARDON BROOKS, the son of Rev. Edward Brooks and Abigail Brown, his wife, was born at North Yarmouth, in the State of Maine, Jan. 6. 1767. His father, a native of Medford, Mass., where he was born, (according to the College Records,) Oct. 31, 1734, graduated at Harvard College in 1757, sustained the office of Librarian from 1758 to 1760, and, upon the decease of Rev. Nicholas Loring, in July, 1763, received an unanimous call to become his successor in the Ministry at North Yarmouth. The invitation being accepted, he was ordained July 4, 1764, on which occasion it is stated that "one hundred and sixteen dollars and sixty-six cents were expended for an Ordination dinner; a more sumptuous entertainment than has been provided in town, on the 4th of July, since the Declaration of Independence." But "this auspicious morning of Mr. Brooks's ministry," it is said, "was soon clouded by disaffection and discontent," and in March, 1769, he was dismissed from his pastoral relation. The separation has been pronounced advantageous in every respect; and Mr. Brooks, who spent the remainder of his life in his native town, is reported to have been accustomed to say, "that his enemies in North Yarmouth had done him more service than all his friends." His wife was Abigail, the daughter of Rev. John Brown, of Haverhill, granddaughter of Rev. Roland Cotton, of Sandwich, and great-great-granddaughter of the celebrated John Cotton, of Boston. Mr. Brooks died in 1781.

Rev. Edward Brooks was the grandson of Samuel Brooks, who was the son of Caleb Brooks, of Concord, — by his second wife, Ann, — who sold his estate in Concord in 1670, and removed to Medford, where he died July 29, 1696 *He* was the son of Capt. Thomas Brooks, a man of some considerable note in Concord, where he died May 21, (or 22,) 1667. His wife Grace died May 12, 1664.

Of the Hon. Peter C. Brooks we will say a few words, mostly in the language of an obituary which has appeared in the public papers. He was, in early life, a distinguished member of the business community. While yet a boy he was initiated into the maxims, laws, and operations of Insurance, and when he became a man, opened an Insurance Office, in Boston, upon his own responsibility; and it was now, as an underwriter, — generally on marine risks — that he laid the foundation of that wealth for which he was afterwards distinguished. But his prosperity is, unquestionably, attributable to the virtues for which, no less than for his wealth, he was preëminently distinguished — prudence, economy, an ardent love of justice, and an inflexible integrity; these were his prominent characteristics, and these formed the basis of his remarkable success in life. As a man of business he was exact, without being illiberal; conscientious, but not narrow, in his dealings. Honorable and open-hearted in all his transactions, and scrupulous in the performance of every obligation, he enjoyed the unlimited confidence of his fellow citizens. Often called to the discharge of important public trusts, his sober judgment and sagacious foresight obtained for him a more than common share of influence. He was the chosen friend and confidant of Caleb Strong and John Brooks, sharing in their counsels, and participating in their measures for the public welfare. An active member and officer of several religious and philanthropic associations, he was ever among the foremost to contribute of his substance for the promotion of their benevolent designs.

For many years before his death, Mr. Brooks, having withdrawn from public life, and abandoned the pursuits of mercantile life, devoted much of his time and attention to the improvement of his noble estate at Medford. A practical as well as scientific agriculturist, his grounds exhibited the results of his well-directed studies in his favorite science. An original member of the Massachusetts Agricultural Society, his influence was exerted to extend the benefits of that institution, and to elevate the character of the husbandman.

Mr. Brooks was long reputed the wealthiest man in New England; but if so, he was, likewise, the most unostentatious. Proverbially modest and unassuming, there was no indication in his personal appearance or public demeanor that he considered himself exalted above those about him, no assumption of superiority because of his wealth, no manifestations of that foolish pride which wealth so often begets in its possessors. To those who had occasion to borrow and availed themselves of his ability to lend, (and the number of such was not small,) he was uniformly courteous and obliging, never making a time of scarcity an excuse for taking unlawful interest, nor profiting by the necessities of his neighbor for his own aggrandizement.

In private and domestic life Mr. Brooks's character was unexceptionable. To hospitality unlimited was added a deportment at once easy, cheerful, and pleasant, an uniform urbanity — the impulse of a kindly heart — which rendered his company welcome, alike, to old and young.

Mr. Brooks breathed his last, at his residence in Boston, on the evening of the First of January, 1849. His death was unattended by sickness or suffering. It was but the natural decay of the physical powers, the mere suspension of sensation. "He only appeared to grow more weary, and then to drop asleep. His hand became cold, while his feet yet preserved the warmth of life. The Angel of Death had taken him by it as with a friendly clasp, to lead him hence, and his steps took hold of the life eternal.

'All heads must come
To the cold tomb.
Only the actions of the just
Smell sweet and blossom in the dust.' "

Mr. Brooks's children inherit the principal part of his wealth. It suited his disposition better to dispense of his abundance as he journeyed through life, rather than to hoard up his thousands "to buy up mourners" at his decease, by bestowing it upon some great public Institution, or magnificent "Charity." His family connections are they, alone, to whom his property comes, and upon them, alone, rests the responsibility of making a wise and proper use of the ample means now placed at their disposal, for great good or greater evil.

Mr. Brooks's Will and Codicil (the former bearing date Jan. 9, 1844, the latter Feb. 29, 1848,) make mention of the following individuals.

1. His four sons, Edward, Gorham, Peter Chardon, and Sidney.
2. His three daughters, Ann Gorham, the wife of Rev. Nathaniel Langdon Frothingham, of Boston; Charlotte Gray, the wife of Hon. Edward Everett, late President of the University at Cambridge; and Abigail Brown, the wife of Hon. Charles Francis Adams, of Boston.
3. His grandsons.
4. The sons and daughter of his "late brother, Cotton Brown Brooks, Esq."
5. "Mrs. Ann Brooks, of Portland, widow" of his "deceased brother."
6. His "sister-in-law, Mrs. Lydia Phillips, of Andover," and her "seven unmarried daughters, Rebecca Gorham, Lydia, Sarah Wentworth, Susan Lowell, Caroline, Julia, and Amelia, Phillips."
7. His "niece, Mary Brooks Hall."
8. The children of his niece, "the late Mrs. Tinkham, daughter" of his "late brother" Cotton Brown Brooks, Esq.
9. Stephen Gorham, Esq., of Charlestown.

Mr. Brooks makes it his earnest request, in his Will, that his farm in Medford shall be retained in his family as long as possible; and he, therefore, gives and bequeaths the same, to whichever of his sons will take it, "at the rate and estimate of $18,000.00," to be considered as part of said son's portion. And he directs that the eldest son shall have the first choice, and so on, according to seniority; and if neither of his sons is inclined to take the estate on these terms, then it is to be offered to his daughters, in like manner, according to seniority, and upon the same terms. And whichever of his children obtains the said estate, is desired "*not to part with it but upon urgent necessity.*" Thus fondly did the good old man's affections cling to his ancestral domain!

A Historical Sketch of the Second Congregational Church in Attleborough: Delivered at its Centennial Meeting, December 7, 1848. By JONATHAN CRANE, Pastor of the Church. Boston: Damrell & Moore, Printers,—16 Devonshire St. 1849. 8vo. pp. 44.

Early Ecclesiastical History of Whately: being the substance of a Discourse delivered January 7, 1849. By J. HOWARD TEMPLE, Pastor of the First Church. With an Appendix containing Family Records. Northampton: Printed by J. & L. Metcalf. 1849. 8vo. pp. 40.

Such are the titles of two valuable contributions to the Ecclesiastical History of New England.

"Upon the 30th of November, 1748, the Second Church in Attleboro' was constituted, by Rev. Mr. Leonard, Pastor of the First Congregational Church at Plymouth, as the organ of an Ecclesiastical Council, called for that purpose, being a colony from the First Congregational Church in this town, then under the pastoral care of Rev. Habijah Weld, its honored Pastor, almost fifty-five years. The organization was attended with the utmost harmony and kind feeling on the part of those who removed their relation from the First Church, and those who remained." The first Minister was Rev. Peter Thacher, (son of Rev. Peter Thacher, of Middleboro', and grandson of Rev. Peter Thacher, of Milton,) who had, as he says in his sermon at the death of Rev. Mr. Weld, "stood in the relation of Pastor elect, to the brethren and people of God in the easterly part of Attleborough, and preached to them the most of the time, between August 20. 1743, and November 30, 1748; yet, with mutual consent, we all attended the Rev. Mr. Weld's meetings the Sabbaths on which he administered the Lord's Supper." Mr. Thacher having suffered an attack of paralysis, which rendered him incapable of performing the duties of his office, he resigned Oct. 26, 1784, and died Sept. 13, 1785. In 1793 Rev. Ebenezer Lazell, of Bridgewater, was ordained Pastor of the Church, the pulpit having been supplied in the interim by occasional preaching. He resigned Jan. 3, 1797, and removed to the State of New York, where he died. His successors have been, Rev. Nathan Holman, of Sutton, Rev. John Ferguson, of Scotland, and Rev. Jonathan Crane, of Schenectady, N. Y., the present Pastor, who was ordained Oct. 20, 1836.

The Northern part of Hatfield was incorporated into a town by the name of Whately, in April, 1771. Mr. Temple's valuable pamphlet is something more than a mere "Ecclesiastical History;" it is also a *civil* history of the town, giving us the particulars of its settlement, and the names of its first inhabitants, with numerous extracts from the official records. June 4, 1771, the town voted to hire Mr. Rufus Wells, of Deerfield, to preach six weeks upon probation; at the expiration of which time he was invited to a permanent settlement. The Church was organized Aug. 21, 1771, and Mr. Wells was ordained Sept. 25th following. After a ministry of sixty-three years, he died Nov. 8, 1834, in the 92d year of his age. Rev. Lemuel P. Bates, of Southampton, had been ordained, as colleague with Mr. Wells, Feb. 13, 1822, but had been dismissed Oct. 17, 1732, so that the Church was now without a Pastor. The pulpit was supplied by occasional preaching until March 16, 1836, when Rev. John Ferguson, (then recently dismissed from the Second Church in Attleborough,) was settled, and after a ministry of four years, was dismissed June 17, 1840. His successor, the present Pastor, was ordained, Sept. 30, 1845.

The "Appendix" to Mr. Temple's "Ecclesiastical History" contains genealogical sketches of the early settlers of Whately, comprising notices of the families of *Abercrombie, Adkins, Alexander, Allen, Allis, Bacon, Bardwell, Barnard, Bartlett, Belding, Bigelow, Bird, Bragg, Bridgman, Brooks, Broughton, Brown, Burroughs, Byrome, Carly, Carey, Castle, or Castwell, Chapin, Chauncey, Clark, Coleman, Cone, Cook, Cooley, Crafts, Curtis, Cutter, Daugherty, Dickinson, Edson, Faxon, Field, Frary, Gibbs, Gilbert, Giles, Graves, Gray, Grimes, Harding, Harwood, Hatch, Hawley, Hazard, Hibbard, Hill, Ingraham, Jefferson, Kellogg, Lamson, Locke, Loomis, Marsh, Mather, Merrick, Morey, Morton, Mosher, Munson, Nash, Orcutt, Parker, Pease, Pierce, Pratt, Richardson, Rogers, Ruddock, Sanderson, Sartle, or Sartwell, Scott, Sexton, Shattuck, Smith, Snow, Starks, Stiles, Stockbridge, Swift, Taylor, Thompson, Todd, Train, Turner, Wait, Walker, Warner, Wells, White, Winchell, Wood, Woods* and *Wright;* with some other curious information. Seldom have our eyes been gladdened by such an admirable specimen of what every commemorative or centennial discourse *should* be.

The Houghton Association. Report of the Agent to England. 8vo. New York: Jared W. Bell, Printer, No. 178 Fulton Street, opposite St. Paul's Church. 1848. pp. 28.

"Not all is gold that glitters," says the proverb; and if ever the truth of the aphorism were exemplified, such is now the case, in the final bursting of the Houghton bubble. "THE HOUGHTON ASSOCIATION," in solemn convention assembled, upon the 3d of March, 1847, in the town of Worcester, and Commonwealth of Massachusetts, appointed an Agent "to proceed to England and institute such inquiries as would tend to elicit all desirable information concerning the 'Houghton Property,' supposed to be in that country;" or, in other words, to chase the Jack O'Lantern which had so long been deluding the imaginations of half the Houghton race in America. The Agent, Mr. F. M. Rice, of Walpole, N. H., left Boston June 1, 1847, reached Liverpool on the evening of June 13th; remained in England until Oct. 24th; when he sailed for New York, where he arrived on the 9th of November, of the same year. No exertions seem to have been wanting on the part of Mr. Rice to accomplish the objects of his mission. In this Report the members of "The Association" are presented with a detailed account of his adventures, his fruitless researches, his vexatious experience of the mean and niggardly penny-a-word policy of the British Government with regard to the public records, his wild-goose-chases from north to south, from east to west, in pursuit of the millionaire, whose accumulated wealth was to make every mother's son of the name, in New England, a second John Cushing, and with his final sensible abandonment of the pursuit, as hopeless. It is delightful to see how the brilliant colors of the bubble, which, while distance lent enchantment to the view, had been so dazzlingly beautiful, faded away, one by one, as *the bowl of the pipe* came in view, until at last it burst, or, at least, vanished, leaving no trace of the power which had had breath enough to blow to such good purpose. The Agent returns home, makes his report, which is (sorrowfully, without doubt,) accepted by the Board of Directors, who forthwith print the same, for the benefit of future ages, and announce the contemplated dissolution of the Association, after an expenditure of nearly one thousand dollars, without any other return save a mass of genealogical information respecting the thousand and one families in England, who bear the name of HOUGHTON.

An Appendix to this Report contains an account of the family of HOGHTON, OF HOGHTON TOWER, in Lancashire, England, from the time of William the Conqueror to the present day, drawn up with much particularity and minuteness, by Mr. Rice, who received every attention and assistance from the present head of the family, Sir Henry Bold Hoghton, in the prosecution of his researches.

The Wight Family. Memoir of THOMAS WIGHT, of Dedham, Mass., with Genealogical Notices of his descendants, from 1637 to 1840. By DANFORTH PHIPPS WIGHT, M. D. Boston: Press of T. R. Marvin, 24 Congress street. 1848. 12mo. pp. 119.

With the exception of the Genealogy of the Drake Family* alone, we think that this little book is the *neatest* work of the kind which has ever come within our observation — neat in its internal arrangement and typographical execution, neat in its external appearance. Says Dr. Wight in his "Introduction": —

"In the following pages I have recorded all that can now be known respecting my ancestors; commencing with THOMAS WIGHT, who emigrated from England and settled in Dedham in 1637, and closing at the death of my mother — a period of two centuries."

"I regret that I have not more to communicate. Papers, which related to family affairs, and which were existing fifty years since, are now lost. I have gathered up all I could find relating to my progenitors, and have committed it to the press for the gratification of those who may hereafter bear my family name, and, like me, feel a reverence for the memory of ancestral connexions."

"The opportunity for collecting materials for genealogical memoirs is daily lessening. Family papers are often little valued by those to whom they are intrusted. But few persons remain, who have brought down to us, by tradition, the opinions and characters of those who were actors upon the stage of life in bygone days; and time is busily at work in erasing the recollection of events from the memory of the living, and names from the monuments which affection may have erected to prolong their remembrance. At this day the pursuits of the present and the hopes of the future make most men indifferent to the past."

* "Genealogical and Biographical Account of the Family of DRAKE in America. With some Notices of the Antiquities connected with the Early Times of Persons of the Name in England. Printed at the Private Press of George Coolidge, for SAMUEL GARDNER DRAKE, [the compiler of the work,] August, 1845." Boston. 12mo. pp. 51.

Beside the chronicles of "the Wight Family," this little volume contains pedigrees of the families of Brown, of Waltham, and Fuller, of Dedham, Mass.

In conclusion, we would say to all into whose hands this book may come, "*go thou and do likewise.*"

The Rawson Family. Memoir of Edward Rawson, Secretary of the Colony of Massachusetts Bay, from 1651 to 1686; with Genealogical Notices of his Descendants. By Sullivan S. Rawson. Boston: Published by the Family. 1849. 8vo. pp. 146.

This book is *got up* in beautiful style, and embellished with portraits of Secretary Rawson and his daughter Rebecca. We had long looked for its publication, with no inconsiderable anxiety; expecting, from the rumors which reached us from time to time, that we should be gratified with an extended biography of the Secretary. But we must confess that our anticipations have been far from realized. The short notice of him can not, with much propriety, be deemed a "Memoir;" it is an exceedingly meagre sketch of his public services. This we regret the more, because we know that there are abundant materials for a full account of this first progenitor of the Rawson Family in New England. His name is continually to be met with on the pages of our Colonial Records, which alone, if carefully examined, would furnish ample data for a *proper* "Memoir." The volume is almost entirely taken up with the Family Genealogy, which appears to be very complete. One thing we are sorry to observe; and that is, that he who has toiled night and day, who has begrudged neither time nor money, to collect the materials for this handsome volume; who, in fact, has been the prime agent, the main spring, in the whole undertaking, has been prevented, by modesty, from allowing his name to appear upon the title-page. What agency Mr. Rawson has had in the compilation of the work we do not know; but certain it is, that his name has never been heard mentioned in connection therewith, that he is not recognized in this vicinity as the author thereof. Here, the name of Mr. R. R. Dodge alone (now a resident in Cambridge) is associated with the "Memorial of the Rawson Family;" and to his enthusiastic ardor alone is generally ascribed the collection of the facts which are preserved upon its pages.

Naomi; or Boston, Two Hundred Years Ago. By Eliza Buckminster Lee, author of the "Life of Jean Paul." Boston: Wm. Crosby and H. P. Nichols. 1848. 12mo. pp. vii, 448.

Merry-Mount; a Romance of the Massachusetts Colony. [By John Lothrop Motley.] Boston and Cambridge: James Munroe & Co. 1849. 2 Vols. 12mo. pp. 8, 222; 4, 249.

Leaves from Margaret Smith's Journal in the Province of Massachusetts Bay. 1678–9. [By John G. Whittier.] Boston: Ticknor, Reed, and Fields. 1849. 16mo. pp. 224.

We give the titles of these little volumes, not with the intention of raising our humble voice to praise or condemn, but merely because they form an interesting addition to our local literature. Their respective merits have been ably discussed in the public prints and periodical reviews; while fault-finding critics have bestowed their usual pains in detecting and pointing out any trifling anachronism or inaccuracy of style, which, either by accident or design, may have crept into their composition. For our part, we are content to close our eyes to a few errors, and to pardon an occasional anachronism, when we meet with anything so infinitely superior to the disgustingly nonsensical and vapid popular double-columned trash — beneath the weight of which our presses groan — as these "books which are *books*" indeed.

Speech in support of the Memorial of Harvard, Williams, and Amherst Colleges, delivered before the Joint Committee on Education, in the Hall of the House of Representatives, Boston, on the 7th of February, 1849. By Edward Everett. Cambridge: Metcalf & Co., Printers to the University. 1849. 8vo. pp. 28.

We had already read, with much interest, the extracts from this admirable Speech which had found their way into the public prints; and have now been highly gratified with the opportunity afforded us, of perusing it at our leisure. It is, in truth, a most eloquent appeal in behalf of Collegiate education, and one which we are fain to hope will have the desired effect upon the minds of the Legislators of our Commonwealth.

MARRIAGES AND DEATHS.

MARRIAGES.

COTHREN, WM. ESQ., attorney at law, 3 Sept., to MISS MARY J., dau. of the late Dr. Samuel Steele, by Rev. Lucius Curtis. All of Woodbury, Ct.

GREIG, MR. GEORGE, formerly of Kinghorn, Scotland, now of the firm of Elliott & Greig, Boston, to LUCY HAYES, dau. of Robert Waterston, Esq., 26 March, at Boston.

LORD, MR. CHARLES HOWARD, formerly of Kennebunk, Me., now of the firm of Geo. C. Lord, & Co., Boston, to LUCY LORD, dau. of Joseph M. Hayes, Esq., of Saco, Me.; at Saco, 6 June, 1849.

QUINCY, MR. THOS. D., to MISS JULIA C., BRADFORD, dau. of Wm. B. Bradford, Esq., 17 July, all of Boston.

DEATHS.

ABBOT, WILLIAM, Bangor, 26 Aug., æ. 73; Mayor of that city.

APPLETON, DEACON FRANCIS, of Dublin, N. H., died July 17, aged 90 years. His native town was New Ipswich, N. H., from which he came to Dublin, in 1779, when he was twenty years of age. His wife was Mary Ripley, sister of Rev. Dr. Ripley, of Concord, Mass. MRS. APPLETON died in 1840, at the age of 74. In the year 1790, Mr. Appleton and his wife became members of the Congregational Church in Dublin, then under the pastoral care of the Rev. Edward Sprague. In the year 1796, Mr. Appleton was chosen Deacon, and he held the office and punctually discharged its duties during the succeeding thirty-six years. He was a brother of the late Jesse Appleton, D. D., President of Bowdoin College.

In 1831, he resigned his office in the church, under the impression that age and its attendant infirmities justified him in taking such a step. His days were extended far beyond his expectation, and some years before his death he arranged his temporal affairs, as if he were soon to leave the world, making himself at the same time, a life-member of the New Hampshire Bible Society, and of the American Unitarian Association, presenting to each Society the sum of fifty dollars. — *Chr. Regr.*

APPLETON, MOSES, M. D., Waterville, Me., æ. 76 yrs. Doctor Appleton was the son of Deacon Isaac Appleton, and was born at New Ipswich, N. H., March 17, 1773. He graduated at Dartmouth College in 1791, and pursued his professional studies a part of the time with the late Gov. Brooks, of Medford, Mass. He received his medical diploma from the Mass. Medical Society in 1796, when Samuel Danforth was its President. He commenced the practice of medicine in Waterville the same year, where he continued it until within a few years of his death. A citizen of Waterville for more than half a century, he felt a deep interest in its advancement and prosperity. Of his friends and associates, the early settlers of the town, a few only survive him. Uniformly kind to the poor, and generous to those who required his professional services, upright and honest in his character, frank and affable in his disposition and manners, he was loved by his friends and respected for his many virtues. His departure will be mourned by an extensive circle of acquaintances. — *Waterville (Me.) Paper.*

ARNOLD, HON. DUTEE, Warwick, R. I., 13 Aug., æ. 87.

ARNOLD, MR. SETH, Westminster, Vt., 6 Aug., æ. 101 yrs. 10 mos. 3 days.

BRAMAN, MR. JAMES, Berlin, Vt., 4 July, æ. 91 yrs. 8 mos.; a revolutionary soldier.

BRAZER, WILLIAM SEVER, West Point, N. Y., 17 August, æ. 23, son of the late Rev. John Brazer, D. D., of Salem, a graduate of Harvard College in the Class of 1846, and a Cadet at the U. S. Military Academy.

BREWSTER, LOT E., ESQ., Cincinnati, 21 June, of Cholera. He was an early associate of the N. Eng. Hist. and Geneal. Society.

At his residence on Fifth street, below Mound, of the prevailing epidemic, LOT E. BREWSTER, Esq.,* of the firm of Brewster and Woodruff, Auctioneers. The deceased has been long known and highly respected in this community, as an upright and useful citizen and an enterprising and efficient business man. He was, for some two or three years, a member of the City Council, and during a part of the time, presided over that body. The ward which he represented, as well as the city generally, is largely indebted to the measures which he originated or seconded by his influence, and to the indefatigable and earnest spirit and energy with which he habitually discharged his duties.

At the time of his decease, he was *President of the New England Society of Cincinnati*—an institution, to the prosperity of which he has, since its organization, devoted much of his best energy and zeal. Mr. Brewster was a lineal descendant of Elder Brewster of colonial memory, and by those who have intimately known the strong points of his character, he will be long remembered as a worthy representative of that stock of stern and noble virtues. — *Cincinnati Paper.*

BRITTON, ASA, ESQ., Chesterfield, N. H., 20 June, æ. 86; a revolutionary pensioner.

BROWN, MR. STEPHEN, Hamilton, 30 Aug., æ. 91 yrs. and 7 mos.; a revolutionary pensioner.

BURGESS, MRS. PRENTICE, Pawtucket, R. I., 26 Aug., æ. 100 yrs. and 3 mos.

Bryant, John, (an Indian,) Rocky Hill, N. J., 29 June, æ. 86; a revolutionary pensioner.

CASS, MOLLY, widow, Wilmot, N. H., 19 June, æ. 86; aunt of Hon. Gen. Cass, U. S. Senate.

CHAUNCEY, CHARLES, ESQ., Philadelphia, Aug., æ. 70; brother of Nathaniel C., Esq. The deceased was a gentleman of the highest respectability, and his loss will be deeply felt. He was a descendant of the second President of Harvard College, Dr. Charles Chauncey, who was of the Chaunceys of Hertfordshire, of whom was Sir Henry Chauncey, who about 1700 published an elaborate history of that county. Mr. N. Chauncey, above named, has prepared an extensive genealogy of the family in England and America.

COOK, MR. GEORGE, Providence, 10 Aug., of Cholera, æ. 56; a native of Kingston, Ms., and half brother to Hon. Jos. R. Chandler, of Philadelphia.

COOLIDGE, MRS. JEMIMA, Watertown, 18 Aug., æ. 83.

CRUFT, JAMES JACKSON, Boston, 25 Aug., æ. 22, son of John Cruft, Esq., of B., and a graduate at Harvard College in the Class of 1846.

GALLATIN, HON. ALBERT, LL. D., New York, 12 Aug., æ. 88, and was buried on the 15th. He was born at Geneva in Switzerland, Jan., 1761, and graduated at the University there in 1779, arrived at Boston, N. E., 14 July, 1780, with a letter of introduction from the celebrated Duke de Liancourt to the afterwards more celebrated Dr. Franklin. To enumerate the offices he has filled would far exceed our limits, but we should not omit to mention that, in 1782, he was elected Professor of the French language in Harvard College. Like some others, afterwards prominent men, he opposed in Congress, generally, the measures of Washington, but has since been a supporter of them.

GRINDELL, MRS. ELIZABETH, Goshen, N. H., 22 June, æ. 104 yrs., 3 mos., and 9 days. She leaves a descendant of the 5th generation.

HARDWICK, MR. FREDERICK, Quincy, 12 Aug., in his 84th year; a native of Quincy. His father came from Germany about 1752, and settled in that part of the town ever since known as Germantown. He was one of a company who came to establish glass works. The business was commenced, but owing to the loss of their manufactory by fire, and other causes, the undertaking was abandoned, and the undertakers became scattered. A small number of the families remained in this place, and their descendants are numerous. — *Communicated.*

HARRIS, MARY A., South Boston, 13 Aug., æ. 7 months, daughter of John A. and Harriet M. Harris.

HAZELTON, MR. RICHARD, Philadelphia, 9 June, æ. 48 years; formerly of Boston.

HIXON, MR. ISAAC, Medway, 3 Sept., æ. 87; the last revolutionary soldier in the town.

HOLDEN, DANIEL, ESQ., Sweden, Me., 23 July, æ. 85 yrs., 10 mos.; a revolutionary pensioner.

HOW, HALL J., S. Boston, 17 Aug., æ. 58; his wife is dau. of Isaac Waldron, Esq., of Portsmouth, N. H.

JOHONNOT, WILLIAM, ESQ., Windsor, Vt., 3 July, æ. 83.

LEACH, MRS. ELIZABETH, Dunbarton, N. H., 20 June, æ. 102; relict of the late Capt. Joseph L.

LONGFELLOW, HON. STEPHEN, LL. D., Portland, 6 Aug., æ. 73. He was father of the present Prof. L. of Harvard College.

LOUGEE, MRS. MIRIAM, Gilmanton, N. H., 23 June, æ. 92; relict of Joseph L. Her maiden name was Fogg. The Lougees of Gilmanton are said (by the able historian of that town) to be descended from *John*, who was born in the Isle of Jersey, and who, at the age of eighteen, (in "Queen Ann's War,") came to New England. He married Mary, dau. of *Moses Gilman* of New Market, and resided in Exeter, N. H.

LYMAN, HON. THEODORE, Boston, 17 July, (at his country seat in Brookline,) æ about 58. Great have been the losses of the community this year, by that indiscriminate destroyer, death; but well and truly can those who knew GEN. LYMAN exclaim of him, as Browne of Tavistock did of Sidney's sister: —

"Death! ere thou hast slain another,
Fair, and learned, and good as *he*,
Time shall throw his dart at thee!"

MANNING, MR. WILLIAM, Cambridgeport, 25 July, æ. 83; the oldest printer in the state. He was one of the well known firm of Manning & Loring, Spring Lane, Boston. His father was Joseph Manning of Providence, a grad. of H. C. 1751

d. 1808. William was born in Providence, 1766. Mr. Manning was twice married; 1st, to Lydia Brown of Bolton; 2d, to widow Lydia Keith of Charlestown. By the former he had 11 children, and 5 by the latter. Of these 16 children, 8 were sons, several of whom are married and have descendants.

PECK, HON. WM. B., Cannahon, Ill., 22 June, æ. 71; one of the first settlers in that section of the country.

PERKINS, JACOB, (the well known inventor,) Regents Square, London, at the house of his son, 30 July, æ. 83 yrs. and 21 days. He was born in Newburyport. He was a descendant of that branch of the Perkins family early seated at Ipswich. His emigrant ancestor was named JOHN, who was born at Newent, Co. of Gloucester, Eng., in 1590; came with his family to New England, in 1631, in the same ship which brought over Roger Williams. His wife's name was JUDITH, and the names of his children were, JOHN, THOMAS, ELIZABETH, ANNA, LYDIA, and JACOB; all born between 1613 and 1625, probably. From the last named, the subject of this notice was descended. He died in 1700. His residence was near Manning's Neck, in Ipswich. He had by his wife Elizabeth, among other children, MATHEW, born 23 June, 1665, died in 1775, æ. 90. He was the grandfather of the great mechanic, as is supposed. [In Mr. Cushing's Hist. of Newburyport it is said that the inventor was son of *Matthew*, and that said "Matthew died æ. 90." The grandfather and father may have been confounded.]

PERKINS, MRS. JUDITH W., Springfield, 5 Jan. 1848, æ. 78; mother of Rev. Justin P., missionary to Persia.

PHILLIPS, MRS. MARY MAGEE, Boston, 23 June, æ. 59; wife of Hon. Jona. Phillips.

PICKERING, JACOB S., ESQ., Portsmouth, N. H., Cashier of the Rockingham Bank, 27 Aug., æ. 69.

PIERCE, REV. JOHN, D. D., Brookline, 24 Aug., æ. 76 yrs. 1 mo. 10 days. He was born in Dorchester, 14 July, 1773, was son of John Pierce, an honest shoemaker, and the oldest of ten children, six of whom survive. He was ordained at Brookline, 1797, when his ordination sermon was preached by Rev. T. M. Harris. Mr. Pierce married, 1st, Abigail Lowell, of Medway, who died in about three years, viz. 2 July, 1800; 2d, Lucy Tappan, of Northampton, 6 May, 1802, now his widow. They had ten children, all living except one, a son. His emigrant ancestor was ROBERT PIERCE, of Dorchester. The father of Dr. Pierce died in 1833, at the age of 91.

POMEROY, LEMUEL, Esq., Pittsfield, 25 Aug., æ. 71; long one of the most efficient men of business in Western Massachusetts. His emigrant ancestor was from Devonshire, who settled at first in Dorchester, and afterwards in Windsor, Ct. His name was ELDRED, or ELTWOOD, called in our Indian history ELTWEED. He had a son MEDAD, of Northampton, who had a son EBENEZER, who had a son SETH, who was the father of LEMUEL, of Southampton, who was the father of the subject of this notice.
Northampt. Cour.

RUSSELL, MR. JOHN B., Keokuk, Iowa, June, æ. 50; late editor of the Keokuk Despatch, and formerly of Boston.

SMITH, REV. ETHAN, Boylston, Sept., in his 87th year; he had been a minister 60 years. He was author of a work on the Prophecies, and "View of the Hebrews; or the Tribes of Israel in America."

SMITH, MRS. JUNIA LUELLA B., Westbrook, Me., 15 Aug., æ. 40; wife of Hon. F. O. J. Smith, and dau. of the late Dr. Levi Bartlett, of Kingston, N. H.

STANDISH, MR. and MRS. MILES, Middleboro, 27 Aug.; "both were attacked and died on the same day."

STARBUCK, LEVI, ESQ., Nantucket, Aug., æ. 79 yrs. 10 mos.

STARBUCK, ELISHA, ESQ., Nantucket, Aug., æ. 70; he was High Sheriff of the County.

STONE, ABIGAIL MARIA, Cincinnati, 26 July, æ. 76, a native of Berkshire Co.; wife of Hon. Ethan Stone, one of the early adventurers to the Western Territory.

STOTT, MR. JOHN H., Boston, 12 July, æ. 50. Mr. Stott has been long known in this community for his eminence in the art of seal engraving, for his skill in delineating heraldic devices, and drawing and emblazoning coats of arms. His place, we fear, will not soon be filled. He was born in London, and was son of Mr. Christopher Stott of that city; emigrated to this country in 1830, since which time he has resided in Boston.

WARD, MRS. PATIENCE, Quincy, Ill., 12 Aug., of Cholera, æ. 56; wife of Mr. Artemas W., formerly of Newton, Ms.

WARE, MRS. SARAH, Springfield, 8 July, of Consumption, æ. 33; wife of Mr. Addison Ware.

WASHBURN, MRS. DEBORAH, Kingston, 28 June, æ. 89.

WASHBURN, ELI, Hanover, N. H., 30 June, æ. 90; a soldier of the Revolution.

WENTWORTH, MR. N., Canton, 9 July, æ. 88; a revolutionary pensioner.

WHITE, MR. REUBEN, Springfield, 10 Aug., æ. 96; a revolutionary pensioner.

WILLIAMS, MR. EZEKIEL, N. Hartford, N. Y., 30 Aug., æ. 94; a native of Roxbury, Ms.

INDEX OF NAMES AND TITLES.

NOTE. — The same rules have been observed in this index as were observed in that of the last volume. In such an immense number of names and references, entire accuracy can only be approximated.

In indexing the *Freemen* we have been obliged to use some discretion, and what judgment we had, in endeavoring to refer to all those bearing the same name, though sometimes under very different spellings. Where we have added a name in brackets, without the interrogation point, we felt confident that the name so bracketed was the true name; when less positive, the interrogation follows. The names of a great many of the *Freemen* were doubtless written down by a clerk, from hearing them pronounced, to whom many of them were entirely new, and others were imperfectly understood: thus, Flagg may have been recorded *fflack;* Checkley, *Chaulkly;* Cilly, *Sally;* Wright, *Right;* Ward, *Word;* Rice, *Roise;* Adger, *Agar;* Audlin, *Odlin;* and others too numerous to particularize.

It would be as easy to make mistakes of this sort as it was for an Irish clerk to mistake the name of the Publisher of this work, to whom pains had been taken to pronounce the name distinctly several times; yet *when he got his bill*, he found his name written *Dregg!*

The first emigrants here had come from different counties, and though speaking the same language, their pronunciation of names was very different. They were not only strangers to one another, but they were strangers to those who took down their names; and in many instances the scribe had probably never heard of the name before he attempted to write it. Hence it is not at all strange if we have many names in our lists that not only represent *nobody in our days*, but that never did represent *anybody at any time.* Therefore, if genealogists never find or hear of descendants of some of those supposed to have settled in the country, there may be a *very good reason for it.*

C